CULTURE AND PSYCHOPATHOLOGY

Culture & Psychopathology

Juan E. Mezzich and
Carlos E. Berganza,
editors

New York
COLUMBIA UNIVERSITY PRESS

This book is Smyth-sewn and printed on
permanent and durable acid-free paper.

Library of Congress Cataloguing in Publication Data
Main entry under title:

Culture and psychopathology.

Bibliography: p.
Includes index.
1. Psychiatry, Transcultural—Addresses, essays, lectures. 2. Psychology, Pathological—Social aspects —Addresses, essays, lectures. I. Mezzich, Juan E. II. Berganza, Carlos E. [DNLM: 1. Cross-Cultural comparison—Collected works. 2. Mental disorders—Collected works. 3. Psychopathology—Collected works. WM 31 C9681]
RC455.4.E8C833 1983 616.89 83-7391
ISBN 0-231-04874-2

Columbia University Press
New York Guildford, Surrey

Printed in the United States of America
c 10 9 8 7 6 5 4 3 2

Contents

Preface

SOMETIME in 1975, while we were with the Department of Psychiatry and Behavioral Sciences at Stanford University in Palo Alto, California, we conceived the idea of a seminar on "Culture and Mental Health" as an introduction to university life for entering students. We settled on a format of individual student presentations and group discussions of selected readings. Throughout the preparation and conducting of this seminar, we were impressed by the fact that although literature in culture and psychopathology was abundant, it was rather disorganized and dispersed, and it was impossible to find a reasonably updated and suitable textbook. As the term progressed, we found that the readings we had selected and subsequent group discussions generated tremendous interest in both the participating students and the experts invited as resource persons for the various sessions.

Stimulated by these results, we decided to organize a seminar on "Transcultural Psychiatry," addressed this time to graduate students in medicine, anthropology, and other behavioral and social sciences at Stanford. We performed a more complete search of the literature using both manual and computerized procedures. We invited several new experts from Stanford and the University of California to our discussions. Again, the outcome was encouraging.

Both seminars convinced us that there was real need for a compilation of annotated readings on culture and psychopathology to facilitate understanding of where the field was and where it was going.

In concordance with the structure of both seminars, we decided to organize this book along two parallel lines: one cultural and the other psychopathological. The "cultural" portions discuss how such specific sociocultural variables as social class, ethnicity, social mobility, urbanization, and migration, affect mental health and psychopathology in general. The "psychopathology" portions, on the other hand, take us into specific aspects of psychopathology as they are affected by sociocultural variables in general. These parts are preceded by those which deal with conceptual and methodological issues and are followed by one that examines globally psychiatry as a social institution.

Although we believe that the most important schools of thought are represented in these readings, we have favored those articles which sustain a bio-psycho-social approach to psychopathology and employ a systematic methodology. A fuller presentation of the principles and organization of the book can be found in the introductory chapter.

Culture and Psychopathology is addressed to a wide audience, and our experience with the seminars from which the book developed gives us reason to believe that it will be found useful by scholars as well as mental health practitioners, by beginning students and seasoned experts alike.

Juan E. Mezzich
Carlos E. Berganza

Acknowledgments

We wish to express our appreciation to all those people who in different ways helped us to make this book a reality. We are grateful to Drs. Clifford Barnett, Benjamin Paul, Bernard Siegel, and George Spindler from the Department of Anthropology and Dr. P. Herbert Leiderman from the Department of Psychiatry and Behavioral Sciences at Stanford University for their helpful suggestions and encouragement during the planning stage. Silvia Askin-Edgar, M.D., Ph.D., while studying transcultural psychiatry with us, helped search through the basic literature with thoroughness and competence. Dr. Ada Mezzich and Dr. Paul Pilkonis from the Department of Psychiatry and Dr. German Matos from the Department of Anthropology at the University of Pittsburgh read the manuscript critically and made valuable suggestions. Ms. Barbara Good made effective editorial contributions. Special thanks are due to Ms. Lorraine Axelson who with incredible dedication, skill, and graciousness helped with typing and preparing the manuscript for the publisher. Ms. Fara Evans helped with proofreading and various editorial issues. Mr. Gerald Coffman and Ms. Shelley Goodpastor also provided kind assistance in various capacities. Ms. Jennifer Angier and Ms. Barbara Epstein effectively helped with computerized literature searches and Ms. Mary Margaret Maloney competently prepared all the needed artwork. Dr. Vicki Raeburn, Ms. Susan Koscielniak, Mr. Leslie Bialler and the staff at Columbia University Press were always available for consultation. Their enthusiasm for this project helped to overcome all obstacles. We wish to thank our students at Stanford University, the University of Pittsburgh, and Francisco Marroquin University in Guatemala for their stimulating interest and curiosity. And to our families, our gratitude for their constant understanding, advice, and support.

Contributors

The editors are grateful to the following publications for permission to reprint materials used in this book. Some minor editorial changes were made, as deemed appropriate for an anthology of this kind. In some cases, the original reference and footnote formats are slightly altered to conform to the author-date method of citation used throughout this book.

1. "Overview: Foundations of Cultural Psychiatry" by Armando R. Favazza and Mary Oman. From: *American Journal of Psychiatry* 135:293–303, 1978.
2. "The Need for a New Medical Model: A Challenge for Biomedicine" by George L. Engel. From: *Science* 196:129–136, 1977.
3. "Culture and Mental Disease: A Social Labeling Perspective" by Nancy E. Waxler. From: *Journal of Nervous and Mental Disease* 159:379–395, 1974.
4. "Problems of Measurement in Cross-Cultural Research" by George M. Guthrie. From: *Annals of the New York Academy of Sciences* 285:131–140, 1977.
5. "On the Comparability of Meaningful Stimuli in Cross-Cultural Research" by R. Bruce W. Anderson. From: *Sociometry* 30:124–136, 1967.
6. "Handling the Cultural Dimension in Psychiatric Research" by H. B. M. Murphy. From: *Social Psychiatry* 4:11–15, 1969.
7. "Cross-Cultural Perspectives on Early Development" by Jerome Kagan and Robert E. Klein. From: *American Psychologist* 28:947–961, 1973.
8. "Anomalous Reactions to Social Pressure of Israeli and Soviet Children Raised in Family Versus Collective Settings" by Ron Shouval, Sophie Kav Venaki, Urie Bronfenbrenner, Edward C. Deveriux, and Elizabeth Kiely. From: *Journal of Personality and Social Psychology* 32:477–489, 1975.
9. "Identification with Mexican-American Values and Psychological Adjustment in Mexican-American Adolescents" by Manuel Ramirez. From: *International Journal of Social Psychiatry* 15:151–156, 1969.
10. "The Causal Priority Between Socioeconomic Status and Psychiatric Dis-

order: A Prospective Study" by Rance P. L. Lee. From: *International Journal of Social Psychiatry* 22:1–8, 1976.

11. "Urbanization and Psychiatric Disorders: The Hong-Kong Scene" by W. H. Lo. From: *Acta Psychiatrica Scandinavica* 54:174–183, 1976.
12. "Ethnic Groups within Communities: A Comparative Study of the Expression and Definition of Mental Illness" by Daniel Sydiaha, Hugh G. Lafave, and Irvin Rootman. From: *Psychiatric Quarterly* 43:131–146, 1969.
13. "Immigration and Mental Disease" by P. W. Burvill. From: *Australian and New Zealand Journal of Psychiatry* 7:155–162, 1973.
14. "Social Mobility and Psychiatric Disorder: A Re-Evaluation and Interpretation" by Robert J. Kleiner and Odd Stefan Dalgard. From: *American Journal of Psychotherapy* 29:150–165, 1975.
15. "Cultural Conflict in Urban Indians" by Joan Ablon. From: *Mental Hygiene* 55:199–205, 1971.
16. "Culture and the Differentiation of Emotional States" by J. P. Leff. From: *British Journal of Psychiatry* 123:299–306, 1973.
17. "Culture and Psychiatric Symptomatology: A Comparison of Argentine and United States Patients" by Toba A. DeFundia, Juris G. Draguns, and Leslie Phillips. From: *Social Psychiatry* 6:11–20, 1971.
18. "Diagnostic Criteria of American and British Psychiatrists" by Robert E. Kendell, John E. Cooper, A. J. Gourlay, J. R. M. Copeland, Lawrence Sharpe, and Barry J. Gurland. From: *Archives of General Psychiatry* 25:123–130, 1971.
19. "The Social Etiology of Schizophrenia in Immigrant Groups" by C. Bagley. From: *International Journal of Social Psychiatry* 17:292–304, 1971.
20. "Depressive Disorders from a Transcultural Perspective" by K. Singer. From: *Social Science and Medicine* 9:289–301, 1975.
21. "Drug Use and Abuse in Cross-Cultural Perspective" by Marlene Dobkin DeRios and David E. Smith. From: *Human Organization* 36:14–21, 1977.
22. "Cultural Differences in Child Guidance Clinic Patients" by David H. Stoker and Arnold Meadow. From: *International Journal of Social Psychiatry* 20:186–202, 1974.
23. "On the Epidemicity of Amok Violence" by Joseph Westermeyer. From: *Archives of General Psychiatry* 28:873–876, 1973.
24. "Sociocultural and Social-Psychological Factors Affecting Personal Responses to Psychological Disorders" by David Mechanic. From: *Journal of Health and Social Behavior* 16:393–404, 1975.
25. "Cultural Aspects of Psychotherapy" by Eric D. Wittkower and Hector Warnes. From: *American Journal of Psychotherapy* 28:566–573, 1974.
26. "Psychiatry and Folk Healing: A Dichotomy?" by Pedro Ruiz and John Langrod. From: *American Journal of Psychiatry* 133:95–97, 1976.
27. "Cultural Variation in Responses to Psychotropic Drugs: A Progress Report" by H. B. M. Murphy. From: *Confrontations Psychiatriques* 9:163–185, 1972.
28. "Psychiatry in the Soviet Union Today" by John T. Salvendy. From: *Canadian Psychiatric Association Journal* 20:229–236, 1975.

29. "Psychiatric Training and Practice in the People's Republic of China" by Philip D. Walls, Lichun H. Walls, and Donald G. Langsley. From: *American Journal of Psychiatry* 132:121–128, 1975.
30. "Psychiatry in Latin America" by Carlos A. Leon. From: *British Journal of Psychiatry* 121:121–136, 1972.

CULTURE AND PSYCHOPATHOLOGY

INTRODUCTION

Juan E. Mezzich and
Carlos E. Berganza

Definitions

CULTURE IS a Middle English word derived from the Latin *cultura,* meaning tilling. It has many varied and complex definitions, which range from "excellence in the arts and manners" to "the growth of microorganisms in an artificial medium." Its anthropological and sociological meaning, according to *Random House Dictionary of the English Language* (1971), is "the sum total of ways of living built up by a group of human beings and transmitted from one generation to another." According to the *Encyclopaedia Britannica's* (1979) enumerative definition, human culture consists of "language, ideas, beliefs, customs, codes, institutions, tools, works of art, etc." An additional contemporary emphasis has been placed on viewing culture as "cognitive ideology" (e.g., Goodenough 1963). It is this enlarged anthropological conceptualization of culture we shall use in this book, with the inclusion of bordering sociological elements.

Psychopathology is a composite word derived from both the Greek *psyche,* meaning "breath or mind," and the Greek roots of pathology, meaning "the study of suffering or disease." Its definition, according to the *Random House Dictionary,* is "the science of diseases of the mind." We use the term psychopathology broadly in this book, to encompass the development, conceptualization, identification, frequency, manifestations, course, and treatment of mental illness.

But what about the definition of "culture and psychopathology"? Given the separate complexity of the two concepts involved, the study of their interrelationship is clearly formidable, intricate, and exciting. This book is an attempt to delineate, analyze, and understand this relationship.

Early Approaches

It is evident that psychopathology and culture have been linked since antiquity. For example, in the Indian Ayurvedic system of the "Science of Life," which dates back to the last centuries of the pre-Christian era, psychiatry is considered an integral part of medicine. Certain mental disorders were believed to reflect the influence of demonic forces and unfavorable stellar patterns, for which exorcism and astrological procedures were used along with drugs. Traditional Chinese medicine described mental illnesses as maladies of "wind" and used treatment methods similar to those of the Indian system (Gwee 1971). Psychopathology and culture continued to be linked through the centuries and up to modern times.

The best documented early attempts to examine this relationship are represented by the "culture and personality" movement. A precursor to this movement was Sigmund Freud's *Totem and Taboo* (1913), in which he drew parallels between the repetition-compulsion and primary-process thinking of neurotics and psychotics and the magic rituals of elementary societies, from which he assumed originated the need for the tribal horde and social organization. Also of seminal importance to this movement were Carl Jung's *Archetypes of the Collective Unconscious* (1968) and *Symbols of Transformation* (1967), in which he attempted to trace the sources of a patient's fantasies back to mankind's ancient recorded artifacts.

The actual thrust of the "culture and personality" movement came with the interaction between a group of distinguished ethnographers, disciples of Franz Boas, and a group of psychiatrists and psychoanalysts interested in the development of psychodynamic formulations of social processes.

As noted by Mandelbaum (1949), Edward Sapir wrote one of the first anthropological monographs discussing personality formation within the framework of culture, in which he proposed that automatic organizations of an individual's behavior are shaped predominantly by his cultural environment.

In the early 1930s, Margaret Mead showed that although anatomy places some restrictions on sex-role behavior, it is not "destiny." She proposed that the infant possesses a basic temperament that culture molds during the years of growing up.

Ruth Benedict (1934) thought of culture as "individual psychology thrown large upon the screen, given gigantic proportions and a long time span." She suggested that the individual has a personal history in growing up and in adjusting to the demands of the culture, which also has its own independent history.

The psychoanalyst most centrally involved with the "culture and personality" movement was Abraham Kardiner (1939) who worked in New York on these issues with Sapir, Benedict, Linton, DuBois, and other anthropologists. They proposed that each society induces a "basic personality structure" in its members through the primary influence of child-rearing practices, family organization, and subsistence patterns. Second-order shapers of personality structure were "psychological defense systems" represented by religion, taboo systems, rituals, folktales, group ideology, etc.

Another psychoanalyst with considerable influence in the field of psychocultural studies was Erik Erikson (1950) who saw his popularity greatly enhanced with the publication of *Childhood and Society.* Largely as a result of his work with the Dakota and Yurok Indians, he thought that each of the varieties of cultural conditioning contains a built-in wisdom, and that, as in the case of embryology, psychosexual development can be understood as a stepwise epigenetic process with time factors and critical periods.

Bio-Psycho-Social Integrated Approaches

A significant step forward in the development of a more systematic and comprehensive approach to the study of culture and psychopathology was made by Whiting and his collaborators during the 1960s. They used the statistical version of the comparative method developed by George Murdock through the Human Relations Area Files. Whiting (1961, 1964) attempted to elucidate probabilistically cross-cultural indicators of a causal chain between child-rearing practices (e.g., prolonged sleeping arrangement between mother and infant) and personality variables (e.g., masculine identification-puberty rites) and certain cultural norms and events such as postpartum sexual taboo polygyny, and Kwashiorkor (a form of severe protein deficiency in infants). In addition to implementing quantitative and encompassing designs, Whiting's work illustrated specific ways in which physical and biological factors interact with cultural and personality variables.

Anthony Wallace (1961) discussed the importance of considering biological as well as psychosocial factors in the comprehensive study of psychopathology. He pointed out the weaknesses of the bland assumption that mental disorder is caused just by sociocultural and psychological factors, and that one need not consider the various known organic impairments which regularly produce various behavioral manifestations and the evidence for genetic and biochemical complicity in the development of "functional" psychoses. Along the same lines, Katz and Foulks (1969) argued convincingly that environmental and physical factors such as climate, diet, and disease affect not only social institutions, which in turn shape personality, but in many cases influence directly the functioning of the central nervous system, which is the biological substratum of behavior and personality.

Psychiatrist-anthropologist Edward Foulks (1972) studied the Arctic hysteria of the North Alaskan Eskimo by examining the life history of afflicted individuals, personality, psychiatric symptomatology, physical and neurological status, biochemical variables, alterations of biological rhythms, and demographic and environmental information. He attempted to integrate these multiple variables, using a systems approach addressed to extending rather than reducing the chain of events leading to mental disorder. His is one of the best empirical studies to date exemplifying a bio-psycho-social approach to the understanding of psychopathology.

In 1975, Horacio Fabrega, a psychiatrist and anthropologist, conducted a penetrating analysis of the relationship between disease, social behavior, and human adaptation, including the relevant concerns from both the biological and social sciences, and integrated them into a field he termed "ethnomedicine." Shortly afterwards, George Engel, a professor of psychiatry and medicine, challenged the established biomedical model of disease for not sufficiently considering the social, psychological, and behavioral dimensions of illness, and for forcing a choice between two inadequate positions: one that reduces all behavioral phenomena of disease to physicochemical principles, and another that excludes from the category of disease anything that cannot be explained physicochemically. Instead, Engel proposed a bio-psycho-social model of disease that considers all factors contributing to both illness and patienthood. (See article 2).

A bio-psycho-social longitudinal approach is probably the most reasonable and promising for articulating the study of behavior and psychopathology. This is so because of the need both for a comprehensive explanatory framework and for an examination of the importance of the cycles or stages in an individual's lifespan. With such

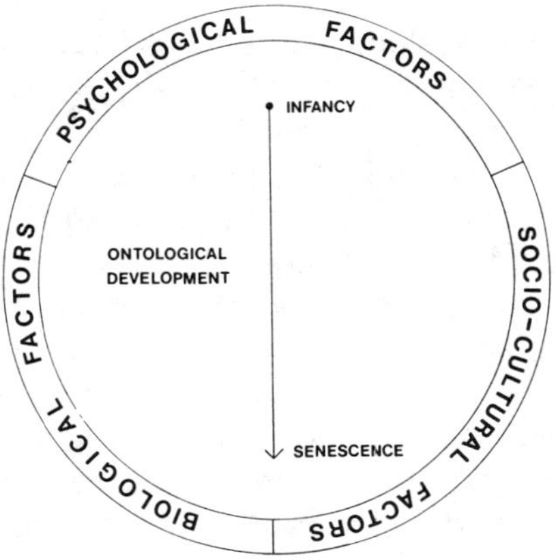

Figure I.1 A Bio-Psycho-Social Integrated Approach.

an approach (see figure I.1), systematic consideration is given to biological, psychological, and sociocultural factors and their interactions as they relate to the individual and his personal, ontological development from infancy to senescence. It is this approach this book takes.

Current Prominent Issues

Several specific issues in the relationship between culture and psychopathology are currently widely perceived as important and pressing:

(1) The need for better descriptive studies in cross-cultural psychopathology

For these studies, there must be developed improved procedures and models for the assessment of cultural as well as psychopathological variables. For example, recent attempts have been made to increase the reliability of the psychiatric evaluation process through the development of structured clinical interviews (e.g., the Present State Examination—Wing et al. 1974) and the use of operational or explicit diagnostic rules (e.g., the Research Diagnostic Criteria—Spitzer et al. 1978). A particularly notable development is the multiaxial diagnostic model, which describes the patient's condition in terms of separate key aspects or axes (Mezzich 1979, 1980). Several versions of this model have been developed in various parts of the world (e.g., Essen-Möller 1961; Wing 1970; Ottosson and Perris 1973; Helmchen 1975; Rutter et al. 1975; Strauss, 1975). One such system is DSM-III (American Psychiatric Association 1980), which has as main features the use of explicit diagnostic criteria and a multiaxial framework. This includes axes on clinical psychiatric syndromes, personality and specific developmental disorders, physical disorders, psychosocial stressors (evaluated according to the sociocultural circumstances and norms for the individual), and adaptive functioning. Such developments are still in a state of flux, and most of the specific procedures available have been generated in certain industrialized countries and their transcultural generalizability is still unclear.

Another important requirement in cross-cultural psychopathological studies is the use of improved investigational designs which consider the multiple variables usually involved and their interactions. These designs call for a more extended use of multivariate statistical techniques in data analysis.

(2) Variance in beliefs about illness, causation, and cure

There is increasing interest in the various ways patients conceptualize the nature of their illness, its etiology, and the appropriate strategies for dealing with it. This information may not only contribute to our understanding of psychopathology, it also appears to be essential for explaining a patient's help-seeking attitudes and behavior. Furthermore, it seems that the most crucial issue regarding compliance with and response to treatment may be the degree of congruence between the patient's and the clinician's concepts about psychopathology and what should be done about it. It is gradually becoming evident that large segments of the population, even in industrialized countries, have concepts about psychopathology considerably at variance with the standard professional notions, which makes the above-mentioned congruence problem both prevalent and critical. For example, Favazza and Oman (1980) noted the following among frequent folk beliefs in the United States: (a) the belief in the "evil eye"—especially in persons with ancestral roots in Italy, Greece, Spain, Iran, India, Mexico, and Czechoslovakia; (b) the hexing belief in "rootwork," particularly in blacks with Southern and rural backgrounds; (c) beliefs in spirit possession among immigrants from Puerto Rico and other Caribbean islands;

and (d) contemporary charismatic Christian beliefs according to which mental illness may be caused by demonic oppression or possession, for which rites of deliverance and exorcism are common treatment techniques.

(3) Problems of working in intercultural settings

Particular demands are placed on mental health professionals working in multicultural areas, including required familiarity with sociocultural factors in the population at large and especially among ethnic minorities, and the need of the professional to deal with his or her own potential ethnocentric biases. Biases are particularly problematic, as they typically involve entrenched and partially unconscious attitudes. Parres (1979), Chairman of the American Psychiatric Association Task Force on Ethnocentricity Among Psychiatrists, conducted a survey of 150 Canadian, U.S., Puerto Rican, and Mexican psychiatrists regarding their relevant backgrounds, experiences, and attitudes. Among his findings were that few psychiatrists had received any planned course content regarding socioeconomic, racial, ethnic, or religious differences during their postgraduate training, and that the majority of psychiatrists expressed a clear preference to treat patients who are relatively young, of the middle or upper-middle class, introspective and articulate, and of racial and ethnic background similar to that of the psychiatrist.

Also, at issue in intercultural settings (especially in large cities) is the relationship between standard mental health professionals and folk healers.

(4) Ethnic minorities: Their assertiveness and access to treatment

It has been noted that the "melting pot" process is actually reversing now. This is a reflection of the increasing assertiveness shown by such minority groups as French-Canadians and Spanish-Americans. That assertiveness is expressed not only as insistence on preserving a particular cultural heritage and way of life but also as a willingness to acquire increasing political power.

Particularly interesting is the case of the Hispanic population in the United States, expected to become the largest ethnic minority group in this country within this decade. In the face of the documented limited access to and underutilization of standard mental health services by this population, interest has been voiced both in and outside this community to demand the development of services more attuned to the ethnic identity and related features and needs of this population (Sanchez 1979).

Overview of the Book

This book is organized into three major sections. The first covers general issues in the field and includes this introduction, and parts 1 and 2. The second section is the most extensive and represents the thrust of the book. It consists of part 3, which pointedly reflects longitudinal concerns; parts 4 and 5, which examine, respectively, specific sociocultural structures and various forms of sociocultural change as they relate to psychopathology in general; and finally parts 6-8, which review, respectively, specific issues in psychopathology and nosology, major psychiatric disorders, and various issues and forms of psychiatric care as they are affected by sociocultural factors in general. The last section of the book is made up of part 9, which reviews psychiatry as a social institution functioning within the framework of a whole nation or geographical region, with focus on those that are non-Western and/or are industrially underdeveloped. Figure I.2 depicts the book's hierarchy and the interrelations mentioned above.

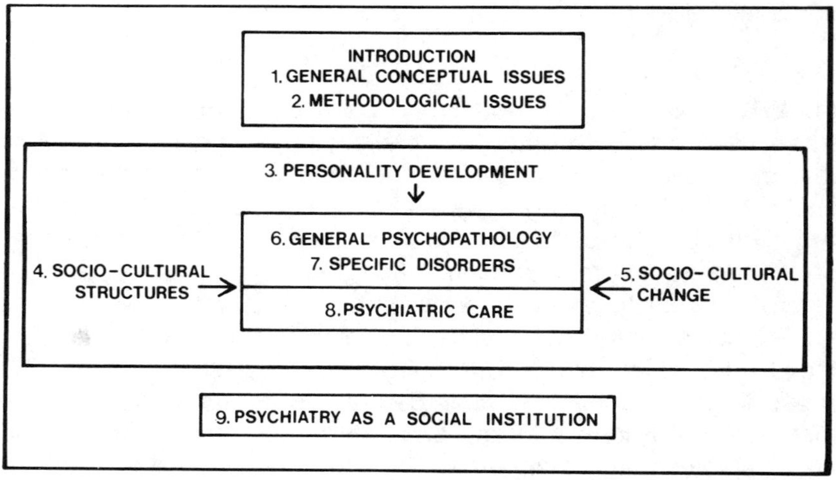

Figure I.2 Organization of *Culture and Psychopathology.*

The articles and the annotated additional references within each part have been identified through manual and computerized searches of the literature. The computerized search focused primarily on *Psychological Abstracts, Index Medicus,* and *Social Science Citation Index* data banks. The following criteria were used for the selection of topical articles: (1) presentation of a fundamental development or position; (2) overview of a broad topic rather than case studies or restricted treatments of narrow issues; (3) use of a systematic methodological approach; and (4) relative recency of the paper.

The major questions addressed are outlined below to provide a glimpse of their content. More detailed introductions to each part and article are presented throughout the book.

Part I, "General Conceptual Issues," examines the crucial ideas articulating the study of culture and psychopathology, teasing out complex notions and placing in perspective the meaning of both early efforts and new developments. It reviews the role and issues of transcultural psychiatry and overviews cultural factors within a comprehensive explanatory framework of psychopathology, with the intent of adding a cultural dimension to the mainstream of psychiatric thinking and work. While acknowledging dissatisfaction with reductionistic biomedical models, it searches for a biopsychosocial reformulation of the notions of disease and medical care, and explores the role of social labeling in the development, course, and outcome of mental illness.

Part 2, "Methodological issues," examines the reliability and validity of measuring instruments, the adequacy of translations (i.e., the equivalence and variance of textual materials across languages), and the need to be sensitive to the potential role of cultural factors in any psychopathological study and the use of appropriate procedures to deal with such factors. This part discusses the requirements for more systematic methodology which include the identification of sources of undesirable variability in cross-cultural assessment and the use of multivariate approaches in design and data analysis.

Part 3, "Personality Development," represents a longitudinal perspective in the study of culture and psychopathology. It deals with the development, conditioning, and course of personality and psychopathology in time as they are affected by sociocultural factors. Topics discussed include the relationship between culture and early cognitive development and the need to consider time frame when assessing this interaction, the relative effects of family vs. collective upbringing and cultural-political systems on children's responses to adult and peer expectations, and the identity conflicts experienced by bicultural adolescents and the consequences on personality orientation and psychological adjustment.

Part 4, "Sociocultural Structures," examines the relations between psychopathology and several specific sociocultural structures, including social class, urban structure, ethnic grouping, and religious identification. Questions addressed here include: What is the causal priority between socioeconomic status and psychiatric disorder? What are the relative effects of parents' social class, subject's social class, and social mobility on psychopathology? What is the relationship between urbanization and mental disorder? How does religion affect the manifestations of stress and psychopathology and how does society cope with them?

Part 5, "Sociocultural Change," reviews the influence of various forms of sociocultural change and their intensity on psychopathology. Specific questions discussed include: What is the impact of international and intranational migration on the mental health of the individuals involved? What connections exist between social mobility in its various forms and psychopathology? What are the mental health consequences of modernization and the conflicts involved in losing a culture and acquiring a new one?

Part 6, "General Psychopathology and Diagnosis," examines various key aspects of descriptive psychopathology, diagnosis, and classification as they relate to sociocultural and international factors. Some of the specific questions addressed are: What is the relationship between culture and the differentiability of basic emotions? What symptomatological contrasts have been reported between countries? What theoretical propositions have been offered to account for them? How can the combined explanatory power of a number of sociocultural variables be elucidated? What is the role of clinicians' diagnostic habits in explaining cross-national differences in rates of mental disorders? What contributions are being made in various regions of the world toward the development of more enlightened and comprehensive diagnostic systems?

Part 7, "Specific Psychiatric Disorders," is the most extensive of the book, as it reviews specialized psychopathology—i.e., discrete psychiatric syndromes and their relations to sociocultural factors. Most of the important broad categories of mental disorder are considered, including schizophrenia, depressive disorder, substance abuse, child behavior disorders, and the so-called "culture-bound" syndromes (a misnomer, given that all psychiatric disorders are cultural to some extent).

Part 8, "Psychiatric Care," discusses the influence of sociocultural factors on the various phases of the psychiatric care process from the individual's attitudes and behavior toward treatment to the implementation and outcome of specific therapeutic modalities. Questions particularly investigated include: How are the subject's beliefs about his condition and his help-seeking behavior shaped by cultural and social variables? What similarities and differences can be discerned among psychotherapies practiced in various parts of the world? How do cultural views on etiology, lifestyle, and political-economic systems influence the psychotherapeutic process? What commonalities can be drawn between Western psychotherapists and traditional healers? How can these comparative considerations be used for the advancement of psychiatric treatment? How can the issue of the coexistence of standard and folk healing systems be constructively addressed? Does culture influence responses to somatotherapies such as psychotropic medication? What is the impact of ethnic factors on patients' expectations and drug metabolism?

Part 9, "Psychiatry as a Social Institution," discusses how psychiatry, including its roots, orientation, service organization, professional personnel and training, and future perspectives, is shaped by the society or country in which it exists. It focuses on non-Western or underdeveloped countries and addresses the following questions: What are the features of psychiatry in a country which is both Marxist-Leninist and industrially developed, such as the Soviet Union? How are mental health services organized in China, a country with a billion people, technologically underdeveloped, and undergoing drastic transformations along a socialist path? What are the health conditions and psychiatric resources in Latin America, a group of countries sharing a combined Iberian and Indian background as well as rich traditions, technological underdevelopment, and political ebullition?

Culture and psychopathology is a field attracting increasing and renewed interest. It appears acutely relevant to major issues confronting the study of abnormal behavior and the provision of mental health services today.

In this book we offer an annotated compilation of major papers in key areas of culture and psychopathology. We are attempting to fill here the need for a book which covers these major areas in a reasonably comprehensive, eclectic, and coherent way.

We hope this volume will stimulate the interest of scholars and clinicians in the field, encourage some of them to look into the possibilities of research, and enrich their professional work through a more differentiated and sensitive practice.

I

General Conceptual Issues

Innovative conceptualizations in mental health and the progressive sophistication of the methods of study of normal and abnormal behavior have revived the interest for greater understanding of the multiple factors involved in the development, manifestations, and handling of mental illness.

Although significant progress has been made in the elucidation of neurobiological variables relevant to psychopathology, there has been fairly generalized disenchantment with a strictly "biological" model as a conceptualization of mental illness. Likewise, purely sociological explanations appear to be quite inadequate. A much more reasonable and heuristic approach seems to be the use of an integrated bio-psycho-social framework to guide inquiries and discussions in psychopathology. This approach involves examining the roles and interaction of genetics, the internal milieu, and the environment; i.e., the biological and the psychosocial.

Within such a comprehensive framework, the study of the relationship between culture and psychopathology is starting a new era, more exciting and innovative, and at the same time more modest in terms of explanatory claims. All this requires critical examination of many conceptual issues.

We have included here a group of articles discussing basic conceptual tenets and problems associated with culture and psychopathology and the very nature of cultural psychiatry as viewed by some of the most articulate workers in the field. The annotated additional references at the end elaborate further on the issues discussed or present alternative viewpoints. Both the articles and the annotated references discuss the role of transcultural psychiatry for understanding human behavior and psychopathology, the implications of incorporating sociocultural concepts within the study of mental illness and the planning of medical care, the issues addressed and the solutions proposed by what Fabrega (1975) calls ethnomedicine, the relevance and complexity of labeling in psychopathology, and the importance of folk conceptualizations of mental illness.

1

Overview: Foundations of Cultural Psychiatry

Armando R. Favazza and Mary Oman

The importance of anthropological and social-psychological insights for the thorough understanding of psychiatric illnesses and their management is rather widely acknowledged and has been the subject of the formulations presented here and in the next article. The following overview by Favazza and Oman certainly endorses, documents, and discusses these notions and then goes one step farther. It attempts to inscribe cultural factors within a comprehensive explanatory framework of psychopathology which explicitly includes neurobiological and personal psychological factors. In so doing, the authors strive to use a broader view of the influence of culture on abnormal behavior, going beyond the restricted and sometimes anecdotal concern exemplified by the traditional focus on exotic "culture-bound" syndromes (which in fact have considerable formal similarities, although do not fully overlap, with psychiatric syndromes recognized in Western societies). Accordingly, the term cultural (instead of cross-cultural or trans-cultural) psychiatry is used.

This scholarly paper overviews a quite recent reformulation of the field as "cultural psychiatry" (see also Foulks et al. 1977), which has the deliberate intention of incorporating the cultural dimension in the mainstream of psychiatry.

THE TRADITIONAL cornerstones of modern psychiatry are biology (the neurosciences) and psychology. Through the influence of epidemiological studies and the community mental health movement, sociology has become a more recent cornerstone, with social class the major variable. Despite the thousands of articles with cultural themes that have appeared in the mental health literature (Favazza and Oman 1977), the study of culture has not yet been established as a cornerstone of psychiatry.

The purposes of this article are to present some of the major conceptual foundations of cultural psychiatry, to acquaint readers with work in anthropology and social psychology that is relevant to psychiatry, and to demonstrate the significance of the addition of the cultural dimension to basic psychiatric concepts. We prefer to use the adjective "cultural" rather than "crosscultural" or "transcultural" because it is more inclusive, less exotic, and does not imply a single methodology. Among the important areas we shall not discuss are socialization (Williams 1972), aging, aggression (Montagu 1968), racism (Thomas and Sillen 1968), drug use (Weppner 1973), immigration, and acculturation (Zwingmann and Pfister-Ammende 1973).

Defining Culture

White, Kroeber, and Durkheim espoused a superorganic theory of culture; i.e., they posited that culture is a phenomenon that can be analyzed without reference to the individuals in whom it is expressed. Thus, suicide can be examined as a social fact explained best by antecedent social factors rather than by focusing on individual motivation. Most scholars have incorporated other theories of culture as well as the superorganic to produce a widely accepted definition of culture. In the words of Kroeber and Kluckhohn

> Culture consists of patterns, explicit and implicit, of and for behavior acquired and transmitted by symbols, constituting the distinctive achievement of human groups, including their embodiments in artifacts; the essential core of culture consists of traditional (i.e., historically derived and selected) ideas and especially their attached values; culture systems may, on the one hand, be considered as products of action, on the other as conditioning elements of further action. (1952: 180)

Psychoanalysis has produced an interesting literature dealing with culture. The bibliography for "Totem and Taboo" (Freud 1913) reveals Freud's wide reading in cultural anthropology. Jung's *Symbols of Transformations* (1967) has many references to archaeology and mythology. H. S. Sullivan founded *Psychiatry,* a journal that has promoted collaborative work with anthropologists. Roheim founded the series now known as *The Psychoanalytic Study of Society*. Robert LeVine (1973) has pioneered in developing a modern psychoanalytic methodology for studying culture. The general thrust of all of these studies has been to enrich our understanding of culture. However, our concept of cultural psychiatry refers specifically to the application of cultural insights to the enrichment of psychiatric practice and our understanding of the human situation.

It is seldom appreciated that culture affects not only individual and group psychology and the social order but also biology (Chapple 1970). Culturally determined mating preferences affect genetic pools (Crow and Felsenstein 1968). Dietary preferences affect nutritional status (e.g., the effect of diet on pellagra). Current research seems to indicate that fundamental operations of the brain might differ radically with cultural background (Paredes and Hepburn 1976). The developing theory of biogenetic structuralism, which, according to Laughlin and d'Aquili (1974), seeks to clarify the concept of cognitive structure by examining the necessary bond between human society and the study of the human CNS, provides an interesting view of schizophrenia. One of the principal themes of physiological anthropology, according to Damon, is "an examination of the way physiological responses of men in stressful environments affect and are affected by culturally defined behavior patterns" (1975:8).

Cultural Dimensions of Psychiatric Concepts

In the following discussions we shall examine some concepts basic to psychiatry. By focusing on the cultural dimension of these concepts we do not mean to imply that psychological, biological, and sociological dimensions are secondary in importance. Rather, we hope to show that the addition of the cultural dimension enriches our understanding of psychiatric concepts and provides an expanded context for successful psychiatric clinical practice. A vital literature on cultural aspects of psychiatry is blossoming (Everett et al. 1976; Westermeyer 1976; Foulks et al. 1977). The number of psychiatrists with doctoral training in anthropology is growing, and there are many more psychiatrists with less formal training in this area. The psychiatry departments at the University of Miami and the University of Hawaii are among the leaders in integrating the anthropological and psychiatric fields.

Understanding Mental Health and Illness

Sapir (1963) noted that cultural anthropology is important because it is constantly rediscovering the normal. Mental illness exists and is recognized in all cultures, from the most simple to the most complex, although its expression and identification vary (Wittkower and Prince 1974; Murphy and Leighton 1965). Some cultures, for example, "tend to mask latent delusional thinking because of their over-all magical configuration" (Benedict and Jacks 1954). In cultures such as our own, which emphasize rationality and scientific objectivity rather than supernaturalism, a psychotic person would find it more difficult to adjust, and his or her symptoms would more likely be identified early.

In relation to mental illness, culture has been considered both etiological (Leighton and Hughes 1961) (through certain child-rearing practices, stressful roles, or culture change) and sympton molding (Wittkower and Prince 1974) (as in the case of the culture-bound syndromes). Dunham (1976) stated, on the other hand, that "it [is] almost impossible to pin down in any conclusive fashion those societal and cultural factors that cause or precipitate specific mental disorders." Mentally ill people may develop a constellation of striking symptoms that frequently can be associated with certain cultural beliefs and practices. These "culture-bound" syndromes have been conceptually categorized into reactions of fear (*susto, latah, imu, koro*), rage (*amok*), and dissociation (trance, possession, *kitsunitsuki*). Our current understanding, according to Wittkower and Prince (1974), is that these syndromes are basically the standard ones described in *DSM-II* (American Psychiatric Association 1968).

The significance of the concept of a culture-bound disorder is that cultural factors are accepted by psychiatrists as important for both understanding and treating such disorders. Because the disorders may be limited to specific, often exotic, cultural groups, the cultural dimension is easily integrated into psychiatric conceptualization. In a modern evaluation, however, cultural factors would be considered in perspective along with other relevant factors. For example, Foulks's monograph on the Arctic hysterias of the North Alaskan Eskimos (Foulks 1972) considered not only cultural traditions but also village demography, the Arctic environment, and psychological and biological functioning. The finding that some cases of Arctic hysteria were related to low calcium levels was seen in the cultural context of Eskimo clothing (which decreases exposure to sunlight) and dietary patterns.

The very process we use to define and identify mental health and illness is linked to our cultural heritage. As Fabrega noted, "At the very least, comparative research findings in human biology and medicine should lead us to appreciate the valuational, arbitrary, and culture-bound bases of what we view as 'normal' (or diseased) biological systems" (1974a: 298). All psychiatric disorders are to some degree culture-bound, but because we are intimately involved in our own culture we find it difficult to look at it objectively. It is just as important to understand the cultural context of the Viennese or American hysterias as it is for the Arctic hysterias.

Child Rearing and Basic Personality

A cause célèbre in the relationship between psychiatry and anthropology occurred in the 1920s (Favazza 1974), when Malinowski, an anthropologist studying the people of the Trobriand Islands, reported that male children there developed hatred toward their mother's brother rather than their father (Malinowski 1927). Some critics of psychoanalysis claimed that because the Oedipus complex was thus shown not to be universal the bedrock of psychoanalytic theory had been shattered. Jones (1925) and Roheim (1950) replied that the Trobriand situation was simply an example of how feelings could be defensively displaced from father to uncle. Over the decades, debate about the universality of the Oedipus complex has lost its sting. The specific complex described by Freud is culturally limited. Freud's major discovery was that of the universal family romance (Hartman et al. 1951). The ethnocentrist might hold that the Viennese complex is primary and that other versions are "merely" variations on a theme. The cultural psychiatrist holds that the family romance concept is primary and that different cultural versions are all equally valid. Thus, the cultural position does not denigrate the findings of psychoanalysis but, rather, seeks to expand their usefulness by linking them to the cultural environment in which people and the symbols live.

World War II stimulated studies attempting to explain adult personality on the basis of child-rearing patterns (Favazza 1974). One prominent theory attributed Japanese character traits to toilet training practices (Gorer 1943). The harshness of toilet training supposedly caused a repressed rage that resulted in such Japanese characteristics as fanaticism, arrogance, sadomasochism, suspiciousness, pedantry, and an obsession with pathological obsenity and anal sexuality (Labarre 1945). Subsequent studies have clearly shown the reductionistic aspects of these theories and their lack of substance (Haring 1956).

Whiting and Child's *Child Training and Personality* (Whiting and Child 1953), written in 1953, has greatly influenced crosscultural studies. These authors correlated ethnographic data from diverse societies with antecedent-consequent factors in individual development. One of their findings was that excessive childhood deprivation could be correlated with pathological reactions and with relevant cultural beliefs. No such correlation could be found for excessive childhood gratification.

Cultural differences in infant motor development have also been studied. A study of Balinese subjects (Mead and MacGregor 1951) related methods of child handling and carrying with a persistently low tonal organization. In Africa, Ganda infants demonstrate remarkable early motor precocity that rapidly declines after age 3 to below Western norms (Ainsworth 1967). Although genetic factors are surely important in these studies, the cultural component cannot be dismissed lightly.

Despite the emphasis of dynamic psychiatry on the importance of the childhood years for adult mental functioning, it is remarkable that fewer than 20 articles on the cultural aspects of child rearing were published in mental health journals before 1950. By placing our psychological and biological insights in a cultural context, the relationship between childhood development and adult personality may become less problematic. An understanding of the process of personality formation would have major implications for preventive mental health programs.

Cognition

Psychiatrists are probably familiar with Piaget's studies of cognitive ontogenesis. Piaget's theories have been tested in diverse cultures (Dasen 1972). The majority of these studies have focused on the principle of conservation and on the concrete operations period (7–11 years of age). Although Piagetian stages of development have been identified in all cultures, there is no indication that all people go through all stages, that the ages for reaching stages conform to the Genevan norm, or that the order of development is invariant (Brislin et al. 1973).

The development of perceptual skills in different cultures has also been studied. Early visual experiences appear to affect the way in which a person perceives his or her environment, e.g., subjects reared in an urban setting (a "carpentered world") tend to perceive angles and visual test illusions differently than do subjects reared in a different visual setting (Segall at al. 1966). Language, art, and crafts may act as cultural mediators that enhance perceptual adaptability. Several studies (Hudson 1960; D'Andrade 1967) have demonstrated that poor performance on perceptual tests may be reversed through instructional programs.

Cognitive anthropology is a relatively new theoretical orientation that, according to Tyler "focuses on discovering how different peoples organize and use their culture. . . . it is an attempt to understand the organizing principles underlying behavior" (1969: 3). Much of the work in this field deals with kinship terminology. Of potential significance for psychiatry is the application of cognitive anthropological techniques to studies of family and psychosocial networks. For example, we are beginning a project in which we will explore the cognitive domains of kinship, friendship, and social relationships among alcoholic patients and significant others in their psychosocial network. Our hypothesis is that networks with high degrees of cognitive sharing in significant domains are more amenable to therapeutic intervention on behalf of a member of the network.

Family and Social Networks

Until quite recently, the intact, nuclear, upper-middle-class family has been regarded as the stereotypic, normal family in the United States. Pattison (1977) reviewed the American family sociology literature and noted four current major types of family structure. The traditional extended family, typical of the American working class and of the very rich upper class, is an interdependent social and economic unit; each nuclear subfamily lives in geographic proximity and depends on the extended kin for major affective and instrumental resources. The weak-dissolving family, typical of slum and ghetto situations, is one in which most kin functions have been taken over by large-scale formal organizations, leaving the nuclear family with few resources and few coping abilities. The isolated nuclear family, typical of the upwardly mobile and geographically mobile middle class, maintains fewer essential family functions but does so with stability, often at the expense of great effort to maintain family cohesion. The modified extended family structure, typical of the successfully adaptive middle and upper-middle class, consists of a coalition of nuclear families in a state of partial dependence.

As we abandon our stereotypic view of family structure, we discover patterns of family process. We discover that the concept of family may be too limiting for maximal therapeutic intervention. A focus on the individual in the context of his or her psychosocial network is a significant aspect of cultural studies.

The concept of social network derives from anthropology. Perhaps the best known studies are those of relationships in African towns (Mitchell 1971) and Boissevain's analysis of various European networks (Boissevain 1974). The mathematical models of social networks developed by European anthropologists have yielded results coinciding with Pattison's clinical findings that normal people have meaningful social networks that include about 25 individuals, while the networks of neurotic people contain about 15 and those of psychotic people about 7 (Pattison 1977). The percent of individuals in a network who interact with others in the network ranges from 30 percent for normal people to 60 percent for neurotic people to 90 percent for psychotic people (Pattison 1977).

The implications of these findings for psychiatry are enormous. In recent years some family therapists have begun network therapy, which includes the nuclear family as well as kin, friends, neighbors, and work associates of family members. This concept dovetails nicely with Caplan's concept of social support systems (Caplan 1974) and heralds an important new therapeutic approach. The orderly expanding focus from individual to family to social network would be expected logically to progress to the community (Henderson 1977). As we gain knowledge about social networks and as we learn to use these networks therapeutically, we can expect a new vitality in community mental health programs.

Sex Roles and Behavior

Freud's brilliant studies of sexual development and behavior no doubt accurately portrayed the Western Victorian era. His concept that anatomy is destiny, however, led many psychiatrists to believe that the Freudian position was universal and that any deviations represented either manifest or latent pathology. Although female psychoanalysts such as Horney and Thompson challenged the concept of inherent male superiority, it was anthropologist Margaret Mead who presented the strongest evidence of the influence of culture on sexual roles.

In 1935 Mead studied the sex-linked behavior of men and women in three tribes living in a 100-mile area of New Guinea (Mead 1935). She observed that Arapesh men and women were, in Western terms, maternal as parents, feminine, and unaggressive. Sex was not a powerful driving force in this culture. Mundugamor men and women, in contrast, were ruthless, aggressive, and highly sexed—they acted like undisciplined and violent Western men. The third group, the Tchambuli, provided a further contrast with Western culture. In this culture women were the dominant, impersonal managing partners and men were less responsible and emotionally dependent. Thus, Mead demonstrated that although anatomy imposes some limitations, it is not "destiny." She recognized two types of deviants—the psychologically inadequate and the cultural. The latter possesses a fundamental discrepancy between his or her innate disposition and his or her society's standards. Mead felt that a society could create deviants by disregarding the totality of human potential and artificially connecting sex with specific approved behaviors, e.g., an individual who is homosexual because of innate temperament may fail to adjust to the accepted standards of a society that accepts only heterosexuality as normal. Forty years after Mead pointed this out, APA voted to remove homosexuality per se from its list of mental disorders.

Kinsey and associates' studies of sexual behavior of American men and women (1948, 1953) presented startling findings that challenged stereotypes about human sexuality. However, a more recent study (Broverman et al. 1972) indicated that sex-role stereotypes are prevalent in our culture and, moreover, that they are widely held by mental health professionals. A troublesome sex-role stereotype is that most desirable traits described as masculine (e.g., aggressiveness, independence, and dominance) are seen as more descriptive of healthy adults. Only a few feminine traits are applied to the description of a healthy adult. Abernethy (1976) pointed out that this negative female self-concept may account for the findings that girls' school performance tends to deteriorate around high school age and that the reported prevalence of mental disorders in adult women is higher than in men (a reversal from the reported childhood prevalence).

Gould (1975) noted that "comparative studies of men and women at different periods in history and others conducted during the same period but in different cultures support the thesis that there are no patterns of behavior peculiar to one sex which cannot be observed in the opposite sex." The implications of this idea for the psychiatrist include recognition of the crippling effect of assumed sex-linked behaviors on human potential and the need for a new understanding of the institution of marriage in the light of changing sociocultural roles for men and women.

Alcohol Use

Most medical and behavioral studies of alcohol use have focused on the pathology called alcoholism and such consequences as traffic accidents, broken families, and liver disease. However, alcohol is a cultural artifact, and the form and meanings of drinking alcoholic beverages are culturally defined (Mandelbaum 1965). There are cultures in which drunkenness and disruption of social life are not inevitable problems, despite a high rate of alcohol consumption. Descriptive studies of alcohol drinking in various cultures are legion. Washburn's *Primitive Drinking* (1961) is a major source. Among well-known case studies are those on North American Indians (Brod 1975). There is evidence that North American Indians were introduced to alcohol by Europeans, who also provided such models of drunken behavior as violence, treachery, and licentiousness.

Intriguing examples of cultural influences on individual reactions to alcohol ingestion are found in MacAndrew and Edgerton's study, *Drunken Comportment* (1969). Most texts regard alcohol as a disinhibitor that releases one's moral brakes, frees the lower brain centers from higher brain controls, and loosens one's curb on instinctual urges. Unguarded behavior then comes to the fore, and released impulses are forcefully expressed. However, there are cultural examples in which the disinhibitor theory does not hold true. Norbeck (1954) described the Japanese fishing community of Takashima as characterized by a puritanical attitude toward sexuality and by the rigid suppression of aggression. During wedding feasts, gambling parties, and the "slambang drunk" of the autumn festival, many inhabitants of Takashima get thoroughly drunk. Instead of a release of aggression and sexuality, however, Norbeck reported good-natured drunkenness, camaraderie, laughter, jokes, songs, and dances, which were considered the inevitable result if not the objective of continued drinking.

Horton's (1943) study of the functions of alcohol in primitive societies and Bales's (1946) study of cultural differences in rates of alcoholism are classic works. Bales concluded that rates of alcoholism are influenced by the degree to which a culture operates to bring about acute needs for adjustment in its members, the sort of attitudes toward drinking that a culture produces in its members, and the degree to which a culture provides suitable substitute means of satisfaction. Horton's hypothesis is that the primary function of alcoholic beverages in all societies is the reduction of anxiety. In 1962 Field reanalyzed Horton's data and concluded that excessive drinking is found in societies that lack stable, permanent, and formal corporate kin groups to provide controls on heavy drinking.

The concept of integrated drinking has emerged from cultural studies. Bacon (1973) defined integrated drinking as "a cultural adjustment to drinking, an adaption and integration of the drinking of alcoholic beverages into the way of life of the group." Societies with high rates of integrated drinking usually have high rates of alcohol consumption as well as widespread participation in and generalized approval of drinking. Thus, a high rate of consumption may be intimately linked with positive group social values and need not be socially threatening. Integrated drinking is not a predictor of drunkenness. Societies showing infrequent drunkenness typically indulge children's dependency needs, use relatively severe toilet training practices, use more permissive than punitive methods of socialization, exert relatively little socialization pressure toward achievement and independence, tolerate adult dependent behavior, engage in communal eating, and relate folktales that tend to describe the world as essentially kind and friendly. When male and female roles are strongly differentiated, sex differences in drinking are more apt to be present.

The marked association in cross-cultural studies of low consumption of alcohol and infrequent drunkenness with the critical acceptance of adult dependent behavior is a finding of interest in connection with the success of AA (Bacon 1973). Although one must be careful not to "overculturalize" the understanding of alcohol drinking because a low incidence of problems with alcohol in a culture *may* be related to physiological metabolic variables (Wolff 1972), neither should one minimize the cultural context in which drinking occurs. Certainly there is a need for clinical cultural studies related to alcohol (Westermeyer 1974) because these may provide an efficacious perspective for the development of programs to treat and prevent the "abnormal, addictive, pathologically compulsive intake of alcohol." Of special interest in this context is Jilek's (1974) psychiatric-anthropological study. He described the apparently successful alcoholism treatment "program" developed by the Coast Salish Indians, which involved the transformation of a religious ceremony into a therapeutic process.

Communication

Psychiatry, more than any other branch of medicine, depends on communication for both diagnosis and therapy. A method of microanalysis of therapeutic conversation has recently been developed by Labov and Fanshell (1977). The psychiatrist must be attentive not only to what a patient says and does but also to the cultural context of the patient's communication (Smith 1966; Hymes 1964;

Hinde 1972). The literature on communication is awesome in complexity and magnitude, encompassing such diverse areas as architecture, semantics, dance, art, anthropology, sociology, ethology, philosophy, cybernetics, urban studies, advertising, mass media, kinesics, proxemics, speech pathology, psycholinguistics, organization theory, psychology, and psychopathology.

Early scholars modeled the study of all languages on the Indo-European. Then, confronted by markedly different Eskimo and American Indian languages, anthropologists pointed out the uniqueness of languages. Whorf (1956) proposed the theory that language forms as well as expresses thought. We are captives of our language structure as reflected in the ways in which we conceptualize such areas as science and art. Sapir (1927) noted that "the 'real world' is to a large extent unconsciously built up on the language habits of the group. No two languages are ever sufficiently similar to be considered as representing the same social reality." An impressive literature exists on the role of lexicon as a determinant of behavior and cultural patterns (Carroll and Casagrande 1958) and, more specifically, on the semantic ramifications of diagnosing disease (Frake 1961).

The United States is a nation of immigrants from many cultures with differing world views, yet, as Scheflen noted, "In America, where there is a common language, these emic differences are often overlooked and are therefore all the more troublesome. Because people speak English, they think they understand each other" (1972: 94). Significant recent studies include those on intelligibility and interethnic attitudes (Wolff 1964), the development of antilanguages that serve to create and maintain subcultural social structures (Halliday 1976), black English (Labov 1972), difficulties in verbal-social interactions created by differences between lay and technical languages (Gumperz 1974), and psychotherapy with bilingual patients (Marcos and Alpert 1976).

The Semantic Differential (Osgood et al. 1957) is an instrument for determining the meanings of verbal concepts, e.g., ethnic variations in the meaning of shame (Marsella et al. 1974). Patients rate concepts on a series of bipolar scales. Through statistical analysis the concepts can then be placed in a three-dimensional meaning space. The Semantic Differential might prove itself clinically relevant as a means of assessing therapeutic progress (Dingman et al. 1969) as well as a clinical research tool (Dick 1969).

Gregory Bateson has had a major impact on psychiatry because of his communication studies. In *Naven* (1936) he developed the concept of schismogenesis—the process of differentiation in the norms of individual behavior resulting from cumulative interaction between individuals. Ruesch and Bateson (1968) described communication as the social matrix of psychiatry. In 1956, Bateson et al. formulated the double-bind theory of schizophrenia, relating disturbed communication to the development of mental disorder.

Psychiatry has focused traditionally on verbal rather than nonverbal communication. It was not until 1952, when Birdwhistell published *Introduction to Kinesics,* that psychiatrists began to appreciate more fully other modes of communication. Spiegel and Machotka (1974) integrated behavioral and esthetic concepts to provide a cognitive theory of body messages. They described research strategies in the study of nonverbal communication, noting that most sociologists follow the principle of somatic exclusion, i.e., "the dispensability of the body as an object for study in sociology has been repeatedly affirmed" (p. 81). Sociologists have developed models in which the communicative act is considered a struggle to achieve social order, e.g., Duncan's (1967) axioms on how symbols create and sustain social order. In general, the sociological literature on communication is relevant to social psychiatry and to the concept of the competent community.

Edward Hall (1959, 1966), whose work derives from cultural, ethological, physiological, and psychiatric studies, has written a series of books on culture as communication. He coined the term "proxemics"—the interrelated observations and theories of man's use of space as a specialized elaboration of culture. He listed eight dimensions of the determination of proxemic behavior: postural-sex identifiers; sociofugal-sociopetal orientations; kinesthetic factors; touch, thermal, and olfaction codes; retinal combinations; and voice-loudness scales. Proxemic analysis is pertinent for understanding not only general cultural behavior patterns but also dyadic and group interactions.

The concept of communication is perhaps the most significant common meeting ground of art and science. The cultural aspects of communication are especially relevant to psychiatrists because they are primary determinants of our codification of reality, our ability to relate meaningfully to others, and our attempts to construct and preserve social order both figuratively and literally (Scheflen 1972).

Therapy

Although the term "shaman" refers specifically to a type of Siberian healer, it has a more generic connotation referring to a role complex undertaken by indigenous healers who use "magical," nonscientific modes of treatment. Every cultural group has its shamans, such as Haitian hungans, Navaho hand-tremblers, West Indian obeah men, and Western faith healers. It is not surprising that some shamanistic practices are similar to scientific therapy, e.g., the use of psychopharmacological agents, psychodrama, catharsis abreaction, environmental manipulation, suggestion, occupational and recreational therapy, and direct ego support (Kiev 1964). Some shamanistic procedures, such as exorcism, bandaging, and magical tricks like sucking out evil spirits, may prove effective if the patient and others in the culture have faith in the shaman's abilities. Frequently shamans are able to mobilize family, social network, and community support for the patient. J. M. Murphy (1964) noted that the effective shaman calls on an entire system of beliefs that are widely held and emotionally accepted by a cultural group, dramatically performs the curing ceremony in a group context, awes the group by his or her extraordinary powers, may act as an agent of a spirit, and actively involves the patient in the treatment by prescribing specific activities. She further noted,

> While shamanism appears to have remarkable strength to accomplish its limited aims, it is weak in encouraging independence and producing insight. The effectiveness of shamanism in removing symptoms and giving release from anxiety rests upon the shaman's ability to demonstrate that he can repeatedly be depended upon for these ends.

Although there are some similarities between the shamanistic complex and psychiatric modes of therapy, there are also marked differences (Prince 1964). Despite demonstrated placebo effects in treatment, psychiatrists are not true shamans in modern garb, and it is doubtful that psychiatrists can use shamanistic magical procedures effectively. A solid literature exists on the magical ideas about mental illness and its treatment that are espoused in varying degrees by cultural groups in Western society. Examples include *espiritismo* (Puerto Rican immigrants), *curanderismo* (Mexican-Americans), and root-work (black Americans). Patients often conceal their beliefs. Therefore, a psychiatrist must ask direct questions to obtain this information. For some patients whose belief systems contain magical concepts the psychiatrist may collaborate with or integrate some of the practices of the native healer in providing treatment (Kreisman 1975; Ruiz and Langrod 1976; Pattison 1977).

In 1959 Spiegel reported on his studies of working-class Irish-American, Italian-American, and Yankee families. In 1976 he reported on the enormous changes in his understanding of ethnic groups, noting that although the literature on economic and social class factors involved in psychiatric treatment is voluminous, there are few studies on ethnic factors. He pointed out the assumption of invariance in the "culture of poverty" and "mental health of the poor" conceptualizations:

> Working-class families are assumed to have the same values and perspectives in life. . . . In my opinion, this view is clearly unrealistic. It fails to take into account the tremendous range of variability in values, roles, and cultural perspectives associated with ethnic background. It neglects the degree to which ethnic families may get caught in conflicting values as they undergo social mobility and social change. . . . When ethnicity is combined with social class variation, the therapist must be something of an anthropologist. . . . He should familiarize himself with the childrearing customs and family relationships of the relevant ethnic group. . . . And he should be able to perceive the degree to which the patient's behavior may be bizarre, deviant or conforming—not just to American middle-class standards—but primarily to the values of his social class, ethnic group, and geographical setting (Spiegel 1976).

In regard to transference and countertransference, Spiegel advocated an approach in accordance with the values of the patient's major group affiliations. The construction of a therapeutic alliance must take into consideration the therapist's age, sex, color, name, accent, costume, ethnic background, and degree of ethnocentrism. The therapist must be prepared to give guidance and advice if the patient comes from a cultural background that emphasizes obedience to authority. A pessimistic attitude toward some groups of patients might be the result of a rigid or stereotyped approach of the therapist, an approach that fails to recognize differing cultural values. The Anglo patient who is five minutes late for therapy might be demonstrating resistance; the Mexican-American who is only five minutes late might be demonstrating a positive attitude toward therapy.

Some of the best examples of the importance of a cultural perspective come from mental health consultation. Successful consultation with subcultural groups and agencies in Western countries and with groups and agencies in foreign countries demands an understanding of cultural, political, social, geographic, and economic parameters (Westermeyer and Hausman 1974). The consultant must be aware of ethnocentric staff attitudes that may interfere with effective agency functioning (Hendrie and Hanson 1972; Yamayoto et al. 1967).

Approaches to the Study of Culture

The psychiatrist interested in interpreting cultural data or in doing research should be familiar with specialized concepts and techniques that have been developed to facilitate the study of culture and cultural processes. The culture-and-personality or psychological anthropology movement originated in the United States at the turn of the century. Franz Boas, Margaret Mead, and Ruth Benedict are the most famous of the early figures in its development. Wallace's (1970) volume on the topic, which emphasizes culture and cognition, the cultural distribution of personality characteristics, the psychology of culture change, and culture and mental illness, presents a more contemporary approach to the field. The most recent overview is that of Williams (1976).

Honigmann (1973) outlined the following general formula of culture and personality research: antecedent general social and cultural conditions (such as maintenance systems of culture, economy, and technology) and antecedent noncultural features of human nature (such as basic physiological and psychological needs, prolonged human infancy, and sexual and aggressive instincts) lead to socially patterned childbearing experiences (such as socialization or enculturation, primary institutions, and disciplines), which lead to socially patterned later-life experiences (such as adult socialization, role learning, and critical experiences), which lead to personality (socially patterned features of overt and covert behavior evident in individuals or groups), which leads to culture and society (patterns of culture, social roles, secondary institutions, and ethos), which lead to feedback (i.e., social and cultural conditions may reinforce or validate personality contents and may function to maintain existing socialization procedures).

A great deal of anthropological research deals with the relationship between personality and culture and society. In some studies culture is seen as instrumental in facilitating individual adjustment; in others individual personality is seen as instrumental in maintaining culture. Anthropological research in these areas has focused mainly on eufunction rather than dysfunction, and explanations are often teleological, i.e., events are explained by subsequent rather than antecedent phenomena (Honigmann 1973). A great challenge for cultural psychiatry is the development of research in culture and personality that focuses specifically on the etiology of mental disorder. Other special approaches of significance to psychiatry include ethnography, emic and etic approaches, the cross-cultural approach, and the study of subjective culture.

Ethnography

Ethnography, a technique of documentation of observed phenomena, employs an accounting method that seeks to describe cultural forms inductively through the examination of a series of cases. Among the tools used by ethnographers are participant observation, interviews with key informants, collection of life histories, structured interviews, questionnaires, projective tests, measures of perception, sorting tasks, written records, recorded folk tales and myths, and linguistic analysis. The emphasis of early ethnographic research on description led to criticism of the approach. Proponents of the personal ethnographic approach point to the current shift of emphasis from description to explanation (Honigmann 1976).

The ethnographic approach has a natural appeal to psychiatrists. The use of life charts or lengthy psychoanalysis are both attempts to understand an individual's current situation in a historical context. Few psychiatrists have undertaken a full ethnographic study of a patient. Perhaps the first step would be for a courageous psychiatrist to study the development of a mental illness within the context of his or her own family. There would be major technical problems with such an undertaking, but these could be overcome, possibly through collaborative work in reporting and interpreting the data. Detailed case reports and books that describe a psychiatrist's observations of a patient (usually in an institution) are, in a sense, partial ethnographies. Ethnographies of noninstitutionalized patients might provide important information about cultural influences on the etiology and course of mental illness. The anthropological literature already contains many ethnological studies of medicine and disease in general (Glick 1967; Foster 1976).

Emic and Etic Approaches

Following the distinction in linguistic studies between the phonemics (a system of describing sound in a culture) and phonetics (a system of describing sounds in all cultures), Pike (1966) proposed that cultural phenomena can be studied by emic and etic approaches. The emic approach studies behavior from within the cultural system in order to discover the structure relevant to the informant, i.e., the informant's principles of classification and conceptualization. An etic approach studies behavior from outside the cultural system; the structure is created by the analyst, whose criteria are considered absolute or universal. An emic approach demands that the researcher abandon stereotypes and preconceived notions and that he or she understand the "true inwardness" of a person's beliefs and practices. Among the widely used techniques for an emic approach are componential analysis, kinesics, generative semantics, semantic information processing, and sociolinguistics. The emic/etic distinction focuses our attention on the ways in which subjects or patients may misinterpret the researcher's or therapist's behavior and vice versa. A major criticism of the emic approach, however, is the difficulty in comparing behaviors across cultures when these behaviors are described in terms uniquely meaningful to members of a particular culture. One method of balancing the two approaches is the embedded emic approach, in which the informant provides the basic structure and criteria of category formation from which the researcher draws his or her analytic data (S. Silverman 1966). This was described by Berry (1969) as the imposed-derived etic approach; it has also been discussed by Goodenough (1970).

Cross-Cultural and Holocultural Studies

Brislin et al. (1973) defined the cross-cultural approach as applied to psychology as "the empirical study of members of various culture groups who have had different experiences that lead to predictable and significant differences in behavior. In the majority of such studies, the groups under study speak different languages and are governed by different political units" (p. 29). Those authors compiled a list of instruments that have been used widely in cross-cultural studies: the cognitive-intellectual tests, including Witkin's Cognitive Style Test, Kohs Blocks, and the Porteus Maze; and the personality-inventory tests, including the MMPI, Locus of Control Scale, the California Personality Inventory, and the Semantic Differential. Projective instruments are difficult to evaluate and are conspicuously missing from this list, despite their widespread use in cross-cultural studies. Brislin and associates noted that evaluation of cross-cultural data invariably profits from advanced statistical techniques, especially when more than two cultures are studied.

Campbell (1969) cautioned researchers to consider plausible rival hypotheses that would explain cross-cultural research results.

In each culture studied the researcher must consider such questions about methodology as, How accustomed are the subjects to taking paper and pencil tests? How accustomed are they to responding to lengthy questions? How representative are the subjects (e.g., were only the most cooperative subjects chosen)? Do the questions have the same meanings for subjects in different cultures? Does a subject's culture influence his or her test or interview behavior?

A great many cross-cultural studies are not particularly valid from a scientific point of view. All too frequently what passes as a cross-cultural study is an impressionistic travelogue in which the author briefly observes or tests some subjects in an exotic locale and then comments on differences from mainstream American or European findings. Some studies are the result of "happenstance"—the researcher happens to be in a foreign cultural setting and decides to do a rapid study. This opportunistic approach is often not as productive as possible because the researcher has not chosen his or her methodology or testing instruments with enough forethought.

An expanded cross-cultural approach is the holocultural, which attempts worldwide correlational studies of all known cultures (Naroll 1973). The holocultural approach in great part arose from Murdock's development of the Human Relations Area Files (HRAF) at Yale University. Materials in the HRAF and in associated publications, such as the *Outline of World Cultures* (Murdock 1975), *Outline of Cultural Materials* (Murdock et al, 1971), and the *Ethnographic Atlas* (Murdock 1967) comprise the world's largest categorized compilation of cultural data. Murdock's *Social Structure* (1965) has led to many studies, almost all of which strive to include four key principles of Murdock's work: (1) a representative sample of all the world's primitive cultures, (2) a test of a prestated hypothesis by means of statistical correlations, (3) a significance test to deal with the "freak sample" or null hypothesis, and (4) an objective, formal, and detailed set of concept definitions leading to objective coding (Naroll 1973).

The cross-cultural survey method has had its share of critics (Vermeulen and de Ruijter 1975). One major problem, especially pertinent to psychiatry, is that most existing societies have not been adequately investigated in regard to key concepts. Naroll (1973) estimated that 4,000 to 5,000 human societies have existed in the past century but that only 100 to 150, depending on the topic of investigation, have been described sufficiently for inclusion in holocultural research.

Subjective Culture

Triandis' concept of subjective culture (Triandis 1972) focuses on variables that are attributes of the cognitive structures of groups of people and refers to a cultural group's characteristic way of perceiving its social environment. Subjective culture is similar to such concepts as cognitive maps, life space, world view, behavioral environment, and mazeways.

The strategy of subjective culture studies is to place people who belong to specific cultural or biological groups in similar situations, present them with various stimuli, and observe their responses. Campbell (1963) cited 80 concepts that can be inferred from consistencies in situations and responses. The most useful of these concepts for the study of subjective culture are associations, attitudes, beliefs, concepts (categorization), evaluations, expectations, memories, opinions, percepts, role perceptions, stereotypes, and values.

The literature on each of these concepts is vast; there are over 3,000 references on the topic of values alone. Opler (1945) viewed values as central themes and dynamic forces that cultural groups use in conceptualizing the world. The most widely quoted study of values is that of Kluckhohn and Strodtbeck (1961). They proposed five basic value orientations: (1) innate human nature, (2) man's relationsip to nature, (3) time focus, (4) the modality of human activities, such as striving and goals, and (5) the modality of man's relationship to others. Kluckhohn and Strodtbeck's instrument limits choices and can distinguish 2,688 patterns of ranking that can be used to differentiate one culture from another. Mazer's psychiatric study of the population on Martha's Vineyard (1976) illustrated how knowledge of a subculture's values can influence the selection of mental health services that would be best accepted by a population as well as the best methodology for establishing these services.

Conclusions

In this article we have reviewed prominent concepts and findings from the field of cultural anthropology in the hope of emphasizing the wealth of relevant information and methodologies available for understanding and dealing with a wide range of problems in mental illness. Culture is a holistic concept whose utility goes far beyond the study of exotic tribes in distant locales. Cultural anthropology is pertinent to the study of industrial society in general and the subcultures of modern society in particular. We believe that cultural psychiatry is a concept that has finally arrived and one that will share a central position in the mainstream of psychiatry.

Cultural psychiatry promises no millennium, no bold new approach. Rather, we see the inclusion of the cultural dimension as an essential integrative component of scientific psychiatry (Kennedy 1973). As an application of knowledge from many disciplines, cultural psychiatry has much in common with psychological anthropology, comparative sociology, and cross-cultural psychology, but its ultimate raison d'être is medical—to further our understanding of mental health and to make more effective our efforts to promote health, to alleviate suffering, and to prevent, diagnose, and treat illness.

2

The Need for a New Medical Model: A Challenge for Biomedicine

George L. Engel

G. L. Engel, using his experience as both a professor of psychiatry and a professor of medicine and his long standing interest in holistic approaches to medical study and care, discusses the limitations of the reductionist biomedical model. He then proposes an alternative conceptualization, which is a bio-psycho-social model of medicine in general and psychiatry in particular. To this purpose he cogently uses the elegant anthropological and epistemological analyses carried out by Fabrega (1975) in search for an ethnomedical science.

Such a comprehensive reformulation of the notions of disease and medical care has rough waters to sail given the entrenchment of the biomedical model, which, as noted by Fabrega (1975b, 1977) has become the folk model of disease in the Western world.

AT A recent conference on psychiatric education, many psychiatrists seemed to be saying to medicine, "Please take us back and we will never again deviate from the 'medical model.'" For, as one critical psychiatrist put it, "Psychiatry has become a hodgepodge of unscientific opinions, assorted philosophies and 'schools of thought,' mixed metaphors, role diffusion, propaganda, and politicking for 'mental health' and other esoteric goals" (Ludwig 1975). In contrast, the rest of medicine appears neat and tidy. It has a firm base in the biological sciences, enormous technologic resources at its command, and a record of astonishing achievement in elucidating mechanisms of disease and devising new treatments. It would seem that psychiatry would do well to emulate its sister medical disciplines by finally embracing once and for all the medical model of disease.

But I do not accept such a premise. Rather, I contend that all medicine is in crisis and, further, that medicine's crisis derives from the same basic fault as psychiatry's, namely, adherence to a model of disease no longer adequate for the scientific tasks and social responsibilities of either medicine or psychiatry. The importance of how physicians conceptualize disease derives from how such concepts determine what are considered the proper boundaries of professional responsibility and how they influence attitudes toward and behavior with patients. Psychiatry's crisis revolves around the question of whether the categories of human distress with which it is concerned are properly considered "disease" as currently conceptualized and whether exercise of the traditional authority of the physician is appropriate for their helping functions. Medicine's crisis stems from the logical inference that since "disease" is defined in terms of somatic parameters, physicians need not be concerned with psychosocial issues which lie outside medicine's responsibility and authority. At a recent Rockefeller Foundation seminar on the concept of health, one authority urged that medicine "concentrate on the 'real' diseases and not get lost in the psychosociological underbrush. The physician should not be saddled with problems that have arisen from the abdication of the theologian and the philosopher." Another participant called for "a disentanglement of the organic elements of disease from the psychosocial elements of human malfunction," arguing that medicine should deal with the former only (RF Illustrated 1976).

The Two Positions

Psychiatrists have responded to their crisis by embracing two ostensibly opposite positions. One would simply exclude psychiatry from the field of medicine, while the other would adhere strictly to the "medical model" and limit psychiatry's field to behavioral disorders consequent to brain dysfunction. The first is exemplified in the writings of Szasz and others who advance the position that "mental illness is a myth" since it does not conform with the accepted concept of disease (Szasz 1961; Torrey 1974). Supporters of this position advocate the removal of the functions now performed by psychiatry from the conceptual and professional jurisdiction of medicine and their reallocation to a new discipline based on behavioral science. Henceforth medicine would be responsible for the treatment and cure of disease, while the new discipline would be concerned with the reeducation of people with "problems of living." Implicit in this argument is the premise that while the medical model constitutes a sound framework within which to understand and treat disease, it is not relevant to the behavioral and psychological problems classically deemed the domain of psychiatry. Disorders directly ascribable to brain disorder would be taken care of by neurologists, while psychiatry as such would disappear as a medical discipline.

The contrasting posture of strict adherence to the medical model is caricatured in Ludwig's view of the psychiatrist as physician (Ludwig 1975). According to Ludwig, the medical model premises "that sufficient deviation from normal represents *disease,* that disease is due to known or unknown natural causes, and that elimination of these causes will result in cure or improvement in individual patients" (Ludwig's italics). While acknowledging that most psychiatric diagnoses have a lower level of confirmation than most medical diagnoses, he adds that they are not "qualitatively different provided that mental disease is assumed to arise largely from 'natural' rather than metapsychological, interpersonal or societal causes." "Natural" is defined as "biological brain dysfunctions, either biochemcial or neurophysiological in nature." On the other hand, "disorders such as problems of living, social adjustment reactions, character disorders, dependency syndromes, existential depressions, and various social deviancy conditions [would] be excluded from the concept of mental illness since these disorders arise in individuals with presumably intact neurophysiological functioning and are produced primarily by psychosocial variables." Such "non-psychiatric disorders" are not properly the concern of the physician-psychiatrist and are more appropriately handled by nonmedical professionals.

In sum, psychiatry struggles to clarify its status within the mainstream of medicine, if indeed it belongs in medicine at all. The criterion by which this question is supposed to be resolved rests on the degree to which the field of activity of psychiatry is deemed congruent with the existing medical model of disease. But crucial to this problem is another, that of whether the contemporary model is, in fact, any longer adequate for medicine, much less for psychiatry. For if it is not, then perhaps the crisis of psychiatry is part and parcel of a larger crisis that has its roots in the model itself. Should that be the case, then it would be imprudent for psychiatry prematurely to abandon its models in favor of one that may also be flawed.

The Biomedical Model

The dominant model of disease today is biomedical, with molecular biology its basic scientific discipline. It assumes disease to be fully accounted for by deviations from the norm of measurable biological (somatic) variables. It leaves no room within its framework for the social, psychological, and behavioral dimensions of illness. The biomedical model not only requires that disease be dealt with as an entity independent of social behavior, it also demands that behavioral aberrations be explained on the basis of disordered somatic (biochemical or neurophysiological) processes. Thus the biomedical model embraces both reductionism, the philosophic view that complex phenomena are ultimately derived from a single primary principle, and mind-body dualism, the doctrine that separates the mental from the somatic. Here the reductionistic primary principle is physicalistic; that is, it assumes that the language of chemistry and physics will ultimately suffice to explain biological phenomena. From the reductionist viewpoint, the only conceptual tools available to characterize and experimental tools to study biological systems are physical in nature (Rosen 1972).

The biomedical model was devised by medical scientists for the study of disease. As such it was a scientific model; that is, it involved a shared set of assumptions and rules of conduct based on the scientific method and constituted a blueprint for research. Not all models are scientific. Indeed, broadly defined, a model is nothing more than a belief system utilized to explain natural phenomena, to make sense out of what is puzzling or disturbing. The more socially disruptive or individually upsetting the phenomenon, the more pressing the need of humans to devise explanatory systems. Such efforts at explanation constitute devices for social adaptation. Disease par excellence exemplifies a category of natural phenomena urgently demanding explanation. As Fabrega (1975b) has pointed out, "disease" in its generic sense is a linguistic term used to refer to a certain class of phenomena that members of all social groups, at all times in the history of man, have been exposed to. "When people of various intellectual and cultural persuasions use terms analogous to 'disease,' they have in mind, among other things, that the phenomena in question involve a person-centered, harmful, and undesirable deviation or discontinuity . . . associated with impairment or discomfort. Since the condition is not desired it gives rise to a need for corrective actions. The latter involve beliefs and explanations about disease as well as rules of conduct to rationalize treatment actions. These constitute socially adaptive devices to resolve, for the individual as well as for the society in which the sick person lives, the crises and uncertainties surrounding disease (Fabrega 1975b).

Such culturally derived belief systems about disease also constitute models, but they are not scientific models. These may be referred to as popular or folk models. As efforts at social adaptation, they contrast with scientific models, which are primarily designed to promote scientific investigation. The historical fact we have to face is that in modern Western society biomedicine not only has provided a basis for the scientific study of disease, it has also become our own culturally specific perspective about disease, that is, our folk model. Indeed the biomedical model is now the dominant folk model of disease in the Western world (Fabrega 1972, 1975b).

In our culture the attitudes and belief systems of physicians are molded by this model long before they embark on their professional education, which in turn reinforces it without necessarily clarifying how its use for social adaptation contrasts with its use for scientific research. The biomedical model has thus become a cultural imperative, its limitations easily overlooked. In brief, it has now acquired the status of *dogma.* In science, a model is revised or abandoned when it fails to account adequately for all the data. A dogma, on the other hand, requires that discrepant data be forced to fit the model or be excluded. Biomedical dogma requires that all disease, including "mental" disease, be conceptualized in terms of derangement of underlying physical mechanisms. This permits only two alternatives whereby behavior and disease can be reconciled: the *reductionist,* which says that all behavioral phenomena of disease must be conceptualized in terms of physicochemical principles; and the *exclusionist,* which says that whatever is not capable of being so explained must be excluded from the category of disease. The reductionists concede that some disturbances in behavior belong in the spectrum of disease. They categorize these as mental diseases and designate psychiatry as the relevant medical discipline. The exclusionists regard mental illness as a myth and would eliminate psychiatry from medicine.

Among physicians and psychiatrists today the reductionists are the true believers, the exclusionists are the apostates, while both condemn as heretics those who dare to question the ultimate truth of the biomedical model and advocate a more useful model.

Historical Origins of the Reductionistic Biomedical Model

In considering the requirements for a more inclusive scientific medical model for the study of disease, an ethnomedical perspective is helpful (Fabrega 1975b). In all societies, ancient and modern, preliterate and literate, the major criteria for identification of disease have always been behavioral, psychological, and social in nature. Classically, the onset of disease is marked by changes in physical appearance that frighten, puzzle, or awe, and by alterations in functioning, in feelings, in performance, in behavior, or in relationships that are experienced or perceived as threatening, harmful, unpleasant, deviant, undesirable, or unwanted. Reported verbally or demonstrated by the sufferer or by a witness, these constitute the primary data upon which are based first-order judgments as to whether or not a person is sick (Engel 1973). To such disturbing behavior and reports all societies typically respond by designating individuals and evolving social institutions whose primary function is to evaluate, interpret, and provide corrective measures (Fabrega 1972, 1975b). Medicine as an institution and as a discipline, and physicians as professionals, evolved as one form of response to such social needs. In the course of history, medicine became scientific as physicians and other scientists developed a taxonomy and applied scientific methods to the understanding, treatment, and prevention of disturbances which the public first had designated as "disease" or "sickness."

Why did the reductionistic, dualistic biomedical model evolve in the West? Rasmussen identifies one source in the concession of established Christian orthodoxy to permit dissection of the human body some five centuries ago (Rasmussen 1975). Such a concession was in keeping with the Christian view of the body as a weak and imperfect vessel for the transfer of the soul from this world to the next. Not surprisingly, the Church's permission to study the human body included a tacit interdiction against corresponding scientific investigation of man's mind and behavior. For in the eyes of the Church these had more to do with religion and the soul and hence properly remained its domain. This compact may be considered largely responsible for the anatomical and structural base upon which scientific Western medicine eventually was to be built. For at the same time, the basic principle of the science of the day, as enunciated by Galileo, Newton, and Descartes, was analytical, meaning that entities to be investigated be resolved into isolable causal chains or units, from which it was assumed that the whole could be understood, both materially and conceptually, by reconstituting the parts. With mind-body dualism firmly established under the imprimatur of the Church, classical science readily fostered the notion of the body as a machine, of disease as the consequence of breakdown of the machine, and of the doctor's task as repair of the machine. Thus, the scientific approach to disease began by focusing in a fractional-analytic way on biological (somatic) processes and ignoring the behavioral and psychosocial. This was so even though in practice many physicians, at least until the beginning of the twentieth century, regarded emotions as important for the development and course of disease. Actually, such arbitrary exclusion is an acceptable strategy in scientific research, especially when concepts and methods appropriate for the excluded areas are not yet available. But it becomes counterproductive when such strategy becomes policy and the area originally put aside for practical reasons is permanently excluded, if not forgotten altogether. The greater the success of the narrow approach the more likely is this to happen. The biomedical approach to disease has been successful beyond all expectations, but at a cost. For in serving as guideline and justification for medical care policy, biomedicine has also contributed to a host of problems, which I shall consider later.

Limitations of the Biomedical Model

We are now faced with the necessity and the challenge to broaden the approach to disease to include the psychosocial without sacrificing the enormous advantages of the biomedical approach. On the importance of the latter all agree. the reductionist, the exclusionist, and the heretic. In a recent critique of the exclusionist position, Kety put the contrast between the two in such a way as to help define the issues (Kety 1974). "According to the medical model, a human illness does not become a specific disease all at once and is not equivalent to it. The medical model of an illness is a process that moves from the recognition and palliation of symptoms to the characterization of a specific disease in which the etiology and pathogenesis are known and treatment is rational and specific." Thus taxonomy progresses from symptoms, to clusters of symptoms, to syndromes, and finally to diseases with specific pathogenesis and pathology. This sequence accurately describes the successful application of the scientific method to the elucidation and the classification into discrete entities of disease in its generic sense (Fabrega 1970, 1975b). The merit of such an approach needs no argument. What do require scrutiny are the distortions introduced by the reductionistic tendency to regard the specific disease as adequately, if not best, characterized in terms of the smallest isolable component having causal implications, for example, the biochemical; or even more critical, is the contention that the designation "disease" does not apply in the absence of perturbations at the biochemical level.

Kety approaches this problem by comparing diabetes mellitus and schizophrenia as paradigms of somatic and mental diseases, pointing out the appropriateness of the medical model for both. "Both are symptom clusters or syndromes, one described by somatic and biochemical abnormalities, the other by psychological. Each may have many etiologies and shows a range of intensity from severe and debilitating to latent or borderline. There is also evidence that genetic and environmental influences operate in the development of both." In this description, at least in reductionistic terms, the scientific characterization of diabetes is more advanced in that it has progressed from the behavioral framework of symptoms to that of biochemical abormalities. Ultimately, the reductionists assume schizophrenia will achieve a similar degree of resolution. In developing his position Kety makes clear that he does not regard the genetic factors and biological processes in schizophrenia as are now known to exist (or may be discovered in the future) as the only important influences in its etiology. He insists that equally important is elucidation of "how experiential factors and their interactions with biological vulnerability make possible or prevent the development of schizophrenia." But whether such a caveat will suffice to counteract basic reductionism is far from certain.

The Requirements of a New Medical Model

To explore the requirements of a medical model that would account for the reality of diabetes and schizophrenia as human experiences as well as disease abstractions, let us expand Kety's analogy by making the assumption that a specific biochemical abnormality capable of being influenced pharmacologically exists in schizophrenia as well as in diabetes, certainly a plausible possibility. By obliging ourselves to think of patients with diabetes, a "somatic disease," and with schizophrenia, a "mental disease," in exactly the same terms, we shall see more clearly how inclusion of somatic and psychosocial factors is indispensable for both; or more pointedly, how concentration on the biomedical and exclusion of the psychosocial distorts perspectives and even interferes with patient care.

(1) In the biomedical model, demonstration of the specific biochemical deviation is generally regarded as a specific diagnostic criterion for the disease. Yet in terms of the human experience of illness, laboratory documentation may only indicate disease potential, not the actuality of the disease at the time. The abnormality may be present, yet the patient not be ill. Thus the presence of the biochemical defect of diabetes or schizophrenia at best defines a necessary but not a sufficient condition for the occurrence of the human experience of the disease, the illness. More accurately, the biochemical defect constitutes but one factor among many, the complex interaction of which ultimately may culminate in active disease or manifest illness (Engel 1960). Nor can the biochemical defect be made to account for all of the illness, for full understanding requires additional concepts and frames of reference. Thus, while the diagnosis of diabetes is first suggested by certain core clinical manifestations, for example, polyuria, polydipsia, polyphagia, and weight loss, and is then confirmed by laboratory documentation of relative insulin deficiency, how these are experienced and how they are reported by any one individual, and how they affect him, all require consideration of psychological, social, and cultural factors, not to mention other concurrent or complicating biological factors. Variability in the clinical expression of diabetes as well as of schizophrenia, and in the individual experience and expression of these illnesses, reflects as much these other elements as it does quantitative variations in the specific biochemical defect.

(2) Establishing a relationship between particular biochemical processes and the clinical data of illness requires a scientifically

rational approach to behavioral and psychosocial data, for these are the terms in which most clinical phenomena are reported by patients. Without such, the reliability of observations and the validity of correlations will be flawed. It serves little to be able to specify a biochemical defect in schizophrenia if one does not know how to relate this to particular psychological and behavioral expressions of the disorder. The biomedical model gives insufficient heed to this requirement. Instead it encourages bypassing the patient's verbal account by placing greater reliance on technical procedures and laboratory measurements. In actuality the task is appreciably more complex than the biomedical model encourages one to believe. An examination of the correlations between clinical and laboratory data requires not only reliable methods of clinical data collection, specifically high-level interviewing skills, but also basic understanding of the psychological, social, and cultural determinants of how patients communicate symptoms of disease. For example, many verbal expressions derive from bodily experiences early in life, resulting in a significant degree of ambiguity in the language patients use to report symptoms. Hence the same words may serve to express primary psychological as well as bodily disturbances, both of which may coexist and overlap in complex ways. Thus, virtually each of the symptoms classically associated with diabetes may also be expressions of or reactions to psychological distress, just as ketoacidosis and hypoglycemia may induce psychiatric manifestations, including some considered characteristic of schizophrenia. The most essential skills of the physician involve the ability to elicit accurately and then analyze correctly the patient's verbal account of his illness experience. The biomedical model ignores both the rigor required to achieve reliability in the interview process and the necessity to analyze the meaning of the patient's report in psychological, social, and cultural as well as in anatomical, physiological, or biochemical terms (Engel 1973).

(3) Diabetes and schizophrenia have in common the fact that conditions of life and living constitute significant variables influencing the time of reported onset of the manifest disease as well as of variations in its course. In both conditions this results from the fact that psychophysiologic responses to life change may interact with existing somatic factors to alter susceptibility and thereby influence the time of onset, the severity, and the course of a disease. Experimental studies in animals amply document the role of early, previous, and current life experience in altering susceptibility to a wide variety of diseases even in the presence of a genetic predisposition

(Ader 1973; Engel 1974). Cassel's demonstration of higher rates of ill health among populations exposed to incongruity between the demands of the social system in which they are living and working and the culture they bring with them provides another illustration among humans of the role of psychosocial variables in disease causation (Cassel 1964).

(4) Psychological and social factors are also crucial in determining whether and when patients with the biochemical abnormality of diabetes or of schizophrenia come to view themselves or be viewed by others as sick. Still other factors of a similar nature influence whether or not and when any individual enters a health care system and becomes a patient. Thus, the biochemical defect may determine certain characteristics of the disease, but not necessarily the point in time when the person falls ill or accepts the sick role or the status of a patient.

(5) "Rational treatment" (Kety's term) directed only at the biochemical abnormality does not necessarily restore the patient to health even in the face of documented correction or major alleviation of the abnormality. This is no less true for diabetes than it will be for schizophrenia when a biochemical defect is established. Other factors may combine to sustain patienthood even in the face of biochemical recovery. Conspicuously responsible for such discrepancies between correction of biological abnormalities and treatment outcome are psychological and social variables.

(6) Even witn the application of rational therapies, the behavior of the physician and the relationship between patient and physician powerfully influence therapeutic outcome for better or for worse. These constitute psychological effects which may directly modify the illness experience or indirectly affect underlying biochemical processes, the latter by virtue of interactions between psychophysiological reactions and biochemical processes implicated in the disease (Ader 1973; Engel 1974). Thus, insulin requirements of a diabetic patient may fluctuate significantly depending on how the patient perceives his relationship with his doctor. Furthermore, the successful application of rational therapies is limited by the physician's ability to influence and modify the patient's behavior in directions concordant with health needs. Contrary to what the exclusionists would have us believe, the physician's role is, and always has been, very much that of educator and psychotherapist. To know how to induce peace of mind in the patient and enhance his faith in the healing powers of his physician requires psychological knowledge and skills, not merely charisma. These too are outside the biomedical framework.

The Advantages of a Bio-psycho-social Model

This list surely is not complete but it should suffice to document that diabetes mellitus and schizophrenia as paradigms of "somatic" and "mental" disorders are entirely analogous and, as Kety argues, are appropriately conceptualized within the framework of a medical model of disease. But the existing biomedical model does not suffice. To provide a basis for understanding the determinants of disease and arriving at rational treatments and patterns of health care, a medical model must also take into account the patient, the social context in which he lives, and the complementary system devised by society to deal with the disruptive effects of illness, that is, the physician's role and the health care system. This requires a bio-psycho-social model. Its scope is determined by the historic function of the physician to establish whether the person soliciting help is "sick" or "well": and if sick, why sick and in which ways sick; and then to develop a rational program to treat the illness and restore and maintain health.

The boundaries between health and disease, between well and sick, are far from clear and never will be clear, for they are diffused by cultural, social, and psychological considerations. The traditional biomedical view, that biological indices are the ultimate criteria defining disease, leads to the present paradox that some people with positive laboratory findings are told that they are in need of treatment when in fact they are feeling quite well, while others feeling sick are assured that they are well, that is, they have no "disease" (Fabrega 1972, 1975b). A bio-psycho-social model which includes the patient as well as the illness would encompass both circumstances. The doctor's task is to account for the dysphoria and the dysfunction which lead individuals to seek medical help, adopt the sick role, and accept the status of patienthood. He must weigh the relative contributions of social and psychological as well as of biological factors implicated in the patient's dysphoria and dysfunction as well as in his decision to accept or not accept patienthood and with it the responsibility to cooperate in his own health care.

By evaluating all the factors contributing to both illness and patienthood, rather than giving primacy to biological factors alone, a bio-psycho-social model would make it possible to explain why some individuals experience as "illness" conditions which others regard merely as "problems of living," be they emotional reactions to life circumstances or somatic symptoms. For from the individual's point of view his decision between whether he has a "problem of living" or is "sick" has basically to do with whether or not he accepts the sick role and seeks entry into the health care system, not with what, in fact, is responsible for his distress. Indeed, some people deny the unwelcome reality of illness by dismissing as "a problem of living" symptoms which may in actuality be indicative of a serious organic process. It is the doctor's, not the patient's, responsibility to establish the nature of the problem and to decide whether or not it is best handled in a medical framework. Clearly the dichotomy between "disease" and "problems of living" is by no means a sharp one, either for patient or for doctor.

When Is Grief a Disease?

To enhance our understanding of how it is that "problems of living" are experienced as illness by some and not by others, it might be helpful to consider grief as a paradigm of such a borderline condition. For while grief has never been considered in a medical framework, a significant number of grieving people do consult doctors because of disturbing symptoms, which they do not necessarily relate to grief. Fifteen years ago I addresed this question in a paper entitled "Is grief a disease? A challenge for medical research" (Engel 1961). Its aim too was to raise questions about the adequacy of the biomedical model. A better title might have been "*When* is grief a disease?" just as one might ask when schizophrenia or when diabetes is a disease. For while there are some obvious analogies between grief and disease, there are also some important differences. But these very contradictions help to clarify the psychosocial dimensions of the biopsycho-social model.

Grief clearly exemplifies a situation in which psychological factors are primary; no preexisting chemical or physiological defects or agents need be invoked. Yet as with classic diseases, ordinary grief constitutes a discrete syndrome with a relatively predictable symptomatology which includes, incidentally, both bodily and psychological disturbances. It displays the autonomy typical of disease; that is, it runs its course despite the sufferer's efforts or wish to bring it to a close. A consistent etiologic factor can be identified, namely, a significant loss. On the other hand, neither the sufferer nor society has ever dealt with ordinary grief as an illness even though such expressions as "sick with grief" would indicate some connection in people's minds. And while every culture makes provisions for the mourner, these have generally been regarded more as the responsibility of religion than of medicine.

On the face of it, the arguments against including grief in a medical model would seem to be the more persuasive. In the 1961 paper I countered these by comparing grief to a wound. Both are natural responses to environmental trauma, one psychological, the other physical. But even at the time I felt a vague uneasiness that this analogy did not quite make the case. Now, two decades later, a better grasp of the cultural origins of disease concepts and medical care systems clarifies the apparent inconsistency. The critical factor underlying man's need to develop folk models of disease, and to develop social adaptations to deal with the individual and group disruptions brought about by disease, has always been the victim's ignorance of what is responsible for his dysphoric or disturbing experience (Fabrega 1972, 1975b). Neither grief nor a wound fits fully into that category. In both, the reasons for the pain, suffering, and disability are only too clear. Wounds or fractures incurred in battle or by accident by and large were self-treated or ministered to with folk remedies or by individuals who had acquired certain technical skills in such matters. Surgery developed out of the need for treatment of wounds and injuries and has different historical roots than medicine, which was always closer in origin to magic and religion. Only later in Western history did surgery and medicine merge as healing arts. But even from earliest times there were people who behaved as though grief-stricken, yet seemed not to have suffered any loss; and others who developed what for all the world looked like wounds or fractures, yet had not been subjected to any known trauma. And there were people who suffered losses whose grief deviated in one way or another from what the culture had come to accept as the normal course; and others whose wounds failed to heal or festered or who became ill even though the wound had apparently healed. Then, as now, two elements were crucial in defining the role of patient and physician and hence in determining what should be regarded as disease. For the patient it has been his not knowing why he felt or functioned badly or what to do about it, coupled with the belief or knowledge that the healer or physician did know and could provide relief. For the physician in turn it has been his commitment to his professional role as healer. From these have evolved sets of expectations which are reinforced by culture, though these are not necessarily the same for patient as for physician.

A bio-psycho-social model would take all of these factors into account. It would acknowledge the fundamental fact that the patient comes to the physician because he does not know what is wrong or, if he does, he feels incapable of helping himself. The psychobiological unity of man requires that the physician accept the responsiblity to evaluate whatever problems the patient presents and recommend a course of action, including referral to other helping professions. Hence the physician's basic professional knowledge and skills must span the social, psychological, and biological, for his decisions and actions on the patient's behalf involve all three. Is the patient suffering normal grief or melancholia? Are the fatigue and weakness of the woman who recently lost her husband conversion symptoms, psychophysiological reactions, manifestations of a somatic disorder, or a combination of these? The patient soliciting the aid of a physician must have confidence that the M.D. degree has indeed rendered that physician competent to make such differentiations.

A Challenge for Both Medicine and Psychiatry

The development of a bio-psycho-social medical model is posed as a challenge for both medicine and psychiatry. For despite the enormous gains which have accrued from biomedical research, there is a growing uneasiness among the public as well as among physicians, and especially among the younger generation, that health needs are not being met and that biomedical research is not having a sufficient impact in human terms. This is usually ascribed to the all too obvious inadequacies of existing health care systems. But this certainly is not a complete explanation, for many who do have adequate access to health care also complain that physicians are lacking in interest and understanding, are preoccupied with procedures, and are insensitive to the personal problems of patients and their families. Medical institutions are seen as cold and impersonal; the more prestigious they are as centers for biomedical research, the more common such complaints (Duff and Hollingshead 1968). Medicine's unrest derives from a growing awareness among many physicians of the contradiction between the excellence of their biomedical background on the one hand and the weakness of their qualifications in certain attributes essential for good patient care on the other (Engel 1973). Many recognize that these cannot be improved by working within the biomedical model alone.

The present upsurge of interest in primary care and family medicine clearly reflects disenchantment among some physicians with an approach to disease that neglects the patient. They are now more ready for a medical model which would take psychosocial issues into account. Sharp challenges to biomedical dogmatism are coming even from within academic circles (Rasmussen 1975; Holman 1976). Thus Holman ascribes directly to biomedical reductionism and to the professional dominance of its adherents over the health care system such undesirable practices as unnecessary hospitalization, overuse of drugs, excessive surgery, and inappropriate utilization of diagnostic tests. He writes, "While reductionism is a powerful tool for understanding, it also creates profound misunderstanding when unwisely applied. Reductionism is particularly harmful when it neglects the impact of nonbiological circumstances upon biologic processes." And, "Some medical outcomes are inadequate not because appropriate technical interventions are lacking but because our conceptual thinking is inadequate" (Holman 1976). How ironic it would be were psychiatry to insist on subscribing to a medical model which some leaders in medicine already are beginning to question.

Psychiatrists, unconsciously committed to the biomedical model and split into the warring camps of reductionists and exclusionists, are today so preoccupied with their own professional identity and status in relation to medicine that many are failing to appreciate that psychiatry now is the only clinical discipline within medicine concerned primarily with the study of man and the human condition. While the behavioral sciences have made some limited incursions into medical school teaching programs, it is mainly upon psychiatrists, and to a lesser extent clinical psychologists, that the responsibility falls to develop approaches to the understanding of health and disease and patient care not readily accomplished within the more narrow framework and with the specialized techniques of traditional biomedicine. Indeed, the fact is that the major formulations of more integrated and holistic concepts of health and disease proposed in the past 30 years have come not from within the biomedical establishment but from physicians who have drawn upon concepts and methods which originated within psychiatry, notably the psychodynamic approach of Sigmund Freud and psychoanalysis and the reaction-to-life-stress approach of Adolf Meyer and psychobiology (Menninger 1948; Romano 1950; Engel 1953; Wolff 1960; Engel 1962). Actually, one of the more lasting contributions of both Freud and Meyer has been to provide frames of reference whereby psychological processes could be included in a concept of disease. Psychosomatic medicine—the term itself a vestige of dualism—became the medium whereby the gap between the two parallel but independent ideologies of medicine, the biological and the psychosocial, was to be bridged. Its progress has been slow and halting, not only because of the extreme complexities intrinsic to the field itself, but also because of unremitting pressures, from within as well as from without, to conform to scientific methodologies basically mechanistic and reductionistic in conception and inappropriate for many of the problems under study. Nonetheless, by now a sizable body of knowledge, based on clinical and experimental studies of man and animals has accumulated. Most, however, remains unknown to the general medical public and to the biomedical community and is largely ignored in the education of physicians. The recent solemn pronouncement by an eminent biomedical leader (RF Illustrated 1976) that "the emotional content of organic medicine [has been] exaggerated" and "psychosomatic medicine is on the way out" can only be ascribed to the blinding effects of dogmatism.

The fact is that medical schools have constituted unreceptive if not hostile environments for those interested in psychosomatic research and teaching, and medical journals have all too often followed a double standard in accepting papers dealing with psychosomatic relationships (Engel and Salzman 1973). Further, much of the work documenting experimentally in animals the significance of life circumstances or change in altering susceptibility to disease has been done by experimental psychologists and appears in psychology journals rarely read by physicians or basic biomedical scientists (Ader 1973; Engel 1974).

General Systems Theory Perspective

The struggle to reconcile the psychosocial and the biological in medicine has had its parallel in biology, also dominated by the reductionistic approach of molecular biology. Among biologists too have emerged advocates of the need to develop holistic as well as reductionistic explanations of life processes, to answer the "why?" and the "what for?" as well as the "how?" (Dubos 1959, 1970; Mayr 1961a, 1974; Bonner 1974; Simpson 1963; Dubos 1965). Von Bertalanffy, arguing the need for a more fundamental reorientation in scientific perspectives in order to open the way to holistic approaches more amenable to scientific inquiry and conceptualization, developed general systems theory (von Bertalanffy 1952, 1968; Laszlo 1972; Dubos 1965). This approach, by treating sets of related events collectively as systems manifesting functions and properties on the specific level of the whole, has made possible recognition of isomorphies across different levels of organization, as molecules, cells, organs, the organism, the person, the family, the society, or the biosphere. From such isomorphies can be developed fundamental laws and principles that operate commonly at all levels of organization, as compared to those which are unique for each. Since systems theory holds that all levels of organization are linked to each other in a hierarchical relationship so that change in one affects change in the others, its adoption as a scientific approach should do much to mitigate the holist-reductionist dichotomy and improve communication across scientific disciplines. For medicine, systems theory provides a conceptual approach suitable not only for the proposed bio-psycho-social concept of disease but also for studying disease and medical care as interrelated processes (Engel 1960; Menninger 1963; Sheldon 1970; Brody 1973). If and when a general-systems approach becomes part of the basic scientific and philosophic education of future physicians and medical scientists, a greater readiness to encompass a bio-psycho-social perspective of disease may be anticipated.

Biomedicine as Science and as Dogma

In the meantime, what is being done and what can be done to neutralize the dogmatism of biomedicine and all the undesirable social and scientific consequences that flow therefrom? How can a proper balance be established between the fractional-analytic and the natural history approaches, both so integral for the work of the physician and the medical scientist (Engel 1972)? How can the clinician be helped to understand the extent to which his scientific approach to patients represents a distincly "human science," one in which "reliance is on the integrative powers of the observer of a complex nonreplicable event and on the experiments that are provided by history and by animals living in particular ecological settings," as Margaret Mead (1976) puts it? The history of the rise and fall of scientific dogmas throughout history may give some clues. Certainly mere emergence of new findings and theories rarely suffices to overthrow well-entrenched dogmas. The power of vested interests, social, political, and economic, are formidable deterrents to any effective assault on biomedical dogmatism. The delivery of health care is a major industry, considering that more than 8 percent of our national economic product is devoted to health (RF Illustrated 1976). The enormous existing and planned investment in diagnostic and therapeutic technology alone strongly favors approaches to clinical study and care of patients that emphasize the impersonal and the mechanical (Engel 1976a). For example, from 1967 to 1972 there was an increase of 33 percent in the number of laboratory tests conducted per hospital admission (McGinnis 1976). Planning for systems of medical care and their financing is excessively influenced by the availability and promise of technology, the application and effectiveness of which are often used as the criteria by which decisions are made as to what constitutes illness and who qualifies for medical care. The frustration of those who find what they believe to be their legitimate health needs inadequately met by too technologically oriented physicians is generally misinterpreted by the biomedical establishment as indicating "unrealistic expectations" on the part of the public rather than being recognized as reflecting a genuine discrepancy between illness as actually experienced by the patient and as it is conceptualized in biomedical circles (Fabrega and Manning 1973). The professionalization of biomedicine constitutes still another formidable barrier (Rasmussen 1975; Holman 1976). Professionalization has engendered a caste system among health care personnel and a pecking order concerning what are appropriate areas for medical concern and care, with the most esoteric disorders at the top of the list. Professional dominance "has perpetuated prevailing practices, deflected criticisms, and insulated the profession from alternate views and social relations that would illuminate and improve health care" (Holman 1976). Holman argues, not unconvincingly, that "the Medical establishment is not primarily engaged in the disinterested pursuit of knowledge and the translation of that knowledge into medical practice; rather in significant part it is engaged in special interest advocacy, pursuing and preserving social power" (Holman 1976).

Under such conditions it is difficult to see how reforms can be brought about. Certainly contributing another critical essay is hardly likely to bring about any major changes in attitude. The problem is hardly new, for the first efforts to introduce a more holistic approach into the undergraduate medical curriculum actually date back to Adoph Meyer's program at Johns Hopkins, which was initiated before 1920 (Meyer 1917). At Rochester, a program directed to medical students and to physicians during and after their residency training, and designed to inculcate psychosocial knowledge and skills appropriate for their future work as clinicians or teachers, has been in existence for 30 years (Schmale et al. 1964; Engel 1967; Young 1975). While difficult to measure outcome objectively, its impact, as indicated by a questionnaire on how students and graduates view the issues involved in illness and patient care, appears to have been appreciable (Engel 1972). In other schools, especially in the immediate post-World War II period, similar efforts were launched, and while some flourished briefly, most soon faded away under the competition of more glamorous and acceptable biomedical careers. Today, within many medical schools there is again a revival of interest among some faculty, but they are few in number and lack the influence, prestige, power, and access to funding from peer review groups that goes with conformity to the prevailing biomedical structure.

Yet today, interest among students and young physicians is high, and where learning opportunities exist they quickly overwhelm the available meager resources. It would appear that given the opportunity, the younger generation is very ready to accept the importance of learning more about the psychosocial dimensions of illness and health care and the need for such education to be soundly based on scientific principles. Once exposed to such an approach, most recognize how ephemeral and insubstantial are appeals to humanism and compassion when not based on rational principles. They reject as simplistic the notion that in past generations doctors understood their patients better, a myth that has persisted for centuries (Engel 1976b). Clearly, the gap to be closed is between teachers ready to teach and students eager to learn. But nothing will change unless or until those who control resources have the wisdom to venture off the beaten path of reliance on biomedicine as the only approach to health care. The proposed bio-psycho-social model provides a blueprint for research, a framework for teaching, and a design for action in the real world of health care. Whether it is useful or not remains to be seen. But the answer will not be forthcoming if conditions are not provided to do so. In a free society, outcome will depend upon those who have the courage to try new paths and the wisdom to provide the necessary support.

3

Culture and Mental Illness: A Social Labeling Perspective

Nancy E. Waxler

The implementation of the notion that sociocultural factors play a significant role in the etiology and course of mental disorders requires the formulation of theories explaining and articulating the processes involved. This is also necessary for substantiating and guiding decisions aimed at improving individual patient care and public health.

An example of such a theory is proposing that social change has a causative role in pyschopathology, as suggested by Leighton (1959) and many others. This role may be quite different in regard to the severe psychoses versus the milder neurotic and adjustment disorders (see part V). Another example is labeling or social response theory. Some interpretations of this theory have been directed to the explanation of the development of mental disorders and this sometimes in a narrow light, excluding the participation of psychobiological factors. Alternative interpretations, such as that cogently discussed by Waxler in the following paper, are convincingly applied to the explanation of course and outcome of illness and quality of patienthood.

OBSERVATIONS MADE by the author in Ceylon (now known as Sri Lanka) and by many practitioners in Africa suggest that the serious psychoses one sees in these peasant systems are of short duration with an excellent prognosis. One systematic study that followed treated schizophrenic patients in the peasant villages of Mauritius has shown that clinical symptoms and social performance after 12 years are significantly better than a comparable group of patients in Great Britain even though the Mauritian treatment was considerably more limited.

Several theories have been developed to explain these kinds of cross-cultural differences in types, rates, and outcomes. Leighton has tied cultural differences to social change, suggesting that more mental illness may occur in rapidly changing societies undergoing industrialization or modernization. Others have suggested that the apparent quick recovery in peasant societies is due to their greater tolerance for deviation. Some have suggested that cross-cultural differences in rates and prognosis are explained by poor epidemiological methods in the peasant societies; the illnesses are there but simply are not counted.

We propose an alternate theory that we feel may better explain the facts. Societies do not cause different rates of mental disorder nor tolerate different degrees of deviance; instead they respond differently to psychiatric illness once it occurs. Differences in societal response, in turn, account for differences in rates and outcome. The social labeling theory of deviance provides concepts and hypotheses that help to explain how different societies may succeed in molding the mentally ill person to match societal expectations.

Of greatest importance in this process are the belief systems of the society and the extent to which the patient has power over his own role as a sick person. In societies such as Ceylon and Mauritius, where beliefs about mental illness center on supernatural causation, where the person is not held responsible for his illness, where his "self" remains unchanged, he can shed the sick role quickly and easily. In contrast, where psychiatric illnesses are believed to involve personality change and personal responsibility, the sick person receives many messages that something is seriously wrong with his self; his self-perception and behavior may conform to these messages and his illness may have a long duration.

The nature of the treatment system, too, may contribute to the patient's outcome. In peasant societies where treatments are highly ritualized and where practitioners are not bureaucratically organized, patients and their family retain control over illness-confirming messages, and the patient may easily drop the sick role and return to "normality." In many Western societies, treatment systems are both comprehensive and bureaucratic, the patient may become engulfed in this system and find little reward and little opportunity for shedding the sick role.

Thus, how societies process the mentally ill person once the illness has been recognized may be a crucial factor in explaining cross-cultural differences in the rates of and prognosis for psychiatric disease.

While studying psychiatric treatments in Ceylon I was surprised by the large number of families reporting that their patient, after having been treated briefly by native and/or Western methods, was now "cured." Further investigation indicated that these judgments were probably valid; after a brief episode of mental illness most patients were able to return quickly and easily to their normal roles (Waxler, In Press).

My observation that psychiatric disease in Ceylon is of brief duration and leaves few residual symptoms is echoed by those who have had experience with mental illness in other primitive and peasant societies. For example, reporting from Africa, German has observed that "acute transient psychoses, characterized by gross disruption of mental function and with an excellent prognosis, are the most common types of psychotic states seen in African hospital practice" (1972:465; see also Tewfik 1958; Jelik and Jelik 1970). The same phenomenon has been reported by Rin and Lin (1962) in an aboriginal group on Taiwan and by others working in quite different peasant cultures. In peasant societies, psychiatric illnesses, at least those that come to the attention of Western doctors, seem to be brief, perhaps florid, but generally the patient returns easily to live in the village.

What accounts for these observations, that in a peasant society like Ceylon the patient who has suffered a psychosis can so easily and quickly return to normal? My thoughts followed these lines. Traditional Ceylonese beliefs about mental illness center upon supernatural causes—demon possession, witchcraft, bad influence of the planets; if a person is supernaturally affected he can be easily treated by prescribed standard rituals carried out by exorcists and priests. The sick person, himself, is not believed to be responsible for the illness; his body or soul may be possessed but his "self" remains unchanged. If he follows the appropriate prescriptions, then it is believed that his symptoms will disappear and he will quickly and easily return to normal. There is no stigma attached to mental illness; no one believes that the patient is "different" and should be treated in a new way after his symptoms have gone. Thus, the way people formulate the illness calls forth certain societal expectations and responses which, in the Ceylonese case, seem to allow the patient to drop the sick role quickly and easily.

This hypothetical explanation of the high rate of cure of mental illnesses in Ceylon focuses upon the beliefs the society holds about mental illness and the consequent response of the society to the person once his symptoms have been noticed. Comparative social psychiatric work, however, has traditionally explained cultural differences in rates and outcome of illness in quite different terms. The most developed and complete formulation that seeks to explain why psychiatric diseases vary in type and incidence across cultures links the incidence of mental illness to social change. Leighton (1959) has suggested that rapid social change results in social disequilibrium and disintegration; when such change occurs there may be, for example, increasing proverty, cultural confusion, secularization, high frequency of broken homes, few and weak leaders, and fragmented networks of communication. These, in turn, may result in alienation, unmet personal needs and higher rates of mental illness in those who cannot or do not "fit" into the new society. Thus, as societies shift, under economic and other pressure, from traditional village systems to urbanized and industrialized systems, more people come to be "at risk" for psychiatric disease. Social disequilibrium, through an intervening process of disrupted personal needs, causes mental illness.

If the social causation theory were to be confirmed empirically we would expect to find that the incidence of psychiatric disease varies with the degree of social disintegration or the amount of rapid social change occurring in the societies compared. Yet the few cross-cultural epidemiological studies meeting requirements of sound methodology have shown that the incidence of the most common psychosis, schizophrenia, may be very much the same in all societies (Lin 1953); problems of methodology and theory prevent any clear statement about the incidence of other types of mental illness (Dunham 1965). Leighton shows that prevalence of mental illness is similar in the Yoruba of Africa and the Canadians of Nova Scotia (Leighton et al. 1963), although there are some tendencies for the more socially "disintegrated" areas of each group to have higher rates. See Kunitz's (1970) critique of the Stirling County study for further analyses of Leighton's findings. However, from these and other studies it is not at all clear that rapidly industrializing and modernizing societies, in contrast to the traditional unchanging peasant and primitive societies, create more mental illness.

A second explanation offered by comparative social psychiatrists for the different rates and outcomes of psychiatric disease in peasant and modern societies is that cultures vary in terms of the amount of deviation they will tolerate. For example, they would argue that the reason I saw so many patients who were "cured" in Ceylon was simply that the range of normal behavior is much wider than it is in the West; a patient who returns to his home may continue to hear voices but this is not deemed to be an indicator of sickness if he, at the same time, can plow the paddy fields. In Western societies, behavior must meet higher standards in order for the patient to be judged cured. This assumption that peasant and primitive societies allow greater laxity in behavior does not fit with my own observations in Ceylon and may be a carry-over from the "carefree savage" days when observers, looking into the peasant society, failed to see the complexity of the normative system. Until there is more empirical evidence (particularly, the incidence of untreated mental illness in the community), the argument that peasants tolerate more deviance than modernized people, thus accounting for the different outcome of psychiatric illnesses, remains unsubstantiated.

Finally, many comparative social psychiatrists, especially those who have attempted epidemiological research in underdeveloped societies, would argue that the reason for findings showing more short-term illnesses and higher cure rates in peasant societies is a methodological one. If surveys were as complete and controlled as say, the Myers and Bean (1968) study in New Haven, one would find much more evidence of psychiatric illness, in Africa or Ceylon, or elsewhere. In other words, the more carefully you look for it the more mental illness you will find. These people would suggest that construction of social psychiatric theories on the basis of most current epidemiological data is fruitless unless and until we can be certain that reported rates accurately reflect the "real" rates of illness in the community.

Each of the above explanations for differences in rates and outcome of mental illness has a certain plausibility, yet none has very strong empirical support. We propose an alternate explanation. Societies do not *cause* different rates of mental disorder nor tolerate different degrees of deviance; instead they do *respond* differently to psychiatric illness once it occurs. Differences in societal response, in turn, account for differences in types of illness and outcome.

Briefly, many peasant societies, like the Ceylonese, do not "make much" of mental illness. Beliefs center on external causation, treatments are routinized, and there is no stigma. When a person becomes ill he is believed to remain basically unchanged as a person. Families, acting on the basis of these societal beliefs, give explicit and implicit messages to the patient that reinforce the normal role. Treatment agents, too, because of their lack of bureaucratic organization as well as the content of their messages confirm the societal expectations. Thus, the sick person is most likely to fulfill these expectations by returning quickly to "normality."

In contrast, in many industrialized societies, when mental illness appears the response of family and those who will treat the patient is to perceive the sick person as now "different." He is often socially rejected; he is encouraged or required to seek treatment (to take the "sick role"); and he may be engulfed in a bureaucratic treatment system in which he has little power to resist illness-confirming messages. Again, the sick person may often fulfill the expectations that others have for him; in this case, however, the messages confirm "sickness."

In presenting brief summaries of these alternative theories we have deliberately not distinguished between different types of mental illness, assuming that the tolerance of deviance notion, for example, applies equally well to patients diagnosed as schizophrenic as it does to those with minor neuroses. With the exception of Murphy and Leighton's work (1965), where there has been concern with examining specific psychiatric syndromes cross-culturally, theories explaining cultural differences in patient careers have usually not been tested empirically at a level at which it was necessary to refine predictions for types of psychiatric syndromes. This is true of the social response theory as well; its current use is to describe the careers of "the mentally ill." One would expect that as empirical work proceeds the theory will be refined to predict the efforts of social responses on those with schizophrenic disorders, alcohol addiction, patients with depressive symptons, etc. We might expect, for example, that the contribution of society's responses to the patient's career is relatively great for the neuroses and perhaps more limited for the severe psychoses.

Labeling Theory: A Social Response Explanation of Cultural Differences

The interpretive model that we have introduced to explain the different experiences of the mentally ill in Ceylon and in Western societies comes from a more general sociological theory called "social response" or "labeling theory" (Lemert 1967; Scheff 1966b; Schur 1971). Labeling theory, we feel, provides concepts and hypotheses that are extremely useful in explaining how different cultures turn out psychiatrically ill people who follow radically different patient careers. We shall introduce some of the more important assumptions of the theory, some of the concepts and hypotheses, and then show how they might be useful in cross-cultural analyses.

Labeling theory concerns itself with the effects of social experiences upon a sick person (or any other deviant) once the illness has occured—that is, with the processes through which the society labels him as "sick." The theory, thus, alerts us to what happens to a person after his symptoms appear. As we have pointed out, this approach is quite different from past social psychiatric theory where concern was with social factors that contributed to the etiology of mental illness. There the focus was on the patient's social background, his position in the community network, or his commitment to the social norms which were, in turn, assumed to be social correlates of psychological factors (such as unmet personal needs or stress) that *caused* mental illness.

In contrast, labeling theory is not interested in explaining the primary cause of the initial psychiatric illness, or "primary deviation." Whether psychiatric illness results from genetic factors, biochemical defects, certain family dynamics, or anomia is not important. What is important is how the society responds to and processes the sick person once the symptoms have occurred. In fact, it is assumed that many such symptoms appear, in many people, at one time or another; yet relatively few of these people find their way to formal treatment systems and into the sick role. The theory predicts that it is the societal response *to* the person with psychiatric symptoms that is the prime determinant of whether he will remain sick and will receive treatment. It is the societal response *to* him that will further determine whether he becomes a "secondary deviant," that is, a person whose major role identification is that of a sick person (Lemert 1967). Thus, the career of the sick person is influenced, not by biological or social factors in his past that cause severe or mild symptoms, curable or noncurable illnesses, but by the ways his family, his neighbors, and most significantly, his doctors respond to him once any sort of symptom occurs.

It is apparent from the vocabulary of labeling theory that illness is seen as something more than just bodily symptoms and personal discomfort. The theory conceives of psychiatric illness as one form of deviation from the social norms; in other words, the sick person has taken on a sick role because he is unable to carry out his normal role obligations. He is unable to work, to go to school, to do what is expected of him as a father or son, for example. These social role disabilities, from the point of view of labeling theory, are the crucial qualities of illness. Bodily symptoms are, of course, not denied importance, but a conceptual distinction is made between clinical diagnosis and social role since it is quite apparent that some clinically ill people are never defined by anyone as being sick and some sick people have few, if any, clinical symptoms.

We have followed this conception of "outcome" of mental illness throughout this paper. That is, we assume that both the patient's clinical symptoms and his ability to carry out his normal social roles are significant for his career as a sick person. However, measures of symptoms at a specified follow-up point are not simply substitutes for measures of role performance since the two factors, following the social response model, are not necessarily highly correlated. Thus, following Brown's example (Brown et al. 1966), we might include as indicators of outcome the presence of delusions, hallucinations, the extent to which these are socially disturbing, as well as whether the person can hold a job, care for children, and get along with family and neighbors. The evaluation of social disturbance, getting along with others, is based on the norms of the patient's own society.

Then, how do the responses of people in a society to a sick person model and sustain that sickness? Once a person is recognized by his family or others as having symptoms of an illness, certain negotiations begin between interested parties as to the patient's status (Balint 1957). Families discuss among themselves and with the patient "what is wrong" and "what is to be done about it." Treatment people also negotiate with the patient and family about the same issues. Once the idea of mental illness is introduced the process becomes one in which all parties begin to introduce subtle expectations into their messages to the patient about *how* he should behave as a sick person (Scheff 1966b). Being mentally ill in the normative or proper way is convenient for all concerned since it makes future interactions predictable and smooth. Thus both families and treatment people may give explicit and implicit messages to the patient that he is, indeed, mentally ill, they expect that he will behave according to the appropriate model of mental illness, and they will reward him for so doing.

What does the sick person do, then, when he receives such messages? When a person with symptoms of mental illness finds himself in what is most often a new and frightening situation, he looks around himself for confirmation and guidance. This search for self-definition is most apparent when the patient has, for example, little information, few alternative roles, low power, and when he receives few messages that disconfirm his illness. Under these conditions he begins to take the sick role; that is, he models his behavior on the expectations of other important people—treatment agents and family—with whom he interacts. They, in turn, have modeled their expectations on beliefs about mental illness in the common culture and their own experiences with such illness.

At the center of the social response theory, therefore, is a well known social psychological mechanism that has been empirically described by such researchers as Sherif (1937), Asch (1951), Milgriam (1964), and many others. When a person finds himself in a new situation—i.e., having symptoms of mental illness—with few internal referents to guide his behavior, he acts upon the expectations of those around him, very often those in authority. The family's and treatment agent's prophecy—that the patient is mentally ill—is thus fulfilled.

Scheff makes the most concise statement of these processes. When a person first experiences symptoms of mental illness, social agents and family members act "in terms of the traditional stereotypes of insanity, [the patient's—amorphous and unstructured rule-breaking tends to crystallize in conformity to these expectations, thus becoming similar to the behavior of other deviants classified as mentally ill, and stable over time" (Scheff 1966b: 82). Thus, through interaction with others, the patient internalizes the proper social role for mentally ill people and acts accordingly.

If all patients having psychiatric symptoms received messages confirming their illness and conformed to the expected role models we would expect very high rates of mental disorder or very long lived illnesses. Labeling theory specifies certain conditions under which the patient is able to resist such labeling and to return to his normal role quickly and easily.

The power and status of the patient and his family, relative to treatment agents especially, are at least in the West a powerful mitigating condition, allowing the patient to avoid remaining in the sick role. We all know of instances in which a high status person's deviant behavior is "normalized", or perhaps reinterpreted as eccentricity, while the same behavior in a low status person is labeled and treated as mental illness. We know, too, that the social class of the patient relative to the doctor is related to the diagnosis and prognosis the pyschiatrist gives.[1] Those lower class patients who receive more serious diagnoses are also very likely to receive messages confirming their illness that they cannot resist.

Not only is the relative power of the patient important in whether he takes the sick role offered but so is the type of deviant behavior he shows (Lemert 1967). If his symptoms are socially "invisible" then it is

1. Two unpublished studies have dealt with these questions: W. Haase, "Rorschach Diagnosis, Socioeconomic Class and Examiner Bias," unpublished doctoral dissertation, New York University, 1955, and S. Lee, "Social Class Bias in the Diagnosis of Mental Illness," unpublished doctoral dissertation, University of Oklahoma, 1968.

much less likely that others will expect him to take the sick role. Only deviant behavior that impinges on other people need be molded into appropriate sick roles (Scheff 1966).

Whether and how the patient has previously been labeled, that is, given a diagnosis or given treatment, is another significant determinant of the way others interact with him and thus how he takes the sick role. Denzin and Spitzer (1966) showed that whether the patient entered the hospital voluntarily or involuntarily influences the staff's predicitions and thus their expectations of his behavior. Rosenhan (1973) has reported that once a diagnositic label is given to a patient—in his case, a pseudo-patient—most of the patient's normal behavior is reinterpreted to conform to the expectations of deviance. Thus normal people admitted to a psychiatric ward without the knowledge of the staff and diagnosed as schizophrenic were reported in nursing notes to be behaving in peculiar ways. Once the impression is formed that the patient is schizophrenic his past life is reinterpreted in accord with the label, and treatment people believe that his future will confirm their expectations (Denzin 1968). The effects of so labeling a patient are particularly strong, according to the theory, when the label in the form of a diagnosis on the medical record is the sole or major bit of information upon which a treatment person must base his decision. This is most common when treatment people see patients in large bureaucratic systems where time and information are in short supply.

Underlying the processes of labeling are the expectations of all people concerned about normative sick-role taking. Thus, the content of beliefs about mental illness held by family, treatment people, and the patient himself are important determinants of the conditions under which the person moves into the role of a secondary deviant, that is, a chronically ill person. Beliefs about mental illness learned through the mass media, jokes and stories, and personal experience, guide the expectations of everyone, including the patient; beliefs and expectations define the proper way for a mentally ill person to be sick. Under many circumtances, to ensure smooth predictable interactions the patient will comply (Scheff 1966).

Implied in labeling theory is the assumption that social responses, being based in the belief and treatment systems of the society, will vary across cultures. Thus, cross-cultural differences in treated illness rates and in the social and clinical outcome for the sick person may be explained in terms of differences in these social processes. A test of the social response hypothesis rests, first, on establishing facts showing that the social and clinical outcome for patients with similar mental illnesses varies across cultures. We shall review one set of findings that supports this argument. Then we shall demonstrate how two important aspects of social response theory—the society's system of beliefs and the structure of its treatment system—can be used to understand differences in the social processing of and thus the treatment outcome for mentally ill people in peasant and modern societies.

Social Response as an Explanation for Clinical and Social Outcome in Two Societies

Recently H. B. M. Murphy and Raman (1971) and Raman and Murphy (1972) reported research designed to examine the observations many people have made, that peasant societies in Africa and elsewhere seem to produce psychotic patients whose prognoses are much better than in the West.[2] Their findings and some of their interpretations lend considerable support to a social response explanation of cross cultural differences.

We shall review these findings very briefly, touching only on issues important in illustrating the theoretical model; readers interested in details of method should consult the original study. Their data came from a 12-year follow-up of psychiatric patients originally treated at the only government psychiatric hospital on the island of Mauritius, an independent state in the Indian Ocean. The Mauritian society is a peasant one, based on a one-crop sugar cane economy; two thirds of the population is Indian and one third African. Although the degree of Westernization is quite limited, British and French colonial control left Mauritius with a psychiatric hospital having the same relative capacity as those in Great Britain. At the time of the study, however, treatment was limited to insulin coma and electric shock; there were no phenothiazines, no psychotherapy, and no aftercare clinics.

A cohort of 94 first admission schizophrenic patients admitted to the hospital in 1956 was followed up 12 years later by home visits. Nurse-interviewers obtained information about course of symptoms and the social performance of patients since discharge. Findings from Mauritius where compared with a follow-up study of schizophrenic patients discharged from three psychiatric hospitals in En-

2. The discussion in this section refers only to schizophrenic patients followed after their first hospital admission.

gland. The latter research, carried out by Brown et al. (1966) used similar sampling methods, and obtained similar data from the patient and his family, although the follow-up period was 5 instead of 12 years.

Our first concern is with the incidence of schizophrenia in the two cultures, the peasant society of Mauritius and the industrial society of Great Britain. Murphy and Raman show that treated age-specific rates of schizophrenia are very similar in the two cultures. Further, the symptoms of patients diagnosed on admission as schizophrenic on Mauritius appear to be no different from symptoms found in schizophrenics in Great Britian.

At the point of entrance into treatment, then, the two societies begin with quite similar characteristics; incidence rates for and types of symptoms of schizophrenic patients are similar. What happens to the patients? Almost all of the findings support the conclusion that clinical and social outcome for treated schizophrenia is better in the peasant society of Mauritius than in Great Britain. In the Mauritian sample 62 percent (or 55 of the total of 86 patients) were classified as being "socially independent with no symptoms" at follow-up; the comparable proportion classified in the same way in the English sample was significantly lower, 49 percent (or 49 out of a total of 100 followed patients). Similar differences between societies were found when the total course of the patient's disorder since the original hospitalization was measured. More Mauritian schizophrenic patients (59 percent of the sample) were able to leave the hospital and return quickly and easily without any further symptoms or treatments to their jobs or household chores. In contrast, fewer (45 percent) British patients were classed as having "no disturbance" or being "symptom-free in the past year." It is interesting to note that the social and clinical outcome differences come largely from the group of patients who do *not* remain chronically ill; 36 percent of the Mauritian sample (32 patients) and 28 percent of the English sample (28 patients) are classified as "chronically disturbed" (in the British study) or having "continuous total or partial disability" or "several episodes of nonfunctioning" (in the Mauritian study). Thus, although rates of chronicity are quite similar, the careers of the nonchronic patients in Mauritius and Great Britain vary. Although psychiatric treatment is admittedly less modern in Mauritius than it is in Great Britain, the outcome for the nonchronic schizophrenic patient in Mauritius is considerably better. Quick return to normality for many patients in this peasant society is assured; the same is not true for similar patients in England.

The social response model suggests an explanation for this set of facts. In fact, Murphy and Raman imply this interpretation when they suggest that the nonchronic English patient "may be 'trapped' within an established sick role by the superficial rationality of society's view of this sickness, whereas the Mauritian patient, with a range of what one would call superstitious explanations for his initial disorder, may more easily find a way of escape" (H. B. M. Murphy 1972:496). On Mauritius mental illnesses are often attributed to supernatural causes, to demons or ghosts that attack at random; the patient is not believed to be responsible nor to be changed in any basic way.[3] Thus, once acute symptoms disappear; i.e., once the supernatural effect has gone, families, neighbors, and treatment people expect that the patient will return to normal; in the face of these expectations the majority of sick people may comply. Further, patients may retain considerable control over how long they retain the sick role since treatment bureaucracies are in their infancy in Mauritius. No one makes home visits; no patient is required to return regularly for outpatient treatment; no local village authority is given responsibility for the patient once he returns home. Thus, few structural supports exist within the treatment system to maintain the sick role beyond the point of hospital discharge. The contrasts with beliefs and treatment systems in Great Britain should be quite apparent.

We have presented the Mauritian data and English comparison data in some detail in order to make concrete the utility of the social response mode. Naturally, we would want more information about Mauritian beliefs and native treatments in order to substantiate the interpretation we have made; further, the findings might be understood in alternate ways. However, the data lead us to the conclusion that the incidence of treated schizophrenia in these peasant and industrial societies is probably the same, yet the outcome for the treated patient is different, even though Mauritian hospital treatments are not as modern as in England. Social and clinical outcome may be dependent upon the response of the society to the sick person, and two response factors are particularly important. First, the cultures differ in beliefs about the cause of mental illness, appropriate treatments, and the proper ways for sick people to take the sick role. Second, these beliefs may have led to reliance on specific types of treatment systems. The comprehensive, integrated and highly available treatment bureauc-

3. Personal communication, from Dr. A. C. Raman, Brown-Sequard Hospital, Mauritius, 1973.

racies in Great Britain may have latent functions that serve to maintain the patient in the sick role once his illness is recognized. Treatment systems like those in Mauritius that are organizationally isolated and not readily available may allow for easy return to normality.

Impact of beliefs on the sick role. While it would be commonly agreed that beliefs about an illness are in some way important for the sick person, social response theory directs our attention to ways in which and places in which these beliefs have their impact. Thus, once a person with symptoms is defined as sick, a series of negotiations begins between him and other interested parties such as families and treatment people. The messages that they give to the patient about how to be sick are representative of the beliefs about illness that are commonly held in the society. Thus, to see the importance of the belief system on the patient's career in different cultures we should examine these negotiation processes.

In our own Western society, it is a common and acceptable belief that once a person has a serious mental illness like schizophrenia he is "changed" for life; he may, in fact, always be schizophrenic, perhaps in a latent way. We see this in newspaper reports that attribute violent acts to former mental patients. The same belief is officially confirmed in a handbook published by the National Institute of Mental Health (1972): "a person does not *have* schizophrenia as he might have an ulcer in his stomach or a cold in his head. He *is* schizophrenic; he *is* the disorder. It pervades his entire being" (p. 5). That this expectation may be communicated from family to patient is supported by Freeman's findings (Freeman and Simmons 1958) that families who believe mental illness is incurable expect little improvement in their patient member, and their expectations are confirmed.

Further, many Westerners believe that interpersonal relationships, especially those in the past, account for later personality defects and mental disorders. We see the impact of this belief in Scheff's description of a patient–doctor negotiation in which the patient proposes several successive formulations of her illness, none of which "matches" the doctor's beliefs about mental disorder (Scheff 1968). All are rejected in subtle ways by the doctor. Not until the patient proposes a formulation that is intrapsychic and links with past interpersonal experiences does the therapist agree. At this point "the therapist's tone and manner change abruptly. From being bored, distant and rejecting, he becomes warm and solicitous. Through a process of offers and responses, the therapist and patient have, by implication, negotiated a shared definition of the situation" (Schur 1971:10). In the process the patient's model for her own mental illness is radically if subtly changed.

The negotiations between the patient and other interested people in Western societies communicate certain expectations about how to be sick in a proper way, one that conforms to the society's beliefs about such illnesses. We would expect that similar negotiations occur in peasant societies, the major difference being the quality of social expectations that are communicated to the sick person.

In many peasant societies beliefs about the prognosis for serious mental illness are in sharp contrast to Western ideas; severe psychoses are believed to be brief, curable, leaving no lasting after effects. This is certainly true for the Sinhalese villagers, and the expectation that mental illness is of short duration is communicated to the patient by native treatment people. When treating mental illnesses attributed to demon possession, the Ceylonese exorcist ties a charmed thread around the patient's wrist, and announces that the thread is protective for a limited period, a week or 3 months. It is understood that many illnesses go away within that period of time. If not, in the more elaborate and major rituals repeated announcements are made by the exorcist that the ritual itself is "conclusive," that the illness of the patient is "now over" (Obeyesekere 1969). The astrologer, to whom many psychiatric patients and their families turn, reinforces these messages by predicting the date on which the cure will be complete. Each of these public predictions acts as a powerful sanction on the patient to conform to expectations. The fact that predictions are ordinarily for short periods, usually 3 or 6 months, may serve to model mental illnesses with short durations. Certainly there is no promise of reward for a chronic sickness.

A belief that mental illness is caused by supernatural agents who often act in an irrationally vindictive way, attacking persons without reason, is common in Mauritius and Ceylon as well as many other peasant societies. The implication of this belief is that the patient cannot be "blamed" for his predicament; his sickness is thus not linked with his own past experience nor can he be expected to take on a new role. These beliefs about the cause of mental illness are also the basis for negotiation between family or treatment agent and the patient, even within what we might assume are very rigidly constructed ritual treatments. For example, Edgerton (1969) reports the process of negotiation between the family of a Tanzanian adolescent boy and a native doctor. After a ritual of divination and prayer the doctor proclaimed that the boy's illness was incurable and probably inherited. This diagnosis, unacceptable to the family, then became the central issue in a long discussion; the boy's father gave arguments why inheritance was an unreasonable cause and finally offered an alternative, witchcraft, an acceptable belief in the society. Then, "the father offered to pay the doctor well if he could identify the witch and the malevolent witchcraft being used, could cure the boy, and then punish the witch" (Edgerton 1969:60). Both parties, having settled on witchcraft as an alternate explanation then carried on with the treatment. The boy improved and his improvement thus confirmed the agreement about the cause of the illness and the belief that cure was possible.

These examples have suggested the important part that negotiations between patients and treatment agents have in translating the society's beliefs about mental illness into concrete expectations for the patient's behavior. Social response theory predicts that the sick person is most likely to conform to these expectations, thus being sick in the way his particular society defines mental illness.

Impact of bureaucracies on the sick role. While the society's beliefs about the mental illness, transmitted in messages to the patient, are important in molding the role that a mentally ill person takes, there are certain conditions under which a patient may resist such messages. One such condition involves the power of the patient relative to the social context in which treatment is given. When the treatment system is a highly organized, integrated, and comprehensive bureaucratic structure, most sick people are powerless to resist illness-confirming messages when they receive them. On the other hand, when the treatment system is not highly structured, the patient retains more power over his patient career and may easily avoid such messages. Thus the organizational structure of treatment systems may reinforce illness, through the expectations about sickness that people in the system communicate to the sick persons.

We shall return to the data from Mauritius and Great Britain to suggest how the treatment systems themselves may model mental illness having quite different clinical and social outcomes. These data will suggest that the greater the patient's contact with treatment agents and the more integrated and comprehensive the treatment system, the poorer the social and clinical outcome for the patient. Thus the nature of the sick peasant's experience within nonbureaucratically organized treatment systems may be one important factor that explains why peasant societies produce psychiatric patients with acute illnesses and good prognosis.

Brown and his colleagues (1966) obtained their sample of first-admission schizophrenic patients from three British psychiatric hospitals. The significant factor for our analysis here is that these three hospitals vary considerably in the extent of treatment offered. The Mapperly Hospital in Nottingham provided the most extended and diverse system of services; the hospital was developed "to form a comprehensive system of the community care intended to assist patients and their families from onset of illness until recovery or death" (Brown et al. 1966:14). Mapperly provides inpatient and day hospital care, 50 specialized outpatient sessions per week, rehabilitation centers, and vocational training. The hospital has direct links with the local town services for the mentally ill. This highly integrated treatment system is similar in goals and structure to the newer community mental health centers in the United States in that it reaches into the community to prevent illness, follows patients to their homes after hospital discharge, and services many and diverse patient needs.

In contrast, the hospitals that provided the remainder of the schizophrenic patients followed in Brown's study do not offer such extensive services. One hospital (Netherne) gives only inpatient services and has 28 outpatient clinics per week and six psychiatric social workers; other agencies with which a patient might have contact, such as the general practitioner or the local mental welfare officers, are independent of the hospital. The third hospital (Severalls) has even fewer services, only nine outpatient sessions, one social worker, and no formal attachments to other agencies. Thus the range of patient services in these two hospitals is considerably less than in the Nottingham hospital.

Although the samples of first admission schizophrenic patients followed from the three hospitals did not differ greatly from each other at the time of admission, nor was their treatment in the hospital significantly different, those patients who were followed from the Mapperly Hospital for a 5-year period after discharge "were under care in the community for about eight times as long as patients from the other two hospitals" (Brown et al. 1966:165).[4]

Thus, knowing that Mapperly Hospital provides a very integrated, available system of treatments to discharged patients, and knowing that the particular patients followed in this research received eight times as much treatment as those from the other two hospitals, we would expect that the outcome for Mapperly patients would be considerably better than for the others as well. This is not true. Measures of social performance, symptoms, and the course of the patient's illness uniformly show that the first admission schizophrenic patients dis-

4. Our discussion of findings from Brown's study refers only to first-admission schizophrenic patients in order to make the clearest comparison with the Mauritius data.

charged from the Mapperly Hospital are either not significantly different upon follow-up from those treated in the other two hospitals, or they are significantly worse; trends are almost always in the negative direction. There is no evidence, then, that what most specialists would judge to be the "best" treatment system produces the "best" outcome.

In fact, if we compare the findings from patients who are discharged from the three British hospitals with those from the Mauritius hospital, we discover that across the four treatment facilities, that is, the three hospitals in Great Britain and one on Mauritius, as the psychiatric treatment given becomes better or more modern the outcome for the patients who are treated becomes worse. The Mauritius hospital, with its limited facilities for following patients and its narrow range of medications, leads to the best outcome; the next best outcome comes, generally, from the two more limited British hospitals; tendencies for the poorest outcome come from the model community mental health center at Mapperly.

Social response theory suggests that the labeling of deviance, in the form of messages to the patient about how to conform to the sick role, is consistently strengthened and reinforced in a large bureaucratic treatment system such as Mapperly and similar Western mental hospitals. In the face of these large comprehensive organizations many patients have little power to resist such messages (Goffman 1961; Rosenhan 1973). In such hospitals staff members have little time with patients, little information about them and their actions are highly routinized. This structure leads to a conservative bias, that is, to a decision that is safe, on the part of treatment agents; for example, a continued drug prescription, further time in the hospital, or a recommendation for another follow-up visit are most likely. Patients, then, receive further confirmation that they are, indeed, still sick.

Sickness may be further confirmed by the reliance of a bureaucratic structure on written records; in this case, then, the patient's diagnosis and prognosis (i.e., his label) recorded on paper may circulate through many hands and may become the sole basis for a treatment person's message to him. The label is the person. Finally, bureaucratic hospital organizations imply highly integrated and available referral systems; it is simple to move patients from one agency to another. Consequently, the option of discharging the patient, in other words, giving the patient confirmation that he is well, is only one of several choices the agent can make.

Thus, in a highly integrated and highly available treatment system such as our Western hospitals, two qualities seem to press sick people to remain in the sick role over a relatively long period of time. First, the patient's power relative to the organization is usually weak. Only those patients with high social status (Myers and Bean 1968), with considerable knowledge of the system, or with strong role alternatives (Dinitz, et al. 1961) may be able to resist the organization's messages. Second, treatment agents' messages most often confirm sickness because lack of both time and information and need for patients to justify their existence call for conservative decisions. As labeling theory suggests, messages about sickness lead the sick person, especially the less powerful sick person, to model his behavior according to the treatment system's expectations.

The effects of such bureaucratic structures upon the messages given to psychiatric patients are not limited to the West. In peasant societies where the services of Western medicine have been modeled on treatment systems in Europe or America, similar, but probably weaker, labeling effects may occur. For example, in Ceylon, Western hospitals are based on the British system; they are government sponsored, serve geographical catchment areas, and provide referral systems for specialized treatment. It is quite clear from some of the psychiatric patients followed there that family and patient control over treatment is diminished when the patient comes in contact with the Western system. Patients are sometimes transferred from one hospital to another without the family's knowledge, treatments may be given without clear explanation either to patient or family, follow-up visits are arranged without choice or discussion. The bureaucratic structure, even in the context of a peasant society, thus may generate the kind of control and thus the kind of messages the patient receives that can make shedding of the sick role more difficult.

These effects are probably even weaker in the Mauritius treatment system where the Western hospital had at the time of Murphy and Raman's study (1971) no after-care clinic, no home visits by hospital staff, and no delegation of treatment or care to a village authority. The fact that the patient, once discharged from the hospital, makes a clean break with the treatment system provides him considerable opportunity to avoid messages of sickness. This fact may, then, partially account for the better outcome of mentally ill patients treated in Mauritius.

In contrast, an examination of the system of indigenous or native treatments in a peasant society such as Ceylon shows how simple it may be for a mentally ill person to avoid receiving further confirmation of his illness from treatment agents. Native treatment people—exorcists, priests, astrologers, Ayurvedic physicians—are not part of bureaucratic organizations. Each is a private practitoner. There are no formal links between treatment people and thus no formal referral systems. Further, there is no system of records, in fact no papers at all, that carry information about a patient from one treatment person to another. Thus, relative to treatment agents the family and patient maintain a powerful position. Specifically, they are in control of the kinds of messages that they receive about the patient's illness. For example, an exorcist must satisfy the family (i.e., give appropriate messages) since his fee may be dependent upon it. An astrologer may recommend a certain treatment person, yet the family is free to select another, or none at all. Of course, there are informal systems of relationships that may exercise certain control over what the family does (and therefore what kinds of illness-confirming messages the patient receives) but it is obviously much easier for the patient to change treatments or to stop treatments entirely than it is in the West.

Further, treatment agents are not pressed toward conservative actions since few native treatment people rely solely on this occupation for income or status; most are farmers or laborers as well. Thus, in Ceylon, where native treatment agents are not professionalized as they are in industrialized societies, their power relative to the patient is less and the patient retains greater control over his own patient career. His goal—to return to "normal"—is thus more easily and quickly reached because he receives fewer and less insistent messages confirming sickness.

Discussion

We began with this question: how can we explain cultural differences in the prognosis of severe mental disorders? We reviewed data showing that first-admission schizophrenic patients treated in the peasant society of Mauritius are much more likely to recover quickly, to return to their jobs or families, and to have no further symptoms than are their counterparts in England. This pattern seems to be true of many peasant or traditional societies. Thus, it appears that the patient's care varies with the culture.

As an alternative to the social causation and tolerance of deviation explanations of these findings, we have proposed a social response model, represented by a sociological labeling theory. In the latter theory, the duration and severity of a patient's illness are explained by the response the society makes to a sick person once his symptoms appear. Any, or many, causal factors—genetic, biochemical, familial—can cause the original symptoms, but it is the society's response that sustains the illness.

Social response theorists have specified in some detail the sociological processes that may serve to sustain illness in one society and discourage it in another. Thus, the theory goes beyond a simple assertion that cultures expect different things of sick people and those expectations are often fulfilled. Instead, the theory focuses on social processes, on how these societal expectations are brought into play. It alerts us to the importance of beliefs about the cause and duration of mental illness and beliefs about the kinds of behavior deemed proper for a mentally ill person. It suggests that these beliefs may determine the expectations that family and treatment agents have for the patients and thus become an important component of their messages to him and the rewards they give for his playing the sick role properly. It specifies the conditions under which his sickness will be attended to or ignored; the frequency and threat of his symptoms and the extent to which his sickness is visible or impinges on others are important conditions. Finally, it provides a way of conceptualizing the extent to which the sick person can resist the society's messages; when a patient has power, relative to family members, treatment agents, and treatment systems he may resist the society's norms for the mentally ill person. Social response theory, therefore, provides a set of concepts and hypotheses that are not tied to any specific culture or cultures, but that serve as a framework for investigating the ways that any society molds mental illness to its liking.

There are certain problems, however, in testing the effects of social responses cross-culturally. When we described the way in which social response theory helps to explain the differences in the career of mentally ill patients across cultures we assumed that the treated incidence of psychosis in a particular society represented primary deviance rates, determined by nonsocial factors. It was implied that social responses to the illness have their effect only after the sick person has been officially recognized as sick. Although this is the easiest assumption to make since most epidemiological data are based on treated incidence rates, it is of course a simplification of the issue. Social responses to a sick person begin to mold his sick-role taking long before he appears as a treated case in the hospital register; incidence rates themselves are the result of social negotiations between patient, family, and society, in which some prospective patients are shunted off the track, labeled as criminals, eccentrics, or even normal.

If social labeling begins early in the patient's career, thus contributing to the treated incidence rates, and if, as in Mauritius there is less labeling, less stigma, less confirmation of illness, why are the treated incidence rates the same there as in Great Britain? Should not these rates be lower, since mental illnesses are not serious deviations? Would not more people with symptoms be treated at home, ignored and never be seen in the hospital? This question is one that cannot be answered until we investigate the negotiation process between patient and family that occurs prior to treatment. Perhaps we would find that the initial social processes that lead to hospitalization in Mauritius and Great Britain are the same (leading to similar treated incidence rates) but that processes after discharge differ (leading to different outcomes).

How do we investigate these initial labeling processes across different cultures? To obtain a complete description of the entire social response process we should begin with the sick person very early in his career, at the point that someone, either himself or others, recognizes that something is wrong. In other words, we should begin with true incidence rates in the community. This, however, creates a problem if we are cultural relativists and assume that each society makes its own definiton of illness. If we are to measure the effect of social responses to mental illness, and to compare these effects across cultures then we must begin with standard definitions of illness that are independent of any particular social group. If we find, then, that each society processes these syndromes differently and patients have careers of different durations, we can fairly attribute the patient career differences to cultural differences in response. This means, then, beginning with nonrelative definitions of illness as Murphy and Leighton (1965) attempted to do, and assuming, with the medical model of illness, that there are syndromes that exist unrelated to a particular society's definitions of illness.

An alternate approach, more compatible with the sociological model, recognizes that each society may create its own definitions of illness, some of which match those in other societies (without assuming that the matching results from basic biological qualities of the illness or social factors). Beiser et al. (1973) has taken the first step in this latter comparative method by showing that the Senegalese illness called O'Dof is very similar to what Western psychiatrists would call schizophrenia. It would then be possible to follow the careers of these particular sick people in the two societies and to attribute different patient careers to variable social responses to the same illness.

We have implied in our discussion of the theory and its applications that peasant or traditional societies discourage prolonged and serious mental disorders and modern or industrialized societies encourage chronicity or episodic recurrence of illness. Data suggest that this may be true of Mauritius, Ceylon and England and the United States. However, if we think twice about the important function that beliefs have in the theoretical system we might expect to find some traditional systems where chronicity is supported by the belief system and thus illnesses are of long, rather than brief, duration. Murphy (1972) reports such findings in data on long-term hospitalization and chronicity in traditional and modern French-Canadian communities in Quebec. Here, it is the traditional French-Catholic community that produces mental illnesses with long durations and impaired social performance; the modern French-Catholic community, on the other hand, is more likely to turn out patients who can return to normal roles with episodes of illness. (Modern Protestant communities showed a mixture of the two outcomes.) Thus, the Mauritius–Great Britain differences are apparent, but in reverse.

We should thus be alerted to the dangers of using such global concepts as traditional society, peasant system, modern society, industrial stage of development and attempting to link these to predictions about incidence and prognosis of mental illnesses. [See M. Singer (1972) for a critique of these categories and the assumptions that underlie them and for an analysis of one society, India, that has both traditional and modern elements, interwoven into a unique whole.] Instead, it appears from Murphy's findings and others we have presented here that we may be able to predict the duration and quality of the mentally ill person's career more accurately by looking in detail at each society's beliefs and expectations about mental illness and at the intervening social processes through which these expectations are acted out. Later, we might find that social expectations are, indeed, related to a cultural state, an economic system, religious values, or a stage in industrialization. Attempting to test such global hypotheses without first examining the internal processes that sustain the sick role seems to be both inefficient and unproductive.

While we have been concerned with the utility of the social response model for understanding cross-cultural differences in the psychiatric patient's career, the model has obvious implications for the practice of psychiatry as well. Stated in its most unadorned form, the theory says that even though doctors, nurses, and family members are motivated to help a patient return to normal as quickly as possible, the social responses of these and other people in the society may actually function to prolong the patient's sickness. This process seems to be most apparent in Western societies where the most modern theories of psychiatry are held and where the most comprehensive hospital and clinic systems have been developed to treat the mentally ill.

Since our treatment systems and the medical professionals within them are implicated, by the theory, in the maintenance of the sick role, does this imply that the solution is to burn down the hospitals, fire the doctors, and let the patients return to the "old" ways—to rely on families, priests, and patent medicines? This solution ignores the fact that psychiatric treatment is beneficial, it does relieve symptoms, and it may cure. Instead, following the notion of labeling theory that the relative power of the patient and treatment system is crucial to the maintenance of the sick role, perhaps patient and family control over his career can be increased without concomitant loss of beneficial therapy, by increasing the participation of the wider community in the operation of clinics and hospitals; by involving more nonprofessionals in patient care; by breaking up monolithic treatment systems into small, unrelated units; or by reducing the extent to which records of patients, on paper or computer tape, circulate through the system. Implied in these organizational changes is the introduction of alternate definitions of illness; the tendency of Western psychiatry to enlarge the types of deviance that it treats (taking the alcoholics from the jails, for example), to feel responsible for prevention of mental illness in the community, and to be concerned with treating the whole life experience of its patients, is countered by alternate community beliefs, for example, that mental illness need not impair the whole person permanently, or even temporarily. Broadening the base of control over treatment systems allows varied and sometimes competing beliefs about mental illness to be represented, and may give patients more power to choose between alternate messages about sickness.

This approach has implications, also, for the introduction of psychiatric teatment systems in underdeveloped, peasant, or primitive communities. It suggests that one should think carefully before establishing a system of highly organized, extensively linked treatment structures; an overburdened hospital ward with limited bed space and no referral options may encourage short-term illnesses.

It suggests, too, the importance of retaining and using indigenous treatments, especially if they call for minimal change in the sick person's role and quick return to normality.

To return to our major concern for researchers interested in explaining why certain societies produce psychiatric illnesses that only briefly disrupt the person's normal life, an examination of the society's expectations for such patients and the ways in which sick people are "processed" is of crucial significance. We feel it strategically important to carry out carefully controlled studies focused solely (through control of other variables) on the social responses to a sick person in order to measure the extent to which these factors can account for long-term social and clinical disability. In the long run, of course, we would not expect that social responses will explain all of the variance in cross-cultural recovery rates. It is obvious that genetic and nutritional factors, treatment availability, and qualities of social life, for example, will have a place in the explanation of outcome. However, social expectations are powerful forces and we should not be surprised to find the significant and perhaps primary part they have in molding the psychiatric patient's career.

Annotated Additional Readings

a) Wittkower, E. D. 1969. Perspectives of transcultural psychiatry. *International Journal of Psychiatry* 8:811–824.
An overview of the field prepared by one of the pioneering and most productive workers in the field. Definitions are offered for main terms and concepts such as culture and mental illness. The author also presents a synthesis of the principal issues that have been studied by transcultural researchers and provides an informative list of tentative conclusions obtained from the literature.

b) Dohrenwend, B. P., and B. S. Dohrenwend. 1974. Social and cultural influences on psychopathology. *Annual Review of Psychology* 25:417–452.
An authoritative overview of the role that culture plays in the prevalence and distribution of mental disorders. After pointing toward the methodological limitations in the field, the authors discuss important aspects of the relationship between culture and psychopathology, attempting to answer in a balanced way such questions as: Are types of psychopathology different in different cultures? Is there more psychopathology today than in the past? Are rates of psychopathology higher in urban than in rural areas?

The authors point out the need for increasing methodological sophistication and suggest the usefulness of moving research in this field from cross-sectional surveys to quasi-experimental studies that exploit contrasts provided by social processes in order to test specific alternative hypotheses.

c) Draguns, J. G. 1973. Comparisons of psychopathology across cultures: Issues, findings, directions. *Journal of Cross-Cultural Psychology* 4:9-47.
A good review of some of the main issues confronting the study of culture and psychopathology. First, sources of differential findings are examined in terms of subject, observer, setting, community, and instruments factors. Then, cross-cultural findings on the incidence, manifestations, patterning, and outcome of mental disorders are examined, suggesting a considerable degree of cultural plasticity along with certain pancultural trends in these parameters. Finally, a reference is made to the relationship between deviant behavior and the characteristics of the normal population in the particular sociocultural setting where such deviant behavior takes place, making a point for the so-called "caricature theory" of psychopathology.

d) Dunham, H. W. 1976. Society, culture and mental disorder. *Archives of General Psychiatry* 33:147-156.
The author, who had neatly teased out with Faris several explanations for the differential urban distribution of schizophrenic patients (Faris and Dunham, 1939), provides a review of mechanisms by which social and cultural factors

may play a role in the development of mental illness. Dunham complements his review with 15 tentative conclusions mainly related to schizophrenia and the psychoses.

e) **Fabrega, H. 1975a.** The need for an ethnomedical science. *Science* 189:969-975.
This is an incisive analysis of the nature and historical roots of the biomedical model, its strengths and limitations, and a justification of the need for a new medical model that takes into account how different cultures think about disease and organize themselves toward treatment.

The paper describes a strategy to develop an ethnomedical paradigm which encompasses concerns relevant to both social and biological sciences. The relation which exists between disease, social behavior, and human adaptation, the primary subject matter of ethnomedicine, is examined at the light of man's unique capacities for symbolization and culture.

This paper offers an excellent preparation and complement, from an epistemological and anthropological perspective, for Engel's article (2).

f) **Eisenberg, L. 1977.** Psychiatry and society: A sociobiologic synthesis. *The New England Journal of Medicine* 296:903-910.
Emphasizing the concerns of the clinician, the author addresses the questions raised by certain uses of labeling theory in the sense that psychiatric diagnoses are mainly labels to legitimate social segregation of people whose behavior is disagreeable and unwanted.

The author calls attention to the interaction of social with psychological and biological factors affecting prevalence, causes, and outcome of human disease. This paper is helpful to put Waxler's article (3) in a clearer and more comprehensive perspective.

g) **Murphy, J. M. 1976.** Psychiatric labeling in cross-cultural perspective. *Science* 191:1019-1028.
A comprehensive review of the perception of abnormal behavior in diverse cultures taking advantage of the author's field experience with the Eskimos of northwest Alaska and the Yorubas of tropical Nigeria. Particularly notable is the documentation offered on the universal detection of several psychiatric disorders.

The author strongly argues against using labeling theory to represent an explanation of the development of mental disorders, although this is neither the only nor the most appropriate interpretation of the theory as Waxler explains. This theoretical paper complements Eisenberg's clinical analysis of labeling theory (f, above).

h) **Towsend, J. M. 1975.** Cultural conceptions and mental illness: A controlled comparison of Germany and America. *Journal of Nervous and Mental Disease* 160:409-421.
A comparison of responses of samples of 100 psychiatric inpatients in Frankfurt and in California to administered questionnaires exploring their concepts about curability of mental illness, characterization of a mentally ill person, and purposes of psychiatric hospitalization as well as their self-

perceptions. The author found that exaggerated stereotypes of the mentally ill were not endorsed by the majority of patients in either sample. On the other hand, the German patients (and also hospital staff) espoused a more fixed and endogenous and less "free-will" conceptualization of mental illness than their counterparts in the United States, and these differences appeared reflected in differential perceptions about proper behavior in the hospital. The author discusses these and related findings in regard to various sociological theories of mental illness. With this perspective, this paper complements the statements by Waxler (article 3) and Murphy (g, above) on labeling theory.

i) **Oetting, E. R. and W. W. Stein. 1966.** Popular medical beliefs and attitudes toward mental illness in Peru. *Human Organization* 25:308-311.
An exploration of attitudes and beliefs about mental illness among professional and subprofessional staff of four psychiatric hospitals in Lima, Peru. The investigators found that those scoring highest on the "humanistic" end of an "ideology scale" consisted almost entirely of psychiatrists, general physicians, and nurses and tended to disregard "bad food" and masturbation as main causes of mental illness. On the other hand, those scoring at the "custodial" end of the scale consisted almost entirely of hospital attendants and most of them agreed that "bad food" and masturbation were principal causes of mental disorder. The latter group appeared to be in line with popular or folk beliefs in Peru. The paper also discusses the influence of these contrasting conceptualizations on the staff's behavior and interaction with patients.

j) **Gaviria, M. and R. M. Wintrob. 1976.** Supernatural influence in psychopathology: Puerto Rican folk beliefs about mental illness. *Canadian Psychiatric Association Journal* 21:361-369.
This paper reports on an investigation of both natural and supernatural etiological factors of psychopathology as conceived by Puerto Ricans living in the Northeast of the United States. Furthermore, it explores the relationship between such conceptualizations and the relative use of standard treatment services and folk healers, and proposes some practical recommendations.

An interesting finding is that the individuals contacted identified two main forms of being mentally ill: the *loco* (crazy) and the *nervous* (characterized by depressive and anxiety symptoms). This information from a "cultural" study may be quite useful to enlighten the current controversy in the mainstream of U.S. psychiatry about the value of "psychosis" and "neurosis" as major classificatory principles for mental disorders.

II

Methodological Issues

In their current developmental stage, each of the behavioral sciences is still in the process of getting organized, struggling among competing paradigms and searching for improved investigational procedures. This situation is even more challenging in the case of the study of culture and psychopathology, where it is the relationship between two complex sets of variables which is of interest. This points out the crucial need to use systematic methodology in this field in order to arrive at trustworthy conclusions.

One of the key methodological tasks involves the identification of and developments for dealing with sources of error and undesirable variability in the process of cross-cultural assessment. Potential sources of error include the subject, the observer, measuring instruments, language equivalence, procedures for integrating the obtained information, etc.

Another major methodological area involves the use of research designs and interpretational frameworks which deal appropriately with the complexity of the situation. This frequently requires multivariate approaches in which several variables are measured on the same subjects and are analyzed conjointly, taking into consideration their interactions. Techniques such as factor analysis for data reduction and elucidation of hypothetical constructs, multiple regression for prediction using a linear combination of several predictors, canonical correlation for finding maximally correlated linear combinations of two sets of variables (say, one sociocultural and another psychopathological), discriminant functional analysis for finding rules separating established groups, and cluster analysis for exploring groupings of individuals or entities on the basis of the similarities of their profiles on a set of relevant variables are all of interest here, and are being gradually explored in cross-cultural research.

A frequent problem in the investigational design of studies on culture and psychopathology concerns the imbalance noted between the use of rigorous procedures in one area and rather cavalier ones in the other. More careful allocation of research resources or collaborative efforts may be helpful in this regard.

The three articles in this part deal with some of the most important methodological issues in the field: measurement, language equivalence, design, and interpretation. Some of the questions explored include: How can we accommodate our measurement instruments to answer the research questions at hand? How do we know we are evaluating the same feature when we are trying to assess it in two different societies? How comparable are verbal and nonverbal stimuli presented across cultures? In which ways can cultural factors influence general research in psychopathology, and what methodological steps may be useful for the various cases under construction?

The annotated additional references concern problems of translation of psychological tests, the stability and generalizability of transcultural findings, the use of physiological measures to increase the validity of cross-cultural evaluations, and issues in the international diagnosis of mental disorders, including the use of structured clinical interviews to improve diagnostic reliability.

4

Problems of Measurement in Cross-Cultural Research

George M. Guthrie

Measurement is a very important issue in systematic research in general, and has particularly intricate connotations in regard to studies on culture and psychopathology. This is so because research questions in this field typically refer to the relationship of two variables or groups of variables—i.e., sociocultural and psychopathological—and adequate solutions to the measurement of each variable are needed.

As required by the subject matter, measurement may involve the use of dimensional or nominal scales. Dimensional scales (i.e., interval and rank) measure quantitative or at least ordered variation (e.g., I.Q. and social class). Nominal scales are composed of a catalog of qualitatively different categories, one or more of which are selected to describe an individual (e.g., for diagnosis according to psychopathological syndromes).

Another set of crucial issues in measurement involves the assessment and enhancement of the reliability and validity of the scales used. The evaluation and improvement of reliability or reproducibility of measurements require the identification of sources of variability and the design of procedures for controlling or minimizing these. Validity involves the fulfillment by the scale of the purposes for which it was developed and used—i.e., to measure what it is intended to measure. This issue is particularly intricate in cross-cultural studies given that it involves definitions of meanings which may be different in different societies.

Significant advances are being made in regard to the measurement of some key variables—e.g., the use of structured clinical interviews which attempt to control several sources of undesirable variability in

psychopathological assessment. Illustrative of this is the Present State Examination (Wing et al. 1974) used for symptomatological evaluation in the nine-country International Pilot Study of Schizophrenia (World Health Organization 1973).

In this article Guthrie stresses the need for relevance of the measurement strategies and procedures to the concepts under investigation. He contrasts issues germane to descriptive vs. experimental cross-cultural research, and pointedly describes measurement issues encountered in the comparative investigation of intelligence, personality, and attitudes. Finally, he notes the need for multiple measurements in studies in this field, which both compounds the measurement issues discussed and requires sophisticated multivariate statistical procedures for data analysis.

IN CROSS-CULTURAL psychological research, we encounter all of the problems of measurement that confront us when we do research at home, plus many other problems that grow out of differences in language and the strangeness of an experimental situation. In both situations, the measurements one makes and the data one collects are determined by the questions one asks or the theories one is testing. Cultural factors are of concern when we ask whether a relationship found in the United States is also present in the Philippines.[1] Merely collecting data on color vision, or conformity, or memory in another country is not cross-cultural research, unless one attempts to relate differences in vision, conformity, or memory to differences in the cultural patterns between at least two societies. Furthermore, if we simply find differences in conformity between Americans and Filipinos we have no basis to choose among an unlimited number of alternative explanations of the differences. As has been pointed out, a difference between two groups is, by itself, uninterpretable.

In both cross-cultural and domestic research, it is convenient to think of Cronbach's (1957) two disciplines of scientific psychology: the descriptive and the experimental. In the former, we are interested in individual differences among people; in the latter, the differences in effects that treatments have on two or more groups whose members have been assigned randomly from a common

1. Because my own experience in cross-cultural research has been in the Philippines, all of my hypothetical examples will involve Americans and Filipinos. This is in contrast to the more abstract Societies A and B that are commonly used. I prefer not to use Society B because I had some unfortunate experiences with them.

source. This does not mean we cannot use experiments in cross-cultural research because people are already assigned to societies; it does suggest we inspect the differences between two treatments applied to each of the groups. The minimum, using this line of reasoning, is then a 2×2 experiment: a treatment and a control applied in two societies in which the interaction term is of great significance.

In either descriptive or experimental work, measurements of cross-cultural differences need to be derived from our conceptualization of how differences in cultural processes have operated. If we conceive of a cultural process as weakening or strengthening a function such as memory, then we measure the function in question and other functions not subject to differential cultural effects in order to make certain that differences are not due simply to test-taking skills. For instance, Guthrie, Sinaiko, and Brislin, (1971) showed that Vietnamese did very poorly on tests of spatial ability but just as well as Americans on tests of numerical ability and perceptual speed; they interpreted the difference in spatial ability as being due to differences in experience of the members of the two societies.

However, if we are interested in the effects of culture on the patterning of sexual or aggressive behavior, then we must compare patterns. People are not more or less aggressive in all of their actions, but rather have different expressions of aggression and different configurations of situations in which they may express aggression. Mischel's (1973) emphasis on the situational specificity of an individual's behavior as opposed to general traits is even more applicable in cross-cultural research. Ethnographic accounts, of course, reflect this state of affairs at a verbal, descriptive level, but we often implicitly deny configurational differences when we try to measure aspects of sexuality or aggression in cross-cultural research.

Descriptive Research

The vast majority of cross-cultural studies are descriptive because they ask, "What are the differences between these two groups?" Differences may be sought in intelligence, memory, aggressiveness, or socialization practices.

But our research can become productive only if we go a second step and ask, "How are these differences related to cultural processes?" For example, merely demonstrating that there is less aggression among Filipino children than among American children is only half the job; we need to go further and indentify the factors which account for this difference. We found (Guthrie and Jacobs 1966), for instance, that Filipino mothers did everything they could to prevent their children from quarreling with neighbors' children because such a fight would lead to great bitterness among parents. There are alternative explanations of the smaller number of quarrels among Filipino than among American children. It is a weakness of the descriptive approach that it is difficult or impossible to choose among alternative explanations.

There are several other problems in such studies: differences found may be due to the measuring instrument, they may be due to the relationship between the subject and the collector of data, or they may be due to sampling biases. We shall examine these difficulties as they appear with different types of measuring procedures designed for different domains of behavior. Descriptive psychologists have traditionally been interested in such characteristics as intelligence, personality, and attitudes within our own society. It should come as no surprise that they carry these interests with them when they go abroad.

Intelligence

Difficulties in this area have been recognized for many years, and recently they have been rediscovered where intelligence tests are used with cultural subgroups within our own society. No test has been designed which has been accepted as a measure of differences in intelligence between two groups whose previous experience has differed markedly. Within-group differences, however, can be measured if we design a new test or reevaluate an established one against the common criteria of test construction. We have, for instance, developed a nonverbal intelligence test for use with Philippine children, the Philippine Nonverbal Intelligence Test (PNIT) (Guthrie, Tayag and Jacobs 1969). With the help of Filipino artists we developed a 100-item test in which the subject points to one of five figures on a card that does not belong with the other four. The test meets many of the criticisms of intelligence tests as applied in and out of the United States: It is untimed, the instructions are simple and do not change, there is no need for words to be exchanged. All of the items present pictures of common objects for Filipino children. Beginning with such simple items as four squares and a circle, the child is asked in his language, "Which one is different, which does not belong with the others?" The instructions may be repeated with the second card. They can even be given in pantomime. The child learns the task with the first three or four items in which five-year-olds show almost 100 percent accuracy. The items are presented in increasing order of difficulty as they go from simple perceptual differences, to differences in function, to differences that require abstract concept formation. Using the total score as a criterion, item analyses can be very simple on programs written to evaluate five-alternative multiple-choice examinations for college students.

These programs provide a comprehensive evaluation of each item including the percentage and mean total score of those who choose each alternative for each item. Carrying out such an analysis separately for age levels and sexes and for different samples enables us to identify items that are culturally biased. The procedure requires hundreds of subjects for each new analysis but it does provide protection against the problems which have beset many attempts at the measurement of intelligence in other societies. Finally, our total scores show a satisfactory rise from one age group to the next and they correlate with school grades as well as IQ tests in American schools.

The PNIT enables us to measure differences within and between groups of Filipinos. The test has also been found by Seymour (1974) to be highly satisfactory in Borneo, which has a very similar environment of plant and animal forms. But it would not be satisfactory for comparisons with children from temperate climate areas or the arid tropics because they would not recognize some of the stimuli. In spite of these limitations, it is still useful for cross-cultural studies like those demonstrating that there are no sex differences in the Philippines where the equality of the sexes is emphasized but there are in Borneo where Islamic traditions are more powerful. It has also been used to determine that height and intelligence are positively correlated in areas of severe malnutrition, but intelligence and height are not related to one another in parts of the world where children are more adequately fed.

Most intelligence tests do not translate satisfactorily because many questions deal with experiences that are not worldwide. But the ability to acquire information is a fundamental component of intelligence wherever one lives. The Information subtest of the Weschler Intelligence Test in its many forms often correlates more highly than other subtests, even Vocabulary, with the total score.

Acting on this observation and with the help of Filipino colleagues, we developed an information test of intelligence (Guthrie 1970) for use in the rural Philippines. We asked such questions as: A woman puts out some wet clothes on a sunny day. Where does the water go that was in the clothes? If the moon rises at 10 o'clock this evening, when will it rise tomorrow evening? What is soap made from? Where does the water in the coconut come from?

Again, there are computer programs which will carry out in a few seconds the scoring and analysis of the preliminary form of such a test providing item difficulties, item-total score correlations, KR20 estimates of reliability, and many other summary statistics. The merit of this approach is that it enables one to develop tests that are meaningful in the experience of the respondents and that avoid the problems of cultural unfamiliarity which intrude when one uses a test developed elsewhere; translated or original. The absence of time limits, the familiar materials, and the simplicity of instructions are all, in our opinion, assets of efforts of this sort.

There is one problem we have not solved in the Philippines. In the process of training at home and at school, Filipino children learn that any answer, no matter how erroneous, is much better than a failure to answer. Accordingly, on a multiple-choice test of abstract reasoning we found the Filipino college students all finished a difficult test in much less than the 20-minute time limit. Scoring revealed that they solved the first few easy items and then guessed the rest so that they omitted no items in the second half of the test; they just got chance scores. Even on the PNIT, we encounter the problem that a child will not examine the alternatives carefully when they start to get difficult for him; he continues answering at the same rate and with the same confident gesture in a silent contract with his society that random answers are preferred to a pause that betrays that one does not know.

One may want to assess other cognitive processes, such as reasoning or memory. Cole's work with the Kpelle (Cole et al. 1971) is a model of the development of measurements that are meaningful within the experience of the subjects.

Personality

Just as is the case with the measurement of cognitive aspects of behavior, personality assessment techniques follow the fashion current at home. A decade ago, the use of projective techniques, especially the Rorschach, declined rapidly both at home and abroad for reasons beyond the scope of this article.

The inkblots would, at first impression, seem to offer a less culturally biased set of stimuli than do inventories either in their original language or translated. The problem with them was that the system of interpretation developed for the test was based on a theory of inner determinants of behavior which meant that interpretive statements could neither be confirmed nor denied. In a broader sense Freudian psychodynamic theory was formulated in a way that could not be confirmed or denied.

Beyond the problems inherent in the way the theory was formulated was the fact that it left little or no place for cultural factors to operate. The basic stages of psychosexual development. oedipal conflicts, the nature of instinctual strivings, the mechanisms of symptom formation were all assumed, even asserted to be universal. Freudian theory was used to explain behavior, as exemplified in the work of Roheim (1950), Kardiner (1945), Wilbur and Munsterberger (1951), and many others. Data from other cultures were not seen as an opportunity to test the universality of Freud's formulations. Even the so-called cultural school of Sullivan, Erikson, etc., shows no effects of data from other societies.

The Rorschach was a method that produced virtually unverifiable statements that, in turn, were expressed in a theory which left no room for cultural differences. As Hartmann et al. (1951) assert with respect to anthropological data:

> It is hardly necessary to emphasize that no data produced and no interpretations advanced have been able, or even seriously set out, to modify our views on the working of the psychic apparatus. Psychoanalytic assumptions on psychic structure and the interrelation of its parts, on the function of psychic energy and its working, on the distinction of degrees or neutralization, of mobile and bound energies, and hence of primary and secondary processes, supply the best, or more precisely, the only set of assumptions which at present permits an explanatory approach to mental functioning.

A second projective test, the TAT, was more clearly a product of white, western society; but the strategy that people would reveal themselves in their stories was not tied to one culture pattern. Accordingly, many variations of the TAT were developed including sets for children and blacks in North America. Lagmay (1966) developed a set of pictures for use in the Philippines that had Filipino faces and backgrounds. Using the Symonds series in original form with Filipino college students, I found that they told Filipino stories about the figures and seemed unaffected by the fact that the pictures were clearly not of Philippine origin. It is possible that many people have seen so many movies made in American or Western

Europe that they are not as influenced by cultural features as one would expect. My experience, at least, led me to doubt that one needs a new set of pictures for each society.

Sentence completion techniques were used productively by Phillips (1966) in Thailand. We were able to take the English version of this test and our own Tagalog version and to develop comparisons of Thai and Filipino responses (Guthrie and Azores 1968), an analysis that seemed to clarify many of the differences in behavior patterns between members of those two societies. We did encounter some interesting problems of translation of even the sentence stems because Tagalog does not always follow the subject-verb-predicate sequence of English. Putting the subject before the predicate tended to shift the meaning in directions we did not want. Maybe we needed a Sentence Beginning Test.

Still another technique that has proven convenient and productive is the ECHO procedure described by Barthol and deMille (1969). Groups of literate subjects are given 20 cards, 10 of which bear the questions, "What is a good thing to do? and Who would approve?," and 10 cards, each asking "What is a bad thing to do; and Who would disapprove?" Teams of three, drawn from the population who answered the questions on the 20 cards are then asked to sort the responses of the entire sample into piles which say approximately the same thing. In this way piles may be generated which say it is a good thing to respect parents, work hard in school, or love God. "Bad thing" statements may generate piles about stealing, killing, or failing to wash one's hands. Pooling the data from several teams and comparing it with data from other samples and other countries gives one some rather remarkable insights into the moral and social emphases of different social and national groups.

Personality inventories have been used abroad since shortly after their appearance here. The Philippines is an especially convenient setting to evaluate inventories because the majority of potential subjects are literate in both English and a Philippine language, and because the Philippine language and culture is Malayo-Polynesian in its roots rather than Indo-European. Meanings, however, can be lost even without translation, as we found when we used Shafer and Bell's Parental Attitude Research Inventory (PARI) (Shafer and Bell 1958) in English with middle-class Manila mothers. The factorial structure of the inventory was different from that found with American mothers even though the items tended to remain on the same individual scales as had been found in the original development of the inventory (Guthrie 1966). Dependency, for instance, a sign of the mother's dominance and the child's weakness in the American setting, turned up as a sign of maternal responsibility and the child's respectfulness in the Philippines.

Because personality inventories are basically measures of attitudes toward oneself, problems of scale construction, bias, and meaning will be deferred for a moment and treated with measures of attitudes.

Attitudes

There are formidable problems of assessment of attitudes which parallel those associated with personality measurement. In our opinion the most severe is response acquiescence or the tendency to agree with an item. Closely related and compounding the problem, is the desire on the part of respondents in many societies to give an answer which they believe will please an interviewer. Various measures of alienation, for instance, are almost always written so that agreement counts for alienation. Measures of modernity often suffer the same shortcoming (Kahl 1968). This problem of response-bias has been studied by many psychologists and some techniques have been developed to control these sources of variance. We have surely passed the point where an investigator can make up a set of statements from face validity considerations and use it uncritically as a measure of attitudes toward such socially significant matters as family planning, sanitation practices, or land reform. Unfortunately, in our opinion, the Guttman index of reproducibility, which is often used to evaluate an attitude scale, will be high when response sets are strongest. One solution we suggest is to present the respondent with pairs of statements judged to be equated for social desirability that express pro and con positions on the issue at hand, and ask him to choose the one which best expresses his view.

There are two major problems in the adaptation and use of attitude or personality scales in cross-cultural research. For cross-cultural purposes, one will ordinarily begin with an established scale and translate it. But the statements of an inventory often cannot be translated so that they mean the same thing even if one has the help of a colleague who is a native speaker of the second language. Anyone undertaking such a project should read Werner and Campbell (1970), Brislin (1970), and Sechrest et al. (1972). The Sechrest paper is an especially good discussion of the problems one can expect to encounter; it is enriched by clarifying examples of English to Tagalog (Philippines) and English to Urdu (Pakistan).

The translation of personality and attitude items is especially difficult insofar as they emphasize emotions and interpersonal relationships. It is in this domain that members of different societies develop unique behavior patterns so that there are no words in a second language to render adequately an important experience in the first language.

The second problem is the extent to which well translated items belong on the same scales as they were in the original instrument. As we pointed out from our work with the PARI (Guthrie 1966), even without translation the same behavioral reports carried different meanings for Filipino than for American mothers. In light of these considerations, we suggest that translated attitude measures be analyzed by the same methods as were used in the development of the original scale. This would include assessing item intercorrelations, item–total score correlations, and the distribution of responses to the alternatives for each item. The scale should also be examined in a matrix of measures of other attitudes and of such distortions as yea saying, and social desirability, or intent to place oneself in an unduly favorable light. This means, essentially, that as with intelligence tests, we build a new scale; the content would be similar, but the method of construction identical.

Developing new scales in each new society we study would appear to reduce comparability from one society to the next. As I see it, there is a tradeoff in which we have to choose between literal accuracy and local validity, between a literally accurate translation of a scale, which may not adequately represent the dimension of behavior under study, and a locally valid measure which reflects the organization of behavior unique to a given society. This is exemplified in the work of Cole on memory (Cole et al. 1971) and, I believe, in our PNIT (Guthrie, Tayag and Jacobs 1969).

Beyond these considerations is the larger issue of the relationships between attitudes and behavior (Deutscher 1973; Calder and Ross 1973). Because social desirability is such a strong determiner of responses to attitude questionnaires, we would suggest that researchers explore behavioral measures. Who cares if a mother's attitudes about infant-feeding practices or family planning are favorable? If babies don't gain weight, and if they continue to gain younger brothers and sisters, then attitude measures are pointless. It would seem to be more productive to specify behavioral indications and to measure them. Furthermore, these can often be assessed unobtrusively. If a rural sanitation program is successful, fewer children should be absent from school due to sickness. If a supplementary school feeding program is accomplishing its objectives the results should show up on a set of bathroom scales rather than attitude scales.

Experimental Research

In this tradition, the investigator is interested in the effects of various conditions he must impose on his subjects, conditions which we call independent variables. In this approach we are not interested primarily in the differences that subjects bring to the experiment; ideally, we would like all of our subjects to come from one litter. Because this is a difficult condition to meet with human beings, an experimenter likes to begin with a relatively homogeneous group of subjects who are then assigned randomly to experimental and control treatments. The less culture the better. But a cultural difference can be studied in this design in a very useful way when it is treated as an independent variable. Of course, the rule of randomization is broken, but randomization remains the rule within societies.

Suppose that we are interested in the effects of cultural differences on the Asch effect. Americans and Filipinos might be assigned randomly in the various conditions of reporting alone, in a pair and in a group of four. We would predict that Filipinos would show a greater effect due to the presence of others than Americans because of the more personalistic qualities of Philippine social patterns. Such a finding is implied by the research of Kubany et al. (1970), who found that the presence or absence of an experimenter changed the performance of Filipino boys on a test considered an analog of achievement motivation. To be a complete example of an experimental study of cultural differences, however, they should have a sample of American boys tested under similar circumstances.

A. P. Hare (1969) studied cultural differences in performance in communication networks of Filipino, American, Nigerian, and South African students. In this social psychological experiment, subjects in groups of five could communicate with one another according to specific rules which produced networks that tended either to give each person equal access to information or to give one or more individuals greater access to information from others. Substantial differences in speed of solution and in preference for different networks were interpreted as indicative of cultural trends which emphasized individuality or cooperation and more or less communication in the interests of agreement and understanding.

This design is not used frequently for reasons that we do not fully understand. It seems simple enough to replicate a classical experiment in social psychology in a different society. Experimenters, however, are quite indifferent to cultural factors. With their penchant for sophomores, it is unlikely that many of them will think to inquire whether their results are limited to their own society.

In another sense, the study of behavior in a second culture is referred to as a *natural experiment.* Considerations of ethics, feasibility, and time make it virtually impossible to vary in a controlled way the kinds of events which we believe to be of fundamental significance in personality development. No one has done real life-extended experiments on the effects of early oral, elimination, or sexual training. They have been studied by Mead in Samoa, and Malinowski in the Trobriands, but by few others. But there is no natural laboratory worthy of the name because a host of other factors vary from one society to another in addition to the one we may be interested in, so that we cannot attribute differences in adulthood unequivocally to a childhood socialization practice. Mead's Samoans may show little adolescent stress because of their breadfruit diet or the proximity of the tropical sea. In a formal sense, these are also antecedents of the conditions of adolescence. Malinowski's reasoning has a different status. If he had not backed down in the face of Jones' Freudian pronouncements, he could have argued that his data constituted an exception to the universal resentment of sons toward fathers.

Although he did not state it as a formal experiment, Malinowski also observed that the inhabitants of another island had a different childrearing practice, which, with environmental factors the same, would enable a test of his theory of the origins of tension between fathers and sons. But he reported with regret that he was never able to follow up that idea.

Polynesian fosterage in which more than half of the children in a community move from one family to another and then to a third would, it seems, provide a superb opportunity to test the significance of stability of parents, a matter that our writers deem of profound importance to a child's development. Similarly the apparent permissiveness of Filipino parents toward homosexual behavior in some sons provided an opportunity not available here to study sexual orientation processes in a setting where the matter is not such a source of anxiety and guilt for all concerned. In both cases, we have the potential of obtaining findings that contradict two of the more fundamental premises of our theories of behavior disorders. Maybe stable parental models aren't necessary; maybe sexual orientation is not fixed at an early age but is something one can change back and forth if the society permits.

The measurements one makes in a cross-cultural project depend on his theory and on the measurement that is current at the time. When she was planning her historic research in Samoa, Mead considered using the GSR, which was becoming popular at that time (Mead 1972). The Cambridge Expedition used contemporary measuring devices. The Rorschach rose and fell abroad as it has at home. Theory and measurement should go hand in hand, but I am of the opinion that a current measurement technique may dictate too frequently the problem one chooses to study. We study modernity because scales are available. We use the Semantic Differential without asking whether it is precisely what we need. Available instruments probably have the effect of distorting or limiting the problems we tackle when we go abroad. We would suggest that more attention be given to making up a measuring technique that is congruent with our theory and with the language and culture pattern of the host society.

In summary, the purpose of cross-cultural research is to test theories and to investigate relationships under more than one configuration of circumstances. We go to another society for this research because the circumstances which we are interested in are too complex and of too long standing to be manipulated experimentally within our own society. But because the new circumstances vary in many and complex ways, we are left with some ambiguity about what cultural factors are important in the processes with which we are concerned. Accordingly, we need to make multiple measurements and deal with the pattern of results by multivariate methods. Furthermore, because the measures themselves inevitably involve the language and other artifacts of a society, it will be necessary to interpret the measures and configurations of scores within the local cultural context. The measures must be developed within each society; the cross-cultural psychologist's skill lies in his knowledge of measurement strategies and not in his mastery of measurement devices.

5

On the Comparability of Meaningful Stimuli in Cross-Cultural Research

R. Bruce W. Anderson

How do we know in cross-cultural research that we are asking the same question of two different sociocultural groups? This is another crucial methodological question in the study of culture and psychopathology, as adequate translations are essential for obtaining interpretable results. Although some empirical investigations of this issue have been carried out, its subtlety and complexity are such that many questions remain unanswered and some others are even awaiting identification and clear formulation.

The following article represents a considerable step forward in clarifying the issues involved. The author proposes that the problem of translation (the replacement of textual material in one language by equivalent textual material in another language) is one of equivalence and variance. Transcultural researchers, therefore, must be concerned with the maximization of equivalence and the concomitant minimization of variance. This issue emphasizes the need for the validation of assessment instruments.

Anderson analyzes this topic by exploring six important problem areas: translation of nonverbal stimuli, stimulus complexity and sample size, stimulus ambiguity, verbal stimuli, back translation, and bilingualism.

This keen review of an important methodological subject should be helpful in sensitizing workers in the field to the intricacies of the translation problem and facilitate the search for solutions.

IN ESSENCE the problem of translation is one of equivalence and variance. The focus of this article is on the problem of maximizing equivalence. Some existing data on translation equivalence are discussed in an effort to destroy some misconceptions and to indicate the needs for empirical data which will help the investigator answer the question: "How do we know we are asking the same question in two or more settings?" Six problem areas are discussed: (1) translation of nonverbal stimuli; (2) stimulus complexity and sample size; (3) stimulus ambiguity; (4) verbal stimuli; (5) back translation, an iterative approach; and (6) bilinguals and bilingualism.

Many investigators are led into cross-cultural research by accident, or as a result of the fascination of foreign things. Others see the crossing of national and cultural boundaries as essential for establishing universal laws of social behavior. Whatever the reasons, sociologists are frequently found making cross-cultural comparisons, and in doing so they come up against the problems of translation whether they are aware of it or not. Indeed, one could argue that part of the concern which sociologists have long manifested about the status of interviewers relative to that of interviewees may be viewed as pertaining to translation problems. In short, translation[1] is involved whenever research requires asking the "same" question of people with differing backgrounds. This is true whether the comparison involves societies using unwritten, tribal languages, nation-states using the "same" language (such as England and the United States), or subcultural groupings within a single society. Many of the differences involved at these various levels of linguistic "exoticism" are matters of degree, not of kind (Haugen 1966).

Further, one may question the correctness of the assumption that the members of the same subculture do not require translation in order that they may understand each other. The frequency with which comments like "I'm sorry, but I don't quite see what you are driving at" occur leads the writer to suggest that this assumption is less valid than it at first appears. Another instance of "hidden need for translation" obtains in the one-culture study where the investigator is not a participant in that culture. Here the need is centered in

1. Since the meaning of "translation" may vary, it seems appropriate to provide a definition of translation as "the replacement of textual material in one language . . . by equivalent textual material in another language." (Catford 1965). The principle is the same whether the replacement involves textual material in two "whole languages" or in two varieties (such as idiolects, or dialects) of the same language.

the probable ethnocentrisms of the investigator and his probable implicit comparisons. Attribution of "home culture meaning" to "host culture stimuli" is the likely consequence of misguided disregard for translation in this context.

In essence the problem of translation is one of equivalence and variance. The focus of this paper is on the problem of maximizing equivalence. The concomitant minimization of variance is dealt with only indirectly. Several questions might be raised at the outset, among them: (1) How does one know he is asking the same question in different settings? (2) What is the minimal level of equivalence necessary for two questions to be considered the same? and (3) What criteria can be established for equivalence? There are no absolute answers to these questions, since the goals of each individual research project will be instrumental in defining criteria of equivalence.[2] Some existing data on translation equivalence and some areas where additional data would be desirable will be discussed below.

Many of the data to be cited are drawn from studies involving personality tests. The reason for this eclecticism is simply that to date psychologists have been more interested in translation problems than have sociologists (Useem 1963; Hertzler 1965; Harsh 1967; Bohannan 1954; H. P. Phillips 1959–1960; Casagrande 1954). Adopting this approach may be justified on the grounds that the specific stimulus content per se is irrelevant to the search for general guidelines for translation equivalence. The use of data involving personality tests has the added advantage of raising the question of "what is equivalent" more sharply than other types of data might. This question is, of course, logically prior to the question of "how much is equivalent."

Focus upon the locus of equivalence properly includes considerations of situational equivalence—such as administration conditions—which are peripheral to the present paper. It also includes the question of response equivalence. The *intra-societal* measurement with (assumed) equivalent stimuli which results in *variant* responses is typically taken as an indicator of individual differences only after some sort of validation. A common means of validating personality instruments is by comparison of responses

2. Catford (1965) discusses the nature of equivalence in translation. His approach, however, deals with formal linguistic criteria and is not directly relevant to the pragmatics of instrumentation for cross-cultural research.

made by subjects who exhibit behavioral differences. Similar findings in cross-cultural comparison are often assumed to indicate *cultural differences* without comparable concern for behavioral validation. If, on the other hand, *equivalent* responses are obtained from a multi-societal investigation they are often uncritically attributed to *cultural universals*. It will be noted that in either of these situations stimulus equivalence is assumed, and conclusions are based on the obtained response equivalence or variance. This paper will be concerned with response equivalence only when it can be used as an index of stimulus equivalence.

It is important to recognize that the question of translation equivalence is a special case of instrument validation. As in the case of other aspects of "the validity problem" the importance of the theoretical matrix within which the instrument in question is embedded should not be overlooked. The assertion that "the goals of each individual research project will be instrumental in defining criteria of equivalence," above, was intended to alert the reader to this fact. Given a single bivariate hypothesis and a single question or instrument for measuring each variable, what can be concluded from findings which appear to support the hypothesis? The present writer is of the disposition that interpretation of such findings (without benefit of additional information) as supportive of the hypothesis, as supportive of the validity of the instrument(s) employed, or as supportive of both instrument(s) and hypothesis would be tenuous at best. The presence of translated instruments should serve to increase, rather than decrease, one's reluctance to accept such conclusions. In discussing ways of improving the quality of translations, as described in the following paragraphs, the reader should understand that the techniques advocated are intended as complementary to traditional validational procedures, not as substitutes for them. Indeed, the use of "translation-equivalent forms" of research instruments provides one take-off point for application of the logic of validation suggested by Campbell and Fiske (Campbell and Fiske 1959; Campbell 1960; Sechrest 1963). This will become particularly obvious to the reader familiar with their work in the discussion of "back translation," below.

The discussion of maximization of stimulus equivalence in cross-cultural research will focus on six problem areas: (a) translation of nonverbal stimuli; (b) stimulus complexity and sample size; (c) stimulus ambiguity; (d) verbal stimuli; (e) back translation, an iterative approach, and (f) bilinguals and bilingualism.

I. Translation of Non-Verbal Stimuli

A non-verbal personality test, such as the TAT or Rorschach, *appears* to avoid the problem of translation except with respect to instructions given during administration. Lindzey (1961) rightly observes that differences in response language in cross-cultural testing by these techniques result in a shift of the location of the translation problem rather than its elimination. The Welsh Figure Preference Test (Welsh, 1959) minimizes these problems of response translation by asking the respondent to indicate whether or not he likes each stimulus—rather than asking for complex responses as with other "projective" tests.

Even with the Welsh test, where the problems of comparing verbal responses in different languages have been effectively eliminated by reducing the content of the responses to a binary choice situation, translation difficulties remain. Consider, for example, Figure 5.1a taken from this instrument. A biology student in any Western European society could clearly and unambiguously interpret this stimulus—and his liking or disliking of it would probably be influenced by his interpretation. Figure 5.1b, on the other hand, has no clearly understood meaning to a Western European—yet an American Indian might well interpret it in terms of the pictographic symbol for "mountain" as can be seen by comparison with Figure 5.2a. It would be naïve to assume that these and similar differences

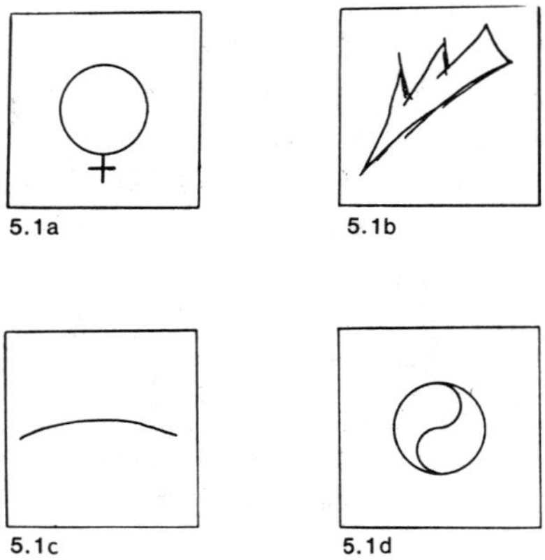

Figure 5.1 Pictures Adapted from the Welsh Figure Preference Test. (Published by Consulting Psychologists Press, Inc. Palo Alto, California. Research edition Copyright © 1949 by George S. Welsh. Released for research use, 1959, by the publishers.)

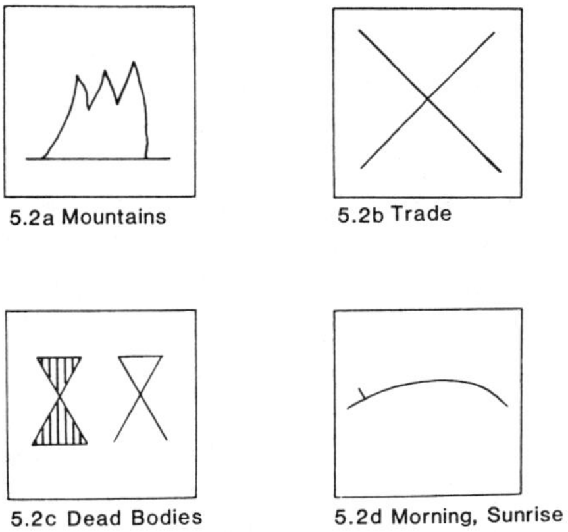

Figure 5.2 Pictures Adapted from "Pictography and Ideography of the Sioux and Ojibway Tribes of North American Indians, by William Tompkins. (In *Universal Indian Sign Language of the Plains Indians of North America* by William Tompkins. San Diego: The Author, 1929, pp. 70–78.

in interpretation which might obtain across societies would not influence responses differentially.[3] Thus, it must be concluded that the use of nonverbal measures changes the nature of the translation problem but does not avoid it.

II. Stimulus Complexity and Sample Size

Hanks, Geertz, and others who have modified the TAT pictures in efforts to gain equivalence across cultures indicate awareness of the need to translate visual stimuli. To undertake the translation of a volume of prose requires a considerable familiarity with the subtleties of both languages involved—even to attain minimal readability. Similarly, modification of visual stimuli requires extensive knowledge of the responses which the original stimulus evoked in the base society and also of the stimulus which will have the same or similar meaning in the second society. Comparison of the sentence "I love you" with the *Kama Sutra* or of one of the Welsh Figure

3. In this connection see Lawlor's (1955) comparison of the responses made by English subjects to those made by West African subjects. Cf. Naumburg (1957).

Preference Test "droodles" reproduced in Figure 5.1 with a TAT picture will immediately suggest one influence of stimulus complexity upon translatability. For the linguistically unsophisticated sociologist the task of finding an equivalent for the shorter, simpler stimulus appears intuitively manageable while the parallel task with more complex stimuli appears hopeless.

Associated with the problem of stimulus complexity is the size of the sample of stimuli. In general, the more complex the stimuli the less practical it becomes to administer a large number of them. Thus the usual number of TAT pictures shown is twenty or fewer. If one out of these twenty pictures is inadequately translated—a situation which appears quite likely given the difficulty of the task—the 5 percent confidence level can no longer be applied to results, regardless of subject sampling procedures employed. Even if all stimuli were satisfactorily translated, the size of the stimulus sample might be considered too small to absorb latent random error. These criticisms imply acceptance of the premise that the original small sample was drawn randomly from some population of theoretically relevant stimuli. This assumption may also be questioned.

III. Stimulus Ambiguity

It is a truism that a useful stimulus must be sufficiently ambiguous that it does not require a single response. One could posit a continuum of ambiguity ranging from questions such as "Are you male or female?", which permit but two answers, to stimuli like the Rorschach blots, which permit a seemingly infinite variety of responses. The problem of the translator, noted by Jacobson[4] in his methodological note on the O.C.S.R. Seven-Nation Attitude Studies, is to faithfully reproduce the ambiguity from one language into the other. The difficulty of this task clearly varies directly with the extent of the ambiguity. How does one know with any certainty if the ambiguity is equivalent in two cultures when it is difficult to describe the

4. Jacobson (1954) and Catford (1965) in distinguishing between various types of untranslatability remark that "Linguistic untranslatability occurs typically in cases where an *ambiguity* (italics in the original) peculiar to the . . . [source language] text is a functionally relevant feature" of the language in question. This explanation goes on to discuss sources of such ambiguity in considerable detail.

nature of the ambiguity in other than purely mechanical terms (i.e., colored, symmetrical blots . . . etc.)?

From the foregoing it can be seen that ambiguity and complexity interact to increase the difficulty of meeting the requirement that equivalent versions permit the same range of responses. Even more difficult is attainment of stimuli which will produce translation equivalent responses with equal probability under controlled conditions. To reduce the problem of translating ambiguities the time honored procedure of precoding responses takes on new significance. A set of predetermined forced choices can often be selected which will define a meaningful response universe in both societies, and the probabilities of the respective choices can be compared, providing data for a rather precise evaluation of the equivalence of ambiguity in the languages in question. With open ended questions, on the other hand, attainment of parallel "double-ambiguity" is virtually impossible. It might be noted in passing that the use of precoded response categories has the added advantages of facilitating use of larger samples of stimuli and of easing the task of employing statistical scoring techniques (Meehl 1954).

IV. Verbal Stimuli

It has been argued, above, that the use of visual stimuli merely modifies the problems of translation, but does not avoid them. With respect to the impact of stimulus complexity and ambiguity, and of the number of stimuli employed, upon translation equivalence, attention has been focused on problems relevant to verbal and visual stimuli alike. In addition there are problems which are almost purely linguistic in nature. Thus, for example, the semantic range of, and overlap between, any two languages is likely to be uneven. The frequent and often necessary perpetuation of foreign words and phrases in English and other languages attests to this fact. These are often situations where nothing short of an extensive essay will adequately translate the meaning, as with *gemütlichkeit.*

Deutscher (1966) provides an interesting illustration of the possible consequences of assuming that the words "friend, *freund,* and *amigo* are equivalent." He observes that, while the German term, *freund,* is limited to really close friends and the English term, friend, is applied to a broader circle of acquaintances, the Mexican usage of *amigo* includes both "direct address and indirect reference to strangers with whom the speaker may have had only the most casual and superficial encounter." The reliability with which these terms are "translation-interchangeable" is quite high. Given this fact, "the conclusion drawn from a hypothetical study of Germans, Americans, and Mexicans must be that Germans are a very unfriendly lot; Americans are quite friendly; and Mexicans are the most outgoing of all peoples when it comes to establishing friendships." Obviously the differences in semantic range noted by Deutscher serve to obscure any conclusions which one might wish to draw with respect to national character from such a study.

The punster's double-meaning provides an illustration of the difficulty encountered in cross-linguistic matching of ambiguities. Phonology is another purely linguistic phenomenon which may influence the translation process, as illustrated by the following excerpt from Catford:

> A Jew has been accused of horse-stealing, and, in court, the following exchanges take place:
>
> *Judge:* Did you steal a horse?
> *Interpreter:* Hot ir gestolen a pferd?
> *Accused:* Ikh hob gestolen a Λ pferd?
> *Judge:* What did he say?
> *Interpreter:* He said "I stole a horse."
>
> The point here is that the interpreter failed to take note of a feature of the accused's speech: namely the Yiddish rise-fall tone, Λ, which occurs on the word *pferd.* Had he done so, his translation might have been "What. Me steal a horse?" (Catford 1965)

The presence of homonyms which may delight the comedian should be included among essentially linguistic phenomena which may cause the translator difficulty. Another is the differential frequency of translation equivalent terms. Thus, "nice" is the English term listed in a bilingual dictionary which approximates the frequency of the Danish word *hyggelig* most closely. It is also the least adequate of the possible translations given in terms of meaning equivalence. Yet another source of difficulty, familiar to all who have studied a foreign language in school, is different grammatical organization. These problems lie beyond the scope of the present paper, for solving them would require considerable linguistic sophistication.[5] This paper seeks, rather, to point out some problems which the linguistically unsophisticated sociologist is likely to encounter in putting his propositions to cross-cultural test and to comment on various heuristics which have been developed for unraveling some of them.

The naïve approach to verbal translation may be illustrated by the reports of Sundberg (1956), Lövaas (1958), and Gough and Sandhu (1964) which pass over the problem with a casual reference to having had a native speaker *(of the non-English language)* do the translating and occasionally having a second bilingual independently check the job done by the first. These writers appear, from their reports, to consider that a person who can read English and who is a native speaker of some other tongue can produce an equivalent to any English document in his native language. To add a second individual with similar qualifications to check the first ignores more problems than it solves as examination of some aspects of the nature of bilingualism, below, will make clear. A more sophisticated means of controlling the quality of translation should be considered before turning to the bilingual as a phenomenon.

V. Back Translation: An Iterative Approach

One way in which a translation can be checked for equivalence is to ask additional bilinguals to start with the translated version and translate it back into the language of origin. Schachter[6] reports an application of the "back translation" technique, but fails to make optimal use of the results. Having obtained one or more back-translated versions of the instrument in the source language the procedure indicated by Schachter was to "eliminate any differences."

---

5. See Catford (1965) and Osgood and Sebeok (1965). Illustrations of the linguistic difficulties encountered in translation may be provided at length. See Savory (1957) (the absence of a precise French equivalent for the English word "home"); Mitchell (1965) (the difficulty involved in translating "aggressive"); Blanc (1956) ("very many," "too many," and other phrases); Hunt et al. (1964) ("may or may not"); Phillips (1959–1960) ("angry," "strange," "day-dreams," and "a 'good' quarrel").

6. Schachter (1954) and Mitchell (1965), indicate that there is "general agreement on how the actual translation of the questions should be made" and proceed to describe the back translation technique as discussed by Schachter. Cf. Casagrande (1954).

A more desirable procedure, first suggested to the writer by Donald T. Campbell, would be to recognize these as alternate forms which approach measurement of the same conceptual realm with somewhat different linguistic irrelevancies. These two, or more, measures might be used to generate added versions in each language through several iterations of the back translation procedure. This process appears costly, and it undoubtedly is more so than a one-step translation, but it appears that the result would permit effective randomization of the effects of language and translation through the use of multiple forms. Further, if a complex personality inventory such as the California Psychological Inventory (Gough 1957) is considered one item at a time the task of exhausting translators' ability to devise new versions, especially without access to other translations or instructions to do other than provide a "true" translation, appears relatively manageable.

Back-translation, when used as an iterative procedure with a new translator for each iteration, will produce a population of items in each language with heterogeneous and random errors. A random sample of items in each language, or use of different versions with randomly selected subsamples of subjects, should provide equivalence save for random error.

VI. Bilinguals and Bilingualism

Another approach to translation equivalence of stimuli suggested by Schachter (1954) and used by Osgood and associates (Osgood et al. 1962) in conjunction with back translation, uses response equivalence of bilingual subjects answering both language versions of the same instrument as an index of stimulus equivalence. Schachter's suggestion was that bilinguals respond repeatedly in both languages while iterative changes in the translated version were made until identical responses obtained. Osgood et al. (1962) apparently use this approach occasionally. An alternate use of bilingual subjects for validation is reported by the Psychological Testing Staff of Sears Roebuck and Co. (1955) in a mimeographed report. Their data show that correlations between English and Spanish versions of the Guilford-Martin inventories administered in standard order with a five-month time gap approach split-half reliabilities for the same scales. These data suggest (a) that the translation is reasonably equivalent to the original, and (b) that the persons responding "think similarly" in both languages.

The findings of Ervin[7] and of Lambert and his associates (Lambert 1955; Lambert et al. 1958) raise issues which cast doubt on the underlying assumption that bilinguals "think similarly" in both languages. Ervin (1964), using the TAT, French bilinguals, counterbalanced order, and a shorter time gap, found systematic differences which could be derived from child-rearing practices and French–American differences in value systems. While her findings may be criticized on methodological grounds, they are clearly suggestive of a "dual personality" in bilinguals. If such exists it is clearly impossible, on the basis of available data, to ascertain the presence or nature of its possible bias producing effects when using bilinguals either as translators or as subjects.

The Lambert studies of bilingualism suggest several variables which should be explored further in order to determine more clearly the nature and influence of bilingualism upon translation. First, these investigations suggest that the order of language learning may have important consequences for the type of characteristics exhibited by the bilingual. This suggests that the predominant utilization by American investigators of bilinguals who have learned English as a second language may introduce errors. Second, the Lambert studies indicate that bilinguals may have a dominant language, one which is preferred or which is easier for them to use. Linguistic dominance tends to be associated with the order of language learning, though this is not always the case. It also appears to be associated with a third dimension of bilingualism—coordinacy/compoundness. These two ideal types are most simply distinguished with respect to relative conceptual independence. If the bilingual utilizes a sort of "common set" of concepts which link his two languages together we term him a compound bilingual. If, on the other hand, such a link is absent and he uses the languages more or less independently, linking them for translation purposes by parallel responses to environmental stimuli, we term him a coordinate bilingual. Lambert and associates clearly indicate that separation of context of language learning increases conceptual independence—a finding which could account for differences between the Ervin data, obtained from persons who probably were compound bilinguals, and the Sears Roebuck findings based on a sample

7. Ervin (1964). For additional discussions of bilinguals and bilingualism see Haugen (1956) and Weinreich (1966). Both of these sources contain extensive bibliographies.

which may have included a significant proportion of coordinate bilinguals.

Summary and Conclusions

This paper raised a question which is basic to cross-cultural research: How do we know we are asking the same question in both settings? Its purpose was not to provide the answer, for at present there is none. Rather its goal was to discuss briefly some of the problems of translation in an effort to destroy some misconceptions and to place in sharper relief the needs for empirical data which will help the investigator answer this question. Many of the studies cited are as insightful as they are incomplete, as rewarding as they are inadequate. The need now is for rigorously controlled research which will pay heed to the different types of problems which have been discussed. One would hope that such research would take the form of self-conscious examination of the adequacy of the translations used in comparative research, as well as in the form of studies specifically directed at further elucidation of problems of translation.

6

Handling the Cultural Dimension in Psychiatric Research

H. B. M. Murphy

The influence of culture is to be considered not only in specific cross-cultural studies but also in attempting to answer a number of general research questions in psychiatry and psychopathology. The way cultural variables affect other variables in such general studies depend on the case at hand: i.e., such influence may refer merely to level of expressiveness and response style but they may also affect the distribution, symptomatology, and course of mental disorders. In any case, it is useful to be sensitive to the potential role of cultural factors in order to be prepared to identify them and then to deal with them appropriately. Required methodological steps may include the use of control groups and procedures addressed to obtain comparable data from different cultures.

H. B. M. Murphy, a prominent member of the well-known trans-cultural psychiatry center at McGill University in Montreal, discusses these issues, reflecting on his vast experience in the field. He pointedly recommends diversification of approaches as a generally wise strategy. Of course, this requires careful planning to avoid compounding errors and getting an overwhelming amount of data and results having obscure interrelations.

IN PSYCHIATRIC research, culture can appear either as a complication which has to be allowed for or as a prime variable which one desires to study, but the problems confronting the two approaches are similar. One type of problem lies in trying to anticipate what level or degree of cultural involvement is likely to be met with. This may be simple to allow for, or so complex that the mixing of subjects of different cultures would make no sense. Another type of problem is in ensuring that the communication with patients carries equivalent connotations as well as equivalent surface meanings. Here problems range from the meanings of single words to the influence and familiarity of a whole setting.

In seeking solutions to such problems, diversification or multiplicity of approaches is recommended, so that no single word or conceptual approach carries too much weight in the results.

There are two main reasons for incorporating culture as one of the studied variables in psychiatric research. One is the desire to correct for the distortions which it imposes on what one hopes is a general formulation regarding psychopathology, nosology or therapy; and in that case it is of little importance which cultural groups are chosen for study, as long as they provide a wide enough range. The other is to see how culture interacts with mental disorder, possibly affecting the distribution, course, symptomatology and outcome of disease, and in that case it is likely that particular cultural groups come to mind. The two purposes require somewhat different approaches, but many of the problems which beset the cultural dimension are common to all, and it is some of these which will be discussed here.

The first half of this paper will concern itself with the ways in which cultural variations can affect psychiatric data; the second will take up some problems in methodology.

Levels of Cultural Involvement

Cultural influences can complicate psychiatric research at various levels or degrees of involvement, and it can be important to anticipate what degree one must be concerned with. Most superficial are those cultural traits which merely need to be discounted for a residual, general relationship to be perceived. Thus, it is necessary to ascertain and then to discount untrue but culturally sanctioned beliefs before one can begin to say what is an individual delusion; but once this is done, familiar relationships between delusion and other indicators of psychopathology will usually appear. Similarly, if a people is highly excitable, as with some Caribbean groups, or unusually slow and heavy, as with the Orcadians from north of Scotland, then the unwary psychiatrist is liable to be deceived into diagnosing an affective disturbance where none exists; but he needs only to learn the local cultural norms in order to be able to discount these traits and to return to normally meaningful diagnoses. Regarding the evaluation of treatment outcomes, a similar situation can arise out of differences in cultural attitudes toward labor, but here again the familiar significance of labor as a measurement of outcome may apply once a simple allowance is made. In one Canadian minority group it is considered quite admirable to be able to live at the expense of the government for a limited period, provided one is still able to be self-sufficient when necessary. To use as a measure of treatment outcome a man's return to formal employment could thus be deceptive in this subculture, at least in the short run, but if instead one used some measure of his return to useful work, perhaps around the house, perhaps helping neighbors, then the picture would become familiar again.

In these illustrations the cultural trait was a general one, found in the sick and the healthy alike, and the eventual method of correction is simple, although it may require some time to ascertain and perhaps to provide a quantifiable means of rating the trait. The matter becomes a little more complex and interesting, however, when one meets cultural traits which apply only or mainly within the sick role, or in relation to some form of deviancy. These are still not true cultural influences on mental health, but they are influences on the way in which health and disease are manifested. A very obvious example of this kind of influence lies in the way in which some cultures encourage or at least permit the reporting and exaggeration of symptoms and weaknesses while other cultures discourage both. Dohrenwend has pointed out that some of the results of the Midtown Manhattan study are probably distorted by the Puerto Ricans in the sample having a different, more exaggerated, method of expressing their symptoms than the other peoples covered. Conversely, Chinese and Japanese stoicism in the face of pain can deceive not only the psychiatrist but the surgeon if the latter is used to Western behavior. In such situations one cannot simply discount the cultural trait as one can, at least theoretically, with the first group of illustrations. Instead, there is the more difficult task of increasing or decreasing the weight given to information. The customary way to approach this problem is to employ members of the same culture to do one's ratings for one, but this is satisfactory at only a relatively elementary level of research. Such assistants are able to report whether patients of the relevant culture exaggerate, for instance, the somatic aspects of their complaints and underplay the purely psychic aspects, but when they are asked to give some quantitative measure to this exaggeration and underplaying it is rare that they can do so. And moreover, unless such people are deeply involved in all aspects of the research, they are unlikely to employ the same diagnostic or the same outcome criteria as the researcher himself does. Hence, it is usually necessary to carry out preliminary studies in order to devise the tools or the comparative weightings which are needed before the main research can go ahead.

The Puerto Rican case just referred to was an example of differences in what is called response style, but the same problem of providing differential weighting can arise in other aspects of psychiatric research as well. For instance, in Canada it was recently discovered that the correlation between occupational status and mental hospitalization rate varies with cultural background (Murphy 1965). It is stronger for people of French origin than for those of British, and for the latter it is still greater than for the German-origin group.[1] In each group the character of the relationship is the same, so that there is no disturbance of the general concept, but if any detailed research into the nature of the relationship between occupational status and hospitalization in different parts of Canada were to be done, one would probably have to make allowances for the proportions of different cultural backgrounds represented in each location.

But still, insofar as basic relationships remain essentially the same between symptom and pathology, treatment and outcome, social variable and distribution of mental disorder, the task of relating cultural variables to one's research at this level remains relatively simple. It becomes much more complex when culture influences the distribution, symptoms, and course of mental disorder. For instance, as was just mentioned, the basic relationship between occupational or social status and mental hospitalization in Canada remains the same regardless of cultural background; only the slope of the curve changes. The same can be said of the relationship between hospitalization rate and age, if one excludes the Indians and Eskimos. But in Singapore these relationships do not hold. Among the Chinese there, the relationship between hospitalization and social class is as one would expect, but not that between hospitalization and age. Among the South Indians in that

1. Under the Canadian Census, "origin" refers, theoretically, to the country of origin of the first ancestor on the male side to arrive in the country. Hence the groups referred to here include members with many generations in Canada, not merely immigrants.

same city, the picture of incidence increasing with age applies in the lower social classes, but not in the white-collar group, and the relationship between mental hospitalization and social class is a most complex one. Among the Malays neither social class nor age yields the expected associations (Murphy 1959b). Since similar differences exist with reference to suicide (Murphy 1954), and since there are good reasons for believing that these hospitalization rates are meaningful in relation to the groups concerned, none of the methods of correction mentioned earlier are likely to permit the relationship between social class and mental hospitalization to be studied sensibly in Singapore, if all cultures are lumped together. One must take the cultural influences fully into consideration here instead of trying to discount them, if one wants to enlarge one's understanding of the relationship between social class and mental disorder as a general phenomenon.

The illustration just given may seem both geographically and conceptually remote from the usual run of psychiatric research, but the problem of deciding what type or degree of cultural influence one should calculate for can arise in quite familiar settings. For instance, the average schizophrenic patient of French origin in Canada, outside of Quebec, stays substantially longer in a mental hospital than schizophrenics of other cultural backgrounds, and schizophrenics of Scandinavian origin remain significantly less time than average.[2] These differences are not due to differences of hospital policy, and neither are they due to the French group sending only their worst cases to hospital while the Scandinavians send mild cases, for the French group have a higher incidence rate of chronic conditions regardless of age and diagnosis, and the schizophrenia rate for the Scandinavian-origin group is significantly below average. Now, when making a comparative study of different treatment programs in Canadian hospitals, and knowing this fact, the researcher can choose to exclude French-origin and Scandinavian-origin patients from his samples and thus hope to eliminate cultural complications without having to ask himself why these differences in hospital stay occur. However, if it is thought that a particular relationship between treatment and outcome is general, it may be desirable to include special samples from these two origin groups, and even to explore what it is that produces these differences in chronicity. The last step would have little relevance to the original research if, say, it were concerned only with the relative efficacy of

2. Own data, unpublished.

different phenothiazines, but if the researcher had started out with a broader concept of treatment, one which included remotivation and working with the patients' families, then it might be relevant indeed.

Translation and Interviewing

The foregoing gives an idea of the variety of cultural influences one may have to plan for in one's research. There are situations where the link between mental disorder and culture is much closer than in the illustrations offered here, for instance with the so-called culture-specific diseases like *latah* and *susto*, and there are others where neglect of cultural differences is well known to cause trouble, as in studies of the interaction patterns within the families of schizophrenics (Sanua 1961). But the rest of this paper will be devoted to the technical question of obtaining close comparability in data from different cultures.

The first point one needs to consider is the elementary matter of ensuring that the words and concepts which one uses have the same meaning in each culture. Most psychiatrists are aware of this problem as it relates to nosology and to the difficulty which they have in ensuring that they know what each other is talking about, when they come from different countries or different medical schools; but it is something more elementary that is intended here, namely the words that patients use or that psychiatrists address to these patients. Problems can arise here even when the different cultural groups share the same language, but they are more obvious and important when different languages are involved.

In translation, the obvious problem is the lack of any word or phrase to convey the intended meaning, but a more serious—because hidden—problem is that of words which seem to fit each other but do not.[3] Nearly every translator and most bilingual psychiatrists will say that "*dépression*" is the French equivalent of the English "depression", but in Montreal Benoist (1964) has shown that they mean different conditions to the general public. The English term suggests to them a rather chronic state, severe, precipitated by remorse or guilt, requiring hospitalization, and occurring rarely. To the French-

3. For a general discussion of the problems of translating a psychiatric interview schedule, see Spilka 1968.

Canadian, however, *dépression* suggests a relatively common state, brought on by working too hard, with somatic components, and disappearing rapidly with rest. In other words, *dépression* is closer to the English-speaking public's concept of "nerves."

Where there is no equivalent term for what one wants to express, it is possible to get round the problem by a lengthier description, but that may still not convey the intended image, because that image is too strange to the subjects. Thus, the English phrase "loss of sense of humor" cannot be translated into French and no related phrase carries quite the same suggestion of the sense of humor being part of the ego. Alternatively, there is the problem that a word or phrase may be normally translatable but may elicit different reactions. To "think about one's death" tends to be taken in Anglo-Saxon psychiatry as a morbid symptom, but French-Canadian patients of all types readily admit to doing this, probably because their religion encourages them to do so and because death is for many of them merely a doorway through which they pass to something else, not a permanent state.

Such differences are not easily realized, even by bilingual people, and one may have to do much probing to find them, though a semantic differential technique can be useful here. But having found such instances, one has still to decide what to do about them. If only two cultures are involved, then it may be easy to abandon some phrase or to alter both versions of a question, but if several cultures are being compared, or if it is desirable to employ a standard rating instrument like the MMPI, this may not be possible.

The ways in which words are used can present just as many problems as the words themselves. The customary psychiatric interview in English tends to be nondirective, using words and phrases which are deliberately ambiguous or neutral insofar as they invite neither a "yes" nor a "no," and cover a wide range of concepts out of which the patient is expected to choose that which touches him most at present. In French it is difficult to be as neutral, and in some other languages or cultures it is virtually impossible to carry out a psychiatric interview without using leading questions most of the time, something which can easily affect the character of the data collected. For instance, if a patient says in answer to the question "How is your mind working?" that he keeps getting senseless thoughts, one would normally give more weight to it than if he gave that answer after he had specifically been asked "Do you sometimes get thoughts which don't seem to make sense?" since (in some cultures, at least) he is quite likely to go searching round in his memory for an occasion that would permit him to say "yes." For this reason it is rarely correct, except in pilot studies, to allow interviewers in different countries to use their own discretion regarding whether they will employ leading questions or not, and regarding whether they can take it for granted that some symptom is absent if the patient does not specifically mention it.

After the words used and the ways in which they are used comes the question of the setting. Most research workers are well aware of the importance of matching both one's samples and one's settings as closely as possible, but it should be kept in mind that after the more obvious physical and social aspects of the setting are matched, there may be cultural factors which unbalance them again. For instance, during an exploration of the equivalence of French and English language interviews, using quite carefully matched samples of paranoid schizophrenics in a French-speaking hospital and in an English-speaking hospital in Montreal, it was found that the samples differed markedly in their answers to the question "How often do you feel angry?" This seemed likely to reflect a cultural difference, but when the same study was repeated with French-speaking and English-speaking patients housed together in a third hospital the difference disappeared. Probably the higher level of largely unexpressed anger in the first sample of French-Canadian schizophrenics was related to the fact that they were in a hospital run by a religious order where acting-out was strongly suppressed. In this instance, the initial interpretation was corrected by adding further samples, but there are other cultural influences of this type which would not be as easily detected. The mere fact of being interviewed alone and without one's family to consult with may be highly abnormal and anxiety-provoking for people from some African and Indian cultures, and achieving equivalence of setting on this point may just not be possible.

Nonverbal Material

Similar problems to these arise if one is using nonverbal cues. Whether it is the subject who is confronted with the nonverbal cue, as in some forms of psychological testing, or whether it is the researcher, as in the observation of ward behaviors, there needs to be a translation of the cue into familiar terms, and culture can determine what these terms will be. In Singapore, Indian students sick with a fever would sometimes roll in their beds, groaning and saying nothing sensible. It took the writer some time to learn that this was not a sign of pain or of febrile delirium, but a culturally accepted expression of regression, indicating that they wanted to be taken into hospital for nursing (Murphy 1959a). Again, with Card VI on the Rorschach, Chinese male students in Singapore made relatively frequent reference to the turtle, whereas Indian and Malay students did not. A first reaction was to treat this as mainly a "texture" response symbolizing defensiveness and rejection of sensitivity in contrast to the rug and fur responses which Western subjects often provide on this card, and such a conclusion seemed to fit the relative inaccessibility and uninvolvement which these Chinese students tended to exhibit. But the turtle has numerous and important symbolic meanings in Chinese culture (longevity, impoliteness, etc.) and reconsideration suggests that interpretation along these lines was also called for.

It is generally agreed today that "culture-free" tests are a myth, and "culture-fair" ones only deserve that title in a restricted sense. But there can be advantages in exploring the latter if they are used with proper precautions. It is nonsense to think that any experience whatever is going to tap concepts which are equally familiar or equally unfamiliar to members of all cultures, and the ability to relate the experience to familiar concepts is going to affect results. During World War II, Gurkha recruits to the Indian army performed quite poorly on Raven's Matrices, a test which depends considerably on the rotation of spacial relationships. Some weeks later, after they had had practice in stripping and reassembling of rifles and machine-guns, a task which needs spatial orientation, they performed very much better.[4] Cattell (1968) recommends that when one employs "culture-fair" tests with a people unused to such instruments, one should retest the same subjects three or four times in order to induce some familiarity, and then throw away all except the last results. Whether this is suitable with all peoples and with other tests is doubtful, but it is certainly worth exploring.

Conclusions

With all the traps described here and with the frequent impossibility of knowing beforehand at what level of complexity a cultural influ-

4. The reference for this interesting observation has unfortunately been lost, but the writer remembers the point distinctly and would be grateful to any reader who could direct him to the original source.

ence will operate, what should be one's general policy in doing cross-cultural research?

The safest approach at the present time can be expressed in the single word—*diversification*.

Whereas the normal goal in most research is simplification, or reduction of one's research efforts to the minimum required to produce the intended results, there is still today a great virtue, for the special field of transcultural psychiatry, in multiplication of both one's approaches and one's methods of analysis. As long as one is not sure that a particular enquiry has the precise meaning intended or will reach the desired goal, it is better to repeat it from a different angle or to employ additional enquiries that will check on it, rather than to strive for economy of effort. In the French translation of the Mental Status Schedule, mentioned above, problems arose regarding items relating to depression and to mental functioning. Because the Schedule had many other approaches to depression, a single translation weakness in that area did not significantly disturb the results, but there were only two items referring to a particular aspect of mental functioning, and when one of these proved difficult to translate in a fashion which would elicit an equivalent response from French-Canadians, it became virtually impossible to know how to construe the results. Regarding the nature or level of cultural influence the same applies. It is an economy of effort to use certain types of mental disturbance as indicative of mental disorder in general, but there is a great risk that different cultures will steer mental disturbance in different directions so that, for instance, psychophysiological disorders may be the best indicators in one people, and psychotic disorders in another. It is an economy of effort, when culture is suspected of complicating one's research, to "control" for it by ensuring that equal proportions of the relevant cultural groups exist in one's different comparison samples; but until the types of cultural influence are known it is safer and potentially much more informative to keep the cultures distinct and to make separate comparisons within each.

Such diversification is costly, and many of the locations where it appears most urgent to allow for culture are those where economies are most pressing. The answer here, insofar as there is any answer at all, is to restrict one's study to two or at the most three clearly distinguishable cultural groups, and more particularly to devote plenty of time to prior examination of one's concepts and proposed techniques. Much of the extra effort which diversification appears to call for can be met by the prior elimination of wasted effort through avoidance of steps which careful consideration would have indicated to be useless. And in this prior consideration, if culture is likely to be a significant variable, lies consultation with suitable authorities on the culture. One of the prime steps in handling the cultural dimension in psychiatric research is to know what "culture" means and to know the psychiatrically relevant features of the cultural group one will be dealing with.

Annotated Additional Readings

a) **Wagatsuma, H. 1977.** Problems of language in cross-cultural research. *Annals of the New York Academy of Sciences* 285:141–150.
A readable review of how the stimulus value of a psychological test may become distorted when translated for application to a different culture. It illustrates the issues involved by discussing the international use of Gough's California Personality Inventory and Adjective Checklist. This paper nicely complements Anderson's article (5).

b) **Finifter, B. M. 1977.** The Robustness of cross-cultural findings. *Annals of the New York Academy of Sciences* 285:151–184.
A cogent and well documented review of the issues involved in the interpretation of cross-cultural findings, with particular focus on the assessment of their robustness (i.e., their stability and invariance under certain modifications of the study conditions).

It examines various attitudes a researcher can take toward the null hypothesis when carrying out and interpreting cross-cultural studies: one striving to find intercultural differences, another trying to establish transcultural universals, and a third tending to suspend judgment until the results and conclusions appear almost obvious and clear cut. The author then considers the types of statistical error associated with such interpretive attitudes.

c) **Al-Issa, I. 1969.** Problems in the cross-cultural study of schizophrenia. *Journal of Psychology* 71:143–151.
A discussion of aspects of the validity of cross-cultural measures of psychopathology with special regard to schizophrenic disorders.

The author discusses physiological responses (e.g., pupillary response to light stimuli, EEG measures) as being minimally and only indirectly influenced by culture in contrast with more heavily culture-loaded conceptual measures such as vocabulary. He then considers the use of physiological variables as baseline indicators for comparing normal and schizophrenic subjects within and across cultures.

d) **Zubin, J. 1969.** Cross-national study of diagnosis of the mental disorders: Methodology and planning. *American Journal of Psychiatry* 125:12–20.
One of the foremost authorities on the interdisciplinary and systematic study of psychopathology provides an overview of the most important methodological problems in the cross-national diagnosis of mental disorders. He also includes a brief description of the structured assessment instruments developed for the pioneering U.S.–U.K. diagnostic project in an attempt to increase interrater reliability.

e) **Wing, J. K. 1971.** International comparisons in the study of functional psychoses. *British Medical Bulletin* 27:77–81.

A short but substantial review of the problems of clinical diagnosis in international studies and of some considerable methodological advances made in this field. The paper discusses early studies and describes improved standardized methods of interviewing and of more reliable classification of the resulting data. The author then focuses attention on the main international diagnostic studies of the 1960s and 1970s: the U.S.–U.K. diagnostic project and the International Pilot Study of Schizophrenia. In both studies, Wing's Present State Examination was used for structurally assessing psychiatric symptomatology.

III

Personality Development

Our approach to the study of culture and psychopathology involves a conceptualization of human behavior, both normal and abnormal, based on the interactive participation of biological, psychological, and sociocultural factors. Another angle of this comprehensive conceptualization involves considering not only the cross-sectional conditioning of psychopathology but also its development and course.

In line with the tremendous impact of workers such as Freud and Harlow, there is great interest in the role of early life experiences in the development of personality, child behavior disorders, and predispositions to later psychopathology. The social and geographical settings of early life experiences—i.e., the norms, values and structures under which such experiences take place and then interplay with psychological development—are the particular subject here. Research in this field is becoming theoretically eclectic and pluralistic and methodologically more sophisticated and empirical. The articles included here reflect this state of affairs and cover some important issues on the effect of cultural variables on psychological development during infancy, childhood, and adolescence. Questions explored include the impact of sociocultural framework on early cognitive development; the influence of national culture and context of upbringing on children's reactions to social pressure; and the identity conflict experienced by bicultural adolescents and its mental health consequences. The additional references deal with cross-cultural aspects of child rearing, mother-child interaction, attachment to inanimate objects, sibling rank, relations between ethnically-different child groups, and aggressiveness throughout the life cycle.

7

Cross-Cultural Perspectives on Early Development

Jerome Kagan and Robert E. Klein

The study of culture and psychopathology places considerable interest in the examination of early child development in regard both to its cross-sectional context and its longitudinal unfolding. Key issues are the impact of external events on the development of psychological patterns in infancy, and then the continuity of such patterns through adolescence and beyond.

The following article addresses directly important aspects of these issues. It represents a collaborative effort of Jerome Kagan, a developmental psychologist from Harvard University, and Robert Klein, a researcher from the Institute of Nutrition of Central America and Panama, located in Guatemala. They report on their studies of youngsters of a small village on the shores of the Atitlan Lake in the highlands of Guatemala as well as from other rural and urban Guatemalan areas, and compare them with a group of U.S. children in Cambridge, Massachusetts.

Their findings suggest that listless, silent, apathetic infants receiving little stimulation from their mothers (busy with heavy responsibilities crucial to the economical survival of the family) still appear as passive, quiet, timid 3-year-olds, but eventually become active, alert, and intellectually competent 11-year-olds cognitively on a par with their U.S. counterparts. In fact, in contrast with U.S. children, preadolescent rural Guatemalans are economically active and responsibly carry out many adult activities. The basic findings seem to support the existence within the child of a developmental drive, probably biologically anchored, which compensates for a previous lack of stimulation.

The points discussed reflect on the interaction between biological and sociocultural factors affecting cognitive development and the need to consider time frame in the evaluation of such interaction.

MOST AMERICAN psychologists believe in the hardiness of habit and the premise that experience etches on the mind an indelible mark not easily erased by time or trauma. The application of that assumption to the first era of development leads to the popular view that psychological growth during the early years is under the strong influence of the variety and patterning of external events and that the psychological structures shaped by those initial encounters have a continuity that stretches at least into early adolescence. The first part of that hypothesis, which owes much of its popularity to Freud, Harlow, and Skinner, has strong empirical support. The continuity part of the assumption, which is more equivocal, is summarized in the American adage "Well begun is half done."

Many developmental psychologists, certain of the long-lasting effects of early experience, set out to find the form of those initial stabilities and the earliest time they might obtain a preview of the child's future. Although several decades of research have uncovered fragile lines that seem to travel both backward and forward in time, the breadth and magnitude of intraindividual continuities have not been overwhelming, and each seems to be easily lost or shattered (Kagan and Moss 1962; Kessen et al. 1970). A recent exhaustive review of research on human infancy led to the conclusion that "only short term stable individual variation has been demonstrated; . . . and demonstrations of continuity in process—genotype continuity—have been rare indeed (Kessen et al. 1970:297)." Since that evaluation violates popular beliefs, the authors noted a few pages later:

> In spite of slight evidence of stability, our inability to make predictions of later personality from observations in the first three years of life is so much against good sense and common observation, to say nothing of the implication of all developmental theories, that the pursuit of predictively effective categories of early behavior will surely continue unabated (p. 309).

The modest empirical support for long-term continuity is occasionally rationalized by arguing that although behaviors similar in manifest form might not be stable over long time periods, the underlying structures might be much firmer (Kagan 1971). Hence, if the operational manifestations of those hidden forms were discerned, continuity of cognitive, motivational, and affective structures would be affirmed. However, we recently observed some children living in an isolated Indian village on Lake Atitlan in the highlands of northwest Guatemala. We saw listless, silent, apathetic infants; passive, quiet, timid 3-year-olds; but active, cheerful, intellectually competent 11-year-olds. Since there is no reason to believe that living conditions in this village have changed during the last century, it is likely that the alert 11-year-olds were, a decade earlier, listless, vacant-staring infants. That observation has forced us to question the strong form of the continuity assumption in a serious way.

The data to be presented imply absence of a predictive relationship between level of cognitive development at 12–18 months of age and quality of intellectual functioning at 11 years. This conclusion is not seriously different from the repeated demonstrations of no relation between infant intelligence quotient (IQ) or developmental quotient (DQ) scores during the first year of life and Binet or Wechsler IQ scores obtained during later childhood (Kessen et al. 1970); Pease et al. 1973). The significance of the current data, however, derives from the fact that the infants seemed to be more seriously retarded than those observed in earlier studies, their environments markedly less varied, and the assessment of later cognitive functioning based on culture-fair tests of specific cognitive abilities rather than culturally biased IQ tests.

Moreover, these observations suggest that it is misleading to talk about continuity of any psychological characteristic—be it cognitive, motivational, or behavioral—without specifying simultaneously the context of development. Consider the long-term stability of passivity as an example. The vast majority of the infants in the Indian village were homogeneously passive and retained this characteristic until they were five or six years old. A preschool child rarely forced a submissive posture on another. However, by eight years of age, some of the children became dominant over others because the structure of the peer group required that role to be filled. Factors other than early infant passivity were critical in determining that differentiation, and physical size, strength, and competence at valued skills seemed to be more important than the infant's disposition. In modern American society, where there is much greater variation among young children in degree of passivity and dominance, a passive four-year-old will always encounter a large group of dominant peers who enforce a continuing role of submissiveness on him. As a result, there should be firmer stability of behavioral passivity during the early years in an American city than in the Indian village. But the stability of that behavior seems to be more dependent on the presence of dominant members of the immediate vicinity than on some inherent force within the child.

Continuity of a psychological disposition is not solely the product of an inherited or early acquired structure that transcends a variety of contexts. The small group of scientists who champion that view of stability—we have been among them—envision a small box of different-colored gems tucked deep in the brain, with names like intelligent, passive, irritable, or withdrawn engraved on them. These material entities guarantee that, despite behavioral disguises, an inherent set of psychological qualities, independent of the local neighborhood and knowable under the proper conditions, belongs to each individual. This belief in a distinct and unchanging mosaic of core traits—an identity—is fundamental to Western thought and is reflected in the psychological writings of Erik Erikson and the novels of popular Western writers. Only Herman Hesse, who borrowed the philosophy of the East, fails to make a brief for personal identity. *Siddartha, Magister Ludi,* and *Narcissus and Goldmund* are not trying to discover "who they are" but are seeking serenity, and each appreciates the relevance of setting in that journey.

A secondary theme concerns the interaction of maturation and environment, an issue that has seized academic conversation because of the renewed debate surrounding the inheritance of intelligence. But there is a broader issue to probe. The majority of American psychologists remain fundamentally Lockean in attitude, believing that thought and action owe primary allegiance to experience and that reinforcements and observations of models set the major course of change. Despite Piaget's extraordinary popularity, the majority of American psychologists do not believe that maturation supplies the major impetus for psychological growth during the childhood years. We have forgotten that many years ago Myrtle McGraw (1935) allowed one twin to climb some stairs and prevented his co-twin from practicing that skill. This homely experiment occurred only a few years after Carmichael (1926) anesthetized some *Amblystoma* embryos to prevent them from swimming. The twin not allowed to climb was behind his partner in learning this skill, but he eventually mastered it. Carmichael's embryos swam perfectly when the anesthetic was pumped out of the tank. In both instances, the organisms could not be prevented from displaying species-specific properties.

Our observations in these Indian villages have led us to reorder the hierarchy of complementary influence that biology and environmental forces exert on the development of intellectual functions that are natural to man. Separate maturational factors seem to set the time of emergence of those basic abilities. Experience can slow down or speed up that emergence by several months or several years, but nature will win in the end. The capacity for perceptual analysis, imitation, language, inference, deduction, symbolism, and memory will eventually appear in sturdy form in any natural environment, for each is an inherent competence in the human program. But these competences, which we assume to be universal, are to be distinguished from culturally specific talents that will not appear unless the child is exposed to or taught them directly. Reading, arithmetic, and understanding of specific words and concepts fall into this latter category.

This distinction between universal and culturally specific competences implies a parallel distinction between absolute and relative retardation. Consider physical growth as an illustration of this idea. There is sufficient cross-cultural information on the age of onset of walking to warrant the statement that most children should be walking unaided before their second birthday. A three-year-old unable to walk is physically retarded in the absolute sense, for he has failed to attain a natural competence at the normative time. However, there is neither an empirical nor a logical basis for expecting that most children, no matter where they live, will develop the ability to hunt with a spear, ride a horse, or play football. Hence, it is not reasonable to speak of absolute retardation on these skills. In those cultures where these talents are taught, encouraged, or modeled, children will differ in the age at which they attain varied levels of mastery. But we can only classify a child as precocious or retarded relative to another in his community. The data to be reported suggest that absolute retardation in the attainment of specific cognitive competences during infancy has no predictive validity with respect to level of competence on a selected set of natural cognitive skills at age 11. *The data do not imply that a similar level of retardation among American infants has no future implication for relative retardation on culture-specific skills.*

The Guatemalan Settings

The infant observations to be reported here were made in two settings in Guatemala. One set of data came from four subsistence farming Ladino villages in eastern Guatemala. The villages are moderately isolated, Spanish speaking, and contain between 800 and 1,200 inhabitants. The families live in small thatched huts of cane or adobe with dirt floors and no sanitary facilities. Books, pencils, paper, and pictures are typically absent from the experience of preschool children, and, even in school, the average child has no more than a thin lined notebook and a stub of a pencil.

The second location was a more isolated Indian village of 850 people located on the shores of Lake Atitlan in the northwest mountainous region of the country. Unlike the Spanish-speaking villages, the Indians of San Marcos la Laguna have no easy access to a city and are psychologically more detached. The isolation is due not only to geographical location but also to the fact that few of the women and no more than half of the men speak reasonable Spanish. Few adults and no children can engage the culture of the larger nation, and the Indians of San Marcos regard themselves as an alien and exploited group.

The Infant In San Marcos

During the first 10–12 months, the San Marcos infant spends most of his life in the small, dark interior of his windowless hut. Since women do not work in the field, the mother usually stays close to the home and spends most of her day preparing food, typically tortillas, beans, and coffee, and perhaps doing some weaving. If she travels to a market to buy or sell, she typically leaves her infant with an older child or a relative. The infant is usually close to the mother, either on her lap or enclosed on her back in a colored cloth, sitting on a mat, or sleeping in a hammock. The mother rarely allows the infant to crawl on the dirt floor of the hut and feels that the outside sun, air, and dust are harmful.

The infant is rarely spoken to or played with, and the only available objects for play, besides his own clothing or his mother's body, are oranges, ears of corn, and pieces of wood or clay. These infants are distinguished from American infants of the same age by their extreme motoric passivity, fearfulness, minimal smiling, and, above all, extraordinary quietness. A few with pale cheeks and vacant stares had the quality of tiny ghosts and resembled the description of the institutionalized infants that Spitz called marasmic. Many would not orient to a taped source of speech, not smile or babble to vocal overtures, and hesitated over a minute before reaching for an attractive toy.

An American woman who lived in the village made five separate 30-minute observations in the homes of 12 infants 8–16 months of age. If a particular behavioral variable occurred during a five-second period, it was recorded once for that interval. The infants were spoken to or played with 6 percent of the time, with a maximum of 12 percent. The comparable averages for American middle class homes are 25 percent, with a maximum of 40 percent (M. Lewis and Freedle 1972). It should be noted that the infant's vocalizations, which occurred about 6 percent of the time, were typically grunts lasting less than a second, rather than the prolonged babbling typical of middle-class American children. The infants cried very little because the slightest irritability led the mother to nurse her child at once. Nursing was the single, universal therapeutic treatment for all infant distress, whether caused by fear, cold, hunger, or cramps. Home observations in the eastern villages are consonant with those gathered in San Marcos and reveal infrequent infant vocalization and little verbal interaction or play with adults or older siblings. The mothers in these settings seem to regard their infants the way an American parent views an expensive cashmere sweater: Keep it nearby and protect it but do not engage it reciprocally.

One reason why these mothers might behave this way is that it is abundantly clear to every parent that all children begin to walk by 18 months, to talk by age 3, and to perform some adult chores by age 10, despite the listless, silent quality of infancy. The mother's lack of active manipulation, stimulation, or interactive play with her infant is not indicative of indifference or rejection, but is a reasonable posture, given her knowledge of child development.

Comparative Study of Infant Cognitive Development

Although it was not possible to create a formal laboratory setting for testing infants in San Marcos, it was possible to do so in the eastern Ladino villages, and we shall summarize data derived from identical procedures administered to rural Guatemalan and American infants. Although the infants in the Ladino villages were more alert than the Indian children of San Marcos, the similarities in living conditions and rearing practices are such that we shall assume that the San Marcos infants would have behaved like the Ladino children or, what is more likely, at a less mature level. In these experiments, the Guatemalan mother and child came to a special laboratory equipped with a chair and a stage that simulated the setting in the Harvard laboratories where episodes were administered to cross-sectional groups of infants, 84 American and 80 Guatemalan, at 5½, 7½, 9½, and 11½ months of age, with 10–24 infants from each culture at each age level.

Before describing the procedures and results, it will be helpful to summarize the theoretical assumptions that govern interpretation of the infant's reactions to these episodes. There appear to be two important maturationally controlled processes which emerge between 2 and 12 months that influence the child's reactions to transformations of an habituated event (Kagan 1971, 1972). During the first six weeks of life, the duration of the child's attention to a visual event is controlled by the amount of physical change or contrast in the event. During the third month, the infant shows prolonged attention to events that are moderate discrepancies from habituated standards. Maintenance of attention is controlled by the relation of the event to the child's schema for the class to which that event belongs. The typical reactions to discrepancy include increased fixation time, increased vocalization, and either cardiac deceleration or decreased variability of heart rate during the stimulus presentation. These conclusions are based on many independent studies and we shall not document them here (Cohen et al. 1971; Kagan, 1971; Lewis et al. 1970).

However, at approximately eight to nine months, a second process emerges. The infant now begins to activate cognitive structures, called hypotheses, in the service of interpreting discrepant events. A hypothesis is viewed as a representation of a relation between two schemata. Stated in different language, the infant not only notes and processes a discrepancy, he also attempts to transform it to his prior schemata for that class of event and activates hypotheses to serve this advanced cognitive function. It is not a coincidence that postulation of this new competence coincides with the time when the infant displays object permanence and separation anxiety, phenomena that require the child to activate an idea of an absent object or person.

There are two sources of support for this notion. The first is based on age changes in attention to the same set of events. Regardless of whether the stimulus is a set of human masks, a simple black and white design, or a dynamic sequence in which a moving orange rod turns on a bank of three light bulbs upon contact, there is a U-shaped relation between age and duration of attention across the period 3–36 months, with the trough typically occurring between 7 and 12 months of age (Kagan 1972).

The curvilinear relation between age and attention to human masks has been replicated among American, rural Guatemalan, and Kahlahari desert Bushman children (Kagan 1971; Konnor 1973; Sellers et al. 1972). If discrepancy were the only factor controlling fixation time, a child's attention should decrease with age, for the stimulus events become less discrepant as he grows older. The increase in attention toward the end of the first year is interpreted as a sign of a new cognitive competence, which we have called the *activation of hypotheses.*

A second source of support for this idea is that the probability of a cardiac acceleration to a particular discrepancy increases toward the end of the first year, whereas cardiac deceleration is the modal reaction during the earlier months (Kagan 1972). Because studies of adults and young children indicate that cardiac acceleration accompanies mental work, while deceleration accompanies attention to an interesting event (Lacey 1967; Van Hover 1971), the appearance of acceleration toward the end of the first year implies that the infants are performing active mental work, or activating hypotheses.

Since increased attention to a particular discrepancy toward the end of the first year is one diagnostic sign of the emergence of this stage of cognitive development, cultural differences in attention to fixed discrepancies during the first year might provide information on the developmental maturity of the infants in each cultural group.

Method

Block Episode

Each child was shown a 2-inch wooden orange block for six or eight successive trials (six for the two older ages, and eight for the two younger ages) followed by three or five transformation trials in which a 1½-orange block was presented. These transformations were followed by three representations of the original 2-inch block.

Light Episode

The child was shown 8 or 10 repetitions of a sequence in which a hand moved an orange rod in a semicircle until it touched a bank of three light bulbs which were lighted upon contact between the rod and the bulbs. In the five transformation trials that followed, the hand appeared but the rod did not move and the lights lit after a four-second interval. Following the transformations, the original event was presented for three additional trials.

During each of the episodes, two observers coded (*a*) how long the infant attended to the event, (*b*) whether the infant vocalized or smiled, and (*c*) fretting or crying. Intercoder reliability for these variables was over .90.

Results

The Guatemalan infants were significantly less attentive than the Americans on both episodes, and the cultural differences were greater at the two older than at the two younger ages. Figures 7.1 and 7.2 illustrate the mean total fixation time to four successive trial blocks for the two episodes. The four trial blocks were the first three standard trials, the last three standards, the first three transformations, and the three return trials.

The American infants of all ages had longer fixation times to the block during every trial block (F ranged for 30.8 to 67.3; $df = 1/154$, $p < .001$). The American infants also displayed longer fixations to the light during every trial block (F ranged from 9.8 to 18.4, $df = 1/141$, $p < .01$). However, it is important to note that at 11½ months, the American children maintained more sustained attention to the return of the standard than the Guatemalans, who showed a drop in fixation time toward the end of the episode. These data suggest that more of the American than of the Guatemalan infants had entered the stage of activation of hypotheses. Since the Ladino infants appeared more mature than the San Marcos children, it is possible that American one-year-olds were approximately three months advanced over the San Marcos children in this cognitive function.

Additional Assessments of Developmental Status

We collected, under less formal conditions in the home, additional information on the developmental status of the San Marcos infant. Not one of the 12 infants between 8 and 16 months reached for an

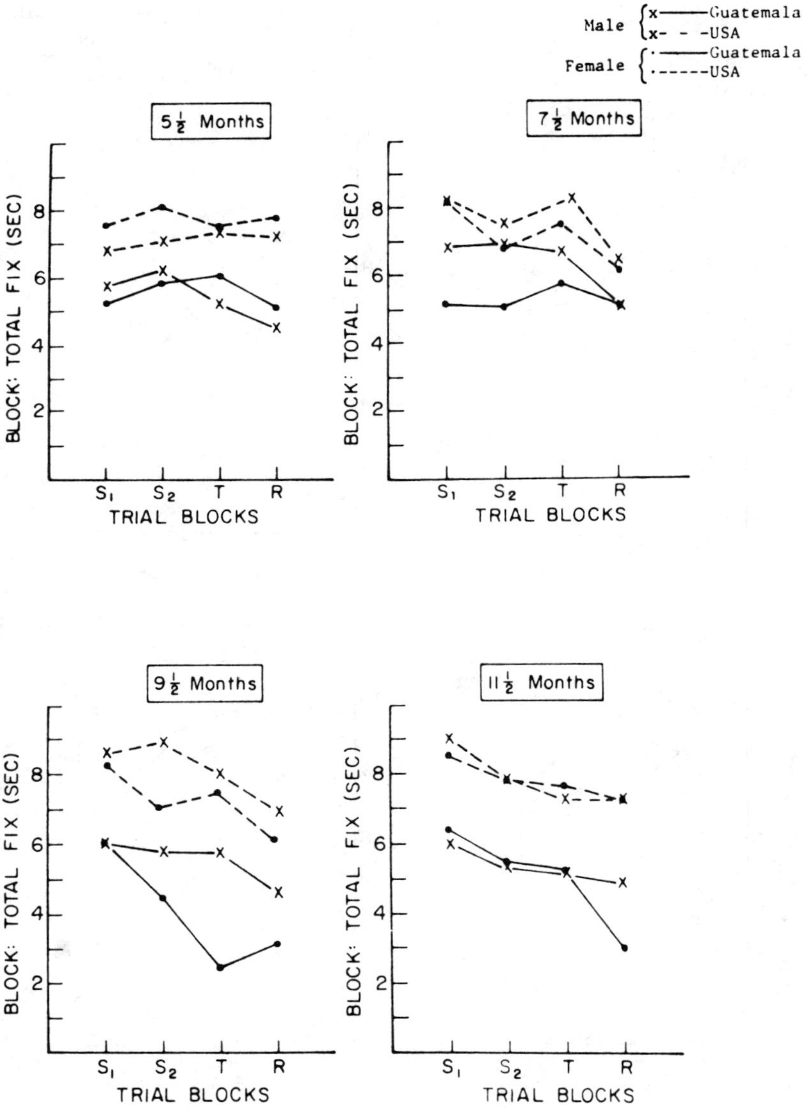

Figure 7.1 Average Total Fixation Time to the Block Episode by Age and Culture.

attractive object they watched being hidden, although many would, with considerable hesitation, reach for a visible object placed close to their hands. Furthermore, none of these 12 infants revealed facial surprise following a sequence in which they watched an object

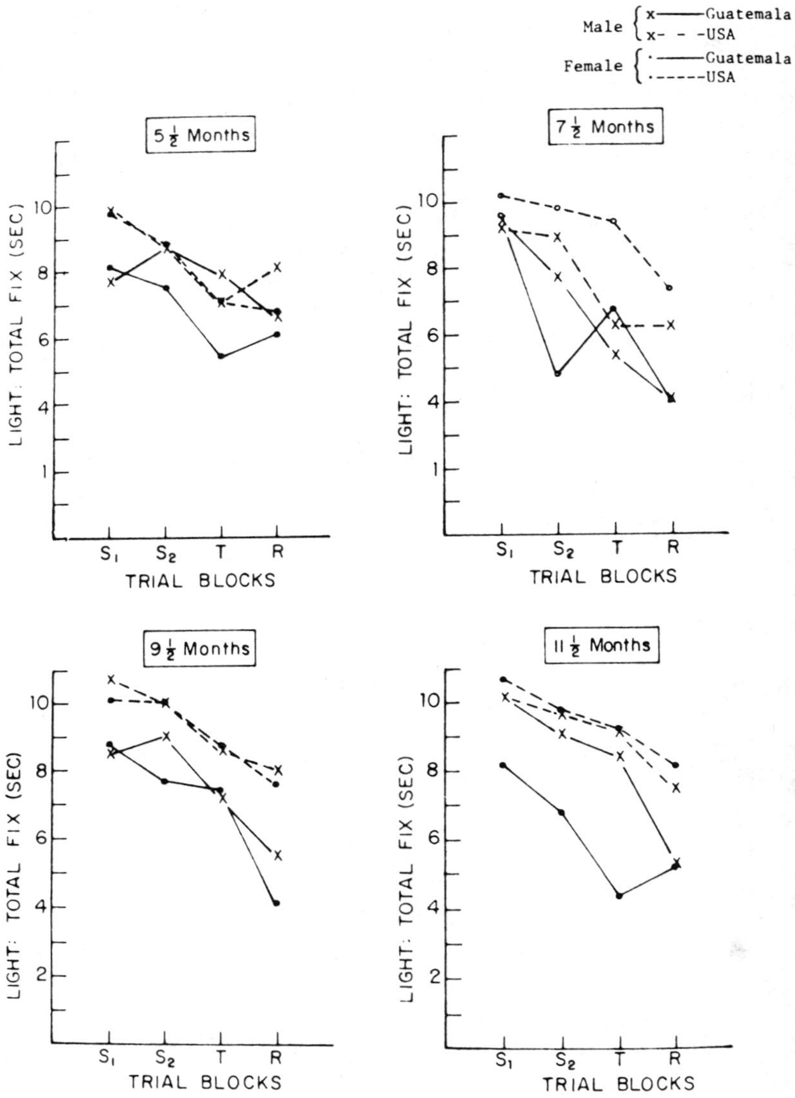

Figure 7.2 Average Total Fixation Time to the Light Episode by Age and Culture.

being hidden under a cloth but saw no object when that cloth was removed. These observations suggest an absolute retardation of four months in the display of behavioral signs diagnostic of the attainment of object permanence.

A third source of data is based on observations of stranger anxiety. Each of 16 infants between 8 and 20 months was observed following the first exposure to a strange male (the senior author). The first age at which obvious apprehension and/or crying occurred was 13 months, suggesting a five-month lag between San Marcos and American infants. Finally, the information on nonmorphemic babbling and the onset of meaningful speech supports a diagnosis of absolute retardation. There was no marked increase in frequency of babbling or vocalization between 8 and 16 months among the 12 San Marcos infants observed at home, while comparable observations in American homes revealed a significant increase in babbling and the appearance of morphemic vocalizations for some children. Furthermore, many parents remarked that meaningful speech typically appears first at 2½ years of age, about one year later than the average display of first words in American children.

These data, together with the extremely depressed, withdrawn appearance of the San Marcos infants, suggest retardations of three or more months for various psychological competences that typically emerge during the first two years of life. With the exception of one 16-month-old boy, whose alert appearance resembled that of an American infant, there was little variability among the remaining children. Since over 90 percent were homogeneously passive, nonalert, and quiet, it is unlikely that the recovery of intellectual functioning to be reported later was a result of the selective mortality of a small group of severely retarded infants.

Resilience of Cognitive Development

The major theme of this article is the potential for recovery of cognitive functions despite early infant retardation. When the San Marcos child becomes mobile at around 15 months he leaves the dark hut, begins to play with other children, and provides himself with cognitive challenges that demand accommodations. Since all children experience this marked discontinuity in variety of experience and opportunity for exploration between the first and second birthday, it is instructive to compare the cognitive competence of older Guatemalan and American children to determine if differences in level of functioning are still present.

The tests administered were designed to assess cognitive processes that are believed to be part of the natural competence of growing children, rather than the culturally arbitrary segments of knowledge contained in a standard IQ test. We tried to create tests that were culturally fair, recognizing that this goal is, in the extreme, unattainable. Hence, the tests were not standardized instruments with psychometric profiles of test-retest reliabilities and criterion validity studies. This investigation should be viewed as a natural experiment in which the independent variable was degree of retardation in infancy and the dependent variables were performances on selected cognitive instruments during childhood. We assume, along with many psychologists, that perceptual analysis, recall and recognition memory, and inference are among the basic cognitive functions of children (even though they do not exhaust that set), and our tests were designed to evaluate those processes.

Tests of recall and recognition memory, perceptual analysis, and perceptual and conceptual inference were given to children in San Marcos, the Ladino villages, an Indian village close to Guatemala City and more modern than San Marcos, Cambridge, Massachusetts, and to two different groups of children living in Guatemala City. One of the Guatemala city settings, the "guarderia," was a day care center for very poor children. The second group, middle-class children attending nursery school, resembled a middle-class American sample in both family background and opportunity. Not all tests were administered to all children. The discussion is organized according to the cognitive function assessed, rather than the sample studied. The sample sizes ranged from 12 to 40 children at any one age.

Recall Memory for Familiar Objects

The ability to organize experience for commitment to long-term memory and to retrieve that information on demand is a basic cognitive skill. It is generally believed that the form of the organization contains diagnostic information regarding cognitive maturity for, among Western samples, both number of independent units of information and the conceptual clustering of that information increase with age.

A 12-object recall task was administered to two samples of Guatemalan children. One group lived in a Ladino village 17 kilometers from Guatemala City; the second group was composed of San Marcos children. The 80 subjects from the Ladino village were 5 and 7 years old, equally balanced for age and sex. The 55 subjects from San Marcos were between 5 and 12 years of age (26 boys and 29 girls).

The 12 miniature objects to be recalled were common to village life and belonged to three conceptual categories: animals (pig, dog, horse, cow), kitchen utensils (knife, spoon, fork, glass), and clothing (pants, dress, underpants, hat). Each child was first required to name the objects, and if the child was unable to he was given the name. The child was then told that after the objects had been randomly arranged on a board he would have 10 seconds to inspect them, after which they would be covered with a cloth, and he would be required to say all the objects he could remember.

Table 7. 1 contains the average number of objects recalled and the number of pairs of conceptually similar words recalled—an index of clustering—for the first two trials. A pair was defined as the temporally contiguous recall of two or more items of the same category. A child received one point for reporting a pair of contiguous items, two points for three contiguous items, and three points for contiguous recall of four items. Hence, the maximum clustering score for a single trial was nine points. As the table reveals, the children showed a level of clustering beyond chance expectation (which is between 1.5 and 2.0 pairs for recall scores of seven to eight words). Moreover, recall scores increased with age on both trials for children in both villages (F ranged from 11.2 to 27.7, $p <$ .05), while clustering increased with age in the Ladino village ($F =$ 26.8, $p < .001$ for Trial 1; $F = 3.48$, $p < .05$ for Trial 2).

No five-or six-year-old in either village and only 12 of the 40 seven-year-olds in the Ladino village were attending school. School for the others consisted of little more than semiorganized games.

Table 7.1 Mean Number of Objects and Pairs Recalled

	Trial 1		*Trial 2*	
Age	*Recall*	*Pairs*	*Recall*	*Pairs*
		Ladino village		
5	5.2	2.1	5.4	2.1
7	6.7	3.3	7.8	3.7
		Indian village		
5-6	7.1	3.4	7.8	3.8
7-8	8.6	3.4	8.3	3.6
9-10	10.3	4.9	10.3	4.3
11-12	9.6	3.4	10.1	3.6

Moreover, none of the children in San Marcos had ever left the village, and the five- and six-year-olds typically spend most of the day within a 500-yard radius of their homes. Hence, school attendance and contact with books and a written language do not seem to be prerequisites for clustering in young children.

The recall and cluster scores obtained in Guatemala were remarkably comparable to those reported for middle-class American children. Appel, et al. (1971) presented 12 pictures to Minneapolis children in Grade 1 (approximately age 7) and 15 pictures to children in Grade 5 (approximately age 11) in a single-trial recall task similar to the one described here. The recall scores were 66 percent for the 7-year-olds and 80 percent for the 11-year-olds. These values are almost identical to those obtained in both Guatemalan villages. The cluster indices were also comparable. The American 7-year-olds had a cluster ratio of .25; the San Marcos 5- and 6-year-olds had a ratio of .39.[1]

Recognition Memory

The cultural similarity in recall also holds for recognition memory. In a separate study, 5-, 8-, and 11-year-old children from Ladino villages in the East and from Cambridge, Massachusetts, were shown 60 pictures of objects—all of which were familiar to the Americans but some of which were unfamiliar to the Guatemalans. After 0, 24, or 48 hours delay, each child was shown 60 pairs of pictures, one of which was old and the other new, and was asked to decide which one he had seen. Although the 5- and 8-year-old Americans performed significantly better than the Guatemalans, there was no statistically significant cultural difference for the 11-year-olds, whose scores ranged from 85 percent to 98 percent after 0, 24, or 48 hours delay (Kagan et al. 1973). (See table 7.2.) The remarkably high scores of the American 5-year-olds have also been reported by Scott (1973).

A similar result was found on a recognition memory task for 32 photos of faces, balanced for sex, child versus adult, and Indian versus Caucasian, administered to 35 American and 38 San Marcos children 8–11 years of age. Each child initially inspected 32 chromatic photographs of faces, one at a time, in a self-paced procedure. Each child's recognition memory was tested by showing

1. The cluster index is the ratio of the number of pairs recalled to the product of the number of categories in the list times one less than the number of words in each category.

Table 7.2 Mean Percentage of Correct Responses

	Americans			Guatemalans		
Delay	*5 yrs.*	*8 yrs.*	*11 yrs.*	*5 yrs.*	*8 yrs.*	*11 yrs.*
0 hours	92.8	96.7	98.3	58.4	74.6	85.2
24 hours	86.7	95.6	96.7	55.8	71.0	87.0
48 hours	87.5	90.3	93.9	61.4	75.8	86.2

him 32 pairs of photographs (each pair was of the same sex, age, and ethnicity), one of which was old and the other new. The child had to state which photograph he had seen during the inspection phase. Although the American 8- and 9-year-olds performed slightly better than the Guatemalans (82 vs. 70 percent), there was no significant cultural difference among the 10- and 11-year-olds (91 vs. 87 percent). Moreover, there was no cultural difference at any age for the highest performance attained by a single child.[2] The favored interpretation of the poorer performance of the younger children in both recognition memory studies is that some of them did not completely understand the task and others did not activate the proper problem-solving strategies during the registration and retrieval phases of the task.

It appears that recall and recognition memory are basic cognitive functions that seem to mature in a regular way in a natural environment. The cognitive retardation observed during the first year does not have any serious predictive validity for these two important aspects of cognitive functioning for children 10–11 years of age.

Perceptual Analysis

The Guatemalan children were also capable of solving difficult Embedded Figures Test items. The test consisted of 12 color drawings of familiar objects in which a triangle had been embedded as part of the object. The child had to locate the hidden triangle and place a black paper triangle so that it was congruent with the design of the drawing. The test was administered to rural Indian children from

2. These photographs were also used in an identical procedure with 12 Kipsigis-speaking 10- and 11-year-olds from a rural village in eastern Kenya. Despite the absence of any black faces in the set, the percentage of items recognized correctly was 82 for this group of African children.

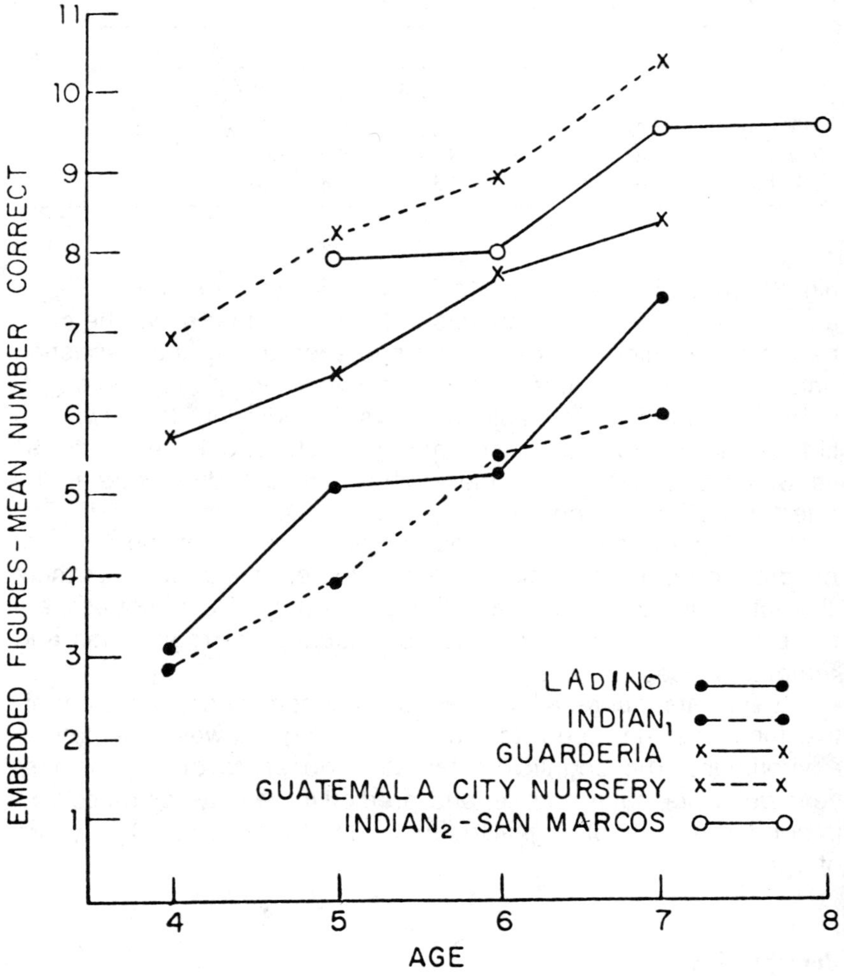

Figure 7.3 Mean Number Correct on the Embedded Figures Test

San Marcos, as well as to rural Indians living close to Guatemala City (labeled Indian$_1$ in fig. 4.2.3), the Ladino villages, and two groups from Guatemala City.

The Guatemala City middle-class children had the highest scores and, except for San Marcos, the rural children the poorest. The surprisingly competent performances of the San Marcos children is due, we believe, to the more friendly conditions of testing. This suggestion is affirmed by an independent study in which a special attempt was made to maximize rapport and comprehension of instructions with a group of rural isolated children before administering a large battery of tests. Although all test peformances were not facilitated by this rapport-raising procedure, performance on the Embedded Figures Test was improved considerably. It is important to note that no 5- or 6-year-old was completely incapable of solving some of these problems. The village differences in mean score reflect the fact that the rural children had difficulty with three or four of the harder items. This was the first time that many rural children had ever seen a two-dimensional drawing, and most of the 5-, 6-, and 7-year-olds in San Marcos had had no opportunity to play with books, paper, pictures, or crayons. Nonetheless, these children solved seven or eight of the test items. Investigators who have suggested that prior experience with pictures is necessary for efficient analysis of two-dimensional information may have misinterpreted failure to understand the requirements of the problem with a deficiency in cognitive competence. This competence seems to develop in the world of moving leaves, chickens, and water.[3] As with recall and recognition memory, the performance of the San Marcos child was comparable to that of a modern urban child of his own age.

Perceptual Inference

The competence of the San Marcos children on the Embedded Figures Test is affirmed by their performance on a test administered only in San Marcos and Cambridge and called Perceptual Inference. The children (60 American and 55 Guatemalan, 5–12 years of age) were shown a schematic drawing of an object and asked to guess what that object might be if the drawing were completed. The child was given a total of four clues for each of 13 items, where each clue added more information. The child had to guess an object from an incomplete illustration, to make an inference from minimal information (see figs. 7.4 and 7.5).

There was no significant cultural difference for the children 7–12 years of age, although the American 5- and 6-year-olds did perform significantly better than the Indian children. In San Marcos, performance improved from 62 percent correct on one of the first two clues for the 5- and 6-year-olds to 77 percent correct for the

3. This conclusion holds for Embedded Figures Test performance, and not necessarily for the ability to detect three-dimensional perspective in two-dimensional drawings.

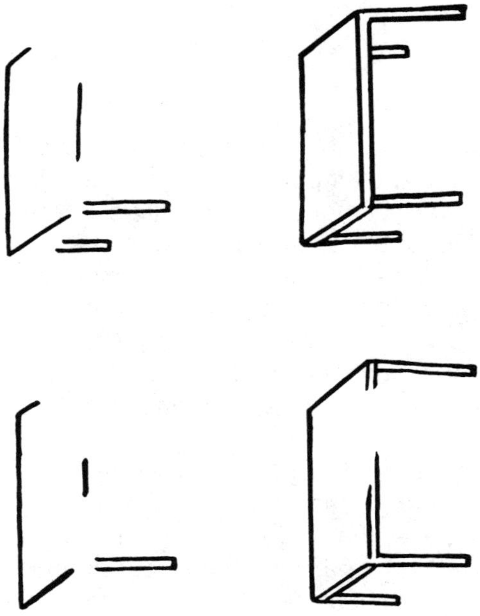

Figure 7.4 Sample Item from the Perceptual Inference Test

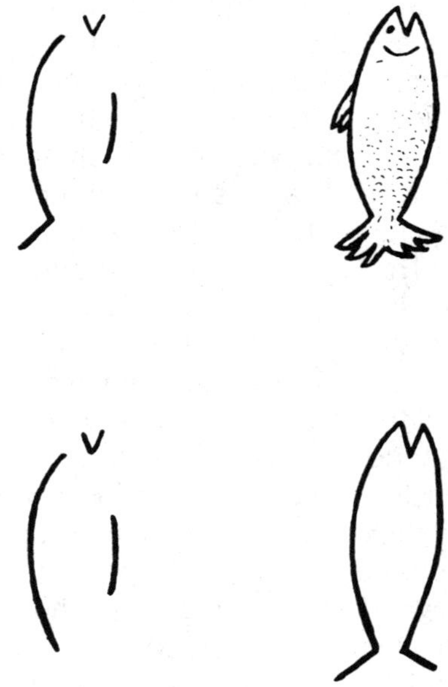

Figure 7.5 Sample Item from the Perceptual Inference Test.

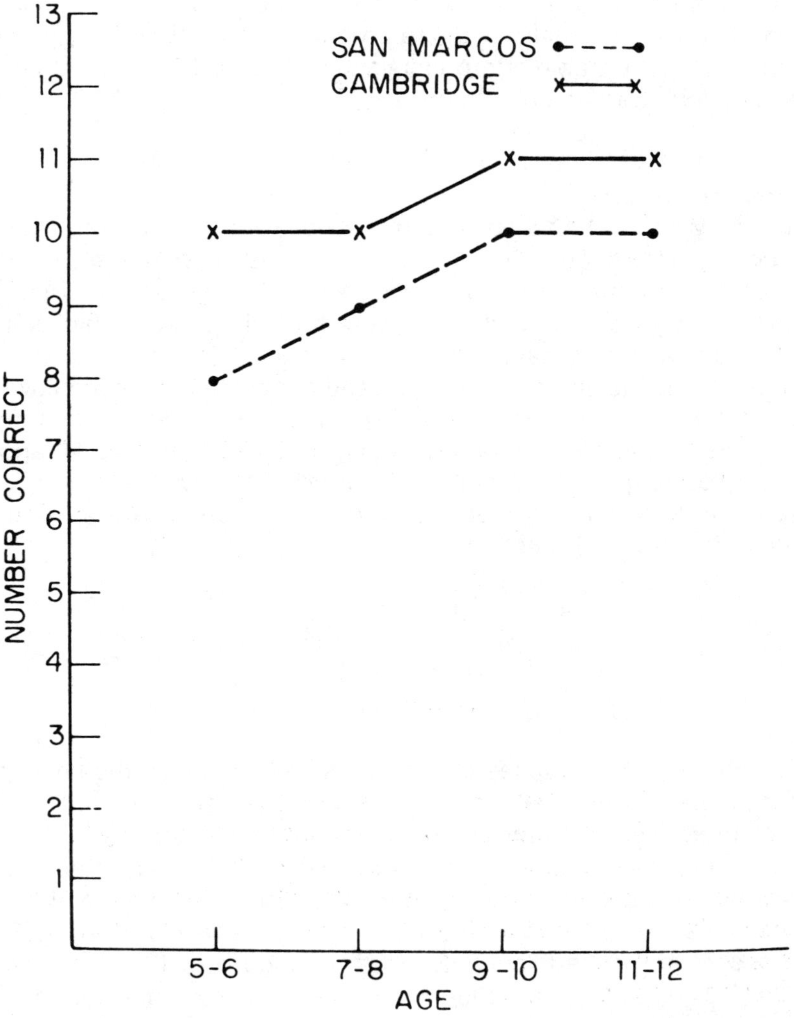

Figure 7.6 Number Correct on the Perceptual Inference Test.

9–12-year-olds. The comparable changes for the American children were from 77 to 84 percent (See fig. 7.6).

Familiarity with the test objects was critical for success. All of the San Marcos children had seen hats, fish, and corn, and these items were rarely missed. By contrast, many American children failed these items. No San Marcos child not attending school, and therefore unfamiliar with books, correctly guessed the book item, whereas most of those in school guessed it correctly. As with memory and perceptual analysis, the retardation seen during infancy did not predict comparable retardation in the ability of the 11-year-old to make difficult perceptual inferences.

Conceptual Inference

The San Marcos child also performed well on questions requiring conceptual inference. In this test, the child was told verbally three characteristics of an object and was required to guess the object. Some of the examples included: What has wings, eats chickens, and lives in a tree? What moves trees, cannot be seen, and makes one cold? What is made of wood, is used to carry things, and allows one to make journeys? There was improved performance with age; the 5- and 6-year-olds averaged 9 out of 14 correct, and the 11- and 12-year-olds averaged 12 out of 14 correct. The San Marcos child was capable of making moderately difficult inferences from both visual and verbal information.

Discussion

This corpus of data implies that absolute retardation in the time of emergence of universal cognitive competences during infancy is not predictive of comparable deficits for memory, perceptual analysis, and inference during preadolescence. Although the rural Guatemalan infants were retarded with respect to activation of hypotheses, alertness, and onset of stranger anxiety and object permanence, the preadolescents' performance on the tests of perceptual analysis, preceptual inference, and recall and recognition memory were comparable to American middle-class norms. Infant retardation seems to be partially reversible and cognitive development during the early years more resilient than had been supposed.

One potential objection to this conclusion is that the tests were too easy for the Guatemalan 11-year-olds and that is why cultural differences were absent. There are two comments that can be addressed to that issue. First, it is not intuitively reasonable to argue that the ability to remember 60 photographs of objects, classify an object from a few sketchy lines, or detect the triangle hidden in a two-dimensional drawing is "easy" for children who rarely see photographs, pencils, crayons, or books. Second, we deliberately assessed cognitive functions that we believe all children should master by the time they are preadolescents. The fact that many 11-year-olds approached the ceiling on some tests is support for the basic premise of this article, namely, that infant retardation does not prevent a child from eventually developing basic cognitive competences.

This result is surprising if one believes that each child is born with a certain level of general intellectual competence that is stable from infancy through adulthood. If, on the contrary, one assumes that each stage of development is characterized by a different profile of specific competences and there is no necessary relation between early emergence of the capacities of infancy and level of attainment of the quite different abilities characteristic of childhood, then these results are more reasonable. There is no reason to assume that the caterpillar who metamorphoses a bit earlier than his kin is a better adapted or more efficient butterfly.

Consideration of why the rural Guatemalan children lagged behind the urban children on some tests during the period five through nine years of age is also important. It will be recalled that on the embedded figures and recognition memory tests the performance of rural children was several years behind both the American and Guatemala City middle-class children. The differences were minimal for the object recall and perceptual inference tests. The approximately three-year lag in performance is paralleled by comparable differences between lower- and middle-class children in urban Western cities. For example, Bosco (1972) found that middle-class first and third graders were able to tolerate smaller interstimulus intervals in a background masking procedure than lower-class children, but that this difference had vanished among sixth-grade children. Similarly, Bakker (1971) compared good and poor readers from urban centers in Holland on a task that required operating simultaneously on two items of information on a temporal integration task. The poor readers performed less well than the good readers at ages six to eight, but were comparable to the good readers during the preadolescent years.

We interpret these results as indicating that the urban lower-class children, like the younger, rural Guatemalans, were not able to mobilize proper problem-solving strategies necessary for task solution, but achieved that level of competence by 11 years of age. Some of these strategies include focused attention, rehearsal of task information and instructions, awareness of and understanding the problem to be solved, maintenance of problem set, and the ability to remember critical information elements in the problem and to operate on that information. It is believed that these functions may emerge a little later in some groups of children than in others, but that they are operative in all children by 11–12 years of age. In a recently completed study with Patricia Engle, we found that among rural Guatemalan children, 5 through 11 years of age, the rate of improvement in performance on three memory tasks (memory for numbers, memory for sentences, and auditory blending) was greatest between 9 and 11 years of age, whereas White (1970), using comparable data from American children, found that the greatest rate of improvement was between 5 and 7 years of age—a lag of about three years.

These data have implications for America's educational problems. There is a tendency to regard the poor test performances of economically impoverished, minority group 6-year-olds in the United States as indicative of a permanent and, perhaps, irreversible defect in intellectual ability—as a difference in quality of function rather than slower maturational rate. The Guatemalan data, together with those of Bosco and Bakker, suggest that children differ in the age at which basic cognitive competences emerge and that experiential factors influence the time of emergence. Economically disadvantaged American children and isolated rural Guatemalan children appear to be from one to three years behind middle-class children in demonstrating some of the problem-solving skills characteristic of Piaget's stage of concrete operations. But these competences eventually appear in sturdy form by age 10 or 11. The common practice of arbitrarily setting 7 years—the usual time of school entrance—as the age when children are to be classified as competent or incompetent confuses differences in maturational rate with permanent, qualitative differences in intellectual ability. This practice is as logical as classifying children as reproductively fertile or sterile depending on whether or not they have reached physiological puberty by their thirteenth birthday.

When educators note correctly that poor children tend to remain permanently behind middle-class children on intellectual and academic performance, they are referring to the relative retardation on the culturally specific skills of reading, mathematics, and language achievement described earlier. That relative retardation is the product of the rank ordering of scores on achievement and IQ tests. The fact that relative retardation on these abilities is stable from age five on does not mean that the relatively retarded children are not growing intellectually (when compared with themselves), often at the same rate as economically advantaged youngsters.

The suggestion that basic cognitive competences, in contrast to culturally specific ones, emerge at different times and that the child retains the capacity for actualization of his competence until a late age is not substantially different from the earlier conclusions of Dennis and Najarian (1957). Although the 49 infants 2–12 months of age living in poorly staffed Lebanese institutions were seriously retarded on the Cattell developmental scale (mean developmental quotient of 68 compared with a quotient of 102 for a comparison group), the 4½–6-year-olds who had resided in the same institution all their lives performed at a level comparable to American norms on a memory test (Knox Cubes) as well as on Porteus mazes and the Goodenough Draw-a-Man Test.

Of more direct relevance is Dennis's (1973) recent follow-up study of 16 children who were adopted out of the same Lebanese institution between 12 and 24 months of age—the period during which the San Marcos infant leaves the unstimulating environment of the dark hut—with an average developmental quotient of 50 on the Cattell Infant Scale. Even though the assessment of later intellectual ability was based on the culturally biased Stanford-Binet IQ test, the average IQ, obtained when the children were between 4 and 12 years of age, was 101, and 13 of the 16 children had IQ scores of 90 or above.

Additional support for the inherent resiliency in human development comes from longitudinal information on two sisters who spent most of their infancy in a crib in a small bedroom with no toys.[4] The mother, who felt unable to care for her fourth child, restricted her to the room soon after birth and instructed her eight-year-old daughter to care for the child. One year later, another daughter was born, and she, too, was placed in the crib with the older sister. These two children left the room only to be fed and, according to the caretaking sister who is now a married woman in her twenties, the two infants spent about 23 hours of each day together in a barren crib. When the authorities were notified of this arrangement, the children were removed from the home and taken to a hospital. By this time the younger child was 2½ and the older 3½ years old. Medical records reveal that both children were malnourished, severely

4. The authors thank Meinhard Robinow for information on these girls.

retarded in weight and height, and seriously retarded psychologically. After a month in the hospital, following considerable physical recovery, both sisters were placed in the care of a middle-class family who had several young children. The sisters have remained with that family for the last 12 years and regard the husband and wife as their parents. One of us (J.K.) tested the sisters five times when they were between 4 and 9 years of age, and recently interviewed and tested both of them over a two-day period when they were 14½ and 15½ years old.

The younger sister has performed consistently better than the older one over the last 10 years. The IQ scores of the younger girl have risen steadily from a Stanford-Binet IQ of 74 at age 4½ (after two years in the foster home) to a Wechsler Full Scale IQ of 88 at age 14. The older girl's scores have also improved, but less dramatically, from a Stanford-Binet IQ of 59 at age 5 to a Wechsler IQ of 72 at age 15. The author also administered a lengthy battery of tests, some of which were discussed earlier. On the Perceptual Inference Test, the percentage correct was 85 for the younger sister and 61 for the older sister. On the Recognition Memory for Photographs, the percentages were 94 for both. On the Embedded Figures Test, the percentages were 92 and 100, and on the recall memory for objects, the percentages were 92 and 83 for the younger and older sister, respectively. Moreover, the interpersonal behavior of both girls was in no way different from that of the average rural Ohio adolescent—a group the author came to know well after seven years of work in the area. Although there is some ambiguity surrounding the competence of the older girl, the younger one performs at an average level on a wide range of tests of cognitive functioning, despite 2½ years of serious isolation.

These data, together with the poor predictive relation between scores on infant developmental tests and later assessments of intellectual functioning, strengthen the conclusion that environmentally produced retardation during the first year or two of life appears to be reversible. The importance of the Guatemalan data derives from the fact that the San Marcos 11-year-olds performed as well, considering the homogeneity and isolation of their childlhood environment. Additionally, there is a stronger feeling now than there was in 1957 that environmentally produced retardation during the first two years may be irreversible, even though the empirical basis for that belief is no firmer in 1972 than it was in 1957.

More dramatic support for the notion that psychological development is malleable comes from recent experimental studies with animals. Several years ago Harlow's group demonstrated that although monkeys reared in isolation for the first six months displayed abnormal and often bizarre social behaviors, they could, if the experimenter were patient, solve the complex learning problems normally administered to feral-born monkeys. The prolonged isolation did not destroy their cognitive competence (Harlow, et al. 1969). More recently, Suomi and Harlow (1972) have shown that even the stereotyped and bizarre social behavior shown by six-month-old isolates can be altered by placing them with female monkeys three months younger than themselves over a 26-week therapeutic period. "By the end of the therapy period the behavioral levels were virtually indistinguishable from those of the socially competent therapist monkeys" (Suomi and Harlow 1972:491).

This resiliency has also been demonstrated for infant mice (Cairns and Nakelski 1971) which experienced an initial 10 weeks of isolation from other animals. Compared with group-reared mice of the same strain, the isolated subjects were hyperactive to other mice, displaying both extreme withdrawal and extreme aggressiveness. These investigators also attempted rehabilitation of the isolates by placing them with groups of mice for an additional 10 weeks, however, after which their behavior was indistinguishable from animals that had never been isolated.

> By the seventieth day after interchange, the effects of group therapy were complete, and animals that had been isolated for one hundred days following weaning were indistinguishable from animals that had never been isolated. (Cairns and Nakelski 1971:363)

These dramatic alterations in molar behavior are in accord with replicated reports of recovery of visual function in monkeys and cats deprived of patterned light soon after birth (Baxter 1966; Chow and Stewart 1972; Wilson and Riesen 1966). Kittens deprived of light for one year recovered basic visual functions after only 10 days in the experimenter's home (Baxter 1966); kittens which had one or both eyes sutured for close to two years were able to learn pattern discriminations with the deprived eye after only moderate training (Chow and Stewart 1972).

If the extreme behavioral and perceptual sequelae of isolation in monkeys, cats, and mice can be altered by such brief periods of rehabilitative experience, it is not difficult to believe that the San Marcos infant is capable of as dramatic a recovery over a period of nine years. These data do not indicate the impotence of early environments, but rather the potency of the environment in which the organism is functioning. There is no question that early experience seriously affects kittens, monkeys, and children. If the first environment does not permit the full actualization of psychological competences, the child will function below his ability as long as he remains in that context. But if he is transferred to an environment that presents greater variety and requires more accommodations, he seems more capable of exploiting that experience and repairing the damage wrought by the first environment than some theorists have implied.

These conclusions do not imply that intervention or rehabilitation efforts with poor American or minority group preschool children are of no value. Unlike San Marcos, where children are assigned adult responsibilities when they are strong and alert enough to assume them, rather than at a fixed age, American children live in a severely age graded system, in which children are continually rank ordered. Hence, if a poor four-year-old falls behind a middle-class four-year-old on a culturally significant skill, like knowledge of letters or numbers, he may never catch up with the child who was advanced and is likely to be placed in a special educational category. Hence, American parents must be concerned with the early psychological growth of their children. We live in a society in which the relative retardation of a four-year-old seriously influences his future opportunities because we have made relative retardation functionally synonymous with absolute retardation. This is not true in subsistence farming communities like San Marcos.

These data suggest that exploration of the new and the construction of objects or ideas from some prior schematic blueprint must be inherent properties of the mind. The idea that the child carries with him at all times the essential mental competence to understand the new in some terms and to make a personal contribution to each new encounter is only original in our time. Despite the current popularity of Kant and Piaget, the overwhelming prejudice of Western psychologists is that higher order cognitive competences and personality factors are molded completely by the environment. Locke's image of an unmarked tablet on which sensation played its patterned melody has a parallel in Darwin's failure to realize, until late in his life, that the organism made a contribution to its own evolution. Darwin was troubled by the fact that the same climate on different islands in the Galapagos produced different forms of the same species. Since he believed that climatic variation was the dynamic agent in evolution he was baffled. He did not appreciate that the gene was the organism's contribution to its own alteration. Western psychologists have been blocked by the same prejudice that prevented young Darwin from solving his riddle. From Locke to Skinner we have viewed the perfectibility of man as vulnerable to the vicissitudes of the objects and people who block, praise, or push him, and resisted giving the child any compass of his own. The mind, like the nucleus of a cell, has a plan for growth and can transduce a new flower, an odd pain, or a stranger's unexpected smile into a form that is comprehensible. This process is accomplished through wedding cognitive structures to selective attention, activation of hypotheses, assimilation, and accommodation. The purpose of these processes is to convert an alerting unfamiliar event, incompletely understood, to a recognized variation of an existing familiar structure. This is accomplished through the detection of the dimensions of the event that bear a relation to existing schemata and the subsequent incorporation of the total event into the older structure.

We need not speak of joy in this psychological mastery, for neither walking nor breathing is performed in order to experience happiness. These properties of the motor or autonomic systems occur because each physiological system or organ naturally exercises its primary function. The child explores the unfamiliar and attempts to match his ideas and actions to some previously acquired representation because these are basic properties of the mind. The child has no choice.

The San Marcos child knows much less than the American about planes, computers, cars, and the many hundreds of other phenomena that are familiar to the Western youngster, and he is a little slower in developing some of the basic cognitive competences of our species. But neither appreciation of these events nor the earlier cognitive maturation is necessary for a successful journey to adulthood in San Marcos. The American child knows far less about how to make canoes, rope, tortillas, or how to burn an old milpa in preparation for June planting. Each knows what is necessary, each assimilates the cognitive conflicts that are presented to him, and each seems to have the potential to display more talent than his environment demands of him. There are few dumb children in the world if one classifies them from the perspective of the community of adaptation, but millions of dumb children if one classifies them from the perspective of another society.

8

Anomalous Reactions to Social Pressure of Israeli and Soviet Children Raised in Family Versus Collective Settings

Ron Shouval, Sophie Kav Venaki, Urie Bronfenbrenner, Edward C. Devereux, and Elizabeth Kiely

School age is a period of intense socialization for children. The influence that culture and social institutions have on character formation during this period appears to be considerable, particularly in regard to the individual's social behavior, attitudes and values.

One aspect of the cultural framework that has received attention in regard to personality development is the dominant socio-political system, as exemplified by Rollins' (1974) comparison of the attitudes of children raised in the Soviet Union and in the United States.

In the following article, Shouval et al. add another dimension to the inquiry, namely the immediate matrix of upbringing (family versus collective) studied along with the cultural-political system (Israeli versus Soviet), in regard to their relative impact on children's responses to adult and peer expectations. This study is inscribed within the formida-

ble contribution of Urie Bronfenbrenner's group at Cornell University on the role of specific systems in child development.

THIS EXPERIMENT investigates reaction to social pressure among Israeli (*n* = 400) and Soviet (*n* = 353) 12-year-olds brought up in family versus collective settings (kibbutz in Israel, boarding school in the USSR). Soviet children showed higher levels of conformity than their Israeli age-mates. Cultural differences, sex differences, and effect of threatened social exposure were greater for youngsters raised in collective settings than for those brought up in their own homes. Kibbutz-reared children did not react in the same way as products of Soviet group upbringing. Israeli children generally did resemble Soviet age-mates in reacting similarly to pressure from peers versus adults, but they differed sharply from their Soviet counterparts, as well as from children from 10 other countries, in giving their most moral responses when neither their parents nor their friends would know of their action.

This study reports the results of an experiment on the effects of social pressure on children from two societies with widely differing systems of child rearing, both between and within cultures. Samples have been drawn from two contrasting child-rearing environments. The first is the conventional context of the home; the second, also found in both societies, is the children's collective. In Israel this setting is represented by the kibbutz; in the USSR it appears in most pronounced form in the boarding school. Under both collective arrangements, children sleep outside the home, the children's peer group constitutes a major context and instrument of upbringing, and substantial responsibility for child rearing is vested in an upbringer specially selected for the task—the *metapelet* in the Israeli kibbutz and the *vospitatel* in the Soviet boarding school.

Thus the design of the study focuses on two major contrasts and their interplay. It permits an assessment of the relative impact of culture as against context of upbringing on children's reaction to social pressure. In addition, the results are examined in the perspective of data from a dozen countries in which the same experiment on effects of social pressure has now been carried out. These nations are concentrated in Eastern and Western Europe, but also include Japan, Canada, and the U.S.

Experimental Procedure[1]

Children in classroom settings were asked to respond to a series of conflict situations under three different conditions: (a) a *base* condition, in which they were told that no one would see their responses except the investigators conducting the research; (b) an *adult* condition, in which they were informed that the responses of everyone in the class would be posted on a chart and shown to parents at a special meeting scheduled for the following week; and (c) a *peer* condition, in which the children were notified that the chart would be prepared and shown a week later to the class itself. The order of the last two conditions was counterbalanced.

The conflict situations consisted of 30 hypothetical dilemmas such as the one shown in table 8.1. Other items dealt with such situations as going to a movie recommended by friends but disapproved by parents, standing guard while friends put a rubber snake in the teacher's desk, joining friends in pilfering fruit from an orchard with a no trespassing sign, running away after breaking a window accidentally while playing ball, etc. In short, each time the child was confronted with choosing between some conventional standard of "moral" behavior presumably approved by adults and some mildly "antisocial" or at least mischievous action urged by his or her peers. Information on the development of the measuring instrument, factorial structure, and procedures employed for ensuring equivalence across structures (e.g., back translation) is provided in earlier publications (Bronfenbrenner 1967, 1970a).

Each response was scored on a scale from −2.5 to +2.5, a negative value being assigned to the behavior urged by age-mates. To control for a positional response set, scale direction was reversed in half of the items. The situations were divided into three alternate forms of 10 items each. Under any one condition a child could obtain a score ranging from −25 to +25, with zero representing equal division between behavior urged by peers and adults. Split-half reliabilities for the 10-item forms (based on American samples only) ranged from .75 to .86 under different experimental conditions; the reliability of the total score (i.e., sum across all three conditions) was .94. All reliability coefficients are corrected for length of test by the Spearman-Brown formula.

1. The experiment was designed by Urie Bronfenbrenner in collaboration with E. C. Devereux, G. F. Suci, and R. R. Rodgers. For more detailed accounts, see Bronfenbrenner (1967, 1970).

Table 8.1 The Lost Test: An Example of Hypothetical Dilemmas Given to Children in 12 Cultures

You and your friends accidentally find a sheet of paper which the teacher must have lost. On this sheet are the questions and answers for a quiz that you are going to have tomorrow. Some of the kids suggest that you not say anything to the teacher about it, so that all of you can get better marks. What would you really do? Suppose your friends decide to go ahead. Would you go along with them or refuse?

Refuse to go along with my friends			*Go along with my friends*		
absolutely certain	fairly certain	I guess so	I guess so	fairly certain	absolutely certain

A measure of orientation toward adults versus peers is thus obtained for each of the three experimental conditions. The *base* score is taken as the point of departure for gauging the effects of social pressure. The *adult* score is presumed to reflect most directly the child's view of his parents' norms for the appropriateness of his behavior. The *peer* score is interpreted as a function of the expectations of age-mates. The three scores can also be combined in various ways. The *total* score across the three conditions measures the general tendency of the child to subscribe to adult- versus peer-approved alternatives. The difference between adult and peer scores (A − P) measures the extent to which children give more adult-approved responses when told their answers will be known to parents rather than to peers; thus the score reflects the perceived discrepancy or convergence of adult and peer standards and expectations. Finally, a second and statistically independent difference score, and one that turns out to be particularly significant for the Israeli–Soviet contrast, is the difference between performance under the base condition and under the two experimental conditions taken together. Expressed as the difference between the latter and the former (E − B), this score reflects the extent to which children shift their response toward (or away from) claimed conformity to conventional moral values when told their answers will become known to others, whether peers or adults.

Rationale and Hypotheses

Our theoretical speculations about the outcome of the cross-cultural comparison were hardly a priori, since they were heavily influenced by the fact that half of the data had already been analyzed and previously published. The so-called "dilemmas experiment" had been carried out several years earlier with two samples of Soviet sixth-graders (Bronfenbrenner 1967, 1970a), one drawn from three different boarding schools in Moscow, the other from three regular day schools in the same or similar neighborhoods. The responses of the Soviet children were compared with those of their age-mates from three American schools.

The experimental results were consistent with the major hypotheses proposed for those investigations. Three dealt with the cross-cultural contrast between the Soviet and American children, the remaining four with differences anticipated within Soviet society between pupils attending boarding school and those attending day school.

In the former category, the first hypothesis was based on the strong emphasis in Soviet upbringing, both in the home and in the school, on the development of conventional virtues such as obedience and propriety (Bronfenbrenner 1962, 1970b). It was therefore anticipated, and strongly confirmed, that Soviet children would obtain markedly higher scores under all three experimental conditions. Indeed, there was not only a marked difference in mean score between the Soviet and American samples (averaging from 12 to 15 points), but scarcely any overlap in the two distributions.

The second and third hypotheses took as their point of departure the fact that in the USSR, in contrast to the U.S., an explicit effort is made to use the peer group as an agent for socializing the child and bringing about an identification with the values of the adult society (Bronfenbrenner 1962, 1970b). On this basis, a different pattern of response to the three experimental conditions was predicted for American and Soviet children. The former were expected to obtain their highest score under pressure from adults, the lowest when told that their answers would be seen by their friends, with the base condition falling in between. In contrast, Soviet youngsters were expected to react similarly to pressure from parents and peers, in each case shifting their reponses in the direction of claimed conformity to conventional moral standards, and thus scoring lowest under the base condition. In terms of difference scores, the Americans should obtain a significantly higher mean on A − P, the Soviets on E − B. The results were in the predicted direction, but reliably so only in the case of the E − B score.

In approaching the Soviet-Israeli comparison, we anticipated differences very similar to those obtained in our earlier comparison involving the U.S. It was clear both from the research of others (e.g., Eisenstadt 1951, 1967) and from our own exploratory interviews and observations that, especially in comparison with the USSR, Israeli society was essentially Western in orientation. Its values were certainly less moralistic and more pluralistic than those of the USSR and child-rearing practices appeared to vary accordingly. There was every reason to expect, therefore, that Israeli children—at least those raised in the family as against collective settings—would exhibit a pattern of response similar to that of their American agemates. It follows that the three hypotheses bearing on Israeli–Soviet differences in the present study are exactly parallel in form to their predecessors in the American-Soviet comparison. The only change is the substitution of the adjective *Israeli* for *American*. The hypotheses follow.

Hypothesis 1. In comparison with Soviet youngsters, Israeli children should obtain significantly lower scores on conventional morality under all three experimental conditions.

Hypothesis 2. Israeli pupils should show a greater discrepancy in response to pressure from adults than in response to pressure from peers, with a higher score under the former experimental condition than the latter.

Hypothesis 3. Whereas Soviet children obtained their lowest scores under the base condition, thus producing a significant and positive E − B difference, for the Israeli sample the average score on the base condition should fall midway between the other two, with the result that the E − B difference should approach zero.

Given the fact that we had already seen half of our data, all three of the foregoing hypotheses would seem assured of a high probablity of support. We therefore hasten to reassure the reader that, for two of the three hypotheses, the results not only failed to support the predictions, but came out exactly opposite in direction. The source of the error turned out to be not methodological but substantive: the mistake of equating Israeli society with American, or, for that matter, with any other.

But we are getting ahead of our story. We have yet to consider a second set of hypotheses bearing on the differential impact of upbringing in the family versus the collective. Here again, half of the data were already available to us: namely, the comparison of reactions to social pressure on the part of pupils from Soviet boarding schools and day schools. But inferences to the corresponding Israeli contrast between kibbutz- and family-reared children proved equivocal. An understanding of the difficulty requires a brief account of the derivation of the general hypothesis pertaining to the boarding versus day school contrast in the original study. This hypothesis had been developed in the course of previous research on socialization in the American family (Bronfenbrenner 1961a, 1961b). The underlying assumption was that exposure to divergent influences in the course of growing up makes it easier for the child to resist pressure to conform. Thus, a child who has been brought up by a single socializing agent (e.g., one parent instead of two) is likely to become not only more dependent but also more anxious at the prospect of differing from his sole source of emotional support. In contrast, a child raised by more than one upbringer is more apt to learn that "you can't please everybody" and that deviation does not jeopardize one's major source of security. As a result, the child reared by multiple agents may not subscribe as fervently to his upbringers' values but is more likely to remain true to his own views, whatever they may be, when these are subjected to pressure for change.

The contrast between boarding school and day school was seen as an opportunity to test the impact of what might be called *pluralistic* versus *monistic* socialization at yet another level. Pupils in Soviet boarding schools are subject to a highly homogeneous pattern of socialization with minimum exposure to extraneous forces. In contrast, children attending regular day schools in the USSR, as in the U.S., go home after school, where they are subject to strong family influences. As a result they are given substantial exposure to two rather different systems of socialization instead of only one.

Within this frame of reference, four hypotheses had been formulated and tested in the original study (Bronfenbrenner 1970a). First, children raised primarily in a boarding school were expected to show stronger adherence to conventional moral values than their age-mates attending regular day schools. Second, given the fact that in the Soviet boarding school the peer collective is relied upon especially heavily as an agent of discipline, the difference in reaction to pressure from adults versus peers should be even smaller for children raised in that setting than for those being brought up in families. In other words, the boarding school pupils should react to pressure from peers in the same way as they react to pressure from adults. In statistical terms, the A − P difference should be closer to zero for boarding than for day school children. Third, if, as hypothesized, children brought up in a single socialization setting are not as likely to develop their own, internalized norms of behavior, then the boarding school pupils should obtain their lowest scores, that is, be most ready to deviate from conventional moral standards, under the *base* condition, when their answers will not be shown to anyone they know. Again, in statistical terms, the E − B score should be higher for children reared in boarding schools than for those brought up in their own homes. Fourth, these differences within Soviet society, while significant, should nevertheless be smaller in magnitude than the differences between the U.S. and the USSR; in other words, intercultural variation should exceed intracultural. By and large, the results gave support to all four hypotheses.

Can we expect the same four relationships to obtain for the contrast between Israeli children raised in the family versus those raised in the kibbutz? The answer to this question hinges on the validity both of the underlying theory and of the analogy between the two pairs of settings in each country. Even if we assume that exposure to a single rather than two or more socializing agents or contexts does increase the child's susceptibility to social pressure, is it correct to regard upbringing as less pluralistic in the kibbutz than in the family? In discussing this issue with experts on kibbutz education, we learned that it is a question on which reasonable men can differ. There were those who argued, and cited historical documentary evidence, that principles and methods of kibbutz upbringing had their roots in socialist and communist ideology and practices; for example, the work of Makarenko (1952, 1955), on which much of Soviet collective upbringing is based. Thus, the distinctive features of the classroom collective in the USSR, including the subordination of individual desires to group goals, group cohesiveness, and group criticism were also to be found (to be sure, in a less intense form) in the *kvutsa*, the children's peer group in the kibbutz.

The counterthesis, sometimes offered by the very same kibbutz experts, stressed the divergent course of socialist ideology in the USSR and Israel, which has resulted in marked differences in the theory and practice of collective upbringing in the two countries. In the Soviet educational system, it was argued, the individual has significance only as a member of a collective. In the kibbutz, while collective goals and values are respected, the rights and opinions of the individual are also protected, and indeed supported, much as they are in the rest of Israeli society. Moreover, kibbutz children have more extensive contacts with their parents than do children in the Soviet collectives, and the influences of parents may pull in different directions from those of the *metapelet* and the peer group. As a result, kibbutz children should exhibit a pattern of reaction to social pressure more closely resembling that of other Israeli youngsters than of Soviet pupils, including those attending boarding schools.

These differing conceptions of Israeli reality lead to alternative sets of hypotheses regarding the results of our experiment. One set, stressing the continuity in the theory and practice of collective upbringing in Soviet communist society and in the Israeli kibbutz, predicts a pattern of differences between kibbutz- and family-reared Israeli children similar to that previously found for the contrast between boarding and day school pupils in the USSR. The second set of hypotheses emphasizes the commonality of values and methods of child rearing within Israeli society and hence anticipates little difference in reaction to social pressure on the part of children raised in the family versus the kibbutz. It is clear that the two sets of hypotheses are mutually exclusive and reflect different assumptions about the empirical realities of socialization in contemporary Israel. In the absence of definitive data, we shall arbitrarily state the first set only, which presumes an analogy between the family versus kibbutz comparison in Israel and the day versus boarding school comparison in the USSR. This set of hypotheses follows.

Hypothesis 4. In Israel, as in the USSR, children raised primarily in collective settings should show greater conformity to conventional moral values than their age-mates who grow up in families. In terms of experimental measures, this means that the mean for the total score across all three conditions should be higher for kibbutz children than for those brought up in their own families.

Hypothesis 5. In Israel, as in the USSR, children growing up primarily in collective settings should tend to react in the same way to peers as to adults. In statistical terms, the A − P difference should be smaller for kibbutz-reared than for home-reared children.

Hypothesis 6. In Israel, as in the USSR, children growing up primarily in collective settings should be most likely to claim conformity to conventional moral values when told that others, either adults or peers, will know of their answers. In statistical terms, the E − B score should be higher for kibbutz-reared than for home-reared youngsters.

Hypothesis 7. The difference across settings within each society should be smaller than the differences between countries.

The last hypothesis is included to complete the parallelism with the previous comparison between the USSR and the U.S.

Statistical Design

In both countries the basic research design took the form of a Latin square with experimental treatments constituting the three rows, classrooms appearing in the columns, and test forms assigned with the restriction that each form appear only once in each column and twice in each row. This basic pattern was repeated four times in each sample, twice for setting (family vs. collective) and twice for sex (boys vs. girls). In the USSR 6 sixth-grade classrooms in the vicinity of Moscow were used in each setting for a total of 353 children; in Israel 9 sixth-grade classrooms were used for each setting for a total of 400 children. The kibbutz sample was selected so as to ensure equal representation from each of the three major kibbutz federations; the children from the family setting were drawn from schools in predominantly middle-class neighborhoods in Tel-Aviv.

In order to equate for varying numbers of boys and girls in each classroom, the cell entries used for the primary analysis of variance were the mean scores obtained by all boys or girls in a given classroom under a particular experimental condition. In this mixed model, classrooms and forms were treated as random variables; culture, context of upbringing (family vs. collective), experimental treatment, and sex of child were treated as fixed effects.

To interpret the results, the reader must bear in mind that a high mean score signifies a reported readiness to conform to conventional, adult-approved moral standards; a low score indicates readiness to engage in the mischievous or antisocial activity being urged by the peers described in the term itself. This does not mean, however, that the behavior in question is necessarily approved or disapproved by the particular adults or peers who supposedly get to see the child's responses under the experimental conditions. Indeed, it is the purpose of the experimental procedure to reveal to what extent and in which direction the adults and peers in the child's world, as the child sees them, do in fact influence his or her responses in a given situation.

Results

Table 8.2 shows the mean scores obtained by children from each country and setting under each of the three experimental conditions, as well as the total score across the three conditions, expressed as an average. Subsequent tables present the mean differences and accompanying significance levels bearing on the several hypotheses. Thus table 8.3 shows means, mean differences, and significance tests relevant to the question of whether children in the two societies and the two upbringing settings vary in their general tendency to conform to conventional moral standards across all three experimental conditions. Since reliable classroom differences in total score were found in both countries, the appropriate error term used for testing the two main effects and their interaction was the mean square for classrooms within settings.

Turning to the cross-cultural comparisons, which appear in the last column of table 8.3, we find clear support for Hypothesis 1, that

Table 8.2 Average Response to Social Pressure Under the Three Experimental Conditions

	Experimental condition			
Upbringing Setting	*1: Base*	*2: Adult*	*3: Peer*	*4: Average score*
Israel				
Family				
Girls	2.54	1.04	.44	1.34
Boys	3.00	1.39	.60	1.66
Both sexes	2.77	1.22	.52	1.50
Collective				
Girls	2.58	2.75	1.65	2.33
Boys	1.93	.85	−.41	.79
Both sexes	2.26	1.80	.62	1.56
USSR				
Family				
Girls	12.36	12.89	13.26	12.84
Boys	11.25	12.08	11.38	11.57
Both sexes	11.81	12.49	12.32	12.20
Collective				
Girls	15.11	17.02	16.90	16.34
Boys	12.54	14.21	13.18	13.31
Both sexes	13.82	15.62	15.04	14.83

Note. A higher score indicates a greater adherence to conventional moral standards.

the Soviet children are much more prone to subscribe to adult-oriented alternatives than their Israeli counterparts. This difference obtains in both family and collective settings, but, as indicated by the reliable interaction effect appearing in the lower right-hand corner of the table, it is larger in collective than family settings; in other words, the tendency for Soviet youngsters to outdo their Israeli age-mates in giving moral answers was especially marked among the children raised in collective settings in the two countries.

With respect to the overall influence of family versus collective upbringing, although the main effect (bottom entry in column 3) is significant, it is critically qualified by the above-mentioned interaction. As can be seen in the first column of table 8.3, Israeli children, in contrast to their Soviet counterparts, showed no difference in score as a function of upbringing; whether raised in the kibbutz or at home, they responded similarly to the series of dilemmas. The effect was further qualified by sex. An additional analysis of variance (not shown) revealed that a significant difference existed in both countries for girls but not for boys: Girls raised in a collective setting

Table 8.3 Means and Mean Differences on Overall Conformity to Conventional Moral Values (Average Score) by Culture and Upbringing Setting

	Culture			
Upbringing Setting	*1: Israel*	*2: USSR*	*3: Israel plus USSR (M)*	*4: Israel minus USSR*
Family	1.50	12.20	6.85	–10.70***
Collective	1.56	14.83	8.20	–13.27***
Family plus collective *(M)*	1.53	13.52	7.53	–11.99[a]***
Family minus collective	–.06*	–2.63**	–1.35[b]**	2.57[c]**

Note. A higher score indicates higher conformity.
[a] Column effect: difference between cultures.
[b] Row effect: family vs. collective setting.
[c] Interaction effect: Culture × Setting.
* *ns.*
** $p < .05$.
*** $p < .01$.

conformed more than those brought up at home. This means that the results of our experiment provide support for Hypothesis 4, *but for girls only.*

It is instructive to look at this same interaction from the viewpoint of sex differences. It signifies that in both countries girls exceeded boys in conformity, *but only when the children had been brought up in a collective setting.* Whether in the USSR or Israel, daughters reared at home did not differ significantly from sons. In other words, in both countries sex differences in conformity were greater for children reared collectively than for those brought up in their own families.

In tables 8.4 and 8.5, the effects of experimental treatment are analyzed. Since these appear in the three rows of a Latin square design, the appropriate error term used was the discrepancy or residual mean square. As already indicated, the two degrees of freedom for rows were broken up and analyzed separately. The first was the difference between means under the adult and peer conditions, shown in table 8.4; the second, the shift from the base condition to the other two, shown in table 8.5.

The data of table 8.4 do not conform to our expectations. Contrary to Hypothesis 2, which predicted a significant shift for Israeli children in moving from adult to peer conditions, the first three A – P differences in column 1, while slightly positive, were all nonsignificant.

Table 8.4 Mean Differences in Adult Minus Peer Conformity Score by Culture and Upbringing

	Culture			
Upbringing Setting	*1: Israel*	*2: USSR*	*3: Israel plus USSR (M)*	*4: Israel minus USSR*
Family	.70	.17	.43	.53
Collective	1.18	.58	.88	.60
Family plus collective *(M)*	.94	.37	.65	.57[a]
Family minus Collective	–.48	–.41	–.45[b]	–.07[c]

Note. All values are nonsignificant.

[a] Column effect: difference between cultures.

[b] Row effect: family vs. collective setting.

[c] Interaction effect: Culture × Setting.

More critical for our hypothesis, they were statistically indistinguishable both in sign and magnitude from the corresponding scores for Soviet children shown in column 2. Consistent with this fact, no associated cultural differences in column 4 were reliable. Hypothesis 2 must therefore be rejected.

The results presented in table 8.4 are similarly negative with respect to the contrast between family and collective upbringing. Whether they had been brought up in family or collective, neither Israeli nor Soviet children differed in their ways of responding to pressures from adults versus peers. Hypothesis 5 must therefore be rejected.

None of the foregoing findings was qualified by sex of child; that is, the results were negative for both girls and boys.

In summary, the results for the A − P scores contradict the relevant hypotheses (2 and 5) on all counts. The expected differences across both culture and setting failed to appear. Instead, much to our surprise, the pattern of response for Israeli children was identical to that previously exhibited by Soviet youngsters; namely, for both groups, changing the source of pressure from adults to peers did not produce any change in response. The unexpected similarity between Soviet and Israeli children is all the more remarkable, since in most other societies in which the dilemmas experiment has been conducted, changing the source of pressure had produced a significant shift, with higher scores occurring under the adult condition. The finding that Israeli and Soviet children share the same atypical response pattern suggests the existence of some common feature in their sys-

Table 8.5 Mean Differences in Experimental Minus Base Conformity Score by Culture and Upbringing Setting.

	Culture			
Upbringing Setting	*1: Israel*	*2: USSR*	*3: Israel plus USSR (M)*	*4: Israel minus USSR*
Family	−1.90*	.60	−.65	−2.50*
Collective	−1.05	1.51*	.23	−2.56*
Family plus collective *(M)*	−1.48*	1.06*	−.21	−2.54[a]**
Family minus collective	−.85	−0.91	−.88[b]*	.06[c]

Note. All values without asterisks are nonsignificant.
[a] Column effect: difference between cultures.
[b] Row effect: family vs. collective setting.
[c] Interaction effect: Culture × Setting
* $p < .05$.
** $p < .01$.

tems of socialization. We shall give further consideration to this possibility in the discussion to follow.

Results contradicting another initial hypothesis appear in table 8.5, which deals with the remaining difference score, that between the base condition and the two experimental conditions taken together. The pattern for Israeli children does indeed depart from the Soviet profile, but not in the expected fashion. Consider first the combined means shown in row 3: In terms of our theoretical analysis, the mean on the base condition for Israeli children was expected to fall midway between the adult and peer conditions, with the E − B value approaching zero. Instead, it was in the base condition that Israeli children obtained their highest score; far from being zero, the E − B difference was reliably negative, thus standing in sharp contrast to the significant positive value of the corresponding score for the Soviet sample. In substantive terms, this means that whereas Soviet children were most willing to say they might deviate from conventional moral standards when told that no one else would see their responses (except, of course, the investigators), it was under this same condition that Israeli youngsters gave their most moral answers. Moreover, in this respect the Israeli children differed not only from their Soviet counterparts, but from children in virtually every other society in which the dilemmas experiment has been carried out. Hypothesis 3 must therefore be rejected.

As indicated by the last entry in column 3, however, there was, as expected, a significant main effect associated with the setting in which the child was raised. In both countries, the tendency to give more moral responses under social pressure than under the base condition was greater for children brought up in collective settings that for those raised at home. The data thus support Hypothesis 6. An additional analysis (not shown) revealed that this trend was particularly marked for girls. In both countries, it was girls raised in the collective who were most likely to shift their responses in the direction of conventional moral standards when threatened with social exposure.

Finally, the data shown in tables 8.2–5 lend support to Hypothesis 7. In general, it is clear that the overall cultural differences that differentiate Soviet and Israeli children in their claimed conformity to conventional moral standards are of far greater magnitude than the within-culture differences associated with upbringing, sex, or experimental treatments.

Discussion

To illuminate the interpretation of our results, we now present them in the context of data from other countries in which the same experiment has now been carried out.[2] The cross-cultural findings are shown in table 8.6. The countries are listed by rank of the average total score (column 1) obtained by the children in each sample across the three experimental conditions. The fact that Soviet youngsters lead the list, whereas both Israeli samples are in the bottom third of the array, dramatizes the magnitude and social significance of the contrast in response by the children of these two nations. The reader will also be struck by the clustering of communist nations at the top of the distribution. Garbarino and Bronfenbrenner (in press) will examine the relation across 13 countries between the average total score obtained in the dilemmas experi-

2. The authors are indebted to the following colleagues who conducted the experiments in their respective lands: *Hungary*, Sandor Komlosi, Pecs Teachers College; *Czechoslovakia and West Germany*, Franz Banhegyi, Institute of Psychology, Bratislava, and University of Cologne; *Poland*, Edda Flexznerowa, University of Warsaw; *Japan*, Kazuo Aoi, Tokyo University; *Canada*, James Jenks, University of Alberta, and Geoffrey Mason, University of Victoria; *Holland*, Meindert Slagter, State University of Groningen; *Scotland*, Halla Beloff, University of Edinburgh; *Switzerland*, Kurt Luscher, University of Bern.

Table 8.6 Dilemmas Experiment: Means for Experimental Conditions in Various Cultures

	Experimental Condition				
Country	*1: Average score*	*2: Base*	*3: Adult*	*4: Peer*	*5: Adult minus peer*
USSR					
Boarding	14.83.	13.82	15.62	15.04	.58
Day	12.20	11.81	12.49	12.32	.17
Hungary	14.06	13.28	15.17	13.74	1.43
Czechoslovakia	9.46	10.36	10.38	7.64	2.74*
Poland	6.14	6.94	7.60	3.90	3.70**
Japan[a]	3.76	3.77	4.62	2.90	1.72*
Canada[b]	2.92	3.58	4.27	.91	3.36**
West Germany	2.83	1.79	4.43	2.26	2.17*
U.S.	2.22	2.43	2.96	1.27	1.69*
Israel					
Kibbutz	1.56	2.26	1.80	.62	1.18
City	1.50	2.77	1.22	.52	.70
Holland	1.18	1.27	2.10	.16	1.94
Scotland	.40	1.31	1.77	–1.89	3.66**
Switzerland[c]	–2.09	–1.59	–.76	–3.91	3.15**

[a] Based on two experiments.
[b] Based on five experiments.
[c] Swiss children were on the average one year older than children in other samples.
* $p < .05$.
** $p < .01$.

ment and an index of sociopolitical pluralism developed by Vincent (1971). The index, derived from a factor analysis of the political characteristics of 121 nation-states, is based on such features as the presence of constitutional limitations on the executive, competitive elections, freedom for opposition parties, etc. The correlation between the two measures was a significant –.89; in substantive terms this means that the less pluralistic the political structure of the country, the more likely are its school children to subscribe to conventional moral values.

The contrasting position of Soviet and Israeli children in this cross-cultural perspective underscores the unequivocal support obtained for Hypothesis 1. Soviet youngsters, whether raised in family or collective, clearly conformed to conventional moral values in far greater degree than their Israeli counterparts.

With respect to Hypothesis 2, however, Soviet and Israeli children not only failed to differ as predicted, but as evidenced in column 5 of table 8.6, exhibited a characteristic in common that distinguished them from their age-mates in all the other countries in which the experiment has been conducted: The A − P scores for both countries were the lowest in the entire distribution. In other words, both the USSR and Israel stood out in the tendency for children of the two countries to respond in the *same* way to pressure from peers as to pressure from adults.

How is one to understand this unexpected result? With the benefit of hindsight, we came to the realization that the USSR and Israel share a common characteristic as societies that distinguishes them from the other countries in our international sample; namely, both exhibit an overriding national concern involving all segments of the population, including both old and young. In the case of the USSR, an uncompromising and ever-present communist ideology binds children and adults to the same set of political and social beliefs and behavior patterns (Bronfenbrenner 1970b). In Israel, a country committed to a differing set of democratic values and a pluralistic system of government, the unifying issue has simply been one of national survival.

This pattern of sociopolitical similarity, though admittedly post hoc in its derivation, permits a reconciliation of the paradoxical performance of Israeli and Soviet children in the dilemmas experiment. Although the sharply contrasting ideologies and social systems in the two countries lead to a marked difference in conformity (Soviet youngsters being much more ready to subscribe to conventional moral values), the fact that in both countries various segments of the society, including old and young, are united in a single overriding national commitment, creates a situation in which social pressure from peers acts in the same direction as social pressure from adults.

In summary, the interpretation of our paradoxical results leads to the formulation of a new hypothesis: *The discrepancy between norms for the behavior of children held by adults and by peers is likely to be smallest in societies that are characterized by an overriding national concern involving all segments of the population.* This hypothesis was not anticipated in our study and hence requires cross-validation in further research.

Our third cross-cultural hypothesis also suffered a sharp reversal; contrary to expectations, Israeli children obtained their highest scores under the base condition; that is, they gave their most moral answers when told that no one they knew would see their responses. Moreover, as can be seen from the middle three columns of table 8.6, Israel was the only country in which this pattern occurred. In all other nations, children gave most conventional moral responses when threatened with social exposure to adults.[3]

In seeking an explanation for this anomalous pattern of response, we were led to a consideration of parental expectations and patterns of child rearing in Israel. A dominant theme in Israel, even since before the establishment of independence in 1947, has been the strong readiness of the early settlers and (to a lesser degree) of the present settled population to undergo a personal "change." They held the conviction that some aspects of the Jewish self-concept and patterns of relationships to others had been a product of long centuries of rootlessness and lack of independence in the *Galut* (exile) years. Many Galut values came to be scorned and despised; a Galut Jew was seen in stereotype as one who acted in fear and self-abnegation, lacking self-confidence and assertiveness. The young Israeli has found it difficult to understand the supposed passivity of many Jews of Europe who were executed by the Nazis. The literature and lore of contemporary Israel glorifies the creation, after centuries of subjugation, of Jewish self-defense organizations that culminated in Hashomer, Haganah, and the present Israel Defense Forces. The history the Israeli lives by today stresses active resistance to oppression, as exemplified by the uprising of the Maccabees, the defense at Masada, and the struggle for independence of the past several decades. In the economic sphere, there occurred an assertive adoption of new techniques and new social structures, such as the moshav and the kibbutz. New trade union forms and innovative social security policies were evolved. Creative, different, nonconformist methods of achievement have become the expected and the norm.

The settlers sought to become self-supportive and independent of the good graces of others. Subservience was frowned on, and their children and youth were encouraged to independence, even from the parents (Eisenstadt 1951, 1967). The ideal was the active, alert, and autonomous child. The parents did not intend to create rebels, but they did welcome signs of independence and self-assertion in their chil-

3. One other exception has come to our attention. In five replications of the dilemmas experiment with Canadian samples, one carried out by Geoffrey Mason in Victoria, British Columbia, also produced lowest scores under the base condition. Since we are not familiar with the cultural background of the children, we are not in a position to offer any interpretation comparable to that given for the Israeli case.

dren. Feeling that they themselves were still products of the Galut, they were more or less tolerant of directions the children set, even if they could not always follow or understand.

In recounting the symbols men live by, the concept of the *Sabra* or young Israeli, born not in the Galut but in Israel, serves as a useful example. This native-born Israeli is considered to have the same characteristics as the fruit of the cactus, the Sabra: hard and prickly outside, soft and sweet inside. Regardless of the correctness of the analogy, it does serve to illustrate the concept held by parents and the self-concept of the children. Israeli youngsters are not especially conformist, and their parents seem to enjoy this quality in them, feeling it to be the best equipment they can give to the next generation. The concern for the autonomous child, especially prominent in the kibbutz, has permeated contemporary Israeli culture (Tsur 1972).

We suggest that the results of the dilemma experiment in Israel can be understood against this background. Parents do not want their children to be "plastic" or "soap," to use a current Hebrew phrase, and children are not intimidated when told their parents will know what they are doing. On the contrary, we suspect they believe their parents like them to be independent. Evidence in support of this generalization comes from a cross-cultural study currently being conducted by the authors on children's perceptions of the roles of their socializing agents. Israeli parents are described as encouraging autonomy more than their counterparts from the other cultures studied, which include the U.S., Great Britain, and Switzerland.

Another possible interpretation of our results is that Israeli children, being told parents will know, adopt a posture of self-assertive, even aggressive, defensiveness. A term current in Israel is *davkah*, which connotes a kind of negativism. A person when pushed might do just the opposite "just because." This interpretation reflects nonconformism toward parents, whereas our first explanation implies nonconformism encouraged by parents. These interpretations need not be mutually exclusive.

In another part of our research, Israeli teachers were asked to fill out the dilemma items as they would like their pupils to answer. Their responses were peer-oriented, little different from the children's own answers. In contrast, Soviet teachers had endorsed the conventional moral alternatives. When Israeli children were also asked to state how they felt their teachers would like them to answer, they selected more adult-oriented alternatives. Thus teachers' expectations were actually more peer-oriented than children perceived them to be. This may reflect the ambivalence of adults as well as of children about the role of independence in the young—independence even from the adults who foster this orientation.

From this point of view, both Soviet and Israeli children are seen to be the products of socialization pressures. The Soviet child learns to conform to moralistic values, but the Israeli child in no less degree also learns to conform—paradoxically, in the direction of nonconformity to authority. Peter Kelvin, in a perceptive discussion of socialization and conformity, speaks directly to this phenomenon: "The paradox is this: socialization, in the broadest sense, consists of learning the norms of one's society and coming to conform to them; however, one of these norms and a very fundamental one, is the *norm of non-conformity*" (1971: 217).

Bronfenbrenner, in contrasting Soviet and American approaches to upbringing, suggested that "the Russians have gone too far in subjecting the child and his peer group to conformity to a single set of values imposed by the adult society" (1970b:165). The results for Israel show no less involvement of parents in the child's world, but the involvement reflects peer-oriented values, stressing autonomy from the pressure of adults.

In summary, in their response to social pressure, Israeli and Soviet children appear to differ in a manner that reflects the distinctive fundamental values of each society. In the case of Israel, childhood is thought of as a time of mischief and adventure that prepares the young person for an adult role emphasizing self-confidence and independence, whereas in the USSR, childhood is a time for learning the discipline and obedience required by communist ideology. Our results indicate that both societies are developing in their children in significant measure the characteristics that each values most.

Turning next to our hypotheses, on the effects of collective upbringing, we must first take note of a negative conclusion. The expectation that children raised on the kibbutz would exhibit a pattern of response similar to that observed in products of Soviet group upbringing is clearly unsupported. In their reaction to social pressure, kibbutz children were far more similar to their compatriots raised in conventional families than to Soviet youngsters, whether attending boarding schools or day schools. Yet the contrast between familial and collective upbringing showed some continuity across the two societies, especially for girls. The tendency observed in the USSR for collectively raised children to conform more to conventional values was also evidenced in the Israeli kibbutz, but in girls only. In both countries the tendency to give more moral responses under threat of social exposure was greater for children raised in collective settings than for those brought up at home, but this trend was stronger for girls than for boys. Looking at these same findings from the viewpoint of sex differences, the tendency in both societies for girls to exceed boys in conformity was found only among children raised in collective settings and, in these settings, it increased under threat of social exposure.

From one perspective, the foregoing findings lend support to our general hypothesis that the effects of social pressure will be greater for children brought up primarily in a single socialization setting, in this case a collective, than for children raised in two contexts simultaneously, that is, family and school. For what our results tell us is that cultural differences, sex differences, and effects of threatened social exposure were all greater for children raised in collective settings than for youngsters brought up at home. But these same results, looked at another way, indicate that the effects of family versus collective upbringing vary by culture and sex of child; specifically, the impact of the setting contrast was more powerful in the USSR than in Israel and greater for girls than for boys. Why should this be the case?

Addressing first the qualifying factor of culture, we begin by noting that the Israeli kibbutz and the Soviet boarding school, while both involving the children's collective as the primary setting of upbringing, differ significantly in the extent to which the family also plays a significant role. Thus children in Soviet boarding schools visit their parents, or vice versa, only once a fortnight, whereas youngsters in the kibbutz see their families for extended periods every day and engage in extensive interactions with them. The effect of all this contact is reflected in patterns of parent–child interaction. In a companion study to the present one (Devereux et al. 1974), the subjects of the present research were asked to describe the frequency of various parent behaviors in the spheres of both affection and discipline. Out of 12 variables, 8 showed no difference for families of kibbutz- versus city-reared children. Both groups saw their parents as equally supportive, although city families were perceived as exercising greater discipline.

In sum, it is clear that in terms of family involvement the Israeli kibbutz is a less pure example of collective upbringing than the Soviet boarding school. Under these circumstances, it is not surprising that the impact of the contrast between family and collective upbringing on children's reactions to social pressure was greater in the Soviet than in the Israeli sample.

The tendency for mode of upbringing (family vs. collective) to have a greater impact on girls than on boys does not invite as ready or reliable an explanation. To be sure, there is evidence from experiments on social compliance (Asch 1956; Kilham and Mann 1974; Sheridan and King 1972) that female subjects are more likely to conform than males, and Bronfenbrenner (1961b) and others (Mischel 1970) have documented differences in socialization practices toward boys and girls consistent with the development of greater social dependency in the female. For example, in our earlier study of kibbutz child-rearing patterns (Devereux et al. 1974) it was shown that kibbutz boys were exposed to the influences of both father and mother somewhat more than kibbutz girls; hence, the kibbutz socialization setting may be more pluralistic for boys than for girls. But in the absence of direct evidence relating child-rearing antecedents to response in the dilemmas experiment, any explanation must remain purely speculative.

In conclusion, our attempt to examine experimentally the effects of social pressure on children from two societies with widely contrasting systems of child rearing both between and within cultures has lent support to several of our original hypotheses but also generated new ones. In the first category, the markedly greater conformity of Soviet youngsters is consistent with the general proposition that the less pluralistic the political structure of a society, the more likely are its children to subscribe to conventional moral values. An unexpected finding of similarity of reaction to pressure from peers versus adults on the part of Israeli youngsters led to the formulation of a new hypothesis that discrepancy between norms for behavior held by children and adults is likely to be smallest in societies that are characterized by an overriding national concern involving all segments of the population. A comparison in both countries of children reared in family versus collective settings yielded results generally consistent with our thesis that youngsters brought up primarily in a single socialization setting are more susceptible to social pressures than children reared in multiple contexts within and outside the family. The fact that the impact of collective versus family influence was greater in Soviet than in Israeli society was traced to the greater involvement of parents in the lives of kibbutz children than in the lives of Soviet boarding school pupils. Probably in part for this same reason, kibbutz children, contrary to the stated hypotheses, did not exhibit a pattern of response similar to that found previously for products of Soviet collective upbringing. Rather, they behaved like their home-reared Israeli compatriots in showing a unique reaction to social pressure; unlike children from every other nation in which the dilemmas experiment has been carried out to date, they gave their most moral responses under the base condition, when neither their parents nor their friends would know of their answers. This result is interpreted as reflecting the emphasis placed in Israeli society and socialization on the development of moral autonomy and independence of action on the part of children and youth, an orientation that contrasts dramatically with the values and methods of upbringing in the USSR. Thus both societies emerge as successfully inculcating in their children the distinctive qualities that each highly prizes.

9

Identification with Mexican-American Values and Psychological Adjustment in Mexican-American Adolescents

Manuel Ramirez, III

Adolescence is a developmental period characterized by rapid physiological and psychological changes that create a sense of crisis in the individual. The search for personal identity is probably one of the main tasks of adolescence, as suggested by Erik Erikson (1959).

Although there is much to be clarified about how culture intervenes in the modeling of the character during this critical developmental period, it appears that cultural factors influence not only the temporal conditions of the phenomenon, but also the kinds of stresses and pressures the individual encounters in his travel to adulthood.

Of particular interest is the crossroads situation of bicultural adolescents who experience, in addition to their developmental identity crisis, an identification conflict between the original and the new culture. The way this conflict is handled by the individual and crystallizes into a particular personality orientation and social relations pattern seems to have considerable bearing on his psychological adjustment.

Ramirez empirically examines the identification dilemma and its mental health consequences as experienced by Mexican-American adolescents who are pulled between the mainstream Anglo culture and the Mexican culture embodied in a population conspicuously proud and assertive in their ethnic distinctiveness.

Child (1943) and Madsen (1964) have observed that persons who are caught between two cultures experience severe value conflicts.

Child's study of second-generation Italian-Americans revealed that they typically adopted one of three reactions to these conflicts: (1) *the rebel,* characterized by the desire of the individual to establish himself as an American and disassociate himself from the labels of the folk cutlure; (2) *the in-group,* a tendency to strive for affiliation with the folk culture and to express hostility to the symbols of the American group; (3) *the apathetic,* an attempt to escape conflict by distorting memory or perception so that the arousal tendencies to seek affiliation with either group are reduced. Child further discovered that both rebels and in-groupers experienced certain difficulties in interpersonal relationships which were a consequence of the particular type of reaction they had adopted. The in-groupers typically reacted with hostility toward the out-group (Americans at large and other national minorities) thus, their relationships with non-Italians were usually unfavorable. Rebels, on the other hand, were resentful of the Italian group in general and suffered severe interpersonal conflicts with parents and other family members.

The results of recent studies of Mexican-Americans show that reactions they exhibit to value conflicts are similar to those which were observed by Child (1943). Madsen (1964, 1965) identified two groups of Mexican-Americans—the conservative and the anglicized, which correspond very closely to Child's in-groupers and rebels respectively. The conservatives are described as being hostile toward the Anglos and rebel Mexican-Americans and also suspicious of individuals outside the family group. Madsen states that the anglicized Mexican-Americans experience the highest degree of anxiety, fear, and guilt. They tend to become alienated from their parents and usually suffer severe health problems such as dizziness, vomiting, fever and memory loss. Anglicized females also tend to adopt masculine behaviors and interests, abandoning their traditional role of submissiveness, whereas anglicized males may adopt feminine interests, thus rejecting the "machismo" ideal of the culture.

The research of both Child and Madsen then, seems to have established that the value conflicts faced by bicultural individuals leads them either to identify with the folk culture or to reject it. In addition, their findings indicate that the reaction adopted by the individual may create certain interpersonal as well as intrapersonal conflicts which affect his psychological adjustment.

This study attempted to identify Mexican-American adolescents who had adopted the rebel or anglicized reaction (R) and the in-group or conservative reaction (I-G). It also sought to identify adjustment problems (as defined by the Bell Adjustment Inventory) which R and I-

G *S*s might be experiencing. It was predicted that: (1) R *S*s would report having more conflicts with their parents (e.g., they would score higher on the Home Adjustment scale); (2) R *S*s would report having more health problems (e.g., would obtain higher scores on the Health Adjustment scale); (3) R *S*s would report experiencing guilt, anxiety, and nervousness (e.g., higher scores on the Emotionality scale); (4) I-G *S*s would reveal experiencing difficulties in relating to others outside the family group (e.g., score higher on the Submissiveness scale) and would give evidence of being suspicious and hostile (e.g., score higher on Hostility scale); and (5) it was expected that I-G males and females would be better identified with their sex roles than R *S*s (I-G males would score higher on the Masculinity-Feminity scale than R males and I-G females would score lower than R females).

Method

Subjects

The *S*s were 100 Mexican-American senior high-school students of the third generation and of the lower-middle socioeconomic class between the ages of 13 and 18. There were equal numbers of males and females.

Procedure

Identification with Mexican-American Values. All 100 *S*s were administered a 29-item attitude scale of Mexican-American values. The items were responded to on a 7-point scale ranging from agree very much (7) to disagree very much (1). The items could be categorized as follows: (1) loyalty to the family; (2) strictness of child rearing; (3) respect for adults; (4) separation of the sex roles; (5) male superiority; and (6) time orientation. The scale was developed by the author and it has been narrowed down from an original 100 items by selecting only those which discriminated best between Mexican-Americans and non-Mexican-Americans. The original item pool was composed of items drawn from the following sources: The Parent Attitude Research Instrument (Schaefer and Bell 1958), the Traditional Family Ideology Scale (Levinson and Huffman 1955), the California F Scale (Adorno et al. 1950), a scale of Mexican family values constructed by Diaz-Guerrero (1955), and items made up by the author. Some of the work involved in the development of the scale has been reported elsewhere (Ramirez 1967).

Rebels and in-groupers. The 10 *S*s who had made the highest scores on the attitude scale were labeled as I-Gs (e.g., greatest agreement with the Mexican-American values) and the 10 who made the lowest scores were classified as Rs (characterized by a rejection of the Mexican-American values).

Psychological Adjustment. All *S*s in both the R and I-G groups were administered the 200 item Bell Adjustment Inventory (revised student form). The items on the inventory were responded to with Yes, No or Don't Knows. The inventory is made up of six scales as follows: (1) *Home Adjustment* (high scores reflect tension in the home due to inability to relate well to parents); (2) *Health Adjustment* (high scores reflect either a history of health problems, a preoccupation with one's body or both); (3) *Submissiveness* (high scores lack confidence in meeting people in groups, entering groups by themselves or taking the initiative in social situations); (4) *Emotionality* (high scores suggest volatile feelings, feelings of guilt also anxiety and nervousness); (5) *Hostility* (high scores do not trust others, they are critical of other persons and have the feeling that others are unfriendly towards them); and (6) *Masculinity-Femininity* (high scores indicate greater preference for masculine activities than is typical of the sex, while lower scores indicate a greater preference for typically feminine activities and roles).

Results

Table 9.1 lists mean scores and standard deviations obtained by the four sub-groups on the attitude scale; table 9.2 lists those items which discriminated best between R and I-G *S*s. Also included in this table are item means and discriminatory powers (D.P.s).

Table 9.1 Means and Standard Deviations of *S*s Who Scored in the Upper and Lower 10 percent of the Attitude Scale

	Upper 10%		*Lower 10%*	
	M	*SD*	*M*	*SD*
Sex				
Males	158.4	9.00	86.2	7.90
Females	156.0	8.85	76.7	7.64

Table 9.2 Summary of Item Analysis

Rank	*D.P.*	*Item*
1	6.0	It doesn't do any good to try and change the future because the future is in the hands of God.
2	5.0	All adults should be respected.
3	4.6	Even if a child believes that his parents are wrong he should obey without question.
4	4.4	The word of an adult should never be questioned.
4	4.4	Relatives are more important than friends.
6	4.0	It helps a child in the long run if he is made to conform to his parent's ideas.
6	4.0	For a child the mother should be the dearest person in existence.
8	3.8	Some equality in marriage is a good thing but by and large the husband ought to have the main say so in family matters.
8	3.8	The place for the woman is in the home.
10	3.7	Women think less clearly than men and are more emotional.

The Bell Adjustment Inventory data revealed that R males (Mean = 18.8, SD = 1.6) and females (Mean = 15.2, SD = 3.8) scored higher on the Home Adjustment scale than I-G males (Mean = 7.6, SD = 2.3) and females (Mean = 7.4, SD = 1.5). This was also the case for the Health Adjustment scale on which R males (Mean = 8.4, SD = 3.4) and females (Mean = 12.0, SD = 1.9) again scored higher than I-G males (Mean = 5.4, SD = 2.7) and females (Mean = 6.6, SD = 1.4). R males (Mean = 13.8, SD = 7.0) and females (Mean = 16.4, SD = 5.1) also obtained higher scores on the Emotionality scale than I-G males (Mean = 8.6, SD = 5.6) and females (Mean = 13.6, SD = 5.1). Results of the Submissiveness scale showed that R males (Mean = 17.4, SD = 9.2) scored higher than I-G males (Mean = 6.6, SD = 3.5) while I-G females (Mean = 21.0, SD = 7.3) scored higher than R females (Mean = 15.4, SD = 9.6). The same was true for the Hostility scale in which R males (Mean = 11.0, SD = 3.7) scored higher than I-G males (Mean = 10.4, SD = 3.4) while I-G females (Mean = 11.8, SD = 3.3) made higher scores than R females (Mean = 10.4, SD = 3.4). Scores for R males (Mean = 20.0, SD = 2.6) and I-G males (Mean = 19.0, SD = 3.9) were similar on the Masculinity-Femininity scale, but R females (Mean = 12.1, SD = 3.5) made higher scores than I-G females (Mean = 7.8, SD = 2.7).

Comparison of mean raw scores for the four sub-groups on each of the scales of the inventory with normative data revealed that scores obtained by both R males and females on the Home Adjustment scale were within the unsatisfactory and poor range respectively. The mean score of the R females on the Health Adjustment scale was also indica-

Table 9.3 Summary of Analysis of Variance of Bell Adjustment Inventory Raw. Scores Obtained by R and I-G *SS*

Scale	*Id F*	*Sex F*	*Id × Sex F*
Home	53.08**	2.10	1.71
Health	11.76	3.84	1.00
Submissiveness	1.00	2.62	4.58*
Hostility	1.00	1.00	1.00
Emotionality	1.58	2.15	1.00
M-F	3.15	42.30	4.43

*P < .05
**P < .005

tive of maladjustment. The score of the I-G females on the Submissiveness scale is interpreted as extreme submissiveness in interpersonal relationships. All other mean scores obtained by the sub-groups fall within the average range.

Results of the 2 × 2 analysis of variance performed on the data of the adjustment inventory are presented on table 9.3. The *F*s for the degree of identification with Mexican-American values (Id) variable were significant for the Home and Health scales supporting predictions 1 and 2. *F*s for Submissiveness, Hostility and Emotionality were not significant, thus failing to support predictions 3 and 4.

Two one tail *t* tests were performed on the M-F scale results. The findings showed that there were no significant differences between the scores of the males of the I-G and R groups (t = .42). The *t* for the females was significant (t = 1.94) < .05). These results then partially support the fifth prediction made by the author.

Discussion

The results of this study, for the most part, confirmed the findings of both Child (1943) and Madsen (1964, 1965). Mexican-American adolescents who have adopted either the rebel or in-group reaction reported experiencing interpersonal as well as intrapersonal conflicts which appear to be specific to their mode of conflict resolution.

Rebels indicated that most of their difficulties center around their relationship with their parents. They agreed with items which stated that their parents do not understand them[1] (Number 194),

1. These items have been abbreviated to conserve space.

that they have had to leave the home in order to avoid conflict (Number 127) and also that their fathers do not share their ideal of manhood (Number 139). Thus, as Child and Madsen had observed, when the young bicultural person adopts American middle class values discord arises between himself and his parents.

The fact that R *S*s do not consider their fathers to be their ideal of manhood is particularly significant in the case of the R males, since one would expect that they would, then reject their fathers as models for identification. Sommers (1964) has indeed discovered that R bicultural persons experience severe identity problems, because they reject parental figures whom they consider to be inferior.

The higher scores obtained by the R *S*s on the Health Adjustment scale supported Madsen's observations. R *S*s, in general, tended to agree with items indicating that they frequently had digestion difficulties (Number 122), headaches (Number 33), insomnia (Number 38), and that they had to guard their health carefully (Number 171). These findings are also in keeping with those of Fried (1959), which have shown that people undergoing cultural transition exhibit psychosomatic problems. Since Americanization has influenced the female role far more than it has the male role (Ramirez 1967), one would expect that they would be experiencing the most instability and stress, thus it is not surprising that the R females obtained the highest scores on this scale.

As predicted R *S*s scored higher on the Emotionally scale than did I-G *S*s. This reinforces the results of the Health Adjustment scale, thereby indicating that R *S*s are probably experiencing intrapersonal conflicts. They agreed with items on this scale which revealed that they frequently felt nervous (Number 118), depressed (Number 13), and guilty (Number 152).

Females from the I-G group had the highest scores on the Submissiveness scale. This finding can be explained in two ways: (1) the authoritarian nature of the culture which emphasizes submissiveness to authority—this is particularly true for the females who hold the most subordinate roles in the culture (Ramirez 1967); (2) the Mexican-American's reluctance to become involved with others outside his family group (Madsen 1964, 1965). This latter explanation is also supported by the higher Hostility scores obtained by the I-G females. They agreed with items indicating they were suspicious of others, e.g., there are people talking behind my back (Number 124), there are many people I can't afford to trust (Number 15), and people are unfriendly to me (Number 25). This hostility score also reflected resentfulness and anger towards others. They agreed with the following items: there are many saps in the world (Number 61) and people have accused me of being too critical of them (Number 51).

Contrary to expectations I-G males did not score higher than R males on the Submissiveness and Hostility scales. With respect to the submissiveness results it may be that R males are behaving submissively because they fear alienating Anglos and, thus, jeopardizing their goal of full participation in the Anglo society. I-G males, on the other hand, may have suppressed their anger towards the members of the outgroup because they fear retaliation from Anglo authority figures who are presently their teachers and employers. It is evident that future research in this area must utilize instruments which will distinguish between expressions of submission and hostility to Anglo and Mexican-Americans and which will tap suppressed information. Perhaps a projective test, similar to the Thematic Appreception Test would be appropriate.

Results of the Masculinity-Femininity scale only partly confirmed the author's expectations. R females did indeed make higher scores than I-G females indicating that they have adopted masculine interests, but R males obtained slightly higher scores than I-G males, reversing the prediction which had been made. This result could have been due to the fact that this particular scale was not sufficiently sensitive to masculine and feminine interests as defined by the Mexican-American culture. Another possiblity is that I-G Mexican-American males, like Mexican males, are experiencing difficulty in superseding the maternal stage (Diaz-Guerrero 1955). The need for additional research in this area is obvious.

In summary, then, the results of a personality inventory have, for the most part verified hypotheses derived from anthropological data obtained by way of interviews and observation. Bicultural individuals experience a variety of adjustment problems which, in turn, appear to be related to the reaction they adopt to value conflicts experienced in the process of cultural transfer. The severe interpersonal conflicts with parents and other members of the family reported by R *S*s may be related to the health problems and stress they are experiencing. Cleveland and Longaker (1967) have proposed an explanation which seems appropriate here. Whenever the person who finds himself caught between two opposing sets of values decides to reject one of the sets he becomes overwhelmed by feelings of guilt and self-derogation. This occurs because the values rejected are associated with a person important to the *S*, usually a parent. Cleveland and Longaker thus, argue for intensive family studies in behavior disorders associated with value conflicts. The results of the present study certainly give validity to this argument.

Acknowledgment

The author would like to thank Mrs. Barbara Petersen for her help in collecting the data.

Annotated Additional Readings

a) **Caudill, W. A., and C. Schooler. 1973.** Child behavior and child rearing in Japan and the United States. *The Journal of Nervous and Mental Disease* 157:323–338.
A systematic study summarizing observed differences in the behaviors of Japanese and U.S. children at various developmental periods, and the role of different child-rearing practices in shaping children's behavior.

The U.S. mother tended to encourage her baby to be active and vocally responsive, while the Japanese mother acted in ways which she believed would soothe and quiet her baby. The responses of the infants appeared to be in line with behavioral expectations of the two cultures: Assertiveness in the U.S. culture and restrain in the Japanese culture.

b) **Zern, D. 1972.** The relationship between mother–infant contact and later differentiation of the social environment. *Journal of Genetic Psychology* 121:107–117.
An examination of the concept that early mother–infant experiences play a determining role in the extent and kind of social differentiation of the developed individual. The author uses a design derived from Whiting's (1961) cross-cultural approach to the study of human behavior. This approach on one hand examines in a relatively large sample of different societies the correlation between certain psychological variables, and on the other hand evaluates the same correlations in a sample of individuals within a particular society.

Zern's study suggests that the extent of physical togetherness between mother and child during the first years of life influences the degree and quality of differentiation of social figures in the grown-up individual. Several alternative explanations are discussed. In a recent extension of this research, Zern (1976) provides further evidence supporting the relationship under consideration.

c) **Hong, K. M., and B. D. Townes 1976.** Infants' attachment to inanimate objects. *Journal of the American Academy of Child Psychiatry* 15:49–61.
Investigates the relationship between infant attachment to inanimate objects (which has potential relevance to broader social behaviors) and child-rearing practices (which eminently reflect cultural tenets) through a mail survey of three groups of families: those of U.S.-born medical residents training in the U.S., Korean-born residents training in the U.S.,and Korean residents training in Korea. The incidence of infant attachment to blankets and pacifiers was highest in the U.S.-born and -reared group, lowest in the Korean-born and -reared, and intermediate in the Korean infants reared in the U.S. It was also found that a greater number of the Korean infants slept in the same room with their mothers, experienced more physical contact with them, particularly at bed time, and were breast-fed longer than the U.S. infants.

d) Whiting, B. B. 1974. Folk wisdom and child rearing. *Merril Palmer Quarterly* 20:9–19.
Likely factors underlying the perceived unpreparedness of parents raising children in contemporary industrialized Western societies are reviewed. Among those factors are geographical mobility of young mothers (which limits access to their own mothers and their advice), intermarriage of members of culturally contrasting groups, rapid social change, and young mothers lack of exposure to caring for infants and young children. The author notes that this situation seems to have produced an explosion of literature on how to raise a child. She makes a case for the usefulness of folk wisdom in this area and discusses some ways in which folk exerience and knowledge can be transmitted and enhanced to help young parents to deal more naturally with their child rearing responsibilities.

e) Muensterberger, W. 1974. Some reflections on multiple mothering, cross-culturally. *Psychosocial Process* 3:57–71.
A look at the issue of the effects on personality development of multiple mothering, in which more than one person is responsible for the child's immediate care and well being. From his own observations on the Thai culture and his psychoanalytic practice, as well as from reports from various parts of the world, the author notes the considerable frequency with which multiple mothering occurs. He examines this vis-à-vis the psychoanalytic assumption that mother is the key figure during the pre-oedipal phases of the child's development and offers some comments on the potential interference of multiple mothering with an individual's ability to maintain lasting relationships later on in life.

f) Leiderman, P. H., B. Baba, J. Kagia, H. C. Kraemer, and G. F. Leiderman 1973 African infant precocity and some social influences during the first year *Nature* 242:247–249.
An evaluation of the mental (perceptual-sensory) and motor (neuromuscular) functioning of sub-Saharan infants at two-month intervals, from 1 to 15 months of age. By comparing the obtained scores on the Bayley Test with previously established standards for U.S. black and white and U.K. white infants, it was found that the African infants performed significantly better than their U.S. and U.K. counterparts on both mental and motor scales.

Multiple regression analysis was then used to assess the potential contribution of specific environmental factors to the explanation of the mental and motor scores of the African infants. The authors found that at least 25 percent of the variance of these scores could be accounted for by combinations of specific social and demographic variables, primarily by the economic status of the infant's family and, in the case of motor functioning also by the presence of older individuals (available additional caretakers) in the household.

9) Hartog, J. 1974. A transcultural view of sibling rank and mental disorder. *Acta Psychiatrica Scandinavica* 50:33–49.
A discussion of the role that sibling rank may have in the development of personality and behaviorial maladjustments. Hartog reviews various theoretical views on this issue and offers an interesting analytical model focused on

the articulated influence of family dynamics (i.e., parental responses) and cultural values and expectations.

h) Kagan, S., and M. C. Madsden 1972. Rivalry in Anglo-American and Mexican children of two ages. *Journal of Personality and Social Psychology* 24:214–220.

A carefully designed experimental study comparing the rivalry (behavior intended to lower the outcomes on a peer) among groups of Anglo-American and Mexican children of ages 5–6 and 8–10, measured under four choice conditions. The authors found that the older groups were significantly more rivalrous than the younger groups, that the Anglo-American children were significantly more rivalrous than the Mexican children, and that the difference between cultures tended to increase with age. Regarding the choice conditions, rivalry was greatest for all groups when accompanied by both relative and absolute gains.

i) Lambo, T. A. 1971. Aggressiveness in the human life cycle within different sociocultural settings. *International Social Science Journal* 23:79–88.

An overview of the development and expression of aggressiveness through various life stages, with an examination of the relationship between aggressive traits and behavior and identifiable sociocultural phenomena. The author draws heavily from his own observations on African children and emphasizes psychoanalytic interpretations of the issues discussed.

IV

Sociocultural Structures

We next examine the cross-sectional role of specific aspects of sociocultural structure and change in the genesis and manifestations of mental disorder. We deal with the interrelations between psychopathology and sociocultural structures, including among these social class, urbanization, ethnic grouping, and religious identification.

Social class is a tremendously important variable in the study of psychopathology, as there is hardly any other that correlates more pervasively with a wide range of aspects of the clinical condition. Lee (article 10) reports on a prospective study of the causal priority between socioeconomic status and psychiatric disorder. An annotated reference compares the role of parental social class, the subject's social class, and social mobility in psychopathology.

The incidence of psychopathology associated with the urbanization process and the distribution of mental disorders across city sections are intriguing issues. Article 11 describes the apparent impact on psychopathology of the Hong Kong urbanization experience. An annotated reference deals with Dunham's classical review of both differential urban distribution of mental illness and alternative explanations for it.

Ethnic groups are cultural structures par excellence. Their interrelations with psychopathology are complex, as such groups can have a significant role in the development and phenomenology of mental disorders both by themselves as well as by representing a minority in a larger society. Article 12 compares the prevalence and conceptualization of mental disorder between French and non-French communities in two Canadian towns. Several annotated additional references elaborate further on this topic.

Religious identification is one of the key aspects of a culture. It can affect both the manifestations of stress and mental illness as well as the ways in which a society attempts to cope with them. One annotated additional reference in this chapter compares Muslims and Christians in Lebanon, and another deals with Catholics, Protestants and Jews in New York City.

10

The Causal Priority Between Socioeconomic Status and Psychiatric Disorder: A Prospective Study

Rance P. L. Lee

An inverse correlation between social class and prevalence of mental disorders (especially schizophrenia) has been fairly well documented in the sociologic and psychiatric literatures. However the question of which causes which has remained highly controversial. Some studies have provided support to the hypothesis that mental illness causes the person to fall down in the social class scale, while others have offered evidence suggesting that lower social status causes mental illness. Of course, it is also possible that these two variables reinforce each other. In any case, the direction or pattern of causation is an issue with serious theoretical implications for the understanding of mental illness and considerable practical consequences for the design of prevention and treatment strategies.

Lee addresses the issue in question using a longitudinal approach (rather than the most frequent purely cross-sectional one), in which he assesses the individual's own social class mobility (rather than the more problematic intergenerational mobility). Although the measures used for psychiatric disorder and social status were relatively weak, the overall design (differential in cross-lagged panel correlations) makes the study quite interesting.

THE METHOD of "Differential in Cross-Lagged Panel Correlations" was employed to evaluate the causal priority between socioeconomic status and psychiatric disorder. The panel data were collected from a sample of 132 noninstitutionalized household heads residing in 12 Canadian rural communities in 1952 and in 1962–63. We found that socioeconomic status was more likely to have causal priority over psychiatric disorder than the reverse. This finding held separately among men and among women. It is suggested that the social causation hypothesis may be more plausible than the social drift hypothesis.

Over the last few decades, sociologists and psychiatrists have been greatly interested in the relationship between mental illness and social environment. There exists, however, a controversial issue: do social-structural forces predispose to mental illness? Or do mental disorders cause changes in social-structural characteristics? To shed light on this issue, the present paper attempts to focus on one aspect of social-structural forces: namely, changes in socioeconomic status. This selection is primarily due to the fact that the "causal" direction between mental illness and socioeconomic status is frequently discussed but not yet well understood.

Many social-epidemiological studies have supported the finding that there is an inverse relationship between socioeconomic status and mental illness (Dunham 1961; Faris and Dunham 1939; Hollingshead and Redlich 1958; Mishler and Scotch 1963; Srole et al. 1962). This finding, however, can be interpreted with two competing hypotheses: (1) *social causation,* i.e., the indigenous forces of socioeconomic status influence the precipitation of mental illness; (2) *social drift,* i.e., the mentally disordered tend to move into the lower strata as a result of the mental disability. Then which of these two hypotheses is the more plausible?

The pioneering work of Faris and Dunham (1939) supported the social causation framework by presenting some indicators of the stress of social isolation within a disorganized area in the city. Tietze et al. (1941) asserted that the differential distribution of schizophrenic patients by social class cannot be accounted for by the downward movement of those who were already ill. Jaco (1959) discovered that more intergenerational downward mobility appeared in communities with high rates of mental illness, and argued that the indigenous conditions indicative of inducing isolation within given communities may be precipitants of schizophrenia. Hollingshead and Redlich (1958) noted that a substantial proportion of schizophrenics were in the same class as their families of origin, while very few schizophrenics were in a class lower than that. Turner and Wagenfeld (1967) compared the intergenerational occupational mobility of schizophrenic males with that of a nonpatient sample, and found that the fathers of the patients were overrepresented at the lowest occupational level, but to a lesser degree than the patients. These studies supported the social causation hypothesis.

The above writers have merely shed light on one side of the issue. While Clausen and Kohn (1959) have found an approximately equal mobility among schizophrenics and controls, Lystad (1957) found that the first-admission schizophrenics in New Orleans were more downwardly mobile than their controls. Dunham (1964) reported that schizophrenics in his Detroit sample showed no significant downward or upward mobility patterns, but in a later study of male schizophrenics, Dunham et al. (1966) concluded that "it is the nature of disease that determines the class position of the schizophrenic, at least by the measure of occupation and education, and that it is not the class position that influences the nature of the disease." In their community study of Midtown Manhattan, Srole et al. (1962) argued that the various psychiatric symptoms interfere with the life adjustment of the person and hence lead to downward mobility. The social drift hypothesis was hence supported by these studies.

The above studies have apparently contributed contradictory findings to the question: which causes which? These inconsistent findings may be due to many possible sources of potential error. Mishler and Scotch (1963), for example, have mentioned three: the case finding procedures are not independent of social class, the diagnostic procedures are not independent of social class, and the measurement of social class is unreliable. Taking into consideration these possible sources of error, the present paper attempts to add knowledge to the understanding of the "causal priority" between socioeconomic status and mental illness. Is socioeconomic status more likely to be causally prior to mental illness? Or is it the other way round?

It is noted that previous studies largely worked with cross-sectional data. Since the time-order between variables cannot be discovered, it is difficult to analyze the direction of causality in such studies. As Rinehart (1966) has demonstrated, "in the absence of longitudinal information, selection of either interpretation (i.e., social causation or social drift) would have to be based on purely arbitrary criteria". A special feature of the present paper is that it works with over-time data, rather than data at one point in time. It is thus able to provide a more logical and accurate analysis of the causal relationship between socioeconomic status and mental illness.

Furthermore, most of the previous studies primarily used the socioeconomic status of parents as the point of origin for measuring the status mobility of the respondents. They analyzed the intergenerational mobility rather than the mobility of an individual's own socioeconomic status. Since this panel study reexamined the same respondents at different points in time, we could therefore measure the individual's own socioeconomic status mobility in relation to his own changes in mental health status over a period of time.

Method of Procedure

The present study used part of the data collected by an interdisciplinary team, directed by Alexander H. Leighton, in the Stirling County Project in 1952 and in 1962-63 (Hughes et al. 1960; Leighton 1959; Leighton et al. 1963). Leighton and his associates described in detail their methodological procedures, which were essentially the same for both 1952 and 1962-63 surveys. We would like to summarize some of the research procedures and then incorporate our methodological approach into the particular problem under study.

Stirling County is located in one of the Canadian Atlantic Provinces. It is a rural and small-town region with a total population of 20,000. The county contains approximately 100 place-name areas, and consists of two main ethnic groups, English and French Acadian. In addition, there are several small black communities and a scattering of Micmac Indian families.

In 1952, a 211-item structured questionnaire was administered by Leighton's research team to a stratified probability sample of 1,015 male and female *household heads* in the county as a whole. These household heads might or might not have been receiving psychiatric care, but they were *not institutionalized* then. Ethnic composition was one of the major criteria for stratifying the county population.

The questionnaire was intended to elicit sociocultural as well as psychiatric information. For psychiatric information each respondent was asked about health history as well as a series of neuropsychiatric screening questions. Many additional data were gathered, however, both for psychiatric and sociocultural purposes. These psychiatric data from different sources were combined into protocols on each of the sample respondents. The project psychiatrists then evaluated and described the symptoms of psychiatric interest in the protocols. Each respondent might have had multiple symptoms. The 1952 Diagnostic and Statistical Manual of the American Psychiatric Association was used as the standard method of symptomatic classification and description, rather than diagnosis. This evaluation procedure was thus relatively independent of socioeconomic background. Each symptom pattern was also judged and rated in terms of the time and duration of presence, the amount of impairment on the respondent's normal life functioning, and the degree to which the psychiatric evaluator was confident in describing the respondent with this particular symptom category.

Leighton and his associates undertook a resurvey in 1962–63. A sample of 404 was drawn from the *adult* population of 12 communities in the county. Of these 404 respondents, 252 constitute a representative sample of household heads, while the remaining 152 consist of people followed up from 1952 plus some non-heads of households who were added in order to get comparative information. The questionnaire schedules used in the resurvey were designed to elicit the same type of information that had been gathered in 1952 plus additional data on changes that had occurred during the ten years.

In both surveys, the case-finding procedures were made as independent as possible of socioeconomic background. By comparing the two samples, we found that 132 individuals were interviewed at both times. The present panel study analyzes the changes in socioeconomic status and mental health of these 132 adults over the decade. It should be noted, however, that these individuals may not constitute a representative sample of the county population.

Psychiatric Disorder. To summarize all the symptomatology reported in the protocol, the Stirling County Project psychiatrists constructed a four-point (ABCD) "caseness" rating scale. The scale expresses the confidence felt by the evaluators that the individual is, or at some time has been, a psychiatric case (i.e., manifesting one or more of the specific psychiatric conditions described in the 1952 APA Manual). The method of psychiatric evaluation involves an agreement of judgments made by a panel of psychiatrists. The inter-rater reliability was found to be highly satisfactory (Leighton et al. 1963).

This caseness scale, however, is cumulative over time as it is based upon "life time" symptomatology. It is not appropriate for the purpose of the present panel study, which attempts to investigate the internal shifts towards mental deterioration as well as improvement. With the help of Drs. Morton Beiser and Alexander H. Leighton, we have introduced a new composite index of "Psychiatric Disorders," which refers to the extent that a person is *currently* in need of psychiatric attention. It is based on the number and types of current symptom patterns within the last six months, the amount of impairment caused by each symptom pattern, and the degree of confidence on the part of the psychiatric evaluator for assigning such symptom categories. This overall index of psychiatric disorder is of three degrees: high, medium, and low. Among the various symptom patterns, Mental Deficiency and Brain Syndrome receive more weight than the others. Examples for a high degree of current psychiatric disorder are Brain Syndrome with significant impairment and high confidence; Brain Syndrome with significant impairment but medium confidence, plus Psychophysiologic and Psychoneurologic symptoms. Examples for a medium degree are: Brain Syndrome with significant impairment but medium confidence; Psychophysiologic plus Psychoneurologic, both with high confidence but either one with negligible impairment. Examples for a low degree are: Psychophysiologic plus Psychoneurotic, both with high confidence but negligible impairment; no symptoms at all.

Our Psychiatric Disorder Index and the ABCD caseness scale differ in at least two ways: the ABCD scale is a "lifetime" measure while our index is based on "current" symptoms only; and the ABCD scale is a probability statement of being a case while our index also implies the degree of disability due to mental disorder. Nevertheless, both are overall estimates of mental health status. They share certain common properties but are, or course, not identical. We tested the relationship between these two measures on the basis of the 1952 survey data, and found that the association was strong and positive. The Somers' d coefficient is .43. In other words, if the rank order for two individuals on the ABCD scale were known, then they would have a 43 percent greater chance of being in the same order than in a different order on the psychiatric disorder index. To control on sex and age (60 and over, 40 to 59, and under 40) separately, we found that the association was positive in all subgroups, and that it was particularly strong among females ($d = .46$) and among those of age 60 or over ($d = .53$).

Socioeconomic Status. Most of the social epidemiological studies of psychiatric disorder have used occupation and/or education as measures of socioeconomic status. The household heads or adults in the present study, however, were unlikely to change their educational levels over time. Furthermore, as suggested by the Stirling County Project researchers, the various classifications of occupation may not be meaningfully applicable for the measurement of socioeconomic status in a rural population. Hence, we decided to use eight indicators concerning the material style of life or the living conditions of the respondents. Five of these indicators were taken from responses to questionnaire items about household possessions including lighting facilities, food refrigeration, toilet facilities, clothes-washing, and heating facilities. The remaining three indicators were interviewer ratings of the quality of interior furnishings, house type, and room–person index. Each of these indicators was dichotomized, and all were then summed to form a Likert-type scale, the score of which varies from 0 to 8 and indicates the degree of socioeconomic status. In view of the trend of modernization and technological process, however, we could expect that many more individuals would be on the upper end of the scale in 1962-63 than were in 1952. In other words, a particular score in 1952 may not have had the same subjective value to the same individual in 1962-63. Instead of taking the absolute values, we therefore transformed them into a set of standard scores, and then collapsed such scores into three categories (high, medium, low) by taking the 33rd and 67th percentiles as cutting points. An individual's socioeconomic status is hence defined by his relative position to other sample respondents at a particular point in time.

Statistical Model. To detect which of the two variables (socioeconomic status and psychiatric disorder) is more likely to have causal priority over the other, we employed the method of "Differential in Cross-lagged Panel Correlations" developed by Pelz and Andrews (1964). The basic logic of this method is to measure the differences in the diagonal (i.e., cross-lagged) relationships between two variables on the basis of over-time data.

Since both socioeconomic status and psychiatric disorder variables in the present study are measured on the ordinal level, we used Kendall's Tau-c to measure their cross-sectional as well as longitudinal relationships. Our decision was based upon several considerations: Tau-c is a *symmetrical* measure of association between variables measured on *ordinal* levels; its statistical value ranges from −1 to +1 for equal or unequal number of rows and columns; its application does not require the assumption of no ties on either variable; and Kendall has developed a partial rank correlation method (P. Kendall 1954; Siegel 1956). Lastly it should be underscored that since we could not claim that the present sample is random or representative, we did not conduct any statistical test of significance (Selvin 1957).

Findings

Before we report the causal priority, we first present the cross-sectional relationship between socioeconomic status and psychi-

Table 10.1 Socioeconomic Status and Psychiatric Disorder in 1952 (*N* = 132)

Psychiatric Disorder	*Socioeconomic Status* Low		Middle		High	
	N	%	*N*	%	*N*	%
High	7	13.7	3	7.3	2	5.0
Medium	11	21.6	8	19.5	8	20.0
Low	33	64.7	30	73.2	30	75.0
Total	51	100.0	41	100.0	40	100.0

atric disorder among the 132 sample respondents in 1952 and in 1962-63. The data distribution in tables 10.1 and 10.2 obviously show that there was an inverse relationship between socioeconomic status and psychiatric disorder in 1952 as well as in 1962-63. In other words, the lower the socioeconomic status, the higher the degree of psychiatric disorder; and vice versa. These findings are therefore consistent with the general findings in most social-epidemiological studies with respect to the socioeconomic-status and mental-illness relationship at one point in time.

Figure 10.1 summarizes the results from our application of the method of "differential in cross-lagged panel correlations" to the overtime data. It was found that the inverse relationship between socioeconomic status and psychiatric disorder was stronger in 1962–63 (tau-c = −.18) than it was in 1952 (tau-c = −.08); socioeconomic status had a higher degree of stabilitiy (tau-c = −.63) than had psychiatric disorder (tau-c = −.13) over the decade; the diagonal relationship between socioeconomic status in 1952 and psychiatric disorder in 1962–63 (tau-c = −.16) was stronger than was that between psychiatric disorder in 1952 and socioeconomic status in 1962–63 (tau-c = −.13). However, since the diagonal

Table 10.2 Socioeconomic Status and Psychiatric Disorder in 1962–63 (*N* = 132)

Psychiatric Disorder	*Socioeconomic Status* Low		Middle		High	
	N	%	*N*	%	*N*	%
High	14	25.5	2	5.4	4	10.0
Medium	21	38.1	12	32.4	14	35.0
Low	20	36.4	23	62.2	22	55.0
Total	55	100.0	37	100.0	40	100.0

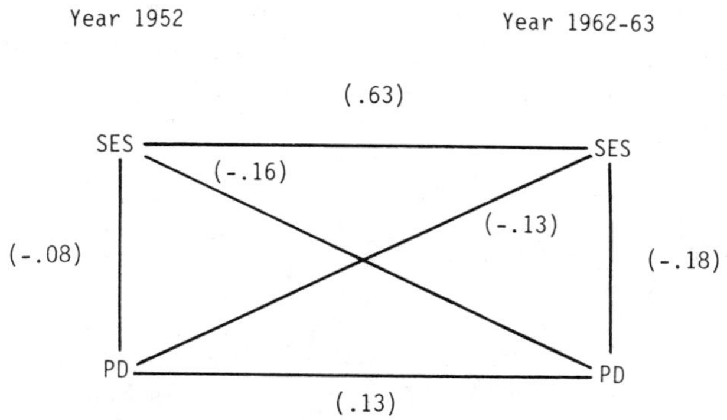

Figure 10.1 Causal Priority Between Socioeconomic Status (SES) and Psychiatric Disorder (PD). Figures in parenthesis are Tau-C Coefficients.

relationships were inevitably contaminated by the lagged self-correlations for each variable, it would be erroneous to draw a conclusion of causal priority by comparing the two diagonal correlation values. In order to free the diagonal relationships from this constraint, we used partial correlation. The Kendall partial rank correlation coefficient for the relationship between socioeconomic status in 1952 and psychiatric disorder in 1962–63, controlling on psychiatric disorder in 1952, was found to be .15; while that for the relationship between psychiatric disorder in 1952 and socioeconomic status in 1962–63, controlling on socioeconomic status in 1952, was .10. The former coefficient is greater than the latter one. We hence conclude that socioeconomic status is more likely to have "causal priority" over psychiatric disorder. The hypothesis of social causation may be more plausible than the hypothesis of social drift.

Since sex as a variable is of overwhelming concern to most psychiatric researchers and may intervene in the causal links under study, we elaborated the causal priority between socioeconomic status and psychiatric disorder separately among men ($N = 56$) and women ($N = 76$). It was found that the Kendall partial rank correlation coefficient between socioeconomic status in 1952 and psychiatric disorder in 1962–63, controlling on psychiatric disorder in 1952, is .13 for men and is .16 for women; while that between psychiatric disorder in 1952 and socioeconomic status in 1962–63, controlling on socioeconomic status in 1952 is .08 for men and is .13 for women. The partial relationship between socioeconomic status in 1952 and psychiatric disorder in 1962–63 is greater than that between psychiatric disorder in 1952 and socioeconomic status in 1962–63 among the male as well as the female adults under study. We hence found that the original finding concerning the causal priority of socioeconomic status over psychiatric disorder held among both men and women.

Summary and Discussion

The present paper evaluates the causal priority between socioeconomic status and mental illness on the basis of a secondary analysis of the panel data collected by the Stirling County Project from a sample of 132 noninstitutionalized household heads residing in twelve Canadian rural communities. The concept of psychiatric disorder was measured by a composite index of current psychiatric symptoms which were classified on the basis of the 1952 APA Manual, while the socioeconomic status scale was composed of eight items concerning the material style of life of the respondents. This study therefore focused on the causal relationship between an adult's own socioeconomic status mobility and his own mental health changes over a decade.

The method of "Differential in Cross-lagged Panel Correlations" and Kendall's tau-c measure of association were used to detect causal priority. The analysis showed that socioeconomic status was more likely to have causal priority over mental illness, and that such a finding held separately among male and female adults. It is therefore suggested that the social causation hypothesis may be more plausible than the social drift hypothesis.

It should, however, be underscored that the above analysis of causal priority does not really demonstrate the *causal* relationship between socioeconomic status and psychiatric disorder. At best, it gives results to support the interpretation that some indigenous forces (e.g., social isolation and psychological stress) within socioeconomic status may precipitate the occurrence of mental illness. As Russell (1929) and Blalock (1961) have asserted, causal laws are applicable only to a completely isolated system. Apparently it becomes very difficult to make causal inferences on the basis of the present panel data which were collected in a natural setting. Although we have attempted to examine the "causal" relationship by controlling for sex, other extraneous influences (e.g., age and ethnic groups) are not excluded. Furthermore, our analysis does not preclude the possiblity of feedback or circular causation, i.e., socioeconomic status and psychiatric disorder may mutually influence each other in the process of change.

In the present paper, the concept of socioeconomic status was measured by several items concerning the material style of life, while the concept of psychiatric disorder was measured by a general index. But both concepts are by no means unitary. Different dimensions of socioeconomic status (e.g., occupation, income, education, and residence) may have different patterns of causal relationship to different types of mental illness (e.g., psychophysiological, psychoneurological, sociopathic, schizophrenic, and brain syndrome). Moreover the study was conducted in rural communities, but the pattern of causal relationship may not be the same in the urban setting. More specific studies are hence needed.

As many social scientists have demonstrated (Harris 1963; Kendall 1954; Zeisel 1957), the methodological problems of unreliability and invalidity are much more serious in panel studies than in experimental research of cross-sectional surveys. The findings in the present study of panel data may be partially, if not entirely, a product of measurement errors. This problem may become more serious in view of the small sample size and the relatively weak associations among the variables under study.

The problem of validity in respect of the measurement of psychiatric disorder in the present study deserves special attention. As mentioned, the psychiatric symptoms of respondents were judged and defined by the project psychiatrists in the Stirling County Project. What is "real" for the psychiatrists, however, may not be for the members in local communities. The subcultural difference between project psychiatrists and respondents may be a possible source of error in this study. This problem becomes more serious in view of the fact there are group differences in modes of expressing distress, including some that involve problems of response bias (Dohrenwend 1966).

Acknowledgments

This paper derives from the Stirling County Study, which has been supported by the Milbank Memorial Fund, the Carnegie Corporation of New York, the Dominion Provincial Mental Health Grant of Canada, the Ford Foundation, and most recently MH 12892-00 of the

National Institute of Mental Health. The paper was expanded from an earlier presentation read before the 24th Annual Meeting, The World Federation for Mental Health, held in Hong Kong from November 22 to 24, 1971. The late Professor Edward A. Suchman, Dr. Robert Chin, and Dr. Robert Avery gave valuable suggestions. I am also indebted to the support and comments from Dr. Alexander H. Leighton and his staff in the Department of Behavioral Sciences, Harvard University School of Public Health. Secretarial help was given by the Department of Sociology, University of Pittsburgh, while I was there in 1972–73.

11

Urbanization and Psychiatric Disorders—The Hong Kong Scene

W. H. Lo

In a world of persistent growth in population the development of rural areas into urban centers is a continuous and widespread process. Along with urbanization, quite frequently there are associated phenomena such as overcrowding and acceleration in the pace of life. As these phenomena have been found, at least impressionistically, to be related to increased mental health problems, there is considerable interest in assessing the association between urbanization and psychopathology.

Hong Kong offers almost a natural setting for exploring the issue in question, as it has experienced an intense urbanization process during the past three decades, reflecting a marked increase in its population within a quite reduced and fixed usable area. Lo reports on the changes in the amount and composition of psychiatric morbidity associated with Hong Kong's urbanization process. This longitudinal study made extensive use of census information and regular clinical-administrative data from Hong Kong's Mental Health Service (facilitated by Lo's directorship of this Service) in addition to a cross-sectional survey of global psychiatric symptomatology (without syndromic differentiation) in the general population.

INDICES WERE used to portray the rapidity and intensity of urbanization Hong Kong had undergone in the past two to three decades. Next the preliminary result of a psychiatric survey was quoted as an estimate of mental ill-health in Hong Kong. Data were obtained from the Mental Health Service to show the increasing demand for psychiatric care for the past 25 years. Attempts were made to analyze the basic composition of the new patients attending a psychiatric center during this period.

High-density living associated with urbanization in Hong Kong was found to generate a high level of emotional strain, and psychiatric ill-health was as prevalent as that in New York. Neuroses were on the increase and psychiatrists were being consulted on a wider variety of problems. Provision of mental health care in future should take the changes in the composition of psychiatric populations into consideration.

Urbanization is an overused word and many people use this term without assigning it any precise meaning. It may refer to the expansion, distribution, and composition of the city population and produces both positive and negative effects. Psychiatrists and related professionals are more concerned with the negative aspects of urbanization since urban living has been alleged to generate a high level of emotional strain. Much depends, however, on the rapidity and intensity of the process. In this respect Hong Kong is unique in that it has become highly urbanized within the past two or three decades as well as in its special sociocultural background and its geographic situation. The total land area of Hong Kong is about 400 square miles but only a little more than one-fifth is immediately usable. Geographically it is divided into Hong Kong Island, Kowloon, and New Territories.

Materials and Methods

In this paper three indices are used to portray the urbanization process: the growth and density of the population, the expansion of the industrial force, and the increase in Gross Domestic Product per capita. The last two are closely associated with industrialization, which in the Hong Kong scene goes hand in hand with urbanization. These as well as other control data were supplied by the Census and Statistics Department, but reliable figures have been available only since 1961 when the first census was conducted.

The preliminary findings of a recent psychiatric survey are quoted as an estimate of the prevalence of mental ill-health in Hong Kong. This was conducted in 1974 with the author's participation. Data are obtained from the Mental Health Service to show the increasing demand for psychiatric care in the past 25 years. Attempts are made to analyze the basic composition of the new patients attending the Hong Kong Psychiatric Centre in the past 15 years; this is one of the units of the Mental Health Service, and provides full-term outpatient and day patient facilities for Hong Kong Island and through the center admission to inpatient hospital/unit takes place.

Results

Growth and density of population (land and floor area). These are shown separately in tables 11.1, 11.2 and 11.3, respectively.

The rapid population growth in the late 1940's and early 1950's was due to a flood of immigrants from China and by 1961 (when statistics became available) the district of most intense urbanization had

Table 11.1 Growth of population

Year	*Population*
1841 (When it became a British Colony)	5,650
1945 (When it was occupied by Japanese during World War II)	650,000
1949 (Political changes in neighboring country)	1,857,000
1961 (1st Full Census)	3,133,131
1966 (By-Census)	3,785,300
1974	4,248,300

Table 11.2 Population density: land area (persons/km^2)

District	*1961*	*1966*	*1971*
Hong Kong Island	13,303	13,637	12,809
Kowloon	38,979	47,505	42,860
New Territories	384	397	468

Table 11.3 Population density: floor area (gross floor area/person in ft^2)

District	*1971*	*1974*
Hong Kong Island	124	202
Kowloon	72–101	141
New Territories	—	—

already shifted from Hong Kong to Kowloon. The increase in gross floor area per person indicates the extent to which high rise residential flats are being built.

Expansion of manufacturing sector. Industrialization may be said to begin after World War II, when the influx of immigrants brought with it capital which was used to build up textile and later other industries. Industry gained momentum during the Korean War (1950–1953) and further development can be seen by the expansion of the manufacturing section in table 11.4.

Increase in GDP per capita. Gross Domestic Product (GDP) is a measure of growth of national income. More specifically GDP at market prices is the sum of consumption expenditure, gross domestic capital formation and exports of goods and services less imports of goods and services. Thus, the increase in GDP per capita as shown in table 11.5 is the positive effect of industrialization and urbanization.

With this remarkable increase in GDP per capita in the past one to two decades, the living standard of the people of Hong Kong is the second highest in Asia.

Hong Kong Psychiatric Survey, 1974

This survey was conducted by an ecological group from the Australian National University with the author's collaboration. Eighty

Table 11.4 Industrial force

Year	*No. of persons in industry*	*Percent of whole population*
1961	*594,679*	*19*
1966	*649,710*	*17.82*
1971	*855,141*	*21.72*

Table 11.5 GDP per capita (HK$)

Year	*At current market price*	*At constant market price of 1966*
1961	1,915	2,098
1966	3,061	3,061
1971	5,149	3,875
1974 (forecast)	8,018	4,518

items including two psychiatric scales (the Langner Scale and the Bradburn Scale) were administered to 116 randomly selected neurotic patients currently attending the psychiatric outpatient clinics as well as to a sample, 3983 in number, of the general population. Prior to this survey, a pilot study was done in order to validate these two scales, which were designed in the West and purported to measure degree of mental impairment and well being. This pilot study showed that despite cultural differences and translation discrepancy they could be applied to Hong Kong. Only the results on the Langner Scale are quoted here. The Langner Scale (Langner 1962) is composed of 22 questions on specific psychophysiological and psychic symptoms which lead to impairment in life functioning. It was first used in the Midtown Manhattan Study and later in several other surveys. As shown in table 11.6 the score on this scale correlates very well with the clinical grading.

A comparison is made in table 11.7 between the sample representative of the general population and the neurotic patients in the Psychiatric Survey with regard to their scores on Langner's Scale.

If the score of 7 or more on the Langner Scale is taken as the cutting off point for fairly certain "psychiatric impairment," then 11.8 percent of the Hong Kong population would have "psychiatric impairment."

Table 11.6 Neurotic patients currently attending psychiatric clinics (n = 116)

Clinical grading	*Mean score in Langner's Scale*
I (Symptoms remitted)	5.56
II (Mild symptoms)	7.59
III (Moderately severe symptoms)	9.87
IV (Severe symptoms)	11.73
V (Totally incapacitated)	13.00

Table 11.7 Comparison of general population sample and neurotic out-patients

Langner's score categories	*General population Neurotic sample (n = 3983)*	*Out-patients (n = 116)*
0–3	68.3%	14.04%
4–6	19.9%	13.16%
7+	11.8%	72.81%

Table 11.8 Comparison of findings of surveys

Sample location	Sample size	4 or more symptoms	7 or more symptoms	10 or more symptoms
Midtown Manhattan	*1660*	*31.2%*	*11.2%*	*3.7%*
Hennepin (A rural town in Illinois)	*1456*	*16.6%*	*5.9%*	*2.3%*
Hong Kong	*3983*	*31.7%*	*11.8%*	*3.8%*

Furthermore, table 11.8 compares this finding with the Midtown study (Langner, 1962) and the Hennepin study (Summers, 1971).

The above findings suggest a similar prevalence of psychiatric impairment in Hong Kong and New York.

Increases in number of patients in Mental Health Service

Table 11.9 shows the increases of outpatients and inpatients in the past 25 years. Calculated from these figures, it can be seen that in the past 25 years the number of new outpatients has increased 10 times (by 987 percent), new admissions 4.5 times (by 446 percent) and re-admissions 18 times (by 1,821 percent). Furthermore, the Mental Health Service began to have day patients in 1961. The admissions to day hospitals were 142 in 1961 and 464 in 1974—i.e., a 3.3 times increase. During this period the population increase was only 2.3 times (229 percent).

Composition of patients attending Hong Kong Psychiatric Centre (HKPC) during the past 15 years

Figures are given for 5-year intervals to simplify tabulation.

Sex distribution. Throughout this period the sex distribution in the gen-

Table 11.9 Patients statistics of Mental Health Science

Year	New out-patients	Old out-patients	New admissions	Re-admissions
1949	*306*	–	*419*	*148*
1954	*468*	–	*749*	*274*
1959	*752*	–	*1,024*	*473*
1964	*1,433*	*2,846*	*1,353*	*942*
1969	*2,628*	*9,109*	*1,470*	*2,177*
1974	*3,019*	*14,606*	*1,868*	*2,695*

Table 11.10 Sex distribution

Year	General population M	General population F	Patients attending H.K.P.C. M	Patients attending H.K.P.C. F
*1961	1,586,900 (50.08%)	1,581,700 (49.92%)	414 (58%)	300 (42%)
*1966	1,818,800 (50.10%)	1,811,100 (49.9%)	490 (54.8%)	404 (45.2%)
*1971	2,057,200 (50.85%)	1,953,500 (49.15%)	584 (58.3%)	418 (41.7%)
1974	2,185,200 (51.43%)	2,063,500 48.57%)	256 (54.2%)	216 (45.8%)

*Difference between the general population and the patient population is statistically significant ($P < 0.01$).

eral population was about equal, but in the patient population males were overrepresented (table 11.10).

Age groups. When the distribution in various age groups of the general population and of the patients attending HKPC are compared, it is found that although the percentage of people aged 65 and over in the general population has almost trebled in the past 15 years (3.2 percent in 1961 and 9.2 percent in 1974), their constitution in the patient population has not even doubled (2.5 percent in 1961 and 4 percent in 1974). In 1974 the percentage of children (aged below 16) was about 35.2 percent but they constituted only 10.4 percent of the HKPC cases.

Educational levels. The changes in educational levels in the general population and the patient population are tabulated below for comparison (table 11.11).

If illiterate and primary education as a group are compared with secondary and post-secondary as a group, then the increased education levels in the patient population reflect those of the general population.

Table 11.11 Education levels

	General population in Hong Kong Island			*Patients attending H.K.P.C.*		
Education Levels	*1961* *n = (1,004,875)*	*1966* *(1,006,600)*	*1971* *(996,183)*	*1961* *(663)*	*1966* *(858)*	*1971* *(960)*
Illiterate	37.3%	34.7%	28.3%	22.6%	27.0%	29.5%
Primary	42.1%	39.6%	39.1%	60.8%	43.9%	43.5%
Secondary	17.6%	21.8%	27.8%	14.9%	24.5%	24.2%
Post-secondary	3.0%	3.8%	4.8%	1.6%	4.7%	2.8%

Table 11.12 Types of living quarters

Living quarters	*General population in HK Island (1974)* (n = 222,940)*	*H.K.P.C. patients (1974) (n = 1,002)*
Hut or squatter	20,716 (9.3%)	101 (10.1%)
** Resettlement estates & low cost housing	16,639 (7.5%)	166 (16.6%)
Housing Authority Society	17,174 (7.7%)	66 (6.6%)
** Private-owned or rent	163,022 (73.1%)	571 (60%)
Others	5,387 (2.4%)	98 (9.8%)

* Data available for 1974 only.
** Difference between the general population and the patient population is statistically significant ($P < 0.01$).

Living quarters. These can be classified into the types shown in table 11.12. Some of these require a brief description. The "resettlement estates" were hurriedly built to provide accommodation for 50,000 people who became homeless after a big fire in 1953. Each estate consisted of 6- and 7-story H-shaped blocks and an all-in room of 120 ft^2 for a family of more than four persons with communal toilets and washing rooms. The resettlement program, with some improvements in quality, was continued to help solve the acute housing problem of the poor. The "low-cost housing" provides better accommodation than the resettlement estates. A living space of 35 ft^2 is allowed for an adult and there are independent private facilities. The "housing authority society" provides high rise estates which are like small townships with all the necessary facilities. Each flat is a self-contained unit for an individual family of higher income group but the space for each unit is still comparatively small, about 300–400 ft^2. As shown in table 11.12, people living in the resettlement estates and low-cost housing are over-represented in the patient population.

Diagnosis. The diagnoses of the Hong Kong Psychiatric Centre cases are given in table 11.13.

There has been a tendency for schizophrenia and confusional state to decrease and neuroses and affective psychoses to increase in their percentage composition of patients attending the HKPC.

Onset-duration of illness before attending is shown in table 11.14. It seems that the percentage of patients with duration of illness less than

3 months has been decreasing and that of 3 years and over increasing.

The proportion of new outpatients admitted to hospital or day centre is shown in table 11.15. Considerable variation can be seen.

Facilities provided by Mental Health Service

Before 1949 there was no special treatment for the mentally ill in Hong Kong. Patients were sent to the "lunatic asylum," which provided only custodial care, and the problem of overcrowding was

Table 11.13 Diagnosis of H.K.P.C. cases

Diagnosis	*1959 (n = 406)*	*1964 (n = 840)*	*1969 (n = 979)*	*1974 (n = 472)*
Schizophrenia	31.5%	31.4%	27.3%	26.5%
Affective psychoses	3.7%	7.9%	7.9%	8.3%
Organic psychoses/dementia	7.4%	8.3%	10.2%	8.9%
Acute brain syndrome (Confusional state/delirium)	1.5%	3.9%	1.6%	0.2%
Neuroses	31.5%	26.7%	24.9%	37.1%
Others	24.4%	21.8%	28.1%	29.0%

Table 11.14 Duration of Illness on attending

Duration of illness on attending	*1959 (n = 406–50*)*	*1964 (n = 840–61*)*	*1969 (n = 979–130*)*	*1974 (n = 431–41*)*
< 1 month	17.7%	31.5%	24.2%	15.3%
1–3 months	20.2%	17.3%	11.7%	13.5%
3–6 months	10.4%	9.4%	9.4%	10.9%
6 months–1 year	14.0%	9.3%	8.0%	9.5%
1–2 years	11.5%	14.5%	15.8%	14.4%
2–3 years	9.3%	5.1%	7.3%	11.4%
> 3 years	16.9%	12.3%	23.5%	25.1%

* The mentally retarded were excluded.

Table 11.15 Proportion of new out-patients admitted

	1959 (n = 406)	*1964 (n = 840)*	*1969 (n = 979)*	*1974 (n = 472)*
Per cent admitted as in-patients	12.8%	35.8%	26.3%	14.2%
Per cent admitted as day-patients	1.2%	8.2%	3.7%	8.1%

solved by periodic transfers of patients to China. This convenient solution was put to an abrupt end by the founding of the Peoples' Republic of China. At this time a qualified psychiatrist, the late Prof. P. M. Yap, became available and was appointed the first Medical Superintendent of the mental hospital. Now the mental health care is provided by the Mental Health Service, the structure of which is shown in table 11.16. All the psychiatric facilities shown in the table were opened within the last 15 years.

Discussion

The three indices used, namely the growth and density of the population, the expansion of the industrial sector, and the increase in

Table 11.16 Facilities of Mental Health Service

Mental Health Centers (out-patient and day center)	*Psychiatric Hospitals (in-patients)*	*Psychiatric units (in-patients, out-patients and day center)*	*Psychiatric Clinics (out-patient)*
Hong Kong Psychiatric Centre (Headquarters of Mental Health Service) (1971[a])	Castle Peak Hospital (1,921 beds) (1961[a])	Kowloon Hospital Psychiatric Unit (67 beds) (1971[a])	Queen Elizabeth Hospital Psychiatric Clinic (1962[a])
Yaumatei Psychiatric Centre (1967[a])	Lai Chi Kok Hospital (300 beds) (1974[a])	[c]Queen Mary Hospital Psychiatric Unit (15 beds) (1971[a])	Tsuen Wan Psychiatric Clinic (1961[a])
	[b]Siu Lam Psychiatric Centre (200 beds for mentally ill offenders) (1972[a])	[d]United Christian Hospital Psychiatric Unit (28 beds) (1974[a])	Miscellaneous Sunday Psychiatric Clinics
	[b]Siu Lam Subnormal Hospital (200 beds for the severely subnormal) (1972[a])		

[a] Year of opening.

[b] The Mental Health Service provides visiting psychiatrists to these two institutions.

[c] Run by the University Psychiatric Department.

[d] Run by a subsidized hospital.

GDP per capita, should be able to portray the rapidity and intensity of urbanization in Hong Kong in the past two to three decades.

Indeed, rapid growth of population associated with intense urbanization has given Hong Kong the highest urban density in the world, and due to the physical and geographic limitation, high rise residential flats are gradually replacing the squatter huts and resettlement estates built earlier. There are few open spaces and public amenities. Unsatisfactory living quarters cause much stress; this can be seen in the over-representation of dwellers in the resettlement estates and low-cost housing in the patient population (table 11.12). In view of this and other adverse factors such as pollution, impersonality, and social disorganization, a high prevalence of psychiatric ill-health can be expected and is confirmed by the finding of the psychiatric survey in which 11.8 percent of the population scored 7 or more items on the Langner Scale. Leighton et al. (quoted by Stoller 1969) find that societies undergoing rapid change have been shown to be more likely to show social, including family, disorganization with an increase of deviant behavior, psychoneuroses, and psychosomatic disorders, though not psychoses. This is compatible with the manifold percentage increase in patients attending the Mental Health Service and the changing patterns of diagnoses. As shown in table 11.13, psychiatrists are being consulted on a wider variety of problems. The category under "Others" included diagnoses such as antisocial disorder, personality disorder and drug dependence.

Despite the manifold percentage increases of outpatients and inpatients in the Mental Health Service, the absolute numbers of patients seeking psychiatric attention are still relatively small compared with many Western countries. Several explanations are possible. First, the Chinese seem to show a higher tolerance of psychiatric symptoms. Second, there is still significant stigma attached to mental illness, which thus deters people from attending psychiatric clinics. Third, neuroses often present with somatic complaints which would bring patients to private practitioners. The latter can charge whatever fees they consider fit and continue to treat their clients with whatever diagnosis as long as they like.

Males are significantly overrepresented in the patient population attending the Hong Kong Psychiatric Center. In fact, this discrepancy is even more marked in our inpatient population, where males constitute about 60 percent this year. This percent is in contrast to the finding of Western countries. Cultural factors appear to be responsible. Despite a gradual change in females' social roles in recent years, women are still fully occupied with domestic work and caring of the children. Their odd behavior, when present, would likely escape scrutiny and unless incapacitated or disturbed, they would not be encouraged to see psychiatrists.

The number of old-age patients has been on the increase, although not reaching the extent of population increase in the age group of 65 and over. This may mean that the Chinese still pay sufficient respect and attention to the aged members in their family. Adolescents and young people (aged 16-24) continue to constitute an increasing percentage in both the general population and the psychiatric outpatients. The latter present with a greater variety of problems, mainly related to maladjustments. The highest proportion in the general population is in the age group below 16 years, but even with availability of part-time psychiatric service, it appears that the demand has not been great.

Better educated people should be more aware of their psychological symptoms and make greater use of the facilities in the Mental Health Service. In terms of percentage this has not been the case during this period, probably because they were better off financially and sought treatment from private practitioners instead. Moreover, with better provisions of psychiatric facilities (table 11.16) and higher education levels (table 11.11), the duration of illness from onset to attendance should become shorter. But this has also not been the case (table 11.14). It is likely that with the advent of effective psychotropic drugs, the early and mild cases would respond to the treatment given by general practitioners. Also, long-standing cases previously coped with solely by the family are now brought to the psychiatric clinics for the first time. In other words, when there are factors acting in opposite directions, the effects tend to cancel out each other.

As regards admissions to the mental hospital and day centers, these were mainly determined not only by the severity of the patient's condition but also by the overcrowding of the hospital and vacancies of the centers.

In Hong Kong, there are still deficiencies of professional manpower and residential facilities. Our psychiatric bed ratio is now 0.5 per 1,000 population. Obviously, assessment of future needs should be based on the observable trends in mental health care, the composition of psychiatric populations, the structure of the whole medical service, the availability of sites, and the likely effect of other developments. The findings quoted in this paper should be helpful in the planning of psychiatric facilities and delivery of psychiatric service in Hong Kong.

12

Ethnic Groups Within Communities: A Comparative Study of the Expression and Definition of Mental Illness

Daniel Sydiaha, Hugh G. Lafave and Irving Rootman

Ethnic groups are characterized by their sharing common cultural, racial, religious, and linguistic features. On a worldwide scale, with the expanding communications media, there is increasing awareness of ethnic diversity and growing recognition of the complexity and richness it involves. Furthermore, ethnic groups are acquiring increasing importance in many areas of the world because of the cultural pride and political assertiveness shown by certain minority groups such as the French-Canadian and the Mexican-American.

One of the long-standing concerns in cross-cultural psychopathology has been the clarification of the relationship between ethnic groups and mental disorder. Most of the studies have been inconclusive. Sydiaha, Lafave and Rootman empirically examine the relationship of ethnicity and other social structures with the prevalence and popular conceptualization of mental illness. Their design involved the comparison of French and non-French populations in two Canadian towns: one where the majority of the people were of French descent and Roman Catholic, and the other where the majority were neither French nor Roman Catholic. Their interesting results point out the need to elucidate not only ethnic groups as such but also their majority vs minority status.

TWO EARLIER papers (Lafave et al. 1967, Rootman et al. 1968) described studies of two communities which were "matched" on a number of economic and geographical factors, but which differed in ethnic composition. One of these communities was composed primarily of "French" inhabitants, the second was not. A comparison of the towns showed differences in epidemiology of mental illness, as well as in attitudes toward, and knowledge about, mental illness.

This paper takes the analysis of the data one step further: It examines differences between French and non-French samples within each of the two communities. The purpose of this analysis is to assess the relative importance of three sets of "cultural" factors, which might be called "traditional culture," "local culture," and "societal culture." Traditional culture is used here to refer to such factors as language and religious practices. Thus, if this factor were operative, a person of French ancestry would hold the same views regardless of whether he lived in Saskatchewan or in Quebec province. Local culture is used to refer to factors which develop out of a local set of circumstances, or incidents affecting the formation of attitudes. Societal culture refers to the influences which bear upon the total population, and which tend to produce a "homogenization" of attitudes and beliefs.

Depending upon the relative importance of these three sets of factors, it is possible to deduce three hypotheses about the effects of ethnic differences:

Hypothesis One: Assuming "traditional" culture to predominate, one would predict that cultural sub-groups (for example, French) would have similar attitudes and values, regardless of their place of residence. In relative terms one would expect that differences among cultural sub-groups within the same town would be *greater* than differences for the same cultural subgroup between towns.

Hypothesis Two: Assuming "local" culture to predominate, one would predict that cultural subgroups drawn from different places would *not* have similar attitudes and values. In relative terms, one would expect that differences among subgroups within the same town would be *less* than differences for the same subgroup between towns.

Hypothesis Three: Assuming "societal" culture to predominate, one would predict no differences between subgroups, provided the subgroups were drawn from the same societal or national milieu. In a sense this "null" hypothesis has been rejected by the differences reported in the two previous papers.

The study was designed to compare four groups of subjects, namely, French and non-French communities. The analysis included data on epidemiology of mental illness, as well as attitudes and knowledge concerning mental illness in the community. In addition to this ethnic breakdown, analysis will also be reported according to other socially meaningful classifications, including religious background, social class, length of residence and place of birth. The analysis reported here will be confined to those results obtained and reported in the two previous papers.

Procedure

Details of data collection are presented in the previous reports. A brief summary follows.

Setting

The two towns used for the study are referred to as Cloverdale and DeLis, in the southern part of the province of Saskatchewan and approximately 45 miles from each other. According to the 1961 census, about 70 percent of DeLis is of French descent, and 80 percent are Roman Catholic. Although French can be spoken by the majority of the town's inhabitants, there is evidence that English language assimilation has changed the character of the town, making it dissimilar from a town of comparable size in the province of Quebec. However, on the whole, the community does seem to have a distinctive French character, reflected in its institutional life.

In contrast, Cloverdale is neither French nor Roman Catholic. According to the 1961 census, only 13 percent of its 2,500 inhabitants were French in origin and only 26 percent Roman Catholic.

But aside from the ethnic and religious differences, the towns are similar in many respects. Closely situated, they are subject to the same climatic conditions and are apparently comparable in topography and soil fertility, both critical considerations in communities dependent upon agricultural conditions for their existence. They were settled about the same time, are approximately the same size, equidistant to cities, and similar in recent rates of population growth. Their age and sex compositon are almost identical. In addition, both towns are located in the same health region and are served by the same Psychiatric Services personnel.

Method and Samples, Attitude Survey

Ten percent simple random samples from the two communities were interviewed by three interviewers, one of them bilingual. There was about a 65 percent response rate in both towns and approximately the same (about 12 percent) refusal rate in each. The interview schedule was partially based on one developed by Dr. Shirley Star, excerpts of which were previously used in Saskatchewan by Cumming and Cumming (1957). In order to elicit frank responses from interviews, most questions were open-ended.

Ethnicity was defined for this study in terms of respondents' personal frames of reference. A series of questions was asked in an attempt to have the respondents classify themselves ethnically. The questions were: (1) What is your nationality? (2) What is your ancestry? (3) Of what descent are you? (4) What is your national origin? (5) To what group do you belong? On the basis of an overall assessment of responses to these questions, respondents were classified. In the case of mixed ancestry, the father's origin was used as the basis for classifying the person as French or non-French. This is in accord with procedure followed in the Canadian census.

In addition to ethnicity, respondents were also classified according to religion, income, length of residence in the community, and contact with mental patients.

Indices for the Survey Data

Three indices were constructed using items on which statistically significant differences were obtained between the Cloverdale and DeLis samples reported previously. These were (1) index of contact, (2) index of general knowledge, and (3) index of specific knowledge.

The "index of contact" was composed of two items: "Have you known anyone who was in a mental hospital?" and "Have you known anyone who was mentally ill?" Both of these were followed by the question, "Was this person an Acquaintance? Friend? or Relative?" For purposes of the index, a person was given a score of zero for the response "no" to each question, a score of 1 for the response "Yes, an acquaintance," a score of 2 for the response "Yes, a friend," and a score of 3 for the response "Yes, a relative." That is, theoretically, scores on the index range from zero (answered "no" to both questions) to 6 (answered "yes, a relative" to both questions). All persons in both samples were scored using this system. Results using this index were similar to those reported in the previous paper. That is, taking the median as a cutting point, a higher proportion of DeLis respondents fell below the median than was the case for respondents from Cloverdale (61 percent vs 40 percent).

As for the "index of general knowledge," respondents were scored by assigning a score of zero to a "don't know" response or to no response at all, and a score of 1 to any other response. That is, once again a person's score on the index could range from zero (answered "don't know," or did not answer to all six items) to 6 (gave the response to each question). Again, after all persons in both samples were scored using the index and broken at the median, the results were as indicated without using such an index. That is, a higher proportion in DeLis scored low in the index than was the case in Cloverdale (61 percent vs 21 percent).

Three items were used in the "index of specific knowledge" ("What psychiatric facilities are available here?" "Is there a clinic in your town?"; and "How are people referred?"). On each item a "knowledgeable" response was scored "one" and an "unknowledgeable" response "zero," giving a range from zero to three on the index. Once again, there was a correspondence between the scores on the index and differences described in the earlier paper. That is, in DeLis a high proportion scored low or were low on knowledge about specific facilities available (92 percent vs 27 percent).

Method and Samples, Epidemiological Survey

Rate of first admission to psychiatric facilities was used as the basic epidemiological index. Inpatient data consisted of the records of all patients from the two towns admitted to provincial psychiatric facilities since 1926. This year was chosen because it marked the opening of the provincial mental hospital in the southern part of the province, i.e. the Saskatchewan Hospital at Weyburn. The towns chosen for the study are in the catchment area for the Saskatchewan Hospital at Weyburn (about 100 miles away) and, as a result, the largest proportion of inpatient admissions are to this hospital.

The inpatient facilities which have handled the remaining cases are the psychiatric wings at the Moose Jaw General Hospital, the Regina General Hospital, and the University Hospital in Saskatoon.

Case finding of inpatients produced a sample of 85 patients from Cloverdale and 69 from DeLis. All 154 files were coded independently by two persons to obtain information about background, symptomatology, diagnosis, and patient careers.

The outpatient data consisted of the records of all persons from the towns admitted to provincial outpatient facilities since 1950. From 1950 to 1954, the psychiatric clinic administered by the Saskatchewan Hospital at Weyburn met monthly in Cloverdale but accepted patients from the entire area, including DeLis. In 1955 the administration of the clinic was taken over by the psychiatric wing of the Moose Jaw Union Hospital, and in 1963 it reverted back to the Saskatchewan Hospital. Since the latter year, the clinic has been staffed by a bilingual psychiatrist, social worker and psychiatric nurse, and has been meeting weekly in Cloverdale and bimonthly in DeLis. In addition to these sources of outpatient data, practicing psychiatrists in the province were contacted, and the records of other provincial outpatient facilities more remote from the towns were examined. However, the majority of cases were found through the study of clinic records kept at the Saskatchewan Hospital and the Moose Jaw Psychiatric Wing.

Samples obtained included 59 cases from Cloverdale and 19 cases from DeLis. As with the inpatient data, files were coded independently by two persons to obtain information about background, symptomatology, diagnosis, and patient careers. For both sets of data, inter-coder reliability was over 90 percent. The data were transferred to IBM cards and analyzed using computer facilities. In the majority of cases, the "χ^2" test was used to assess significance. In the few instances where the number of cases was too small, the Fisher's exact probability test was employed. The .05 probability level was chosen as the criterion for rejection of the null hypothesis.

Results

Each section begins with a statement of results reported in previous studies, followed by results obtained by comparing subsamples within each of the two towns.

Also, to shorten presentation, only statistically significant results are reported.

Attitude Survey

The Cloverdale and DeLis samples were divided according to: (1) Ethnic background (French vs non-French); (2) Religion (French-Catholic vs non-French-Catholic vs non-French Protestant); (3) Income (above and below median income for both towns combined); (4) Length of residence (above and below median for both towns combined, and (5) Contact with persons having mental illness (above and below median for both towns combined).

Previous finding: Respondents from DeLis less frequently reported contact with persons having illness and seemed to be less informed about the nature of mental illness.

Comparison among groups within Cloverdale and DeLis

(1) *By Ethnicity*

(a) French and non-French groups in Cloverdale reported more "above median" contact with mental illness than was the case in DeLis (90 percent vs 44 percent for French and 57 percent vs 34 percent for non-French groups respectively).

(b) Non-French respondents in DeLis had less general knowledge about mental illness than their counterparts in Cloverdale (41 percent vs 81 percent above the median score).

(c) Regarding specific knowledge about mental illness, French respondents in Cloverdale and non-French respondents in DeLis reported less knowledge (40 percent vs 76 percent above median scores for French and non-French in Cloverdale; 3 percent vs 76 percent above median scores for non-French in DeLis and Cloverdale respectively). *Thus, lack of specific knowledge tends to be associated with the minority element in each community; it tends not to be a function of ethnic or community factors as such.*

(d) Non-French respondents in DeLis less frequently gave "qualified" responses when asked whether mental illness is hereditary (12 percent for non-French in DeLis compared with 39 percent for non-French in Cloverdale). In other words, the non-French group in DeLis took a more dogmatic positon with regard to the question. This difference was not obtained for the French groups in the two communities.

On the whole, few differences among ethnic sub-groups in the two communities were obtained. Of those obtained, none was attributable to ethnic (i.e., French vs non-French) factors. Rather, the differences tended to occur for non-French groups in the two towns. Since the label "non-French" incorporates a variety of ethnic labels, it is clear that ethnic factors cannot explain the differences obtained.

(2) *By Religion*

(a) French Catholic respondents in Cloverdale reported fewer contacts with persons having mental illness than their counterparts in DeLis. (No contact reported in 15.2 percent and 5.4 percent respectively.)

(b) Non-French Catholics and non-French Protestants in DeLis have less general knowledge about mental illness than their counterparts in Cloverdale. (High scores were obtained in 43 pecent and 35 percent in DeLis, 89 percent and 80 percent in Cloverdale.)

(c) This difference between towns also holds for non-French Protestants for the index of specific knowledge. (High scores obtained for 34 percent of the sample in Cloverdale and none of the sample in DeLis.)

Again, the pattern of results is distinctly regional, and no differences were found among religious groups in either community.

(3) *By Income*

(Income was found to be significantly lower among DeLis respondents. Consequently, it was considered necessary to compare income groups on attitudes and conceptions of mental illness, to establish whether community differences were attributable to differences in income.)

Seven statistically significant differences were obtained. These differences were distributed as follows:

(a) In Cloverdale, high income respondents gave more qualified answers to the question about the hereditary basis of mental illness (39 percent vs 24 percent). The opposite was true in DeLis (zero vs 33 percent).

(b) In DeLis, high income respondents had more specific knowledge about mental illness than did low income respondents (73 percent vs 27 percent).

(c) Considering low income respondents only, those from DeLis compared with those from Cloverdale had less specifc knowledge (73 percent vs 94 percent), less general knowledge (23 percent vs 71 percent), and less frequently knew whom to go to if someone became disturbed (24 percent vs 37 percent).

(d) Considering high income respondents only, those from DeLis were more certain about the hereditary basis of mental illness than was the case for Cloverdale respondents (100 percent vs 61 percent).

In other words, of the seven differences obtained, three were associated with income differences and the remaining four with regional differences.

(4) *By Length of Residence*

(Length of residence was considered relevant for this analysis since it was presumed to reflect the influences of "local" culture. In other words, if attitudes and conceptions are shaped by local circumstances, then differences in length of residence should be associated with differences in attitudes and conceptions.)

The five statistically significant differences obtained were distributed as follows:

(a) No differences were obtained between short and long term residence groups in either DeLis or Cloverdale.

(b) Considering short-term residents only, Cloverdale respondents indicated more general knowledge about mental illness than was the case for DeLis respondents (78 percent vs 44 percent).

(c) Long-term residents: Cloverdale respondents, compared to DeLis respondents, indicated more contact (62 percent vs 35 percent, more general knowledge (79 percent vs 38 percent), more specific knowledge (39 percent vs 9 percent), and better articulated conceptions about a person in a mental hospital (differences were obtained on several items).

In a sense, these results give partial support to the local culture hypothesis: Although regional influences can be thought of as accounting for the differences between long-term residents in the two towns, one would also have expected differences between long- and short-residence respondents. Such was not the case. One possible explanation is that regional influences shape attitudes and conceptions, but that this shaping occurs within a relatively brief period of time.

(5) *By Contact with Persons Having Mental Illness*

(Contact with mental illness was considered relevant to control for in this analysis, since the previous work had shown that in 1962 fewer patients from DeLis than from Cloverdale were admitted to psychiatric facilities. On the other hand, more patients with psychiatric illness from DeLis than from Cloverdale were admitted to general hospitals. It was inferred from these results that DeLis citizens were prone to deny the occurrence of mental illness, and to treat it more casually by sending the person to a general hospital rather than a psychiatric center. Consequently, DeLis respondents reported less frequent contact.)

The following results were obtained:

(a) There were no statistically significant differences between high and low contact groups, either in DeLis or in Cloverdale.

(b) Considering high contact respondents only, those from Cloverdale had more general knowledge about mental illness than did those from DeLis (67 percent vs 22 percent).

(c) Considering high contact respondents only, those from Cloverdale were more uncertain as to the hereditary basis of mental illness than were respondents from DeLis (48 percent vs 8 percent).

These results suggest that contact per se cannot be considered a significant factor in accounting for differences. The two significant differences described above are considered incidental, and appear to be specifically associated with circumstances in each of the towns.

Epidemiology: Inpatient Data

For the inpatient data, the Cloverdale and DeLis samples were divided according to (1) Ethnicity (French vs non-French), (2) Religion (French-Catholic vs non-French-Catholic vs non-French-Protestant), (3) Social Class (Blishen 1964) (Blishen classes I, II, III vs classes IV, V, vs classes VI, VII), (4) Birthplace (those born outside Canada), and (5) Time Period (1926–1941 vs 1942–1951 vs 1952–1961 vs 1962–1963).

Previous Findings: Since the inception of mental hospital treatment facilities in the region (1926), a higher proportion of inpatients entered from DeLis than from Cloverdale. DeLis patients are more frequently diagnosed as paranoid schizophrenic and alcoholic. Symptoms observed are more frequently described as being "hallucinations" for DeLis patients.

Comparisons among Groups within Cloverdale and DeLis

(1) *By Ethnicity*

Table 12.1 indicates a trend for the minority group in both towns to have a higher incidence of psychiatric disorder. Thus, for Cloverdale the average rate of psychiatric admissions for the French group over all years shown is 1.47 per thousand and for the non-French group 1.09 per thousand.[1] For DeLis, the rate of admission for the non-French

1. When the admission rates are considered for various time periods, the pattern does not appear to be as consistent in Cloverdale as in DeLis. In the latter, the admission rate for the non-French group is consistently higher than for the French group, whereas in Cloverdale this is the case for only two of the four time periods shown (1942–1951, 1962–1963).

It should be realized, of course, that the rates shown in table 12.1 are approximate, since the possibility remains that some cases were missed in the file search, some cases may have been misclassified with respect to ethnic background, and that the approximations of the population size for the various time periods were not accurate. Taking these limitations into account, however, the most plausible interpretation suggested by these results is that minority groups in both towns tend to be more subject to admission to a psychiatric inpatient facility than the majority group. This finding is consistent with those of other investigators (Rose, 1955; Dunham 1961).

Table 12.1 Psychiatric First Admissions to Inpatient Facilities by Ethnic Background (Average rate per 1,000 population)

	Cloverdale						*DeLis*					
	French			*Non-French*			*French*			*Non-French*		
	No. of First Admits	*Av. Pop. Size*	*Av. Rate*	*No. of First Admits*	*Av. Pop. Size*	*Av. Rate*	*No. of First Admits*	*Av. Pop. Size*	*Av. Rate*	*No. of First Admits*	*Av. Pop. Size*	*Av. Rate*
1926–1941	3	98[a]	2.04	15	1,195[a]	0.84	8	832[a]	0.64	16	332[a]	3.31
1942–1951	1	157[b]	0.64	19	1,487[b]	1.28	6	850[b]	0.71	5	314[b]	1.59
1952–1961	3	216[c]	1.39	31	1,942[c]	1.59	17	957[c]	1.78	8	392[c]	2.04
1962–1963	4	355[d]	5.97	4	2,247[d]	0.89	2	1,077[d]	0.93	2	480[d]	2.08
Overall	11	202[e]	1.47	69	1,718[e]	1.09	33	929[e]	0.96	31	380[e]	2.21

[a] Mean of 1941 population figures and 1926 figures as estimated from 1931 census data.
[b] Mean of 1941 and 1951 population figures.
[c] Mean of 1951 and 1961 population figures.
[d] Estimated mean for period based on 1951-1961 growth rates.
[e] Mean of estimated period means.

group is 2.21 per thousand and only .96 per thousand for the French group.

With regard to diagnosis and symptoms, only one statistically significant difference was obtained: Non-French patients from DeLis were more frequently diagnosed as paranoid schizophrenics (91 percent) than were non-French patients from Cloverdale (13 percent). Other differences between and within towns for alcoholism and hallucinations were not statistically significant.

(2) *By Religion*

Comparing the three religious groups in each of the two communities, only one statistically significant result was obtained: Considering only patients who were non-French Protestants, those from DeLis were more frequently diagnosed as paranoid schizophrenic compared with patients from Cloverdale. This single result obtained from 15 comparisons was considered to be of only incidental significance. Religious factors appear not to be associated with incidence of mental illness, as indicated by these results.

(3) *By Social Class*

A comparison of respondents in three social classes in each of the two communities produced two statistically significant results: Compared with middle class patients from Cloverdale, middle class patients from DeLis were more frequently diagnosed as paranoid schizophrenics or as alcoholics. In other words, the regional differences obtained for the towns seemed to concentrate in the middle classes.

(4) *By Place of Birth*

Relating diagnosis and symptomatology to place of birth gave two statistically significant differences:

(a) Within Cloverdale, patients born outside of Canada more frequently were observed as having hallucinations.

(b) For patients born elsewhere in Canada (i.e, other than in DeLis or Cloverdale), patients from DeLis were more frequently diagnosed as paranoid schizophrenics.

These two results were considered of only incidental importance since these were the only two results obtained from a total of 15 comparisons made.

(5) *By Time Period*

When patients were compared in terms of the four time periods, the following results were obtained:

(a) Within the Cloverdale sample there were statistically significant differences among the four time periods in the proportion of patients observed as having hallucinations.

(b) Within the DeLis sample, there were statistically significant differences among the four time periods in the proportion of patients diagnosed as paranoid schizophrenics.

(c) For the earliest time period (1926–41) a higher proportion of DeLis patients (compared with Cloverdale patients) were diagnosed as paranoid schizophrenics.

(d) For the time period 1952–1961, a higher proportion of patients from DeLis (compared with Cloverdale) were diagnosed as alcoholic.

It is difficult to interpret these diverse results in any meaningful way as supporting a theory about cultural factors in the epidemiology of mental illness. According to these results, the frequency with which diagnostic categories occur may be expected to vary with time and place.

Epidemiology: Outpatient Data[2]

Previous Findings: Compared with DeLis, a higher proportion of the Cloverdale population made use of outpatient facilities. A higher proportion of outpatients from DeLis were described as exhibiting hyperactivity, and diagnosed as mental defectives.

As was the case for the inpatient data, in both towns the overall use of outpatient facilities was greater for the minority group (see table 12.2). In Cloverdale, the rate of use for the French group over the period 1950–1964 was 3.84 per thousand compared to 1.41 per thousand for the non-French group; in DeLis the rate for the non-French group was 1.05 per thousand versus 0.89 per thousand for the French. However, only in Cloverdale was this difference consistent over time in that the admission rate for the minority group was higher in all time periods. On the other hand, in DeLis the rates for the French and non-French groups were identical in one time period (1950–1954), slightly higher for the French group in the second period (1955–1962), and higher for the non-French group in the third period (1950–1964). However, it should be remembered that clinic facilities have been less active in DeLis than in Cloverdale so that changes over time in DeLis are less meaningful. The overall conclusion to be drawn from these results is that the use of outpatient psychiatric facilities tends to be associated with minority group status.

Regarding differences in diagnosis and symptomatology, only one statistically significant difference was obtained: Non-French patients from DeLis more frequently were described as being hyperactive when compared with their counterparts from Cloverdale.

2. The outpatient data were not subjected to the same comparisons as were the inpatient, for a number of reasons: (1) Since there were only 19 outpatient cases from DeLis, some of the subgroups were extremely small; (2) Data for outpatient cases were much less complete; (3) Fewer differences between DeLis and Cloverdale out-patients were obtained in the previous research.

Table 12.2 Psychiatric First Admissions to Out-Patient Facilities by Ethnic Background (Average rate per 1,000 populations)

	Cloverdale						*DeLis*					
	French			*Non-French*			*French*			*Non-French*		
	N	*Av. Pop. Size*[a]	*Av. Rate*	*N*	*Av. Pop. Size*[a]	*Av. Rate*	*N*	*Av. Pop. Size*[a]	*Av. Rate*	*N*	*Av. Pop. Size*[a]	*Av. Rate*
1950-1954 (clinic run by Saskatchewan Hospital)	3	237	2.64	2	1,766	0.23	0	886	0.00	0	342	0.00
1955-1962 (clinic run by Moose Jaw Psychiatric Wing)	7	292	3.00	21	2,060	1.27	5	1,003	0.62	2	425	0.59
1963-1964[b] (clinic run by Saskatchewan Hospital)	5	349	9.55	16	2,304	4.63	7	1,099	4.25	4	497	5.37
Overall	15	239[c]	3.84	39	2,043[c]	1.41	12	996[c]	0.89	6	421[c]	1.05

[a] All population figures estimated on the basis of 1951 and 1961 census.
[b] Data complete for only first half of 1964.
[c] Mean of average population sizes for three periods.

Conclusions

The results reported here provide no clear evidence for the importance of ethnic factors in the expression of mental illness or in community attitudes and conceptions about mental illness. That is to say, there were no results specifically associated with French patients and respondents in both towns and which were different than non-French patients and respondents. Thus traditional culture per se does not appear to be a direct factor in accounting for differences among communities in incidence and in knowledge about mental illness.[3]

Some differences between non-French groups in the two communities were obtained which, in a sense, can be thought of as indirect evidence for ethnic influences. However, the ethnic label "non-French" constitutes a heterogeneous grouping of patients and respondents with only one common feature: Practically all members of this particular "non-French" category speak the English language. This definition, which is basically a negative one, provides no basis upon which to develop an explanation of community attitudes as related to ethnic variables.

The one distinctive pattern which emerges from these results is the "minority group" pattern: Minority groups in both communities tended to have a higher incidence of mental illness, and the non-French minority in the French community tended to be the most uninformed in its attitudes and conceptions about mental illness. Again, this pattern can be thought of as an indirect ethnic influence, or as implying ethnic causation in reverse.

On the whole, the results obtained are most consistent with a "local culture" interpretation of community differences. Thus, most of the results described above involved regional differences between sub-samples in the two towns. In other words, most of the statistically significant differences were obtained for subgroup comparisons between towns, rather than within towns. The implication

3. It should be pointed out that a methodological problem is created by the use of subsamples of the original study samples, as was done in this study. The problem is that the reduction of sample sizes increases the standard error term for testing statistical significance of differences in proportions. This factor reduces the likelihood of obtaining statistically significant differences, including differences between ethnic subsamples. In defense of this procedure, however, it should be pointed out that this small sample bias applies equally to comparisons between regional subsamples. In other words, the conclusions are unaffected by the small subsamples, since there were more statistically significant regional differences than ethnic differences.

here is that the way in which a community defines and reacts to mental illness is determined by a particular set of local historical circumstances, and that these circumstances influence most people to think and act in the same way.

As a concluding note, the reader should be reminded that advocates of the ethnic hypothesis might be inclined to doubt the wisdom of selecting DeLis as a study population for this research. As indicated in the introduction, the town shows evidence of acculturation in spite of its "French" cultural emphasis. For this reason, the survey has been repeated in a less acculturated community situated in the province of Quebec. The results of this survey will be reported elsewhere.

Acknowledgment

The authors gratefully acknowledge the contributions of the following research assistants: Rosemary Duckworth, R.N.; Joanne Ball, Mary McCaron, and G. McEachern, R.P.N. Thanks are also due to the Psychiatric Services Personnel of the following institutions which made their files available to us: Psychiatric Wing, Moose Jaw Union Hospital; Munroe Wing, Regina General Hospital; Psychiatric Wing, University Hospital, Saskatoon: and the MacNeill Clinic, Saskatoon.

The project was supported by Canadian National Health Grant number 607–7–67.

Annotated Additional Readings

a) **Birtchnell, J. 1971.** Social class, parental social class, and social mobility in psychiatric patients and general population controls. *Psychological Medicine* 1:209–221.
A carefully designed study of parental social class, current social class, and social mobility evaluated in a large sample of male referrals to psychiatric services and in a sample of men randomly selected from the general population in northeastern Scotland. The author found that most psychiatric patients, especially the psychotics, were, relative to the general population, downwardly mobile in social class. The social mobility of the neurotic patients seemed to correspond with that of the general population. This paper complements article 10.

b) **Dunham, H.W. 1969.** City core and suburban fringe: Distribution patterns of mental illness. In S. C. Plog, and R. B. Edgerton, eds. *Changing Perspectives in Mental Illness*. New York. Holt, Rinehart and Winston.
A classical review of the issues of differential urban distribution of mental illness and the city core causality of psychopathology. The author examines the changes that took place in U.S. cities over a 30 year period and the associated changes in urban patterns of mental illness. He presents information showing that a high schizophrenic rate in a subcommunity of the city developed over the study period. He concludes that the mobility of the schizophrenics themselves was the main factor accounting for the particular distribution of schizophrenia cases in the community.

c) **Uhlenhut, E. H., R. S. Lipman, M. B. Balter, and M. Stern. 1974.** Symptom intensity and life stress in the city. *Archives of General Psychiatry* 31:759–764.
The study of the relationships between psychopathology and basic demographic variables such as age, sex, marital status, social class, and ethnic grouping are among the basic foci of social and cultural psychiatry. On the other hand, the association between stressful life events and psychiatric symptomatology has been widely studied during the past decade and a half, and has become one of the most documented and heuristic items in psychiatric epidemiology.

This article surveys a community, investigating the relationships between symptomatology and a number of demographic variables and the intermediary role played by stressful life events. The sound sampling technique used and the sophisticated multivariate statistical methodology employed are this intriguing study's conspicuous strengths.

d) **Warheit, G. J., C. E. Holzer III, and S. A. Arey. 1975.** Race and mental illness: An epidemiologic update. *Journal of Health and Social Behavior* 16:243–256.
Evidence is presented on the relationship between race (black vs white) and

mental illness from a large epidemiologic study in the southeastern United States. Blacks had higher mean scores than whites in all 5 scales used to assess mental illness. However, when controlled for age, sex, and socioeconomic status in multiple regression analyses, the variable race was statistically significant in only two of the equations predicting psychopathology. Socioeconomic status appeared to be consistently the strongest correlate of mental illness.

e) **Heiman, E. M., and M. W. Kahn. 1977.** Mexican American and European American psychopathology and hospital course. *Archives of General Psychiatry* 34:167–170.
An examination of the symptomatology and hospital course of all Mexican-American and European-American patients admitted over a 3-month period to the inpatient component of a mental health center in the U.S. Southwest. In line with previous investigations, this study found that Mexican-American inpatients exhibited more disturbed and bizarre behavior than their European-American counterparts. However, these differences were considerably reduced when controls for sex and social class were imposed. This study, which used analysis of variance for determining the influence on gross psychopathology of demographic variables, individually and in combination, shows the importance of taking into consideration the interactions among such sociocultural variables.

f) **Fabrega, H. Jr., J. D. Swartz, and C. A. Wallace. 1968.** Ethnic differences in psychopathology. I. Clinical correlates under varying conditions. *Archives of General Psychiatry* 19:218–226.
A study carefully designed to compare the psychopathological manifestations of three groups of schizophrenic patients hospitalized in state institutions in Texas: Anglo, Negro, and Mexican-American. Comparisons were carried out under three different conditions: (1) random, (2) with social class held constant, and (3) when individuals of the groups were matched on age, sex, estimated IQ, number of previous psychiatric hospitalizations, and years of education. The extent of significant differences between groups decreased as the analysis moved from conditions 1 through 3. However, even under condition 3, involving extensive matching, important differences were noted, especially when the Mexican Americans were compared either to the Anglo or to the Negro Americans. This paper, along with the Heiman and Kahn's study, emphasizes the importance of controlling for demographic variables in cross-ethnic research.

g) **Ablon, J. 1973.** Reactions of Samoan burn patients and families to severe burns. *Social Science and Medicine* 7:167–178.
Differential responses to stress and coping resources were found between members of different ethnic groups. Ablon vividly describes reactions to both severe burns and death of loved ones in a Samoan community trapped in a fire in the San Francisco area. These reactions were characterized by striking stoicism and cooperation with health personnel, which markedly differed from reactions to similar disasters reported for other groups in the United States.

Furthermore, few emotional disorders seemed to have derived from the disaster among the Samoan survivors. The author discusses specific Samoan cultural patterns which appeared to have underlaid the described responses to stress.

h) Srole, L., and T. S. Langner. 1969. Protestant, Catholic and Jew: Comparative psychopathology. In S. C. Plog, and R. B. Edgerton, eds. *Changing Perspectives in Mental Illness.* New York: Holt, Rinehart and Winston.
A report from the Midtown Manhattan Study, which attempted to determine the prevalence of mental illness among people living in a large and heavily populated urban area. The report particularly compares the degree of psychological impairment noted among members of three religious groups. Using parental religion as criterion, Jews showed less psychopathology than either Protestants or Catholics. These differences seemed to remain after controlling for socioeconomic status. Degrees of parental religiosity and religious mobility in relationship to degree of psychopathology were also explored.

i) Katchadourian, H. 1974. A comparative study of mental illness among the Christians and Moslems of Lebanon. *The International Journal of Social Psychiatry.* 20:56–67.
The author reports here on the rates and diagnostic distribution of mental illness among the two major religious populations of Lebanon. The study focuses on treated psychiatric patients as reported by their attending psychiatrists and therefore its reflection of differential rates of psychopathology is likely to be tainted by differential availability of services for the two religious populations involved. In any case, the mental illness rates obtained are informative and their breakdown by diagnostic category, sex, and treatment setting are especially interesting.

V

Sociocultural Change

After examining such sociocultural structures as social class and ethnic groupings, we turn now to various forms of sociocultural change.

The relevance of sociocultural change to psychopathology is denoted by the widely accepted influence of life stressors on mental disorders. This is reflected in the inclusion of psychosocial stressors as one of the axes of DSM-III, the new U.S. psychiatric diagnostic system (American Psychiatric Association 1980). DSM-III further considers that the judgment of stress severity should take into account the amount of change in the individual's life caused by the stressor.

Migration is a form of sociocultural change of great interest, whether it is international or intranational, as it frequently involves adjustments to the loss of roots and of a social network, stresses related to the relocation process, and the challenge of facing a new culture. Article 13 reviews the evidence about the relationship between various aspects of immigration and psychopathology, and an annotated reference formulates four migratory theories and evaluates them empirically, while another deals with psychiatric morbidity among refugees.

Given the clinical importance of social class, it is not surprising that interest has been raised by social mobility as another form of sociocultural change. Article 14 reviews the literature regarding the connections between social mobility and psychiatric disorder, and an annotated reference involves a longitudinal study examining various forms of social mobility and their relations to psychopathology.

The challenges to the cultural identity and mental health of individuals and groups posed by a new culture are discussed in article 15, while an annotated reference analyzes the impact of "modernization" and the introduction of a new culture on the traditional way of life and the personality development of the youth of subarctic Canadian Indians.

13

Immigration and Mental Disease

P. W. Burvill

Immigration and its potential impact on mental health has long been an intriguing topic. The importance of this issue is growing, along with the increasing development and availability of more efficient transportation systems across the world. Enhancing the interest and complexity of the issue is the plurality of factors involved in the process of migration. Each is interesting in its own right: e.g., loss of roots and of the social network available in the place of prior residence, social isolation in the new place of residence, the acculturation challenge.

Burvill presents a documented review of the relationship between immigration and psychopathology. He emphasizes the need to control for age, social class, and other demographic data, and points out the differential effects of time or number of generations since the initial migration, and discusses intranational vs international migration, and the particular case of the refugees. He also indicates the usefulness of looking at the rates of specific psychiatric disorders vs. psychopathology in general, a degree of sophistication which is only recently becoming feasible, owing to the development of more reliable instruments for psychiatric evaluation and diagnosis.

IN THE introductory remarks of the U.S. 1880 census, it was stated that "the extraordinary ratio of insanity among the foreign born has attracted wide attention" (Locke et al., 1960). Before the 1930s papers were regularly published indicating that the immigrant sections of the United States and Canadian populations had proportionately two to three times more patients in mental hospitals than the native-born sections (Murphy 1961). This was before due attention was paid to standardization of rates for age and other factors.

Malzberg and Lee (1956), in reviewing the literature on the relationship of immigration and mental disorder, including their own studies, concluded that most differences associated with migration "have been based on scanty or otherwise inadequate data, and even the fact of high incidence of mental illness among migrants is not firmly established, much less the theories as to cause."

The classic paper of Odegaard (1932) showed that the incidence of mental disorder as measured by admissions to mental hospitals was higher among the Norwegian-born in Minnesota than among the native born in that state, and also was higher than the hospitalization rates in Norway. Malzberg (1940), in his study of first admissions to all institutions for mental disease in New York State, 1929–31, reported "that the foreign-born had a higher rate of first admissions that the native-born," a finding which he greatly modified in later studies.

In a study of all 1939–1941 age-standardized first admissions to all psychiatric institutions, including private, in New York State, Malzberg and Lee (1956) found: (a) migration from overseas was associated with almost no excess of mental hospitalization over the native-born; (b) migration from other states of the United States into New York was accompanied by a marked excess of mental hospitalization as compared with those born in the state; (c) the incidence of such hospitalization was higher in those migrants who were outside of New York State five years previously than those who were within the state at the time, an exceptional proportion of the former appearing to have been admitted within a year of their arrival. E. S. Lee (1957) came to the same conclusion analyzing first admissions in New York State for 1949-1951. Lee (1963), utilizing once again the first admissions to New York State hospitals for 1949–1951, introduced controls, not only for sex and age, but also for education, occupation and marital status. His conclusions were the same as his 1957 paper, namely that the rates for those migrating between states were considerably higher than for nonmigrants, and that rates for foreign-born whites were intermediate between rates for the two groups of native-born. A similar finding was reported by Locke et al. (1960) for all first admissions to Ohio Public Mental Hospitals for a 4½-year period from 1948–1952. Malzberg (1964) reported a higher rate of hospitalization among the foreign-born in Canada for 1950–1952 than among the native-born. However, when factors such as differences in age distribution and the density of population were considered, the rate for the foreign-born proved to be in excess by only 4 percent and was not statistically significant.

Reports of immigrants having *less* mental hospitalization than natives have come from Israel (Sunier 1956) and Singapore (H. B. M. Murphy 1961). However, the Israeli data were crude, not being standardized for age or anything else. In the Singapore study the native rates exceeded immigrant rates for most ages, but conclusions drawn must be somewhat limited by the fact that population estimates rather than census figures had been used.

Krupinski and Stoller (1965) analyzed all first admissions for 1962 to Victorian State Mental Institutions and outpatient clinics, specific for diagnosis, standardizing for age, and dividing all their immigrant patients into four broad groups according to their country of birth, namely, those from Britain (including Eire), West Europe, Eastern Europe and Southern Europe. They did not find any difference in the overall rate of immigrant breakdowns as compared with the Australian born. This result was similar to that of the Commonwealth Immigration Advisory Council (1961), although the latter body was concerned only with migrants who had been in Australia less than five years—an arbitrary definition of a migrant which was criticized by Krupinski and Stoller (1962). However, Krupinski and Stoller demonstrated a higher incidence of certain categories of mental illness among particular migrant groups, confirming most of the original trends described by Cade and Krupinski (1962) based on admissions to only one psychiatric hospital.

J. Kraus (1969 a, b) found differentially high rates of certain psychiatric illness among particular migrant groups admitted to New South Wales hospitals in 1967. It is not clear from the papers whether the quoted rates were standardized for age. This study has been criticized by Stoller and Krupinski (1969) on important methodological issues, including the fact that Kraus was unfortunately not able to use the generally accepted epidemiological procedure of using first admissions only, and assumed a constant relationship between first admissions and readmissions in all the groups studied. Victorian data has shown, however, that the relationship is different for specific groups of origin, and that rates of first admissions do not necessarily correspond to those of all admissions (Krupinski and Stoller 1965). As such, it is difficult to know what significance to place upon his results.

Some studies of mental health in the community, as opposed to studies based on mental hospital admissions, have specified findings among immigrants. Neither psychoneuroses in adults nor behavior disorders in adolescents were present to a significantly higher degree in the foreign-born than in the Australian-born in Heyfield (Krupinski et al. 1970). Srole et al. (1962) using the figures from Hollingshead and Redlich's (1958) New Haven Study, after making certain necessary adjustments for age differences, found no significant differences between the rates of mental illness in the foreign-born and the native-born. In the Midtown Manhattan Study (Srole et al. 1962) the authors investigated many hypotheses regarding mental health differentials among immigrants. These included whether there were any differences: (a) between first, second, third and fourth generation immigrants, and (b) between immigrants who arrived in America in their childhood, in their youth, or at an older age (hence having different degrees of self-determination in the initial move to migrate).

With one exception, they showed that there was no convincing evidence that immigrants had more mental ill health than the native-born. However they tended to qualify their conclusions with such statements as "however, reanalysis of the data in the light of the overlooked complexities suggested that (a) at the very least, the data do not warrant rejection of the chapter's major hypotheses; and (b) with considerable probability the data seem to support these hypotheses." The one exception was the detection of much more psychiatric illness in immigrants from a rural lower socioeconomic origin than among immigrants from an urban middle socioeconomic origin and among the native-born. Before accepting the conclusions of this study, one should first consider the implications of the devastating criticisms of the whole Midtown Manhattan Study by Gruenberg (1963).

Refugees

There is a basic difference between an immigrant and a refugee. The first has a free choice, which means many possibilities of motivation; the refugee has no choice (Eitinger 1958). Many studies throughout the world have demonstrated high rates of psychiatric illness among refugees and concentration camp survivors—Krupinski et al. (1973) list 28 relevant references. The age standardized incidence of schizophrenia in patients of the Victorian Mental Health Department over the years 1961–68 has been five times as great in Eastern European immigrants (many of whom would have been refugees) than amongst Australian-born and British, and twice as high as that for the Southern and Western European immigrants. However the authors attributed the high rate among Eastern Europeans to their more severe war experiences, not specifically mentioning the word refugee. Eitinger (1960 a, b) discussed in detail the psychodynamics of mental disease in refugees generally, and the symptomatology of such in refugees in Norway.

The Hungarian uprising of 1956 provided a unique opportunity to study refugees who were *suddenly* moved from one environment to another. Of 82 consecutive Hungarian refugees referred to the Maudsley Hospital for psychiatric disorders, Mezey (1960 a, b) found 50 percent suffered from a personality and neurotic disorder, 28 percent from an affective disorder, 17 percent from a schizophrenic disorder and 5 percent from an organic disorder. Mezey stated that, except in affective disorders, it was difficult to ascribe etiological importance to the stresses of immigration, as opposed to preexisting maladaption, in the causation of psychiatric disorder.

Krupinski et al. (1973), in an intensive survey of a sample of Eastern European refugees who had arrived in Australia prior to 1955, showed that they were not a homogeneous group either in terms of their past war experiences or psychiatric illness among two groups, the Jews and the Poles, Russians and Ukrainians, were proportionate to the severity of their war experiences. The Jewish refugees, possibly because of genocidal selection during the war and further selection on migration, had the lowest rate of schizophrenia of all refugees, though the rate was still several times higher than that of the Australian population. Most of the Jews had neurotic symptoms. A third refugee group, from the Baltic countries, Czechoslovakia, Hungary, and Yugoslavia (predominately Croatia) had suffered least from Nazi persecutions and had left their countries before the Communist takeover. Their high rate of psychiatric disturbances was considered to be related not to their war experiences, but to be associated rather with the loss of social status and the stresses of migration.

Internal Migration

Evidence of possible relationships between internal migration and mental disorder does exist, but it is mixed and inconclusive with the weight in favor of migrants having raised rates of mental hospitalization, but with no indication whether this would derive from self-selection or from the social change which is presumed to be experienced (Murphy 1961). The best known study on this subject is that of Malzberg and Lee (1956), analyzing age standardized first admissions into all New York mental hospitals for 1939–41. They showed that migration from other states of the United States into New York State was accompanied by an excess of mental hospitalization as compared with those born in the state, this applying to both sexes, urban and rural dwellers, and to both whites and Negroes. Similar conclusions were made by Lee (1963), for New York State first admissions during 1949–1951, by Malzberg (1967) with similar admissions for 1960–61, and by Lazarus et al. (1963) for first admissions to mental hospitals in New York State, Ohio and California in 1950. Lazarus et al. (1963) found that in contrast to the varying patterns of foreign born/native differentials, the differentials were all wider for the in-state/out-of-state comparisons.

Findings in the *opposite* direction have been reported by Odegaard (1945), Astrup and Odegaard (1960) and by Jaco (1954). Jaco's results did not refer to total mental hospitalization and have been severely criticized on methodological grounds by Murphy (1961) and Malzberg (1967). Odegaard (1945), in a study covering all first admissions to mental hospitals in Norway for 1926–35, showed that Norwegians migrating within Norway had lower admission rates than those who remained resident in their district of birth, the only exception being those who migrated into Oslo. Astrup and Odegaard (1960) reported similar conclusions utilizing first admission mental hospitalizations for two 15-year periods, 1916–30 and 1931–45. By contrast, the admission rate was higher among foreign-born inhabitants of Norway despite the fact that 60 percent of them had migrated from the neighboring country of Sweden, which has a language and culture not dissimilar to Norway. However, Astrup and Odegaard considered their results to be in line with those of Malzberg and Lee (1956) "for the migration to Oslo is the only type within Norway comparable to the migration to New York." Migration to a metropolitan area of the main city of a country may have a different sigificance for mental health from migration elsewhere (Murphy 1961).

A number of mental health surveys have dealt with, or mentioned, internal migration. Tietze et al. (1942), in their Baltimore Study, concluded that there was an inverse relationship between the prevalence of mental health problems and the duration of residence in their house, but no such relationship with the length of residence in the city. They felt that the reason for their findings probably lay somewhere between the two extremes: (a) the mobile families were on the move for reasons not associated with their mental make-up, and their adjustment difficulties and personality disorders of every kind were the result of moving around; and (b) families with a tendency to mental deviation may not adjust well wherever they find themselves and hence change their residence more often than do more stable people. However, Thomas (1956) pointed out that the method of conducting the survey was probably such as to exclude from final consideration the most mobile section of the population. Bremer (1951), in his Northern Norwegian Community Study, showed that migrants had a significantly higher rate of mental abnormality than those normally resident there, but pointed out that his immigrant group was an exceptionally selected one.

Martin et al. (1957), in their investigation of the incidence of mental disturbance in a new housing estate outside London, found the new estate dwellers to be less mentally healthy than they had anticipated. Symptoms were present more frequently in the more recently migrated than in the longer settled. Contrasting results were obtained in other new-town studies, Wilner et al. (1960) in Baltimore, Taylor and Chave (1964) in Harlow New Town, and Hare and Shaw (1965), which all set out to compare the physical and mental health of people in a new town or a new housing estate with that of a comparable population in an older urban area. They all reached the conclusion that there was no difference between the two populations in the prevalence of neurotic ill-health. After considering the various implications of these findings, Hare (1966) concluded that the special conditions of the new towns or the strain of moving there did not influence neurotic ill-health. Hall (1966) in a Sheffield study was unable to demonstrate the precipitation of psychiatric illness by moving from house to house in previously well adjusted personalities.

Noreich (1965) reviewed the literature on vagabonds and wanderers. In a study of Norwegian vagabonds, who constituted a small and diminishing part of the population, he showed higher frequency of psychosis among the males than would be expected.

Types of Mental Breakdown

Many studies based on first admissions to mental hospitals have analysed their results globally as mental disorder without specification to diagnostic category. The mental hospital admission rates for schizophrenic disorders have been recorded as being very considerably higher in immigrants than in the native population (Odegaard 1932; Murphy 1955; Malzberg and Lee 1956; Krupinski and Stoller 1965). A more discreetly raised admission rate for immigrants has been reported for depression (Roberts and Myers 1954; Murphy 1955), for organic disorders (Odegaard 1932; Roberts and Myers 1954) and for neurotic illness (Roberts and Myers 1954). Murphy (1961) listed the following psychiatric disorders which have been ascribed as being associated with 'social change'—mild depression, schizophrenia, arteriosclerotic psychosis, paranoid tendencies, epidemic hysteria and acute confusional states, although he pointed out that the latter two were relatively rare. Krupinski and Stoller (1965) found that in Victoria mental retardation and senile brain disorders occurred less frequently in immigrants than in the Australian-born population; that alcoholism did not appear to depend upon immigration, although there were marked differentials in the amount of alcoholism between various broad migratory groups; that there was a high incidence among immigrants of schizophrenia, especially among the Eastern Europeans, who have had the greatest degree of exposure to severe war experiences; that depressive states were more common in immigrants, especially among the British and Eastern European populations; and among all immigrant adolescents, except those from Southern Europe, a high incidence of personality disorders was beginning to show up.

The relative absence of reporting of a high incidence of neurotic and personality disorders among immigrants has possibly been due to the fact that most studies related to first admissions to mental hospitals, which would have an excess of psychotic disorders among their admissions. A relatively high rate of neurotic and psychotic reactions has been found among immigrants into Israel from Asia, and of personality disorders among male immigrants from North Africa, but most immigrants to the State of Israel were refugees (Halevi 1963; Maoz et al. 1966). Finlay-Jones and Burvill, as part of a wider study, are currently estimating the prevalence of minor psychiatric morbidity among immigrants, both at the general practitioner level and among those living in private residences in the Perth community. A disporportionately high suicide rate among refugees has been repeatedly observed (Ruesch et al. 1948; Murphy 1955; Pfister-Amende 1955) and among immigrants in America (Dublin 1963) and in Australia (Whitlock 1971; Burvill et al. 1972). However, Straus and Straus (1953) in Ceylon and Murphy (1954) in Singapore found differential suicide rates for the various ethnic groups in the mixed populations in these areas. There is conflicting evidence regarding the incidence of attempted suicide in immigrants in Australia. Krupinski et al (1967) found a higher incidence of suicide attempts in Victoria among non-British female immigrants than among the British and Australian-born. Edwards and Whitlock (1968), based on their own work in Brisbane, and citing work done in Melbourne and Tasmania, concluded that immigration was not a significant cause of attempted suicide. Ewing et al. (1971) found a much higher incidence of attempted suicide in Perth among immigrants than in the Australian-born.

The Effect of Time

The assumption that the longer migrants live in a given area, the better the resulting adaptation, and consequently the lower the incidence of mental disease would become (Malzberg, 1967), has been supported with respect to immigrants in Canada (Malzberg, 1964) and to internal migrants in New York State (Malzberg and Lee, 1956), these all being based on first admissions to mental hospitals. Burvill et al (1972) found increased standardized suicide rates with increasing periods of residence in Australia among all immigrants, undifferentiated by actual country of birth. However, suicide may come at the end of mental illness which has been present for longer periods than that among first admissions to hospital. Burvill et al. (1973) have found that, among immigrants to Australia from Britain, those who suicided within the first seven years of arrival adopted methods more akin to those prevailing in Britain than in Australia, but that those who had been resident in Australia for longer periods used methods more like those of the Australian-born. It was suggested that the latter was a possible index of assimilation into the Australian culture.

Odegaard (1932) concluded that the power of resistance to the strain of immigrant life was weaker in the female sex, at least in regard to the development of mental diseases, this being most marked during the early period of immigration, during which adaptation was probably more difficult for women than for men. By contrast, Malzberg and Lee (1956) postulated that whereas the initial ability to bear the early stresses of migration was about the same for both sexes, adjustment to the environment could, in the long run, be more difficult for females. Krupinski et al. (1965) found the peak incidence of admission for female immigrants to be after seven to fifteen years of residence in Australia, in contrast to one to two years for males. They considered one factor in the late onset of mental illness in the females was the termination of the mother's formal role in the family when the offspring had become adult, independent and assimilated. This was especially so in the female non-British migrants, a high proportion of whom did not speak English even after several years of residency in Australia, so that eventually the mother became the only non-assimilated person in the family, with resulting isolation and diminution of her role as mother and wife.

Schaechter (1965), in a study of female migrants, found that the shorter the time interval between arrival in Australia and admission to a pyschiatric hospital, the higher the percentage of patients with previous psychiatric histories. Krupinski et al. (1965) attributed the early breakdown of male immigrants to premigration mental disorder or instability, although Krupinski and Stoller (1966) pointed out that the influence of stresses of migration could not be absolutely disregarded.

In summary, it would appear that the relationship between the development of mental illness and the time of immigration is determined by several factors: the presence or absence of premigration mental illness or severe personality disturbance; the sex of the individual; the degree to which environmental circumstances in the new country are a major contributing factor; and, in the case of immigrants from countries speaking a language different from that of the host country, the ability to learn the new language together with the amount of family support available.

Nature–Nurture as an Aetiological Determinant

Evidence of whether differential rates of mental illness in immigrants compared with native-born derives from self-selection, or from the social and personal stress which is presumed to occur with immigration, is mixed and inconclusive. The above-mentioned studies of the effect of time on the mental breakdown of immigrants provide evidence of both self-selection and social stress as contributing factors. Parker et al. (1969), in a detailed examination of the utility of the "cultural shock" concept and several alternative social-psychological factors in explaining variations in rates of mental illness among different migratory status groups, found little evidence for "cultural shock" as an explanatory model. Astrup and Odegaard (1960) stated that it was their impression that social and personal stress did not tend to be specific for migrant or non-migrant situations, but was more likely to be related to prior life experience which was a specific problem for *particular* persons. It depended upon the individual nature–nurture situation of each human being, whether he was vulnerable or resistant towards migrant or nonmigrant stress, or to neither of them, or possibly to both. In this state of flux, the authors considered that statistical studies can, under favorable circumstances, contribute by exploring and mapping out the currents along which the individuals are most likely to navigate or drift.

Odegaard (1932) found a higher degree of psychotic illness among Norwegian immigrants in Minnesota which he felt was not due to any difference in stock or race, but must be traced back to the fact that they were immigrants rather than that they were Norwegians. However, he felt that it was likely that people predisposed to become schizophrenics immigrated more readily than those likely to develop manic-depressive psychosis. The evidence showed that in many cases the patient, at the time of immigration, was not only schizoid but actually presented a schizophrenic psychosis. Similarly, Mezey (1960), in his study of Hungarian refugees into Britain following the Hungarian uprising in 1956, concluded that in those who developed a psychiatric illness in Britain, their maladaption had been a major reason for leaving Hungary, and that in the two-year period covered by the investigation stresses of immigration did not play an important causal role in schizophrenic illnesses, but did in the affective disorders.

The existence of an inverse relationship between psychiatric admission rates and the size of immigrant groups has been recognised (Leading Article 1967), and demonstrated for the immigrant population in New South Wales for mental hospital admission rates (Kraus 1969a, b). These and other findings (Malzberg 1964; Murphy 1965) are in line with the hypothesis that the larger the immigrant group the more likely it is to provide its nationals with a supportive, and hence psychologically prophylactic, sociocultural milieu (Kraus 1969b). Where Chinese lived in relatively large numbers on the Pacific coast in British Columbia, they had a low incidence of mental disorder, whereas the incidence was higher in Ontario where the Chinese were few and scattered (Murphy 1965). A similar situation was outlined in Malzberg's (1964) study where the French formed the majority in the Province of Quebec, but a minority in Ontario.

A recent conference on mental health in foreign workers (Verhaegen 1972) reported several investigations which revealed a sense of isolation among the immigrants. The reasons varied between homesickness, strange customs and diet, and lack of religious support. However, the most important factor seemed to be unwelcoming and irresponsible behavior on the part of the host country, which increased the sense of insecurity of the immigrants and forced them to remain in small groups of their own.

Considerations of Methodology

Good detailed accounts of methodology used in the study of migration and mental illness are to be found in publications by Malzberg and Lee (1956), Lazarus et al. (1963), Thomas and Locke (1963), Lee (1963), and Parker et al. (1969) and of internal migration by Malzberg (1967). Traditionally, first admissions to mental hospitals have been used in the statistical analysis of the relationship between immigration and mental illness. Although this usage is far from ideal it is generally conceded that it is by far the *best available* methodology for the usage of mental hospital statistics for this purpose. Srole et al. (1962) are of the opinion that the *best available* does not necessarily imply *good enough* for the kinds of generalizations drawn from them. Malzberg and Lee (1956) discuss in detail certain qualifications concerning the finding of first admissions being higher for migrants than non-migrants, based on the situation in New York State. Studies of the mental health of immigrants are required which are based on criteria other than hospital admissions—e.g., studies at general practice level and as part of community surveys. Mental hospital admission and psychiatric outpatient attendence studies pose numerous difficulties regarding their relevance, including whether to use first admissions or all admissions, whether it is a real first admission as opposed to merely a first admission to that particular psychiatric service, and whether mental hospitalization admissions and outpatient attendances are used differently by immigrants of different countries of origin and of different socioeconomic status to that of the host country. Furthermore, mental hospital admissions, and to a lesser extent psychiatric outpatient attendances, tend to be disproportionately weighted towards major psychiatric disturbance rather than to neurotic/personality disorder which forms the vast bulk of all psychiatric illness. It is of interest to note that in Victoria a study has been conducted comparing immigrant patients seen in one of the Victorian Mental Health Authority hospitals, with a sample of those admitted to the casualty of a general hospital (Krupinski 1973).

It is now axiomatic that all rates quoted in studies of immigrants versus non-immigrants must be age-standardized. Lazarus et al. (1963) and Lee (1963) have discussed some of the statistical problems encountered in these standarization techniques. As well as immigrants differing from the native-born with respect to age, it has long been known that they also differ with respect to average social class, predominant type of residential milieu, years of schooling, ratio of single to married, all of which have been shown to be associated with mental hospitalization rates (Murphy 1961). In consequence, the possibility exists that if these factors were to be controlled, the immigrant/native difference in mental hospitalization rates would disappear completely. Such a disappearance has not yet convincingly been demonstrated, but Murphy (1961) quoted two papers which have pointed in the expected direction (Malzberg 1955; Clark 1948). Parker et al. (1969) documented evidence suggesting the importance of incorporating social psychological variables into the design of studies of social factors in mental illness. They considered that such global variables as "migration" and "social status" might be too varied in their situational context and effects to order data on mental illness and other forms of deviant behavior. Similarly, Murphy has pointed out that maybe the most useful result of the work of Malzberg and Lee (1956) has been to lead us to question the validity of using migration as a single concept in sociopsychiatric studies.

Practically all studies of immigration and mental illness have been of first generation immigrants; Srole et al. (1962) detailed theoretical arguments to support their hypothesis that from first generation to fourth generation immigrants there would be diminishing frequencies of mental pathology. Their results showed the opposite, viz., that any differences between the four generations disappeared almost completely when age and parental socioeconomic status were standardized. From clinical experience it might be expected that the second generation immigrants from non-English speaking parents, especially Italians and Greeks, might have a higher rate of psychiatric morbidity than the first generation, being caught between the conflicting set of values and behavior patterns of their parents and those of their peers. This would be expected to have disappeared by the third generation.

There appears to be a dearth of such studies apart from the Midtown Manhattan Survey. Unfortunately the latter did not classify the four generations specific for country of origin.

Thomas (1956), in a critical review of the concept of migration and mental disease, says "migrants variously defined do indeed differ from nonmigrants, also variously defined, in respect to the incidence of mental disease, and the weight of evidence favors an interpretation that migrants represent greater risks than nonmigrants. But many exceptions have been noted, many ingenious attempts have been made to explain it away. Closer examination of both generalizations and exceptions show so many inconsistencies in definitions, so few adequate bases of control, so many intervening variables, so little comparability to time and place, that the fundamental cause of the discrepancies may well be merely a nonadditive nature of the findings of the different studies."

14

Social Mobility and Psychiatric Disorder: A Re-evaluation and Interpretation

Robert J. Kleiner and
Odd Stefan Dalgard

The relationship of social class with mental illness (especially with such disorders as schizophrenia) has been well documented for some time. However, there are a number of issues pending clarification such as the causal direction of the relationship (although bidirectionality is plausible) as well as the underlying factors and intermediate processes.

Kleiner and Dalgard review the evidence supporting the proposition that upward and/or downward social mobility are correlated with psychopathology, which is relevant to the clarification of the casual directionality mentioned above. The authors also consider the importance of the initial status of the individual. Finally, they review the concept of "anomie," defined by Merton (1957) as disjunction between means-ends relations in society, and examine its linkage to social mobility.

IN EPIDEMIOLOGIC studies of mental illness or psychiatric disorders, social psychiatric and social scientific research has been concerned with the relationship of rates of these disorders to various demographic and social structural variables, for example, age, sex, social status, marital status, or migration. Each of these variables constitutes a classification system with its categories usually having no implicit or explicit etiologic connection with mental illness.

One need only enumerate the categories within each variable to become aware of this point. For example, with age, we speak simply of the number of years that one has lived; with sex, we speak of men and women; with social status, we refer to the number of years of education or the type of work one does; or with migration, one usually talks of a person being born in one part of the world or country and subsequently moving to another, or having been born in a particular place and remaining there. There is nothing in these categories to suggest why mental illness rates should be low, medium, or high. Yet, these variables are constantly the object of study for the epidemiologist and are always invoked to explain the differential distribution of mental illness in a given population.

The explanations of "why," the correlations between these variables and rates of illness, derive from the particular theoretic assumptions the investigator makes about what these categories or classes mean to him. Usually, these assumptions are not tested empirically and depend for their acceptance on their "common sense" quality or the compelling logic of the explanation. The authors of this paper would like to draw attention to the concept of "social mobility" which has not been studied to the same degree as the other concepts and is only recently becoming increasingly the focus of study. This concept is of particular interest because there is also a body of sociological theorizing that is concerned with this issue and its ramifications, particularly as it relates to suicide.

For the purposes of this paper, the concept of "social mobility" will refer to changes in the status level of an individual from a baseline defined in terms of the status position of his parents, or in terms of his own status at an earlier time. In addition, social mobility may be defined operationally in terms of educational and occupational mobility.

Psychiatric disorder or "mental illness" is difficult to define. However, without defining the term, we may still delimit the kinds of data to be included under this rubric. The studies to be reviewed embrace mental illness and emotional instability as diagnosed by judgments of qualified medical and nonmedical personnel, making use of clinical interviews, psychologic tests, and scores of questionnaire checklists or psychosomatic and neurotic symptoms. Although "casting such a wide net" raises many problems of its own, the existing level of knowledge concerning the nature and limits of "mental illness" (and mental health) does not warrant a constriction of the definition to include only medically diagnosed cases. In addition to the problem of inadequate knowledge of the nature of these disorders, recent studies by Leighton, Srole, Pasamanick, and others, show that large numbers of undiagnosed and untreated "cases" exist in the community population, raising questions about the generalizing value of incidence and prevalence studies of medically diagnosed cases.

Having defined our basic terms, we turn now to a consideration of the issues we wish to discuss. Our purpose is several fold: first to review some of the literature concerned with social mobility and mental illness that has appeared in recent years and in which the authors have not made as much use of broader more macrotheoretic considerations in planning their research or organizing their analyses; second, to briefly summarize the theoretical formulations of Emile Durkheim and Robert Merton with respect to the concept of "anomie" and suggest their potential relevance for the problem at hand; third, to present some of the results of studies carried out by the authors that bear on this question; fourth, review selected readings that illustrate how cultural values of minority groups with respect to social mobility in the United States may make the group member more vulnerable under certain conditions and less vulnerable under other conditions. These findings support the discussion of the relevance of Durkheim's and Merton's views for mental illness and are consistent with the findings of the authors as well. Lastly, we will discuss the implications of these findings for social action.

Review of the Literature

In a review of the literature, Kleiner and Parker (1969) state that "research in this area has been concerned mainly with two questions: 1. Can the high rates of mental disorder, often reported for the lower socioeconomic groups, be explained by the "downward drift" of sick individuals into a lower socioeconomic position? This question is concerned with mobility as a manifestation of "social selection." 2. To what extent is social mobility (including considerations of direction and degree) related etiologically to mental disorder? This is concerned with the "social causation" hypothesis.

With regard to the first question, if the high rates in the lower class can be explained on the basis of "downward drift," then the experiences associated with lower class life per se, might have little relevance for mental disorder. This question has been discussed many times, since the early studies of Faris and Dunham (1939) and of Tietze et al. (1941) reported that the inverse relationship between schizophrenia and social class could not be explained by mobility into the lower socioeconomic class. Using "place of residence" as a criterion of status position, Lapouse (1956) also found evidence that "for first admissions of schizophrenics to state hospitals from Buffalo, the concentration in the low economic areas is not the result of downward drift from higher areas. Nor is there any evidence that the concentration in the poor areas is the result of a recent migration into those areas of mobile men who live alone." More recent studies by such investigators as Hollingshead and Redlich (1954) also fail to support the social selection concept.

Although there is impressive evidence tending to refute the "downward drift" hypothesis, other studies tend to support it. Lystad (1957) found that schizophrenic patients tended to be significantly more downwardly mobile than a comparable group of nonmentally ill individuals. In their study of a nonhospitalized population in New York City, Rennie et al. (1957) reported that a relatively high proportion of the sample having severe psychiatric symptoms had been downwardly mobile.

Further analyses of these same data by Langner and Michael (1963) confirmed Rennie et al.'s conclusion that the downwardly mobile were characterized by the poorest mental health, and the upwardly mobile by the least mental impairment. Nonmobile individuals were between these two groups. These findings applied to "psychotic types" but not to "neurotic types." The latter, in fact, were most often upwardly mobile and least often downwardly mobile. In contrast to the studies mentioned above, these data depended on symptom inventory scores in a general community population. In studies carried out in England, Morris (1959) and Goldberg and Morrison (1963) reported a heavy concentration of schizophrenic patients in the low status group but noted that the fathers of these patients were more randomly distributed throughout all classes. More recent studies all show a disproportionately large number of downward mobile individuals among the mentally ill relative to "normal" controls.

The weight of the evidence presented, thus far, clearly shows that the mentally ill are characterized by higher rates of downward mobility. One may ask to what extent is upward mobility related to mental disorder? Rennie el al.'s findings (1957) indicate the least impairment for the upward mobile. However, Hollingshead and Redlich (1954) noted that although there was no significant relationship between mobility and mental disorder, most of the patients who did change social position were, in fact, upward mobile. Hollingshead et al. (1954) explored mobility and diagnosis at two different status levels. At the lower status level, they found no relationship between mental illness and mobility; but at the higher status position, neurotics were more upwardly mobile than nonpatients, and schizophrenics were the most upwardly mobile of all groups.

Of considerable interest to this discussion is the study of a Negro population by Parker and Kleiner (1966). Their data showed that the downward mobile had the highest rates of illness while the upward mobile had the lowest. However, when controlling for status position, they showed that *both* the downward mobile at the low end of the scale and the upward mobile at the high end had significantly higher rates than their respective nonmobile status peers. Thus, the two studies using status controls report that downward mobility is associated with mental disorder at the upper end of the scale. Clearly, status controls are necessary in studies of mobility.

There has been considerable theorizing to the effect that individuals who have experienced social mobility are more likely to be confused as to their reference groups and their self-identity, thus experiencing concomitant interpersonal difficulties (Blau 1956). Ruesch (1946) reported that people who had been "social climbers" tended to be more subject to chronic psychosomatic disorders than those who had not been socially mobile, or who had been downwardly mobile. Warner (1937) and Lipset and Bendix (1963) speculated that high social mobility in our society was related to disturbed interpersonal relationships and mental illness.

This explanation seems to account for findings relating social mobility to various forms of deviant behavior, such as racial prejudice, high concern over health, and radical political voting behavior (Greenbaum and Pearlin 1953; Litwak 1956; Lopreato 1967). Several additional studies (Parker and Kleiner 1966; Parker et al. 1969) determined directly the sociopsychologic correlates of the mobility experience. In other studies, high goal striving stress, poor integration with reference groups and low self-esteem characterized the upward mobile at the high end of the occupational scale *and* the downward mobile at the low end relative to their respective nonmobile peers.

It has been suggested in the literature that status inconsistency is psychologically disturbing, since social roles and expectations associated with one status position may conflict with those of another (Lenski 1967). Using this assumption, Lenski (1954) predicted, and found (in four separate countries), that high status inconsistency was associated with radical political voting. Jackson and Burke (1965) showed that particular patterns of inconsistency were associated with different types of deviant reactions. Although Parker and Kleiner (1966) reported that status inconsistency was not significantly related to mental disorder, a particular pattern of inconsistency (for example, high education and low occupation) was so related. As discussed earlier, this pattern was associated with a high aspiration–achievement discrepancy, for example, high stress and frustration.

The literature summarized above strongly suggests that downward mobility is associated with mental disorder. Other studies, particularly those using status controls, have also shown that upward mobility is associated with mental disorder. It can be concluded that a wide variety of deviant behavior, including mental disorder, is associated with social mobility regardless of direction. Studies have also been cited that show some of the sociopsychologic variables that intervene in this association.

An issue that has been raised consistently in the literature concerns social selection and social causation. Social selection would be considered operative if it could be shown that individuals drifted into a status position because of prior mental illness. This widely held view is used to explain the high concentration of downward mobile individuals in psychiatric populations. On the other hand, social causation would attempt to explain high rates of mental disorder in a given class as being due to socialization experiences in that class.

The concentration of downward mobile individuals at a given class level is often used to affirm social selection and deny social causation. However, the assumption that illness preceded mobility is an unwarranted inference. It is also possible to hypothesize that mobility preceded and is etiologically related to mental illness. Myers and Roberts (1959) emphasize that the class III patients relative to class III controls experienced more upward social mobility, higher goal striving stress, and social rejection prior to their illness. As noted previously, Parker and Kleiner (Parker and Kleiner 1966; Parker et al. 1969) found that mental illness was associated with downward mobility at the low end of the scale, and upward mobility at the high end of the scale. It is very difficult to entertain the hypothesis that people "drifted" up because of prior mental illness. "The evidence presented does not resolve the question of temporal priority. The resolution of this question awaits relevant longitudinal studies."

Anomie as Viewed by Durkheim and Merton

Durkheim (1951) noted that suicide rates tended to increase during periods of economic depression and of prosperity. The existence of high rates in both types of situations indicated that physical deprivation or poverty in itself was not the most important contributory factor. He concluded that each type of economic crisis situation was accompanied by disturbances in the "collective order" in which the individual was involved. Durkheim reasoned that the structure of human nature made the individual's needs and desires "insatiable" unless subject to an "external regulatory force." Normative regulation by the society (or significant social groupings to which the individual belonged) provided this restraining force on aspirations.

Without this normative regulation, the society could be characterized as "anomic." Durkheim reasoned that during an economic crisis, society was distrubed (that is, status transitions disrupted the individual's integration with social groups that had previously provided consensus about the range of legitimate striving). When the regulatory force was shattered, the individual experienced "deregulation" or anomie. The downwardly mobile individual in this situation would have to reduce his requirements, his desires, and so on. Durkheim postulated a similar process operating in the upwardly mobile person: the disturbance in group relations occasioned by the transition in status would weaken the restraint on the individual's aspiration.

The failure to perceive realistic limitations in social situations would cause continual striving for unlimited goals. In both instances, weariness and disappointment would result from the "futility of an endless pursuit" and constituted the preconditions of anomic suicide. Using more modern sociological terms, Merton (1957) called these social groupings the significant reference groups that supplied the individual with guidelines for judging his performance and setting realistic aspiration levels.

In Merton's own view of "anomie," he explicitly defines the term as the "disjunction between means-ends relations" in society. In other words, society (or one's particular significant reference groups) socializes the individual to aspire to specific goals. But the means, presumably available for realizing these goals, may be inaccessible to the individual due to social structural barriers that prevent the individual from making use of them. Thus, the individual is functioning within an anomic situation.

By defining the concept in strictly sociological terms, he has avoided the sociopsychologic aspects that are intrinsic to Durkheim's discussion. He then goes on to state that this disassociation between means-ends gives rise to stresses or tensions toward deviance, the particular form of deviance being a function of the manner in which the individual resolves the state of affairs. For example, he might devalue the goals, emphasizing the adhering to the means as a form of ritualism. Or, he might deemphasize means and emphasize the goals, seeking alternate and perhaps illegal means to goal achievement.

Without belaboring the far-reaching effects Merton's conception has had on the area of social deviance from the point of view of the social activist or the social scientist, suffice it to say that mental illness was assumed to derive from the individual's devaluing of both the means and ends, thereby manifesting withdrawal and isolation behavior.

Social Mobility, Anomie, and Mental Illness

In comparing Durkheim and Merton with respect to their use of the concept of anomie, social mobility means for Durkheim disruption and breakdown of normative systems regardless of the direction of mobility, and concomitant psychologic confusion and dissatisfaction. For Merton, on the other hand, social mobility could not easily be linked theoretically to anomie without invoking additional assumptions and formulations.

Parker and Kleiner (1966), utilizing Merton's definition of anomie, established that their psychiatric population, in the context of a closed system (or in a state of disassociated means-ends relations), *perceived* an open system, experienced high goal striving stress, dissatisfaction with one's achievements, and low esteem when compared with a community population with no known psychiatric history. These findings served to show that mental illness was linked first to the lack of agreement between the specific state of affairs and the perception of that state of affairs, and the concomitant motivational characteristics of the individual in the situation.

It has also been mentioned earlier in this paper that Kleiner and Parker found upward mobility relative to nonmobiles at the high end of the status scale, and downward mobility relative to nonmobiles at the low end of the scale to have higher rates of mental disorder. These findings were obtained when mobility was defined in terms of education or occupation. In addition, in the community population, the motivational characteristics of the two socially mobile groups differed from the nonmobiles in the same ways that the population differed from the community population. Lastly, it should be mentioned that the downwardly mobile usually had higher rates of psychiatric disorder than the upwardly mobile, and it was also found that the greater the social mobility, or distance moved, the higher rates of illness as well.

It was clear to these investigators that the perception of the opportunity structure and the motivational characteristics of the patients, and of the two socially mobile groups in the community were identical with those characteristics that Durkheim attributed to upwardly and downwardly mobile individuals and considered to be anomic. Thus, in the context of Durkheim's work, his use of anomie and the concomitant psychologic effects were linked to suicide, but in the present context they are linked to mental illness.

Pursuing this observation further, Kleiner and Parker (1969) sought to determine if the socially mobile individuals were less integrated with and less subject to the normative control of significant social groups. Using the black population included in their earlier study, degree of ethnic identity among the socially mobile and nonmobile groups provided the measure of integration necessary to confirm Durkheim's description of these groups. These authors found that the upwardly mobile, relative to the nonmobile at the high end of the status scale, and the downwardly mobile, relative to the nonmobile at the low end of the scale, were characterized by weak or ambivalent ethnic identity, whereas the nonmobile at both points on the status scale showed positive identification. At the same time, they found that the two socially mobile groups, relative to the nonmobile groups, tended to deny that their racial membership constituted a barrier to goal achievement, had higher status aspirations, and devalued their achievements. All of these characteristics were found to be more prevalent among the psychiatric population than among the community sample. Clearly, these findings demonstrate the relevance and usefulness of Durkheim in this area of investigation.

Concurrent with the research activities of Parker and Kleiner (1966), Dalgard (1971) was studying the relationship of social mobility to rates of psychiatric disorder in Norway. He also came to the conclusion that the research findings reported in the literature were somewhat inconclusive, suggesting that this state of affairs could be due to the problem of definition of terms, or to the different meaning that social mobility might have with respect to stress and selection factors in different societies. With these considerations, he chose to study the problem in Norway, stating that the findings should be interpreted in the context of Norwegian social conditions.

He selected as his psychiatric population 325 male patients hospitalized for a functional disorder. All of these patients were residents of Oslo and had been first admitted during the period 1951–1955. His control sample consisted of 325 "normal" residents of Oslo living there during the same period of time. The names of the community sample were drawn from election files of the parliamentary election in 1953. The two samples were matched in terms of age, occupation, marital status, and place of residence in the city. The occupational status of the fathers of both samples was obtained. The discrepancy between the occupation of the individuals in the sample and their fathers was used as the measure of social mobility.

He found that both the downwardly and upwardly mobile groups had higher rates of psychoses than the nonmobile group, with the downwardly mobile showing higher rates than the upwardly mobile. In further analyses, controlling for the status of the individuals in the samples, the upwardly mobile in the high status groups showed higher rates of psychoses than their nonmobile status peers. In addition, he found that as the social distance moved by the mobile individual increased, in either direction, the rates of illness increased in both directions as well. Dalgard explained the data in terms of role conflict deriving from anomie and social mobility as Durkheim suggested.

In two earlier papers (Dalgard 1967, 1968) that led to this research effort, he found that high status migrants to Oslo and low status natives of Oslo manifest high rates of psychoses. These findings suggested that social mobility might explain the finding he obtained in the study of migration and mental disorder better than the factor of migration itself. In addition, status inconsistency was also ruled out as a practical explanatory concept. Thus, despite Dalgard's initial hesitation about generalizing beyond Norwegian society, his findings are precisely the same as those obtained by Parker and Kleiner in the United States.

On the basis of the findings reported above by Parker and Kleiner, these investigators sought to explain differential rates of mental illness by migratory status in terms of social mobility and the concomitant sociopsychologic factors. In the first of their two studies concerned with this issue, Kleiner and Parker (1969) snowed that the rates of illness were higher for natives of Philadelphia (those socialized in this urban environment), than for southern migrants (those socialized in the southern section of the United States). They hypothesized that the natives would show higher rates of both upward *and* downward mobility, that is, be the high risk groups. Consequently, the natives in contrast to the migrants would also (1) perceive a more open means-ends relation, (2) deny more readily that race is a barrier to achievement, (3) manifest weaker or more ambivalent ethnic identification, (4) have higher status striving, (5) devalue their accomplishments to a greater degree, and (6) have lower self-esteem. The data supported all of these expectations.

In a second paper by Parker et al. (1969), the investigators ruled out culture shock as an explanatory variable for explaining differences in rates of illness between natives and migrants, and between migrants from urban areas and migrants from rural semi-urban areas. In the latter case, rates were higher for urban migrants from the south to Philadelphia than for those migrating from less urbanized sections. These authors again hypothesized that the urban migrants would be characterized by higher rates of downward *and* upward mobility, and would show the social motivational characteristics enumerated above. The data supported these expectations as well.

Culture Values, Anomie, and Mental Illness

It has been shown that in the black community, in the context of an anomic social and cultural system, blacks that perceive an *open* opportunity system, have *high* goal striving stress, *devalue* their achievements relative to their close reference groups, have *low* self-esteem and manifest *high* rates of mental disorder. Buerkle and Kleiner (1966) and Kleiner and Stub (unpublished research) have gathered data which show that black youth who, in the context of an anomic situation, perceive a *closed* system, do *not* have traditional middle class aspirations and striving, have *high* positive self-esteem, and *low* risks for mental disorder, but are *high* risks for juvenile delinquency. We have used the phrase "in the context of an anomic social and cultural system" without indicating the particular measures used in support of this statement. In view of the emphasis, in Western European society, on education as a means to occupational and income success, the correlations between education and occupation, and between education and income may be considered two different measures of anomie.

In view of the findings summarized above it is possible to state one's expectations about relative incidence of mental illness and delinquency from the characteristics of one's ethnic culture and the socioeconomic characteristics of the particular ethnic group. For example, if there exists a black lower class culture that fosters the belief that the opportunity system is closed, then the motivational characteristics of lower class individuals will not include the traditional middle class emphasis on the success ethic; their self-esteem will be intact; the risk of mental illness will be low and the risk of delinquency will be high.

On the other hand, to the extent that black persons reject this culture and identity with the larger white society, they will perceive a relatively open opportunity structure, have high goal striving motivation, low self-esteem, and be a relatively high risk for mental illness. It is for this reason that in an unpublished study McCarthy and Yancey say they would expect higher self-esteem among the lower class blacks than among the middle class blacks. The latter would show a greater prevalence of symptoms of psychosomatic stress and lower self-esteem than middle class whites.

Placing the issues of anomie, social mobility, social motivation, and deviance in the context of "Minority Group 'Culture'" is not new, but relatively little research has been carried out, despite the plethora of writing and commentary on the subject. Frazier's (1957) theme focuses on the sociopsychologic aspects of the marginal position of the socially mobile black, that is, between the black community and the white middle class. The characteristics associated with this situation are similar to those found for the mentally ill in the work summarized above. He does not deal clearly with the "culture" issue, except with occasional references to "folk culture." One attempt to deal empirically with the issue compares Anglo-Americans, blacks, and Mexican-Americans with respect to their educational aspirations for their children, and the amount of education they would be satisfied with for their children (Heller 1967). The educational aspirations were highest for the Anglo-Americans, next highest for the blacks, and the Mexican-Americans had the lowest aspirations. Implicit in the discussion of these data is the assumption that the differing emphases on education can be explained in ethnocultural terms. Actually, Heller states this very explicitly elsewhere (Heller 1970).

The degree to which a given culture engenders the view that specific avenues to goal achievement are inaccessible appears to have profound consequences for the social mobility, social motivation, and psychiatric risk for a given ethnic group. It is also important to determine the degree to which this view of society is correct. Heller's (1967) data show that Mexican-Americans have lower education aspirations for their children and are satisfied with less because they don't have the financial resources to keep their children in school beyond the ninth grade. This would suggest that Mexican-Americans do not perceive the social system to be anomic. Moore and Cuellar (1970), however, write that Mexican-Americans in the southwest discourage their youth from entering into the larger society and its emphasis on status striving and ambition, because they believe the system does not allow Mexican-Americans to succeed. The youth would be doomed to failure and frustration if they were not protected from the effects of an anomic system. To the extent to which this view pervades the Mexican-American community, they would not be part of the total society and would not necessarily manifest mental illness or psychosomatic disorders.

There is very little empirical literature showing the rates of distribution of mental illness among Mexican-Americans. Karno and Edgerton (1970) come to the same conclusion in reviewing the meager material although they also point out that the few studies available show relatively low rates among Mexican-Americans. Moore and Cuellar (1970) also comment on the paucity of material on both mental illness and crime. They mention that there seem to be higher rates of adolescent arrests and convictions for gang behavior and narcotics. However, it still needs to be determined if this is a function explicitly of visibility to the police and labeling processes or of the sociopsychologic aspects of the youth and their culture.

Although tentative, these findings show that where cultural emphases indicate a closed opportunity system, mental illness is low and juvenile delinquency is high, as was found for blacks. It is also significant to point out that any number of sources in the literature say there is relatively little correlation between educational achievement of Mexican-Americans and their occupational or income achievements in the cities, indicating, from our point of view, an anomic social situation. There are other writers who, while admitting to these findings, feel that this only appears to be true because the socially mobile disappear into society and give up their ethnic identity. Clearly, these issues need much more systematic empirical investigation.

A number of writers have suggested that social mobility among Mexican-Americans is frowned upon by this ethnic group because successful mobility means leaving the community. Therefore, those who enter into the status striving and related motivation in terms of the larger society are in fact deviants from the point of view of the Mexican-American community itself. This does not appear to be true of the black community, where social mobility seems to be generally accepted and encouraged, but with the caution that blacks should not forget their origins. With recent efforts to provide more opportunities for blacks, both through planning and the enactment of new laws, it is possible that many blacks will redefine the means-ends relations of society as being more open than before. It would appear that if this revised estimate exaggerates the true state of affairs, rates of mental illness will increase. The situation may be very different for Mexican-Americans because there are still laws in a number of states imposing heavy restrictions and indignities on these people.

In reviewing the literature for Indians there seem to be several parallelisms with Mexican-Americans. For example, according to Wax (1971), Indians in general do not encourage their youth to enter the larger society either and they deemphasize ambition and the striving ethic as well. These also signify to them moving out of the community. This action is rejected and stigmatized by the tribe. Thus, the act of moving into the white middle class society is being deviant for most of the Indian tribes, just as it is among Mexican-Americans. The reasons for rejecting such actions is not simply because it means the dissolution of the ethnic culture and community, but because such actions are also doomed to failure since opportunities for success and fulfillment of ambitions are considered to be closed to Indians. Again, we may suggest that to the degree to which the Indians internalize this view of society, there should be relatively little mental illness or associated disorders. There does not appear to be any firm literature to speak of on this question. One may contrast this situation with that for the Cherokee Indians and their allied tribes in Oklahoma. These particular tribes emphasize education and the success ethic despite the "obvious" barriers to such fulfillment that exist for them. Wax, in discussing these issues, observed that this preoccupation with education and success borders on the "neurotic" obsession, and "is difficult to understand." Again, there are no empirical data on this question. From our vantage point, the use of the term "neurotic" may be quite appropriate although Wax may not really have intended to use it in the technical sense.

Concluding Remarks

In the first section of this paper, concerned with past research on social mobility and mental disorder, a wide net was cast to bring together whatever might, in some way, relate to this problem, including references to the relationship of social mobility to interpersonal disturbances or problems. This was considered necessary, in part, because the volume of material has been quite limited and more tenuous than suggested by the review. This was not considered necessary in subsequent sections because of the recent research that has yielded consistent theoretical and *empirical* results. These findings have shown the relevance of more macrotheoretic formulations for explaining the obtained correlations between social mobility and mental illness. The particular relevance of Durkheim and Merton has been especially important in this endeavor. The focal concepts have included "anomie" and the derivative sociopsychologic factors which are the perception of the means-ends relations, integration with significant social groups to which one belongs, status and goal striving, evaluation of one's achievements, and one's self-esteem.

In this article, we have presented findings which indicate that social mobility is significantly related to functional psychiatric disorders. More specifically, the rates of illness have been higher for the upwardly and downwardly mobile populations relative to the socially stable or nonmobile population. The downwardly mobile show higher rates than the upwardly mobile; however, the upwardly mobile at the high status levels and the downwardly mobile at the low status levels are the particular high risk groups. We have also shown that as the distance moved in the upward and downward direction increases, the rates of illness increase in both conditions. These findings have led to additional research which has shown that rate differentials between differing migrant and native groups can be explained in terms of social mobility and the associated sociopsychologic characteristics enumerated above.

The literature reviewed and included in this paper has concentrated exclusively on work done in the Western World and points to the high risk associated with social mobility and status striving in this sphere. One can draw a few conclusions from these observations which have far-reaching implications. Clearly, the societal emphasis on status and status striving brings with it increasing risk for mental illness as long as the means-ends relations are not accessible to all participants of that society. If access to the means are available to some and not to others, the problem of realistically estimating one's chances and opportunities for success, with this ethic, will always be problematic, not to mention the inequities built into such a situation.

It is difficult to conceive a totally open system whereby status goals and social mobility are available to all since there will always be some who must be at lower levels. Social mobility also means the loosening and straining of one's ties to significant social groups that ordinarily provide support, meaning, and belongingness. Perhaps we should consider different social arrangements in which social status, status striving, and social mobility as motives for individual behavior may be set aside. Lastly, we have also indicated that to consider deemphasizing status orientation in the present societal arrangement increases the risks of other forms of deviance or social problems.

15

Cultural Conflict in Urban Indians

Joan Ablon

Rural life seems to facilitate the preservation of traditional cultural values, while urban areas are the banners of the level of technological development and "modernization" attained by a given country. This contrast enhances and adds a new dimension to the impact of internal migration and changes in cultural context on the behavior and mental health of the people involved. More specifically, the move of members of certain ethnic groups from a rural area to a large city, in which they are minorities, involves an actual or potential loss of old culture as well as adaptational challenges that conflict with their traditional values.

Ablon provides a vivid description of the vicissitudes of American Indians leaving their rural reservations to live in a large city. Using her anthropological insights and her familiarity with clinical services, the author elucidates the contrasts between the gregarious and sharing way of life typical of the reservation and the highly individualistic and competitive behavioral patterns prevalent in the mainstream of large cities in the United States.

THE URBAN American Indian frequently shares many characteristics of poverty with other urban immigrants, but brings to the city a particular ethnic identity with associated cultural values that may all but preclude successful urban adjustment. An examination of the life style and adjustment patterns of the urban Indian offers an unusual opportunity for observing the effects of new economic and social stresses on a person whose ego strength has been sorely damaged by a lifetime of poverty, social and cultural disorganization, and cultural conflict.

Few published studies look at "mental health" of American Indians in terms of actual identified psychiatric problems or mental retardation (Leighton 1968; Martin et al. 1958). Investigations on this subject have been inhibited by several factors, including the relative isolation of Indian communities from the agencies and resources of the mainstream American society and the fact that problems of individual deviance that would be identified and labeled as "mental illness" in an urban or semi-urban area are dealt with on the reservations within a context of vastly differing cultural expectations of behavior and performance.

During the last several years a number of papers have pointed up the fact that problems of cultural identity have resulted in widespread personal and social alienation, depression, anxiety, and tendencies for withdrawal among Indian children and adolescents (Saslow and Harrover 1968). For the adult population, studies are generally lacking except for a small number dealing with specific problems such as suicide, alcoholism, and crime.

Many emotional difficulties that may be observed among Indians may in part be a reflection of stresses caused by severe economic deprivation and social disorganization. Therefore, the functional scope of mental health concerns must include the total arena of the Indian's economic and sociocultural adaptation and confrontation with the mainstream of American society (Leon 1968).

Migration from Reservation to City

Most Indian reservations are economically depressed areas. Employment opportunities are meager or nonexistent, and problems of physical and mental health, housing, and education are staggering. For this reason, thousands of Indians, like other migrants from rural areas, have come to the city seeking employment, education, and a new life for themselves and their families. The greatest impetus for Indian relocation during the past fifteen years has come from federally sponsored programs providing employment assistance and vocational training in major cities throughout the Midwest, Southwest, and West Coast.

The data on which this paper is based were collected in various cities of the San Francisco Bay Area. The three relocation areas of San Francisco, Oakland, and San Jose share an Indian population estimated to be from 12,000 to 20,000 persons, representing more than 100 tribal groups from across the country.[1] The migration of more than half of this population has been sponsored by the Bureau of Indian Affairs, while the others have come on their own initiative and resources, drawn by the diversity of employment and educational opportunities available in this area.

Relocatees generally appreciate the many conveniences and diversions of urban life, but find it hard to tolerate traffic, the crowds, the many buildings pushed together and the everpresent white man's laws restraining them in ways they cannot comprehend. Most will readily say that they came to the city to seek jobs and schooling, not to become whites or to stop being Indians. Were jobs and educational opportunities available on their home reservations, most would return as soon as possible.

Few Indians who come seeking employment have training for specific job skills, and most qualify only for irregular and low paying jobs. Some now have the opportunity to enter new programs designed by industry specifically for members of minority groups. During the past ten years an increasing number of young single people have been coming directly from reservations and off-reservation boarding schools for federally sponsored vocational training and a look at the big city.

Most Indians live in working class neighborhoods made up of diverse ethnic and racial groups. Indians tend to limit their social contacts to other Indians. There are many active pan-Indian social, political, and recreational organizations in the Bay Area, but probably less than one-half of the Indian population is touched by these. Because people are dispersed over large areas and often tend to stay within their own kinship or friendship circle, it is difficult to speak of a viable "Indian community" in the sense of a widespread network of relationships (Saslow 1968).

The following case example portrays some of the common problems that Indian families encounter in the relocation experience.

---

1. There are no existing accurate census figures for the Indian populations of any of the large metropolitan areas of the country. The Bureau of Indian Affairs will not attempt to give exact figures for the relocatees coming through their programs who remain in relocation areas because they generally do not have comprehensive follow-up data.

Charlie and Rhoda Two Arrows: Turmoil and Withdrawal

The Teton Dakota were formerly one of the typical nomadic Plains Indian tribes of the Siouan language family. Today, they live chiefly on reservations in North and South Dakota. Common problems plaguing the reservations are inadequate housing, poor sanitation, excessive drinking patterns, and general family and social disorganization.

Rhoda and Charlie Two Arrows, the names are fictitious, both full-blood Teton Dakota, were in their early thirties during their six years in San Francisco. Rhoda was one of four children who grew up in a family where traditional values and discipline were honored. She went to reservation day and boarding schools until the completion of the twelfth grade, after which she moved to a nearby town to live with a sister and work as a waitress. There she first met Charlie Two Arrows.

Charlie grew up on the periphery of the reservation and was exposed to a traditional but disorganized early home life. His mother died when he was young, and his father remarried a woman who joined him in a pattern of continual drinking that soon depleted the money from the lands of his first wife. Charlie attended a public school until sixth grade and then began the round of hard farm work that has characterized his life to the present.

After their marriage, Rhoda and Charlie lived with Charlie's father. It was a hard life for Rhoda because her father-in-law drank heavily, and she had farm chores to do besides taking care of the household and a growing family of three children. The Two Arrows decided on an impulse to relocate to "sunny California" because they heard there was eternally good weather there and because it was the farthest relocation area from the reservation that they could choose. They planned to save up enough money to buy some land and cattle and then return.

Charlie came to San Franciso with no special skills, but the Bureau of Indian Affairs got him a job in a factory as a machinist. He was reputed to be one of the top workers in the factory, even though he soon initiated a pattern of going on a week's binge every two or three months. He was always careful to call in as ill to cover himself at work and so never got into serious employment difficulties because of his continued drinking. He did, however, lose money for those days missed, since he did not receive sufficient benefits to cover those periods.

The Two Arrows lived in three apartments during their stay in San Franciso. Two years before they returned to the reservation, they moved into the public housing project in which they lived during the twelve months of interviews with them.

Rhoda had two more children in San Franciso and experienced three periods of acute illness during which she was hospitalized. At these times Charlie would often drink heavily, and welfare officials were called in several times, much to Charlie's later chagrin, because of his drunkenness or his "abandoning" the children. On the reservation, grandparents, aunts and uncles, or cousins are ready sources of short- or long-term babysitting, and most Indian women sorely miss such family support.

This couple lived almost completely in an Indian universe despite the immensely diverse population around them and the many cumbersome new rules of white society that dictated their daily life. Rhoda was active for a time in a local Indian Center, but she noticed that the more active her participation the more inclined Charlie was to drink, so she lessened her activities. Charlie did not care to go to Indian gatherings, because he feared that in a group situation pressure to drink would be brought upon him by other Indians.

The Two Arrows' three school-age children had considerable difficulty in the San Francisco school system. They could not understand the teachers' urgings to apply themselves to materials that had little relevance to their lives. They were frightened by the aggressive black students who made up almost one half of their classes. They seemed to withdraw almost totally from the situation. They did not read well and, as the years went by and their alienation from the total school experience deepened, found themselves further and further below the class reading level.

The Two Arrows' contacts with the Bureau of Indian Affairs were frequent and involved. The Bureau was called in repeatedly when Rhoda was in the hospital and Charlie was having problems with his drinking and coping with the care of the children. During the last years, Rhoda called the Bureau office only occasionally to say that things were going well and that she would be eternally grateful that the Bureau had brought them out here. Although not liking the bustle and red tape of urban living, she felt it was all worth it to get away from her father-in-law and to have such conveniences as running water, a washing machine, and easy heating.

The facts of personal and family disorganization among the Sioux are well documented in the anthropological literature. Macgregor (1961–1962) has noted that the Sioux man particularly has suffered from the loss of the meaningful economic and social roles that he enjoyed in the dramatic Sioux lifestyle of old. The woman now may be thrown into the position of the key family figure, causing additional psychological and social difficulties for the man. Rhoda and Charlie exhibited very different personalities and the general pattern of their family roles and behavior typifies this problem of contemporary Sioux. Rhoda was a handsome woman who bore herself with great pride, was gregarious, and enjoyed many kinds of activities. It was her strength and determination that held her family together throughout their many crises in San Francisco.

Charlie, on the other hand, was a very shy person, sensitive about his Indian identity and quick to take offense at imagined criticisms of Indians. He referred frequently to his lack of education. He was able to support his family; however, he was beset with many insecurities about himself and his worth. Charlie seldom spoke and appeared to loosen up only when in the presence of certain known Sioux or when drunk. Beneath his quiet exterior was the latent drinking problem that could surface any day, usually a Friday payday, when he just would not come home from work.

When Charlie returned from a drinking period, he was very remorseful. Because the Two Arrows were nominal Catholics, Rhoda twice attempted to send Charlie to a priest for counseling after his shamefaced return. On both occasions the priest did not have time to see him until a week or more had passed, and by then Charlie had refused to talk to anyone about his problem. Once, in the middle of the night, Rhoda called the well-liked minister of a local Indian Protestant church. He came over immediately and talked to Charlie. This minister once said that every man in his congregation had had a drinking problem at one time, so he was well accustomed to this sort of counseling. He felt that one reason many white ministers are unable to reach Indians is that they are afraid to counsel persons with serious drinking problems, and this sort of interaction is frequently an essential one with Indian parishioners.

Charlie, and to a lesser degree, Rhoda, held strongly to the important Sioux value placed on sharing and the giving of hospitality, which was difficult, given Charlie's salary. His father came out to stay with them almost every winter, and a variety of other relatives and friends would also drop in and remain for weeks at a time. These houseguests did little but drink and watch television during their prolonged stays, and rarely did any of them contribute to the grocery bill.

Life for the Two Arrows in San Francisco seemed to be an almost continual round of crises caused by unexpected expenses and family illness, by their impulsive, erratic behavior, and by their inability to meet the demands of white society.

Charlie finally found himself seriously involved in what seemed to him to be an incomprehensible maze of traffic offenses. While drunk one night he was picked up and booked on drunk driving and hit-and-run charges. When he sobered up the next day, he did not remember committing any of the crimes with which he was charged. Charlie was released pending trial, and when he got home he informed Rhoda that all this was too much for him; he had decided they would go home. On the federal reservation area he would be safe from state reprisals. In the next few hours they packed the most essential of their belongings, crowded the children into the car, and left. Their flight to San Francisco from the reservation had not freed them from economic or psychological struggles. They had lived in the land of promise six years, and returned without the money they had come to save. Moreover, Charlie was a wanted man. At present they are resettled with Charlie's father on his lands and Charlie is doing wage labor where he can find it. Rhoda harbors in her heart the hope of another relocation, but it is doubtful that Charlie could be roused to leave the reservation again.

The Unique Cultural and Historical Background of Urban Indian Problems

American Indians bring a peculiar cultural heritage to the urban world. Most Indians are basically tribal men who leave the primary, kin-oriented relationships of a closed reservation community to enter a highly individualistic metropolitan milieu. Many fundamental Indian values not only are incompatible with those of American culture but work directly in opposition to the principles on which the modern competitive capitalistic order is based.

It is this great value disparity that sets Indians apart from most other migrants now entering our cities. Indians are generally noncompetitive, except in certain circumscribed situations, and will avoid competitive activities and aggressive action when possible.

They tend to withdraw in the face of conflict. Indians traditionally have regarded the good person as one who shares his money and property with others. A man's reputation was based on what he gave away, not on what he kept. Budgeting and putting away resources for a later day for oneself is improper if others are in need. The functional time dimension is the present, thus the deferring of goals and gratifications that we take for granted in our future-oriented white world is very hard for Indians to comprehend.

Members of our middle class society have come to see themselves as objects to be shaped to fit the requirements of complex modern culture and to be changed to seek goals that hold promise of rewards. Indians do not regard themselves as malleable entities. Their frame of reference is a stable social and moral system that is fixed in the universe. The shift to the highly competitive, individualistic existence of modern urban life is an adjustment that many persons have not been able to effect.

The relationships that most Indians have had with representatives of the white world often have been unpleasant and inauspicious for potential urban adjustment. While the various reservations have differed in the details of their federal administration, the Bureau of Indian Affairs policy has been paternalistic and many programs have been ill-planned, ill-administered, and inconsistent. The pre-emption of the decision-making process by government planners has resulted in communities that are dependent, hostile, and factionated in the seeking of those few semblances of native power that are available. Two chief pathological symptoms of the long-term crippling of Indian communities have been a deeply entrenched dependency and widespread and chronic drinking.

State and local agency personnel as well as whites that Indians encounter in areas peripheral to reservations often have treated them in a patronizing or discriminatory manner. Therefore, the Indian may regard his new white urban neighbors and workmates with distrust and cynicism. Indeed, it seems safer to the Indian to limit his dealings to his own tribesmen, if possible, or at least to other Indians.

Indians encounter a variety of novel problems in the city. Reservation Indians depend on the federal government for many services that are delivered in legal association with federal trusteeship of Indian lands. Indians frequently pay little or no rent; they receive free medical and dental care from the U.S. Public Health Service. In contrast, city living entails seemingly endless bills. Such matters as money management and efficient impersonal interaction with business functionaries are fearsome arts to be learned.

Indians who come to urban areas through federal programs receive money and services from the Bureau for a limited period of time. When referred to community agencies they may not be sufficiently aggressive to pursue such assistance. Often, their shyness and reticence about speaking of their personal problems with non-Indian strangers is regarded as resistance. Also rigid time-fixed appointments cause difficulty for many Indians. If there is one Indian employee working in a community agency, Indians generally will seek him out for services. Indian OEO centers and those private agencies established by such religious-based organizations as the American Friends Service Committee that have tried to develop a special understanding of their Indian clients, have been the chief agencies contacted by Indians for welfare and personal services.

Agency personnel agree that the chief problems Indians struggle with in the city are employment, marital discord, and difficulties with the law. Dysfunctional drinking patterns frequently are found in combination with any or all of these. Excessive drinking generally is regarded to be the largest single mental health problem of reservation Indians, and the widespread drinking problems found among Indians in the city appear to be carried from the reservations rather than being any new response to anxieties caused by the urbanization experience. Indeed, some persons relocate to the city specifically to escape family and peer group pressures that force drinking activities on them as a social propriety of reservation life.

Conclusion

The difficulties in separating pathological personality characteristics from culturally determined responses to social expectations or to stress become apparent in the case example of the Two Arrows family. Common Indian social patterns still passed through the generations, such as the sharing of money and goods and the offering of endless hospitality, as well as such typical responses to stress as heavy drinking, acting out, and withdrawal may be native coping mechanisms that are expected or tolerated on the reservation but are highly maladaptative in the city.

The cultural and historical heritage of American Indians frequently contributes to the following kinds of situations that are potentially dysfunctional for urban adaptation and that lead to perpetual individual and family crisis states:

1. An inability or unwillingness to manage or budget available finances results from: (a) cultural values that emphasize sharing and hospitality to extended family and fellow tribesmen; (b) a present-oriented time dimension; and (c) little experience in paying for the many kinds of services that are necessary in the urban situation.

2. Difficulties in relating to community agencies in effective ways to utilize available services result from long-standing apprehension and ambivalence in dealing with whites. Traditionally valued personality characteristics such as noncompetitiveness, a dislike of aggressive action, and withdrawal in the face of unpleasant situations may preclude such effective interaction with whites.

3. Patterns of alcohol consumption alleviate anxiety but lead to marital conflict, loss of jobs and money, and difficulties with the law.

4. An inability to provide adequate supervision for children in times of crisis frequently results from the absence of the traditional large extended family.

5. A psychological and physical withdrawal of children from the school experience may be caused by cultural conflict, lack of interest because of perceived irrelevance of materials offered them, and discomfort in the threatening and alienating white and black social situation of the school.

The poverty of underdeveloped reservations has brought about a continuing migration of American Indians to urban areas. A clear understanding by community agencies of the unique cultural characteristics that Indians bring to the city and of how these characteristics affect their adaptation is imperative for working effectively with this sizeable new urban ethnic group.

Annotated Additional Readings

a) **Kuo, W. 1976.** Theories of migration and mental health: An empirical testing on Chinese Americans. *Social Science and Medicine* 10:297–306.
The author conceptually teases out four constructs of variables theoretically underlying the phenomenon of migration—social isolation, cultural shock, goal-striving stress, and cultural change. He then empirically assesses the correlation between these concepts and some psychopathological indices. Additionally, he elucidates a significant intermediary role for certain sociological factors such as social class and intercity mobility, which documents the intricacy of the issues involved. This reference and the next complements article 13.

b) **Krupinski, J., A. Stoller, and L. Wallace. 1973.** Psychiatric disorders in East European refugees now in Australia. *Social Science and Medicine 7:31–49.*
Reports on a survey of psychiatric morbidity among eastern European refugees living in Victoria, Australia, divided into three groups according to ethnicity and severity of war experiences: (1) Jewish refugees, who suffered the worst persecution, (2) Poles, Russians, and Ukranians, whose suffering was intermediate, and (3) Balts, Czechs, Hungarians and Yugoslavs, who suffered the least. For the first two groups positive correlations were found between certain indices of psychopathology and severity of war experiences. Besides that, special morbidity patterns obtained for each of the three groups appeared to be related to their particular war experiences, socioeconomic status, and migration stresses.

c) **Odegaard, O. 1975.** Morbidity and social mobility in an upper class educational group. *Acta Psychiatrica Scandinavica* 52:36–48.
An examination of the relationship between psychiatric admission rates and social mobility in various forms, including intergenerational and intraindividual upward and downward shifts in socioeconomic status, as well as intergenerational change of occupation within the same social group. The paper addresses these issues on the basis of a 50-year follow-study of high school graduates, using Norway's National Case Register of hospitalized psychoses. It is both this kind of register and the population stability observable in Scandinavian countries which make feasible such remarkable longitudinal studies. This reference complements article 14.

d) **Tan, E.-S. and R. C. Simons. 1973.** Psychiatric sequelae to a civil disturbance. *British Journal of Psychiatry* 122:57–63.
This is a report of the demographic characteristics, symptomatology, and diagnoses of the 58 patients with riot-related psychopathology at the psychiatric unit of a university hospital following the bloody rioting between the Malay and Chinese components of the population of Kuala Lumpur, Malaysia, in May 1969. Compared with patients seen in the unit under usual conditions, the

patients with riot-related symptoms were of lower social class, and were more exclusively identified with their ethnic community and less well integrated into the multi-ethnic greater society. In addition to generally recognized psychiatric syndromes, many patients presented short-lived psychotic disorders with a strong affective component. Most patients appeared to recover with supportive crisis intervention and medication.

e) **Wintrob, R. M., and S. Diamen. 1974.** The impact of culture change on Mistassini Cree youth. *Canadian Psychiatric Association Journal* 19:331-341.
A sensitive analysis of the effect of culture change derived from "modernization" on the youth of the Mistassini Cree Indians from a sub-arctic region of Quebec. The authors examine the five-year course of the interaction between culture change and the traditional way of life of the Mistassini Cree population, and delineate the types of cultural identity roles being adopted by its youth.

f) **Minde, K., and R. Minde. 1976.** Children of immigrants. The adjustment of Ugandan Asian primary-school children in Canada. *Canadian Psychiatric Association Journal* 21:371–381.
A detailed and systematic study of the psychological and academic adjustment of a group of 51 children whose Asian familes were forced to emigrate from Uganda to Canada. A quarter of all the children presented significant psychopathology and 50 percent experienced academic difficulties. The psychopathology of the children was found to be significantly correlated with the family's drop in socioeconomic status. This study evaluates the effects of a drastic form of sociocultural change, i.e, forced migration, on children's performance and mental health.

VI

General Psychopathology and Diagnosis

Various key aspects of general psychopathology, diagnosis, and classification will be examined here as they relate to international and sociocultural factors. In dealing with psychopathology and diagnosis, descriptive approaches to abnormal behavior will be emphasized given the likelihood of the multifactorial nature and causation of mental disorders.

Some methodological developments in psychopathological assessment during the past decade are worth noting here because they have improved the scientific status of psychopathological evaluation and have therefore enhanced the possibilities of conducting reliable and useful cross-cultural comparisons in this field. These developments include the systematizaton of the clinical information-gathering process through structured clinical interviews (e.g., the Present State Examination described by Wing, Cooper, and Sartorius, 1974) and the operationalization or explication of rules for assigning patients to diagnostic categories (e.g., the computerized CATEGO system described by Wing et al. 1974, and the Research Diagnostic Criteria formulated by Spitzer et al. 1978). Welcomed for their efforts to decrease undesirable variability, these methodological developments should be considered cautiously in cross-cultural research, not only because there is still ample room for improvement in the areas they cover, but most especially because of their risk of ethnocentricity given that they have been typically generated in industrialized countries (mostly England and the United States).

The articles here progress from the elementary to the complex, moving along the steps of the diagnostic evaluation process. First, the relationship between the differentiation of emotional states and culture is examined in article 16, using data from the World Health Organization's (1973) International Pilot Study of Schizophrenia, and the U.S.–U.K. Diagnostic Project (Cooper et al. 1972), the two most important international diagnostic studies completed to date. Then, article 17 compares psychiatric symptomatology in patient samples from the Argentine and the United States. The study of diagnostic habits, and their role explaining differences in rates of mental disorders is the subject of article 18, which is based on the U.S.–U.K. Diagnostic Project.

The annotated references deal with complementary topics on symptomatology, diagnostic habits international classification systems, and structurally innovative diagnostic models developed in various parts of the world.

16

Culture and the Differentiation of Emotional States

J. P. Leff

The experience and manifestation of emotions and their external perception and rating across sociocultural lines is a basic issue in the study of culture and psychopathology. Within that general topic, the differentiability of specific emotions or affects such as anxiety and sadness is important given that such elementary subjective experiences and behaviors are used for describing the condition of the individual at the symptom, syndrome, and clinical entity levels, on which a number of clinical decisions are based.

J. P. Leff empirically evaluates the differentiability of certain emotions across various cultures using data from the W.H.O. International Pilot Study of Schizophrenia and the U.S.–U.K. Diagnostic Project.

The design of Leff's study is quite elegant and facilitates quantification. However, some of its basic assumptions require pondering, such as that a high correlation between two emotions or symptoms implies low ability of the people involved to differentiate one from the other. An alternative explanation would be that the two symptoms are nosologically and epidemiologically related in the population in question. Also to be kept in mind is that the differences found between industrially developed and developing countries could be related to social class differences, a possibility that is only partially and indirectly ruled out in this study.

THE EXPERIENCE of another person is never directly available to us, just as our own experiences cannot be directly experienced by other people. "We're all of us sentenced to solitary confinement inside our own skins" (Tennessee Williams). We can use empathy to get closer to another person's experience; in other words we imagine ourselves in the same situation as he is in and credit him with the feelings we would then experience. However, it is invariably our own experience that we use as the yardstick. We judge another person's experience from his behavior, of which speech is one of the most informative parts. If another person says, "I see a man," and there is indeed a man in our shared visual field, then both of us assume we are sharing a common perceptual experience. When there is no external referent, as in the statement "I feel sad," the assumption of a common experience rests on more tenuous grounds. We can sometimes look to an external situation, like the loss of a close relative, to confirm that we understand the statement in the same way. But on many occasions there is no readily understandable link between a person's mood and the situation in which he finds himself. In judging a person's mood we also depend a great deal on nonverbal accompaniments of emotional states, but these are known to vary from culture to culture and from individual to individual. The movements used to express emotion, particularly those of the face, are so complex that very few attempts have been made to describe and categorize them accurately. There is a paucity of studies of this kind between Charles Darwin's pioneering work of 1872, which attempted to show the similarity of emotional expression throughout the races of mankind, and the recent work of Ekman and Friesen (1968) and Grant (1970). The few systematic studies in the intervening century do not support an invariable pattern of expression accompanying specific emotions. However, Ekman et al. (1969) found that subjects from literate cultures accurately identified emotions from photographs of the face, although subjects from preliterate cultures showed much less agreement.

No doubt because of the difficulties involved in measuring these aspects of emotion, a great deal of time and attention has been lavished on the physiological changes that accompany emotional states. Scientific measures of these have been developed: the forearm blood flow, the galvanic skin response, and others. It has been found that such measures do not distinguish between experientially different emotions like anger and fear (Frankenhaeuser 1971). Findings of this kind have led to a concept of arousal, which is measurable in physiological terms and is common to a variety of emotional states. Thus a quantitative approach to the physiological accompaniments of emotional states has led us back to the experience of emotion as the key differentiating factor. This point has been elegantly illustrated in a series of experiments by Schachter and others (1962). Subjects were injected with adrenaline to produce a state of physiological arousal. Some were informed of the expected somatic effects and reported little emotions. Others were kept in ignorance of the effects of the injection and then reported experiencing an emotion which corresponded to the situation they were placed in. Those who were in company with a stooge who was trained to act euphorically felt happy and those who were with a stooge trained to act angrily felt anger.

Not only do these experiments show that the differentiation of emotion occurs at a quite different level from the physiological events, but they emphasize the formative effect of the social environment on the experience of emotion. The effects of one's social environment, or in a broader sense one's culture, can be seen in the relationship between language and experience. A problematical question is whether a particular experience is available to someone who does not have the words to define it. Roger Brown (1956) points out that a range of experience may be differentiated in the lexicon of one language and undifferentiated in another. For example, many Pacific island languages fail to distinguish blue and green. Among the Navaho Indians one word stands for both grey and brown, while Shona (a language of Rhodesia) groups together the reds and purples. In the case of colors the situation is particularly clear because special tests exist for color-blindness which do not entail the use of color names. These tests measure a subject's ability to pick out a figure in color A from a background in color B. Such tests show that the lack of linguistic distinction between two colors is certainly not due to an inability to perceive differences between colors. The full range of color-perceiving apparatus is present in the Pacific islanders. It is rather that linguistically and practically they do not make as much use of its differentiating ability as some other peoples. This link between linguistic categories and practical usage is well illustrated by the extensive vocabulary of types of snow possessed by the Laplanders. They have many different words for the different kinds and conditions of snow, and such distinctions are of particular importance to them. An Englishman has words for snow, ice, slush, and frost, and these constitute his linguistic range for frozen water on the ground. If the importance of the Laplander's distinctions were pointed out to him he would surely be capable of appreciating the refinement of perception involved.

But until his eyes are opened to the differentiation and its practical implications, the Englishman will go on seeing all the different varieties of snow as one indivisible continuum.

Words that refer to closely related concepts, like the different varieties of snow, are often similar in sound. Brown (1956) asserts that the closer in sound two words are, the less likely are the concepts to which they refer to be differentiated.

In considering the differentiation of emotional states we have less evidence to aid us than with colors or varieties of snow, because, as pointed out above, there are no reliable external referents. Nor are there any scientific measures available to help us. We are left with the words used to categorize emotion. However, a study of these alone can be quite revealing.

The following discussion draws extensively on the work of Sir Aubrey Lewis in tracing the roots of the word "anxiety" (A. Lewis 1967). The Greek root of "anxiety" is the word 'αγχω which meant to press tight, to strangle. There are a number of Latin words with the same root—*angustus, ango, angor, anxius, anxietas, angina*—and they all contain the notion of constriction and discomfort. The French word *angoisse,* from which anguish is derived, was defined in the nineteenth century as a feeling of constriction in the epigastric region with difficulty in breathing and great sadness. It is clear that this phonetically related group of words embodies some at least of the somatic accompaniments of emotional arousal. From the previous discussion we can appreciate that words for denoting emotion whose meaning largely relates to these somatic accompaniments cannot be used to distinguish a variety of emotional states with any clarity. Further evidence for this poor differentiation of the vocabulary of emotion at some stage in its historical development is provided by Old English, a language which was current up to the middle of the twelfth century. In this language the word *ange* meant to be in trouble and to suffer affliction, while *anger* had a now obsolete meaning of trouble or sorrow. It is of interest in this respect that the modern Icelandic word *angr* means grief or sorrow. Thus we find that emotions we consider as distinct, namely, anger, fear (anxiety) and sadness, at one stage in the development of English were all represented by words which derived from the same hypothetical Indo-Germanic root *Angh.* The closeness in sound of the various words for emotional states at this earlier stage in their development suggests that they referred to closely related concepts.

We are now in the position to postulate a scheme for the historical development of the words that denote emotional states. At an early stage one word, presumably something phonetically similar to *Angh* in the case of the Indo-European languages, denoted the somatic accompaniments of emotional arousal. No more than one word was necessary to stand for the pattern of physiological events because it is the same whatever the characteristics of the arousing situation. Later the word came to denote the emotional experience as well as the somatic accompaniments. The focus of meaning shifted to the experience of emotion, and the somatic meaning faded into the background. Eventually the root word split up into a number of phonetically related variants, as the global emotional state was differentiated into several smaller categories.

Such an exposition would be unjustifiably speculative if it rested solely on the fossil record, as it were, of etymology. But the evolution of language, being a social process, has occurred much more unevenly than the evolution of animal species, and there are plenty of living fossils available. One reason is that a language and its verbal categories have to be learned afresh by every individual, and the relevant information is not uniformly available even within a single culture. Bernstein (1958) points out that a middle-class child is the object of much attention so far as his development as an individual is concerned. He learns to differentiate his experience to a much greater degree than the working-class child. Bernstein states that the way in which the working class use language limits the verbal communication of feelings so that the latter tend to be as undifferentiated as the language. There is support for this in the reported finding that people of lower class and poorer education tend to express emotional distress in somatic terms (Crandell and Dohrenwend 1967).

Apart from class distinctions within a culture, cross-cultural differences are striking. For example, in a number of African languages a single word stands for both being angry and being sad. This does not mean that anger and sadness are not experienced by Africans, but only that these two emotions are not clearly distinguished linguistically. Statements that depression rarely occurs in Africans (Carothers 1953) have been made, but are as fallacious as the assumption that the Englishman cannot match the Laplander's perceptual differentiation of the different qualities of snow once these have been pointed out to him.

The link between a culture and the verbal categories of its language is worth exploring further. Brown states that once we have learned what is distinctive and what is equivalent in a man's speech we have a key to his thought and to the culture he represents. Verbal categories reflect the modes of thought of a culture. Whorf (1956) points out that we have a false view of the unanimity of modes of thought in different cultures because modern European languages are all Indo-European dialects which have been historically transmitted from what was long ago one speech community. These modern dialects have long shared in building up a common culture. However, when we contrast our language with Semitic, Chinese, Tibetan, or African languages, the divergence in analysis of the world becomes more apparent.

A unique opportunity to test the propositions put forward above arose with the institution of a cross-cultural study of mental illness by the World Health Organization. This study, known as the International Pilot Study of Schizophrenia (IPSS), has as its main aim the comparison of the clinical features of schizophrenia in nine different centers (World Health Organization 1973). The centers involved were picked to ensure the inclusion of at least some developing countries as well as the more developed ones; the nine centers are sited in Aarhus (Denmark), Agra (India), Cali (Colombia), Ibadan (Nigeria), London (England), Moscow (USSR), Taipei (Taiwan), Washington (United States), and Prague (Czechoslovakia). It can be seen that four of the countries, India, Colombia, Nigeria and Taiwan, fall into the developing group. In order to ensure comparabilitiy of data, a semi-structured interview schedule was developed to elicit the mental state of the patients. This is known as the Present State Examination (PSE). It was originally constructed and developed in English and studies of its reliability were carried out (Wing et al. 1967; Kendell et al. 1968; Sartorius et al. 1970). For the purposes of the IPSS, the PSE had to be translated into the seven other languages spoken by the psychiatrists and their patients in the various centers. These were Chinese, Czech, Danish, Hindi, Russian, Spanish and Yoruba. The original English version of the PSE was translated into local languages in the individual centers. The translation was then given to another person who translated it back into English. The English back-translations were then assessed by English-speaking psychiatrists, who compared them with the original version and removed any inconsistencies from the translated version.

In each center, the majority of patients selected were given a diagnosis of schizophrenia, but there was a small proportion (about 14 percent) with a diagnosis of affective psychosis, and a smaller group (about 9 percent) who suffered from a variety of neurotic conditions. The author interviewed virtually all the patients from the London Center who constituted the IPSS sample.

Each center contained from two to seven psychiatrists who participated in the IPSS. Each psychiatrist had to undergo a period of training in the use of the PSE before contributing patients to the study. Regular checks were made on the inter-rater reliability within each center, and this was shown to be extremely high for most of the areas in which the patient reported his symptoms. It was somewhat lower for the observations of the patient's behavior made by the psychiatrists during the interview. The pooled intra-class "r" for all centers for the individual items of the PSE varied from 0.96 to 0.47, with a median of 0.77 (W.H.O. 1973).

Inter-center reliability was assessed by getting the psychiatrists from the various centers to rate 25 filmed and videotaped interviews recorded in different centers. The reliability on individual symptoms was generally high, reaching a maximum of 0.84. As with the intra-center comparisons, the ratings of patients' responses to questions had a much higher reliability than ratings made of observed behavior. These figures indicate that the psychiatrists' ratings of patients' responses to questions are reliable enough to be compared within centers and between centers.

The PSE aims to cover the full range of mental symptoms and is divided into a number of different areas for convenience. Three of these are of particular interest for the purposes of the present study, Anxiety, Depression and Irritability. The standardized questions to be asked in each of these areas are set out in the Appendix.

Each question has scoring instructions on a scale of 0, 1, 2, where absence of the symptom rates 0, and presence rates 1 or 2 according to specific criteria of frequency or intensity or a combination of the two. The scores in each section can be simply added together to give a total, so that each patient has a total score on Anxiety, on Depression and on Irritability. In the original PSE the psychiatrists' subjective ratings of affect were also available, but these were omitted from the totals in this study because of the lower reliability demonstrated for these assessments.

The scores on the three sections of interest for this study were utilized in the following way. The correlation coefficients between the scores on Anxiety and Depression, on Depression and Irritability, and on Anxiety and Irritability were calculated for all the patients in each center. These three correlations exhaust the possible combinations of the three section scores. Our contention is that if two different emotions are always reported by a patient as being present to the same extent, or are always reported as being absent together, then the differentiation between them is poor. Conversely if one emotion is always present when the other is absent, and vice versa, then the differentiation is extremely good. Hence a correlation coefficient of +1 between the scores on two different emotions represents the least possible discrimination between those emotions, while a correlation of −1 represents the greatest possible discrimination.[1]

It was predicted from the postulated scheme of the development of the vocabulary of emotion that there would be significant variaton in the degree of emotional differentiation between different countries. In particular it was predicted that the developed countries would show a greater differentiation of emotional states than the developing countries.

Results

The correlation coefficients between the emotions for the different centers are shown in table 16.1. The level of significance of the values is also indicated.

To test the hypothesis put forward above, the correlation coefficients between the various emotions were transformed into Z

Table 16.1 Correlation coefficients between the emotions for the various centers (IPSS)

Center	*No. of patients*	*Anxiety: Depression*	*Depression: Irritability*	*Anxiety: Irritability*
Aarhus, Denmark	129	.39‡	.05	.13
London, England	127	.23*	.25†	.18
Moscow, USSR	140	.32‡	–.10	–.01
Prague, Czechoslovakia	122	.56‡	–.13	–.17
Washington, U.S.	132	.37‡	.34‡	.21*
Agra, India	140	.51‡	.05	.05
Cali, Colombia	127	.33‡	.16	.36‡
Ibadan, Nigeria	145	.50‡	.43‡	.26*
Taipei, China	137	.62‡	.29†	.39‡

* $p < 0.05$; † $p < 0.01$; ‡ $p < 0.001$.

1. Alternatively it could be argued that a correlation coefficient of zero represents the greatest differentiation and a correlation coefficient of −1 represents a lack of discrimination equivalent to a correlation of +1. When the results are recalculated on this basis the difference between the developed and developing countries on Depression:Irritability is no longer significant, while the significance of the difference on Anxiety:Irritability is reduced to $p < 0.05$. The scores on Anxiety:Depression are not affected.

Table 16.2 Average Z scores for the developed and developing countries (IPSS)

	Anxiety: Depression	*Depression: Irritability*	*Anxiety: Irritability*
Developed countries	.40	.08	.07
Developing countries	.55	.25	.27
Critical ratio	2.62†	2.79†	3.47‡

† $p < 0.01$; ‡ $p < 0.001$.

scores, and the average Z scores for the five developed and four developing countries were compared using the Critical Ratio. This gives a measure of the significance of the difference between two Z scores. These results are presented in table 16.2.

It can be seen that for each of the three sets of correlations the average Z score was significantly higher for the developing than for the developed countries, thus confirming the hypothesis.

Once this was established, it seemed to be of considerable interest to study a group of subjects from a developing country living in a developed country. It was thought that contact with a culture in which emotions were relatively well-differentiated might have an educative effect. Negro people living in America were selected for study because although they are of African origin their language of upbringing is English. Hence it might be possible in this group to sort out the effects of language and culture. The group of American Negros included in the IPSS was too small to be subjected to statistical analysis, but a much larger group was available from another source.

The U.S.–U.K. project (Cooper et al. 1972) has been carrying out comparisons of British and American psychiatric patients, using the eighth edition of the PSE, of which the W.H.O. edition is a shorter version. In fact, the questions covering the area of interest of this paper are identical in the two schedules. Moreover, the research psychiatrists working in the U.S.–U.K. project have had very similar training in the use of the PSE to those involved in the IPSS. It was therefore considered justifiable to compare data collected in the two projects.

Data were available for 55 Negro patients collected from nine psychiatric hospitals in the New York area. These patients were not entirely comparable with the IPSS sample in terms of diagnostic distribution, as there was a smaller proportion with psychosis (60 percent), and of these a smaller proportion suffered from schizo-

Table 16.3 Correlation coefficients between the emotions for American patients (U.S. : U.K. project)

	No. of patients	*Anxiety: Depression*	*Depression: Irritability*	*Anxiety: Irritability*
New York negroes	55	.57‡	.70‡	.47‡
New York whites	55	.33*	.27	.07
Critical ratio		1.54	3.01†	2.24*

* $p < 0.05$; † $p < 0.01$; ‡ $p < 0.001$.

phrenia (45 percent). The results for the Negro group are shown in table 16.3.

The Negro group shows high correlations in all three areas. In fact it differs significantly from the Washington sample on the correlation between Depression and Irritability and from the London sample on all three correlations. The difference between the Negro group and the Washington sample could be explained by a difference in the distribution of the social classes, particularly in the light of Bernstein's emphasis on the links between social class and the use of language.

To investigate this possiblity, the 55 Negro patients were matched exactly on social class, age and sex with 55 white patients collected from the same hospitals in the U.S.–U.K. project. The results for this group of matched white patients are also shown in table 16.3. The correlation coefficients do not differ significantly from those of the Washington patients, an additional check on the comparability of the IPSS and U.S.–U.K. data. However, as shown in the table, the correlations between Depression and Irritability, and Anxiety and Irritability are significantly higher among the New York Negro patients than among the matched group of white patients. The matching procedure ensures that this difference cannot be connected with the social class distribution of the samples.

To throw further light on any association with social class, the London data were analyzed using the social class of the patients' fathers. This measure was chosen rather than the patients' social class because of the drift down the social scale that schizophrenics exhibit, and because the strongest influence on a child's development of language is presumably its parents' use of language. The children of skilled workers were compared with the children of unskilled workers. There was no significant difference between the two sets of correlation coefficients.

Discussion

The hypothesis tested, namely that developed countries show a greater differentiation of the emotions than developing countries, was arrived at after a fairly lengthy theoretical argument. It was supported by data from the IPSS, a study which was conceived and designed with quite different objectives in mind.

The countries which showed the highest correlations in all three areas were Nigeria and China, indicating that their patients achieved the lowest degree of emotional differentiation as defined in this study. Some confirmation of this finding comes from the problems encountered in translating the PSE into the various languages. The words "depression," "anxiety" and "tension," were found to be particularly difficult to translate into either Yoruba or Chinese. Leighton et al. (1963) also noted that depression was an unfamiliar concept among the Yoruba and encountered difficulties in finding Yoruba words with which to describe the subjective feelings meant by the term. The Yoruba words used in the PSE for "depression" and "anxiety" are translated literally as "the heart goes weak" and "the heart is not at rest." It is evident that they refer to the somatic accompaniments rather than the emotional experiences themselves.

It is clear from the above that there is a strong link between the availability of the appropriate words for the various emotions and the ease with which people distinguish between the experiences. However, it is not sufficient for the words to be available in the language. Their correct use had also to be learned. The findings from the comparison of the New York whites and Negroes strongly suggest that the Negroes, though English-speaking, do not use the discriminatory capacity of the available words to nearly the same extent as the whites. The learning of the verbal expression of the differentiation of emotional experiences must be far more restricted in the Negroes than in the white population, although they are living side by side. The results of a study by Davitz (1969) complement these findings. He asked a sample of Ugandan adolescents to write descriptions of three emotional states, Happiness, Sadness and Anger. For each state, the subject was asked to think of a time when he experienced the emotion, to describe the situation briefly, and to describe his experiences as fully as possible. Half of the subjects wrote in Luganda and the other half in English. The descriptions of each emotional state were analyzed for content, using a number of categories such "discomfort," "expressive behavior," "move away from others." It was found that the reports written in English differed very little from those written in Luganda. Davitz concluded that the content of the emotional reports was not influenced by the language of report *per se*. It is perhaps not very startling to find that in learning a second language one does not adopt the modes of thought of the culture whose language it is. It is much more surprising to find that people of African origin living side by side with people of European origin and using their language for centuries still retain some evidence of their cultural origin in their use of the borrowed language.

One final and fundamental question remains to be raised. What is it about the culture in the developed countries that leads to a greater differentiation of the emotions? There is only room here for very tentative suggestions, but it is possible that cultures which emphasize the importance of the individual rather than of the group, such as the extended family or the tribe, are more conducive to the development of the person's sense of identity. His relationships with other people are likely to be less prescribed in form and more individual. Under these circumstances one might expect that his emotional reactions would develop in the direction of greater differentiation.

Summary

The level of experience at which emotional states are differentiated is discussed. The possible development of the vocabulary of emotion is traced, and it is hypothesized that developed countries show a greater differentiation of emotional states than developing countries. This hypothesis was confirmed using data from the International Pilot Study of Schizophrenia, which includes five developed and four developing countries. Data from another transcultural study, the U.S.–U.K. Project indicated that a group of American Negro patients showed significantly less emotional differentiation than a matched group of white American patients.

Acknowledgment

This paper is based on the data and experience obtained during the International Pilot Study of Schizophrenia, a project sponsored by the World Health Organization and funded by the World Health Organization, the National Institute of Mental Health (United States) and the participating field research centers. A full list of all investigators and staff is presented in Volume 1 of the Report of the IPSS, WHO, Geneva, 1973.

My thanks are due to Dr. J. R. M. Copeland of the U.S.–U.K. Project (funded by N.I.M.H. grant No. NH 09191) for permission to use the data from this project, and to Miss Jane Gourlay for performing some of the analyses on them.

The views expressed in this paper are the author's own and do not necessarily represent those of all the IPSS collaborating investigators nor the stated policy on decisions of WHO.

Appendix

Extract from Eighth Edition of the PSE (W.H.O. version)

Anxiety

8.4 Are there times when you feel very anxious and frightened although you don't know why, and there is no obvious reason for it? Or feel that something terrible is going to happen but you don't know what? Suggested probes.
Have you had times in which you felt shaky, your heart pounded, or you had difficulties in getting breath when this was not due to exercise? Or any similar feelings (sinking feeling in stomach, clammy hands, dry mouth, etc.).

8.5 Rate severity and constancy of autonomic anxiety attacks accompanying fear.

8.6 Have you had attacks of fear or panic when you simply had to do something to end it? What was it like? How often have you had such attacks in the past month?

Depression

7.01 Have you been very miserable, low-spirited or depressed during the past month?

7.02 Have you cried at all? How often?

7.03 Have you felt like crying or wanted to cry, without actually weeping? (How often?)

7.04 Do you find yourself brooding over gloomy topics, unpleasant thoughts like disease and death, which happen to other people?

7.05 Do you find yourself brooding over the thought of death or illness, which might happen to you?

7.06 How do you see the future?

7.07 Have you ever felt that life isn't worth living?

7.08 Did you try to give yourself an injury in the past month (apart from suicidal thoughts)?

7.09 Do you stay depressed most of the time or does your mood vary?
7.10 What does this depression feel like? Rate presence of depression of a special quality, e.g. "like heavy black cloud over my head."
7.11 Did you ever think of ending your life at all? How often? During past month?
7.12 Have you tried to commit suicide in the last month?

Irritability
5.1 Have you been getting angry with things or people in the last month?
5.2 Do you get angry with yourself?
5.3 Do you show that you are angry? Can other people tell that you are angry?

17

Culture and Psychiatric Symptomatology: A Comparison of Argentine and United States Patients

Toba A. De Fundia, Juris G. Draguns and Leslie Phillips

A comprehensive description of the clinical condition of a psychiatric patient includes consideration of symptoms, work and social functioning, and associated biological and psychosocial factors. Although not adequate by itself, the description of psychiatric symptomatology, subjective and/or observable manifestations of disturbance in thought, perception, affect, speech, motor behavior and general appearance is essential to the characterization of a psychiatric patient as such.

The authors compare in the following article the symptomatology of samples of psychiatric patients hospitalized in public institutions in Argentina and the United States. Particularly interesting is their evaluation of the samples along the passivity-activity dimension proposed by the Mexican psychiatrist and psychologist Diaz Guerrero to characterize the psychological contrast between the general populations of Mexico and the United States. This evaluation leads the authors to examine the applicability of their conceptualization of psychopathology in a given society as a caricature or exaggeration of the local pattern of normal behavior. This conceptualization appears to refer most effectively to the notion of cultural pathoplasticity—i.e., the influence of cultural framework on the form and, especially, the content of psychopathology.

ON THE planes of theory, research, and clinical practice, recent years have witnessed a growing recognition of the impact of cultural variables upon psychopathology (e.g., Benoit 1964; Brody 1966; Ellenberger 1960; Jakovljevic 1963a; Leighton and Hughes 1961; Murphy 1969b; Murphy and Leighton 1965; Opler 1959; Opler 1967; Wittkower and Rin 1965). One of the manifestations of this increasing concern has been in the form of actual empirical comparisons of psychopathology at two or more geographically removed distinct sites. Typically, such investigations have been focused on cultural groups maximally contrasted on such axes as Western versus non-western or traditional versus technologically advanced (e.g. Gaitonde 1958; Hitson and Funkenstein 1959; Jakovljevic 1963b; Kimura 1965; Murphy et al. 1967; Murphy et al. 1963; Schooler and Caudill 1964; Yap 1960). Much less work has been done in comparing maladaptive manifestations of cultures only moderately different from each other (e.g., Hendin 1964; Page 1966; Saenger 1968; Zubin and Klietzman 1966). Our purpose is to contribute toward this, as yet sparse, store of knowledge by investigating the psychiatric symptomatology of patients in two countries of the Western Hemisphere, similar in many important respects, yet different in the Hispanic versus Anglo-Saxon sources of their cultural tradition, those of Argentina and the United States.

Our interest in this comparison, moreover, goes beyond mere exploration. Rather, we have embarked upon this study with the objective of ascertaining the applicability of certain formulations of the Mexican psychologist and psychiatrist, Diaz Guerrero (1967) to contrast in psychopathological manifestations of hospitalized patient groups in the two countries. Specifically, Diaz Guerrero proposed that two qualitatively different modes of coping with stress are inculcated in the respective socialization practices of Spanish-speaking and English-speaking countries of the Americas: in the former, a serene, passive, resigned acceptance of life's circumstances and in the latter, an active, forceful attack upon the source of frustration.

The passive-active dichotomy, originally designed to capture the essence of culture contrast between Mexico and the United States, has been found heuristically useful in a number of investigations of normal personality patterns in several other Latin American countries (e.g., Hereford et al. 1967). Independently of Diaz Guerrero's conceptions, Havighurst (1963) concluded, upon a collaborative study of adolescents in Buenos Aires and Chicago by means of a variety of paper-and-pencil measures, that their results might best be accommodated by a construct akin to the activity-passivity dimension.

The question now arises whether the contrast in passivity-activity, hitherto observed in samples of psychiatrically unimpaired individuals, can also be demonstrated upon comparing psychiatric patients of the same two nations. This expectation guided us in a preliminary study (Draguns et al. 1964, 1966) with small samples of partially matched Argentine and United States patients that yielded promising results; differentiating symptoms of Argentines expressed withdrawal while those in the United States tended toward crystallization of hostility and explosiveness.

Promising though these findings were, they were based on small samples and their matching on a number of social characteristics was less than totally successful. In the present study, we have set out to replicate these results in more adequately equated samples whose size should be sufficient for conclusive statistical analyses. In addition to this basic goal, we have embarked to extend the procedures and measures of this comparative intercultural study in the following three directions:

1. We have formalized the dimension of passivity-activity and incorporated this axis specifically as an added avenue of intergroup comparison.

2. We have separately analyzed intercultural differences in symptoms and precipitating circumstances for groups of male and female patients.

3. Finally, as a subsidiary feature of the present study, we have undertaken a preliminary exploration of the character of sex differences in our central variable, that of symptomatology, within each of the two countries.

Moreover, the concern of the present study has not been limited to the passivity-activity dimension. Rather, a comparison of the two patient populations has been attempted over the entire range of symptomatology. By doing so, we endeavored to increase the similarity of this investigation in methods and measures to a series of other interrelated studies by the present authors and their associates concerned with the effect upon overt psychiatric manifestations of culture (Draguns et al. in press), ethnicity (Brockington et al. 1969; Draguns et al. 1967; Lancer 1962; Schooler and Caudill 1964) acculturation (Nachson et al. in press), socioeconomic class (Nuttall and Phillips 1969; Saks et al. 1970), social mobility (Nuttall and Phillips 1969; Saks et al. 1970), and social competence (Draguns et al. 1964, 1966, 1970; Phillips et al. 1966, 1968; Zigler and Phillips 1960, 1962).

Procedure

Measures. In the interpersonal and developmental framework applied to psychopathology (Phillips 1968) two kinds of data are considered crucial for the complete description of maladaptive patterns of behavior: premorbid pattern of adaptation, as indexed in the spheres of education, occupation, and marital status and subsumed in the term "social competence," and the character of clinical malfunctioning as expressed through discrete manifestations and more general groupings of symptomatology. In this study, we have tried to take into account both of these classes of variables. We have done so by equating the groups of patients from the two cultures in the component indices of social competence or premorbid adaptation, in order to observe the culturally mediated variations in symptom manifestation.

Preparatory to matching, indices were obtained from hospital records concerning each patient's years of schooling completed, marital status, occupations exercised by him for the longest period of time within the last five years, his age, and psychiatric diagnosis.

The psychopathological manifestations of the members of our several samples were recorded by means of equivalent Spanish-language and English-language versions of the Symptom and Temperament Checklist, developed at the Worcester State Hospital by one of the present authors (Leslie Phillips). This instrument allows for the recording of 178 psychiatric symptoms and 27 temperaments, yet is sufficiently flexible to allow for the inclusion of any new and unanticipated symptoms should such be encountered in a different cultural milieu. As yet, we have not faced this necessity, however.

The raw symptom information obtained in this manner was investigated in the present study in two ways: distribution of discrete symptoms was compared across cultural lines as was that of more inclusive categories of symptomatology. To expand on the last point, the symptom clasifications of role (turning against self, turning against others, avoidance of others) and sphere (thought, action, affect, and somatization) were constructed. Role in this content, pertains to the interpersonal varieties of symptomatology and sphere to those or organismic channels of expression. Table 17.1 provides the operational definitions of each of the above divisions of this two-dimensional scheme of classification.

Table 17.1 Age, social, and diagnostic characteristics of United States and Argentine patients

		Argentine men	*U.S. men*	*Argentine women*	*U.S. women*
Age	Mean	31.89	32.51	29.27	30.00
	S.D.	11.48	11.28	8.01	9.19
Years of schooling	Mean	8.46	8.49	10.45	10.66
	S.D.	4.26	4.28	3.23	2.17
Marital status	Married	12	13	11	15
	Widowed	0	0	1	2
	Separated	5	8	5	8
	Divorced	0	4	3	2
	Single	37	29	22	15
Occupational level	1 (Highest)	1	1	2	0
	2,3	8	5	6	2
	4	9	7	11	8
	5	13	16	6	8
	6	10	12	7	8
	7 (Lowest)	9	10	2	2
	8 (Students)	2	2	2	5
	9 (No work history, housewives)	2	1	6	9
General diagnosis	Involutional and manic-depressive	5	5	6	6
	Schizophrenic reaction	21	21	8	7
	Psychoneurotic	10	10	19	19
	Mental deficiency (with psychosis)	1	1	0	0
	Personality disturbance	4	4	5	6
	Transient situational personality disorder	0	0	1	1
Specific diagnosis	Manic-depressive reaction				
	Manic	1	1	2	2
	Depressive	3	3	4	4
	Mixed	1	1	0	0
	Schizophrenic reaction				
	Manic	1	1	2	2
	Depressive	3	3	4	4
	Mixed	1	1	0	0
	Schizophrenic reaction				
	Simple, undifferentiated	13	13	4	4
	Paranoid	6	6	3	3
	Schizo-affective	3	3	1	0

Table 17.1 (continued)

	Argentine men	*U.S. men*	*Argentine women*	*U.S. women*
Mental deficiency (with psychosis)	1	1	0	0
Psychoneurotic				
Anxiety, phobic	3	3	6	5
Dissociative	0	0	1	1
Obsessive-compulsive	2	0	2	0
Depressive	5	7	9	13
Anorexia nervosa	0	0	1	0
Personality disturbance				
Inadequate, schizoid	1	1	2	3
Chclothymic, continually unstable	1	1	3	3
Paranoid	1	1		
Sexual deviation	1	1	1	1
Alcohol addiction	10	10	2	2
Anti-social	1	1		
Dysocial	1	1		
Adjustment reaction of adolescence	0	0	1	1

For each patient, his dominant role and sphere were ascertained. In the case of role, the procedure used for this purpose was simple: the number of symptoms included in each of the three roles being approximately equal, the role in which the patient had the largest number of symptoms was deemed to be his dominant one. As for sphere dominance, the procedure was similar in rationale, but more complex in computational detail. The examination of table 17.1 reveals that the number of symptoms included in various spheres was markedly unequal. For this reason, the dominant sphere for each patient was established upon computing z scores for all four spheres according to the formula: $z = (x - \bar{x})/\sigma$. The patient's highest z score established his dominant sphere.

In addition to role and sphere dominance computed in all of the interrelated cultural, ethnic, and social competence studies enumerated earlier, the dimension of passivity-activity was explicitly included as an empirical dimension of appraisal. To this end, two advanced graduate students of clinical psychology in the United States[1] familiar

1. Appreciation is expressed to Harvey Black and Bennett Tittler, both of The Pennsylvania State University, who performed these ratings. The help of Harvey Black in matching subjects is also gratefully acknowledged.

with the pertinent theoretical formulations by Diaz Guerrero (1967) undertook to sort independently symptom and temperament descriptions of the checklist into three piles: passive, active, and indeterminate. The specific symptoms on which both of the raters agreed were retained for the purposes of this study. By means of this procedure, passive and active symptoms were identified; dominance patterns for either of these two styles of coping were established exactly as in the case of roles.

On the basis of these techniques, comparisons were carried out between Argentina and United States in discrete symptoms, dominant roles, spheres, and coping styles for male and female patients separately. Each of these analyses was undertaken by means of the chi-square procedure. An analogous set of operations was carried out within each of the two cultures, to establish differences in symptom variables between men and women.

Subjects. Two pools of subjects were used in this study. In Argentina, we succeeded in obtaining, from hospital records and through interviews, social competence, symptom, diagnostic information on 63 male and 49 female psychiatric patients hospitalized in public facilities in Buenos Aires and Cordoba in 1966 and 1967. These data were collected by members of the psychiatric staff of their respective institutions, all of them Argentine in nationality.

In the United Staes, we drew upon a pool of analogous data gathered on patients at the Worcester State Hospital under the direction of one of us (Leslie Phillips). There were over 400 men and over 200 women in this pool of subjects all of whom underwent psychiatric hospitalization between 1963 and 1966. Formal scoring of the requisite data was performed by specially trained nonprofessional personnel. Interviews and entries into hospital records were carried out by the regular psychiatric staff of the institution.

In both countries, subjects available for the comparison were nonchronic patients most of whom were experiencing their first admission to a psychiatric hospital. Patients outside of the range of 17 to 55 years of age, as well as those with diagnoses of organicity or mental retardation, were routinely excluded.

Practical considerations prevented us from obtaining either a representative or a random sample of patients in their respective communities. In view of this, the best precaution against spurious and artifactual findings appeared to be individual matching of patients of the two countries in those variables that might constitute sources of intergroup variation extraneous to culture: the component indices of social competence, age, and psychiatric diagnosis. In practice, we attempted to find for each of the Argentine patients his closest available counterpart

Table 17.2 Symptoms included in the several spheres, rules, and coping styles

Thought (35):	
Poor time, place, or person orientation	Fears of injury
Perplexed, mixed-up	Fear of failure
Obsessive doubting, can't make decisions	Feels threatened
Obsessions	Suspiciousness, ideas of reference, ideas of persecution, paranoid ideas, feels influenced
Phobias	Ideas of grandeur, omnipotence, genius, special ability
Feels going crazy or mentally ill	Sexual preoccupation
Depersonalization, feelings of unreality, things changing	Feelings of sexual inadequacy
Confused	Afraid of opposite sex, afraid of own masculinity of feminity
Bizarre ideas	Feels perverted
Delusions	Guilt, self-accusatory, self-critical, feels "evil," "sinful"
Hallucination (unspecified)	Depreciatory ideas against self
Auditory hallucinations	Suicidal ideas
Visual hallucinations	Fears of own hostile impulses
Olfactory hallucinations	Fears someone will be hurt or killed
Tactile hallucinations	Feels someone else may hurt or kill another
Evasive, guarded	Threatens assault
Free-floating anxiety, vague fears	Fears of committing an abhorred act (sexual or aggressive)
Afraid	
Action (21):	
Compulsions	Assaultive
Excessive drinking	Charged with murder or manslaughter (or attempt)
Drug addictions other than alcohol, takes narcotics	Rape (or attempt, other than technical rape)
Eats a lot, voracious eater	Exhibitionism, indecent exposure
Doesn't eat, refuses to eat, anorexia	Voyeurism
Suicidal attempt	Pedophilia
Irresponsible behavior	Fetishism
Running away	Incest
Doesn't work, although physically able; neglects home chores	Sexual or anal compulsions
Robbery, stealing, breaking and entering	Homosexuality
Firesetting	

Affect (9):
- Apathetic, listless, indifferent, doesn't care, not interested
- Tense, nervous, anxious, upset, sensitive, apprehensive, troubled, uneasy
- Restless, excited
- Emotional turmoil, agitated
- Temper outbursts, tantrums, violent explosive temper
- Depressed, despondent
- Elated, euphoric, exaggeration of wellbeing
- Mourning
- Mood swings

Somatization (21):
- Bodily concerns
- Tremors, tics, tremulous
- General fatigue, weakness, lacks energy, chronically exhausted
- Migraine and tension headaches, pains in head
- Insomnia, disturbed sleep
- Blackouts, fainting speels, aura, "nervous seizures"
- Musculoskeletal reactions
- Asthma
- Respiratory reactions (other than asthma)
- Peptic ulcer-like reactions, ulcerative colitis, ulcer
- Anorexia nervosa
- Vomiting, nausea
- Diarrhea
- Constipation
- Other gastrointestinal reactions
- Heart attack
- Other cardiovascular reactions
- Nervous system reactions
- Unusual sensations in head
- Dizziness, trouble with equilibrium

Against others (22):
- Threatens assault
- Temper outburst, tantrums, violent explosive temper
- Excessive drinking
- Drug addictions
- Eats a lot, voracious eater
- Irresponsible behavior
- Running away
- Doesn't work, although physically able; neglects home chores
- Lying, malingering
- Robbery, stealing, breaking and entering
- Firesetting
- Destructive, maniacal-like outbursts
- Assaultive
- Charged with murder or manslaugher (or attempt)
- Rape (or attempt, other than technical rape)
- Exhibitionism, indecent exposure
- Voyeurism
- Pedophilia
- Fetishism
- Incest
- Sexual or anal compulsions
- Homosexuality

Avoidance of others (18):
- Excessive daydreams, fantasies, lives in dream world
- Olfactory hallucinations

Table 17.2 (continued)

Poor time, place, or person orientation	Tactile hallucinations
Perplexed, mixed-up	Evasive, guarded
Feels going crazy or mentally ill	Afraid, scared
Depersonalization, feeling of unreality, things changing	Suspiciousness, ideas of reference, ideas of persecution, paranoid ideas, feels influenced
Confused	Feels perverted
Bizarre ideas	Apathetic, listless, indifferent, doesn't care, not interested in anything
Hallucinations (unspecified)	Withdrawn, socially isolated
Auditory hallucinations	
Visual hallucinations	
Against self (19):	
Obsessive doubting, can't make decisions	Depressed despondent
Obsessions	Elated, euphoric, exaggeration of wellbeing
Phobias	Mourning
Guilt, self-accusatory, self-critical, feels "evil", "sinful", "sexual," religious	Mood swings
Depreciatory ideas against self	Compulsions
Suicidal ideas	Doesn't eat, refuses to eat, anorexia
Fears of own hostile impulses, of hurting or killing someone	Suicidal attempt
Fears of committing an abhorred act (sexual or aggressive)	Migraine and tension headaches, pains in head
Tense, nervous, anxious, upset, sensitive, apprehensive, troubled, uneasy	Insomnia, disturbed sleep
Active orientation (24):	
Talks to self	Destructive, maniacal-like outbursts
Overtalkative	Assaultive
Talks loudly, shouts	Promiscuous
Restless, excited	Excitable
Emotional turmoil, agitated	Impulsive
Temper outbursts, tantrums	Irritable
Overactivity, uninhibited pacing	Overdemanding

Suicidal attempt	Driven, hard-working
Excessively busy, engrossed in plans and projects	Derogatory
Threatens assault	Domineering
Robbery, stealing, breaking and entering	Bullying
Firesetting	Hostile, aggressive
Passive orientation (25):	
Excessive daydreams, fantasies, lives in a dream world	Stays in bed, sleeps a lot
Preoccupied	Withdrawn, socially isolated
Stupor	Aversion or apathy toward sexual activity
Evasive, guarded	Does not eat, refuses to eat
Not interested in opposite sex	Neglects own health
Does not believe he can be helped	General fatigue, weakness
Does not believe he has a problem	Indecisive
Mute, untalkative, whispers	Lazy, does not like to work
Feels incapable of work	Passive dependent, helpless
Apathetic	Self conscious
Obsessive doubting, obsessions	Shy, ready to retreat into self
Depressed, despondent	Does not work though physically able
Psychomotor retardation	

in years of schooling completed, occupational level, according to the scheme developed by Warner et al (1960), martial status, as well as age and psychiatric diagnosis. A total of 54 pairs of men and 42 of women were matched in this manner. Table 17.2 contains information on the results of this procedure. It will be seen that intercultural correspondence was close in age, years of schooling, and in the inclusive nosological categories, as well as the specific syndromes, of the Kraepelinian diagnostic system. The degree of matching in marital status and occupational level is somewhat less satisfactory, reflecting possibly certain sociological incompatibilities of the two countries compared (Cuevillas 1967). One may note in this connection the low proportion of divorced individuals in our Argentine samples and the higher representation of small-scale businessmen entrepreneurs in that country. In any case, even these discrepancies appear relatively minor and do not make our two samples altogether incomparable.

Results

Symptomatology in the Two Countries. Findings obtained upon comparing Argentine and United States groups in the distributions of dominant roles, spheres, and coping styles are presented in table 17.3. It is worth noting that cultural differences were found in five of the six comparisons performed. With the exception of role dominance in women, Argentine and United States patients were demonstrated to differ in the interpersonal character, the organismic mode, and the manner of coping with the world, as expressed through their symptomatology. The last finding is of particular interest as it bears out the expectations with which our research was initiated. The nature of these differences conforms to Diaz Guerrero's formulations (Diaz Guerrero 1967) and parallels the results obtained in the two countries with normal subjects (Havighurst 1963).

Outside the passive-active dimension, avoidance of others is the role disproportionately encountered among male Argentines. In the United States there is a more even distribution of the three roles among men. In sphere, Argentine male patients exceed their counterparts in North America in both thought and affect; the opposite is true of somatization. The array of findings in sphere with women is different in the following respects: a greater frequency of thought dominance among Argentines, coupled with virtual absence of ac-

Table 17.3 Dominant roles, spheres and coping styles in Argentine and United States groups

	Men		*Women*	
	Arg.	*U.S.*	*Arg.*	*U.S.*
Role				
Against self	16	13	28	22
Against others	5	8	1	3
Avoidance of others	30	19	9	11
Indeterminate	3	14	4	6
	$\chi^2 = 10.59$ ($p < 0.05$)	$\chi^2 = 1.92$ (N.S.)		
Sphere				
Thought	19	14	30	9
Action	11	12	3	12
Affect	18	11	2	11
Somatization	6	17	7	10
	$\chi^2 = 7.88$ ($p < 0.05$)	$\chi^2 = 23.47$ ($p < 0.001$)		
Coping style				
Active	20	32	8	21
Passive	34	22	34	21
	$\chi^2 = 5.34$ ($p < 0.05$)	$\chi^2 = 9.10$ ($p < 0.01$)		

tion, and overrepresentation of affect among patients in the United States.

On the plane of individual symptoms, listed in tables 17.4 and 17.5 separately for men and women, the differentiating characteristics of Argentines bespeak withdrawal and diminution of activity level. Moreover, the list of symptoms in which Argentines exceed their counterparts in the United States is free of aggression contemplated, perceived, or expressed. By contrast, North American patients bring to the fore an elaboration of ideational or overt activity that is often aggressively directed either against self or others. On a more formal plane, five of the nine symptoms overrepresented among Argentines are classified as passive while none of the North American symptoms fall into that category. At the same time, three of the eleven symptoms in that group are designated active. In the two female groups, the trends are similar, with 9 out of 28 Argentine symptoms passive and only one active and, conversely, no passive and one active symptom in the equivalent groups in the United States.

Differences along the dimension of passivity-activity do not, in any case, exhaust the scope of intercultural contrasts obtained.

Table 17.4 Symptoms differentially distributed in male Argentine and United States patients

	χ^2	*p.*	*Higher in:* *Arg.*	*U.S.*
Formal thought disturbance				
Excessive daydreams	13.03	0.0001	√	
Poor judgment	3.72	0.05		√
Poor insight	22.98	0.001		√
Tangential, loose, illogical	9.93	0.01		√
Confused	8.41	0.01		√
Delusions	12.2	0.001		√
Stupor	19.96	0.001	√	
Feels others misunderstand him	12.71	0.001	√	
Feelings of sexual inadequacy	6.15	0.05	√	
Threatens assault	7.42	0.01		√
Affect and mood disturbance				
Shallow, dull, bland affect	13.55	0.0001		√
Feels incapable of work	6.63	0.01	√	
Tense, nervous, anxious	4.16	0.05		√
Restless, excited	5.30	0.05		√
Depressed, despondent	9.53	0.01		√
Formal behavior disturbances				
Psychomotor retardation, slow	4.59	0.05	√	
Running away	5.98	0.05	√	
Aversion or apathy toward sexual activity	3.98	0.05	√	
Temperaments				
Irritable, gets angry	3.79	0.05		√
Bitter	5.50	0.05	√	
Pessimistic	4.43	0.05	√	

Three additional trends might be worth articulating. First, in contrast to the aggressive symptoms of United States patients, sexual disturbances are selectively encountered among Argentine patients, especially women. Second, under the heading of formal thought disturbance, we find expressions of cognitive deficit in Argentina (e.g., poor attention, poor orientation in time and space) and those of cognitive restructuring in the United States (e. g., delusions). Third, we take note of the greater frequency of social referents in the symptoms of Argentines, particularly women, as exemplified by "feeling misunderstood," "lonely," "seeking approval and support." Combining this impression with the findings on Argentine patients' passivity, it would appear that Argentines withdraw more from the

Table 17.5 Symptoms differentially distributed in groups of Argentine and United States female patients

	X^2	p.	Higher in: Arg.	U.S.
Formal thought disturbance				
Excessive daydreams	6.26	0.05	√	
Poor insight	9.86	0.01		√
Poor attention, distractible	14.86	0.001	√	
Preoccupied	8.35	0.01	√	
Tangential, loose associations, illogical	5.73	0.05	√	
Obsessive doubting, can't make decisions	27.16	0.001	√	
Feels "going crazy"	18.97	0.001	√	
Delusions	4.06	0.05		√
Auditory hallucinations	8.12	0.01		√
Nightmares	17.41	0.001	√	
Thought content				
Free floating anxiety	12.05	0.001	√	
Fear of failure	27.56	0.001	√	
Feels misunderstood	24.74	0.001	√	
Suspiciousness, ideas of reference	11.16	0.001		√
Sexual preoccupation	13.86	0.001	√	
Feelings of sexual inadequacy	9.10	0.01	√	
Afraid of opposite sex	3.95	0.05		√
Does not believe she can be helped	5.56	0.05	√	
Lonely, fears loss of a relationship	6.86	0.01	√	
Seeks approval and support	6.86	0.01	√	
Affect and mood disturbance				
Feels incapable of work	19.34	0.001	√	
Apathetic, listless, indifferent	7.94	0.01	√	
Tense, anxious,nervous	6.11	0.05		√
Formal behavior disturbance				
Aversion toward sexual activity	6.70	0.01	√	
Untidy, slovenly, unkempt	4.76	0.05		√
Temperament				
Excitable	6.94	0.01	√	
Hostile, aggressive	4.73	0.05		√
Indecisive	20.57	0.001	√	
Jealous	22.78	0.001	√	
Passive-aggressive	6.94	0.01	√	
Pessimistic	14.77	0.001	√	
Self-conscious, difficulties Dealing with people	7.38	0.01	√	
Shy, ready to retreat into oneself	9.14	0.01	√	

world of activities and things than they do from people; perhaps the opposite trend operates among the United States patients.

Sex Differences. To turn to the subordinate objective of our study, we examined differences between men and women in each of the two countries in specific symptoms, as well as dominant roles, spheres, and coping styles. With this goal in mind, we made the male and female groups comparable in both size and biographical characteristics. This was done by reducing the male samples to the number of the smaller female group and by selectively eliminating from the comparison those individuals of the male group whose educational, occupational, age, marital, or diagnostic characteristics contributed to discrepancies between the original two samples. Thus equalized, the groups yielded findings that are presented in tables 17.6 and 17.7.

To summarize these results, it is readily apparent that sex differences are better delineated and more pronounced among Argentines than among North Americans. In the former country, women tend toward Turning Against Self and Thought as avenues of symptom expression; their discrete symptoms also connote ideational self-deprivation. By contrast, Argentine men selectively turn to Avoidance of Others and Affect as their characteristic symptom categories; the trend of their discrete symptoms bespeaks social withdrawal and dis-

Table 17.6 Dominant roles, spheres, and coping styles of male and female patients in the two countries

	Argentina		*United States*	
	Male	*Female*	*Male*	*Female*
Roles				
Against self	16	28	9	22
Against others	5	1	7	3
Avoidance of others	21	9	14	11
Indeterminate	0	4	12	6
	$\chi^2 = 14.73$ ($p < 0.05$)	$\chi^2 = 9.41$ ($p < 0.10$)		
Spheres				
Thought	12	30	11	9
Action	9	3	9	12
Affect	15	2	9	11
Somatization	6	7	13	10
Coping Styles				
Active	15	8	27	21
Passive	27	34	15	21
	$\chi^2 = 2.54$ (N.S.)	$\chi^2 = 1.75$ (N.S.)		

Table 17.7 Symptoms differentially distributed in groups of men and women in Argentina and the United States

	χ^2	*p.*	*Higher in:* Men	Women
Argentina				
Obsessions	4.06	0.05		√
Amnesia, fugue state	5.52	0.05	√	
Delirium tremens	5.10	0.05	√	
Stupor	6.55	0.01	√	
Tense, nervous, anxious, upset	4.99	0.05	√	
Restless, excited	3.89	0.05	√	
Depressed, despondent	5.81	0.05		√
Bizarre dress	4.21	0.05	√	
Untidy, slovenly, unkempt	5.48	0.05	√	
Self-inflicted injury	7.99	0.01	√	
Anorexia nervosa	5.97	0.05		√
General fatigue, weakness	7.04	0.01		√
Excitable	4.43	0.05	√	
Immature	4.43	0.05		√
Jealous	7.14	0.01		√
United States				
Bizarre ideas	3.95	0.05	√	
Visual hallucinations	4.21	0.05	√	
Delirium tremens	4.11	0.05	√	
Anorexia nervosa	3.86	0.05		√
Psychosomatic symptoms, general	8.86	0.05		√

organization of thought. The same tendencies appear, albeit in a much attenuated form, among the United States groups of male and female patients.

Discussion

Two themes emerge from the foregoing presentation of our findings. First, differences of considerable scope and magnitude exist in the symptomatology recorded in two countries only moderately different from each other; Argentina and the United States. Secondly, the character of these differences is by no means fortuitous; rather, it shows more than a casual degree of correspondence with contrasts theoretically postulated and empirically obtained for the normal segments of the population in the two nations.

The very fact of the existence of these differences carries implications for the currently active enterprise of determining international comparability of diagnostic judgments (Fabrega and Wallace 1967; Lin 1959, 1967; Pichot 1966). Our results, as well as those of a number of other intercultural investigations (Draguns et al. 1964; Draguns et al., in press; Kimura 1965; Saenger 1968; Wittkower and Rin 1965) demonstrate that diagnostically and socially matched groups of patients presented markedly different pictures on the plane of symptoms. From this, it is not far-fetched to infer that diagnostic categories, as applied in the two countries, are expressed through different manifestations. In the light of this conclusion, it appears to be highly desirable that future epidemiological comparisons of psychopathology in two or more countries include information on symptoms observed, as well as syndromes diagnosed.

To integrate this suggestion with the concepts and measures applied in the study, we might recall a recent series of investigations (Phillips, Browerman and Zigler 1966, 1968; Zigler and Phillips 1960, 1962) specifically devoted to ascertaining the nature and extent of the relationships between symptoms and diagnosis. To paraphrase the findings of these studies, specific symptoms showed little relationship and diagnostic categories, the association of roles and spheres with diagnostic judgements was considerably higher, and best results were obtained when social competence, together with the variables of role and sphere dominance, were related to the components of the diagnostic system. All of these results were gathered in a culturally uniform environment. For intercultural comparisons, culture characteristics would appear to be an additional term to be included together with social and symptom variables, in order to magnify the relationship between these component characteristics and diagnosis.

Our findings, however, do not only bear on the existence of intercultural differences, but, as noted, on their nature. In particular, we take note of the differences on the passive-active axis that conform both to the findings of Havighurst et al. (1963) and to the theoretical formulations by Diaz Guerrero (1967).

The concordance among these bodies of information strengthens the case for what we would like to call the "caricature theory" of culture's relation to psychopathology (Phillips and Draguns 1969). Within this formulation, psychopathological behavior is only seemingly outlandish, senseless, and bizarre; what it represents is the culturally shared mode of behavior that is applied in a wrong way, at the wrong place, and at the wrong time. Certainly, the pervasiveness of contrasts along the passive-active axis that have repeatedly emerged from a number of recent intercultural investigations of the English-speaking versus Spanish-speaking countries of the Western Hemisphere (e.g., Diaz Guerrero 1967; Havighurst and Dubois 1963) argues persuasively for the need for further research, within and across the "normal" and "abnormal" populations of the several cultures, along this heuristically fruitful organizing principle.

At the same time, we recognize that our findings went beyond the activity-passivity dimensions. These observations, at this point, remain isolated and in need of both a theoretical framework and a parallel set of findings on normal subjects drawn from the same two milieus. Only after such information is obtained will we be in a position to determine the limits of usefulness of the view of psychopathology as a caricatured exaggeration of the culture within which it occurs and as a revealing, if distorted, mirror of its milieu.

So far, our discussion has been predicated upon the implicit assumption that our findings objectively and automatically reflect patient characteristics in the two countries. In actuality, these results represent the products of a complex set of cognitive and social processes in which the patient, the psychiatrist, the hospital, and the community have participated. The psychiatrist's function in this transaction is a dual one: as an expert in recognizing and classifying psychopathology and as an agent of his society, called upon to identify instances of inappropriate and ineffective deviance. It might be fair to assume that the former component of his professional behavior has a higher degree of intercultural constancy than the latter, affected as it is by socially patterned norms of deviance, selective expectations and perceptions. In this connection, one might recall the recent study by Sandifer et al. (1969) who demonstrated the effect of these variables upon psychiatric judgment in two countries as similar as the United States and the United Kingdom. In addition to the psychiatrist, the hospital milieu, through its nurse and attendant agents as well as through patient group pressure, differentially reinforces or inhibits symptom manifestation. The behavior therapy literature (e. g., Ayllon and Michael 1959) has contributed illustrations and demonstrations of this influence; nothing is as yet known about the variation of these effects across cultures. Finally, let us not overlook the fact that the preliminary determination of who is a mental patient takes place in the community, at the hands of nonprofessional observers and associates in the patient's immediate environment. Again, it is gratuitous to assume that these decisions are uniformly made in several countries. Each of the variables enumerated is a potential subject for intercultural study, either as a discrete variable or as a component in a more inclusive research design. Pending the realization of these projects, we are left with a facet of an as yet incomplete structure, pointing to the striking differences in the patient descriptions of biographically, socioeconomically, and diagnostically matched sets of hospitalized patients in the two countries. As such, these findings are a function of both the procedure of data gathering and the mode of intercultural comparison. In our case, we elected to rely upon the method of individual matching, a technique which, on the one hand excludes sources of subject variation extraneous to culture, yet, on the other hand might cause some sources of intercultural differences to be overlooked. More concretely, our equating groups across cultures in diagnosis might have resulted in obscuring differences in the distribution of diagnostic categories in the hospitals of the two countries. A more global methodology, such as that of Saenger (1968), who compared across culture lines the gross incidence of symptoms and syndromes of total clinic populations might well be a useful adjunct to our work, based on relatively miniature and artifically equated groups. In making this suggestion, we echo the recommendation by Murphy (1969b—article) for diversification on an indispensable strategy in transcultural research in psychopathology; only through a pooling of a variety of complementary research approaches will definitive information emerge concerning the phenomena explored in this study.

18

Diagnostic Criteria of American and British Psychiatrists

R. E. Kendell, J. E. Cooper, A. J. Gourlay, J. R. M. Copeland, L. Sharpe, and B. J. Gurland

A diagnosis constitutes a summarized formulation of the clinical condition of the patient. Its purpose is not only to facilitate communication among clinicians and researchers, but also to promote the organization of clinical information, the prediction of important clinical events such as course of disorder and treatment response, and the advancement of causative research and theory development.

Traditionally, the psychiatric diagnostic process has involved the use of rather loose interview and data collection procedures and connotative diagnostic criteria, which have yielded low inter-rater agreement or reliability on diagnostic judgments made even within the same cultural milieu. In an effort to increase reliability, more systematic assessment procedures, such as structured clinical interviews and explicit denotative diagnostic criteria, have been developed in recent years. These developments have been quite helpful although they have not solved all problems. The situation is particularly intricate on the international scene, as cultural factors play a role not only in how the patient manifests his or her disorder but also in how observers perceive, interpret, and integrate verbal communications and behavioral expressions of psychopathology.

The authors, from London and New York, present an experimental study aimed at comparing diagnostic habits in two societies which are

closely related by culture and language and have similar degrees of technological development.

VIDEOTAPES OF diagnostic interviews with eight patients, three American and five English, were shown to large audiences of trained psychiatrists in the eastern United States and in different parts of the British Isles. The diagnoses made by these audiences were compared and for some patients there were major disagreements between them. The overall pattern of diagnostic differences between the American and British raters indicates that the American concept of schizophrenia is much broader than the British concept, embracing not only part of what in Britain would be regarded as depressive illness, but also substantial parts of several other diagnostic categories—manic illness, neurotic illness, and personality disorder. These serious differences in the usage of diagnostic terms have important implications for transatlantic communication, and indeed for international communication in general.

There are striking differences between the diagnostic contributions of first admissions to the mental hospitals of the United States and those of England and Wales (Kramer 1961), but these differences are greatly reduced when cohorts of patients admitted to hospital in the two countries are examined by a single team of psychiatrists using consistent diagnostic criteria (Cooper et al. 1969; Cooper 1970). These findings imply that there are systematic differences between the diagnostic criteria used by American and British psychiatrists and that, in particular, the former have a broader concept of schizophrenia and the latter a broader concept of manic depressive illness. If this is so, one would expect American and British psychiatrists to make different diagnoses when both are confronted with the same patients, and there is indeed some evidence that this occurs.

Sandifer et al. (1968) showed films of diagnostic interviews of a series of American patients to small groups of psychiatrists in London, Glasgow, and North Carolina and found systematic differences between the three centers. The British psychiatrists tended to diagnose manic depressive illness more readily, and the North Carolina psychiatrists tended to diagnose depressive neurosis more readily, and all within national differences were overshadowed by these cross-national differences. In a similar study Katz et al. (1969) showed a videotape of a diagnostic interview of a young woman, an aspiring actress, to two different audiences—42 American psychiatrists at the 1964 annual meeting of the American Psychiatric Association and 32 English psychiatrists at the Maudsley Hospital in London. A third of the American audience regarded this woman as schizophrenic, a third regarded her as neurotic, and the remainder regarded her simply as having a personality disorder. By contrast 60 percent of the English audience made a diagnosis of personality disorder and no one diagnosed schizophrenia.

The studies described here were conceived against this background. Our intention was to define more closely the areas in which the diagnostic criteria used by American and British psychiatrists differ from one another by showing videotapes of diagnostic interviews with varying types of patients, both British and American, to large representative audiences of psychiatrists on both sides of the Atlantic.

Method

Eight videotapes were used. Each was an unstructured diagnostic interview lasting between 20 and 50 minutes. Five of the patients (A, B, C, D, and E) were English and three (F, G, and H) American. Some were chosen in the expectation that they would highlight diagnostic differences between the two countries, others were chosen because their symptomatology was typical of a well-known stereotype. Together they portrayed a wide range of symptoms and a variety of different clinical problems.

In the British Isles five of the tapes were rated by an audience of 30 to 40 psychiatrists mainly from the Maudsley Hospital, London, and the other three (patients A, B, and F) were seen by 200 psychiatrists drawn from all over the country. This large group was obtained by holding a series of all-day meetings in different regions—two in London, two in Scotland, two in Ireland, and one each in Birmingham and Manchester. Apart from some overrepresentation of clinicians trained at the Maudsley Hospital, and the inevitable problem that only those with an interest in diagnosis offered to participate, this group can reasonably be regarded as broadly representative of British psychiatry. In the United States it proved harder to obtain a representative sample and eventually raters were obtained mainly from the New York Psychiatric Institute and the staffs of other state, city, and private hospitals supplying the New York metropolitan area. Audiences were also assembled, though, in Baltimore, Boston, and New Jersey and a few raters were obtained at the 1968 annual meeting of the American Psychiatric Association. Altogether over 450 psychiatrists participated; two tapes (patients A and F) were rated by over 120 psychiatrists and the others were rated by between 30 and 60.

All British raters were required to possess a Diploma in Psychological Medicine and American raters to have completed a psychiatric residency. Both were also required to have a minimum of four years experience in psychiatry and the average for both groups was between 12 and 15 years experience. Nearly all the British raters had received both their medical and their psychiatric training in the British Isles. Half the American raters, however, had obtained their initial medical qualification abroad (mostly in Central Europe), but over 90 percent had received their psychiatric training in the United States. A higher proportion of the British raters were from university departments or the psychiatric departments of general hospitals, and a correspondingly higher proportion of the Americans were from state hospitals. These differences are probably due to the different manner in which raters were obtained in the two countries. More of the American raters, on the other hand, had received a formal training in psychotherapy, and more were currently in private office practice. These latter differences probably reflect, or even underreflect, genuine differences between the two countries.

Apart from explanations of a few slang phrases and allusions that might have been unfamiliar on the far side of the Atlantic, raters were given no information other than that provided by the videotapes. After seeing each tape every audience was required to complete three sets of ratings. The first, Lorr's Inpatient Multidimensional Psychiatric Scale (IMPS) (Lorr and Klett 1967) consists of a series of 89 ratings, mainly on 9-point scales, which are defined in nontechnical language and cover most of the varieties of abnormal behavior likely to be manifested in an interview. The second was a check list of 116 technical terms, culled from both American and British sources and including most of the terms, like retardation, blocking, flattening of affect, and so on, commonly used by psychiatrists to describe abnormalities of speech and behavior. Lastly, raters were required to make a diagnosis. As the main purpose of the study was to compare the two sets of diagnoses it was necessary for a common nomenclature to be used. For this reason every rater was provided with the psychiatric section of the 8th edition of the *International Classification of Diseases* and asked to restrict himself to terms included therein. (*ICD* 8 is very similar to the American Psychiatric Association's *Diagnostic and Statistical Manual of Mental Disorders,* ed. 2 which was in fact modelled on *ICD* 8.) In addition to this main diagnosis, provision was made for a subsidiary diagnosis, and also for an alternative diagnosis, if either or both were felt to be needed by the rater. Finally, raters were invited to make a personal diagnosis, using whatever terminology they wished. Because the information that can be included in a 40-minute videotape is necessarily limited it was anticipated that raters might often feel that some vital piece of information was lacking, and so be unable to make a confident diagnosis. For this reason a 5-point confidence scale was attached to the main diagnosis. In fact, these fears proved to be largely unjustified; over all eight tapes 84 percent of American raters and 85 percent of British raters made confidence ratings of either 1 ("the patient's behavior or description of his subjective experience is pathognomonic") or 2 ("on the evidence provided this is by far the most likely diagnosis").

Results

This communication is concerned primarily with Anglo-American diagnostic differences. An account of the relatively minor differences between psychiatrists within the British Isles is published elsewhere (Copeland et al. in press) and an analysis of the IMPS and checklist ratings is to be published shortly.

PATIENT A. This 34-year-old English housewife had a long history of mild depressive symptoms and had recently developed a florid psychotic illness in which both schizophrenic and affective elements were prominent. She described feeling wonderfully happy and feeling that she was being forced to dance and sing and that radio programs were purely for her benefit; and then a few days later feeling "dirty and nasty" and thinking people were laughing at her because she was in hell. Table 18.1 lists the diagnoses given to her by 128 American and 211 British psychiatrists. In each country the majority regarded her illness as schizophrenic, mostly either as paranoid schizophrenia or as a schizo-affective psychosis. However, a significant minority (27 percent) of British clinicans regarded her illness as an affective disturbance and a further 11 percent, by

Table 18.1 Diagnoses Given to Patient A

	American Psychiatrists (N = 128)	*British Psychiatrists (N = 211)*
Schizophrenia	112 (88%)	148 (70%)
Hebephrenic	5	25
Catatonic	2	1
Paranoid	60	43
Acute schizophrenic episode	7	28
Latent	0	1
Residual	1	1
Schizo-affective	26	42
Unspecified	11	7
Affective Psychoses	9 (7%)	56 (27%)
Involutional melancholia	2	1
Manic depressive, manic	1	16
Manic depressive, depressed	2	9
Manic depressive, circular	4	17
Reactive depressive psychosis	0	1
Unspecified	0	12
Other Diagnoses	7	7
Alternative Diagnosis of Affective Psychosis	11 (9%)	23 (11%)

listing an affective psychosis as an alternative diagnosis, implied that they regarded this as a serious possibility. The corresponding American figures were lower (7 percent and 9 percent, respectively).

Patient B. This patient was a 33-year-old Londoner with more straightforward symptoms. He had heard voices (talking about him and plotting to kill him) intermittently for several years and had had frequent admissions to hospital. He was also a heavy drinker and commented that he could always get rid of his voices by having a few drinks. For this man the American and British diagnoses were very similar (table 18.2). The majority, 83 percent of the British group and 76 percent of the smaller American audience, regarded him as a schizophrenic. In each case, however, there was a dissenting minority who regarded his illness as an alcoholic psychosis; 11 percent of the American and 6 percent of the British audience made a diagnosis of alcoholic paranoia and a further 15 percent of the American audience and 21 percent of the British listed one of these as an alternative diagnosis.

Patient C. This was a 37-year-old Cockney laborer who, like patient A, had both schizophrenic and affective symptoms. At the

Table 18.2 Diagnoses Given to Patient B

	American Psychiatrists (N = 46)	*British Psychiatrists (N = 205)*
Schizophrenia	35 (76%)	171 (83%)
Hebephrenic	0	5
Paranoid	32	159
Acute schizophrenic episode	0	3
Latent	1	0
Residual	0	1
Schizo-affective	2	3
Paranoid State	5 (11%)	15 (7%)
Paranoia	4	9
Involutional paraphrenia	0	1
Unspecified	1	5
Alcoholic Psychosis	5 (11%)	12 (6%)
Alcoholic hallucinosis	4	9
Alcoholic paranoia	1	3
Other Diagnoses	1	7
Alternative Diagnosis of Alcoholic Psychosis	7 (15%)	44 (21%)

time of interview he was euphoric and talkative and revealed an elaborate series of grandiose delusions, centered on the belief that he was "King David," but he was prone to marked fluctuations of mood and had had periods of deep depression in the past. Again, most raters in both countries regarded him as a schizophrenic but again a significant minority (20 percent) of the British raters regarded him as a manic depressive and a further 17 percent gave this as an alternative diagnosis (table 18.3). By comparison, only 8 percent of the American raters even considered an affective illness as an alternative to schizophrenia.

PATIENT D. This patient was an unhappy 50-year-old woman who felt, with some justification, that her family were treating her as a servant. She had been admitted after a suicidal attempt and wept during the interview. She also had a longstanding fear of crowds and enclosed spaces and always spent much of her time cleaning and polishing her house. There was almost universal agreement that she had a depressive illness (table 18.4) but less agreement over what kind of depression it was. The majority (79 percent) of American raters favored a diagnosis of involutional melancholia; 42 percent of the British raters did likewise, but nearly as many (39 percent) regarded her as a manic depressive while the remaining 19 percent thought she had a depressive neurosis. In addition,

Table 18.3 Diagnoses Given to Patient C

	American Psychiatrists (N = 39)	*British Psychiatrists (N = 30)*
Schizophrenia	37 (95%)	23 (77%)
Hebephrenic	0	1
Paranoid	32	15
Acute schizophrenic episode	1	3
Residual	1	0
Schizo-affective	2	3
Unspecified	1	1
Manic Depressive Psychoses	0	6 (20%)
Manic depressive, manic	0	2
Manic depressive, circular	0	4
Other Diagnoses	2	1
Alternative Diagnosis of Affective Psychosis	3 (8%)	5 (17%)

about 40 percent of both American and British raters made a subsidiary diagnosis of either a neurotic illness or an anankastic personality disorder.

PATIENT E. The last of the five English patients presented a less familiar problem. She was a married woman of 25 years of age who described herself with some accuracy as having "gone back to being six." She denied knowing the date or how old she was and behaved and spoke in an absurdly childlike manner, clutching an empty egg carton and asking only to be allowed to sit on her husband's knee and be cuddled. She described how this remarkable behavior had been precipitated by the threat of her husband's arrest on a criminal charge and also gave a history of an earlier

Table 18.4 Diagnoses Given to Patient D

	American Psychiatrists (N = 29)	*British Psychiatrists (N = 31)*
Involutional melancholia	23 (79%)	13 (42%)
Manic depressive, depressed	1	12 (39%)
Reactive depressive psychosis	2	0
Depressive neurosis	2	6 (19%)
Schizophrenia, schizo-affective type	1	0
Subsidiary Diagnoses		
Anxiety, phobic or obsessive-compulsive neurosis	5	6
Anankastic personality	6	6

"breakdown" when, as a nursing student, she had been required to assist at a delivery. The attitudes of the American and British audiences to this problem were very different. Eighty-five percent of the American raters regarded her as a schizophrenic (table 18.5) though there was no consensus on the type of schizophrenia involved. Only 7 percent of the British audience agreed with this diagnosis; 52 percent of them thought that she had a personality disorder and 38 percent thought that she had a neurotic illness. In fact, the most common diagnoses were hysterical neurosis and hysterical personality, so 76 percent of the British raters were agreed that she was a hysteric. In contrast, only one American rater mentioned the term hysteria.

PATIENT F. This 30-year-old bachelor from Brooklyn had been hospitalized briefly several times, had no close friends, and had rarely held a steady job. He described having once had a hysterical paralysis of his arm and gave a vivid account of the fluctuations in his mood and morale and of his willingness to abuse alcohol or drugs whenever the opportunity arose. Table 18.6 shows the diagnoses made by 133 American and 194 British psychiatrists. Again, there is a striking difference between the two; 69 percent of the American audience, but only 2 percent of the British audience, di-

Table 18.5 Diagnoses Given to Patient E

	American Psychiatrists (N = 27)	*British Psychiatrists (N = 29)*
Schizophrenia	23 (85%)	2 (7%)
Simple	1	0
Hebephrenic	2	1
Catatonic	2	0
Paranoid	2	0
Acute schizophrenic episode	4	0
Residual	1	1
Schizo-affective	7	0
Unspecified	4	0
Neuroses	1 (4%)	11 (36%)
Anxiety neurosis	0	1
Hysterical neurosis	1	10
Personality Disorders	1 (4%)	15 (52%)
Schizoid	1	0
Hysterical	0	12
Antisocial	0	1
Unspecified	0	2
Other Diagnoses	2	1

Table 18.6 Diagnoses Given to Patient F

	American Psychiatrists (N = 133)	*British Psychiatrists (N = 194)*
Schizophrenia	92 (69%)	4 (2%)
Simple	0	1
Catatonic	1	0
Paranoid	27	1
Latent	8	0
Residual	3	0
Schizo-affective	33	1
Unspecified	20	1
Personality Disorder	10 (8%)	146 (75%)
Paranoid	1	2
Affective (cyclothymic)	1	8
Explosive	0	2
Hysterical	4	105
Asthenic	0	2
Antisocial	1	8
Unspecified	3	19
Affective Psychosis	10 (8%)	7 (4%)
Neurosis	19 (14%)	37 (19%)
Alcoholism or Drug Dependence	2	0

agnosed some form of schizophrenia. The most common American diagnoses were schizo-affective psychosis and paranoid schizophrenia, but many of the psychiatrists concerned indicated that pseudoneurotic schizophrenia, a term not recognized in the International Classification, was the diagnosis they would normally have made. Only three British psychiatrists even mentioned this term. Instead, 75 percent of the British audience made a diagnosis of personality disorder, and the majority specified that this was of hysterical type. By comparison, only 8 percent of the American group diagnosed a personality disorder of any kind.

The striking differences between the American and British diagnoses for the previous patient (E) might perhaps be discounted on the grounds that her behavior, and the situation that had precipitated it, were both unusual and that, in any case, the diagnostic discrepancy summarized in table 18.5 was derived from a comparatively small number of raters. But neither of these pleas can be made here. The general tenor of the patient's history and his behavior in the interview were familiar enough to psychiatrists on both sides of the Atlantic and both groups of raters were large. For this reason the discrepancy was studied in more detail.

If the patient's account of his problems had been vague and incomplete, or if the interviewer had left important areas uncovered, the raters would not have been able to make confident diagnoses and the discrepancy would lose much of its significance. But this does not seem to have been the case: 83 percent of both the American and the British audiences made ratings of 1 or 2 on the 5-point confidence scale, and when the two audiences were compared again after excluding all those who had rated 3, 4 or 5, the discrepancy was as great as ever: 68 percent of the Americans, but only 2 percent of the British, diagnosed schizophrenia; 79 percent of the British, but only 6 percent of the Americans, diagnosed a personality disorder. An examination of the alternative diagnoses offered pointed to the same conclusion: 59 percent of the American audience and 62 percent of the British audience offered no alternative diagnosis, a further indication of their confidence in their main diagnoses. Of the 92 American psychiatrists who regarded the patient as schizophrenic, only three offered a personality disorder as an alternative; and of the 146 British psychiatrists who regarded the patient as having a personality disorder, only three mentioned schizophrenia as an alternative. In short, the majority of American psychiatrists was confident that the patient was schizophrenic and did not seriously consider any other diagnosis; the majority of British psychiatrists, on the other hand, insisted that he simply had a personality disorder and that there was really no question of his having a psychotic illness.

Because of this persisting discrepancy, the personal information provided by all participating psychiatrists was analyzed in an attempt to identify types of psychiatrists particularly prone to make a diagnosis of schizophrenia rather than personality disorder, or vice versa. Age, length of psychiatric experience, country of medical qualification, and formal psychotherapeutic training exerted no significant influence. In the United States there was a significant ($P < 0.05$) tendency for raters who had either been trained in, or were currently working in, state hospitals to diagnose schizophrenia more commonly than those from university departments or other settings, but by far the most important variables were which country the rater worked in, Britain or America, and which he had received his psychiatric training in. The two could not be distinguished because they were nearly always the same.

Patient G. This patient was a 26-year-old American who spent most of the interview describing his illogical and incomprehensible schemes for world domination. He rocked in his chair, giggled repeatedly, and twice stopped speaking in midsentence and stared blankly for several seconds before continuing. This tape was seen by 34 psychiatrists in each country and their diagnoses are listed in table 18.7. Nearly everyone agreed that he was schizophrenic but there was much poorer agreement on the type of schizophrenia involved. Eight of the nine subtypes recognized in the International Classification were mentioned and none commanded a majority of either American or British raters.

PATIENT H. The last patient was an American woman of 47 who regarded herself as the queen of England. She was flippant and preoccupied with her sexual needs and her speech was full of puns and slang associations. Her symptomatology had prominent schizophrenic and manic components and she gave rise to a similar pattern of diagnoses to patient A. That is, in both countries the majority diagnosis was schizophrenia, of either paranoid or schizo-affective types, and in both there was a dissenting minority who felt she had a manic-depressive illness (table 18.8). Again, like patient A, the proportion of American raters diagnosing schizophrenia was higher than that of the British raters (78 percent vs 66 percent), and the proportion diagnosing an affective psychosis correspondingly lower (22 percent vs 34 percent).

Comment

Three different patterns of diagnostic agreement or disagreement are portrayed by these eight patients. Patients B, D, and G all exhib-

Table 18.7 Diagnoses Given to Patient G

	American Psychiatrists (N = 34)	*British Psychiatrists (N = 34)*
Schizophrenia	33 (97%)	32 (94%)
Simple	0	1
Hebephrenic	11	12
Catatonic	0	8
Paranoid	15	7
Acute schizophrenic episode	3	0
Residual	0	1
Schizo-affective	1	0
Unspecified	3	3
Other Diagnosis	1	2

Table 18.8 Diagnoses Given to Patient H

	American Psychiatrists (N = 60)	*British Psychiatrists (N = 41)*
Schizophrenia	*47 (78%)*	*27 (66%)*
Hebephrenic	*5*	*6*
Catatonic	*1*	*0*
Paranoid	*17*	*10*
Residual	*1*	*0*
Schizo-affective	*12*	*11*
Unspecified	*11*	*0*
Affective Psychoses	*13 (22%)*	*14 (34%)*
Manic depressive, manic	*8*	*7*
Manic depressive, depressed	*1*	*0*
Manic depressive, circular	*1*	*5*
Unspecified	*3*	*2*
Alternative Diagnosis of Schizophrenia	*6 (10%)*	*8 (20%)*
Alternative Diagnosis of Affective Psychosis	*7 (12%)*	*5 (12%)*

ited symptoms which were fairly typical of classical stereotypes and for all three there was substantial agreement between American and British psychiatrists. For patient B agreement was very close, not only for the main diagnosis of paranoid schizophrenia but also for the alternative diagnosis of an alcoholic psychosis. Similarly, there was almost complete agreement that patient D had a depressive illness and that patient G had a schizophrenic illness. There was poor agreement, however, both between and within countries, on the variety of depression or schizophrenia involved. Patients A, C, and H all exhibited a mixture of schizophrenic and affective symptoms and had been chosen for that reason. All three were regarded as schizophrenic by the majority of both American and British raters, but for each between 20 percent and 34 percent of the British audience made a diagnosis of an affective psychosis (mainly manic-depressive illness) and a further 15 percent or so suggested this as a serious alternative to schizophrenia. A few American psychiatrists did the same, but in each case the proportion was much lower. Patients E and F had originally been included to offset a preponderance of psychotic patients rather than to highlight any particular diagnostic problem but, in the event, it was these two who gave rise to the most serious disagreement. For both, the majority of American psychiatrists diagnosed some form of schizophrenia while British psychiatrists diagnosed either a personality disorder or a neurotic illness.

The difference between the American and British diagnoses for patients A, C, and H are consistent with the many other indications (Kramer 1961; Cooper 1970; Gurland et al. 1970) that American psychiatrists have a broader concept of schizophrenia and British psychiatrists have a correspondingly broader concept of manic depressive illness, and are not of sufficient magnitude to prevent the majority diagnosis from being the same on both sides of the Atlantic. The problem is familiar, and of manageable proportions. The same cannot be said of the almost total disagreement revealed by patients E and F, which has more serious implications. The basic design of the study ensured that all raters were provided with exactly the same information and it has already been shown that both sets of raters had confidence in their conflicting diagnoses. The different interpretations placed on patient E's behavior might perhaps be discounted, for reasons that have been discussed previously, but the same cannot be done for patient F. The essential features of his problem—a long history of failure to develop lasting relationships or to cope with the demands of everyday life, but without florid psychotic symptoms—were commonplace. Perhaps significantly, Katz et al.'s aspiring actress (1969) showed these same general characteristics and the majority of English raters considered that she had a personality disorder; while a third of the American audience regarded her as schizophrenic.

In a situation such as this, where two groups of equally experienced psychiatrists, both provided with the same data, disagree as to whether or not a patient is schizophrenic there is a natural temptation to ask who is right. It is important to realize, though, that in our present state of knowledge such a question is not only unanswerable, it is inherently meaningless. Schizophrenia, like all other varieties of functional mental illness recognized in our nomenclature, is defined in terms of its clinical picture. In Scadding's terminology (Scadding 1963), its defining characteristic is its syndrome, and so the decision whether or not an individual patient has schizophrenia can only be made by the "Hippocratic procedure" of comparing his symptoms with those of the illness and deciding whether the resemblance is adequate. In consequence, though one may discuss whose concept of schizophrenia is more useful, or closer to Bleuler's original description, one cannot meaningfully discuss which is right, for we have no external criterion to appeal to—no morbid anatomy, no etiological agent, no biochemical or physiological anomaly.

But disagreements as glaring as this have serious implications. Diagnoses are the most important of all our technical terms because they are the means by which we identify the subject matter of most of our research. They identify the types of patients who received the drug we were assessing, or whose family dynamics or sodium metabolism we were studying. If these terms are used by different groups of psychiatrists in widely differing ways, the two will, at best, fail to communicate with each other, and may well actively mislead one another.

The fact that these Anglo-American differences have arisen in spite of a common language and numerous cultural and professional ties has unhappy implications for international communication in general. Certainly the opportunities for groups of psychiatrists who lack these advantages to diverge from one another without realizing it must be much greater. Only recently have attempts been made to study differences in diagnostic criteria on this wider stage, and so far only two multinational comparisons have been reported, both based on written case histories rather than on films or videotapes. In the first of these (Shepherd et al. 1968), a World Health Organization pilot study involving a small number of distinguished psychiatrists from eight different countries, cross-national differences were no worse than those within a group of British psychiatrists. However, in the second (Rawnsley 1967), which involved larger groups of psychiatrists from the United States, the United Kingdom, and the Scandinavian countries, several systematic differences were detectable. American psychiatrists had a propensity for diagnosing schizophrenia where Europeans diagnosed a depression or a paranoid psychosis: Scandinavian psychiatrists used the term psychogenic psychosis to describe patients others regarded as neurotic; and American and Swedish psychiatrists diagnosed cerebral arteriosclerosis and their British, Norwegian, and Danish counterparts diagnosed an affective disorder. Significantly, these differences emerged in spite of the fact that the study was based solely on written transcripts, and these eliminate one of the most important sources of variation, the observer's own perception of psychopathology.

There is probably no easy way of removing entrenched differences in diagnostic usage of the kind that have been demonstrated here. If psychiatrists detected the same abnormalities in patients to whom they attributed different diagnoses the problem would be relatively simple. Patients could be identified by their symptoms instead of by diagnosis, and different schools of psychiatry might even be persuaded to agree on common definitions for their diagnoses. But in this study at least the evidence (to be reported in detail elsewhere) is that American and British psychiatrists often detect quite different symptoms in patients whom they diagnose differently. Patient F, for instance, was rated by 67 percent of the American audience as having delusions, by 63 percent as having passivity feelings, and by 58 percent as showing thought disorder. The corresponding percentages for British raters were 12 percent, 8 percent, and 5 percent, a contrast every bit as striking as the difference in diagnosis. Even the IMPS ratings, which are couched in nontechnical language and purport to be straightforward descriptions of deviations from normal behavior, showed several significant differences, with American raters perceiving more symptomatology in all areas, particularly in those with a strong schizophrenic connotation. Whether clinicians make different diagnoses because they perceive different symptoms, or whether they perceive different symptoms because they have already recognized a familiar illness is an important and intriguing issue. But either way the fact that serious perceptual differences are involved makes it very difficult for someone who has been trained in one frame of reference to change to another.

Probably the most important cause of the Anglo-American discrepancies revealed here is that the American concept of schizophrenia has expanded greatly in the last 30 years without any corresponding enlargement of the British concept. The reasons for this divergence are complex, but the greater influence of the psychoanalytic movement in North America, and influential teachers on both sides of the Atlantic, have probably been more important than any factual discoveries. The evidence provided by these and earlier videotape studies (Sandifer et al. 1968; Katz et al. 1969) and comparisons of hospital populations in London and New York (Cooper et al., Cooper, 1970; Gurland et al. 1970) make it clear that the concept of schizophrenia held on the east coast of the United States now embraces not only part of what in Britain would be regarded as depressive illness but also substantial parts of several other diagnostic categories—manic illness, neurotic illness and personality disorder (figure 18.1).

Only less important differences can also be seen. The diagnoses given to patients E and F (tables 18.5 and 18.6) indicate that British psychiatrists are more prone to use the term hysteria than their American counterparts, a finding presumably related to the omission of hysteria from the American Psychiatric Association's

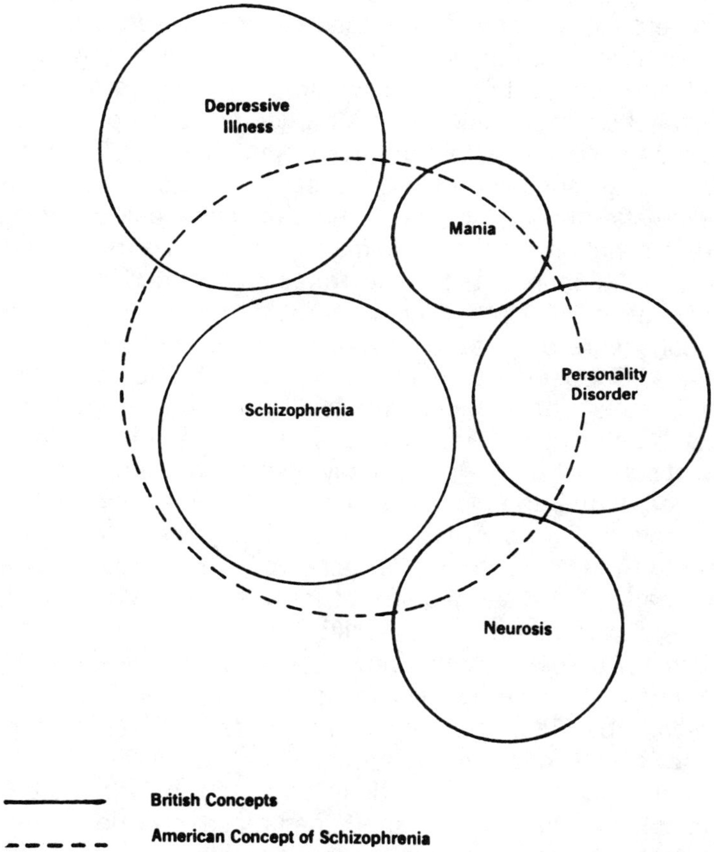

Figure 18.1 The differences between American and British Concepts of Schizophrenia.

1952 classification (DSM 1). Similarly, the diagnoses given to patient D (table 18.4) and the results of the hospital population comparisons referred to above (Cooper et al. 1969; Cooper 1970) indicate that American psychiatrists diagnose involutional melancholia in middle-aged women whom many British psychiatrists would regard as manic depressives. Of all these differences, the overlap between that American psychiatrists diagnose involutional melancholia in middle-aged women whom many British psychiatrists would regard as manic depressives. Of all these differences, the overlap between probably represents the most serious problem, particularly where ambulant patients are concerned.

Although, as was stressed above, no concept of schizophrenia can be either right or wrong it does seem, at least to a European observer, that the diagnosis is now made so freely on the east coast of the United States that it is losing much of its original meaning and is approaching the point at which it becomes a synonym for functional mental illness. Seven of the eight patients in this study were diagnosed as schizophrenic by over two thirds of the American psychiatrists, although between them they presented a variety of different symptoms and problems. Similarly, in a recent random sample of 192 patients below the age of 60 admitted to public mental hospitals in New York City, 82 percent of those with nonorganic conditions were diagnosed as schizophrenic by the hospital psychiatrists (Cooper 1970; Gurland et al. 1970). But doubtless the situation looks very different when seen through North American eyes and any major changes in either the British or American concepts of schizophrenia will probably occur only after, and as a consequence of, therapeutic innovations or biochemical or physiological discoveries. Changes currently taking place in the American concept of mania illustrate this quite well. The diagnosis of mania was in danger of disappearing, at least in New York, until lithium salts were introduced as a specific treatment of manic illnesses. The interest aroused by this new drug has, however, caused patients who five years ago would have been regarded as schizophrenics to be diagnosed now as manic depressives in order that they may be given lithium salts (Lipkin et al. 1970; Gattozzi 1970).

Finally, one last issue needs to be raised. Although the British raters, at least of tapes A, B, and F, can reasonably be regarded as geographically representative of British psychiatry, the same is not true of the American raters, the majority of whom worked in or near New York. At present we do not know how representative New York psychiatrists are of American psychiatry as a whole, but there are a number of indications that their concept of schizophrenia may be broader than that of their colleagues elsewhere. The 1968 tables of first admissions to public mental hospitals compiled by the Biometry Branch of the National Institute of Mental Health show that, for the whole of the United States, 18 percent of admissions are diagnosed as schizophrenics, or 31 percent of all admissions other than organic brain syndromes and addictive states. For California and Illinois, two large states of similar size and population distribution to New York State, the corresponding proportions are very similar. For New York State, though, they are considerably higher—25 percent and 52 percent. These high percentages might, of course, be due to a higher prevalence of schizophrenia in New York, but they certainly raise the possibility that schizophrenia is diagnosed more readily there. The preliminary results of videotape comparisons between New York and other centers on the Pacific coast and in the Midwest suggest the same. It is probably also significant that several of the ideas that have been instrumental in enlarging the American concept of schizophrenia, like the introduction of the concept of pseudoneurotic schizophrenia (Hoch and Polatin 1949) and the dictum that "even a trace of schizophrenia is schizophrenia" (Lewis and Piotrowski 1954) originated in New York, and so can be expected to have been more influential there than elsewhere.

It is possible, therefore, that future work will show that these comparisons between predominantly New York psychiatrists and British psychiatrists have given a misleadingly alarming picture of overall Anglo-American differences. It is important to realize, though, that if this does happen an equivalent communication difficulty will necessarily be revealed between New York psychiatrists and their colleagues elsewhere in the United States. The magnitude of the diagnostic disparity, and hence of the communication problem, would not be affected, only its geographical location—within the United States instead of between the United States and Britain. In view of the confusion which inconsistent diagnostic criteria can cause, the sooner this question is answered the better.

Acknowledgment

This work was supported by Public Health Service grant no. MH-09191 from the National Institute of Mental Health.

Without the help of the hundreds of psychiatrists, British and American, who rated these videotapes for us, and the hospitals and university departments who allowed us to use their facilities, this study could not have been carried out.

Annotated Additional Readings

a) **Opler, M. K., and J. L. Singer. 1959.** Ethnic differences in behavior and psychopathology: Italian and Irish. *International Journal of Social Psychiatry* 2:11–23.
Differences in the symptomatic expression of psychopathology between Irish and Italian schizophrenic patients, matched for demographic variables and hospitalization history, are presented. The relationships between the differences found and the characteristics of each culture are analyzed using a psychoanalytic framework.

b) **Rin, H., C. Schooler, and W. A. Caudill. 1973.** Symptomatology and hospitalization: Culture, social structure, and psychopathology in Taiwan and Japan. *Journal of Nervous and Mental Disease* 157:296–312.
An investigation of symptom patterns presented by psychiatric patients admitted to Japanese and Taiwanese hospitals. The authors competently use various multivariate statistical analyses to clarify the questions at hand. First, factor analysis is employed to reduce the number of symptoms and to elucidate psychopathological constructs underlying them, which are then compared across the two samples. Multiple regression and multivariate analysis of variance, as well as path analysis, are also used to assess and describe the combined influence of various sociocultural variables on the previously obtained psychopathological factors.

c) **Draguns J. G., L. Phillips, I. K. Broverman, W. Caudill, and S. Nishimae. 1971.** Symptomatology of hospitalized psychiatric patients in Japan and in the United States: A study of cultural differences. *The Journal of Nervous and Mental Disease* 152:3–16.
"A comparison of symptoms, dominant roles (turning against self, turning against others, avoidance of others) and spheres (thought, affect, somatization, action) between U.S. and Japanese hospitalized psychiatric patients.

The authors define and explain psychopathological differences between these two groups in the light of "social caricature" concepts, which propose that maladaptive behavior is essentially a self-defeating exaggeration of behavior considered normal within the sociocultural environment of the individual. This reference and the previous one complement well article 17.

d) **Saenger, G. 1968.** Psychiatric outpatients in America and the Netherlands: A transcultural comparison. *Social Psychiatry* 3:149–164.
A systematic comparison of the symptomatology and functioning of psychiatric patients seen in some outpatient clinics in the Netherlands and the United States. The focus on outpatients is rather unusual.

U.S. clinics appeared to see more than 10 times as many patients diagnosed as schizophrenic than did the Dutch clinics, but comparisons of symptoms suggested that these differences were due mainly to contrasting diagnostic habits. On the other hand, Dutch clinics saw a much higher proportion of hysterical neurotics than did the U.S. clinics. U.S. patients had more feelings of inadequacy, loneliness, and social isolation. Depressed patients in the Netherlands more often presented apathy, guilt feelings, and psychomotor retardation than their U.S. counterparts, who more often displayed agitation and suicidal ideation.

e) **Sandifer, M. G., A. Hordern, G. C. Timbury, L. M. Green. 1968.** Psychiatric diagnosis: A comparative study in North Carolina, London, and Glasgow. *British Journal of Psychiatry* 114:1–9.
A cross-national study of diagnostic styles using clinical filmed diagnostic interviews plus complementary written information on 30 psychiatric patients quasi-randomly selected from admissions to a North Carolina hospital. Forty-three diagnosticians in North Carolina, four in London, and four in Glasgow appraised the clinical information offered and each independently formulated a psychiatric diagnosis. The major findings were a greater use of neurotic (especially neurotic depressive) diagnoses by North Carolina psychiatrists, a greater use of personality disorder by Glasgow psychiatrists, and greater use of manic depressive by both U.K. groups of diagnosticians. This paper is an interesting complement to article 18.

f) **Surawicz, F. G., and M. G. Sandifer. 1970.** Cross-cultural diagnosis: A study of psychiatric diagnosis comparing Switzerland, the United States and the United Kingdom. *International Journal of Social Psychiatry* 16:232–236.
A continuation of the above study. For this report, 10 filmed diagnostic interviews and complementary written information were selected from the 30 used in the previous study. The psychiatric diagnoses formulated by a group of Swiss psychiatrists were compared with those previously made by U.S. and U.K. psychiatrists. In the diagnosis of schizophrenia and grouped affective disorders, Swiss and U.S. psychiatrists tended to show frequencies similar to each other and slightly higher than those of U.K. psychiatrists. The latter group diagnosed manic-depressive disorders more frequently than either U.S. or Swiss psychiatrists.

g) **Kendell, R. E., P. Pichot, and M. Von Cranach. 1974.** Diagnostic criteria of English, French, and German psychiatrists. *Psychological Medicine* 4:187–195.
An international study of diagnostic habits among English-speaking psychiatrists of three European countries, using 27 videotaped diagnostic interviews of psychiatric patients hospitalized in London. The findings suggested that English, French, and German psychiatrists have similar concepts of schizophrenia, neurotic illness, personality disorder, and alcoholism, but differ greatly in their concept of affective illness, particularly manic-depressive disorder. English psychiatrists appeared to have much broader concepts of both neurotic and psychotic depression and of mania than the French, with German psychiatrists in an intermediate position, closer to the French. This paper and the two preceding ones, complement article 18.

h) **Murphy, H. B. M. 1974.** Differences between mental disorders of French Canadians and British Canadians. *Canadian Psychiatric Association Journal* 19:247–257.

In contrast with preceding readings, this paper reviews several reports comparing two major Canadian populations. Particularly interesting are the symptomatological contrasts among schizophrenic and depressive patients. French Canadians presented more symptomatology in general and those diagnosed as schizophrenic exhibited more abundant complaints about family, friends, and associates. Depressive British Canadians presented more difficulties in thinking and concentration while their French-Canadian counterparts presented a higher frequency of somatic symptoms. After discussing these and other contrasts, the author offers some practical recommendations for the differential evaluation and care of these two groups of patients.

i) **Sartorious, N. 1976.** Classification: An international perspective. *Psychiatric Annals* 6:358–367.

The chief of the Division of Mental Health of the World Health Organization (WHO) reviews several major issues on international diagnosis. He outlines the development and role of the International Classification of Diseases, including its section on mental disorders. This classification, which has been accepted by most countries of the world, has as a main purpose to provide statistical data about groups of cases. The author then describes some aspects of WHO's program on standardization of psychiatric diagnosis, classification, and statistics. This includes various seminars which started in 1965 and have dealt with several major psychiatric syndromes and the psychopathology of childhood and old age. It also includes the preparation of an international glossary. Finally, the author discusses both the implications of the classification of mental disorders for public health as well as some continuing lines of research toward more satisfactory models for psychiatric classification.

j) **Mezzich, J. E. 1979.** Patterns and issues in multiaxial psychiatric diagnosis. *Psychological Medicine* 9:125–137.

Multiaxial diagnosis represents an innovative model which essentially consists in systematically formulating the patient's condition according to separate variables, aspects, or axes—such as symptomatology, level of social functioning, associated physical disorders, and psychosocial stressors. The multiaxial diagnostic model has attracted considerable attention on the basis of its potential both to describe and to handle more effectively the complexity of the clinical condition and to articulate a multi-theoretical approach to psychiatry and medicine in general.

The model is being incorporated into various national diagnostic systems and is under consideration for the tenth revision of the International Classification of Diseases. It is noteworthy that the preparation of various versions of the model has been to a large extent an international enterprise, with specific multiaxial diagnostic systems developed in Sweden, England, Germany, Japan, and the United States. This paper reviews multiaxial systems from various parts of the world and points out major issues in their conceptualization and methodology.

VII

Specific Psychiatric Disorders

In the previous part we discussed general issues in the expression, perception, and diagnosis of mental disturbance. In this one we move in the direction of specialized psychopathology to look at specific psychiatric syndromes or disorders as they relate to a variety of sociocultural factors.

Psychiatric symptoms, such as hallucinations, agitation, insomnia, and compulsions and other clinical features, do not happen at random. They are usually seen clustered into higher order categories such as obsessive-compulsive disorder and schizophrenia. Although there is by no means universal agreement on the characterization and stability of these syndromes, studies in recent years have shown that at least certain major psychiatric disorders, such as schizophrenia and depression, have been detected wherever they have been thoroughly looked for. Considerable variations in their incidence and especially their particular manifestations and course have also been noted. A variety of causative factors, including biological, psychological, and social variables, have been plausibly postulated for most psychiatric disorders. Within such a multidisciplinary framework, this chapter focuses on sociocultural factors as they influence and interact with the rates, manifestations, and outcome of specific psychiatric disorders.

The articles presented in this chapter cover many broad categories of psychiatric disorder, including schizophrenia, depressive disorder, substance abuse, child behavior disorders, and the so-called "culture-bound syndromes."

The editors' introductions preceding the articles contain a brief standard description of the psychiatric disorders under consideration for the benefit of the reader unfamiliar with them, without pretending to suggest that they are fixed categories when in fact the conceptualization and definition of many of them are very much in a state of flux.

A number of additional annotated references are provided containing alternative views as well as studies conducted in various cultures, which complement the articles presented in full.

19

The Social Aetiology of Schizophrenia in Immigrant Groups

Christopher Bagley

The first article presented in this chapter on specific psychiatric disorders and their sociocultural correlates, deals with schizophrenia. This seems to be in order given the centrality of this disorder in psychopathology: conceptually most challenging, one of the most serious mental disturbances an individual can experience, and a tremendous public health problem.

Schizophrenia, having at the time the misnomer of "dementia praecox," gained lasting nosological identity when Emil Kraepelin separated it from another major functional psychosis, manic-depressive illness, in 1896. Reflecting current notions, the glossary of the Ninth Revision of the International Classification of Diseases (Clinical Modification) defines schizophrenia as "A group of psychoses in which there is a fundamental disturbance of personality, a characteristic distortion of thinking, often a sense of being controlled by alien forces, delusions which may be bizarre, disturbed perception, abnormal affect out of keeping with the real situation, and autism. Nevertheless, clear consciousness and intellectual capacity are usually maintained." More explicit and denotative diagnostic criteria for this and other psychiatric disorders can be found in the U.S. Diagnostic and Statistical Manual of Mental Disorders, 3d Edition (DSM-III) (American Psychiatric Association, 1980). The above statement and reference are mentioned here only to provide a guide to the reader unfamiliar with the notion of schizophrenia and not to suggest that discussions on the conceptualization and nature of this disorder are not still going on.

As for most psychiatric disorders, especially the severe ones, multifactorial causality seems to be most likely. Evidence for a strong although limited role of biological factors, including genetic ones, has been provided (e.g., Kety 1976). Research on psychosocial factors is also active. In the following article, sociologist Christopher Bagley presents an interesting study on the contribution to the causation of schizophrenia of certain sociocultural factors—i.e., ethnic minority status, social change, and status striving in a climate of limited opportunity.

STUDIES OF the incidence of schizophrenia in a variety of cultures (Lin 1953: Lin and Standley 1962) suggest that, in contrast to conditions like psychoneurosis or suicide, the proportion of schizophrenics in any community is relatively stable. The various studies reviewed by these authors suggest that the rate of schizophrenia is between 0.4 and 0.9 percent. Mayer Gross et al.(1960) suggest that the most reliable estimate of incidence is the figure given by Luxenburger for Germany of 0.85 percent. Similar findings are reported in the review by Yolles and Kramer (1969). This finding of the relative stability of rates of schizophrenia between cultures has an implication for understanding the aetiology of the disease. It carries the implication that endogenous rather than exogenous factors are of major importance in the emergence of the illness.

There are grounds, however, for supposing that although constitutional and hereditary factors may be of major importance in schizophrenia, factors in the environment can play a subsidiary, and sometimes a primary, role in the emergence of the disease. The most reliable evidence on the influence of external factors on schizophrenia is that concerning organic trauma and illness of the central nervous system. There is considerable weight of clinical evidence showing that schizophrenia can follow such events in the absence of a premorbid personality or a heredity indicative of schizophrenia (Davison and Bagley 1969). The evidence on the influence of factors in the social or interpersonal environment is less clear, and most studies in this area have not been methodologically adequate. A notable exception is the study by Brown and Birley (1968). Studies of the social environment have to tackle the difficult problem that the illness itself may create changes in the individual's environment which may be mistaken for social precursors of the disease. Brown and Birley, using a methodology designed to cope with this problem, did in fact show that social factors had an important role in the onset of schizophrenic symptoms.

Although the rate of schizophrenia is relatively stable between cultures, epidemiological studies have shown marked differences in rates between subcultures within a single culture. The review of American studies by Sanua (1969) suggests, for example, that the rate of schizophrenia is markedly higher in the foreign-born than in the native-born, and is particularly high in American-born Negroes. The evidence on these subgroups within society is particularly interesting, for it suggests the possibility that in these cases there may be social causes or precipitants of schizophrenia associated with the status of the ethnic or immigrant minority in society. An important clue to possible social causes of schizophrenia in Negroes in America has been proved by the work of Parker and Kleiner (1966). The object of these two authors was to test the relation of the degree of psychosis and neurosis to "goal-striving" in the Negro population. A random sample was made of wards with a high proportion of Negroes. Negro subjects thus obtained were given a mental health assessment, and assigned to a "community" or healthy group, or to an ill group. A second sample of mentally ill Negroes was obtained from clinics, psychiatrists and hospitals. These procedures gave 1,489 subjects in the community or healthy sample, and 1,423 in the mentally ill sample. All subjects were given questionnaires on attitudes to goal striving, by Negro interviewers.

The results of this procedure showed clear and significant differences with regard to goal-striving, between the mentally ill and the community samples. The mentally ill had higher levels of aspiration—i.e. , set themselves higher goals—than the non-mentally ill. Significantly more of the mentally ill denied being a negro constituted any barrier to achievement: "Almost every clinical study of psychopathology among Negroes indicates that the Negro who is not identified with other members of his group, or who aspires to 'be white', is relatively more prone to manifest various forms of mental ill health."

The mentally ill had significantly more "low self-esteem," which was related to the large gap between an internalized ideal and perception of the self's success. There was a significant and positive correlation between the number of psychiatric symptoms and lower self-esteem. The highest rates of mental illness were found in those who were upwardly mobile. The findings in this respect are consistent with the anomie theory of Durkheim and Merton:

> Individuals at the highest level, who have risen in the occupational status hierarchy despite the considerable barriers facing the Negro, are

probably characterized by chronic achievement striving and dissatisfaction with self—an inability to reduce their strivings even after they have achieved considerable success. This continued achievement striving suggests the anomic effects of the differentially restricted opportunity structure the Negro faces in American society. A high level of goal striving in the context of a relatively restricted opportunity structure apparently takes its psychological toll.

More goal-striving was found in the psychotics (a more seriously mentally ill group) than in the neurotics. Men were more often mentally ill, and younger rather than older men. The authors conclude:

Despite the relatively closed nature of the opportunity structure for the Negro in American society, the patients were more prone than the community respondents to perceive the system as open. Along with this perception, they rigidly maintained high levels of goal-striving stress. The existing dysfunctions involved high levels of goal-striving orientation in the context of an objectively limited opportunity structure."

The study by Brown and Birley (1968) is also of particular interest in that, although it did not deal with ethnic or cultural minorities, it dealt with a carefully diagnosed group of schizophrenics. Parker and Kleiner's study does not deal with schizophrenia specifically, although the group of "psychotics" in this study obviously contains a large number of schizophrenics. Brown and Birley studied "life crises" in a 13-week period preceding the onset of schizophrenic symptoms, and took great care to define whether the events were independent or only possibly independent of the possibly insidious onset of symptoms.

"Since," the authors say, "we believed that for schizophrenic patients at least emotional arousal as such is important as a precipitating factor, we include changes and crises which might be expected to give rise to marked negative *or* positive emotion in many people." The events they considered were: (1) Role change for the subject, e.g., leaving school, changing job. (2) Role change for close relatives or household members, including e.g., admission to hospital with serious physical illness. Similar changes in close relatives or household members including death. (4) Residence change in subject, his family, or household members. (5) Forecast of change, e.g., subject being told that his firm will move to another town. (6) Valued goal fulfillment of disappointment, e.g., offered house to rent at price he could afford. (7) Other dramatic events, e.g., house burgled; witnessing a road accident; relative or friend involved in accident; arrest of relative or friend.

The number of events in the recent history of 50 schizophrenics was compared with the number of events over the same time period in a general population comparison group of 325. The 50 schizophrenics had significantly more events in the three weeks prior to the onset of symptoms than their controls.

Three hypotheses.
The foregoing review of literature suggests three exploratory hypotheses.

(1) Ethnic and cultural sub-groups in society will have rates of schizophrenia which may differ from those of the major culture.
(2) Social events, in the form of the life changes described by Brown and Birley, and probably other social factors in the environment, such as poverty and poor material environment, may be precipitants of schizophrenia in sub-cultures within society to a greater extent than in schizophrenic individuals in the major culture.
(3) The phenomenon observed by Kleiner and Parker of "goal-striving in a climate of limited opportunity" will apply to black minorities in cultures other than America.

The first hypothesis is tested by means of an epidemiological study of mental illness in the Camberwell area of London, and the second two hypotheses by a detailed enquiry into the background and aspirations of three matched groups, West Indian schizophrenics, West Indians in the community, and English-born schizophrenics. The numbers in this second study are small (27 in each group), and besides providing an initial test of the stress hypothesis, the study aims to provide methodological baselines for a much larger study, of the type carried out by Parker and Kleiner.

The Prevalence of Schizophrenia in Ethnic Subgroups

This study utilizes data available from the Camberwell Cumulative Psychiatric Register (L. Wing et al. 1967; 1968). This Register records all contacts, both in-patient and out-patient, of the population in the defined geographical area of Camberwell, South London.

A large number of hospital and clinical records are systematically checked to provide this information. The prevalence study is based on contacts in the two-year period 1967 and 1968 and refers to individuals aged 15 to 64. It excludes patients who were in hospital at the beginning of the two-year period, so that long-stay, chronic patients are not included. The schizophrenics located by this study are thus patients whose illness has appeared for the first time, or who have relapsed after a previous recovery, or who are maintained in the community by means of out-patient treatment. Two types of referral were excluded—night emergency admissions, and referrals for brief psychiatric consultation from general hospital wards—because in a large proportion of such cases demographic data were not collected. The variations in prevalence rate between the ethnic groups in the present study (table 19.1) are very similar to those in a previous study (Bagley 1969a) which collected similar data over a different time period, and used slightly different methods of case definition. Because long-stay patients are not included in the present study, the prevalence rates are lower than the incidence rates found in other epidemiological studies. As Yolles and Kramer (1969) pointed out, different prevalence studies (as opposed to incidence studies) are not comparable with one another, being specific to the population examined. What is important in such prevalence studies is the variation in rates between subgroups *within* that population.

Table 19.1 shows the prevalence rates of schizophrenia and of all mental illness in the various ethnic groups living in the area considered. There are some striking differences. The schizophrenic rates in West Indians (the Caribbean group), Africans, Indians and Pakistanis, and individuals from the Old Commonwealth (Australia, Canada, New Zealand and South Africa) are much higher than in individuals born in Britain. The rates in Africans and those from the Old Commonwealth are particularly high.

There are two kinds of model one can invoke to account for these findings: the stress model, and the migration model. In the first account, mental illness including schizophrenia is the result of the stresses of adaptation, and perhaps also of the additional stress of housing and job discrimination that colored people face. The second model would suggest that some migrants have a predisposition to mental illness, and migrate in order to escape from a culture in which they are deviant. The evidence on colored immigrants in Britain (Bagley 1968 and 1969a; Hashmi 1969) strongly favors the stress model. There are stringent regulations restricting the entry of

Table 19.1 Prevalance Rates of Schizophrenia in Different Ethnic Groups

	Males		Females		Males		Females	
Ethnic Group	*Schizophrenics/ population at risk*	*Rate**	*Schizophrenics/ population at risk*	*Rate*	*All psychiatric cases/population at risk*	*Rate*	*All psychiatric cases/population at risk*	*Rate*
British-born	62/67,680	0.916	61/74,400	0.82	623/67,680	9.21	1,108/74,400	14.69
Caribbean	14/3,740	3.74	6/4,010	1.50	49/3,740	13.10	68/4,010	16.96
Irish	1/2,770	0.361	3/2,890	1.04	51/2,770	18.4	50/2,890	17.3
Cyprus and Malta	0/1,070	0.0	0/1,050	0.0	5/1,070	4.67	15/1,050	14.28
Africa	12/370	30.83	1/330	3.03	21/37	56.76	10/330	30.3
India and Pakistan	1/340	2.94	0/330	0.0	7/340	20.59	7/330	21.21
Old Commonwealth	5/200	25.0	1/190	5.26	20/200	100/0	8/190	42.1
All other foreign	1/1,210	0.83	1/1,670	1.2	18/1,210	14.83	29/1,670	17.36

Old Commonwealth indicates Canada, Australia, New Zealand, and white South Africa and Rhodesia.
*Period prevalence rate calculated by number of patients/number at risk times 1,000.

colored people to Britain, and emigration for such individuals requires considerable long-term planning, the accumulation of capital, and the acquisition of skills. These are precisely the qualities which the schizoid personality lacks.

Krupinski's study of British and European migrants to Australia (1967) illustrates the probability that some individuals may be mentally ill before migration. He found that the mental illness rates in immigrants in Victoria, Australia, were much higher than those in the native population. The mentally ill fell into two groups, (a) unstable, single men emigrating from Western Europe who broke down in their first year in Australia, and who were probably schizophrenic before emigration; (b) migrants from Southern and Eastern Europe who broke down after being in the new culture for a year or more, and in whom stress played a part in the aetiology of the illness, relating to the lack of acceptance found by the immigrant in the host culture.

It is very easy for white residents in Old Commonwealth countries to migrate to Britain, and there is no evidence that there are any stresses of adaptation for an Australian or New Zealander in English culture. We would hypothesize that mental illness in such individuals is the phenomenon observed by Krupinski in British migrants to Australia in reverse; it reflects an attempt to escape from a culture in which they are deviant. Mental illness in Africans and West Indians is almost certainly the result of stress, in the same way that mental illness in Southern and Eastern Europeans in Australia is the result of the problems of adaptation.

The high rate of mental illness in Irishmen has been discussed elsewhere in detail (Bagley 1969a). Despite the high rate of mental illness in the Irish there is a dearth of diagnosed schizophrenia in Irish males. We have shown (Bagley and Binitie 1969) that significantly more Irish alcoholics display some schizophrenic symptoms than a matched group of English alcoholics, suggesting that alcoholism can "mask" schizophrenic symptoms in Irishmen. The higher rate of schizophrenia in Irish women, who do not tend to be alcoholic, is in keeping with this finding.

The absence of schizophrenia in the Cypriot and Maltese population (in fact, the population at risk is very largely Cypriot), as well as the low rate of mental illness in Cypriot males, is extremely interesting. This finding would suggest a high degree of group cohesiveness and successful adaptation in Cypriots. There is very little ethnographic evidence on Cypriots in London, and it would be interesting to investigate this hypothesis.

Table 19.2 Proportion of Total Cases of Psychiatric Disorder Who Are Schizophrenic, by Ethnic Groups

Group	*Number of schizophrenics*	*Total No. of mentaly ill*	*Percent of mentally ill who are schizophrenic*
British	123	1,731	7.11
Caribbean	20	117	17.09
Irish	4	101	3.96
Cyprus and Malta	–	20	0.0
Africa	13	31	41.93
India and Pakistan	1	14	7.14
Old Commonwealth	6	28	21.43
All other foreign	3	47	6.38
Total	170	2,089	8.14

Table 19.2 shows the proportion of schizophrenics in the total population of the mentally ill in the various ethnic groups considered. The proportion is particularly high for West Indians, Africans and those from the Old Commonwealth. Schizophrenia is a disease involving very serious impairment of an individual's capacity to adapt to his environment, and it is virtually impossible for a schizophrenic to exist in an urban community without coming to the notice of the authorities (Dunham 1965). The fact that schizophrenia is a relatively frequent diagnosis in West Indian and African patients suggests that there may be a similar excess of milder psychiatric states (depression, anxiety, etc.) which do not come to the notice of the psychiatric services. This possibility does not seem so likely for the Old Commonwealth group, and it may be here that, as we have suggested, people with schizoid personalities tend to emigrate to Britain. It is interesting to note in this context that in the "other foreign" group—mostly German and Polish refugees of lengthy domicile—rates of schizophrenia are not particularly high, and the proportion of schizophrenics in the total mentally ill population in this group is the same as in the British-born.

Another possibility which must be considered is that the finding of an excess of schizophrenics in the West Indian and African population is the result of diagnostic biases on the part of examining psychiatrists. This hypothesis is currently being tested by Rwegellara, using some of the clinical material used in the present study. Rwegellara (1969) has found that the modal period between arrival in the country, and onset of the schizophrenic illness in Africans is 3–4 years. For West Indians there is a bimodal distribution, the peaks being 5–6 years after emigration, and at 10 years after emigration to Britain. There appeared to be some relationship between being joined by family, and subsequent onset of illness. These findings implicate stress rather than selective factors in the aetiology of the illness.

Social Stress and Schizophrenia in West Indians

A special study has been made of potentially stressful factors in the background of West Indian schizophrenics. These factors are (a) the life crises defined by Brown and Birley (1968); (b) chronic environmental hazards; and (c) the stresses of competing for upward occupational mobility in a social system which motivates all members to strive, but provides specific blocks to mobility (i.e, through racial discrimination) for certain groups of individuals.

Twenty-seven West Indian schizophrenics have been studied, and have been compared with a similar number of West Indians in the community who have never had a psychiatric consultation, and with a similar number of English-born schizophrenics. The West Indian patients were individually matched with the other two groups for age, sex, occupational class, marital state, amount of education received,[1] and father's occupational class. Matching was carried out on these last two variables in order to try and avoid the possibility suggested by Dunham (1966), that the association of a gap between desired and achieved occupation and psychosis is a function of the downward mobility of the schizophrenic, and not a possible contributory cause of it. All subjects in this study were male, and the presence of schizophrenia was assessed by the presence of two or more of the primary symptoms defined by W.H.O. (1957).[2]

In studying life crises, similar methods and definitions to those used by Brown and Birley have been used, except that we present in table 19.3 only "fully independent" events. The differences are in the direction and of the magnitude predicted by Brown and Birley's study, but because of the small N, the excess of life crises in the

1. Education was matched in three groups: statutory minimum education; secondary schooling beyond statutory minimum; and secondary education beyond minimum, plus some college education.

2. English subjects were interviewed by the writer, and the West Indian subjects by a Nigerian psychiatrist.

Table 19.3 Life Crises Independent of the Onset of Schizophrenia in Three Weeks Prior to the Onset of the Illness

Number of events	*West Indian schizophrenics*	*West Indian community controls*	*English schizophrenics*
None	13	19	15
One or more	14	8	12
Total	27	27	27

West Indian schizophrenics vs. West Indian community controls, $P < .1 > .05$, N.S.
West Indian schizophrenics vs. English schizophrenics, $P > .1$, N.S.

three weeks prior to the onset of schizophrenic symptoms is different from the number of such crises in the community controls at the 10 percent level only. On this evidence, life crises appear to have some association with schizophrenia but are independent of ethnic categcry.

The following environmental stresses have been considered: (1) overcrowding—a density of two or more per room; (2) poverty—household income after allowances for rent, at less than 140 percent of the Supplementary Benefit Scale (see Bagley 1969b for definitions); (3) bathroom and toilet facilities shared with other households; (4) accommodation built before 1914; (5) insecurity of tenure under the 1965 Rent Act (i.e., furnished rented accommodation); (6) subject's usual working day more than 12 hours long. Table 19.4 shows that the West Indian patients have significantly more of such environmental stresses than the English patients, but not more than the West Indian community controls. These stresses, then, are associated not with schizophrenia, but with membership of an ethnic subgroup. This picture of the economic and housing conditions of West Indians is in keeping with the findings of Davison (1966).

The goal-striving stresses have been defined as follows: (1) Subject perceives an open opportunity structure (responding "often" rather than "occasionally" or "hardly at all" to the question "It has been said that if a man works hard, saves his money, and is ambitious, he will get ahead. How often do you think this really happens?"—Parker and Kleiner 1966: p51); (2) subject has aspirations for a son to receive higher education; (3) subject has aspirations for a son's occupation at least three grades higher than father's occupation. For this comparison the Registrar General's six grades of occupation were used—professional and executive; intermediate professional; white collar clerical; skilled blue collar; semiskilled blue collar; unskilled blue collar. For example, if a skilled blue collar

Table 19.4 Chronic Environmental Hazards

Number of hazards	*West Indian schizophrenics*	*West Indian community controls*	*English schizophrenics*
None	7	9	16
One or more	20	18	11
Total	27	27	27

West Indian schizophrenics vs. West Indian community controls, $P > .1$, N.S.
West Indian schizophrenics vs. English schizophrenics, $P < .02, > .01$.

father wanted his son or hypothetical son to become a doctor, this represented an occupational aspiration for his son three steps above his own; (4) subject has occupational aspirations higher than present occupation—"What kind of job do you think your talents and ability fit you for?" High aspiration was taken to be present if subject aspired to a job two grades above the one he was most recently doing. As in (3), the Registrar General's occupational grades were used for this comparison. Thus for example, a building laborer who aspired to the job of skilled carpenter would have occupational aspirations two grades above his own.

These four indices of goal-striving are derived from Parker and Kleiner's study (chapters 3, 4 and 5), and are intended to provide some measure of the degree to which the subject perceives an open opportunity structure, and the degree he would like to see himself and his children rise in the social structure. In using these measures as an index of stress we are making the assumption that for the Afro-British the opportunity structure is *not* open—that there are significant barriers, in the form of racial discrimination—against upward occupational mobility. There is very good evidence from the P.E.P. report on racial discrimination (1967) that this is in fact so.

Table 19.5 shows the number of goal-striving stresses faced by the three groups. The West Indian patients have significantly higher scores on this index of goal-striving than either the English patients, or the West Indian community controls. In other words, goal-striving is significantly associated with schizophrenia in West Indians. These findings are in keeping with the findings of Parker and Kleiner about Afro-Americans.

It is interesting here to note Lowenthal's (1967) finding that although West Indian immigrants in New York comprise one-eight of the Afro-American population in that city, they provide one-third of Afro-American professionals in New York. There is evidence from Lowenthal's study for supposing that desire for economic advancement is a very

Table 19.5 Goal Striving Score

Goal striving score	*West Indian schizophrenics*	*West Indian community controls*	*English schizophrenics*
None	5	11	12
One or more	12	6	5
Total	17	17	17

West Indian schizophrenics vs. West Indian community controls, $P < .05$
West Indian schizophrenics vs. English schizophrenics, $P < .01$

strong motive in West Indian migration, and we can assume that it is highly probable that West Indians in Britain have similar economic motives.

The difference in the items measuring goal-striving between the West Indian and the English patients is interesting in that the English patients do not have to face any discrimination on grounds of color. They do have to face discrimination on grounds of class however, and it is known that the father's occupational status is a significant determinant of his son's occupation (see, for example, the evidence in Runciman and Bagley 1969). Beetham (1967), who made a comparative study of the occupational aspirations of young English and West Indian workers, suggested that West Indians had, by and large, failed to be socialized in the predominant norms prevailing in the English working class, norms which suggested that if one had working class origins, occupational striving would be of little avail.[3] The present findings suggest that a significant subgroup of West Indians may perceive British social structure to be "open," and have high vocational aspirations for themselves and their sons.

The social structure in which the Afro-Briton lives has an ambiguous hold on him. In the first place he is required to perform the duties of a citizen, and faces pressures to internalize the values of the dominant ethnic group. He is not, however, allowed admission to working class subcultures; it is indeed amongst such subcultures that racial prejudice is most prevalent (Bagley 1969c). He is not socialized in the norms of the subculture which inform the working class individual that the opportunity is by no means open—that although one's skin is white, one's collar is blue. The Afro-Briton is motivated to succeed by the formal processes of socialization in society; his motivation may have

3. It is pertinent to enquire what effects blocked opportunity has on members of white working class subcultures; the answer seems to be, high delinquency rates. Cf Bagley (1965, 1968 and 1969d).

been reinforced by his experiences in West India, which have led him to emigrate in the search for occupational advancement.

Many Afro-Britons are in what we might describe as a "double-bind" relationship with society, which like an eccentric parent offers inducements for a particular kind of behavior, while at the same time punishing or at least discouraging the logical outcome of such inducements. He must strive, but he may not succeed.[4]

Writers about psychosis in immigrants (see the reviews by Bagley 1968, and Sanua 1969) have suggested that the schizophrenic pictures often have a paranoid coloring. One can easily understand how this happens. The aspiring Afro-Briton has a very positive desire to succeed occupationally, and to achieve good living conditions. Yet he is constantly aware, if he exposes himself to the open market for jobs and housing, that he is being discriminated against (see P.E.P. 1967 for elaboration of this point). Knowledge of discrimination is profoundly disturbing for the individual, for although in some situations discrimination is obvious, in others it is not. The flat may have just been let, the man hired may have better qualifications as well as a white skin, but the applicant cannot be sure of this. He may come to hold the suspicion, sometimes the certainity, that members of the white power structure have malicious designs against him. To the extent that this is not always true his beliefs are paranoid.

These points can be illustrated by a case history. The patient is a 39-year-old man with five children. He came from the Caribbean in 1958, and received some schooling beyond the statutory minimum. After working for two years as an omnibus conductor he obtained a clerical post in the government service. He applied for promotion, but his supervisor would not allow him to take professional examinations which would have given him higher status, on the grounds that the likelihood of his passing these examinations was small. He deeply resented this. He was buying a small and dilapidated house by means of a mortgage. He was repaying this mortgage over 12 years at a rate of interest well above the market rate. In order to meet his mortgage payments he also worked in the evenings as a cleaner. At work he developed the suspicion that certain employees were deliberately avoiding him (which was probably true) and also that they were trying to poison him and kill him by means of electric currents (which was not true). A "life crisis" before the onset of these symptoms was the arrival of a younger brother from the Caribbean who both increased the fam-

4. We have also used this kind of "double bind" model in trying to explain the high rates of violence in Bantu communities in South Africa (Bagley 1969d).

ily's overcrowding problem, and presented the patient with the humiliating task of explaining why the rosy picture of life and prospects painted in his letters home was not in fact true. This man had high occupational aspirations for himself and his sons, and despite his paranoia about certain individuals, still maintained a belief in the possibility of advancement through striving.

The findings we have presented suggest that social factors can influence the onset of schizophrenia; this illness has quite marked differences in prevalence between different groups. As to aetiology, life crises can be of special significance in bringing about the onset of symptoms. These crises are the final precipitants of schizophrenia in individuals whose long-term life experiences (and perhaps their constitution as well) have predisposed them to the disease.

Summary

Three hypotheses have been tested, using material from an epidemiological study of mental illness in ethnic minorities in a London Borough.

(1) Ethnic minorities will have different prevalence rates of schizophrenia than the major population. This hypothesis is supported.

(2) Social stress as defined by Brown and Birley will play a significant role in the emergence of schizophrenia in West Indians. This hypothesis is partially supported.

(3) "Status striving in a climate of limited opportunity" (Parker and Kleiner) will be significantly associated with schizophrenia in West Indians. This hypothesis is supported.

20

Depressive Disorders from a Transcultural Perspective

K. Singer

Depression is a very complex and multiform phenomenon, which can range from a basic human experience to a serious psychiatric disorder with considerable public health importance.

Depressive disorders have been found in virtually all areas of the world where they have been looked for, although with some variation in incidence and prevalence. The existence of a universal core depressive syndrome composed of sadness, disturbed sleep, fatigue, feelings of emptiness in life, and loss of interests is becoming widely recognized. However, questions about the presence and frequency of less central manifestations of a depressive disorder are only gradually being answered.

In the following article, K. Singer, professor of psychiatry at the University of Hong Kong, conducts a penetrating and thorough review of the literature on the intercultural frequency and manifestations of depressive disorders. His conceptual and methodological recommendations for improved comparative research on depression are quite useful.

GENERAL REVIEWS of the transcultural aspects of depressive disorders have been made (Stainbrook 1954; Benedict and Jacks 1954; Opler 1956; Krapf 1959, Wittkower and Rin 1965; Yap 1965; Lenz 1964; Montagu 1967; Wittkower and Hugel 1968; Pfeiffer 1970). There has, however, been no detailed, systematic examination of the main problems involved, which are: (1) to identify the variations in frequency and symptom patterns of depressive disorders occurring across cultures, (2) to identify the cultural elements that account for such variations and to determine their *modus operandi,* (3) to identify similarities in frequency and symptom patterns occurring across cultures, and to determine the reasons for these and (4) from a knowledge of the differences and similarities to devise improved and universally valid conceptual models of depressive disorders.

It is the purpose of this paper to summarize and evaluate the work so far carried out relating to the foregoing problems, to attempt to come to some conclusion regarding the state of current knowledge, and to indicate some requirements for future research in this field.

The term depressive disorders will be used to include psychotic and endogenous depressions, neurotic and reactive depressions and involutional melancholia. For the definition of culture, one may refer to Kroeber and Kluckhoh (1952) who have listed 160 definitions in English. In this article the physical correlates of culture, e.g., nutrition, physical diseases, genetic factors, will not be considered.

Incidence and Manifestations

1. Major ethnic and cultural groups

Africa. Much of the interest has focused on this region. On the whole early reports based mainly on hospital samples indicated that depressive illness was rare in Africa (0.38 percent of hospital population) and that when it occurred it was light and fleeting, that ideas of sin and of guilt and suicide were rare while confusional and paranoid features were common and that mania was commoner than depressive illness (Laubscher 1937; Smartt 1956). This atypical pattern of depression which we will refer to as the "primitive" pattern has also been reported in other preliterate cultures. However, the prevalence of hospitalized depressives in Zambia was found to be similar to that in Europe (Shelley and Watson 1936) while in a field survey in Ghana (which excluded hospitalized depressives) a prevalence of 19.7 percent of affective disorder was reported (Tooth 1950), a figure comparable to the Western one.

More recent and more reliable studies have thrown doubt on early beliefs that depression is rare in Africans. It has been found to be common in Nigeria (Lambo 1960, Asuni 1969), Senegal (Collomb 1965, 1967), Ghana (Field 1960; Weinberg 1965), Ethiopia (Torrey 1966; Marinko 1966), Sudan (Elsarrag 1968; Cederbad 1968), and South

Africa (Gillis et al. 1968). Figures for hospitalized depressives range up to 23 percent of the population. Differences in manifestations were noted by these authors: in Nigeria a predominantly somatic presentation and recently a changing symptomatology attributed to westernization, in Senegal a predominance of somatic and paranoid symptomatology and of mania (Diop 1967), in Ghana a high frequency of self-accusations of witchcraft and in Sudan more shame than guilt feelings. However the reports for Ethiopia and South Africa indicated that the picture of depression there resembled the western pattern.

The studies mentioned are of single cultural or ethnic groups in which tacit comparison is made with European findings. A careful cross-cultural study on psychiatric disorders in distinctly different ethnic groups using uniform diagnostic criteria was carried out by Leighton, Lambo and their co-workers (Leighton et al. 1963). They surveyed psychiatric illness in selected population in Nigeria and compared the data with those previously obtained by Leighton and his colleagues in Nova Scotia. They concluded that depressive illness was commoner in Africans than was formerly believed and that many of its symptoms could be identified. However the concept of depression as a syndrome was unknown and there was no word for depression among the Yoruba. The only symptoms missing that were commonly seen in the West were guilt and self-recrimination. German (1972) has pointed out that depression is now diagnosed more freely in Africans in the absence of guilt feelings or spontaneous admissions of being depressed.

The Arab countries. In Lebanon a low prevalence of hospitalized depressives has been reported (Katchadourian and Racy 1969). Reports on depressive symptomatology have been contradictory, some affirming that the picture approximated the western and others the "primitive" pattern. The latter has been reported for the Arab East in general (Racy 1970) and in Iraq (Bazzoui 1970). A Western pattern was reported for out-patients in Cairo (Okasha 1968), while in a special study there on guilt feelings in depressives, Christians (Coptic) showed no greater frequency of these than Moslems (El-Islam 1969).

The Indian subcontinent. In India regional differences have been reported. A high prevalence of depression has been found in field surveys in North India (Dube 1964; Sethi and Gupta 1970) ranging from 9 to 16.7/1000 population. In West Bengal a prevalence rate of 2.9/1000 was found in a rural community (Elnager et al. 1971). In South India depression was reported to comprise only 1.3 percent of patients in a psychiatric hospital (Rao 1966) but no data on the prevalence in the general population are available.

As regards manifestations, in the north Teja et al. (1971) reported that guilt feelings were prominent in a sample of clinic patients, but Hoch (1963) found these were rare while somatization was prominent. The latter pattern was also reported for southern Indian hospitalized patients (Rao 1966, 1970). In western India also, a similar picture was found (Bagadia et al., 1970).

The Far East. In *China* no data are available on the prevalence of depression in the general population. Chu and Lin (1960) published data on hospitalized patients in Peking admitted during the years 1933-1943. Diagnosed manic-depressive psychosis comprised 22.1 percent of total first admissions. The ratio of manic-depressive psychosis to schizophrenia was 1/1.5. Recent reports indicate that the prevalence of manic-depressive psychosis is low, ranging from 2–5 percent (Taipale and Taipale 1973; Sainsbury 1974). Suicide is said to be very rare in the Chinese People's Republic (Taipale and Taipale, 1973).

Among the Chinese in *Indonesia* a high prevalence of depression was observed, in contrast to its rarity in the Indonesians (van Wulfften-Pathe 1936; Osterreicher 1950). This was reaffirmed by Pfeiffer (1966) who also remarked on the high frequency of hypochondriasis in Chinese depressives.

Lin (1953) in *Taiwan* carried out a careful census type investigation and found a point prevalence rate for manic-depressive psychosis of 0.4/1000. In Hong Kong, Yap (1965) studied depressive symptomatology retrospectively in Chinese in-patients. He concluded that the clinical features paralleled those described in the West, but that ideas of guilt and unworthiness were infrequent and mild, and delusions of sin were absent. Later he reversed his position and was extremely sceptical of reported differences (Yap 1971). Singer (1972) found that depressive disorders were infrequent (7 percent of admissions) and mania rare in the hospitalized population in Hong Kong.

In *Thailand* Tongyonk (1972) found that somatic symptoms were commoner among Asian depressive patients seen in private practise than Occidentals there. Asian patients focused more on headache, dizziness and labile blood pressure and Occidentals on complaints affecting the extremities and skin.

In *Japan,* type examinations (Kato 1969) showed a prevalence rate for affective psychosis of 2/1000. Kimura (1965) found that guilt feelings were encountered with equal frequency in Japanese and German depressives contrary to previously held beliefs that they were absent in the Japanese (Seligman 1929). However he also found differences in the direction of guilt feelings. The Japanese were guilty towards their parents, ancestors, fellow-workers; the Germans towards children and God.

In *Korea* a field survey in rural areas (Yoo, 1961) found a prevalence rate of manic depressive psychosis of 0.3/1000.

In *Hawaii* Beaglehole (1939) found among mental hospital admissions that native Hawaiians had a higher frequency of schizophrenia compared with depression. Kinzie et al. (1973) studied the point prevalence of depressive symptoms of University students of Japanese, Chinese and Caucasian ancestry using the Zung Self-Rating Depression Scale. Contrary to previous assumptions they found that Asians, particularly females, had significantly higher prevalence of depression than Caucasians. They hypothesized that Asian American students in being more introverted, reserved, deferential and "turning towards the self" produced more depressive symptoms under stress.

In *Indonesia,* Pfeiffer (1966) reported depression to be infrequent and mania common in hospital and in private practice. In a cross-cultural study comparing Indonesian and German depressives he also found the former to typically show hypochondriasis, self-absorption and agitation while the latter manifested the classical picture of melancholia with performance conflict, feelings of guilt and suicidal tendencies (Pfeiffer 1971). The two samples however differed in social status.

Australasia. Kidson (1967) and Kidson and Jones (1968), who carried out field surveys in tribes in Central and Western Australia, noted that the depressive illnesses they diagnosed bore no resemblance to what they understood as endogenous depression and that guilt and self-recrimination were absent. A similar pattern of symptomatology was reported by Burton-Bradley (1965) in New Guinea. He further maintained that the response to group disapproval in these people is a distinctive response of shame, which he described as a simple, short-lived depressive reaction and the counterpart of the European reaction of depression.

In New Zealand Foster (1962) found that the rates for manic depressive psychosis in mental hospital admissions were higher in Europeans than in Maoris.

The Western Hemisphere. Silverman (1968) cited a number of studies generally indicating a lower frequency of depression among Negroes in the United States as compared with Whites. These conclusions were based on hospital statistics. McGough et al (1966) has reported however that with availability of better treatment facilities and introduction of racial integration in the psychiatric hospital the pattern of psychiatric illness among Negroes in the Southern States has changed. The proportion of Negro patients with psychotic depression and to a lesser extent psychoneurotic depression has risen to equal and in some cases to even exceed that of white patients.

Tonks et al (1970) found that Negro in- and out-patients in New Haven in the lower social classes showed less guilt than whites did.

Among North American Indian tribes, a high frequency of depressive illness was reported in the Mohave by Devereaux (1961) and in the Dakota Sioux by Johnson and Johnson (1965). The reports were based on field impressions.

In South America, Stainbrook (1954) reported that depressive illness and guilt feelings were rare in hospitalized Bahians in Brazil, but added that depressive illness was much more frequent in private hospital patients. Delgado (1967) comparing reports from the countries of South America concluded that depressive states were commonly encountered in the Indians of the Altoplano in Argentina and that agitation was more prominent in jungle than in rural Indians.

In the Caribbean mania was reported to be almost twice as frequent as depression in hospitalized patients (Royes 1961) and periodicity and guilt feelings were reported to be rare and hypochondriasis common in depressive states (Despinoy and Camelio 1967). Similar findings were reported for Haiti (Bordeleau 1963). In an impressionistic study comparing Negroes and East Indians in Trinidad in which guilt reactions were ascertained, Rubin (1959) found that the Christian Negroes reacted with guilt when they thought they had done something wrong in private or in public while the nor Christian East Indians reacted with shame.

Western cultures. A number of surveys on the prevalence of psychiatric illness including depressive disorders have been carried out in the last 20 years in Europe and North America. These will be considered briefly for purposes of comparison with non-Western findings.

Silverman (1968) in a comprehensive epidemiological review selected seven community surveys, six in Europe and one in the United States, for assessment. She found that the point prevalence rates for depressive disorder ranged widely from 0.2 to 38.4/1000 population. As regards period prevalence rates, in a further four surveys carried out in the United States and Canada, Silverman found that these ranged from 0.8 to 3.0/1000 population. These studies are not strictly comparable because of wide differences in age structure, period of survey and diagnostic criteria, and especially because of the inclusion of varying proportions of depressive neurosis. The last point is highlighted in another study, a survey of the urban population of New York City, in which 236/1000 population were classified in the depression symptom group (Srole et al. 1962).

Studies on affective disorders in general practice in the United Kingdom have been reviewed by Rawnsley (1968) who found the prevalence rates for psychotic depression to range from 2.4 to 6.0/1000 per annum.

In mental hospital and clinic patients the prevalence for depressive disorders was also found to vary widely, for example, from 0.46/1000 in Maryland in 1963 (Silverman 1968) to 3.6/1000 population aged 15 and over in Aarhus County, Denmark in 1958 (Juel-Nielsen et al. 1961). First admissions for depressive psychosis ranged from 0.07 to 0.3/1000 population in the United States (Silverman 1968) which compares with a much higher rate of 2.4/1000 population found in Bristol (Kramer et al. 1961).

As regards lifetime morbidity risk, on the basis mainly of Scandinavian studies, a range of 4.2/17.0 in males/1000 births, and 6.2/28.0 in females/1000 births have been found (Rawnsley 1968).

Cross-national differences in the observed prevalence of depressive disorders have been studied. The much higher admission rates for affective disorders in England and Wales compared to the United States (Kramer et al. 1961) have been attributed to variations in diagnosis and admission practice in the two countries (Cooper 1972). A similar pattern of difference between Germany and the United States has been reported and explained in the same way (Neidermeyer 1967).

In support of real differences in prevalence among Western communities, the high prevalence reported in the Hutterites of North America (Eaton and Weil 1955) has been contrasted with the very low prevalence in a group of North Swedish parishes (Book 1953). However, with regard to the Hutterites Silverman (1968) has shown that when the cases active at the time of the survey are separated from the recovered cases, the period prevalence rate is found to be an unremarkable 0.9/1000 for the year. As regards the very low rate of 0.2/1000 found in Sweden the population surveyed was only about 9000. The evidence in favor of really wide differences in prevalence is therefore not convincing.

Little work has been done on possible cross-national differences in the symptomatology of depressive disorders in Western communities. An example is Saenger's (1968) study which compared symptomatology in psychiatric out-patients in the Netherlands and the United States. The author concluded that in the former apathy, psychomotor retardation and guilt were more often reported to be present, a finding which he attributed to the Calvinist background of the people.

Silverman concluded that in very general terms, the prevalence rates for depressive psychosis were under 1/1000 population in community surveys except in some Scandinavian countries where they were higher. The prevalence rates for depressive neurosis were generally 2–3 times greater than the rates for psychosis.

From the foregoing it is obvious that statements about comparative prevalence and manifestations cannot be made with assurance without studies of matched communities by single teams using uniform methodology. The range of findings even in Western communities is wide and this makes tacit comparison with non-Western findings hazardous.

2. Subcultural differences

Subcultural differences are dealt with briefly for comparative purposes. Due regard needs to be given for differences within the same culture due to social variables like social class, education, age, and sex if social influences are not to be mistaken for the cultural.

Non-Western cultures. Reports of regional differences in prevalence of depressive disorder in India and Africa have already been mentioned.

A higher prevalence in the upper *social classes* was observed among hospitalized Bahians in Brazil (Stainbrook 1954), the Chinese in Taiwan (Lin 1953) and out-patients in Cairo (El-Islam 1969). Hes (1960) found the illness commoner among Western than Oriental immigrants in Israel. Lambo (1960) noted a higher prevalence in westernized Africans. In contrast, Gillis et al. (1968) in their survey of Cape colored people in South Africa found a preponderance of psychiatric disturbance of all types in the lowest social class. As regards *religion* Katchadourian (1974) in Lebanon reported that the incidence of depression was equal among Christians and Muslims but that there was a preponderance of manic reactions in Muslim males.

Western cultures. Bagley (1973) has comprehensively reviewed the literature on the relationship between depression and *social class* and concluded that a relationship exists between depression and higher occupational status. He suggests three possible causes for this phenomenon: diagnostic biases in some cultures which fail to recognize symptoms of depression manifested by lower class patients, a personality link between striving for success and predisposition to depression and an association of certain class positions with stresses leading to depression.

Enquiries into *urban–rural differences* in mental hospital admissions have usually shown a higher rate of depression in urban areas (Malzberg 1959: Wechsler 1961).

As regards the influence of *age* there is general agreement that depressive disorders are rare till adolescence when it usually makes its first appearance. Therefore its frequency increases with age till it peaks in the 55–65 age group and then it declines somewhat (Silverman 1968). Changes in symptomatology and possibly in course and aetiology may occur with increasing age (Post 1968), the illness tending to become more severe, protracted and frequent.

The influence of *sex* on the morbidity of depression is established. Depression is almost always found to be commoner in women, who usually predominate over men by 2:1. This predominance is much greater in the younger age groups. In women the incidence is highest in the fourth decade whereas in men the peak is reached only in the sixth decade. After the age of 65 depressive illness is equally common in both sexes (Kendell 1970). Sex-related differences in symptomatology have been reported. On the Hamilton Rating Scale women showed more anxiety and agitation and men more retardation and initial insomnia (Hamilton 1967). Schwab et al. (1968) also observed that depressive women tended to somatize and men to experience personal despair.

Studies generally indicate that depression is more frequent in the *married* (Schwab et al. 1967; Silverman 1968).

The evidence on the influence of *religion* is conflicting. The older German literature regarded manic depressive psychosis as particularly frequent in Jews. A higher prevalence in Jews than in Christians was found in hospital admissions in New York City (Malzberg 1962). Studies in Palestine however did not report an unusually high prevalence (Hes 1960; Maoz et al. 1966). European Jews consistently showed a higher admission rate than Oriental Jews in Israel (Halevi 1963; Miller 1967) but the samples were not controlled for social class. Fernando (1966, 1969) studied differences between Jewish, Catholic and Protestant out-patient depressives in East London. He found that Jews were significantly less hostile than Catholics and less intropunitive (guilt-ridden) than Protestants.

3. Variations across time

Non-Western cultures. Little reliable information is available but the trend in reports on depressive illness in the last 20 years, especially among Africans, is towards a Western rate of morbidity and pattern of symptomatology. Prince (1967) has equated the remarkable increase in the reported prevalence in sub-Saharan Africa since 1957 with the gaining of political independence in Africa. Before 1957 observers mostly employed in colonial governments consistently found a very low rate of depression. After 1957 and up to 1965 there were 21 papers all reporting that depression was commonly found. The author suggested that observers may have been biased by the racial prestige factor: depression has popularly been regarded as a characteristic of sensitive and intellectual peoples.

Lin et al. (1969) compared the findings of two successive census type studies carried out at an interval of 15 years in three communities in Taiwan. The authors concluded there was no significant change with time in the prevalence rates of the various psychoses but that a significant increase in non-psychotic disorders, especially psychoneuroses, had occurred.

Western cultures. In England and Wales, first admissions of depressive illness to psychiatric hospitals increased by about 75 percent for both sexes in 8 years (1952–1960) while first admissions for schizophrenia remained steady during the same period (Registrar General 1964). Varga (1968) who compared depressions treated in a university psychiatric hospital in Budapest in 1910 with those in 1960 found that the proportion of illnesses diagnosed depressive had considerably increased in the latter year. By contrast, Kramer et al. (1961) showed that in the United States first admissions to public psychiatric hospitals of affective psychosis decreased steadily since 1940, while admissions of psychoneuroses and personality disorders increased.

Changes in the symptomatology of psychotic depression over the period 1910–1960 have been reported from Austria (Lenz 1964) and Germany (Lauter and Schon 1965) on the basis of analyses of case histories. In general there was a decrease in expressions of guilt and self-reproach with the passage of time. There was a change particularly in the content of guilt, from religious preoccupation to social and family concerns. Similarly Ancherson noted that in Norway depressive ideas had become less dramatic, taking the form of guilt over social slips and failures and being usually void of religious content. It is difficult to see however how reliable comparisons of symptomatology across time can be made without uniformity in methods of assessing and recording symptoms.

4. Comparative aspects of suicide

Suicide has been regarded as a mortality of depression (Silverman 1968). There is also a tendency to use the suicide rate as an index of the prevalence of depression for comparative purposes.

Non-Western cultures. Dublin and Bunzel (1933) showed the wide variations in the attitudes towards suicide which prevail among primitive peoples affecting the prevalence of suicide. Among the groups for whom no cases of suicide were reported were the Yahgans of Tierra del Fuego, the Andaman Islanders, the Zuri of New Mexico and the Aborigines of Western and Central Australia. By contrast the Kamachadals of Siberia, the Cherokee Ojibway and Navajo Indians and the Melanesians committed suicide for relatively trivial reasons.

Later studies have reported very low suicide rates (less than 1/100,000 population) in African and Muslim countries (Laubscher 1937; Asuni 1962; Gobar 1970) but some recent reports (Fallers and Fallers 1960) have indicated an incidence approaching western figures. A moderate to high suicide rate has been reported for some Oriental countries, e.g., Hong Kong (Yap 1958) and Southern India (Rao 1966). Among American Indians overall, the suicide rate is slightly higher than the national average of 11/100,000 (Resnik and Dizmang 1971) but the frequency varies from reservation to reservation and is significantly higher for instance among the Apache.

Western cultures. Comparative studies were carried out by Hendin (1960, 1964) who showed that trends in suicide rates in the period 1910–1960 failed to show a consistent pattern. The highest rates tended to be from Austria, Denmark, Sweden, and Switzerland; the lowest from Iceland, Spain, and Italy. Estimates of the contribution of mental illness and of depressive disorders to the suicide problem have varied widely. Sainsbury (1968) from a review of the literature concluded that nearly half of all suicides had an affective disorder of the manic-depressive type and that at least 15 percent of people with this diagnosis would die from suicide.

It is clear that comparative ratings of suicide must be interpreted with extreme caution. The reporting and recording of suicides are enormously influenced by attitudes and sociological variables. Suicide rates cannot therefore be used as a general index of the frequency of depressive illness for transcultural studies.

Influence of Culture

A vast literature is extant on the influence of culture on mental disorders, mostly contributed by analytically-oriented cultural anthropologists and social psychiatrists among whom beginning from the

1920's the "culture and personality" approach was much favored (Linton, 1945: Hallowell, 1954).

We will consider the cultural factors that have been postulated to influence depression under three headings: (1) factors generating or reinforcing depression, (2) factors counteracting depression and (3) factors altering its manifestations or determining their choice.

1. Factors generating or reinforcing depression

Early formative influences. Cultural variations in the components of child training, such as amount of breast feeding and coddling, time of weaning, degree of independence training and of parental severity, and the use of symbolic sanctions vs physical punishment, have all come under scrutiny (Benedict 1946; Swanson et al. 1952; Whiting and Child, 1953; Honigmann 1954; Sears et al. 1957; Gold 1958; B.B. Whiting 1963). The role of such factors in personality formation and in predisposition to depression has been formulated into various psychopathological hypotheses to account for cultural variations in depressive disorder; these will be considered later. It may be noted at this stage that in spite of the voluminous literature the evidence of a relationship between cultural variations in child-rearing practices and depressive disorder remains tenuous (Cumming 1961). Even intensive studies in the West on factors like parental deprivation, birth order, and parental age have not yielded sufficient evidence to support the view that early environment is of aetiological importance. However considerable methodological difficulties are involved so that it would be premature to conclude that such factors are irrelevant (Granville-Grossman 1968).

Culture change. The impact of cultural change on mental disorder including depression has been widely studied. (Spindler 1955; Fabrega 1969). Criteria that have been used to indicate culture change include industrialization, urbanization and westernization; breakdown of family traditions and other social institutions; changes in values, ideas, and attitudes; acculturation, and migration. Murphy (1965) gives an example of a psychiatrically relevant classification of the sociocultural environment.

The evidence with regard to stressful influence of culture change is conflicting with studies in favor (Kluckhohn and Leighton 1946; Thompson 1950; Murphy 1961) and against (Hallowell 1952) the hypothesis. Alternative hypotheses favoring other than a simple straight relationship between culture change and breakdown have been proposed. Thus it has been suggested that during a transitional stage of culture change personality disintegration occurs but is followed by reintegration at a new level of functioning (Spindler and Goldschmidt 1952) or that cultural change tends to produce social disintegration only in a vulnerable population with a high rate of psychiatric disorder (Leighton 1965).

Studies of the relationship between migration and mental illness have been reviewed (Fabrega 1969; Murphy 1965). As regards depressive disorder, the evidence for such a relationship was found to be inconclusive.

Social cohesion. A number of studies have purported to show that depressive illness is more frequent in persons who belong to societies with a high degree of social cohesion. Social cohesion pertains to the intensity of interaction which takes place in a group and the degree to which its members share its values and feel themselves involved in social expectations. The social cohesion theory of depression has overtones with interpersonal psychoanalytic theories, such as that of Fromm-Reichmann (1959), according to which depression tends to occur in individuals from large closely knit families.

On the basis also of communication theory, Cohen (1961) suggested that every group requires its members to conform and keep within bounds potentially disruptive forces directed toward the group, if it is to remain intact and the individual is to receive rewards from his membership in it. In a cohesive group if a member cannot repress, deny, or displace potentially threatening feelings, he may apply to himself the censure which he knows the group would apply to him if his feelings were expressed. Hence the greater the cohesiveness of the group the more the individual is liable to feel guilty, withdrawn, and become depressed if he is not living up to group expectations. In accordance with these postulates it was hypothesized that a high frequency of depression will be found in highly traditionalized and tightly knit groups, in the upper social strata, and among professional and executive groups who have strong group affiliations (Chance 1964). No study has however been designed to test the hypothesis satisfactorily.

Support for the social cohesion hypothesis was seen in the work of Eaton and Weil (1955) among the Hutterites. The Hutterites consist of about 9000 members and are an Anabaptist religious sect who through isolation and endogamy have zealously preserved their tradition of communal cooperation, with stress upon duty, conformity, and responsibility. It was reported that the ratio of schizophrenia to affective disorder among them was 0.23 whereas in nine other studies it was greater than unity. The high rate of depressive disorder was attributed to the high degree of social cohesion, whereas a low degree of social cohesion would, it was suggested, give rise to a relatively high rate of schizophrenia. However Silverman (1968) has pointed out that the actual period prevalence rate of depression for the Hutterites was 0.9/1000 per annum, which was not high.

Further support for the social cohesion hypothesis was claimed by H.B. Murphy et al. (1967) on the basis of a study in which authors used a questionnaire to ask psychiatrists in 30 countries to rate on a scale their estimates of the frequency of a "basic depressive disorder" in their own societies. The authors concluded that a high prevalence of depression was primarily related to a high level of cohesion in the community as well as to Western rather than non-Western cultures. They went on to develop the view that feelings of guilt were bound up with Christianity, within which tradition intensity of religious involvement was associated with strength of guilt feelings. Such an association was not found in other religious groups, the members of which tended to project their distress outside. The study in fact provides no valid data for such conclusions.

Miscellaneous. A hodgepodge of other cultural elements operative mostly but not exclusively in non-Western societies, has been suggested to be stressful and to contribute to depression but no evidence is available from which conclusions may be drawn. One example is *role deprivation* whereby certain categories of individuals are denied or deprived of a psychologically satisfying or significant life role. This has been seen to be the case with women, particularly barren women, the aged and siblings other than first rank in Eastern traditional societies. The opposite practice, *the imposition of roles* for which individuals are ill-prepared, e.g., in arranged early marriages, has also been thought to be harmful. Other stressful cultural systems include those which incur *deprivation of basic gratifications,* e.g., excessive taboos on sex, those which *canalise energy into wasteful channels,* e.g., time-consuming rites, and those which *inculcate enervating sentiments,* e.g., supersitions producing fears.

The rigidity and authoritarianism of the *traditional family structure* in certain Eastern societies have been postulated to foster an over dependency in interpersonal relations which ill-prepare the individual for responsibility. The specific structure of Japanese families which requires reverence, piety, and a sense of duty on the part of sons toward their parents has been invoked (Kimura 1965) to account for the high prevalence of guilt feelings toward parents in Japanese male depressives, which are absent in their German counterparts. Similarly the patriarchal family structure of the Hutterites is seen to contribute to a high frequency of depression and guilt feelings (Eaton and Weil 1955).

A number of other cultural elements are seen to be generally inimical to mental health. One is *value saturation,* which refers to the phenomenon where individuals become excessively imbued with the goals and values of the culture. Thus excessive valuation of aggressiveness may lead to what may be regarded as aggressive psychopathic behavior. Another is *value polymorphism,* which refers to the coexistence in the culture or individual of conflicting values which may arise in societies which are complex or which fail to provide clear strategies for role changes. Various aspects of social organization such as *anomie, social rigidity,* and *minority status* are also seen to contribute to mental ill-health.

2. Factors counteracting depression

Rituals and beliefs. Lindemann (1944) remarked that guilt feelings and acute grief can be counteracted by religious belief. Fernando (1969) saw in the confession of Roman Catholics a means of relieving guilt. Kiev (1964) among others was impressed by the psychotherapeutic value of some rituals and magical and religious beliefs in primitive societies. Cultures may provide "cathartic strategies" such as carnivals, feasts, games and dances, and "status-reversal rituals," by which the powerful are temporarily humiliated by the weak, which alleviate psychological tensions and convert the purposeless unadaptive behavior of subjects under duress into socially sanctioned ones (Wittkower 1971).

Many pre-literate societies have mourning rituals which may provide a much more intensive working through of object-loss than is possible with the inhibited mourning of the West (Stainbrook 1954). The value of institutionalized orgies of grief following death was stressed by Tooth (1950) on the basis of his observations in Ghana. Similarly Kidorf (1963) saw in Jewish mourning rituals a means of alleviating guilt.

Extended family system. Stainbrook (1954) suggested that non-Western societies with an extended family structure may have a lower incidence of depressive reactions than Western societies with the more restricted conjugal family. He hypothesized that in the extended family with its multimothering group, the child would have greater opportunities to seek rewards and avoid punishments and frustrations. Object-loss would be less threatening both in early and in later life because of availability of multiple external sources of gratification. Whiting (1959) suggested that guilt is less prominent in cultures characterized by extended families. Fernando (1969) found that Jewish depressives were less guilt-ridden than Protestant depressives and attributed the difference mainly to the closer kinship ties in Jewish families.

Status provision. Adequate status provision for certain categories of individuals such as the aged, postmenopausal women and adolescents in some non-Western societies is seen to account for the lower frequency of depression in these groups compared with the West. The rising incidence of suicide with increasing age in Western societies is interpreted as being consonant with the hypothesis that role deprivation is related to a higher frequency of depression in the aged. The finding that the incidence of suicide remains constant with increasing age in societies that esteem their aged—e.g., in Peking in 1922 (Gamble and Burgess 1921) and in Nigeria more recently (Asuni 1962)—is taken as confirmatory evidence for the role deprivation hypothesis.

Other cultural factors which have been postulated to have a mitigating effect on depression, such as *permissiveness in early childhood training* and *lack of inhibition of aggression,* are considered in the section on psychopathological hypotheses.

3. Factors altering manifestations or determining their choice in depression

Cultural sick role. Parsons (1951) has described the characteristics of the sick role. Brody (1964) has pointed out that societies define the sick role in various ways, that such differences may be reflected in the presenting complaints and that without such considerations one cannot meaningfully assess the absolute frequency of sickness across cultures.

Culture may define the sick role predominantly in somatic terms on the basis of prevalent ideas of disease, as appears to be the case in lower social classes, illiterate and primitive groups. Psychological distress may then find expression in somatization and hypochondriasis. The sick role for depressives may be totally denied, as apparently so with African societies which have no word for depression in their language, and with the Hutterites, where depression is regarded as "divine testing." The depressive sick role may on the other hand be culturally sanctioned: in South American tribes depression may take the form of "susto," the so-called "fright disease," believed to originate from loss of soul following sudden impressions or bewilderment. The sick role may be exploited, as in parts of Africa where emotional instability qualifies for priesthood (Tooth

1950). Finally the sick role may be shaped by the attitude of the community to the helping profession, as among the Japanese (Caudill 1959).

Beliefs. Prevailing beliefs may determine the choice of depressive symptoms. Thus sexual disorders are said to be common presenting complaints in India and have been linked with beliefs relating the quality and quantity of semen to health, various foods, and innumerable social and ritualistic practices (Carstairs 1956). Another symptom prevalent in India is a sensation of burning in the whole or parts of the body. According to Chakraborty (1971) the origin of this symptom can be traced to folk beliefs derived from the Ayurveda, the ancient Indian system of medicine, in which "burning" of the body is a main component of the diseases described.

Among the Arabs, Racy (1970) observed that impotence was a common disorder, often associated with backache. He related these symptoms to beliefs concerning seminal fluid similar to those held by Indians.

Among Chinese depressives the high frequency of hypochondriacal complaints, if confirmed, may be related to ideas about the nature of health, sickness, and healing derived from traditional Chinese medicine, philosophy, and religion. These appear to lead to a heightened awareness and preoccupation with the functions of the body and may predispose the depressive to hypochondriasis and somatization (Singer 1974).

In Africa, beliefs in bewitchment have been related to depressive illness manifesting with spontaneous self-accusations of witchcraft (Field 1960). Belief in demoniacal possession in various cultures is generally accepted to lead to states of possession. Similar supernatural beliefs may account for the high incidence of dissociative, hysterical, and confusional symptoms reported in preliterate cultures.

Western cultures may not be free from beliefs which influence the manifestations of depression. The Judaeo-Christian tradition with its ideas of sin and belief in a punishing God may be related to the prevalence of delusions of sin and guilt feelings.

Factors altering the observed prevalence of manifestations include *community tolerance,* availability of *treatment facilities,* and *semantic problems.* Even within Western societies depression carries different connotations for doctors and for patients (Benoist et al. 1965) and the semantic problems are multiplied in comparative work. Other cultural elements apparently altering manifestations are those that affect the process of *symptom identification, referral,* and *assessment* and will be dealt with in the section on sampling and diagnostic problems.

Psychopathological Hypotheses

Psychopathological hypotheses proposed to explain cultural variations in depressive illness have usually been within the framework of psychoanalytic theory. The popular view (Wittkower and Hugel 1968; Collomb 1965; Burton-Bradley 1965) is that depression is rare in non-Western, especially primitive, communities, and that when it occurs it is characterized by a rarity of guilt feelings and a high frequency of somatization, hypochondriasis, paranoid symptoms, and confused, excited, manic, and aggressive behavior.

Ego development

Lack of frustration at the oral stage due to extreme permissiveness in child-rearing has been postulated for the alleged rarity of psychotic depression in developing societies, especially the African (Wittkower and Hugel 1968). This hypothesis has also been used to explain a supposedly *high* prevalence of depression in Ghana (Weinberg 1965; Kraus 1968) and Nigeria (Staewen and Schonberg 1970). It is claimed that the abrupt weaning which follows extreme permissiveness predisposes depression.

Superego development

A number of variations on the theme that in non-Western societies the superego is weakly developed have been postulated.

"*Projection* instead of repression is the main defence mechanism employed in primitive cultures" (Benedict and Jacks 1954: Wittkower and Hugel 1968: Carothers 1953).

A threatening conscience is externalized in superstitious beliefs and practices. Furthermore, encouragement of a sense of social belongingness through ceremonials and rituals leads to the development of a predominantly collective or class superego and a weak individual superego. Plentiful use of the projective mechanism accounts for the high frequency of paranoid delusion, hallucination, agitation, excitement, aggressive and hysterical behavior and mania.

"Deficient internalization of external authority leads to a lack of sense of responsibility and low incidence of depression."

In the West the decline of manic depressive psychosis in the United States has been attributed to rapid replacement of the "inner-directed" society, characterized by responsibility, guilt, and introjection with the "other-directed" society, characterized by group security and support (Arieti 1959). Sense of responsibility has been postulated to be positively correlated to depression (Hitson and Funkenstein 1959; Schwab et al. 1968). Africans in Ghana have been surmised to have a high sense of responsibility, leading to a high frequency of depression (Weinberg, 1965). However no criteria or quantitative measures of sense of responsibility have been introduced to verify these postulates.

"Lack of inhibition of aggression accounts for the low incidence of depression."

An association between aggression and depression is implicit in psychodynamic theories of depression (Freud 1925; Abraham 1960; Kendell 1970). A low incidence of depression is said to be found in communities and groups where aggression may be readily expressed, e.g. primitive cultures, soldiers in combat, young males, and where the homicide rate is high. However, what little transcultural work that exists does not support the hypothesis of an inverse relationship between aggression and depression. Naroll (1965) using ratings compiled by anthropologists on primitive tribes found no significant correlation between frustration level and a suicide measure in 58 cultures. Palmer (1966) found not a negative but a positive relationship between homicide and suicide in 40 primitive societies.

"Non-westerners lack a *sense of guilt.*"

The concept of guilt occupies a prominent place in psychoanalytic theory. Guilt feelings are regarded as a fundamental characteristic of depressive illness, so much so that doubts have been expressed whether depression with guilt is the same disease as depression without guilt (Murphy et al. 1967). Psychoanalytically oriented workers have inclined to the belief that guilt is a prominent component of depression, that the latter is also rare. Two issues are involved: (a) whether guilt is in fact rare in non-Western cultures and (b) whether guilt is a necessary component of depressive illness.

Studies that purport to show a rarity of guilt feelings outside the West (Murphy et al. 1967; Leighton et al. 1963) suffer from methodological shortcomings. The few that have been carried out recently in which guilt feelings were specifically compared have found a high frequency in non-Western depressive, e.g., in the Japanese (Kimura 1965), the Indian (Teja et al. 1967), and the Arab (El-Islam 1969). It is probable that non-Western cultures differ not in frequency but in content of guilt feelings. Observations in the past of a low frequency of guilt were probably based on a biased interpretation of content. Semantic problems are involved, for non-Western cultures are said to suffer from shame (whose sanctions are external) rather than guilt (whose sanctions are internal). But the criteria for separating guilt from shame are difficult to define and the two have more similarities than differences.

As regards the question whether guilt is a necessary component of depressive illness this is a matter of agreement on the definition.

Evaluation

Difficulties in work on the relationship between cultural factors and depressive disorder stem from the conceptual issues and methodological problems of cultural research.

Research has employed *conceptual frameworks* which are oversimplified, lack explictness and definitional precision, and employ a limited number of theoretical orientations. The culture illness sequence has usually been treated as a linear, self-contained system of causality, whereas a more appropriate model would be a sophisticated system embracing a large array of interlocking variables, with overlapping sequences and feedback mechanisms, and subject to the modifying effect of intrusive external elements. The complexity of the problem is such that no matter how sophisticated the analysis straightforward conclusions can rarely be drawn.

Conceptual formulations have been ambiguous: there is no agreement, e.g., as to how concepts such as cultural disintegration are to be defined and measured. "Guilt" and "shame" are concepts too vague to be productive of reliable empirical research. Social cohesion as a concept is ambiguous and shifting in meaning. Psychodynamic interpretation has been contradictory, e.g., concerning the effect of permissiveness in child training on depressive disorders in African societies. Such ambiguity prevents proper testing of many postulates in transcultural psychiatry. A number of postulates are testable but untested, e.g., that mourning rituals can alleviate depression, that certain belief systems can aggravate or alleviate guilt, and that the cultural sick role can modify depression.

The problems of *sampling* in psychiatric epidemiology are well known and they are of greater magnitude when cross-cultural comparisons are attempted. As regards depressive disorders in non-Western cultures generalizations have been made, with few exceptions, from hospital and clinic populations, who are a highly selected group. Selection on the basis of disturbed behavior would appear to adequately account for the low frequency of depression and high frequency of mania, as well as the high frequency of aggressive, confused, excited and paranoid behavior in hospitalized depressives in underdeveloped countries. Thus when field studies are carried out depressive symptoms appear to be not uncommon.

The problems of sampling differ according to the requirements of research. In studies on the incidence and symptomatology of depressive illness cross-culturally, representativeness of the samples is essential. The problems of obtaining representativeness are formidable and in studies of causal relationships between culture and depressive disorders it is sufficient to achieve comparability of samples. Indeed this is actually preferable when the composition of the two populations is widely divergent. For testing of descriptive hypotheses, random sampling is the best. To overcome the problem of generalizing from the study of one small community, replication in a number of communities is necessary. The shortcomings of sampling procedure are reduced when the investigator is explicit about his procedure. Adequate sampling applies not only to selection of subjects but also to selection of cultures, institutions, practices, relationships, and other cultural phenomena.

Another problem is *diagnosis*. It is impossible to achieve comparability in cross-cultural work in depressive disorders without a common basic terminology, defined indicators of illness, and agreement on the norm. Fundamentally the difficulty stems from lack of knowledge of the nature of depression and its aetiology, and the consequent lack of a generally accepted classificatory system. Depressive illness has therefore been described under a variety of other rubrics which makes comparison of findings reported in different cultures impossible. In comparative work diagnostic difficulties are amplified by linguistic problems, investigator bias, and unreliability in interpreting alien symbols of behavior.

Some reduction in diagnostic discrepancies may be achieved by the use of standardized procedures for diagnosis such as described in the WHO 10 year plan of research in psychiatric epidemiology (Shepherd et al. 1968) and of standardization procedures for interview (Wing et al. 1974). There is need for objective methods of assessment, behavioral and physiological, in transcultural work.

Functional equivalence is another problem in cross-cultural work which has often been ignored. This refers to the observation that in different cultures apparently similar phenomena—symbols of communication and behavior, values, social systems—may have different functions and significance: conversely different cultures may use different symbols to communicate similar phenomena or different systems to achieve similar ends.

Finally an outstanding problem in transcultural research is *interpretation*. In research which seeks correlations between cultural variables and mental illness, the large number of variables and the complexity of interrelationships require sophisticated methods of analysis, but even then the interpretation of causal sequence can only be suggestive. Any interpretation is usually subject to potential fallacies because a number of alternative explanations often present themselves. There is need for extending research to rule out such alternative hypotheses and to test hypotheses arising from the consequences of interpretations.

Methodological requirements

A more sophisticated frame of reference is required for study of the culture–depressive illness sequence which will take into account the complex interaction of a much larger number of variables.

In studying depressive disorders cross-culturally we need to cast the net wider than hitherto and study phenomena simultaneously at several levels of organization. An example is the scheme suggested by Fabrega (1974b) whereby depression may be studied at the following levels: (1) the biological, e.g., neurochemical changes, (2) the functional, e.g., emotional changes, (3) the behavioral, in the cultural context, e.g., crying, and (4) the meaning that culture assigns to the phenomena of depression. Studies at several levels of organization clarify problems of terminology and are relevant to issues such as the significance of form versus content in psychiatric disorder, the relation between depressive disorder and other illnesses, such as the neurotic, and the degree to which all these illnesses share a common basis.

Obviously we should avoid the pitfalls of previous work and use improved methodology. There is need for more precise formulations in aims and methods of research and for use of the explanatory, experimental, and prospective models in place of the merely descriptive. There is need above all to obtain the facts of differences in phenomena relating to depressive disorders in different cultures before making generalizations; hitherto it has been the other way round.

Research designs should encompass graded comparisons of a wide variety of cultures instead of being confined to comparisons of two extremes of cultures. They should extend cross-cultural comparisons to intra-cultural comparisons along similar dimensions as well as to cross-cultural comparisons along other dimensions. Due regard needs to be given for the control of social variables like social class, education, age, and sex if social influences are to be separated from cultural.

Conclusion

Investigations to date on the role of culture in depressive disorders have been unsophisticated. There is insufficient evidence to support the prevalent view that depressive illness in primitive and certain other non-Western cultures has outstanding deviant features.

The putative rarity of depressive disorders and of depressive affect in depressives in non-Western cultures appears to be due to the unrepresentativeness of the samples studied and the use of an excessively narrow definiton that overemphasizes guilt feelings and the verbalization of depressive affect for diagnosis. The reported rarity of suicides in some non-Western communities cannot be taken as a reliable indicator of the magnitude of the problem of depression for comparative studies. The alleged increase in morbidity with increasing complexity of civilization probably reflects an increase in availability of psychiatric facilities and a broadening of concepts of psychiatric disorder.

The prevalence of shame feelings in depressives of certain non-Western cultures, in contradistinction to guilt feelings in the Western is an artifact of a problem in semantics and in interpretation of symbols of speech and behavior by alien observers.

The pronounced somatization and hypochondriasis in depressives outside the Western culture is probably mainly due to self-selection for treatment, consequent upon a somatic orientation of disease and interpretation of the sick role that are found in illiterates and those of the lower social classes irrespective of culture. It is possible however that cultural beliefs which inculcate an unhealthy preoccupation with the functions of the body, as traditionally found in the Orient, play a pathoplastic role in the genesis of these symptoms.

The frequency of persecutory ideas, confused and excited behavior and mania is understandable in terms of bias conferred by selection of disturbed patients for hospitalization where facilities are under-developed. But it is also possible that the preponderance of hysterical and confusional symptoms is due to conditioning of dissociative reactions by cultural beliefs in spirit possession and other supernatural influences.

That culture influences the content of symptoms such as of guilt, delusions and somatization cannot be disputed. That culture may infuence the form in which depressive illness manifests, e.g., a predominance of somatization in one culture, depressive affect in another, and so on, is a plausible supposition, but one which has yet to be unequivocally demonstrated for each type of manifestation and for each culture. The evidence does not support the view that culture influences the morbidity of depressive disorders. When careful field surveys are carried out, the prevalence rate of depressive disorder has generally been found to be well within the range reported in the West. One also gains the impression that similarities considerably outweigh differences across cultures. A conglomeration of features—depressive mood, diurnal variation, fatigue, insomnia, loss of interest, weight loss, periodicity, and the biphasic nature of the illness—appears to be found consistently in all cultures. The concept of depressive disorder as it is held in the West emerges as universally valid.

In the comparative approach, a constant sensitivity to and an objective evaluation of cross-cultural *differences* may still provide rewarding insights and can only advance our knowledge of psychogenesis. Even more important perhaps is the need to clarify *similarities,* in order to provide a basis for the development of a truly international and scientific psychiatry. The difficulties of such work are great. Whether the effort is worthwhile is a question which cannot be answered till we have a better knowledge of the weights to be assigned to the various physical, sociological, and psychological variables that interact to produce depressive disorder. In any case it would be unwise to embark on further comparative work without closer attention to problems of methodology. Alternatively, researchers may perhaps be more fruitfully occupied testing hypotheses about the nature, distribution, and consequences of depressive disorders in their own cultures.

21

Drug Use and Abuse in Cross-Cultural Perspective

Marlene Dobkin De Rios
and David E. Smith

Substance use, abuse and dependence are major concerns of the World Health Organization and of mental health professionals everywhere. The current revision of the International Classification of Diseases defines nondependent abuse of drugs as cases where a person is under medical care because of the maladaptive effect of a drug that he has taken on his own initiative to the detriment of his health and social functioning. Drug dependence is characterized further by compulsion to take a drug on a continuous or periodic basis in order to experience its psychic effects and sometimes to avoid the discomfort of its absence.

It is becoming increasingly clear that the above phenomena are determined not just by pharmacological factors but also by a number of physiological, psychological, and sociocultural variables in reciprocal interaction. Thus an adequate explication of their nature seems to go beyond narrow biomedical conceptualizations and requires the participation of such ethnomedical concepts as those discussed earlier in article 20.

De Rios and Smith present in the following article an illuminating cross-cultural review of the use of psychoactive drugs and of the role and meaning of such use for the individual and the community. Their conclusions challenge many established tenets on the understanding and social regulation of drug use.

ANDREW WEIL (1973) has suggested that the desire to alter human consciousness is a basis human psychologic characteristic. Bourguignon, an anthropologist, and her colleagues, during a decade of cross-cultural research on altered states, have analyzed a global ethnographic sample of 488 societies. The data show that 90 percent of the societies in question are reported to have one or more institutionalized, culturally patterned forms of altered states of consciousness (1973). As Bourguignon points out, it is likely that we are dealing with a psychobiological capacity available to all societies, and that indeed "the vast majority of societies have used it (altered states of consciousness) in their own particular ways, and have done so in primarily a sacred context" (1973:10–11).

We shall examine one aspect of cross-cultural altered states of consciousness—namely, drug induced ones—to seek continuities and discontinuities in sacred, ritualized drug use. We shall focus both on traditional non-Western societies as well as contemporary industrial ones such as the United States. Our interest includes the current increase in American ritualistic drug use (ranging from the heroin needle ritual, the cocktail party, or the marijuana smoking ritual at rock concerts) as it correlates with the evidence from traditional societies of the world. In so doing, we hope to obtain a cross-cultural perspective on an issue of great importance and controversy in American society today. This perspective presumes a certain familiarity with the drug abuse question in general. We hope to provide philosophical underpinnings in understanding cross-cultural variations in a definition of drug use and abuse.

The Lack of Drug Abuse in Traditional Society

De Rios (1975b) has stressed that conceptualization of drug abuse in traditional societies of the world does not exist as it does in industrial ones like our own. In her own monograph on the non-Western use of hallucinogenic agents, prepared for the U.S. National Commission on Marijuana and Drug Abuse in 1971, she surveyed a dozen societies of the world, chosen with respect to levels of sociocultural integration and geographic distribution. She found that when ritual use of psychoactive plants was found in such societies, little if any abuse occurred. Other writers such as

Schultes (1972) and Harner (1973) have been in general agreement that when ritual use of psychoactive plants is found, little if any abuse could be said to obtain. Generally speaking, the particular powers of psychoactive substances were early acknowledged to belong to special realms that were constrained with taboos, rituals, and proscriptions. Any individual daring to embark upon a hallucinogenic journey had to be properly prepared. The sacred nature of plant hallucinogens as used in non-Western society, to be spelled out in detail here, attests to the maturity and experience of man in traditional society in dealing with substances that were not viewed as amenable to mundane, secular use.

In a study conducted by Blum in 1959, based on the Human Relations Area File, data on psychoactive drug use was correlated with material culture, social structure and belief systems. That author reiterated the real problems that historically have occurred with regard to Western perception of native drug use. Cultural blinders on the part of many early travelers, missionaries, botanists, and even anthropologists, emanating as they did in large part from Europe and America where culturally approved drugs such as alcohol and tobacco were used, did not adequately prepare those investigators for a sensitivity toward the use of exotic drugs; in turn, such substances were often shrouded in ritual secrecy. In Blum's analysis of over 250 societies then available for statistical manipulation, he found much of the HRAF data to be incomplete and inaccurate. De Rios' procedure in 1971 was to utilize the excellent drug libraries available in California, a good portion of which data was not coded in the HRAF. She chose a dozen societies of the world which, for the most part, had been studied prior to European influences upon them. In some instances, drug cults arose in direct response to acculturative pressure. Societies were chosen ranging from hunters and gatherers, to pastoralists, to incipient agriculturalists, to peoples of ancient civilizations, as well as a drug-using peasant society in northern Peru studied by her in 1967. She presented general ethnographic data describing each society's psychoactive plant use. A series of drug-related themes emerged from this compilation, which serve to test a variety of propositions in societies where psychoactive drug use continues to be important cross culturally; in addition, these working hypotheses provide a means of examining the art and artifacts of extinct peoples who we have reason to believe used mind-altering plants in order to suggest possible magico-religious interpretations of such materials (de Rios 1974, 1977, in press a, in press b).

Some General Comments on Drug Use in American Society

When we turn to the evidence on drug oriented industrialized societies such as that of the United States, we find that the use of psychoactive drugs is a major way in which people alter their consciousness. The psychoactive drugs used to achieve this alteration are quite varied, ranging from legal sedative-hypnotics such as alchohol, legal stimulants such as caffeine and nicotine, to illicit substances which include marijuana, heroin, and LSD. Smith (1975) has described various psychoactive drug patterns in the United States as experimental, recreational, ritualistic, compulsive, and medicinal, with the latter category including those individuals who self-medicate because of underlying psychological problems such as depression, or use psychoactive drugs to facilitate performance in achieving a particular goal.

The ritualistic pattern of American drug use expanded greatly in the 1960s with the popularization of Timothy Leary's LSD theme, "Turn on, tune in, and drop out," particularly in the youth counterculture. Ritualistic drug use has increased in magnitude and is used to achieve a wide variety of objectives including the expansion of cosmic consciousness, enhancement of feelings of religiosity, and attempts to gain better self understanding in both an individual and group context. This pattern of ritualistic drug use, however, is considered destructive by most of American society. For example, Jaffe states; "the term drug abuse will be used in its broadest sense, to refer to the use, usually by self-administration of any drug in a manner that deviates from the approved medical or social patterns within a given culture" (1975:224). As Szasz (1975) has pointed out, licit versus illicit definitions of drug use and abuse are spurious, if indeed we turn to the health implications of psychoactive substances in general. He argues that use and avoidance of drugs are not matters of health and disease, as we are conditioned to believe, but questions of good and evil—the latter basically being a religious issue. Szasz claims that drug abuse in contemporary America has to do with disapproved or prohibited patterns of drug use without regard to the actual harmful effect of the substance involved, since many legal substances are indeed highly toxic and dangerous.

Common definitions of abuse suggested by Webster, such as "to use wrongly, to misuse; wrong or bad or excessive use; bad, unjust or corrupt custom or practice" present us with semantic and political difficulties which have to be considered in this light. When we talk about a corrupt custom or practice, or one that is wrong or excessive, we are, of course, dealing with value laden terminology which can lend itself to an ethnocentric focus. This issue will be examined more fully later on. However, at this point, we would like to define drug abuse in terms of health related criteria, as being the use of a psychoactive substance in a fashion that seriously interferes with an individual's economic, health, or social functioning. We suggest that much of current ritualistic drug use in American society is destructive only in that it deviates from accepted social and cultural norms. In fact, this ritualistic drug use may be beneficial to the individual and the group in which interaction occurs. We suggest that ritualistic drug use, although criticized and rejected by the dominant culture in the United States, in fact is a very central part of the behavior of people in traditional societies, receiving at the same time positive social valorization. As the cross-cultural evidence to be reported on shows, ritualization of psychoactive drug use often enhances group goals, contributes to social cohesion, reaffirms belief systems, and performs a host of adaptive functions for the group.

In addition to ritualization, we are also interested in the sacralization of drug use. In this context, definitions of the sacred, which include the act of setting apart, creating awesomeness or exaltation—all the opposite of a mundane, secular focus—seem to be a rubric under which a cross-cultural analysis of psychoactive drug use will yield some interesting continuities.

In many traditional societies where ritualized drug use has occurred without evidence of abuse (either in terms of negative health considerations or social mores), the introduction of foreign drugs such as distilled alcohol, without any accompanying ritual, caused subsequent abuse that was of major social, political, and economic consequence.

We would like to make a twofold analysis: de Rios' findings with regard to drug use in traditional societies of the world will be presented, paying particular attention to epistemological and religious structures which correlate cross culturally with plant psychoactive use. Political variables will be analyzed in an attempt to understand the differential reception and perception cross culturally of mind-altering substances. Smith's analysis of the sociological and medical aspects of contemporary American drug use will provide us with continuities and discontinuities in understanding problems of drug abuse in Western societies such as our own.

The Anthropological Evidence

The societies upon which the following analysis is based include the Australian aborigines of the central Australian desert, the reindeer herders of Siberia, the Huichol Indians of Mexico, the New Guinea highlanders, the Plains Indians of the United States, the Jivaro of the Amazonian rain forest, the Fang of northwestern equatorial Africa, the Aryans of northern India, the Aztec, the Maya, the Inca, and the Mestizos of north coastal Peru. The major finding of de Rios' report reiterates the role of cultural variables, such as belief systems, values, attitudes, and expectations which structure one of the most subjective experiences available to man—a notion first explored by Wallace in 1959. The role of antecedent variables of a biological, psychological, social-interactional, and cultural nature are primary in interfacing with the consequent effects of psychoactive drugs, permitting us to predict a drug effect cross culturally, be it in a traditional or industrial society. Certainly, any psychoactive drug effect is a complex interaction between pharmacological, physiological, psychological, and sociocultural variables (de Rios 1975b). One cannot understand a particular drug pattern merely by focusing on the pharmacological variables alone.

Based on the data, some important themes connected to the use of plant hallucinogens can be delineated. A number of explanations can be cited to explain the derivation of near cultural universals with regard to psychoactive plant use. Such universals may be coincidental, or due to direct borrowing of belief systems related to drug use from one society to another. It is also possible that the biological parameters of psychoactive drugs, such as the so-called psychedelic group, afford a united stimulus acting upon man's central nervous system. Physiological effects such as increased pulse rate or psychophysiological effects such as altered time and visual perceptions, may find their way into such a mytho-poetic theme as "out-of-body" or "aerial voyage." Explanations dealing with instrumental or expressive behavior present yet another mode of argument. The former behavioral pattern acts to change nature, while the latter is a reflection of man's inner states, which in Western scientific approaches are seen as projections outward onto nature. LaBarre (1975) has written about this recently and he dismisses most of the global beliefs linked to hallucinogenic ingestion as individual psychodynamic states related to animistic superstitions, derived through drug induced accessibility to the unconscious.

Still another explanation is possible, owing in large measure to the publication of Carlos Castaneda's works (1968, 1971, 1972, 1974). The anthropologist, among others, has been forced to reexamine his data from the point of view of epistemology, to query his own basic assumptions about the nature of the so-called real world and the possible ethnocentrism of coding mechanisms in his language and scientific culture which may rule out alternate explanations. From Castaneda's general impact on epistemology, social scientists now are wary of simplistic suggestions that there is no such thing as witchcraft or that natural spirit forces do not exist other than as a poetic search for meaning which characterizes religions in general—a stance which earlier they might have given in to under the influence of those scientific paradigms guiding their work. By these comments, we do not necessarily wish to go on record for the existence or nonexistence of such phenomena, but rather to argue for an agnostic posture which makes clear the concept that we are perhaps, in Castaneda's approach, victimized by our culture and its consensual validations in our attempt to understand and define patterns of psychoactive drug use.

Hallucinogenic Themes in Traditional Society

The overriding themes connected to plant psychedelic use cross culturally include the following:

(1) Altered perception of time and its symbolic coding in religious precepts; a relationship between man's perception of the slowing down of time, or else its enormous acceleration during the hallucinogenic effect—and its influences on the so-called *in illo tempore*. Referred to by Eliade in his cross-cultural studies of myth and symbol (1957), this eternal mythical present is periodically reintegrated by man in traditional society by means of his religious ceremonials.

(2) The relationship between the animal kingdom, a spiritual hierarchy within it, and a perceived spiritual hierarchy among men, best seen in the phenomenon of shamanistic familiars acquired through drug ingestion. A corollary of this theme deals with the correspondence between human spiritual power and man's relationship to a hierarchy of animal familiars; further, shamanistic transformation into animal familiars is associated with plant hallucinogenic use.

(3) Spiritual animation of plant hallucinogens, microscopic or macroscopic in dimension, coded in myth or visionary experience. The plant animators are deemed to be repositories of supernatural power, or links to spirit forces.

(4) Death and resurrection. As dissolution of ego boundaries commonly ensue upon plant hallucinogenic use, a frequently recurring theme deals with man's crossing over into realms of the dead, with the subsequent phenomena of renewal, rebirth, or resurrection. This is particularly found in puberty rites related to hallucinogenic ingestion.

(5) Paranormal phenomena such as telepathy, precognition, and psychokinesis are closely associated with plant hallucinogenic ingestion cross culturally. Whether or not cerebral lateral dominance is affected by such pharmacological stimuli, with ensuant threshold states for these paranormal phenomena linked to right brain activity (the passive mode, in Deikman's terminology [1973]) remains an open question, but one to which anthropologists will have to attend in future research (see also Marsh and Chemtob 1974).

The foregoing themes, while drawn from the data, by no means present us with an exhaustive list. Hopefully, however, they provide some interesting pathways for those anthropologists interested in symbolic systems, especially those who may not have paid particular attention to the presence of a unified stimulus—hallucinogenic plant drugs—as they affect man's central nervous system in a patterned fashion and their symbolic elaboration in a finite number of ways.

Political Variables and Plant Psychedelic Drug Ingestion

Perhaps the most important finding of de Rios' research with regard to the drug abuse question deals with the cross-cutting variable of political structure. Harner was the first to point out hypothetically in a personal communication (1970) that as societies grow in structural complexity, we should expect to find a change in the use, and access for use, of plant hallucinogens. The data point out quite clearly that with growing segmentation, status differentiation, and elite formation in stratified societies, plant hallucinogenic use becomes less likely among all segments of society. Rather, such plants are usurped and reserved by elite segments, who incorporate them into sumptuary laws. The Inca response to coca (a CNS stimulant, but one possibly mixed with other plant hallucinogens in

Precolumbian times) illustrates this theme nicely. About 150 years prior to the Spanish intrusion, Inca nobility began to promulgate myths concerning the origin of coca, a plant drug of great regional antiquity. Such myths had as their purpose the justification of the usurpation of the coca plant from common usage, converted now to a reward system linked to the authority structure of the evolving Inca state administration. De Rios (1974) argued for similar phenomena with regard to the use of Maya psychoactive flora and fauna. Data on the Aztec, too, show rather stringent measures used to control yet another psychoactive substance, alcohol. In summary form, as societies change from an egalitarian status, where goods and services are shared and exchanged, and as man enters into hierarchical orderings, drug use, too, undergoes changes. In traditional societies, drug use tends to be communally oriented while in stratified societies, drug use seems to have been eliminated from widespread use. It is possible that the belief that man is able to bewitch and cause his enemy's death, commonly associated with the power of hallucinogenic plants, presents a danger to members of stratified or state society. The concept of state society generally is associated with the total control of legitimized power, with all other attempts at power being subject to regulation. If a peasant shaman in a state society were permitted use of drug plants that all segments of society believed bestowed power to bewitch a state ruler or administrator, legitimate power itself may have been in jeopardy. As suggested by Wasson and Wasson (1957), it may be that in the history of Western civilization, ancient oracular use of hallucinogens disappeared because of this threat to state power. As mentioned earlier with regard to the Inca, their sumptuary laws limiting the use of coca for the Inca, his nobility, and favorites, illustrates this principle. Among the Aztec and Maya, such usurpation of drugs by higher ranking segments may very well explain the quick demise of drug knowledge upon culture contact, when a specialized caste of drug users was eliminated. This esoteric kowledge did not again diffuse to the folk level where it surely originated. The implication of loss of drug knowledge is interesting to examine. We might speculate that reports of drug use historically tend to be most complete in traditional societies where hallucinogenic plants are in general use rather than among large populations in advanced civilizations, where only special castes may have employed the drug for communal or private ends.

It is worthwhile recapitulating the correlation between the cultural value placed on revealed knowledge with the readiness of a given society to attribute supernatural powers to hallucinogenic plants. In such societies where, for one reason or another, man holds that only first-hand experience is the true path to knowledge, such plants have been received with great acclaim and awe. As soon as hierarchical functionaries intercede between man, proposing doctrines concerning religion and specific pathways of access to the supernatural, such plants either fall from popular use or else are arrogated from folk segments. When such plant drugs have been used for religious goals, they conveyed to man his own personal vision of the supernatural, while at the same time, they reaffirmed his society's collective vision of truth and knowledge. In those societies where plant hallucinogens have played a central role, ethnographers describe beliefs of the drug user that he can see, feel, touch, and experience the unknown—which is filtered through a cultural screen of expected visionary experience. As with Buber's dictum regarding the I-Thou relationship between man and the supernatural (1970), the central commandment of such societies seems to be to make the secular sacred. Here the notion of a set-apart state of consciousness is often in focus.

Thus, the very nature of religious systems as they have evolved sets the stage for distinctive response to the power believed conferred upon the drug user by these potent plants. Shamanistic religion, in particular, which focuses on man's direct revelatory experience of the supernatural, is widely influenced by the visionary properties of hallucinogenic plants. As stratified societies develop, hierarchies of intermediaries interceding between man and the supernatural tend to view such plant potentiators as truly dangerous to the commonweal.

If we turn to the question of drug abuse and employ definitions enmeshed within a specific sociocultural matrix, such as those presented by Jaffe (1975) or Webster, we can argue that terminology such as "to use wrongly; bad or excessive use; corrupt or unjust custom" must be viewed clearly to emanate from a particular ethnocentric social context rather than from the perspective of a value free one. To use wrongly, for example, may simply be the way of determining under what circumstances just who it is that is entitled to access to drugs and ensuant states of consciousness. One can suggest in this context that all state level societies must deal with issues of control over consciousness states as part of the ideological control and influence upon its members. Bad or excessive use, again, becomes a matter of who is defining such use. While there are many potential psychological, physiological, and social problems connected to psychoactive drug use in industrialized, American society, we find that in traditional societies of the world, ritualization of such use sidesteps many difficulties encountered by Western drug users. Plant drugs in traditional society tend to serve cultural goals; general recognition of a spiritual hierarchy of individuals favored by factors of personal maturity, power, or just plain experience in dealing with their access to their unconscious (but most generally conceptualized as realms of recognized spirit forces) provides drug users with guidance in the specific drug experience. This contrasts dramatically to patterns of use of psychoactive substances in Western industrialized societies of the world. Certainly, European observers of drug use in traditional New World societies acknowledged that such substance use did not threaten native cultures as constituted. Recent cytogenetic studies of peyote use, too, remove the spectre of unharnessed physiological damage ensuant upon hallucinogenic ingestion (Dorrance et al. 1975).

Blum has written that there is no drug abuse in traditional society because drugs are not used for escape. Here again, we must consider questions of epistemology. De Rios' data (1974, 1975a, 1975b) on nonindustrial societies show that drug use is merely a means to a socially approved end, such as contacting the supernatural, either to control its forces, or else to place oneself at the mercy of forces seen to be more powerful than man. Generally, drugs have been used to reconfirm the integrity, values, and goals of a culture. In most cases, drug use is controlled by ritual rather than legal means. The individuals who utilize such plants do so only after periods of careful apprenticeship or guidance, with specific expectations of visionary content. Much of the shaman's behavior while under the effects of such drugs is influenced by the cultural conditioning to which he is subject during much of his formative years. Most often, an experienced shaman guides the session, utilizing nonverbal aspects such as music (de Rios and Katz 1975) and olfactory aids to evoke specific types of visionary content. Drugs are rarely taken by the lone individual for personal, introspective quests. Rather, even in the hands of an individual shaman (a common enough occurrence), they are used to serve specific cultural ends such as healing, divining the future, ascertaining the prognosis of a disease, protecting the community from its enemies, and the like. The use of drugs for culturally defined negative purposes in traditional society generally has taken the form of witchcraft activity aimed at harming enemies for a fee. From a Western cognitive framework, what is often titled hedonistic aspects of drug use generally entails the enhancement of social interaction between strangers or members of a social group. In all cases, where members of a society merely lounge around and indulge in a plant brew or snuff, we tend to find Euroamerican influences, cultural disorganization, and concomitant problems of alienation and alcoholism present.

Moreover, in traditional societies where plant hallucinogens have been used, they often take on the aspect of a learning experience. Among rain forest Amazonian hunters and gatherers such as those described by Cordova-Rios (1971), learning the ways of animals to permit greater success in the hunt has been a major function of the use of one plant hallucinogen, ayahuasca. No doubt other peoples in the past have used such plants because of their ability to heighten sensory perception and permit the recall of information perhaps only partially or incompletely understood or accessible to them through normal channels.

In this way, plants are used to reaffirm a society's mapping of the supernatural, permitting individuals to partake of such beliefs both visually and emotionally. The use of plant hallucinogens for the reduction of private anxiety, the dampening of personal problems, or as a general escape from social pressures, occurs only rarely in the literature, except in the face of dire acculturative stresses. For the most part, in the societies described, drugs are used in a magico-religious context of ceremony, either to celebrate or contact the realm of the supernatural, heal illness, diagnose its cause and determine its prognosis, divine the future, or promote social solidarity among men.

Blum's study (1959) presents us with some interesting summary statements, although his population cases often dwindled down to a handful. For one thing, males rather than females predominate in the use of hallucinogens. In most cultures, children are prohibited from using the plant, although this is far from a cultural universal. Further, in Blum's words, when there is a "hierarchy of jurisdiction," group use of plants is far more prevalent than individual use. In addition, when bellicosity is extreme, the society approves of the use of hallucinogens. Both in traditional society as well as industrial ones, hallucinogens fulfill multiple social functions. Blum's conclusions are that an increase in social complexity (such as in the realm of social organization, stratification, and differences of authority within a society) leads to a variation in individual behavior. This, in turn, would contrast dramatically with the use of plant hallucinogens in non-Western society, where even when shamans were the rare drug users, the society was cognizant of its use and approved of the shaman's role as psychopomp and defender of the commonweal. Certainly, the kinds of drugs used within a society vary with that society's complexity; as a corollary, the more complex the society, the more we can anticipate internal variety in drug use and view with regard to its use.

Ritualistic Drug Use in Contemporary American Society

As described by Smith (1975) and Dennis Jaffee (1964), ritualistic drug use in the United States, particularly among the young and within the counterculture, has greatly increased in the ten year period between 1965 and 1975. In fact, originally the youth culture and the drug culture were synonymous. Needless to say, in recent years there has been a movement by some segments of the counterculture away from drugs to alternate ways of modifying waking consciousness, including Transcendental Meditation, involvement in the Jesus movement, and in eastern esoteric psychologies among a host of others. Early explanations of youthful interest in drugs include factors such as religious searches, curiosity, the need to conform to peer group values, a "dare" factor, rebellion against authority, a search for identity and mystical experience, as well as escape from intolerable circumstances (Unwin 1970). As Smith (1975) has stressed, there is a need to distinguish between drug use and drug abuse in contemporary America, which interfaces well with the cross-cultural analysis presented above. Again, returning to our definition of drug abuse as individual involvement with psychoactive substances to the point where it seriously interferes with the individual's health, economic, or social functioning, Smith (1975) sees sociocultural factors in rapidly changing American society as primary in understanding drug use. Given these many changes taking place during the last decade and a half in the political and social arena of American society, Smith argues that many elements of youthful protest and alternative lifestyles are potentially adaptable as valid by the society as a whole; this, in turn, may lead to a reassessment of American values and goals. Toffler's book *Future Shock* (1970) is often cited because it emphasizes that recent changes among youth and in American society, in general, are an extension of a much broader, sweeping process moving through society. Even deviant behavior, such as illicit drug use, may be futuristic rather than abusive within Toffler's model. Slater, another writer of the contemporary American scene (1971), characterizes segmental differentiation in American society, between what he calls the old and new cultures as follows:

> The old culture when forced to choose, tends to give preference to property rights over personal rights; technological requirements over human needs; competition over cooperation; violence over sexuality; concentration over distribution; the producer over the consumer; secrecy over gratification; Oedipal love over communal love and so on. The counter-culture tends to reverse all these priorities [Slater 1971:75].

Smith (1975) has argued that ritualistic patterns of American youthful drug use should be examined within Slater's context. Such young people see drug taking activity as a means of giving coherence to life's experiences. It is interesting to note here that the ritualization of hallucinogenic substances in American society has led to a diminution of problems such as the ubiquitous "bad trip" phenomenon. Smith has commented that many young people still use LSD. Street drug analyses tend to show high quality and purity as well as low cost, with concomitantly few bad trips reported. Thus in drug abuse clinics, fewer individuals are seen than in the past, leading perhaps to false conclusions that hallucinogenic drug use is fast diminishing. Although epidemiological estimates may be difficult under the circumstances of illicit drug use, we must stress the possibility that the ritualization of certain types of drug use in American society, in fact, has decreased its dangers. Certainly, it is clear that within the last decade, as Dennis Jaffee (1964) has stressed, illicit drug use in certain youth subcultures has been transformed from a deviant act—practiced in ghettos and bohemian subcultures—to a major symbol of the differences between the generations. In a forthcoming paper, we will detail aspects of the ritualization of drug use among contemporary American youth. We are particularly in agreement with Rappaport (1971) who argues that ritual is an information exchange device which communicates cultural, ecological, and demographic data across the boundaries of local social groups, which at some level becomes important in the planning of social strategies. As Rappaport points out, information transferred during rituals, which is held to be sacred, is likely to be accepted as true, even by conflicting parties. This focus on the function of ritual cross culturally is quite useful in explaining the large corpus of relatively unified belief systems among American youthful drug users in the late 1960s–early 1970s, despite variations of an urban, regional, and social class nature.

Relating these comments to the cross-cultural data presented above, there are some fascinating dimensions to be explored within the drug ritual, the use of music as a guide, the antecedent variables and so on. With regard to contemporary American drug use, any future study of drug related rituals would have to pay detailed attention to these components of the function of ritual.

From a cultural evolutionary point of view, once we find the post-industrial state emerging, it is possible to agree with Margaret Mead (1970) that the concept of culture has generational components with regard to contemporary America. Thus, the youth culture distinguishes itself from the parental generation just as a pastoral society might be easily distinguished from a horticultural one. Drug use adheres to generational differences in terms of psychoactive drugs of preference. Alcohol, tobacco, and hypno-sedatives of one generation may contrast with the hallucinogens and amphetamines of another. The asymmetry of political power, aligned with the perseverance of traditional values, perhaps explains some of the contemporary conflicts with regard to drug abuse in contemporary America.

Conclusion

In summary, we see that particulars of the definition of drug use and abuse are clearly contextual and derive from a structural overview of industrial society. In fact, we suggest that the major danger of certain patterns of ritualistic drug use in American society is that the individual may be arrested for violating laws based on sociocultural norms which derive from less than clear-cut negative health considerations. It is well worth exploring how the pattern of ritualistic drug use among American youth may be both of benefit and of value to individuals in their interacting group.

22

Cultural Differences In Child Guidance Clinic Patients

David H. Stoker and Arnold Meadow

The study of the distribution and manifestations of psychiatric disorders in children and adolescents has lagged considerably behind that for adults, given the relatively incipient knowledge on the psychopathology of earlier age groups. The recently increasing interest in these groups is reflected by the greater differentiation in the classification of child and adolescent behavior disorders noted in the current version of the International Classification of Diseases in comparison to that in the 1968 version. Given the tremendous importance of the family in the life and development of the child, understanding of child psychopathology requires consideration of the structural patterns, particular stresses, coping mechanisms, and psychopathology of the surrounding family. Crucial sociocultural variables typically reach the child through the family.

In the following article, Stoker and Meadow contribute to the systematic clarification of the psychopathology and family processes of Mexican-American vs. Anglo-American children through a study conducted in child guidance clinics in the Southwest. Of particular interest is their examining not only the distribution of diagnostic categories but also elementary symptom behaviors which turned out to be quite revealing of specific cultural influences on psychopathology.

A HOST of anthropological, sociological, and psychological researches have pointed to major cross-cultural differences in the distribution, frequency, and types of psychopathology, as well as in basic personality structures (For example: Benedict 1958; Cohen 1961; Moffson 1954; Opler 1959 and 1967; and Tooth 1950). There have been some explorations of the differences in psychopathology and personality between Anglo-American and subjects of Latin-American cultural backgrounds (Abel and Calabrisi 1951, Jaco 1959; Kaplan 1954, 1955, 1956; O. Lewis 1949, 1951, 1959a and b, 1961, 1964; Meadow et al., 1967).

Previous studies have shown wide and consistent differences in the psychopathology of adult Mexican-American and Anglo-American clinical groups (Stoker 1963; Meadow and Stoker 1965; Stoker et al., 1969).

The present study investigated Mexican-American and Anglo-American child guidance clinic files to determine the patterns of psychopathology, cultural and family dynamics which might give further insight into the previously demonstrated differences in adult patients.

Method

Subjects

Case files of Mexican-American and Anglo-American child patients were randomly selected from three child guidance clinics.[1] All cases were current within two years of the investigation. All cases of organic pathology or mental deficiency were discarded and only cases of functional psychopathology were retained.

The Mexican-American and Anglo-American case files were matched in total gross yearly income of patients' families, a rough approximation of socioeconomic class, in order to minimize the effects of socioeconomic discrepancies on possible differences in psychopathology and family interaction patterns.

The final sample consisted of 152 Mexican-American and 152 Anglo-American case files, matched for income. Each cultural group consisted of 76 male and 76 female cases. For comparative purposes, the descriptive characteristics of the samples are presented in table 22.1. And the diagnoses of the samples in table 22.2.

---

1. The authors are indebted to the staffs of the Jane Wayland Child Centre of Phoenix, Arizona, the Community Guidance Center of San Antonio, and the Child Guidance Clinic of Tucson, Arizona for making their files available.

Table 22.1 Characteristic of the Four Samples Expressed in Frequencies and Percentages of the Samples

SECTION A: Age When First Seen at Clinic

	Mexican-American				*Anglo-American*			
Age Groups	*Boys*		*Girls*		*Boys*		*Girls*	
	N	%	N	%	N	%	N	%
4–6	6	8	4	5	8	11	8	11
7–9	11	14	11	14	22	29	12	16
10–12	25	33	13	17	20	26	16	21
13–15	26	34	28	37	21	28	29	38
16–18	8	11	20	27	5	6	11	14
Totals	76	100%	76	100%	76	100%	76	100%
Mean Age when first seen	11.78		12.83		11.36		11.78	

SECTION B: Distribution of Gross Yearly Family Income

Income groupings	*Mexican-American*				*Anglo-American*			
	Boys		*Girls*		*Boys*		*Girls*	
	N	%	N	%	N	%	N	%
0000–0999	5	7	4	6	15	20	5	7
1000–1999	8	11	16	21	9	12	8	11
2000–2999	20	26	13	18	8	11	20	26
3000–3999	18	24	17	22	14	18	8	11
4000–4999	14	18	18	24	17	21	20	26
5000–5999	7	9	3	4	9	12	11	14
6000–6999	3	4	3	4	4	6	0	0
7000–7999	0	0	1	1	0	0	3	4
8000–8999	0	0	0	0	0	0	1	1
9000–9999	1	1	0	0	0	0	0	0
Totals	76	100%	76	100%	76	100%	76	100%
Matching groups								
0000–2999	33	43	33	43	33	43	33	43
3000–5999	39	51	39	51	39	51	39	51
6000–and above	4	6	4	6	4	6	4	6
Totals	76	100%	76	100%	76	100%	76	100%

SECTION C: Religion

	Mexican-American				*Anglo-American*			
	Boys		*Girls*		*Boys*		*Girls*	
	N	%	N	%	N	%	N	%
Catholic	71	97	62	94	16	27	9	16
Protestant	2	3	4	6	41	68	45	77
Jewish	0	0	0	0	1	2	1	2
Other or none	0	0	0	0	2	3	3	5
Totals	73	100%	66	100%	60	100%	58	100%
Unknown or not stated	3		10		16		18	
Grand Totals	76		76		76		76	

Table 22.1 (continued)

SECTION D: Sibling Position

	Mexican-American				*Anglo-American*			
	Boys		*Girls*		*Boys*		*Girls*	
	N	%	N	%	N	%	N	%
1. Position in entire family								
Oldest	24	32	20	28	25	34	27	36
Nonoldest	46	61	47	66	41	55	35	37
Only	5	7	4	6	8	11	12	17
Totals	75	100%	71	100%	74	100%	74	100%
Unknown or not stated	1		5		2		2	
Grand Totals	76		76		76		76	
2. Position among same six sibs								
Oldest	28	37	37	49	17	23	27	37
Nonoldest	32	43	26	34	29	39	25	34
Only	15	20	14	17	28	38	21	29
Totals	75	100%	76	100%	74	100%	73	100%
Unknown or not stated	1		0		2		3	
Grand Totals	76		76		76		76	

SECTION E: Current Marital Status of Parents

Same mother and father	45	63	41	60	42	58	38	53
Same father – stepmother	1	1	2	3	2	3	2	3
Same mother – stepfather	4	5	7	10	6	8	10	14
Parents divorced	7	10	5	7	14	20	10	14
Separated	4	5	2	3	3	4	5	7
Father deserted	5	7	9	13	0	0	0	0
One parent deceased	6	8	2	3	4	6	6	8
Father unknown	1	1	1	1	1	1	1	1
Totals	73	100%	69	100%	72	100%	72	100%
Unknown or not stated	3		7		4		4	
Grand Totals	76		76		76		76	

SECTION F: Birthplace of Mexican-American Parents

Father born in Mexico, mother in the United States	9	21	11	26
Mother born in Mexico, father in the United States	3	7	1	2
Both parents born in Mexico	4	9	4	10
Both parents born in the United States	27	63	26	62
Totals	43	100%	42	100%
Unknown or not stated	33		34	
Grand Totals	76		76	

Table 22.1 (continued)

SECTION G: Referral Source

	Mexican-American				*Anglo-American*			
	Boys		*Girls*		*Boys*		*Girls*	
	N	%	N	%	N	%	N	%
Private M.D. or Psychologist	9	14	15	19	15	20	10	16
Private clinic	0	0	0	0	2	3	0	0
Public clinic	2	3	3	4	2	3	1	2
Residential agency	0	0	0	0	5	7	3	5
Juvenile Court	7	11	2	3	4	6	5	8
School	18	28	27	35	25	34	17	28
School nurse	1	1	3	4	1	1	0	0
Public health	1	1	2	3	1	1	1	2
Welfare	5	8	4	5	2	3	0	0
Self	2	3	1	1	7	9	7	12
County hospital	1	1	4	5	0	0	0	0
Probation department	16	24	13	17	3	4	12	20
Non-clinical public agency	2	3	1	1	2	3	0	0
Neighbor, friend, or relative	0	0	1	1	4	6	3	7
Hospital (other)	0	0	1	1	0	0	1	2
Special education	2	3	1	1	0	0	0	0
Totals	66	100%	76	100%	74	100%	60	100%
Unknown or not stated	10		0		2		16	
Grand totals	76		76		76		76	

SECTION H: Staff Recommendations

Institutionalization	18	29	9	14	12	17	11	14
Foster home placement	0	0	0	0	3	4	1	1
Therapy for patient	10	16	17	26	16	24	14	19
Therapy for mother	0	0	3	4	3	4	6	8
Therapy for patient and mother	4	6	5	7	5	7	10	13
Therapy for patient, mother and father	9	13	4	6	9	13	12	16
Continue probation	0	0	3	4	1	1	1	1
Referral to other agency	8	13	5	7	3	4	7	9
Therapy for patient and father	1	2	0	0	1	1	1	1
Placement with relative	4	6	1	1	0	0	0	0
Interpretation of problem to parent close case	3	5	5	7	3	4	5	7
Special education	1	2	1	1	0	0	0	0
Therapy for mother and father but not patient	0	0	2	3	8	12	0	0

Table 22.1 (continued)

SECTION H: Staff Recommendations (continued)

	Mexican-American				*Anglo-American*			
	Boys		*Girls*		*Boys*		*Girls*	
	N	%	N	%	N	%	N	%
Return to home	1	2	0	0	0	0	0	0
Further evaluation	0	0	1	1	0	0	0	0
None	4	6	13	19	6	9	8	11
Totals	63	100%	69	100%	70	100%	76	100%
Not stated or not readily determinable	13		7		6		0	
Grand Totals	76		76		76		76	
SECTION I: Case Outcome								
Closed due to lack of interest	16	27	22	36	25	36	10	16
No need for treatment – closed	4	7	4	7	4	6	7	10
Probation continued	0	0	3	5	0	0	2	3
Placed in foster home	0	0	0	0	0	0	1	2
Institutionalized	13	23	10	17	7	10	9	14
Closed–improved	6	11	6	11	10	15	11	17
Closed–unimproved	1	2	2	3	6	9	2	3
Referral accepted	4	7	6	10	10	15	10	16
Referral not accepted	4	7	3	5	0	0	1	2
Placed with relatives	2	4	1	2	0	0	0	0
Returned to home	0	0	0	0	1	1	1	2
Interpretation to parent–closed	3	5	2	3	0	0	3	5
Special education	1	2	1	2	1	1	1	2
Family moved—case closed	3	5	0	0	5	7	5	8
Totals	57	100%	60	100%	68	100%	63	100%
Not stated or not readily determinable	19		16		8		13	
Grand Totals	76		76		76		76	
SECTION J: Parents' Drinking Behavior								
Mother has occasional binges	0	0	1	1	0	0	2	3
Mother is chronic alcoholic	1	1	0	0	3	4	6	8
Father has occasional binges	4	5	3	4	5	7	5	7
Father is chronic alcoholic	12	16	15	20	7	9	8	11

Table 22.2 Diagnoses of the Four Child Guidance Samples in Terms of Frequencies and percentages of the Separate Samples

	Mexican-American				*Anglo-American*			
	Boys		*Girls*		*Boys*		*Girls*	
Schizophrenic Reaction	N	%	N	%	N	%	N	%
Childhood	2	3	0	0	2	3		
Chronic Undifferentiated	0	0	3	4	0	0	2	3
Simple	0	0	0	0	0	0	0	0
Schizo-affective	0	0	1	1	0	0	0	0
Total Schizophrenic	2	3	4	5	2	3	3	4
Neurotic Disorders	1	1	8	11	7	8	9	13
Personality Pattern Disturbances								
Sociopathic personality	3	5	2	3	3	4	1	1
Schizoid personality	3	4	3	4	5	6	6	8
Emotionally unstable personality	5	6	5	6	0	0	6	8
Passive-aggressive personality passive-aggressive type	22	27	6	8	11	13	9	12
Passive-aggressive personality passive-dependent type	2	3	8	11	11	13	5	7
Passive-aggressive personality aggressive type	0	0	0	0	2	3	0	0
Passive-aggressive personality dependent type	2	3	0	0	0	0	0	0
Inadequate personality	3	4	2	3	8	11	1	1
Other	6	7	3	4	5	6	4	4
Total Personality Pattern Disturbances	46	58%	29	39%	45	56%	32	41%
Personality Trait Disturbances								
Adjustment reaction of childhood	12	15	5	6	10	13	11	14
Adjustment reaction of adolescence	4	4	8	11	4	5	8	11
Special symptom reaction	2	3	10	13	2	3	1	1
Total Personality Trait Disturbances	18	22%	23	30%	16	21%	20	26%
No Psychiatric Diagnosis	13	16%	12	15%	6	9%	12	16%
Grand Totals	76	100%	76	100%	76	100%	76	100%

Procedure

A list of 73 symptomatic behaviors was constructed through preliminary reading of a number of case histories.[2] In addition, data describing family structure and family interactions were collected and are referred to on following pages.

The investigators read each case record and noted the presence or absence of each variable. Case material consisted of psychiatric evaluations, social history reports and, in numerous cases, therapy progress notes.

In order to assess the inter-rater reliability of the procedure, the two investigators independently read and assessed ten case records. The independent ratings were then compared to ascertain the degree of agreement between the two individual, independent assessments of identical data.

Results

The raw data consisted of the frequency of occurrence of each symptomatic variable within each of the four sex-culture samples. Table 22.3 shows the frequencies for each variable within sex-culture samples and table 22.4 shows the distribution of variables for the total Mexican-American and Anglo-American groups.

The frequency of each variable in a group was compared separately to the frequency of each variable in each of the other three groups and (between the total Mexican-American and Anglo-American samples) by means of the Chi-square test. The symptoms and characteristics which differentiated, at or beyond the five percent level of confidence, each group from every other groups are presented in tables 22.5–8. Those variables which differentiated the total Mexican-American sample from the total Anglo-American sample are presented in table 22.9.

The two investigators agreed over 98 percent of the time in placing symptoms in their appropriate categories. In no case was there more than one disagreement per symptom category across all subjects, indicating no systematic rater bias.

2. The preliminary cases, which also served as practice cases for the investigators, were not included in the sample case studied. Psychological test data were also collected and will be reported in a future paper.

Table 22.3 Frequency of Occurrence of Symptoms Within Each Sex-Culture Group and Within the Total Samples

	Mexican-American		*Anglo-American*		*Total Mexican-American*	*Total Anglo-American*
	Boys	*Girls*	*Boys*	*Girls*		
1 Academic problems	15	10	20	17	25	37
2 Agitation	8	14	0	0	22	0
3 Acting out	4	1	2	0	5	2
4 Attempted suicide	2	13	0	3	15	3
5 Affect hunger	0	1	7	10	1	17
6 Anxiety	10	12	32	41	22	73
7 Aggressive behavior	20	13	16	7	33	23
8 Bites nails	5	5	14	19	10	33
9 Compulsive behavior	0	1	6	9	1	15
10 Cruelty	2	1	2	2	3	4
11 Crying spells	3	21	3	8	24	11
12 Day dreaming	6	2	3	3	8	6
13 Dependency	17	13	10	9	30	19
14 Depressions	12	30	8	10	42	18
15 Disrupts class	3	0	5	4	3	9
16 Demands own way	4	4	1	5	8	6
17 Drinking	5	0	1	3	5	4
18 Dropped out of school	8	5	1	3	13	5
19 Destructiveness	13	6	6	5	19	11
20 Enuretic	6	8	28	21	14	49
21 Erratic school work	8	5	4	7	13	11
22 Failed grade(s)	9	6	6	10	15	16
23 Fights	26	10	11	3	36	14
24 Feels parents don't love him	2	3	4	5	5	9
25 Flat affect	4	4	6	12	8	18
26 Grimaces	0	3	2	1	3	3
27 Guilt	2	5	5	11	7	16
28 Hallucinations	3	4	0	0	7	0
29 Homosexual behavior	6	5	3	0	11	3
30 Hurts self	3	1	0	0	4	0
31 Hyperactivity	18	7	11	3	25	14
32 Hostility	34	23	12	15	57	27
33 Impulsivity	15	6	5	2	21	7
34 Indifference	6	0	2	2	6	4
35 Immaturity	11	16	5	13	28	18
36 Inappropriate affect	0	4	0	3	4	3
37 Infantilization	1	1	5	8	2	12
38 Irritability	7	7	0	2	13	2
39 Lack of motivation	2	0	0	2	2	2

Table 22.3 (continued)

	Mexican-American		*Anglo-American*		*Total Mexican-American*	*Total Anglo-American*
	Boys	*Girls*	*Boys*	*Girls*		
40 Lying	6	9	6	13	15	19
41 Masturbation	1	2	11	4	3	15
42 Malicious mischief	7	2	5	2	9	7
43 Narcissism	5	4	0	0	9	0
44 Nervousness	6	9	23	19	15	42
45 Nightmares	4	3	9	15	8	24
46 No or few friends	5	7	27	22	12	49
47 Negativism	18	6	3	5	24	8
48 Obesity	1	8	4	3	9	7
49 Obstinate and defiant	18	5	4	5	23	9
50 Passivity	16	10	5	5	26	10
51 Poor self-control	4	0	4	2	4	6
52 Preoccupied with sex	3	4	2	8	7	9
53 Poor social relationships	5	3	25	15	8	40
54 Phobias	9	6	12	10	15	22
55 Ran away from home	13	18	8	11	31	18
56 Stealing	27	8	10	12	35	22
57 Sucks thumb	1	2	8	9	3	16
58 Soiling	4	1	3	0	5	3
59 Sexual acting-out	4	13	7	11	17	18
60 Swearing, obscene language	3	2	0	1	5	1
61 Shyness	0	4	3	5	4	8
62 Short attention span	2	1	5	2	3	7
63 Sleep pattern disturbance	3	10	9	9	13	18
64 Somatic complaints	6	27	9	11	33	20
65 Suspicious-distrustful	2	7	1	1	9	2
66 Stuttering	3	1	1	1	4	2
67 Suicide threat	3	6	2	2	9	4
68 Truancy	13	3	5	7	16	12
69 Temper tantrums	17	13	7	16	30	23
70 Tics	1	2	4	0	3	4
71 Violent behaviors	4	22	0	2	6	2
72 Doesn't work to capacity	7	6	7	4	4	11
73 Wants attention	0	4	7	4	4	11
74 Withdrawn	4	7	9	13	11	22

Table 22.4 Frequency of Symptoms Within Each Sex-Culture Group and Total Samples Expressed in Terms of Percentages

	Mexican-American		*Anglo-American*		*Total Mexican-American*	*Total Anglo-American*
	Boys	*Girls*	*Boys*	*Girls*		
1 Academic problems	20	13	26	22	17	24
2 Agitation	11	18	0	0	15	0
3 Acting out	5	1	3	0	6	3
4 Attempted suicide	3	17	0	4	10	2
5 Affect hunger	0	1	9	13	1	11
6 Anxiety	13	16	42	54	15	48
7 Aggressive behavior	26	17	21	9	22	15
8 Bites nails	7	7	18	25	7	22
9 Complusive behavior	0	1	8	12	1	10
10 Cruelty	3	1	3	3	2	3
11 Crying spells	4	28	4	11	16	8
12 Day dreaming	8	3	4	4	6	4
13 Dependency	22	17	13	12	20	13
14 Depressions	16	39	11	14	28	13
15 Disrupts class	4	0	7	5	2	6
16 Demands own way	5	5	1	7	5	4
17 Drinking	7	0	1	4	4	3
18 Dropped out of school	11	7	1	4	9	3
19 Destructiveness	18	8	8	7	13	8
20 Enuretic	8	11	37	28	10	33
21 Erratic school work	11	7	5	9	9	7
22 Failed grade(s)	12	8	8	14	10	11
23 Fights	34	13	14	4	24	9
24 Feels parents don't love him	3	4	5	7	4	6
25 Flat affect	5	5	8	16	5	12
26 Grimaces	0	4	3	1	2	2
27 Guilt	3	7	7	14	5	11
28 Hallucinations	4	5	0	0	5	0
29 Homosexual behavior	8	7	4	0	8	2
30 Hurts self	4	1	0	0	3	0
31 Hyperactivity	24	9	14	4	17	9
32 Hostility	45	30	16	20	38	18
33 Impulsivity	20	8	7	3	14	5
34 Indifference	8	0	3	3	4	3
35 Immaturity	14	21	7	17	18	12
36 Inappropriate affect	0	5	0	4	3	2
37 Infantilization	1	1	7	9	1	8
38 Irritability	9	8	0	3	9	2
39 Lack of Motivation	3	0	0	3	2	2

Table 22.4 (continued)

	Mexican-American		*Anglo-American*		*Total Mexican-American*	*Total Anglo-American*
	Boys	*Girls*	*Boys*	*Girls*		
40 Lying	8	12	8	17	10	13
41 Masturbation	1	3	14	5	2	10
42 Malicious mischief	9	3	7	3	6	5
43 Narcissism	7	5	0	0	6	0
44 Nervousness	8	12	30	25	10	28
45 Nightmares	5	4	12	20	5	16
46 No or few friends	7	9	36	29	8	33
47 Negativism	24	8	4	7	16	6
48 Obesity	1	11	6	4	6	5
49 Obstinate and defiant	24	7	6	7	16	7
50 Passivity	21	13	7	7	17	7
51 Poor self-control	5	0	6	3	3	5
52 Preoccupied with sex	4	5	3	9	5	7
53 Poor social relationships	7	4	33	20	7	28
54 Phobias	12	8	16	13	10	15
55 Ran away from home	17	24	9	14	21	12
56 Stealing	36	11	14	16	24	15
57 Sucks Thumb	1	3	11	11	2	11
58 Soiling	5	1	4	0	3	2
59 Sexual acting-out	5	17	9	14	11	12
60 Swearing, obscene language	4	3	0	1	4	1
61 Shyness	0	5	4	7	3	6
62 Short attention span	3	1	7	3	2	5
63 Sleep pattern disturbance	4	13	12	12	9	12
64 Somatic complaints	8	36	12	14	22	13
65 Suspicious-distrustful	3	9	1	1	6	1
66 Stuttering	4	1	1	1	3	1
67 Suicide threat	4	8	3	3	6	3
68 Truancy	17	4	7	9	11	8
69 Temper tantrums	22	7	0	21	15	15
70 Tics	1	3	5	0	2	3
71 Violent behaviors	5	3	0	3	4	2
72 Doesn't work to capacity	9	8	8	7	9	8
73 Wants attention	0	5	9	5	3	7
74 Withdrawn	5	9	12	17	7	15

Table 22.5 Symptomatic Behavior Found More Frequently in the Mexican-American Girl $P(X^2)>.05$

Spanish-American Girls — Spanish-American Boys
Attempted suicide
Crying spells
Depressions
Obesity
Sexual acting-out
Somatic complaints
Spanish-American Girls — Anglo-American Boys
Agitation
Attempted suicide
Crying spells
Depressions
Hostility
Immaturity
Irritability
Ran away from home
Somatic complaints
Suspicious-distrustful
Spanish-American Girls — Anglo-American Girls
Agitation
Attempted suicide
Crying spells
Depressions

There were a total of 1,009 symptoms in the Mexican-American samples and a total of 1,014 symptoms in the Anglo-American samples, suggesting that differences between the samples can be assumed not to be due to disproportionate frequencies of symptoms in sex-culture groups.

Discussion

Description of Samples (Table 22.1)

Section A: Age When First Seen at Clinic

A Chi-square comparison of the frequency of ages over and under 13 between the two total samples was significant beyond the .01 level. The mean age for the Mexican-American girls was over a year greater than the other three samples. It appears that the Mexican-American

Table 22.6 Symptomatic Behavior Found More Frequently in the Mexican-American Boys $P(X^2)>.05$

Spanish-American Boys — Spanish-American Girls
Fighting
Hyperactivity
Hostility
Impulsivity
Negativism
Obstinate and defiant
Stealing
Truancy
Spanish-American Boys — Anglo-American Boys
Agitation
Dropped out of school
Fighting
Hostility
Impulsivity
Irritability
Negativism
Obstinate and defiant
Passivity
Stealing
Temper tantrums
Spanish-American Boys — Anglo-American Girls
Agitation
Aggressive
Fighting
Homosexual behavior
Hyperactivity
Hostility
Impulsivity
Negativism
Obstinate and defiant
Passivity
Stealing

girl tends not to develop difficulty until she gets close to puberty. At this time relationships with parents become intensified, and in some cases, sexualized. There is also a great deal of pressure on Mexican girls to share household duties at this age. The data indicate a far larger percentage of Mexican-American girls of 16 to 18 years of age (27 % as opposed to 11 % of Anglo girls).

Section B: Distribution of Gross Yearly Family Income

Section B of Table 22.1 shows the distribution of income among the four samples. Within the $1,000 categories there is considerable

Table 22.7 Symptomatic Behavior Found More Frequently in the Anglo-American Girls $P(X^2)>.05$

Anglo-American Girls — Spanish-American Girls
Affect hunger
Anxiety
Bites nails
Compulsivity
Enuretic
Flat affect
Infantilization
Nervousness
Nightmares
No or few friends
Poor social relationships
Anglo-American Girls — Spanish-American Boys
Affect hunger
Anxiety
Bites nails
Compulsivity
Enuretic
Flat affect
Guilt
Infantilization
Nervousness
Nightmares
No or few friends
Poor social relationships
Sucks thumb
Withdrawn
Anglo-American Girls — Anglo-American Boys
Temper tantrums

inequality between groups so that there perhaps is not really adequate matching.

The second part of the Section shows perfect matching by using larger categories. Large income categories were used to increase the size of the samples while sacrificing some accuracy of matching. Nevertheless, the groups are roughly matched on the basis of gross yearly income.

Section C: Religion

The large majority of the Mexican-American cases (97% of the Mexican-American boys and 94% of the Mexican-American girls) were Roman Catholic. The most prevalent religion in both Anglo-American samples was Protestantism. It is thought that the religion figures represent fairly adequate and accurate samples of the incidence of the various religions in the normal population.

Section D: Sibling Position

In a previous study by Stoker (1963), the sibling positions of Mexican-American and Anglo-American hospital patients were compared. When the sibling position of the patient was defined in terms of his position relative to the total number of siblings in his family, no difference between the number of oldest children and the expected frequency of oldest children was found. However, when the sibling position of the patient was defined in terms of his position relative to his same-sex siblings, it was found that, for both male and female Mexican-American schizophrenic patients, there was a significantly greater proportion of schizophrenics occupying the first sibling position in the Mexican-American sample.

Table 22.8 Symptomatic Behavior Found More Frequently in the Anglo-American Boys $P(X^2) > .05$

Anglo-American Boys — Spanish-American Boys
Affect hunger
Anxiety
Bites nails
Compulsivity
Enuretic
Masturbation
Nervousness
No or few friends
Poor social relationships
Sucks thumb
Wants attention
Anglo-American Boys — Spanish-American Girls
Academic problems
Affect hunger
Anxiety
Bites nails
Enuretic
Masturbation
Nervousness
No or few friends
Poor social relationships
Anglo-American Boys — Anglo-American Girls
Aggressive
Fighting
Hyperactivity

Table 22.9 Symptomatic Behavior Found More Frequently in the Total Samples as Compared to Each Other $P(X^2) > .05$

Total Mexican-American Samples	*Total Anglo-American Samples*
Agitation	Affect hunger
Attempted suicide	Anxiety
Crying spells	Bites nails
Depressions	Compulsivity
Dropped out of school	Enuretic
Fights	Flat affect
Hallucinations	Infantilization
Homosexual behavior	Masturbation
Hostility	Nervousness
Impulsivity	Nightmares
Irritability	No or few friends
Narcissism	Poor social relationships
Negativism	Sucks thumb
Obstinate and defiant	Withdrawn
Passivity	
Run away from home	
Somatic complaints	
Suspicious and distrustful	

A similar finding is suggested by the second portion of Section D of table 22.1. Forty-nine percent of the Mexican-American girls were the oldest female children in the families. The same figure for the Mexican-American boys was 37 percent. Both of these figures are considerably higher than those in the corresponding Anglo-American samples. The observed frequency of oldest and nonoldest children in each sex-culture sample was compared with the corresponding frequencies which would occur by chances. This was done on all four groups for both the patient's position in the entire family and his position in same-sex siblings. The results of the Chi-square analysis (table 22.10), show that the only significant difference was found in the same-sex sibling analysis in the Mexican-American girl samples.

Three alternative explanations of the findings suggest themselves. First, Ramirez (1960) has described the sudden weaning of the child in the Mexican culture. He indicates that the child is consistently breast-fed until the arrival of the next child when the close, almost symbiotic relationship is broken. This rupture may, in part, account for the differences in the frequency of psychopathology in the oldest child as compared with children in other sibling positions, but only for families which have only two children. In larger families, each child but the last would undergo the same process. This hypothesis would also fail to explain why only female first children and those which are first of sex seem to show more psychopathology.

A second hypothesis is that since the first-born or oldest child is subjected to more difficulties and stresses during enculturation, it is more probable that he should become ill rather than his younger siblings. The oldest Mexican-American child is the first one that has to attend schools in the new Anglo culture, and his experiences should make it easier for the rest of his siblings to adapt. This hypothesis again would fail to explain why the significant differences are found only in the female child when she is the oldest of her same-sex siblings.

A third hypothesis is that of the excessive responsibility of the oldest female child in the Mexican-American family. Since excessive responsibility is not necessarily a disruptive force during personality formation, the following factors must also be considered. First, the Mexican-American mother is often overburdened with household work and with the care of numerous children. The oldest girl is very often unprepared to take over much of the care and responsibility for household affairs, because of her age and relative immaturity. Secondly, conflict between husband and wife may lead the husband to sexualize his relationship with the oldest girl. Although there is, as yet, no direct evidence of a greater number of incestuous relationships in the Mexican-American culture, it is the authors' general impression from therapeutic experience with the Mexican-American patient and from reading many case histories, that there is a differential amount of covert father-daughter incest-like behavior in the culture. A third factor that must be taken into account is that marital conflict within the Mexican-

Table 22.10 Results of Chi Square Analysis of Sibling Position Data: Comparison of Observed and Expected Frequencies

	N	Chi Square	P
Mexican-American Girls			
a. Position in entire family	71	1.494	N.S.
b. Position in same-sex sibs	55	5.488	.05
Mexican-American Boys			
a. Position in entire family	99	.616	N.S.
b. Position in same-sex sibs	78	.958	N.S.
Anglo-American Girls			
a. Position in entire family	75	1.406	N.S.
b. Position in same-sex sibs	59	.548	N.S.
Anglo-American Boys			
a. Position in entire family	95	.212	N.S.
b. Position in same-sex sibs	65	.538	N.S.

American family may place the oldest daughter in a particularly vulnerable position due to the fact that she, since she has many of the duties and responsibilities of her mother, may represent to the father much that is like her mother. The anger of the father may be easily transferred to his oldest daughter. In general, it appears that there is differential stress on the oldest female child in the Mexican-American family which may play an important etiological role.

Section E: Current Marital Status of Parents

There are no particularly wide differences in current marital status of the parents of the patients. However, the incidence of the desertion of the father in both the Mexican-American samples stands out distinctly ($X^2 > .001$). It is possible that these children were exposed to even more desertions than the data indicate since no data were obtained on the desertion or abandonment of stepparents or foster parents. The physical or psychological desertion of the father in the Mexican-American culture may be an important etiological factor in the psychopathology of children in this group, and may indicate more overt marital conflict between Mexican-American parents.

Section F: Birthplace of Mexican-American Parents

Section F of table 22.1 indicates the birthplace of the parents of the Mexican-American children. In both the Mexican-American samples, there were many more cases in which the father was born in Mexico and the mother in the United States than cases in which the birth places were reversed. This suggests a pattern of a more acculturated woman marrying a less acculturated male. Although the direction of the differences is not clear in all cases, the obtained ratios vary significantly from the normal population according to the 1960 census on persons of Spanish surname.

Section G: Referral Source

Mexican-American patients tend to be referred by welfare and charitable organizations; Anglo-American children, by contrast, tend to be referred by their parents (self) and by private practitioners or private clinics. Thus Mexican-American families are more likely to come into contact with a non-clinical social agency. It is possible that marital conflict and low income bring the Mexican-American family to the attention of agencies which deal with marital counseling and allied problems. From there the child himself may be referred to a child guidance clinic. Anglo parents tend to take the child to a private practitioner who will then refer the child to the clinic; they more often make direct contact with the clinic. Perhaps the Anglo-American family is less likely to tolerate the psychopathology of the child himself and to perhaps disregard the existence of psychopathology within the entire family structure. Twice as many Mexican-American children were referred by the probation department.

Section H: Staff Recommendations

The rate of recommended institutionalization for Mexican-American boys was 29 percent higher than the other three groups. This suggests a particular response of aggression and hostility in the Mexican-American boy, an acknowledgment by staff that strict controls are needed. And reflects their more frequent contact with the law. Summing the number of recommendations for therapy for parents *without* collateral therapy for the child, one finds a rate of 21 percent in the total Mexican-American sample and 38 percent in the total Anglo-American sample. This suggests that staff members may recognize that the role of intrafamilial psychopathology is more important in Anglo children. Staff recommendations which terminate services to the patient without recommendations for further treatment or for referral to another agency amount to 27 percent in the total Mexican-American sample as opposed to 19 percent in the total Anglo-American sample. This finding suggests that the psychopathology of the Mexican-American child is situational in nature and may therefore be dealt with by means other than psychotherapeutic treatment. Correspondingly, there is a higher rate of recommendations for direct discharge from the clinic and for termination of clinic services. Finally, when one sums the staff recommendations which involved the patient in therapy, including those which specify collateral therapy with the parents, the rate is 42 percent in the total Mexican-American sample. This may indicate that psychotherapeutic treatment of the child is deemed more necessary in a higher percentage of Anglo cases.

Section I: Case Outcome

There is a higher rate of dropping out of therapy in the Mexican-American sample although the differences are not statistically significant. More Anglo cases were closed with the statement that the patient had improved. These data suggest that psychotherapy, conceived and practiced by Anglos, may not be suited to the therapeutic needs of Mexican-American patients or that their need is not for traditional psychotherapy.

A comparison of case outcome classified generally as "positive" and as "negative" was significant at the .01 level. Thus it appears that there is a high probability for a Mexican-American child not to profit from the general services of a child guidance clinic.

Section J: Drinking Patterns

The data show less drinking in the mothers of the Mexican-American patients as compared with the mothers of the Anglo-American patients. Drinking, as many authors have suggested, in Mexican males is a particularly disruptive factor in family life. It is possible that the Mexican-American wife consciously avoids drinking because she sees it as an extremely undesirable and even dangerous form of social conduct. The brutality of the drunken Mexican-American husband toward his wife and children has been well-documented in therapeutic practice (18 percent of the Mexican-American fathers were chronic alcoholics as opposed to 10 percent of the Anglo-American fathers).[3]

It is possible that the behavior of the drunken father is etiologically related to psychopathology through the mechanism of fear and anxiety in mother and child.

The Distribution of Diagnoses

Table 22.2 indicates a higher rate of neurotic disorders in the Anglo-American sample, suggesting a basic difference in psychopathology between the two groups although the difference is not statistically significant. In the three remaining groups of diagnoses there are no significant differences between the samples.

Within the subtypes of disorders, the most notable difference is found in the incidence of the passive-aggressive personality disturbance—27 percent in the Mexican-American male sample, and a much higher frequency of this disorder in the total Mexican-American sample. Major differences are more clearly revealed in the discussion of symptomatology to follow.

The Symptomatology of the Mexican-American Girl

Inspection of Table 22.5 shows considerable difference in the psychopathology of the Mexican-American girl as compared to the three other sex-culture groups, a consistent pattern of symptomatology consisting of primary symptoms of *attempted suicide, crying spells, depressions,* and *agitation.* This finding is identical to the results of a study of Mexican-American female adult hospital patients

3. It must be pointed out that there may be more alcoholism in fathers of patients who are not seen at child guidance clinics in the Mexican-American population as compared to the Anglo-American population. Such a difference in the frequency of heavy drinking in the normal population may explain the obtained difference.

(Meadow and Stoker 1965), indicating an agitated depressive condition in which there is considerable disturbance of affect.

Correspondingly there are also significantly frequent symptoms that tend to associate with such a condition; for example, *somatic complaints,* and *obesity.*

Depression in the Mexican-American Girl

Gibson (1964) reported that many Mexican-American children around the ages of six to eight undergo a serious depression. The present data show that depression in the Mexican-American girl sample exceeds depression in the Anglo-American girl sample by a ratio of three to one, and that depressions in the total Mexican-American sample outnumbered depression in the total Anglo-American sample by a ratio of more than two to one. Gibson related the depression in the Mexican-American child to feelings of deprivation and anger in early life. Three alternative explanations for such anger and depression suggest themselves. First, the typical pattern of child rearing in the Mexican-American culture is characterized by abrupt weaning of the child at the birth of the next child. Secondly, there also is a general rejection of most of the children in the family due to various economic, social, and interfamilial patterns of disruption. It is probable that during this period extreme hostility arises toward the parents. Clinical experience with Mexican-American patients and the current research suggests that depression in these cases differs from depression in Anglo-American patients. Adult Mexican-American patients experience a depressive mood, agitation, and feelings of anger, differing quite sharply from the Anglo-American patient who typically feels heavy guilt, self-depreciation, and accompanying depression. A third possible hypothesis is that there is a greater tendency in Mexican society and in the Mexican-American subculture to react to external shame rather than to internal guilt. That is to say, controls are externalized (Lewis 1964), as contrasted with the typical Anglo-American child rearing pattern which places emphasis on personal conscience and on repressive defenses.

Comparative Lack of Hostility Expression

The Mexican-American boy shows more aggressive, acting-out types of behavior than the Mexican-American girl. There is a very discrete role expectation for the female child in the Mexican and Mexican-American family. She is expected to be a "little mother," to serve the needs of the male members of the family, to follow her mother about the house and learn the household duties, and to almost completely repress the expression of many personal needs. Parents voice a feeling that all female children are inherently bad and wicked and the

Mexican-American father often fears that his daughter will embarrass him socially.

Anglos tend to view the Mexican-American mother as an all-giving figure. There is perhaps some truth in this stereotype, since the expected role of the Mexican mother is to be warm, giving, a good housewife, and to be completely subservient to the male members of the family. She is to take charge of the female children and to rear them in her own image. The Mexican-American wife thus finds herself expected to restrict the expression of her dependency needs and to give to her children and husband, increasing the likelihood that she will either consciously or unconsciously reject her children.

This pattern often results in an attempt to impress upon the daughter the same denial of gratification which has been imposed by her own mother. The anger of the child toward the inconsistent and sometimes rejecting behavior of the mother is a predictable reaction.

The Mexican-American father may be a physical threat to the female child. He is sometimes drunken, cruel, and abusive. The hostility which the female child feels cannot be expressed directly because of the fear of direct retaliation by the father and by cultural prohibitions against hostility expression in females.

The Symptomatology of Mexican-American Boys

Table 22.6 shows a symptom pattern distinguished by *fighting, hyperactivity, impulsivity, negativism, obstinate and defiant attitude, stealing, truancy, dropping out of school and temper tantrums.* This pattern indicates a more direct expression of hostility and symptoms indicating severe intrapsychic conflict or serious disturbance of personality functioning rarely in evidence. Hostility and tension tends to be discharged quickly and effectively. This particular point was also validated in the study of hospitalized Mexican-American psychiatric patients (Meadow and Stoker 1965).

Hostility, Acting Out and the Problem of Authority

Clark (1959) and Burma (1954) state that the young boy in Mexico appears to have no expected role to play. He is given little structure by the family and left to the street and to whatever activities please him. However, his hostility is directed outside of the family because of the male-female sex difference between him and his mother and because of his inability to express hostility toward his father.

The relative ease of the relief of tension in this group is consistent with the double standard of behavior that exists more noticeably between male and females in the Mexican-American culture. The externalized super ego allows rebellion, coupled with hostility with little anxiety and guilt. The Mexican-American boy tends not to directly act out his hostility suggested by the frequency of *dropped out of school.* This is consistent with the incidence of a passive-aggressive character structure which is frequently found in clinical experience with Mexican-American male outpatients and in the present data.

Another possible source of Mexican-American difficulty in dealing with authority figures may be that the Mexican peasant has always lived in a position of servitude and subordination to his "betters" in society. The relationship between authority figures and those beneath them in Mexico has been largely of an exploitative type. The well-known *patron* system is another example of this general pattern and certainly this pattern has been continued by elements of Anglo society.

The authoritarian relationship is repeated again in the entire family organisation. Children are expected to obey without question. The reason for one's having authority in the Mexican family is based almost exclusively on the variables of age and sex. In the traditional Mexican family, the father is the supreme ruler, the highest authority. Next in line is the mother and, after her, the oldest male child, resulting in a rather clear-cut division of male power over female.

The School Dropout Pattern

The present data indicate that there are significantly more cases in the Mexican-American group of boys dropping out of school. This particular datum is made somewhat more impressive by the fact that the majority of children in this sample were not old enough to be able to legally drop out of school.

The dropout pattern is an important one not only for the welfare of the child himself but for the entire geographic area in which he lives. In the Mexican-American culture in particular, even more so than in the Anglo-American culture, a constant threat to economic security is posed by the lack of jobs for unskilled workmen. If then such a particular segment of citizens continues to produce an abnormally large percentage of poorly educated children, the economic problems of not only the subcultural group but of the entire area become intensified. Industry will not move to areas where it will be unable to secure a complement of trained or potentially trainable workers, completing the cycle of poverty.

Psychopathology of the Total Mexican-American Sample

Essentially the same patterns of symptoms as were found in the analyses of the symptomatology of the four sex-culture samples are also found in the analysis of the total Mexican-American sample (table 22.9). One finds the agitated, depressive symptomatic component and the aggressive and affect-discharging component.

The total Mexican-American sample showed *aggressiveness, destructiveness, fighting, hostility, impulsivity, obstinate and defiant attitude, stealing, and swearing.* This pattern of symptoms is most clearly indicative of a far-reaching problem in the Mexican-American child with hostility and its expression. The important difference is in the direction of the expression of the hostility. The Mexican-American children tended to handle hostility by "acting out." It has been noted that Mexican-American children are extremely well-behaved toward individuals in authority, that they are usually quiet and unobtrusive, and that they appear well controlled by their parents. Hostility is not directly expressed within the family but through antisocial acts.

A pattern of irresponsibility in the Mexican-American child is suggested by the significantly high frequency of *impulsivity, indifferent attitude, passivity,* and *truancy.* In Mexican-American adult males the pattern of irresponsibility is seen in the more florid form of the "macho" pattern with its drinking, gambling, promiscuous behavior, and nonsupport of family. The pattern may result from the lack of goal direction and role expectation for the younger male child. Controls within the family are exceedingly strict but, because of the lack of direction over the behavior of the child outside family life, he is relatively free to express hostility. The Anglo-American child differs because controls are more internalized and are therefore carried over into behavior outside of the home.

The higher frequency of *running away from home* is perhaps symptomatic of the inflexibility of the Mexican-American family pattern and of the overall tendency of Mexican-American children to withdraw from conflict. Clinical experience has shown this to be a major method of reducing anxiety in Mexican-American patients and may also represent a method of expressing hostility toward parents.

Although *dependency* did not statistically differentiate the Mexican-American samples from the Anglo-American samples, its greater frequency in the Mexican-American samples and its relationship to *passivity* is of central importance. The studies of Mexican and Mexican-American child-rearing patterns have agreed that the culture supports a family structure which does little to meet the dependency needs of children. The one major specific agreement in all of the studies reviewed is that there is a sudden weaning of the child from the mother upon the birth of the next child. Certainly in such a "Culture of Poverty" as Lewis (1961) describes the Mexican culture, and in a population which tends to give birth to many children, the sudden and rather traumatic weaning of the child from the mother is undoubtedly more frequent.

Behaviorally one finds in the present samples an underlying dynamic of passivity and dependency which, especially in the Mexican-American male child, is punctuated by rather severe outbursts of hostility, manifested by *stealing, lying, truancy, drinking, violent behavior, fighting* and so forth.

School teachers in Tucson frequently describe the good manners and compliant disposition of their Mexican-American students and express surprise at their quick outbursts of temper and their rather serious episodes of antisocial, acting-out behavior.

The Symptomatology of the Total Anglo-American Sample

Because it is not the purpose of this paper to discuss in detail psychopathological reactions in the Anglo-American groups but rather to describe the psychopathology of the Mexican-American as compared to the Anglo-American, it will suffice to indicate that the psychopathology of the total Anglo-American sample consists of a neurotic pattern of adjustment, showing the symptomatic correlates of *anxiety, nail biting, enuresis, nervousness* and so forth. (See tables 22.7–.9).

Secondly, the comparison also shows the symptoms of *poor social relationships* and *no or few friends.* These two symptoms are characteristic of a pattern of disturbance in interpersonal relationships, suggesting a more serious disruption in personality functioning in the Anglo-American children as compared to the Mexican-American children. These major and important differences are not artifacts of the sex comparisons, since they are shown in the comparison of the total samples.

There is six times as much *infantilization* in the Anglo-American sample. The most direct explanation of this phenomenon, in a descriptive sense, is that there is a strong regressive component to the psychopathological reaction of the Anglo-American child. This finding is consistent with the hypothesis of the extratensive nature of the Mexican-American personality structure as contrasted with the intratensive and intropunitive nature of the Anglo-American personality structure. Psychological dynamics in the Anglo-American child are, by contrast, organized not around giving overt expression to inner needs and impulses, but directed toward the repression of impulsivity. The psychopathological result may often be regression to earlier forms of satisfying activity and to more active fantasy life.

Summary

The present study concerns itself with a comparison of the psychopathology, psychological and familial processes, and therapeutic treatment of Mexican-American and Anglo-American children seen in three child guidance clinics.

Case files of Mexican-American and Anglo-American children were randomly selected from the files of three child guidance clinics in the Southwestern part of the country. Cases of organic pathology or mental deficiency were discarded, yielding a final sample of 152 Mexican-American and 152 Anglo-American cases, divided evenly between male and female cases. Each case was matched roughly for gross yearly family income.

A list of 74 symptomatic behaviors was constructed through reading a number of case histories. The investigators closely examined each matched case record for the presence or absence of each variable. The two investigators independently assessed the content of 10 case records, showing high agreement between raters.

The frequency of each variable in each group was compared to the frequency in every other group by means of the Chi-square test. A similar comparison was also made between the total Mexican-American and total Anglo-American samples. The results of the analysis thus indicated which symptoms were found significantly more frequently in each group as compared separately with each other group.

In general, the data indicated significant and consistent differences in psychopathology between the four different sex-culture samples. The findings were related to culturally determined aspects of family structure, family interaction, role conflicts, and personality structure.

Acknowledgment

This research was supported in part by NIMH Grant 2 RC-580 (240) to Arnold Meadow at The University of Arizona.

23

On the Epidemicity of Amok Violence

Joseph Westermeyer

The so called "culture-bound" syndromes, including "amok," "koro," "latah," "susto," "piblokto," "wihtigo," and certain possession and trance states, used to be the major concern of transcultural psychiatry. As is evident from the material presented across this book, the scope of cultural psychiatry has expanded considerably to cover the whole field of psychopathology in a compatible and integrated way with interdisciplinary biopsychosocial approaches to the field. Nevertheless, the above listed syndromes are still of high interest as they clearly demonstrate the pathoplastic and pathogenic effects of culture.

Two interesting and relatively recent developments in the study of "culture-bound" syndromes have been the elucidation of certain similarities between these syndromes and standard diagnostic categories such as hysterical dissociation and depersonalization states, and their epidemiological examination from historical and biopsychosocial viewpoints.

The following report is an excellent example of contemporary approaches to "culture-bound" syndromes, in which Westermeyer presents a penetrating analysis of the epidemiology of amok, one of the most fascinating of these conditions.

AMOK, a Malaysian word meaning "to engage furiously in battle," has settled into an established niche among psychiatric syndromes (Adams 1950–1952; Arieti and Meth 1959; Lehmann 1967; Pfeiffer

This study was supported in part by Ford Foundation funds administered through the Office of International Programs at the University of Minnesota. Dr. H. B. M. Murphy contributed to its organization and content.

1970; West 1967). Contemporary literature regarding amok often relegates it to the past; and indeed, most papers on the subject were written some decades ago (Abraham 1912; Amir 1939; Ellis 1893; Galloway 1923; Gimlette 1901; Norris 1849; Oxley 1849; Rasch 1894; Van Loon 1927; Van Wulffton-Palthe 1933). However, reports since World War II from the Philippines (Zaguirre 1957), Papua and New Guinea (Burton-Bradley 1968), Malaysia (Esser 1961), Indonesia (Kline 1963), and Laos (Westermeyer 1971; Westermeyer, in press; Westermeyer 1972) indicate that amok continues to occur in southeast Asia.

Older writers, and even some later ones, categorize amok as a bizarre culture-bound form of psychopathology which remains endemic within certain societies. A few recent studies have turned from an emphasis upon psychopathology to an emphasis on the interaction between several specific psychological and social variables (Burton-Bradley 1968; Westermeyer 1972). Most recently, the changing cultural role of amok over time has been investigated (H. B. M. Murphy 1971). This present paper questions the solely endemic nature of amok and suggests that amok can be viewed as an epidemic phenomenon.

Data

Laos

Elderly informants in Laos reported that amok events occurred decades ago prior to World War II. These earlier episodes involved the use of bladed weapons. In recent decades, amok involving knives, machetes, and swords have been notably infrequent (Westermeyer 1972).

Beginning in 1959, amok involving the use of grenades first appeared near the capital city. This first grenade-amok case occurred at a money-raising temple festival (or *boun*). Based on reports from a family member and family friends, the event occurred as follows:

> A few weeks prior to his amok outburst, this 26-year-old, single Laotian soldier began to express fixed, rigid opinions and to be irritable in his relations with friends and relatives. At a temple festival, he had a public argument. A short time later, he threw a grenade into the crowd at the temple, killing four people and wounding 20. He was readily apprehended and hauled off to prison; there he alternated between

shouting incoherently and mumbling to himself. After several months of further mental deterioration in prison, he was released to his home.

In the several years following this event, the number of grenade-amok cases gradually increased in the entire province (Vientiane). They became so frequent that, late in 1966, the Prime Minister of Laos declared a suspension of all *bouns* for the remainder of the Buddhist calendar year. Around this time also, grenade-amok events were reported from adjacent parts of the country (Luang Prabang and Xieng Khouang provinces). In addition, the events came to be reported in a variety of settings besides the *boun,* including army camps, private homes, a marketplace, a movie theater, a public street, a parking lot, and a national exposition.

A peak in the number of cases was reached in 1966 when the author collected 20 reports of amok episodes from the newspaper, radio, and informant reports. Subsequently, the number fell to half that amount each year. The Vientiane police reported seven mass slayings by grenade during 1970. Except for the first case (described above), none of the subsequent amok persons were known to be psychotic.

I have studied 20 cases of amok in Laos; 18 of these events involved the use of grenades (Westermeyer 1971; Westermeyer, in press; Westermeyer 1972). Only two cases, from the same geographic location and time period as the other 18 cases, did not involve the use of grenades. Interestingly, both of these cases involved bladed weapons, the traditional weapon for amok homicide, rather than guns (the weapon most commonly used for other kinds of homicide) (Westermeyer 1972).

Thailand

During the last few years, cases of grenade-amok have begun to appear in the *Bangkok Post,* a Thailand newspaper. Early in 1971, these cases came mostly from north and central Thailand (areas closest to Laos):

> *Chiang Mai; Feb 14, 1971.* A village chief threw a grenade into a group of students, one of whom he accused of flirting with his wife. Eight students were wounded. The village chief took flight.
>
> *Korat; Feb 8, 1971.* Four youths wanted to ride a bus chartered to take 20 students on a tour. An argument ensued. Suddenly, one of the four threw a grenade into the students. Eight died, and 12 sustained wounds. The four were apprehended soon afterwards.

Later in the year, on Nov 14, a grenade incident was reported further south in Bangkok itself.

Philippines

In 1957 Zaguirre wrote regarding amok, "Incidence in the post-war (World War II) personnel of the AFP (Armed Forces, Philippines) appears to be alarmingly far more frequent than during the pre-war period" (Zaguirre 1957). His first case occurred in 1947. Following this, the incidence of amok increased gradually, and reached a peak of five cases in 1953, after which they leveled off at two or three cases per year. Case reports indicated use of automatic weapons (Thompson submachine gun, carbine), as well as the traditional bladed weapons.

Malaysia

Several papers regarding amok in Malaysia were written by European physicians in the first few decades of this country (Ellis 1893; Galloway 1923; Gimlette 1901; Van Loon 1927; Ellis 1901; Fitzgerald 1923; Fletcher 1908). These authors reported at the time that amok violence was becoming notably less frequent. The amok persons presented in these case reports from Malaysia employed traditional bladed weapons.

Spread to Foreign Nationals

Foreign ethnic groups have fallen prey to amok violence after taking residence in regions where amok prevailed. For example, amok violence among ethnic Chinese has been reported in Singapore (Burton-Bradley 1968; Kline 1963) and in Indonesia (Van Wulffton-Palthe 1933; Kline 1963), though there have been no such reports from mainland China. The Tamil from India were also felt to be liable to amok outbursts in Malaysia, (Burton-Bradley 1968; Fletcher 1908), and one report averred that the Dutch in Indonesia have at times gone amok (Fletcher 1908), however, no actual cases of amok by Tamil or Dutch have been documented in the literature.

Comment

Epidemic Characteristics

Grenade-amok appeared in Laos during 1959, and gradually increased until 1966. After that it decreased and appears now to have reached a steady plateau. A similar picture emerged in the

Philippines after World War II; it, too, involved the use of a nontraditional weapon, the automatic gun. These recent appearances of amok "epidemics" contrast markedly with reports from Malaysia earlier in this century, when such violence gradually decreased until only a rare "sporadic" case was encountered.

In all of these countries the increases and decreases in amok events are more than chance events occurring in a Poisson distribution. Moreover, the shift from traditional bladed weapons to a single type of modern, highly destructive ordnance suggests a fashion or "communicability" in which a specific weapon becomes the culturally prescribed implement. (However, the changeover in weaponry is not a sharp one; the bladed weapons formerly prescribed by cultural dictate continue to be used infrequently.)

In addition to changes of amok incidence within a given ethnic group, there are other evidences of "transmission" from one population to another. For one, the grenade-amok noted for over a decade in Laos has recently made its way into Thailand, progressing from north to south. Also, "exposure" of foreign ethnic groups (such as the Chinese, and perhaps the Tamil and Dutch) to amok behavior in Malaysia-Indonesia has resulted in amok violence among them, though they do not ordinarily demonstrate such behavior in their lands of origin.

Thus, amok violence has certain features which suggest that it may be thought of as being an "epidemic" phenomenon. Its incidence waxes and wanes over time, building gradually over years to a peak, followed by a plateau, and finally ending with a decline in which occasional cases may yet occur. Also, it can be "transmitted" (or "learned," or "communicated") from one location to another, either within the same country or across national boundaries, and from one ethnic group to another. Interethnic "communicability" may be greater when two adjacent ethnic groups share many cultural traits (as with the Thai and Lao) or where they inhabit the same land (as with the Malayo-Indonesians, Chinese, Tamil, and Dutch).

Historical Correlates

If indeed amok violence follows an epidemic pattern, we should then search for variables which appear to contribute to its increase and/or decrease. Since most social behavior follows upon a multitude of complex prior events, one is not likely to discover simple causation for amok violence. Nonetheless, these few cross-cultural case studies do suggest historically correlated patterns.

Increased rates of amok in the Philippines, Laos, and Thailand have been associated with the following: (1) armed internal conflict between parties of divergent ideology; (2) increased exposure to foreign mores and values; (3) influx of manufactured goods; and (4) widespread availability of modern military ordnance. In sum, these have been periods of momentous political, social, and economic upheaval.

In a thorough historical review of amok, H. B. M. Murphy reports an increase of its incidence in the Malay Straits during the early years of the nineteenth century (Murphy 1971). This was a time when European powers were assuming hegemony over the area and were introducing foreign workers (Chinese and Indian) into the area. Cultural traditions were being replaced by economic innovations and a foreign political structure. Later in the nineteenth century and early in the twentieth, amok declined in this area during a period noted for its economic and political stability.

Psychodynamic Hypotheses

Common explanations for amok violence include the following: (1) The amok individual is projecting his rage on his reference group; (2) amok violence is an alter form of suicide in areas where suicide is not approved; and (3) "shame" cultures (as opposed to "guilt" cultures) are prone to amok behavior.

The first argument is a tautology. The second does not take into account the fact that many amok persons escape or are captured alive, nor the fact that suicides do in fact occur in these countries (and considerably more often than does amok).

The third argument grows out of latter-day psychoanalytic writings and has recently been applied to amok violence (Weidman and Sussex 1971). The theory states that cultures with amok violence elicit socially conforming behavior from their members by externalized "shame" rather than by internalized "guilt." Supposedly then, the distraught person in a "shame" culture is more apt to express rage or act destructively against his society rather than against himself. However, this hypothesis does not readily explain the epidemic nature of amok violence, nor the absence of amok females, nor the diversity of social controls in countries with amok episodes. Moreover, the guilt–shame hypothesis, derived by Western thinkers and applied to Western societies, has not been sufficiently operationalized to allow cross-cultural validation or invalidation. (Experience among Asian and American peoples suggests to me that, if the guilt–shame hypothesis could be operationalized, differences would probably occur among various cultures along a spectrum rather than in an all-or-none fashion. I further suspect that wide variation would occur among individuals, with fairly narrow mean or median differences among cultures.)

The Psychosocial Perspective

As noted above, amok outbursts seem to increase during times of political, economic, and sociocultural upheaval. The son questions what the father believes; career choices can be washed away in a moment; security becomes unknown; the future cannot be predicted. It is a time when men are bereft of their traditional ways, as new influences undermine the old. Men are frustrated, but cannot channel hostility into efforts against a common foe or toward a common goal.

As has been noted by other students of amok violence, the amok person himself has not been well equipped to manage social turmoil. He has come from peasant or lower-class origins, and has had little or no formal education. Often he has traveled a distance from his home, away from his extended family and familiar village. Following a "loss...of a person or an object upon which an individual depends for his safety or security" (Weidman and Sussex 1971), he withdraws socially for some minutes, days, or weeks. Suddenly he appears with a lethal weapon, at a time and place where people tend to congregate. He may die by his own hand or at the hands of his captors; often he escapes or is captured and imprisoned.

Thus, the right combination of individual susceptibility and sociocultural flux must co-exist in time and place for the amok outcome to occur. In addition to individual and social variables, a third variable should be present; amok violence as a behavioral alternative must be prevalent in the society. If it does not occur as an alternative to an individual, it is highly unlikely that he will spontaneously invent this kind of behavior (though he may be more apt to innovate new weaponry or new social contexts). However, given an awareness of this kind of behavior, either in his own ethnic group or in an adjacent one, he may act in this way—especially if subject to the psychosocial variables known to precede amok violence.

The Laos case, in which the first amok person to use a grenade later became psychotic, suggests that the amok innovator may be more likely to be psychiatrically disabled than his more reality-oriented successors. Subsequent amok persons during the Laotian epidemic did not have the evidence of major mental illness possessed by the original grenade-amok innovator.

The total absence of amok women from all studies over the last century and a half can perhaps also be understood from the psychosocial perspective. By virtue of their socially subordinate status to men, they have not been so vulnerable to social upheaval; prestige and a reliable social role are available to them in the home. Where stress does mount, their cultures offer behavioral alternatives which channel anger into nondestructive syndromes such as *latah* (Abraham 1912; Van Loon 1927; Murphy 1971; Fletcher 1908). In Laos, where men are expected to keep a "cool heart" in public, women can loudly vent their feelings at home. Thus, women in these cultures appear more able to show hostility in their area (the home); where they cannot do so, the socially prescribed syndromes do not lead to irremediable violence.

Conclusions

1. Amok homicide tends to wax and wane in epidemic proportions over time. In modern times, outbreaks have tended to involve one or another specific type of military ordnance (though traditional bladed weapons continue in use). Under certain circumstances amok homicide may be "transmitted" from one ethnic group to another contiguous ethnic group.
2. Increased rates of amok events may be favored by armed internal conflict, rapid intercultural contact, influx of a foreign technology, and/or availability of military ordnance.
3. Three variables contribute to amok violence: (*a*) the susceptible individual, a young uneducated man away from home who has recently sustained a loss; (*b*) rapid sociocultural change; and (*c*) social awareness of amok violence as a behavioral alternative under appropriate circumstances.
4. In reports from several countries for over a century, no women have been noted among amok slayers. Women are less apt to be "susceptible individuals" in these countries since their geographic and social mobility are limited; and even in times of sociocultural flux, they experience less turmoil in their traditional, home-centered roles as wife and mother.

Annotated Additional Readings

a) **Cooper, J. E., and N. Sartorious. 1977.** Cultural and temporal variations in schizophrenia: A speculation on the importance of industrialization. *British Journal of Psychiatry* 130:50–55.
A theoretical paper in which the authors, two distinguished international psychiatric researchers, pose a thought-provoking hypothesis linking the relatively late development of modern concepts of schizophrenia with social and familial effects of industrialization. They suggest that pre-industrial cultures possessed some social characteristics (still to be found in contemporary developing cultures) which exert comparatively beneficial effects upon the course of schizophrenia, and that these effects are lost during and after industrialization. Furthermore, the authors examine plausible mechanisms by which industrialization could influence the structure of communities and families and the development of individuals to worsen the prognosis of schizophrenia among them.

This paper and the two references annotated next provide useful information complementary to article 19.

b) **Turner, R. J. 1972.** The epidemiological study of schizophrenia: A current appraisal. *Journal of Health and Social Behavior* 13:360–368.
A review of the role of the epidemiological approach in the understanding of different aspects of schizophrenia, including its etiology. Crucial methodological considerations, such as sample representativeness and case identification procedure, are discussed. Some of the most consistent findings produced by epidemiological research, such as the connections between schizophrenia and social class, marital status, geographic mobility, and intergenerational social mobility, are reviewed and the intricate problem of their interpretation is discussed.

c) **Schooler, C., and W. Caudill. 1964.** Symptomatology in Japanese and American schizophrenics. *Ethnology* 3:172–178.
This report used a symptom check-list to compare psychopathological patterns in hospitalized schizophrenics from Tokyo, Japan, and Maryland. The Japanese group had higher scores on assaultiveness, social withdrawal, sleep, and affective symptomatology, while the U.S.A. group was higher on hallucinations, bizarre ideas, and perplexity. The sources of these differences were explored by taking into consideration such differential cultural features as high concern for interpersonal and family decorum in Japan and orientation to pragmatic reality in the U.S.A.

d) **Zung, W. W. K. 1969.** A cross-cultural survey of symptoms in depression. *American Journal of Psychiatry* 126:116–121.
A report on the application of appropriate translations of the Zung Self-Rating Depression Scale, one of the most widely used instruments of its kind, to

samples from six industrially developed countries (Australia, Czechoslovakia, England, Germany, Japan, and Switzerland). The author found that self-ratings of patients independently diagnosed as having a depressive disorder were comparable between countries and differed significantly from scores of normal controls and nondepressive psychiatric patients. Similar findings had been obtained earlier in U.S. samples. The author also found substantial positive correlation coefficients between scale scores and Physicians' global ratings of depression in each of the patient samples, the highest being in England (0.65) and the lowest in Japan (0.43).

This paper and the two others annotated next complement article 20.

e) **Marsella, A. J., D. Kinzie, and P. Gordon. 1973.** Ethnic variations in the expression of depression. *Journal of Cross-Cultural Psychology* 4:435–458.
A systematic study evaluating depressive patterns in three ethnically different groups of college students from the University of Hawaii. Factor analysis of responses to depression inventories was used to elucidate major depressive constructs or dimensions in each of the three ethnic groups. Both similarities and differences in depressive patterns among the groups could be noted. In discussing their findings, the authors proposed a theory suggesting that symptoms are related to extensions of the self, conditioned through socialization experiences.

f) **Mezzich, J. E. and Raab, E. S. 1980.** Depressive symptomatology across the Americas. *Archives of General Psychiatry* 37:818–823.
A comparison of depressive symptomatology and its sociocultural context across Peruvian and U.S. samples of depressive patients. Noteworthy in the design was that both samples were interviewed and evaluated by a bilingual investigator using Spanish- and English-language versions of the same assessment instruments. A basic commonality of core depressive symptoms and signs was found across samples, which also had similar levels of overall depressive severity. However, more complaints and higher scores on somatic symptoms and daily fluctuation of depression were seen in the Peruvian group, while the U.S. group had higher scores on suicidal manifestations. The individual and interactional roles of demographic, sociocultural, and diagnostic variables in explaining these cross-national findings were also examined.

g) **Parkin, M. 1974.** Suicide and culture in Fairbanks: A comparison of three cultural groups in a small city of interior Alaska. *Psychiatry* 37:60–67.
An examination of the rates of suicidal behavior among three ethnic groups in an Alaskan city: Eskimos, Indian Athabascans, and Westernized Caucasians. Natives (Eskimos and Indian Athabascans) were overrepresented among those showing suicidal behavior. Developmental and sociocultural factors contributing to these interethnic differences are discussed.

h) **Derogatis, L. R., L. Covi, R. S. Lipman, D. M. Davis and K. Rickels. 1971.** Social class and race as mediator variables in neurotic symptomatology. *Archives of General Psychiatry* 25:31–40.
The authors of this systematic report contribute to the understanding of the relationship between sociocultural variables and neurotic symptomatology.

The sociocultural variables considered, social class and race, are investigated in terms of both their separate and interactive effects on the levels of five neurotic symptom dimensions as measured with a self-report Symptom Distress Checklist on various samples of anxious neurotic patients obtained in Pennsylvania and Maryland.

i) **Kelleher, M. J. 1972.** Cross-national (Anglo-Irish) differences in obsessional symptoms and traits of personality. *Psychological Medicine* 2:33–41.
Using standardized psychometric instruments (The Leyton Obsessional Inventory, questions taken from the Cornell Medical Index, and the short version of the Maudsley Personality Inventory), the author explores the influence of cultural factors upon obsessional manifestations, based on an examination of Irish and English orthopedic patients of both sexes. The roles of religion and place of origin are discussed. Also commented upon are ways in which the obsessional traits may affect the course of psychiatric disorders.

j) **Wittkower, E. D., and H. Warnes. 1975.** Transcultural psychosomatics. *Canadian Psychiatric Association Journal* 20:143–150.
The authors survey the literature on the "cultural etiological parameter" of "psychosomatic" pathology. Following a detailed analysis of the methodological flaws of many reports in the field, they use certain cardiovascular and gastrointestinal disorders for illustrating cross-cultural differences in rates and discussing some of the potential explanatory factors.

k) **Tseng, W. S. 1975.** The nature of somatic complaints among psychiatric patients: The Chinese case. *Comprehensive Psychiatry* 16:237–245.
A penetrating analysis of the cultural meaning of somatic symptoms experienced by psychiatric patients. The author starts by noting that a distinctive feature of Chinese neurotic patients is that their complaints are predominantly characterized by somatic symptoms rather than psychological ones, and that although such somatic emphasis is very strong among patients from a lower social class, it is also present among patients belonging to the upper social class. Among the sociocultural aspects he considers for explaining such somatic complaints are the following: (1) the influence of patients' knowledge about "problems": Chinese Patients' conception and presentation of problems in somatic terms is probably based on the organ-oriented theory of pathology, which characterizes traditional Chinese medicine; (2) the socially recognized and accepted signal of illness—e.g., in Chinese society somatic illness is a legitimate excuse to request rest and care from others while psychological strain is not; (3) reluctance and resistance to explore emotional problems (in general, the Chinese are not used to discussing their emotions directly with others, particularly if this involves sexual or negative feelings); (4) reflection of an hypochondriacal culture trait. The author illustrates these points with interesting clinical vignettes. This paper is a helpful reading on cross-cultural aspects of neurotic and psychophysiological disorders.

l) **Ikemi, Y., Y. Ago, S. Nakagawa, S. Mori, N. Takahashi, H. Suematsu, and M. Sugita. 1974.** Psychosomatic mechanism under social change in Japan. *Psychotherapy and Psychosomatics* 23:240–250.

A review of major sociocultural changes in Japan since the end of World War II, including the devaluation of traditional family ties, an emphasis on academic achievement and very rapid industrialization, and its accompanying environmental deterioration and pollution. The authors relate these changes to increases in the rates of "psychosomatic" disorders, using bronchial asthma as an example for their analysis.

m) **Brod, T. M. 1975.** Alcoholism as a mental health problem of Native Americans. A review of the literature. *Archives of General Psychiatry* 32:1385–1391. Heavy drinking among American Indians and Eskimos is widely considered a serious public health and community mental health problem. The author critically evaluates the extent to which this heavy drinking among Indian men corresponds to the concept of alcoholism in the dominant culture.

Toward a comprehensive formulation of Native Americans' problem drinking, the author first considers the role of cultural stresses, both deculturation stress involving the loss or devaluation of historical tradition as well as acculturation stress—that is, the demand to identify with the dominant culture. He then reviews the evidence suggesting the presence of cultural factors facilitating alcohol intoxication. He finally proposes, as a key individual motive, that drunkenness can provide short-cut gratification by promoting fantasy solutions to culture-bound problems.

The keen anthropological analysis incorporated in this paper complements well the article on cross-cultural drug use and abuse in article 21 and extends it in regard to alcohol drinking.

n) **Wanberg, K., R. Lewis, and F. M. Foster. 1978.** Alcoholism and ethnicity: A comparative study of alcohol use patterns across ethnic groups. *International Journal of the Addictions* 13:1245–1262.
A well-organized study using reliable assessment instruments to compare alcohol use patterns and related demographic, psychopathological, and social functioning variables among American Indian, Black, Hispanic, and White Anglo patients admitted for alcoholism inpatient care at a mental health center in Denver. The four groups did not differ as to use of alcohol to enhance self, manage anxiety and depression, or as to sustained or periodic use. American Indians and Hispanics had a greater tendency than the other two ethnic groups to drink convivially and gregariously and to show more disruption in social functioning. This appeared to suggest the need for differential strategies in alcoholism treatment for various ethnic groups.

o) **Westermeyer, J. 1974.** Alcoholism from the cross-cultural perspective. A review and critique of clinical studies. *American Journal of Drug and Alcohol Abuse* 1:89–105.
A well-documented analysis of the past and prospective role of clinical studies for the cross-cultural understanding of alcoholism. The author reviews, first, types of clinical studies including those on inpatient alcoholics, inpatients not admitted for alcoholism, outpatient alcoholics, and outpatients not seen for alcoholism. He then assesses the clinical method, covering definition issues, sampling procedures, and research strategies. He finally points out that the

clinical setting lends itself to certain investigations which cannot be done elsewhere, such as the testing of linkage theories between biological, behavioral, and social variables, but cautions against inappropriate generalizations.

p) **Ramanujam, B. K. 1975.** Psychiatric problems of children seen in an urban center of Western India. *American Journal of Orthopsychiatry* 45:490–496.
An outline of the most frequent problems seen in a child guidance clinic in Western India. Close to half of the sample had organic brain syndromes involving mainly perinatal causative factors. Next in frequency was mental retardation, apparently due predominantly to malnutrition and "cultural deprivation." Also conspicuous were learning disabilities and neurotic disorders. The author discusses these disorders in relation to sociopsychological changes taking place in India as it moves from a traditional agrarian structure toward industrialization. An interesting complementary reading to article 22.

q) **Yap, P. M. 1967.** Classification of the culture-bound reactive syndromes. *Australian and New Zealand Journal of Psychiatry* 1:172–179.
A general review of the "culture-bound" syndromes and attempts to organize them within the framework of Western psychopathological concepts. The author describes the "culture-bound" reactive syndromes as forms of psychogenic psychoses and specifically considers koro as a depersonalization state; susto as a fear-induced depressive state; latah as a syndrome of impaired consciousness; malignant anxiety and amok as turbid states; and certain types of possession syndrome and windigo psychosis as syndromes of dissociated consciousness. Although the author's nosological scheme could be modified at the light of recent international nomenclatures, his pioneering work tracing cross-cultural syndromic connections remains useful and illuminating. This reading and the next are excellent complements to article 23.

r) **Carr, J. E. and E. K. Tan. 1976.** In search of true amok: Amok as viewed within the Malay culture. *American Journal of Psychiatry* 133:1295–1299.
The authors' interviewed and evaluated 21 individuals in West Malaysia who were labeled as amok. They found that the subjects' behavior was consistent with both the popular and their own concepts of amok and that they "emphatically insisted" that amok is an illness, which is also in concordance with popular notions. They also found that amok cases were disposed in line with this—i.e., individuals committing murder and assault as part of an amok episode were typically sent by the magistrate not to prison but to a psychiatric hospital for "observation, diagnosis and treatment." The authors also discuss the degree of purposiveness of amok behavior and its ambivalent cultural proscription and sanction.

s) **Edwards, J. G. 1970.** The koro pattern of depersonalization in an American schizophrenic patient. *American Journal of Psychiatry* 126:1171–1173.
A case report of a Westerner who develops what the author calls "a koro pattern of depersonalization" during an episode diagnosed as schizophrenic in a U.S. hospital. Here the author shows how the phenomenology and descriptive psychopathology of koro—i.e., a specific distortion of body image, is quite ubiquitous both across geographical areas and across accompanying or

underlying psychiatric disorders, while its fatalistic interpretation appears to be culturally mediated.

t) **Wijesinghe, C. P., S. A. W. Dissanayake, and N. Mendis. 1976.** Possession trance in a semi-urban community in Sri-Lanka. *Australian and New Zealand Journal of Psychiatry* 10:135–139.
This is an enlightening description of the clinical and epidemiological features of possession trance states. Particularly outstanding is this study's having been carried out as part of a psychiatric morbidity survey of all households in a community. This allowed the opportunity for systematic comparison of the demographic and psychopathological features of the individual experiencing possession trance states to those of the general population.

u) **Uzzell, D. 1974.** Susto revisited: Illness as strategic role. *American Ethnologist* 1:369-378.
Susto, a "culture-bound" syndrome particularly reported in Latin America, is usually described as frightened depression—i.e., it typically follows a severe fright and is behaviorally characterized by listlessness, loss of appetite, and social withdrawal. Effects imputed to this syndrome include death. It has been reported in men and children, but most frequently in women. The author reviews first various levels of analysis of this phenomenon. Then, using data from a field trip to a village in Oaxaca, Mexico, he discusses susto as a strategic role played by the "asustado" to control her or his interactions with the social environment. He proposes that the assumption of this role is not a fully conscious process and that it involves a complex series of transactions between the subject and the surrounding people.

VIII

Psychiatric Care

After having examined the general sociocultural correlates of symptomatology, nosology, and specific psychiatric disorders in the previous two chapters, we turn now to the process through which the subject and society deals with them—i.e., psychiatric care.

Two issues in this area are worth noting at this point. One is the growing plurality of the standard psychiatric armamentarium, which currently includes many forms of psychosocial and somatic therapies. This contrasts clearly with the almost exclusive focus on psychoanalysis during the forties and fifties. The second issue is that the psychiatric care process does not involve just the selection and implementation of a given treatment approach, but actually starts with the individual's perception of his own condition and help-seeking behavior vis-à-vis society's arrangements for dealing with psychopathology.

The first article in this part reviews personal responses to psychopathology, including the subject's conceptualization of his disorder and his care-seeking behavior as these are affected by sociocultural factors. The second article compares various psychotherapies practiced in contrasting cultures and relates them to differential etiological perspectives, lifestyles, and political-economic systems. The coexistence of standard and folk healing systems in large U.S. cities is the subject of the third article, which also reports on an actual experiment attempting their integration. The last full article examines ethnic variations in responses to the currently most important somatotherapeutic approach—i.e., psychotropic medication.

24

Sociocultural and Social-Psychological Factors Affecting Personal Responses to Psychological Disorder

David Mechanic

It seems very appropriate to start the examination of the relationship between psychiatric care and sociocultural factors by looking at the role of these factors at the beginning of the care process—i.e., the individual's help-seeking attitudes and behavior. These attitudes and behavior are to a large extent based on both the individual's conceptualization of his own disorder and the society's arrangements for dealing with this, all of which are heavily influenced by culture.

Until a few years ago, most of the efforts and knowledge in this area were circumscribed to the identification of relationships between specific sociocultural factors and care process variables. More recently, along with the development of medical sociology, attempts have been made to organize the information available into more encompassing theoretical statements, which could facilitate advancement in understanding and planning for action. David Mechanic, a pioneer in these efforts, presents in the following article a cogent statement on the current status and promising perspectives of the study of sociocultural factors and help-seeking behavior.

Supported in part by Public Health Service Grant MH 20708, and a grant from the Robert Wood Johnson Foundation.

SOCIOLOGISTS AND social psychologists have given considerable attention in recent decades to the process leading to the identification of mental disorders in the community and to factors affecting help-seeking. Such work was given impetus almost twenty years ago with the publication of *Social Class and Mental Illness* (Hollingshead and Redlich 1958) and its analysis of social class differences in thresholds for identifying mental disorder and pathways into care. At approximately the same time Clausen and Yarrow (1955), then at the National Institute of Mental Health, in a study of the families of schizophrenic patients, detailed the processes of denial and normalization that resulted in delays in seeking care until the patient's behavior became so bizarre and difficult to cope with that treatment was initiated. A variety of other studies examined the instrumental functioning of mental patients in the community and factors related to rehospitalization (Freeman and Simmons 1963; Dinitz et al. 1962; Brown et al. 1966). These studies were consistent in finding that rehospitalization was related less to instrumental functioning than to the manifestation of bizarre and difficult behavior that significant others found hard to manage.

Medical sociology was then at an infant stage, and these early studies stimulated enthusiasm and interest. They illustrated that sociological methods could be applied to problems of mental illness, its identification and care, and that insights resulted through such investigation that were not apparent from clinical research. It is difficult to believe, but nevertheless true, that until the publication of Hollingshead and Redlich, psychiatrists and other mental health personnel largely ignored social class and the subcultural styles it embodies as important variables in understanding and dealing with mental illness. Although trite today, the demonstration twenty years ago that recognition of symptoms, pathways into care, and response to treatment were related to social class and subcultural patterns was of very great interest.

I have begun this article with a brief historical overview because it illustrates some of the difficulties inherent in understanding the process of personal response today. While in the 1950s and 1960s it was useful to demonstrate the importance of social variables in explaining various processes related to mental illness and its treatment, the task is much more demanding today. It is no longer a revelation that social class, ethnicity, or household structure are correlated with dependent variables of interest. The field is presently grasping for a theoretical framework that ties together disparate studies into a more coherent whole. While the literature abounds in reports of studies illustrating that one or another social variable is associated with recognition of having a problem, with help-seeking, with retention in treatment, or whatever, these reports have a tedious similarity, giving the impression that although the effort is considerable the yield is relatively small. What clearly seems necessary is not more studies in the same vein, but clarification of the theoretical problems, formulation of the issues that remain problematic, and review of the most adequate methodologies that facilitate their clarification. This review, thus, is not a summary of the many studies done but, in contrast, an attempt to specify where we are and where we must go if we are to advance study of personal responses and help-seeking.

Some Theoretical Issues

The areas of concern here fall most properly into an aspect of sociological theory that might be referred to as the study of social selection. Social selection is one of the most pervasive processes characteristic of human communities, and its study concerns the identification of underlying principles of sorting and resorting that continuously go on among social groups. Subareas of the study of social selection include assortative mating, geographic migration, selection related to education, life careers and achievement, and numerous other topics. Social selection ideas have become increasingly important in theoretical conceptions of deviance where attention is directed to the social processes through which particular persons are identified, processed, isolated, and are confronted with restricted opportunity structures (Lemert 1951; Scheff 1966b; Matza 1969).

In making sense of processes of social selection, whatever the subarea of concern, attention is given to the particular characteristics of the individuals and groups involved that make them different in one way or another from others in the community. Attention is also given to the processes by which they interact with others exchanging information about their social characteristics skills and disabilities, and personal inclinations. Efforts must also be made to understand the underlying opportunity structure that makes differential choice possible and that either facilitates or retards certain possibilities. In short, selection problems have personal, interactional, and structural dimensions.

Although social selection is one of the most central processes of social activity, much of sociological investigation views it more as an irritation than as an object of inquiry. Because social selection is such a powerful process, sociologists cannot ignore it, but in order to maintain credibility they must successfully discount it. Thus, students of complex organization, comparing varying types of social structures or management styles, must make a credible case that it is the structural arrangements that are really important in contrast to the types of persons drawn to varying organizations. Investigators of education or other social programs must, in order to be taken seriously, convince us that the effects they observe are related to a specific intervention in contrast to the types of clients drawn to varying kinds of programs. Indeed, some social scientists, recognizing the power of selection, take the position that serious study without the randomization of selection effects is futile. Most curious about all of this is that, despite such widespread recognition of social selection as a powerful and pervasive social process, so few sociologists take selection itself as the object of their theory and inquiry.

It is quite possible to formulate varying hypotheses about selection that have important implications for how we construe social processes more generally and what policy implications we derive from such understanding. Take, for example, the simple instance of a patient seeking the assistance of a physician. One hypothesis about selection is that it basically reflects the magnitude, quality, and seriousness of symptoms. This "rational" concept of medical utilization would lead one to anticipate that characteristics of illness are the main determinant of use of physician services, and that exceptions flow from ignorance, misperception, or poor communication; and, of course, this is the way many physicians view the utilization process. A contrasting hypothesis would maintain that many of the problems brought to a physician resemble similar problems of considerable prevalence that only occasionally lead to care; thus, knowledge of symptoms is not sufficient to make sense of the use of physicians. What may differentiate those who seek care from those who do not is a desire for social support, secondary gain as reflected in release from work or from other obligations, or some other social process quite unrelated to the illness or symptoms.

The perspective taken on a problem as seemingly simple as medical utilization may have important implications for the types of questions asked, as well as a variety of practical concerns. To the extent that the discrepancy between the character and magnitude of illness and utilization is seen as little more than the result of distortions that require correction, then there are few issues of intellectual concern. But the inquiry may also attempt to probe somewhat deeper to examine why people with similar symptoms behave differently, why assistance is sought during some stages in illness rather than others, and why the patient at a particular point in time comes to emphasize a given set of symptoms. The most frequent reason given for seeing a doctor is the common cold. But most people with colds do not consult doctors, and people who consult doctors because of colds on one occasion may not do so on another. An adequate theory must do more than explain a certain proportion of the variance in the dependent variable; it must provide some way of accounting for the diversity of response not only among individuals and groups but within the life history of individuals. It is conceivable, for example, that the common cold is an excuse for visiting a physician in contrast to the primary motivation, and the desire to relieve the stress of a hated job or an unhappy family situation often constitutes the primary motivation. The implication of such a hypothesis, in contrast to the rational theory referred to above, is that eliminating the prevalence of colds in the population is likely to have a less dramatic impact on utilization than might be expected. If the common cold as a justification became less viable, people would find other excuses to seek release from obligations or support.

Methodological Considerations

It is often difficult to pose interesting questions so that they are answerable. Although there are extensive reports and discussions on the "hidden agenda" in medical consultations and numerous attempts to analyze people's deeper motivations for seeking care when they do so for psychological problems (see Balint 1957), it is difficult to investigate these issues in a rigorous and replicable manner. Generally speaking, there are four methodological approaches to understanding how people respond to symptoms and choose pathways for care.

1. Study of Care-Seeking as a Dispositional Variable: One way of attempting to understand why people seek care from psychiatrists or some other type of helper is to attempt to isolate a dispositional trait and examine its correlates and social development. Such dispositional attributes may be measured directly through verbal reports as with a measure of the propensity to seek medical or psychiatric care, or indirectly through the fact that some individuals have sought care from a particular help source and others have not. The fact of having sought help from, for example, psychiatrists defines the disposition, and the investigator then attempts to reconstruct through depth interviews or statistical manipulation of survey or other data both the antecedents and concomitants of such dispositions. Most of the literature has gone beyond simple sociodemographic correlates of particular help-seeking patterns, and almost no direct study has been undertaken of the social development of different dispositions.

There are a variety of interesting issues concerning the social development of help-seeking dispositions that remain highly problematic. For example, there are abundant studies indicating that women report various symptoms more frequently than men and use medical and psychiatric facilities more commonly (Gurin et al. 1960; Srole et al. 1962; Dohrenwend and Dohrenwend 1974; Gove and Tudor 1973; Anderson and Andersen 1972). Many reasons are given by investigators to explain such differences: real differences in the prevalence of psychological disorder; characteristics of the measures used and judgments made of disorders that contain sex biases; women's lower threshold to perceive symptoms; differences between men and women in the willingness to acknowledge the presence of symptoms; and psychobiological differences between men and women. Although each of these various explanations surfaces from time to time, few investigators attempt to devise studies that allow competing hypotheses to be tested. Mechanic (1964) found in a study of the socialization of attitudes toward illness that sex differences in reporting reactions to illness and pain were already apparent in children by the fourth grade, and these increased as children became older. Aggregate data on sex and utilization of medical care suggest that women have higher levels of utilization at all ages except during childhood when it is usually the mother who makes decisions for both boys and girls. However, C. Lewis (1975) has shown that sex differences in using a school health service exist even among young children in an experimental child-initiated help-seeking system. A better understanding of how differences by sex, as well as other important personal characteristics, emerge requires developmental inquiry. It will become clearer, however, that defining help-seeking predispositions is no easy matter and involves the same types of difficulties inherent in other predispositional investigation in developmental psychology, such as in the study of honesty, independence, etc.

2. *Study of the Interaction of Independent Variables Explaining Utilization:* One of the most common approaches to studying help-seeking is to carry out an epidemiological survey and to identify in the survey population those who have sought a particular type of care. Other data from the survey are then used to examine how the characteristics of those who seek care differ from those who do not. Such analysis allows the exploration of interactive effects and more complex models of help-seeking. Mechanic and Volkart (1961), for example, in a study of freshmen students, found that both tendency to adopt the sick role and stress were related to the use of student health services. Stress was more influential, however, among those students with a higher propensity to use medical services in affecting the actual rate of medical utilization. Thus, it appeared that students had differential predispositions to cope by using health services; stress appeared to be the trigger that activated the disposition among those who were high on this variable. Stress probably led to other types of coping behavior among those who had lower dispositions to use medical services. Gurin and his associates (1960), in a national survey of definitions and reactions to personal problems, suggested that different types of factors influence varying aspects of the help-seeking process such as the identification of the problem, the decision to seek care, and the particular type of practitioner consulted.

3. *Study of the Effects of the Structure of the Health Delivery System on Utilization:* Still a third approach to studying utilization is to examine the help-giving organizations and the extent to which they either encourage care among certain groups or impose barriers to such care (McKinlay and Dutton 1974:275-284). Barriers may result from the location of sites of care, economic or other impediments to access, bureaucratic harassment, social distance between client and professional, stigma associated with seeking care, or whatever. Such barriers may further result because of the way in which agencies and professionals define their work and organize their efforts. Beginning with the early study of Myers and Schaffer (1954), showing the varying accessibility of a psychiatric clinic to clients of different social statuses, many studies have illustrated the extent to which agencies express preferences for certain types of clients and how social dissimilarity between clients and professionals results in difficulties in communication and disruption of service.

4. *Studies of Processes of Illness Attribution:* An illuminating approach to the study of the identification and response to symptoms is the investigation of the attribution process itself, and how people come

to make sense and give significance to the experiences they have. One of the most consistent findings in the illness behavior literature is that persons are more likely to take action for symptoms that in some fashion disrupt usual functioning than in other circumstances, and that concepts of health are affected as much by total functioning as by the nature of the symptoms exerienced (Mechanic 1968; Hennes 1972). Persons experiencing changes in usual physical functioning and feeling-states engage in various attempts to make sense of their experience and test various hypotheses about the seriousness of the symptoms they are experiencing and possible causes (Mechanic, 1972). The manner in which attributions are made affects the significance given to symptoms and the types of action pursued.

One of the most interesting dimensions of such attribution processes relevant to the mental disorders is how people come to attribute causality to their experiences, and more specifically the locus of causality. Under what conditions, for example, do people come to view their feelings or behavior as a consequence of a moral failure or as a consequence of an illness for which they are not responsible? Particularly in cases where definitions of mental disorder are imposed on individuals by other members of their social group, decisions must be made as to the extent to which the behavior or attitude of the patient reflects "badness" in contrast to "sickness," and these attributions are very much affected by the sociocultural context (Mechanic 1968).

Attributions of causality have considerable implications for the care provided, for the course of disorder, and may even dramatically affect programs of rehabilitation. For example, during the Second World War soldiers who experienced "breakdown" in combat were evacuated to the back lines, and their disorganized behavior was viewed as rooted in their early childhood socialization. The soldier, wishing to avoid further combat, readily accepted the attribution that the problem was rooted in his personality, and it was difficult to return these soldiers to active duty (Glass 1958). The military later developed a psychiatric policy that defined stress reactions in combat as transient reactions. Although soldiers were given opportunities to rest, the definition of the situation was that this was a reaction in the normal range, and that soldiers were expected to return to active duty. With this policy, many soldiers returned to effective functioning within their units. These policies have now been translated into community care of the mentally ill, and it is apparent that many patients suffering from psychological distress do extremely well with minimal intervention. At times, however, such policies are carried too far and it is assumed that community tenure by itself, without adequate supporting care, can allow disabled persons to function adequately. The basic point, however, should be clear: the manner in which the behavior is conceptualized has an important impact not only on how the person affected sees himself and his efforts at continuing coping, but also on how he is perceived by the community in which he resides.

The study of how people come to understand and conceptualize experiential change is perhaps the area most neglected in studies of reactions and help-seeking. Although a variety of interview studies have been carried out that attempt to reconstruct the attribution process, such retrospective reports may be closer to reconstructions of what took place in light of later experience than accurate descriptions of the attribution process itself. Although such studies as those of Clausen and Yarrow (1955) provide a good intuitive sense of the processes of attribution and normalization, by focusing on patients we lose an understanding of those instances where behavior was normalized and the person concerned did not become a patient. Moreover, retrospective reports may come to emphasize the more dramatic and unusual aspects of the process, neglecting those more mundane aspects. Furthermore, to the extent that the individuals involved are coping with the problem effectively through attributions that normalize unusual feeling-states, they may not experience consciously the extent to which their frames of reference are changing. Davis (1963), in a study of adaptations to having a child with polio, followed families for several years and observed that although they changed significantly in confronting the crisis, they often failed to recognize the extent to which they had changed. Such lack of recognition may be part of the coping process. To the extent that adaptation is smooth and effective, one would anticipate that the actors themselves would not fully recognize the extent to which the situation required them to change.

A Note on Level of Analysis

It is frequently implied that reactions to mental disorder and help-seeking are in some way a unique topic deserving special attention. Although there are some unique aspects to the mental disorders area, at least from a descriptive vantage point, I do not believe that it is particularly useful to dwell on such descriptive variations. If our concern is to develop a better theoretical approach to illuminating how reactions come about and relate to help-seeking, we must not neglect the fact that reactions to physical and psychological changes are part of the same general attribution process, and that many of the same factors are operative whether it is the person himself who is interpreting his feeling-states or behavior or whether such attributions are being made by others in the group (Mechanic 1968). From a help-seeking perspective, mental disorder is different from physical disorder in that the nature of the problem, as it becomes evident, may lead to somewhat different scores on varying dimensions of importance. Thus, any set of symptoms may be evaluated by the extent to which they disrupt normal functioning, their visibility to others, their perceived seriousness, the extent to which they elicit embarrassment, the extent to which treatment is perceived as effective, or whatever. The value on any of these criteria may be very different from one condition to another. Analytically, consideration of how a particular condition falls on relevant dimensions is more helpful than the gross distinction between psychiatric and nonpsychiatric conditions. Similarly, the underlying dimensions of the attribution process are not likely to be very different in situations where the person is defining his own problem in contrast to one where interpretations of the problem are imposed by others.

The problem of identifying mental disorder is further compounded by the fact that much of mental disorder is treated by primary care physicians in contrast to mental health professionals, and that such problems are often presented to helping personnel in physical and psychophysical terms (Gardner 1970; Shepherd et al. 1966). Thus the line between physical and psychiatric illness is not easily defined and, indeed, it is often the attribution process and the factors that affect it that determine the manner in which the symptoms are organized and how they are presented to helping agencies. Certainly, the problem of understanding reactions is simplified if analysis is limited to certain well-defined instances of mental disorder such as schizophrenia. But from a sociological perspective, it is valuable to study a wider spectrum of problems, since the issue of interest is how the person comes to identify a problem, define the nature of the problem, and identify the appropriate helping source, and how he negotiates among the various agencies that play some role in providing care. The process of attribution takes place when the illness situation is still unorganized Balint 1957). To focus on more coherent entities tends to exclude the more ambiguous cases in which the attribution process is at work, and thus misses part of the process that is of sociological interest.

More Specific Issues

In understanding how people come to define a problem and seek appropriate assistance, it is necessary to distinguish a variety of issues in a way that no existing study has effectively achieved. In this section I wish to specify the issues that must be disentangled, the methodological requirements for pursuing them, and problems of measurement that complicate such investigation.

Most of the existing literature in the past decade demonstrates certain continuities in the characteristics of individuals drawn to psychiatric care. Existing studies generally agree that such persons are more likely to be of higher educational and income levels, of urban or suburban residence, of Jewish identification or of low religious participation, and women (Gurin et al. 1960; Kadushin 1969; Boyce and Barnes 1966; Scheff 1966a). At a more analytic level it has been argued that persons more inclined to seek psychiatric care are more likely to have developed vocabularies of distress (Bart 1968), to have a cosmopolitan orientation (Linn, 1967), or to be part of a social circle of others who are friends and supporters of psychotherapy (Kadushin 1969). In short, seeking care for psychiatric problems and remaining receptive to psychotherapy have been seen by a variety of students of the problem as indicative of being part of a subcultural milieu that is encouraging, supportive, and that values the nature of the service given.

To complicate the issue, however, it is necessary to take into account that types of treatment are themselves linked to social movements, and have their own rise and decline over time as the appropriate fashion for a particular subgroup facing life problems or existential dilemmas. Psychoanalysis, for example, developed its roots in urban areas, with many practitioners of urban, middle-class, Jewish origin. It is not surprising, therefore, that this form of therapy attracted persons with certain social characteristics and life inclinations. But as the psychotherapeutic movement grew and developed, it became more heterogeneous in its geographic location and types of practitioners trained; and as these characteristics changed, so did the clients drawn into treatment. Although there is no definitive study, there is every indication that both psychotherapists and their patients are becoming more like the general population than was true twenty or thirty years ago. Thus, the social characteristics of clients drawn to such therapies are likely to change over time, becoming less distinctive. The kinds of results researchers are likely to obtain on the descriptive aspects of the selection of patients depend, in part, on what point in time they take a cross section of a continuing process through time.

At a single point in time, several interrelated issues exist in understanding the significance of sociocultural differences among patients who seek particular types of treatment (Greenley and Mechanic 1975). First, it is necessary to distinguish the extent to which social characteristics are related to seeking treatment because these are also related to the prevalence of certain problems requiring treatment. It is not clear to what extent these social characteristics are related to the occurrence of problems or to the care-seeking process. Second, it is necessary to distinguish the extent to which certain sociocultural processes are related to the inclination to seek care (or dependency on helping sources) as compared with their effect on the use of a particular source of care. It is obvious that Jewish identification, although related in many studies to the use of psychotherapy, does not increase the propensity to use Catholic counselors. Most studies in the literature confuse the issue of generalized sociocultural selection in seeking assistance for mental disorder from the issue of selection of specific forms of help.

The requirements for carrying out a study that allows separation of sociocultural effects on symptoms as compared with seeking help, and on generalized help-seeking propensities as compared with specific inclinations to use psychiatry or some other mode of help, are extremely difficult to meet. First, the researcher must have some way of measuring unorganized psychological distress or morbidity which can be alternatively defined by members of a population. Unfortunately, there are no good measures of health levels that can be applied to community populations, and measures of generalized psychological distress pose a variety of additional difficulties. Second, the study must be so organized that the researcher has access to a variety of alternative helping sources available to the population. Some studies, such as those by Gurin et al. (1960), cover a wide variety of agencies but depend on respondent reports as compared with verified data, and use lifetime prevalence rates that are unreliable. Preferably one would like to study a population during a defined period of risk and under conditions where the help-seeking behavior is verifiable by agency records. Furthermore, to the extent that the study is concerned with issues of functioning, diagnostic assessments made by helping practitioners, and the like, it would be desirable to obtain as much data as possible on performance from sources independent of the respondent, and preferably from records.

A further comment is needed on measures of psychological distress. At present, there are no adequate reliable techniques for identifying psychiatric disorders in the general population, although a great deal of progress has been made in developing a reliable clinical present-state examination with patient populations (Wing et al. 1974). Existing measures such as the Langner 22-item scale and the Health Opinion Survey, based on items from the Army Neuropsychiatry Inventory, confound physical and psychiatric distress and are biased by problems of social desirability response (Dohrenwend and Dohrenwend 1969; Crandell and Dohrenwend 1967; Seiler 1973; Manis et al. 1963; Tousignant et al. 1974; Phillips and Clancy 1970; Dohrenwend et al. 1970). Because of the association between age and physical morbidity, such measures are particularly deceptive when comparing subgroups of varying ages. Similarly, in populations of considerable ethnic and cultural heterogeneity, social desirability may be a source of major biases. Such measures, however, may still be relatively useful in studying populations within limited age ranges and that are not too culturally diverse. In any case, they offer better solutions than the one most sociological studies adopt — completely excluding the measurement of mental health status.

The ideal approach, although usually impossible to implement and extemely expensive, would be to follow on a panel basis a large defined population with access to a definable range of helping services. Although complete control is never fully possible, opportunities for a successful study are increased in a closed panel health care plan, particularly one in a relatively isolated community where treatment alternatives are not readily available or are easily identifiable, and thus can be included in the study. Other alternatives include such self-contained groups as college communities, armed forces units, ships, small isolated communities, and the like. Such a study could monitor the occurrence of distress in the population, the processes by which people identify and make sense of unorganized symptoms, and types of help-seeking from alternative agencies available to the population, such as medical care, mental health practitioners, clergymen, lawyers, special clinics, etc. To the extent that such a study would monitor the help sources themselves and the course of treatment, it becomes possible to separate not only the issues already identified, but also to ascertain whether the factors that facilitate continuation in treatment are separable from those leading to the initiation of treatment in the first place (Levinger 1960).

The cost and difficulties of implementing such a methodology require some compromises. One possibility that has been used in a variety of studies is to compare a random sample of a defined population eligible to use a particular facility with a sample of users (Scheff 1966a; Linn 1967; Greenley and Mechanic 1975). Although one cannot demonstrate a causal sequence using such a methodology, a variety of interesting hypotheses can be examined. Greenley and Mechanic (1975), using such an approach, compared a random sample of a defined population with samples of users of various helping agencies which the population was eligible to use. However, in the case of the random sample, further data were obtained on the use of a wider variety of agencies including those for which special samples were obtained. If the random sample is large, the availability of reported data on help-seeking allows the replication of the analysis within the random sample that was carried out across agency samples. To the extent that comparable results appear, there is reason to have added confidence in the findings. The value of working with a variety of alternative agencies is the availability of data independent of reports by respondents and the possibility of examining sociocultural influences on help-seeking in general as compared with inclinations to use particular types of helpers.

The State of the Literature

Most of the existing literature documents with considerable consistency systematic differences in the sociocultural characteristics of users of particular helping facilities. Only a few studies tangle with the kinds of theoretical issues I have suggested. Kadushin (1969) has perhaps done the most extensive work on attempting to describe how individuals come to perceive that they have a problem, the nature of the problem, whether care should be sought, and what type of practitioner to consult. He analyzes the propensity to use certain types of services in terms of his concept of social circles and indicates that while those of higher social status and of low religiosity tend to consult analytic clinics, lower status persons and those more religious are drawn to religious-based counseling clinics.

Kadushin (1962) has further provided support for the hypothesis that patients tend to seek among alternative helpers those that minimize social distance between patient and therapist.

Although studies by both Scheff (1966a) and Linn (1967) are confined only to use of psychiatric services, they present analyses very similar to the one provided by Kadushin (1969). Scheff infers a subculture attuned to psychiatry on the basis of sociocultural characteristics differentiating users from the population from which they come. Linn (1967), studying the same clinic, more directly measures cultural attitudes and associations with others, and suggests that there is a cosmopolitan subculture characterized by introspection, interest in psychology, and the like, that predisposes individuals to use psychiatric services.

The literature is particularly confusing in differentiating sociocultural characteristics as they affect the occurrence or recognition of distress in contrast to their effect on the use of helping services. For example, epidemiological investigations find that women report more distress than men; help-seeking studies also find that women use more services than men. These studies do not make clear whether sex is important primarily because it is related to rates of symptomatology or whether it has an independent effect on help-seeking behavior. Similarly, the high proportion of Jews found in psychotherapy has been said to result from a high level of introspection (presumably making feeling-states more salient and heightening distress) (Henry et al. 1968), or greater willingness of Jews to express distress and seek assistance (Antonovsky 1972). Few studies differentiate these factors.

Scheff (1966a) was one of very few investigators who attempted to measure psychological problems as intervening variables, basing the measure on a problem list developed from presenting complaints of students when they sought help from a psychiatric clinic. Scheff found that, although the clients' problem levels were related to seeking help, the sociocultural differences persisted when number of problems was controlled. He found, however, that sociocultural selectivity was greater among students with fewer as compared with more problems. One of the difficulties with Scheff's measure was the absence of any indication of severity other than the number of problems reported.

Greenley and Mechanic (1975) have carried out an extensive epidemiological survey as well as a study of students using particular helping agencies in order to examine some of the issues described in this paper. Although they used a wide variety of indicators to measure level of psychological distress, and took severity into account, they find, as do other investigators (Langner et al. 1963; Gersten et al 1974), that simple counting of symptoms or problems gives results comparable to more detailed scaling of severity. The comparability of findings is probably due to the fact that respondents who are more seriously distressed are likely to report a larger number of problems.

Using the Langner (1962) scale as a measure of psychological distress, Greenley and Mechanic could account for very little variance in rates of distress on the basis of social and cultural characteristics of students. Only sex and age had any important effects. They found, however, considerable sociocultural selectivity in the use of psychiatric services consistent with many other studies: in the psychiatric sample there was an overrepresentation of women, older students, students with Jewish identification or no religious affiliation, those from families of high socioeconomic status, and the like. However, those students who used a student counseling service had different and sometimes opposite characteristics. Thus, students coming to counseling were younger on the average than the students in the population from which they came. Only the overrepresentation of women was consistent with selection into the psychiatric clinic. Similarly, they found considerable specific selection into a variety of formal helping sources within the random sample suggesting that much of the social selection into care depends on certain compatibilities between help-seeker and help-provider. The information on use of a variety of formal help-giving agencies, including psychiatrists, counselors, clergymen, general physicians, and the like, allowed them to compare students who sought help from a formal helper as compared with those who did not. When such an analysis is performed there is very little difference on the basis of sociocultural characteristics between these two groups, suggesting that most such characteristics have little relationship to a general readiness to seek help for personal problems.

There are a few other findings worthy of note. The most important single factor affecting the use of psychiatry or counseling services is the level of distress. Although there is significant sociocultural selection, it operates for the most part independently of distress levels. Of the various sociocultural factors, only sex appears to be related in any significant fashion both to the reporting of levels of distress and to the use of helping services. While controlling for distress seems to account for the overrepresentation of women in the psychiatry sample, such controls did not account for the overrepresentation of women in the counseling sample or the overrepresentation of women in the random sample reporting consulting a psychiatrist. Although Greenley and Mechanic found a slight tendency for social selection to be strongest among those least impaired, for the most part social selection appeared to operate in a comparable way at varying levels of distress. Finally, they found that distress played some role in the selection among formal help sources. In general, students seeking care from psychiatry as compared with other sources of help had higher levels of reported distress.

Where Do We Go From Here?

The discussion has ranged over a wide area, suggesting a variety of issues that remain to be clarified about how people respond to indications of mental disorder. I have neglected the literature on other-defined deviance, as in the case of involuntary hospitalization, since these issues have been amply discussed elsewhere (Mechanic 1968; 1969), and growing emphasis in society — as well as in research studies — is being devoted to voluntary processes of care. I should emphasize that many of the considerations here are applicable to "other-defined situations," and the neglect of specific discussion should not suggest that this area offers no further provocative questions for the sociologist. The shift away from involuntary hospitalization and the emphasis on community care, as well as the new emphasis on the rights of the mentally ill, is part of a social movement that is likely to be cyclical in its development. Already there are strong indications of a community backlash to permissive mental health applications, and forces are growing to reinstate at least partially some earlier practices. The politics of the mental health sector have been very poorly studied and require vigorous sociological analysis.

In pursuing further research, the following general frame of reference appears to be a viable starting point. The occurrence of symptoms, particularly when they become visible, disruptive, or incapacitating in some fashion, sets into motion a process of conceptualization in which various attributions are made. The nature of the attribution process is to some extent shaped by the character and magnitude of the symptoms but also by the sociocultural characteristics of the persons and the social circles within which they function. The type of care selected depends on sociocultural predispositions, the assessment of the locus of causality of the problem, the immediate social context, and the character and accessibility of available helping services. In all probability, when conditions are ripe, any of a wide variety of triggering events may help bring individuals to a source of help. Such triggers may include certain crises they confront because of this problem, social influences of significant others, or public information that gives them cues as to the availability of a source of help well fitted to their difficulty. Future efforts will be required to provide data to clarify the framework and further extend it.

25

Cultural Aspects of Psychotherapy

Eric D. Wittkower and Hector Warnes

Psychotherapy is a central and ubiquitous form of psychiatric care. It can be very brief as in crisis interventon and very prolonged as in traditional psychoanalysis, it can be rather informal as in general counseling and very structured as in behavior therapy, and it can be focused on the individual as well as on the family and other groups. Furthermore, psychotherapeutic elements are important in the general interaction between clinician and patient, regardless of the nature of the encounter and the specific treatment used. Of all forms of psychiatric care, psychotherapy is clearly the most influenced by culture, given the prominence that in its implementation play the values and world view of both therapist and patient and the eminently cultural significance of the language used and its subtleties.

In the following article, E. D. Wittkower and H. Warnes review both the similarities and the differences among psychotherapies practiced in various parts of the world, and discuss probable factors underlying the differences noted. They then compare Western and folk psychotherapies and propose the gradual Westernization of psychiatric care in developing countries, a very intricate and controversial issue which is discussed further in the next article.

THIS PAPER deals with the cultural aspects of psychotherapy, that is, with the relevance of cultural factors to its application. A clear delineation of what we intend to cover is required. Psychotherapy, for the purpose of this paper, may be defined as interaction of one person with another (or with others) by verbal means for the alleviation of emotional distress or for change in behavioral dysfunction. In accordance with this definition our paper concerns itself with treatment procedures ranging from those practiced by physicians in industrialized societies to those practiced by traditional healers in developing countries. Questions which will be asked are: Why are certain psychotherapeutic procedures preferred to others in some cultural areas, and to what extent are procedures created, developed, and practiced in the West transferable to other parts of the world? Accordingly, our paper is divided into two major parts: cultural psychotherapy and cross-cultural psychotherapy.

1. Cultural Psychotherapy

Numerous writers have pointed out that despite superficial differences, psychotherapies practiced all over the world have a few common underlying themes. These have been identified by Jerome Frank (1972) as follows:

1. An intense, emotionally charged confiding relationship with a helping person.
2. A rationale of myth which includes an explanation of the cause of the person's distress and which is compatible with the cultural world view shared by the patient and therapist. Also, supplying a conceptual scheme for what seems to the patient to be a group of nonsensical symptoms provides powerful reassurance to him. Essentially, then, the functions of the rationale and ritual, rather than their specific content and form, are what really count.
3. Provision of new information concerning the nature and sources of the patient's problems and alternative ways of dealing with them.
4. Strengthening the patient's expectations of help through the personal qualities of the therapist, enhanced by his status in society and the setting in which he works.
5. Provision of success experiences which further heighten the patient's hopes and also enhance his sense of mastery, interpersonal competence, or capability.
6. Facilitation of emotional arousal, a prerequisite of attitudinal and behavioral changes.

But while such universal features undoubtedly exist, it seems absurd to minimize differences in psychotherapy—differences in intensity, quality, and depth—and to claim, as Fuller Torrey (1972) did, that the techniques of therapy are basically the same whether they are used by a witch doctor or a psychiatrist.

Preferences in the choice of forms of psychotherapy cross-culturally depend on differences in etiologic views and on cultural and ideologic differences.

In many nonindustrialized areas of the world the belief prevails that mental illness is due to supernatural and preternatural forces, that is, to angry deities, soul loss, intrusion (possession) by noxious elements, witchcraft, or sorcery. For patients in whom such beliefs prevail, it is obviously appropriate to turn for help to those who believe themselves, or are believed, to be able to deal with these forces. Consequently, in these countries shamans, priests, traditional healers, medicine men and witch doctors, in the accepted view, are much better qualified to deal with mental illness than scientifically trained doctors. In fact, in these countries, even if psychologically disturbed patients submit themselves to medical help for symptom removal, they may afterwards turn to the traditional healer for effective removal of the assumed cause.

The procedure which these healers adopt consist of administration of plant concoctions (which are often empirically potent), lavages, application of holy oil, imposition of sacrifice, confession, catharsis, application of shock-producing irritants, and many other measures. As regards the psychotherapeutic effects of these procedures the following elements can be identified: (1) rationalization of fears of unknown origin, for example, "Sopono, the smallpox god, has inflicted this on you"; (2) suggestion reinforced by the high prestige of the traditional healer resulting in repression; (3) projection of internal badness onto vicious deities; (4) displacement of internal badness, be it sin or sickness, on the scapegoat or any other sacrificial animals; (5) displacement of target of attack, that is, the killing of an animal in lieu of a person; and (6) penance by sacrifice.

Because in many developing countries individuation has been imperfectly accomplished and reliance on group approval predominates over superego pressure, therapeutic procedures are carried out usually in groups, such as in the Zar cult in Ethiopia and the Pentecostal services in African and Caribbean countries. The psychotherapeutic function and effect of cult ceremonies in many countries have been documented in detail.

Symptoms, symbols, and customs are to be understood within the context and limitations imposed by a particular culture. Doi (1962a, 1962b), a Japanese author, emphasized the need for the Japanese to surrender to authority by submission, dependency, helplessness, and to yield to the wish to be loved which is incongruent with Western thought promoting independence and self-help. Other Japanese cultural traits are a predilection for politeness, obedience, conscientiousness, secretiveness, and ceremoniousness well described by W. LaBarre (1945) and H. M. Spitzer (1947). These cultural traits, which are likely to be derived from traditional Buddhism and family rearing practice, have to be taken into account in psychotherapeutic procedures. Western methods, with values and beliefs which are in covert or overt disagreement with the Japanese national tradition and character, may prove unviable. A gradual change in the Japanese culture may leave the door open to alternative ideologies and practices compatible with the new historical dimension.

It is not only in developing or recently industrialized societies like Japan that culture influences therapy. However, between one industrialized society and another differences in their cultures and world view can be important. For instance, it is hardly surprising that owing to the emphasis on individualism, rational thinking, scientific idolatry, free expression of thought, and tolerance of dissent, psychoanalysis with its free association, free-floating attention, collaborative effort, and scientific theory found a fertile ground in the United States.

Shift of focus from narcissistic self-concern, as evidenced by doing-one's-own-thing attitudes, to a communal orientation led in the United States to a decline in interest in psychoanalysis and a growth of interest in community psychiatry, family therapy, and group psychotherapy. In view of the postulated doctor-patient interaction given in our definition, behavior therapy, at least in the way it is practiced in some quarters, can hardly be regarded as a form of psychotherapy. However, it is likely that different emphasis is laid on the cognitive, emotive-relational and conditioning-autonomic factors according to the personality of the therapist.

Psychoanalysis, for obvious reasons, has failed to gain ground in authoritarian countries such as Soviet Russia up to now and Japan, Germany, and Spain until recently. Russian "pathogenic psychotherapy," German "autogenic training," and Japanese "Morita therapy" are highly structured procedures; they ignore the unconscious, are ego-directed, and have a drill quality. They are "specific step-by-step approaches" aimed at controlling and regulating various psychologic and somatic functions through "training," "preselected words," and goal-directed formulas.

Work therapy, as might be expected, figures prominently among psychotherapeutic measures in the Soviet Union and other communist countries. Ample use is also made of the collective as a therapeutic agent. As Kiev (1968b) points out: "In Marxist theory work is viewed as man's most important activity. It is felt that man's consciousness grows and his relations with other men develop within the framework of economic activities. According to the Soviet Constitution, work is a duty and a matter of honor." Psychoneuroses in the Soviet view are attributable to bad education and bad habits.

The aforementioned pathogenic psychotherapy practiced at the Bechterev Institute in Leningrad therefore has a pedagogic quality. Myasishev (1958), one of the leading members of this Institute, stated: "The psychiatrist is a teacher of life." Analogously, though much more brusquely, a treatment procedure developed in East Germany "drives out" phobic symptoms by forcible exposure of phobic patients to anxiety evoking situations.

The Far East and mysticism have always had an attraction for Germans. Hence it is conceivable that the yoga component in autogenic training and the mysticism in Jung's analytic psychology and in existential psychotherapy may at least in part account for the popularity of these methods in Germany.

Zen Buddhism teaches tranquility of mind, serenity, and acceptance of adversity. Accordingly Morita therapy (practiced in Japan), which is based on Zen Buddhism, aims at acceptance of suffering through isolation, self-confrontation, and partial deprivation. To quote Kimura (1972), Zen Buddhism says: "If you walk in the rain you feel damp and cold. This happens because you feel the rain as something apart from you. If you were to unite yourself with the rain and would not perceive any separation, any duality, between yourself and the water, as the swimmer does immersed in the water, then you would instantly no longer feel cold and damp." "Hence," Kimura continues, "the basic principle of Morita therapy is: surrender yourself with your whole being to anguish and pain."

2. Cross-Cultural Psychotherapy

Problems arise if treatment procedures created, developed, and practiced in one cultural area are transposed to another. In principle any psychotherapeutic method can be transferred from one country to any other country; for instance, yoga practices and some Buddhistic ceremonials have gained popularity in some quarters in the West. But more often than not it is the application of Western psychotherapeutic procedures to non-Western societies which gives rise to difficulties.

Three different views have been expressed on this matter: (a) that psychotherapeutic methods are universally applicable (Berne 1960); (b) that understanding of each individual must be based on assessment of his specific experiences (Alexander and Selesnik 1966); and (c) that identical nationality and cultural background facilitate the psychotherapeutic process (Santoso 1959).

The last two views require discussion. The knowledge of the cultural background of the patient will aid the therapist in his understanding of the patient and will prevent him from inculcating patterns of thoughts and behavior acceptable to the therapist's society but alien to the patient's society.

Even in the West, omitting Eskimos and Indians for a moment, differences in race, religion, social class, and ethnicity between psychotherapist and patient may give rise to difficulties or at least require consideration. This is a little explored but highly important area which is beginning to arouse a great deal of interest and attention. Is it really true, as some authors have alleged, that the middle class psychotherapist is incapable of empathizing with the poor patient and that poor and uneducated patients are unable to introspect and to articulate their feelings? And is it true that prejudice of the psychotherapist, suspicion of the therapist on racial, religious, or ethnic grounds, and differences in world view constitute major obstacles in psychotherapy?

The mother tongue gains a special place of prominence in any psychotherapeutic procedure. "Le language est à la fois le fait culturel par excellence (distinguant l'homme de l'animal) et celui par l'intermédiate duquel toutes les formes de la vie social s'établissent et se perpétuent."[1] This axiological insight is for Lévi-Strauss (1958) the leitmotif of anthropological search and we would suspect, a primal factor in the effectiveness of psychotherapy.

Language is the vehicle that circumscribes and defines the unknown danger, thus reducing anxiety, and brings the deviant (patient) in line with the prevailing social values by neutralizing the pathogenic effect of whatever the suspected cause of his sufferings is. Finer nuances presented in the patient's material may be missed

1. Language is at once the prototype of the cultural phenomenon (distinguishing man from the animals) and the phenomenon whereby all the forms of social life are established and perpetuated.

by the psychotherapist, misunderstandings may occur, and the newly acquired language may be used by the patient for defensive purposes. Should translation from and into local dialects be required, psychotherapy becomes a formidable task.

Difficulties in transplanting Western psychotherapy mount still further if the world view of the psychotherapist grossly diverges from that of the patient. This is the case in dealing with Eskimos, Indians, some Puerto Ricans, and some Mexican-Americans on the North American continent and with the bulk of the rural populations in many parts of South America, Africa, and Asia. Here, as stated before, rational thinking clashes with animistic magic belief; genetic and environmental etiologic considerations contrast with beliefs in supernatural and preternatural forces; expectations of the doctor's role and function widely differ, and suspicion and distrust of the white intruder may be rife.

All over the world patients are apt to trust in the therapist and his methods. If not, as in the practice of Westerners in developing countries, the therapist is likely to fail (Lederer 1959). Further, a psychotherapist may justifiably feel guilty for applying or advising a treatment method which clashes with the prevalent cultural values.

In the face of such a situation workers in the field dispute the possibility of applying a Western type of psychotherapy, erroneously described as insight therapy, to non-Western uneducated persons, claiming that psychoanalytically oriented psychotherapy is applicable only to Westernized members of these societies or postulate at least that profound knowledge of the history, religion, literature, customs, and modes of thinking of the cultural groups whose members are to be treated, are required.

What then can be done to offer the best psychotherapeutic assistance to the indigenous population of developing countries? It may be argued that if the traditional healer fits the needs of the people why should the care of the mentally ill not be left in his hands? It cannot be disputed that especially in the treatment of psychoneuroses the traditional healer is often effective and at any rate the results of Western psychotherapy are not staggering.

The number of trained psychiatrists in developing countries is so small that they have no or little time to spare for psychotherapy. However, time marches on. More and more are the services of European and American psychiatrists requested by the governments of developing countries, more and more scions of these countries undergo medical and psychiatric training in Europe and America and have adopted on return home Western concepts and ideas, and more and more, with progressive Westernization, animistic magic etiologic concepts are replaced by genetic and environmental etiologic concepts in the indigenous population.

For a long time the services of the traditional healers in the treatment of the mentally ill will be indispensable in developing countries. Meanwhile as the world view of the indigenous population undergoes a change toward Westernization, the following interim steps have been suggested:

1. To acquire skills and techniques to overcome the suspicion and distrust of the Western trained psychiatrist (Jilek and Jilek-Aall 1971).

2. To establish collaboration between psychiatrists and traditional healers (Lambo 1966; Bolman 1968).

3. To adapt Western methods to the cultural climate in which they operate, for example, more parameters are expected to be introduced in applying psychoanalysis to certain cultural groups.

4. To explore and develop existing healing methods in that culture, to offer a rationale for their application, and to attempt to integrate them into Western methods.

5. To hand over increasingly, as is the logical course to take, the care of the mentally ill in their own country to foreign-trained indigenous psychiatrists.

In this last case, however, contempt for the traditional healer by the returning psychiatrist and refusal to have anything to do with him are, unfortunately, common.

In brief then it is our opinion that owing to the scarcity of psychiatrists, psychoanalytically oriented psychotherapy is for the time being hardly feasible in developing countries, that it is probably practical though at present unacceptable, and that its application on a substantial scale depends on an increase in the number of psychiatrists capable of practicing it and, of course, on culture change.

Summary

Cross-cultural preferences in the choice of forms of psychotherapy depend on differences in etiologic views and on cultural and ideologic differences. For instance, based on belief in supernatural and preternatural forces, in many developing countries, the treatment of the mentally ill is largely in the hands of shamans, priests, and witch doctors. Among many other factors psychoanalysis has gained ground in the United States because of cultural emphasis on individualism, work therapy in the Soviet Union because of Marxist ideology, and autogenic training in Germany and Morita therapy in Japan because of culturally imposed rigid self-discipline in these two countries.

Application of Western types of psychotherapy to non-Western uneducated persons is difficult. For a long time in developing countries, the services of traditional healers will be needed. The world view of the indigenous population in these countries is undergoing a change toward Westernization. Interim steps to be taken are suggested.

26

Psychiatry and Folk Healing: A Dichotomy?

Pedro Ruiz and John Langrod

The development of comprehensive community mental health centers in the U.S. during the past two decades and the recent findings of the President's Commission on Mental Health have pointed out the underserved condition of many people belonging to cultural minorities who represent sizable segments of the general population. Great difficulties in making the standard mental health services available to such groups and limited effectiveness of the services actually provided to them have been reported. These problems are particularly critical in large cities such as New York and Los Angeles, where a geographical coexistence of two systems of mental health care, one standard and the other folk, have been noted.

In the following paper, Pedro Ruiz, a distinguished bicultural psychiatrist and mental health administrator, and his associate John Langrod, describe the vicissitudes of a university-affiliated mental health center in a heavily Hispanic area of New York City vis-à-vis the issues noted above. They outline the similarities found between the standard and the folk health systems and the challenges posed by their coexistence. Particularly exciting is the experiment they describe integrating these systems through joint meetings and by fostering collaborative attitudes.

THE METHODS and therapeutic value of folk healers have aroused the interest of mental health practitioners for some time. In fact, Kline (1969) and Lubchansky and associates (Lubchansky et al.

1970), after examining the mode of operation of folk healers in Hispanic communites, proposed that their work be incorporated in some manner into the structure of mental health facilities.

Since 1971, the Lincoln Community Mental Health Center, Bronx, N.Y., has independently included folk healers in a system that also encompasses credentialed professionals and a training program for psychiatric residents. Such a leap across established disciplinary boundaries resulted from the convergence of three factors: 1) the innovative character of the community mental health movement, with its mandate for positive action toward enhancing the mental health of a whole community; 2) the unique nature and needs, articulated by strong leadership, of the population served by this center; and 3) the acknowledgment by many professionals employed in the program of their lack of skills in dealing with mental problems in which culture played a significant, if not the key, role.

Cultural Barriers to Communication

There were many well-known obstacles to translating the ideology of the Community Mental Health Centers Act of 1963 into reality. In such ghetto areas as southeast Bronx the going was especially slow and painful. The reactions of this disadvantaged community to the initial impersonality of traditional service delivery resulted in many challenges and confrontations.

The heart of the problem was soon found to lie in the realm of cross-cultural misunderstanding. Much has been written about improving the quality of life in poor communities and thereby improving the mental health of its inhabitants. However, the values and qualities considered "good" by one culture may not be those which are admitted and sought after in another.

For Spanish-speaking people who migrated to New York, the expectations of a better life that brought them here all too often gave way to the realities of prejudice, language barriers, and poverty in a dilapidated area of an indifferent city. The disillusionment and culture shock experienced under such circumstances can create almost unbearable stress, hardly conducive to respect and admiration for the new environment or its institutions. In a perceived hostile environment, the immigrant finds reassurance and relief in closing ranks with his fellow migrants and holding fast to familiar ways.

When stress becomes unendurable, the social network of the Hispanic community often provides access to the system of folk healing as a suitable solution. This was confirmed by Rogler and Hollingshead (1964), who studied the role of spiritualism in families of schizophrenics. The solution to the cultural dilemma confronting us was to blend psychiatry and folk healing into a unique network of treatment programs.

A Comparison of Folk Healers and Psychiatrists

In a classic study of Mexican-American folk healing practices Kiev (1968a) compared the relative merits of *curanderismo* (a Hispanic concept of healing) and dynamic psychotherapy and found both systems beneficial under certain circumstances.

In south Bronx folk healers practice in *centros*—usually store fronts or rented halls where regular meetings are held. Almost all of these are licensed as churches, with a regular congregation and a president who is usually a medium *(espiritista);* several other mediums or mediums-in-training frequently attend. A smaller *centro* may be located in the home of an *espiritista.* When a client comes to a meeting at the *centro* (usually at the urging of, and accompanied by, relatives or friends) he is helped to present his problem by responding to questions posed by mediums. The complaints presented are most often those of persistent physical discomforts. At other times mental stress caused by marital problems or job situations may be examined. No problem is too small to merit attention; the mediums know from experience that even minor complaints or events can be accompanied by great stress. They decide whether "material" or "spiritual" causes are to blame in a given instance.

It is very difficult for a society schooled in the immutable value of scientific theory to understand or accept the therapeutic value of a helping system based on faith in the supernatural. Nevertheless, the trend has been the other way. Nelson and Torrey (1973) pointed out that in the last 25 years psychiatry has taken over many of the "healing" functions of religion. In fact, a close examination of practices in psychiatry and *espiritismo* reveals some striking similarities.

Similarities in Practice

Although they are based on very different bodies of knowledge and belief, both folk healing and psychiatry use suggestion, persuasion, and manipulation in treatment. Group process and family and milieu therapy, which are increasingly employed by professionals, are comparable in a sense to the group approach of the *centros.* Futhermore, the acting out of feelings in the spiritualistic rituals resembles such psychiatric techniques as psychodrama. Transference reactions occur in both settings. Psychiatrists may prescribe psychotropic drugs that must be procured from a pharmacist; folk healers use herbal remedies, perfumes, symbolic objects, special baths—all of which are found in Hispanic *botanicas* (similar to drugstores). Both systems derive a great deal of authority from their ability to state what is wrong with their clients; Torrey (1972) suggested that the very act of naming an ailment is therapeutic to the patient. The very fact that another person can pinpoint an etiological factor can lead to associated ideas in the mind of the client that in turn could produce confession, catharsis, and self-awareness.

Important Differences in Practice

Folk healers are problem oriented, tackling one difficulty at a time. Psychiatrists more often cluster a series of symptoms to arrive at a diagnosis. The folk healer believes that symptoms of distress frequently originate in powers beyond the control of the individual and when externalized relieve the patient in most instances of responsibility for them. In contrast, classic psychotherapists measure symptoms against a series of diagnostic classifications representing different degrees of mental disorders that usually originate in intrapsychic conflicts. The therapist frequently locates causes in the patient's unconscious and encourages and helps the patient to recognize and deal with these inner conflicts. His goal is the reintegration of the individual personality, enhanced by self-awareness.

The *centro* setting is communal and supportive; *espiritistas* and other participants are peers of the individual who is seeking help. They speak his language, especially in the idiom of shared neighborhood experience. If the client is unable to articulate his feelings or respond to questions, mediums find clues in nonverbal communication. On the other hand, psychiatric treatment is most often available only in institutional settings: therapists are almost always from a different socioeconomic class; and even if they speak the patient's language, they may not use words that have meaning for him.

Such general terms as "psychiatrist," "mental health center," "psychiatric hospital" connote mental illness and thus carry a stigma in Hispanic culture. The fear of being considered *loco* (crazy) may be enough to keep patients away. As a member of the *centro,* however, an individual becomes part of a familiar group that may provide empathic understanding and help. Symptoms that could appear alarming to others may often be interpreted as indicating that a person is in the process of developing spiritual powers of his own.

The Dilemma

There is a troublesome question facing the administrator of a mental health program in a predominantly Hispanic ghetto community. How can one combine the findings of modern clinical psychiatry with cultural realities and produce high quality service delivery?

Fitzpatrick and Gould (1970), commenting on the extremely high comparative incidence of Puerto Rican first admissions to state mental hospitals, suggested that what was psychiatrically defined as mental illness may actually be a temporary disturbance in response to pressures of poverty, discrimination, and rapid social change. Conversely, Martinez (1973) warned that too much emphasis on the social and economic factors might lead to the extreme position of denying intrapsychic conflicts in the poor. In addition, Maduro and Martinez (1974) reported that people of Spanish descent who undergo classical psychotherapy can improve symptomatically and also enhance their ethnic identity. We suggest that while psychiatric treatment should be administered within a cultural context and with a knowledge of cultural norms, it is also necessary to avoid stereotyping individuals because they come from a particular culture.

The South Bronx Experience

Our program slowly moved toward a closer relationship with the spiritualist centers operating in our community. Hispanic patients were not readily inclined to confide their spiritualist beliefs to therapists they felt would not understand. However, as professionals became better acquainted with the neighborhood, they could not fail to notice the presence of the *botanicas,* sometimes as many as two or three on a block. In addition, Hispanic patients would sometimes complain that a "spell" had been put on them, or they would report that they had been "talking to God" or felt "possessed" by a bad spirit. At clinical conferences in the center, where cases were reviewed, psychiatrists would invariably note signs indicating some category of mental illness (e.g., paranoid delusions); in such cases, drug therapy usually was recommended. The diagnosis was often some form of schizophrenia, and hospitalization was indicated. Analytic psychotherapy was virtually ruled out as a treatment modality. Unfortunately, hospitalization meant as many as three months away from family and supportive elements in the community and involved risks to an individual's autonomy in an institutional atmosphere. These circumstances made it possible for us to understand how the same client could come to the mental health center for the help in the daytime and visit spiritual centers in the evening.

Were we competing with folk healers? Were we duplicating services? Were folk healers helping or harming our patients? Obviously, we had to know more. Professionals were invited to various *centros* to observe the way folk healers practiced. They saw a built-in "caretaker" system, capable of translating stressful events and deviant behavior into acceptable explanations for their occurrence and offering specific remedies for coping with them. They also discovered the therapeutic value of a set of beliefs that provided social support for persons undergoing emotional disturbance. In this interaction the mental health professionals were able to explain to the folk healers that some of the signs and symptoms attributed to spiritual causes might indicate the presence of an ulcer, a brain tumor, or a serious mental disorder, all of which would require medical intervention.

Implications for Professional Training

In order to familiarize staff and students with folk healing methods, an in-service training program was developed for both professionals and nonprofessionals to sensitize them to cultural factors and their implications in mental health. Discussions of symptoms and treatment goals took place in regularly scheduled seminars where a free exchange of views by practitioners from both systems was fostered. If professionals saw spiritualist premises as somewhat alien, they also could not help but see them as supportive and effective in their cultural milieu. At the same time, spiritualists could obtain first-hand knowledge of diagnostic techniques used by psychiatrists practicing in the community.

To date, the reciprocal interchange in training is carried out informally, with emphasis on health care delivery. However, the next step may be to mount a formal training program for folk healers that would acquaint them with the medical aspects of psychiatric health and illness and perhaps lead to credentialed status on our mental health teams as assistant "therapists."

27

Cultural Variation in Responses to Psychotropic Drugs: A Progress Report

H. B. M. Murphy

In addition to the psychotherapies, other major forms of psychiatric care involve somatic treatment. Prominent in this group is psychopharmacotherapy. Since the discovery of chlorpromazine in France in the early fifties, there has been an explosion of research on psychotropic drugs, first involving antipsychotics and then minor tranquilizers and antidepressants as well as a revival of interest in Lithium. The effectiveness of these drugs for several psychopathological conditions has been responsible in large extent for the boom of biological psychiatry during the past two decades.

Research on the influence of culture on pharmacological treatment has not been nearly as intense as in the case of the psychotherapies. However, patient's expectations and other affective and cognitive factors involved in treatment process and outcome as well as ethnic variations in the metabolism of certain drugs are receiving increasing attention.

H. B. M. Murphy, from the McGill University Transcultural Psychiatry Program, conducted several years ago a seminal international survey of ethnic variations in drug response. Building on it, he later conducted a critical review of a set of clinical trails comparing responses to psychotropic drugs among several ethnic groups, the results of which he presents in the following article.

THE POSSIBILITY that racial and cultural backgrounds affect the ways patients respond to psychotropic drugs made its appearance as soon as it was realized that such backgrounds could affect symptomatology, but the probability of such an influence has for long been considered so slight as to be negligible. There are thousands of drug trials each year which yield apparently no evidence in this direction—though this could merely be because such evidence is not looked for—and clinicians do not even intuitively adjust their choice of drug or dosage in accord with the patient's ethnicity. However, when the literature was searched, some half-dozen studies which gave evidence for such differences were found; and when an international inquiry was circulated asking for further impressions on the subject, a number of respondents indicated belief that they obtained better results with patients of some races than with those of others (Murphy 1969a). Briefly, that review suggested that European clinics obtained better results than North American ones when treating similar patients with standard doses of certain phenothiazines; that within North America paradoxical reactions to some psychotropic drugs were commoner in subjects of one cultural origin than in those of another (though their racial background should have been similar); and that Southeast Asia would be the best location in which to pursue the matter further.

The evidence uncovered by that review, balanced as it was by so large a volume of countervailing argument in the form of apparently negative results, did not appear to be strong enough to justify stating that a racial or cultural influence on drug efficiency exists, but it did at least justify an attempt to reexamine the data of earlier drug trials where patients of more than one culture had been differentiated, insofar as such data could be found. The writer therefore sought access to the records of trials that had taken place in Southeast Asia and also let his interest in similar material be known to colleagues nearer home. These feelers were quickly successful, for the University of Indonesia proved to possess suitable data relating to two phenothiazine trials and a colleague in Montreal drew the writer's attention to some promising results in a trial of anxiolytics there. This article presents the results obtained by re-analyzing data from those two sources and will explore some possible explanations for them.

Indonesians and Chinese

The Department of Psychiatry at the University of Indonesia has built up under the chairmanship of Professor Kusumanto Setyonegoro a tradition of careful and responsible drug research that is unusual in South Asia and that has received recognition by manufacturers seeking to test the appropriateness of their products under Asian conditions. The patients used for such trials are drawn indiscriminately from the many cultural subgroups that Djakarta hosts and are seen either in the University Hospital or in city clinics, but not in a large state mental hospital where the treatment milieu is usually very foreign to the patients' normal experience. The psychiatrists of that Department had the impression that their Asian patients responded to many psychotropic drugs more rapidly than did comparable patients they had treated in Europe or North America, but did not have the impression that there was a significant association between drug effectiveness and culture within their Djakarta patient population. Therefore, although they were willing to provide data on relatively matched samples of patients with specified cultural backgrounds from their earlier drug trial records, they did not expect that there would be significant differences in drug response patterns.

For the first exploration it was decided to use cases of schizophrenia that had been treated with thioridazine (Melleril) and the goal was to compare at least 40 Chinese, 40 Javanese, and 40 of some other Indonesian subculture. To reduce complicating factors it was agreed that the patients should all:

(a) be still diagnosed at discharge as having had schizophrenia;
(b) be within the age range of 16 to 40;
(c) have a history of not less than six months' and not more than five years' disturbance;
(d) be roughly matched for age and sex across the three subsamples;
(e) not be drawn from any hospital or clinic that had an unusual predominance of one or other culture using it.

The last condition was included to avoid having to allow for possible differences in the total treatment setting.

When the data were received it was discovered that some of the patients had been treated unsuccessfully with another phenothiazine before being put onto the thioridazine while others had had no prior phenothiazine, and the pictures for these two groups differed. The patients who had failed to respond adequately to another phenothiazine (usually chlorpromazine) responded less well to the thioridazine than those who came fresh to the latter drug, which is what one would expect, and in this group it was not possible to detect any statistically significant differences between the response pic-

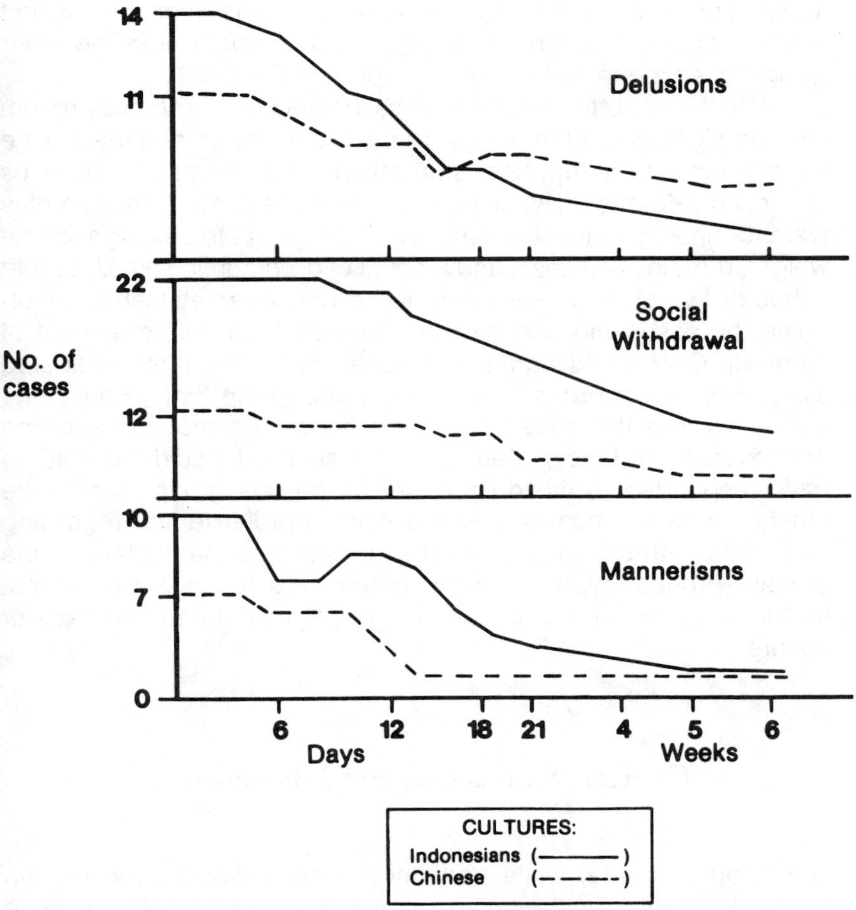

Figure 27.1 Disappearance of Symptoms Over Time. Drug: Thioridazine (Melleril)

ture in one subculture and that in another. In the patients who came fresh to the thioridazine, however, there were significant differences in the response patterns of the two main cultures, as figure 27.1 shows. Owing to the reduction in total sample size it was necessary to combine the two Indonesian subcultures, but when this combined group is compared with the Chinese it is clear that for three classical symptoms—delusions, social withdrawal, and mannerisms—their recovery is better than that of the Chinese patients. (Only patients having the given symptom at the start of treatment or developing it during the treatment period are included in each chart, which explains why the numbers are different each time, and for each patient two half-steps are countable, one when there is first mention of improvement in the specified symptom and the other when it is stated to have wholly disappeared.)

With the doubtful exception of hallucinations, no other symptom showed significant differences in improvement rate and there were no differences in reported side-effects. (Thioridazine produces almost no side-effects when used in moderate doses.) The samples were fortunately quite well matched with respect to sex, age, body-weight, duration of illness, and amount of drug administered, so that although two of these variables had a definite relationship to outcome the associations shown in figure 27.1 were independent of them all. One would normally assume that if the three indicated symptoms had improved more in the one group than in the other and if, as was the case here, there were no symptoms showing the reverse tendency, then the disease itself could be said to have responded to the drug better in the one group than in the other. However, because there is considerable debate regarding what criteria to use in assessing schizophrenia, particularly of the primary process type, it seems better here to state merely that the drug's effect on these specific symptoms differed with race or culture.

Chinese, Sundanese, and Minangkabau

The foregoing data, while permitting a comparison between two races, did not permit the comparison of two cultures with the same racial background, as had been intended, and did not cast light on the relative frequency of side-effects. A subsequent trial of another phenothiazine, trifluoperazine, permitted both these points to be investigated, however. Taking only patients who came fresh to the drug and who had not recently been on any other phenothiazine, it was possible to get samples of two distinct Malaysian groups in addition to a Chinese one. Selection of cases was determined by the same criteria as previously, but matching proved to be more difficult, as table 27.1 illustrates, and the effect of sex, age and education had therefore to be allowed for. We were naturally looking for some replication here of the earlier findings, but since the one drug was of a more sedative and the other of a more disinhibitory character it was recognized that they did not offer the same type of

Table 27.1 Characteristics of Second Djakarta Sample

	Chinese	*Sundanese*	*Minangkabau*
(N)	(22)	(26)	(14)
Sex:			
Male	46%	69%	50%
Female	54%	31%	50%
Age:			
15-19	23%	15%	7%
20-24	23	12	21
25-29	23	39	29
30-39	32	35	43
Education:			
No schooling	–	4%	–
Primary only	50%	50%	14%
Secondary	45	46	86
University	5	–	–
Duration of Illness:			
1-6 months	23%	39%	36%
7-24 months	18	23	14
2-5 years	59	30	50
Mean Weight (kgs):	45	48	48
Mean Daily Dose, 2nd WEEK (mgm):	13.9	11.7	14.3

experience to the patients and therefore might be reacted to differently. Of the two Malaysian subcultures one, the Sundanese, had been well represented among the thioridazine patients but the other, the Minangkabau, had not been.

Once again the method of time sequence used for the new analysis of the data revealed quite substantial differences in the symptomatological improvement shown by the three cultural groups, but the relevant symptoms were not all the same and the divergences were not all in the same direction. As figure 27.2 illustrates, delusions and excitement disappeared much less rapidly in the Minangkabau than in the other two groups, the differences being beyond the 0.001 level of expectation when 21 days is used as the cutting point. With excitement also, the Chinese respond significantly less well than the Sundanese. In figure 27.3, however, one sees that the Minangkabau respond significantly better ($p = 0.05$) than the other two groups as respects two symptoms. Educa-

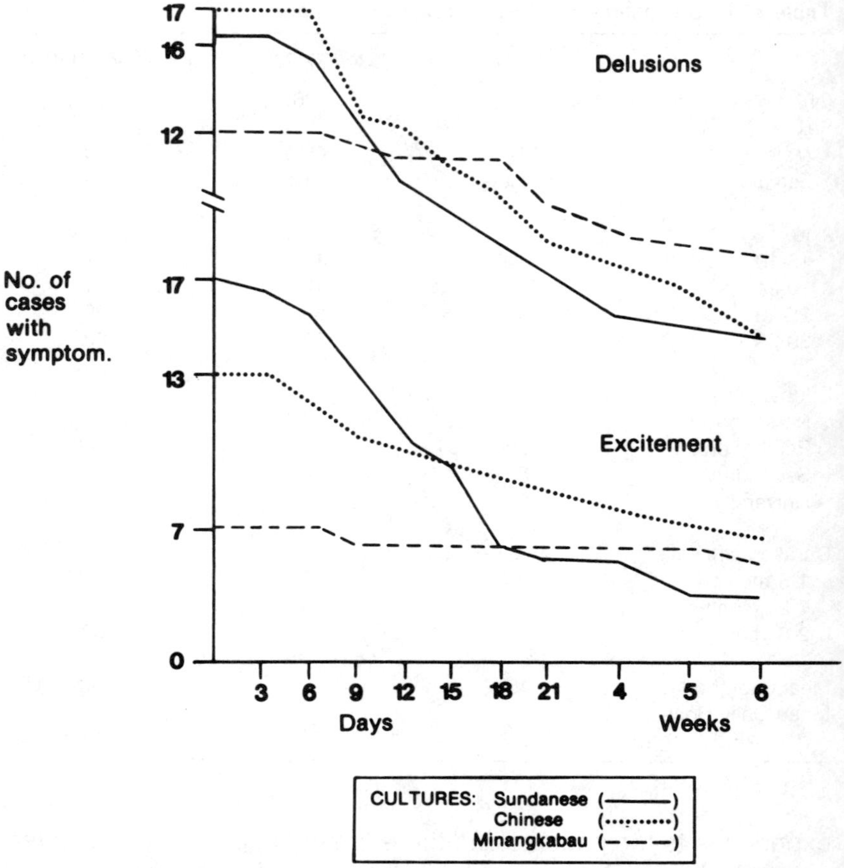

Figure 27.2 Disappearance of Symptoms Over Time. Drug: Trifluoperazine (Stelazine).

tion and age both showed some relationship to improvement on the four cited symptoms, but allowance for these appeared to alter the results on only one, hostility, by suggesting that the difference between the Minangkabau and the other two groups would have been increased had educational levels been more similar. In none of the cited symptoms did allowance for demographic factors appear to reduce the differences, although there were other symptoms where this was the case. Between the Chinese and the Sundanese there was a slight tendency for some symptoms to disappear more rapidly in the latter, but this only reached statistical significance for excitement.

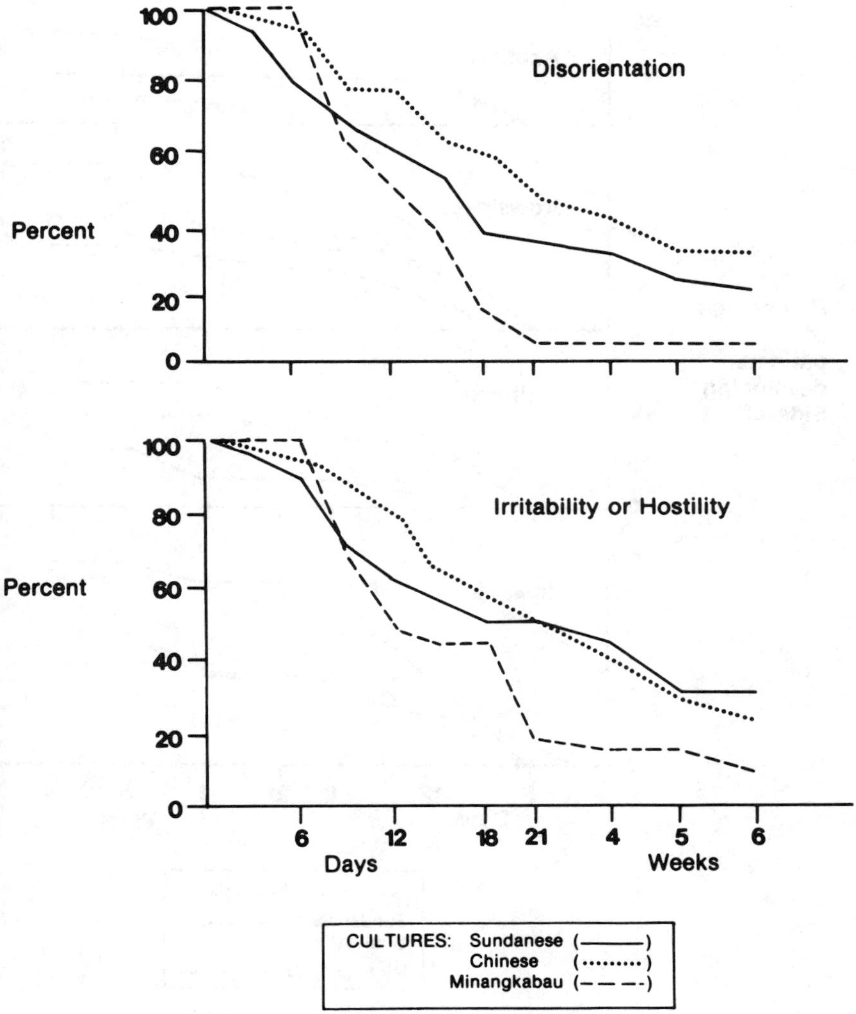

Figure 27.3 Disappearance of Symptoms Over Time. Drug: Trifluoperazine (Stelazine)

So much for symptom changes; what about side-effects? Eleven of these were recorded, and for the majority of them the Minangkabau scored proportionately higher than the other two groups. This is shown for representative categories in figure 27.4 where one sees that the difference applies both to those effects which the patient reports and those which the psychiatrist observes. Therefore, one

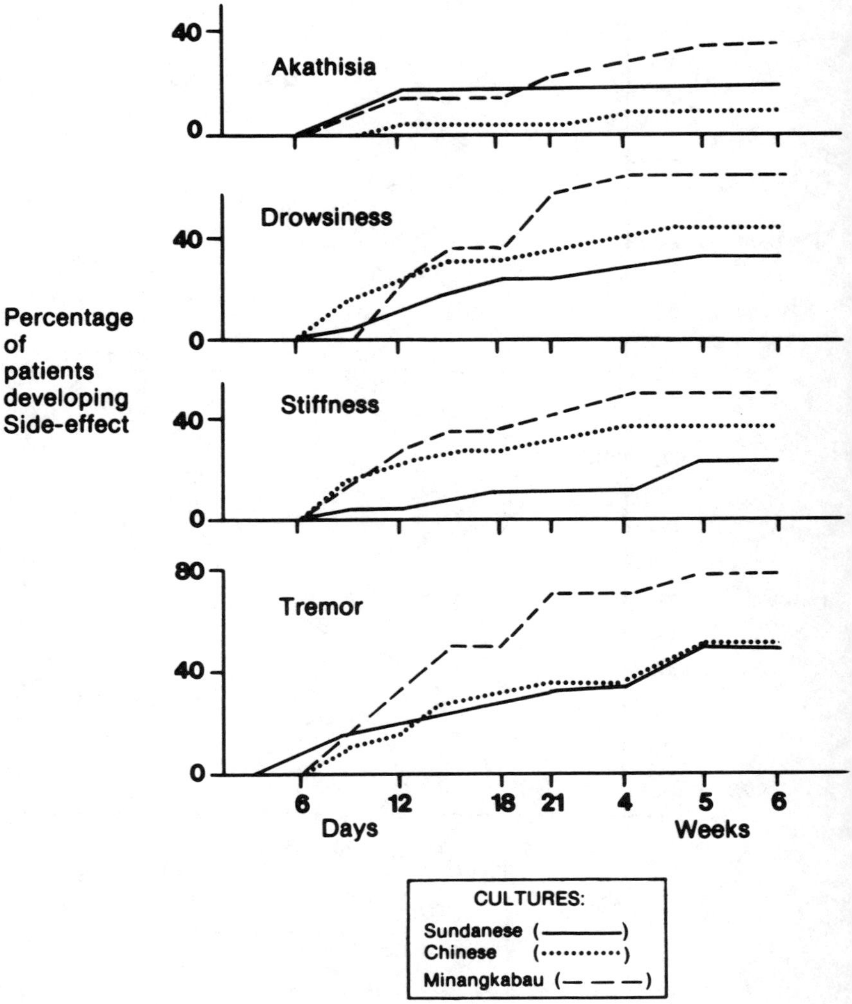

Figure 27.4 Side Effects. Drug: Trifluoperazine (Stelazine)

cannot attribute such difference to a higher complaint level or greater verbal facility on the part of the Minangkabau, and from table 27.1 it is easy to infer that it cannot be attributed to differences in dosage or in body weight either. Accordingly, there is a suggestion here that one is dealing not merely with nonspecific therapeutic effects but with something linked to the drug in question, and since the major differences are not between the two racial groups—Chinese on the one hand and Minangkabau plus Sundanese on the other—but between the Minangkabau and the Sundanese, this is not a finding that can easily be explained in terms of genetic influences on drug absorption and excretion.

French- and Anglo-Canadians

The other source of data lay in the fact that Drs. Heinz Lehmann and Thomas Ban of the Douglas Hospital, Montreal, have for many years been participating in the Early Clinical Drug Trials network and that a recent trial undertaken by the latter had been located not in the hospital itself but in two suburban clinics, one of which served almost entirely French-Canadian patients and the other mainly Anglo-Canadian. When the data came to be analyzed, it was noticed that although there were very slight differences between the two drugs being compared there were quite marked differences between the results reported by the two clinics. The doctors carrying out the actual clinical assessments at these clinics were not the same, but all concerned had been well trained in ECDTU methodology and it seemed quite unlikely that observer error could account for the obtained results. The data were therefore pointed out to the writer and eventually made available for reanalysis.

The drugs being compared were chlordiazepoxide (Librium) and a new anxiolytic, Doxepin. The patients were all suffering from some neurosis, often depressive, and attending the clinics at weekly intervals. While the groups assigned to each drug were well matched, the same degree of matching was not applied to the two clinic groups and hence there were significant differences in sex ratio, mean educational level, and mean social class. For these reasons it was decided before conducting a reanalysis of the findings to draw smaller and more suitable matched samples from the original totals, something which meant excluding males, women with more than a certain amount of education, and those above or below a chosen age range. This reduced the number of patients to be compared and increased the range of chance variation in their drug responses, but since the drugs were so similar in effect their results could be pooled. However, the dosage used was more important, as was duration of illness, and it was decided that these should be allowed for, as is shown in table 27.2, although their effect on the clinical differences eventually proved quite slight. Cul-

Table 27.2 Comparison of French-Canadian and Anglo-Canadian Female Neurotic Patients Treated with Anxiolytics Doxepin and Chlordiazepoxide.

	COMMENCING LEVEL		CRUDE IMPROVEMENT RATING		ADJUSTED IMPROVEMENT RATING		F RATIO (1,36)
	FRENCH	ANGLO	FRENCH	ANGLO	FRENCH	ANGLO	
Brief Psychiatric Rating Scale							
Somatic concern	3.85	3.23	8.0	8.4	6.8	11.1	1.933
Anxiety	4.70	4.38	9.3	9.3	8.8	3.9	2.820
Withdrawal	1.15	1.54	12.0	10.5	11.7	11.1	0.152
Guilt feelings	2.70	4.00**	11.1	3.0	10.9	3.4	5.374*
Tension	4.11	4.38	8.6	6.4	8.2	7.3	0.162
Depression	3.78	4.54*	8.5	5.0	7.9	6.3	0.242
Hostility	2.96	2.85	6.6	11.2	6.7	11.1	1.895
Suspiciousness	1.15	1.77	11.1	12.0	11.2	11.9	0.235
Motor retardation	2.04***	1.08	12.7	10.7	12.6	11.0	0.393
Excitement	1.78	2.23	8.8	7.2	9.5	5.8	1.559

Wittenborn							
Rating Scale							
1. (Task anxiety)	2.78	2.69	10.0	10.2	9.7	10.7	0.236
2. (Foreboding)	2.70	2.23	11.4	8.2	10.8	9.5	0.596
3. (Guilt)	2.11	2.46	10.7	6.4	10.5	6.7	4.800*
4. (Anxiety)	2.74	2.53	10.3	7.2	10.0	7.7	2.762
5. (Demanding)	2.33**	1.38	8.9	9.6	8.7	10.0	0.693
6. (Exploitative)	1.19	1.31	12.0	10.5	11.8	10.9	0.600
7. (Organic)	2.52*	1.69	9.3	10.0	9.0	10.5	0.423
8. (Phobic)	2.30	2.23	9.2	9.5	9.3	9.2	0.006
9. (Obsessive)	1.63	1.69	13.1	6.2	12.9	6.6	27.295***
10. (Compulsive)	1.15	1.85***	12.1	9.0	12.0	9.2	10.233**
11. (Indecision)	2.48	2.00	9.8	3.5	9.6	3.8	16.137***
12. (Avoidance)	2.33	2.31	9.4	10.3	9.2	11.1	0.845
14. (Overactive)	1.48	1.77	9.4	11.4	9.6	11.0	0.580
16. (Misconstruing)	2.37	2.31	8.1	7.4	8.2	7.1	1.095
Factor III (Obsessive-compulsive)	2.69	2.92	7.8	4.9	7.8	5.0	10.806**
SIDE-EFFECTS	–	–	2.00	0.23	2.05	0.13	14.664***

Improvement ratings were obtained by subtracting score at 4th week from score at commencement, with weights added to avoid zero and negative answers. Adjusted improvement ratings were obtained by analysis of covariance allowing for drug dosage and duration of symptomatology. Levels of significance at commencement and in F ratios are indicated by * = 0.05; * * = 0.01; * * * = 0.001. Table omits those scale-incorporated symptoms which were absent from either one of the samples at commencement.

tural or language background of the patients had not been recorded so that these had to be assumed on the basis of which clinic was used, but any error here would tend to obscure differences rather than exaggerate them.

Over most of the symptoms rated in this trial the two patient samples did not significantly differ, particularly if one allows for the fact that when so many variables are measured the 0.05 level of significance is not really acceptable. However, at two points there was a substantial difference, as the F-ratios in table 27.2 show. Obsessive-compulsive traits with an associated tendency to indecision improved much more in the French-Canadian patients than in the Anglo-Canadian, though the commencing levels for these symptoms were quite similar, and side effects were also much more often observed in the French-Canadians than in the Anglos. Due to the nature of the drugs used these side effects were usually not such as the psychiatrist could observe for himself, and it is thus legitimate to ask whether one is not dealing here merely with differences in complaint level, but logic would seem to argue against this. Some of the side effects were not such as a patient would be likely to mention if he had had no sensation on which to base his remark, and on the other hand there is no indication in the main part of table 27.2 that the commencing level of symptoms in the French-Canadians was higher than in the Anglo, something which one would have expected if the former had a general tendency to report abundant symptoms. Figure 27.5 shows the side effects reported by both groups.

Discussion

In each of the three drug trials reviewed here—the only ones which the writer has so far been able to find that permit reanalysis with a focus on ethnicity—the outcomes of treatment have shown a greater association with that ethnicity than would have been expected by chance. This cannot be attributed to different races or cultures producing different symptom constellations for the same disease, since the reanalyses have deliberately focused on single symptoms and avoided global assessments. It also probably cannot be attibuted to differences in treatment setting and personnel, since the Djakarta patients were all treated in the same setting and dis-

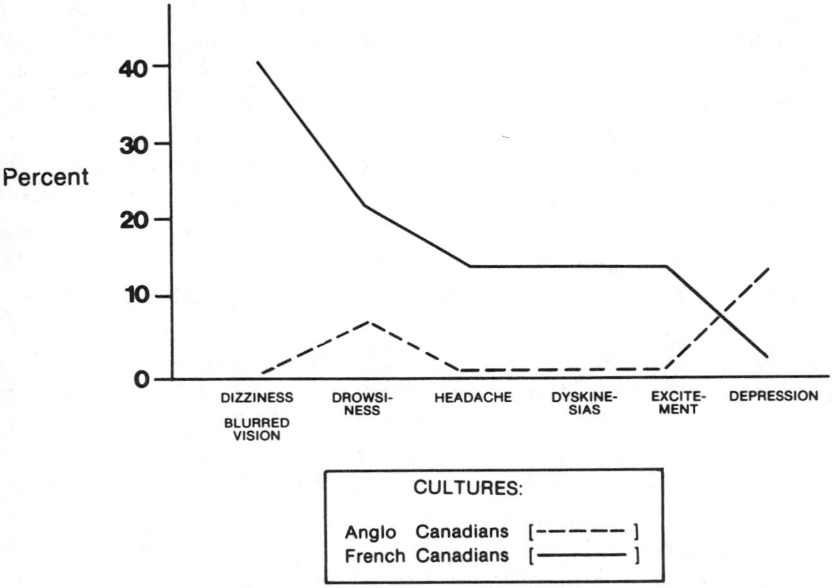

Figure 27.5 Side Effects. Restructured Samples. Drugs: Chlordiazepoxide (Librium) Doxepin

tributed in an unselected fashion among the therapists. Thirdly, rough matching on such outcome-relevant variables as duration of illness, education, and dosage, plus correction for them when necessary during the analysis, makes attribution of the results to these variables unlikely. But there remain many other possible explanations and these now call for closer examination.

Probably the simplest and most easily accepted explanation would be to say that the differences in outcome had nothing to do with the medications provided, but were nonspecific. Recent studies have shown that U.S. Negroes show a better short-term recovery from the functional psychoses than U.S. Whites, regardless of the drug used (Overall et al. 1969), and that the long-term prognosis for schizophrenia in East Indians and Africans is better than that in British patients (Murphy and Raman 1971). One may think of these results as reflecting a racially based difference in the character of mental disease or a culturally based difference in the patients' responses to the nonspecific aspects of the treatment process, without involving specific pharmacotherapies at all. However, in the trials reviewed above, a greater general improvement in one ethnic group than in another was found only with thioridazine. With trifluoperazine the Minangkabau showed significantly less improvement than the other groups in some symptoms but significantly more improvement than the latter in others; and with the anxiolytics the French-Canadians' symptoms do not in general improve more than the Anglo-Canadians'. Moreover, the rate of disappearance of delusions in Chinese patients was significantly more rapid under trifluoperazine than under thioridazine, whereas this symptom disappeared just as rapidly with the latter drug as with the former among the Sundanese. And finally, although speed of recovery in different ethnic groups might be nonspecific, the development of side effects to one drug and no side effects to another is clearly related to the pharmacotherapy, and this also shows marked ethnic variation. Accordingly, if one rules out the possibility of all these results being no more than the extremes of chance variation—a most unlikely fact that can only be ruled out by repeating the trials—then it seems reasonable to conclude that the differences relate to the pharmacotherapy and not to the nonspecific aspects of the disease and setting.

But though the differences probably relate to the pharmacotherapy, this is not to say that they need relate to the specific action of the drugs concerned. The acceptance and absorption of the drugs can vary from one ethnic group to another, and these were not matters which the chosen trials investigated. It is well known that in some treatment settings the patients resist taking their medication, either because they do not believe in it, or dislike its effects, or (in countries where drugs are scarce) in order to sell it to other patients. Moreover, dietary habits can affect the absorption of medication taken by mouth. In the present instances such concealed influences on the absorbed dosage might have affected the thioridazine results and to a lesser extent those from the anxiolytics, but fortunately it seems highly unlikely that they could have produced such results with the trifluoperazine. The Minangkabau could have absorbed higher doses of the drug and hence have experienced more side effects, as was observed, but then we would not have expected them to have retained their delusions longer, unless one is prepared to argue that delusions respond less to the specific drug action than to the nonspecifics or placebo effect of the treatment setting, as has been hinted at by Goldberg et al. (1965). Clearly this is something which should be looked into in any future research on the subject, but since it is ignored in most drug trials we can leave it aside for the present, particularly as Pfeiffer (1969) has shown that Indonesian and Chinese patients treated with intramuscular depot fluphenazine responded no better than those treated with that drug by mouth.

The arguments used against the results being due to differences in absorption of the drugs apply also, up to a point, to the possibility of genetic factors modifying the drug's fate within the body. None of the drugs employed in these trials is known to be affected by genetically variable enzyme systems (Vesell 1969), but since pharmacogenetics is a young science this does not exclude the possibility that some might be. If they were, and if the relevant enzyme system merely affected the availability or excretion of the active form of the drug, then this is essentially the same as affecting its absorption and the above argument applies. However, there is the possibility of the absorbed drug being converted into more than one secondary form within the body, as has been demonstrated for cocaine (Montesinos 1965) and if such secondary forms had different effects on the symptomatology then the results observed with the trifluoperazine could theoretically still be produced, provided there were sufficient genetic difference between the Minangkabau and Sundanese. The major obstacle to a genetic explanation of present findings is that although the Chinese and Indonesians (Malaysians) show clear genetic differences, there is virtually nothing in blood group data, etc. to indicate the presence of such differences between either the Minangkabau and Sundanese or the French-Canadians and Anglo-Canadians.

These considerations leave us with cultural factors as the main possible explanations still to be examined. Culture is known to be able to affect symptomatology and it is easy to imagine how it might affect the patients' response to the nonspecific aspects of the treatment situation, but neither of these types of influence go far enough. In order for culture to be able to produce the present results it is necessary for it to influence either the basic personality structure on which the drugs operate or the way the patients react to the sensations the drugs produce. The latter possibility is probably the easier to accept since it would harmonize quite well with one of the main theories respecting paradoxical reactions to psychotropic drugs, but the former provides wider scope. If one accepts the idea that patients can perceive the effects which drugs induce as either helpful or threatening, as controlling and soothing or as breaking down self-control (Azima and Sarwer-Foner 1961), then it is not too much of an extension to think of culture as helping to determine these perceptions. We are not concerned here with frankly paradoxical reactions, of course, but it seems quite likely that some patients fight the effect of a drug on their minds while others cooperate with it and that such cooperation or resistance is stronger for some aspects of the psyche than for others. If so, then there is nothing inconsistent in the Minangkabau clinging to their delusional systems at the same time as they are becoming more oriented and less hostile under the effect of the trifluoperazine, and nothing inconsistent either in the fact that patients of different cultures should complain in different degrees about the drowsiness or dizziness that a drug induces. Where this hypothesis does get into difficulties is with respect to those side effects that are not so much felt by the patient as observed by the psychiatrist—the tremors, akathisia, etc. One can readily imagine that a certain type of upbringing might make a patient highly sensitive to what is happening in his own mind, but it is difficult to see why such sensitivity should be reflected in the extrapyramidal signs. If it can be confirmed that the latter signs vary in intensity with the patient's culture, as is suggested not only by the present data but by the fuller results of Denber et al. (1961) then sensitization of the patient's awareness seems an insufficient explanation for the variations observed. Is there any other concept relating culture to personality and to psychopathology which fits the data better?

Empirical results suggesting that personality or culture can affect susceptibility to extrapyramidal disturbances have been reported by Makela (1967) and by Bente et al. (1968) but in neither case is there any real indication as to how such an influence would work. Bente's data, deriving from elaborate EEG analyses, are particularly impressive and indicate that we are not dealing here with differences in complaint level or in subjective psychiatric judgments. The most likely explanation for these findings lies in the effect of culture on the mind's watchfulness and attention to stimuli, for Bente's data show that the group which developed the most extrapyramidal disturbances was the one whose "vigilance" pattern on EEG was most reduced by butaperazine. Even this formulation is probably too simple, however, since Pfeiffer and Gebelein (1969) have shown that the type of extrapyramidal disturbance induced by a phenothiazine varies with race or culture. German patients exhibited mainly dyskinetic disturbances such as akathisia and torticollis, whereas Indonesian patients exhibited mainly hypokinetic side effects. All this work is quite recent, however, and it is clear that convincing answers are going to depend on results from a field of psychophysiology that has not yet really been touched. The differences uncovered by Pfeiffer and Gebelein could be racial, but those reported by Bente seem far more likely to be cultural.

Our conclusion at this stage must be, therefore, that although the evidence for a racial or cultural influence on the functioning of psychotropics is impressive, we cannot yet say how this influence works. In view of the fact that Sundanese patients responded equally well to thioridazine and trifluoperazine whereas Chinese patients apparently did much less well on the former than on the latter drug the question has immediate, practical relevance. Such differences need to be tested afresh, and it might also be helpful to search other prior drug trials for overlooked evidence relating to ethnic group.

Acknowledgment

Geigy (Canada) Ltd. kindly defrayed the cost of collecting and abstracting the Djakarta data.

Annotated Additional Readings

a) Mayo, J. A. 1974. The significance of socio-cultural variables in the psychiatric treatment of black outpatients. *Comprehensive Psychiatry* 15:471–482.
An exploration of some of the social and cultural factors that appear to account for the frequently noted underutilization by blacks of urban mental health facilities in the U.S., and how the typically white staff perceive the condition of black patients and respond to their requests for psychiatric care. Upon analyzing patient evaluation and care statistics at a community mental health center in New York's Greenwich Village, the author notes that factors such as language, cognitive style, appearance, and behavior of black patients were likely to be mislabeled as grossly pathological and/or deficient and not amendable to traditional forms of outpatient treatment. This article illustrates some of the issues discussed in article 24.

b) Iwai, H. and D. K. Reynolds. 1970. Morita psychotherapy: The views from the West. *The American Journal of Psychiatry* 126:1031–1036.
A review of the psychotherapy program developed by Professor Shoma Morita of Jikei University in Tokyo for a Japanese form of neurosis called *shinkei-shitsusho,* characterized by escalating cycles of hypochondriacal tendencies, self-consciousness, and social ineffectiveness. The treatment program typically involves hospitalization, a period of absolute bed rest, and then engagement in increasingly tiring and self-monitored jobs, with the understanding that to work well and to behave normally despite the symptoms is the proper course to recovery and to a satisfactory life. Five topics are singled out: (1) the relationship between Morita psychotherapy and Zen Buddhism, (2) the concept of *arugamama* (the acceptance of phenomenological reality "as it is"), (3) absolute bed rest, (4) work therapy, and (5) the efficacy of Morita therapy outside of Japan. This article discusses a form of therapy developed in and for a particular non-Western culture which is now receiving attention in the West and which illustrates issues raised in article 25.

c) Torrey, E. F. 1972. What Western psychotherapists can learn from witchdoctors. *American Journal of Orthopsychiatry* 42:69–76.
The author, well known for his iconoclastic views, elucidates fascinating similarities between Western psychotherapists and witchdoctors, complementing this way Jerome Frank's (1972) work on general commonalities among psychotherapies. Concluding that similar basic principles are held by both modalities of psychotherapy, the author pleads for a learning and reflexive attitude when looking at healing procedures different from our own as a way of enhancing the progress of psychiatric care.

d) Jilek-Aall, L. 1976. The Western psychiatrist and his non-Western clientele. *Canadian Psychiatric Association Journal* 21:353–359.

Using her extensive medical experience with African tribes and Canadian Indians, the author reviews some crucial cultural differences between the typical Western middle-class psychiatrist and nonwestern tradition-oriented patients, and the effects of these differences on psychotherapeutic interaction. She also discusses the responsibility of the psychiatrist working with non-Western patients for acquiring sufficient knowledge of the patient's culture to evaluate appropriately psychiatric disorder, vis-à-vis culturally determined pseudopathological states, and to determine whether an indigenous healer would not be of more benefit to the patient than Western psychiatry. This paper is a useful complement to the discussions presented in articles 25 and 26.

e) **Fabrega, H., and P. K. Manning. 1972.** Health maintenance among Peruvian peasants. *Human Organization* 31:243–256.

An elegant theoretical and experimental examination of health-related behavior of peasants from the Peruvian highlands. The authors note that this people exhibit a pervasive concern with the functioning of their bodies and that their regular use of herbs is addressed to relieve or avoid unpleasant bodily feelings or disturbances. The theoretical analysis of the social aspects of using herbs employs the framework of symbolic interactionism. The experimental study is based on a survey of the associations reported by 40 peasants between each of 18 herbs of frequent local use and each of 18 disturbances that tend to occasion herb usage. For each herb, a profile of its reported specific usage for the 18 disturbances was obtained. A similar profile across the 18 herbs was obtained for each disturbance. On the basis of these profiles, a typology of herbs and a typology of disturbances of them were elucidated. The above issues and findings were interpreted from the perspective of the individual's motivation to maintain his health in the harsh environment of the highlands.

IX

Psychiatry as a Social Institution

Psychiatry as the art and science of diagnosing and treating mental disorders does not happen in a vacuum but within the framework of the views and values, resources and priorities of a given society. It formally constitutes a social institution as it represents the way that society deals with its mentally ill.

Psychiatrists and other mental health professionals as members of a given society are exposed and largely subject to the prevailing cultural ideology and they practice according to its sociopolitical and economic conditions and constraints. For example, a psychiatrist in the Soviet Union will focus efforts on the recovery of the patient's social and occupational functioning as the prevailing ideology holds that the actualization of the person takes place through the fulfillment of socially productive roles. On the other hand, a typical psychiatrist in the U.S. will focus attention on enhancing the patient's autonomy and self-sufficiency, as the prevailing ideology emphasizes individual competition and victoriousness.

Social resources and priorities also crucially influence psychiatric services. For example, in an industrially underdeveloped country, malnutrition and infectious diseases are usually the major health problems. Under these circumstances, such a country will tend to assign to mental health care a very small proportion of its typically meager resources.

The articles here review the roots, orientation, service organization, professional manpower and training, and future perspectives of psychiatry in various parts of the world, with a focus on non-Western and/or industrially underdeveloped countries. The first article examines how the orientation and organization of psychiatry is influenced by the Marxist-Leninist and industrialized sociopolitical system of the Soviet Union. Two other articles deal with various industrially developing countries or regions, all of which show a contact between their rich medical and psychiatric histories and the currently critical and challenging situation of their mental health care systems. Particularly interesting are attempts made in some of these countries to integrate Westernized and folk healing systems.

28

Psychiatry in the Soviet Union Today

John T. Salvendy

The study of psychiatry as a social institution in the Union of Soviet Socialist Republics is of great interest given the prominent position of this country in the world and the conceptual and practical importance of its cultural system.

As it would be expected in any society, basic values and norms in the USSR influence all aspects of life, including psychiatry. For example, the emphasis on socially productive work influences the definition of adaptive functioning, treatment methodology, and criteria for assessing recovery.

In the following article, John Salvendy, a Hungarian-born psychiatrist on the faculty of the University of Toronto in Canada, presents his observations and reflections on the organization of clinical services, professional training, and forensic procedures in Soviet psychiatry, on the basis of his evaluation of the available literature and a visit he made to the Soviet Union during October 1973.

History

THE ORGANIZATION of health care was among the early tasks of the post-revolutionary Soviet government. As a part of this effort, early recognition and treatment of psychiatric and neurological diseases were deemed to be important. In Moscow and Leningrad in 1920 the first network of neuropsychiatric dispensaries was started to provide outpatient treatment. At this time the foundations were also laid for a large number of scientific institutes, psychiatric hospitals, after-care and rehabilitative settings, and facilities for the continuing education of psychiatrists (Degenhardt 1973; Wing 1974). This period of expansion came to an abrupt halt during World War II, when a substantial part of the psychiatric facilities was destroyed or severely damaged. This contributed to the heavy emphasis on the ambulant treatment of psychiatric patients in the Soviet Union as it exists today.

Although from the very beginning the mental health field has been an exclusively medical domain, there has been little interaction between psychiatrists and other medical colleagues. The idea of having a psychiatric department as part of a general hospital has not caught on in the USSR, and it was against considerable resistance that a few such units were established in the five-year plan that ended in 1975 (Degenhardt 1973). Probably the best cooperation has been maintained with neurologists, who have traditionally been treating patients with gross brain damage, such as geriatric populations with senile and arteriosclerotic dementias, epileptics, chronic alcoholics, syphilitic patients, and so on.

Organization

Central planning and tight organization are characteristic of mental health care delivery in the Soviet Union. An excellent detailed description of the facilities involved is available in Lebensohn (1962).

Most psychiatric facilities are under the aegis of the Ministry of Health, but some are under the control of the Ministry of Social Affairs.

As the organizational aspects of Soviet psychiatry have received attention (Allen 1973; Bellak 1969; Degenhardt 1973; Kolb 1966; Lebensohn 1962; National Institute of Mental Health 1969; Singer 1969; Torrey 1971; Yolles 1968), this paper will be limited to a short review. In the outpatient-oriented Soviet psychiatry the dispensary takes a focal place, and the overwhelming majority of patients are treated in these centers. There are about three thousand polyclinics in the USSR which have a neuropsychiatric department, and approximately 150 independent neuropsychiatric dispensaries, mainly in the large cities. These dispensaries have an average catchment population of 300,000–400,000. The staff consists of 15 to 25 psychiatrists and at least as many nurses.

The outpatient service of the neuropsychiatric dispensary receives its patients either from the polyclinics or from followup of patients in the catchment area. The inpatient unit has between 30 and 75 beds and serves as a diagnostic observation unit and as an acute treatment center. Workshops are an integral part of the dispensary, and the patients are engaged in useful, productive work for which they are remunerated. Social and vocational services do not represent a separate department but a separate task, and are carried out by the psychiatrists and/or the nurses. Primary prevention is provided by psychiatrists mainly in the form of lectures and talks to organizations such as schools, factories, and trade unions. Among the main topics are the furthering of group and social values and the dangers of alcohol abuse. A special feature in the set-up of the dispensaries are home visits by psychiatrists and nurses. The catchment area is subdivided so that each doctor and nurse is allotted a small area where, theoretically, they know all acutely ill patients as well as those in need of active follow up. The minimum quota for every psychiatrist is twenty home visits per month to patients who do not show up for their appointments, or where the family has requested a reassessment of the patient.

The Soviet mental hospitals are far less numerous than their counterparts in North America or in Western Europe. They are smaller in size and do not occupy a central role in psychiatric treatment. Emergency teams are either associated with the neuropsychiatric dispensary or are part of the general ambulance service (Torrey 1971). Sanatoria, which are frequently located in resort areas, are used for convalescence, both for physical and emotional illnesses—particularly for the treatment of neuroses. Future planning includes an increase in the number of mental hospitals, but any given facility will be limited to a maximum of 500 beds (National Institute of Mental Health 1969).

Reviewing the rather impressive array of psychiatric facilities available in the Soviet Union, it is nevertheless hard to ignore some intriguing facts. If the official version of the impressive quality and quantity of psychiatric care is true, one wonders why most Western psychiatrists have been shown the same few facilities, and have been exposed to the same small group of Soviet colleagues. Even taking into account the natural tendency of any country to show its best facilities, it is likely that the present facilities are merely showpieces. These doubts will persist until other psychiatric facilities are made available on a larger scale and in greater variety to the Western visitor. After evaluating the literature (Bazelon 1968; Bellak 1969; Field and Aronson 1965; Hein 1968; Kline et al. 1961; Kolb 1966; National Institute of Mental Health 1969; Singer 1969; Torrey 1971; Wing 1974; Yolles 1968) and gathering personal impressions, this author is concerned about the relevance to the everyday practice of the theoretical information conveyed to Western colleagues. Anecdotal comments about staff enthusiasm in a few facilities shown (Gorman 1969; National Institute of Mental Health 1969; Ziferstein 1966b; Yolles 1968) cannot be taken at face value as that behavior was exhibited in carefully selected locations.

Research and teaching are to a large extent separated. There are nine research institutes for psychiatry (the majority being in the European part of the USSR), which operate under the auspices and direction of the Medical Academy of Sciences. Each institute specializes in one particular field, and obtains its patients from an attached mental hospital. Thus, the Institute of Psychiatry in Moscow conducts research into the genetics of schizophrenia, while the Bekhterev Institute in Leningrad is primarily involved in research in psychophysiology, behavior modification, and psychotherapy. Research psychiatrists are fully qualified specialists, who have to obtain a certain academic standing (through thesis presentation and examinations) before they are accepted for their positions or recommended for promotions. They have no teaching obligations. Most of the researchers specialize early in a narrow field. The organization of these institutes is distinctly hierarchical and the prevailing atmosphere is authoritarian. Although research publications seem to be available from all over the world, closest contacts are maintained with the central and East European countries, and particularly with those who are German-speaking.

Most of the training for medical students and, to a lesser extent, for psychiatrists in training is conducted in the 80 departments of psychiatry, which are composed of mental hospitals designated for that specific purpose.

Treatment

Organic approaches to treatment prevail. Most of the major tranquillizers are widely used, both for psychotic and nonpsychotic patients. The dosages are frequently somewhat higher than those given in North America (National Institute of Mental Health 1969). ECT and insulin sub-coma treatment are both used relatively extensively. The use of electro-sleep, which several years ago was widespread, now is not used so much. Among minor tranquillizers the variety is not as rich as in the Western countries, and more of the older sedatives and hypnotics such as barbiturates are used. There is widespread belief that vitamins in small to moderate doses have a "strengthening" effect in various mental disorders, and they are frequently given (mostly by injection) for alcoholics, in various forms of neuroses and in personality disorders (Portnov and Fedotov 1969).

The significance of the "medical model" in the treatment of mental disorders is obvious because psychiatric orientation tends to be more physiological than psychological. Much attention is given to the possibly physiological impairment as an underlying source of psychiatric illness.

Work therapy plays a central role in the rehabilitative efforts of the Soviet psychiatrist. In the light of Marxist ideology it is considered to be the foundation upon which the social readaptation of the psychiatric patient is based (Wortis and Freundlich 1964). The therapeutic workshop, which has very little to do with old-fashioned concepts of occupational therapy, is ubiquitous in the Russian psychiatric network. Most of these workshops are attached to neuropsychiatric dispensaries and mental hospitals, and are directed by a psychiatrist who has the required expertise in work therapy. He is frequently assisted by an economist and a rehabilitation expert or engineer. The patients in these workshops are paid for their labor and produce anything from simple tools to electronic devices.

Psychotherapy, as practiced in the Soviet Union, is a short-term, directive procedure. The therapist assumes an active role in which he advises and guides his patient through his day-to-day problems. He tries to strengthen the patient's self-esteem, reassures him and personally intervenes in his everyday realities. The ultimate goal in treatment is to enable the patient to engage in socially productive work and to function as a "useful" member of society. In order to achieve this the therapist reeducates the patient and clearly conveys to him the moral values and priorities of his Marxist society (Allen 1973; Ziferstein 1966b, 1968,1972). The length of sessions are said to be anywhere from a couple of minutes to a couple of hours, but most seem to be less than half-an-hour.

Psychoanalysis is not practiced as it is considered to be "idealistic," that is, not scientific and certainly not "materialistic." Hypnosis for individuals or in groups is frequently used in the treatment of neurosis and alcoholism. Behavior modification, mainly along Pavlovian lines but also the reciprocal inhibition type, is practiced to a limited extent.

Group psychotherapy or "collective" psychotherapy, as it is called in the Soviet Union, is used in a large variety of instances. Its theoretical foundations originate primarily from the field of education and were strongly influenced by the thoughts of Makarenko. The result has been a major emphasis on education and reeducation, taking advantage of the decisive influence of the peer group collective under the guidance of the therapist, who is their "teacher of life" (Bazelon 1968). Emotional support and guidance are also offered. The most significant criterion of cure in Soviet psychiatry is the "restoration of the patient's ability to function as a member of a collective and to engage in socially productive work" (Ziferstein 1972).

Psychotherapy resembles the more classical type of counselling and guidance given by social workers in North America, as Soviet psychotherapy attempts to be reality oriented, directive, and supportive. This treatment modality, although available to the patient in larger cities, has many pitfalls, both to the therapist and to the patient. The former has little choice but to adopt the prevailing ideological and philosophical dogma and operate within its limits. Assuming this, it is hard not to question either the spontaneity and enthusiasm (National Institute of Mental Health 1969; Ziferstein 1966b, 1968, 1972) of the psychiatrist or his moral authority and sincerity, should he not share these philosophies. On the other hand, the patient is forced, at a time of utmost need, to seek help from a physician who cherishes the collective's values above all and is closely identified as a protector of rigid social mores. There seems to be little room for open and individualized discussion of feelings and thoughts in a setting heavily favoring indoctrination and environmental manipulation.

One wonders about the feasibility and therapeutic effects of the "no fixed appointment, no fixed duration (of individual sessions) approach" in psychotherapy (National Institute of Mental Health 1969; Ziferstein 1966b). It is not necessary to agree fully with Bellak's criticism that "If community mental health services have sometimes been defined as a system of delivering emotional help to the people who need it, much of Russian psychiatry strikes me as a very good postal service with very little to deliver" (Bellak 1969), but it certainly merits careful consideration.

The Professionals

Eighty percent of psychiatrists (and 70–75 percent of all physicians) are women. The medical school begins after eleven years of primary and secondary education, and lasts for six years. Following graduation all physicians are required to spend three years service as general practitioners in an area designated by the health authorities (Degenhardt 1973; National Institute of Mental Health 1969; Yolles 1968).

Information available upon the duration of the psychiatric training is somewhat conflicting. The residency can last anywhere from one to three years, the longer training being a preparation for research careers in one of the designated institutes. This specialty training is mostly given in a mental hospital or a neuropsychiatric dispensary under the supervision of the senior psychiatric staff. At the end of the training there is no national certification similar to that in Canada or the United States. Instead, the candidate is examined and certified by the senior staff of the facility where he got his training. A psychiatrist who wishes to teach or do research has to take an additional two years of research work, at the end of which he has to write a thesis. There is a strong emphasis on continuing education, and every five years three to five months are spent on fully paid post graduate refresher courses.

The average psychiatrist spends six hours a day at work. However, because of the relatively low remuneration (psychiatrists receive only slightly more than a skilled worker, in spite of the fact that a regular "hardship" bonus is added to the salary) a second job in a clinic, hospital or another facility is often taken. Private practice is apparently theoretically legal, but because of the low fees allowed it is neither lucrative nor widespread (Steinberg 1973). Western scientific publications are accessible to psychiatrists working in research and to senior staff of teaching hospitals. Most other psychiatrists and medical students are offered mainly Russian translations often well-edited and with ideological interpretations (Portnov and Fedotov 1969). The impression is that the competence of the research psychiatrist can be favorably compared to his colleagues in the West, but the practicing psychiatrist seems to have a rather narrow field of knowledge (Wing 1974). This is due to a short training, early subspecialization, inadequate exposure to foreign scientific work, and limitations imposed on his therapeutic work by prevailing ideology.

An enormous responsibility is placed on the psychiatric nurse, particularly in the dispensaries. Aside from her traditional role, she also assumes those of the social worker and public health nurse. Her training takes three years and is usually conducted in a mental hospital. Further education through on-the-job guidance and experience and refresher courses after graduation are encouraged. The nurse does a considerable amount of active counselling and guidance, works with the family, the neighbors, members of the patient's collective, whether at work or at school, and is strongly involved in the patient's social rehabilitation (Kolb 1966; National Institute of Mental Health 1969; Singer 1969).

The *feldsher,* or medical technician, receives three years of training in general nursing and one year additional training in the speciality he chooses. In psychiatry he occupies a position between the nurse and the psychiatrist, and his involvement is primarily in the medical aspects of psychiatric treatment.

Many neuropsychiatric dispensaries have on their staff a "narcologist," who is either a psychiatrist or an internist specializing in the treatment of alcoholism (other addictions are said to be rare). Aside from aversive therapies and drug treatment the narcologist checks the work situation and job capacity of the alcoholic. Increasingly, more clinics employ a sexologist who is also a marital counsellor. The psychiatrist in this latter role does not differ in his approach from his other colleagues and he relies heavily on simple advice-giving and rather naïve environmental manipulations. In the treatment of sexual disorders very little behavior modification and none of the Masters and Johnson techniques are being practised. Psychologists are limited to intelligence testing and research and are not involved in any clinical work.

The Patient

Patients in the Soviet Union benefit from a large network of prophylactic and treatment facilities offered free of charge and with a reasonable degree of availability, at least in the large cities. Focal points of intervention, education and treatment are the kindergartens, the schools, the residential settings, the work situation, and the trade unions. Patients experience job security which is unparalleled in most Western countries. This notion represents a strong positive impetus for the rehabilitative effort.

Not all groups benefit equally from the help available, the psychotic patients being rather comprehensively looked after, but the same cannot be said of the neurotic patients and those suffering from personality disorders. Intrapsychic aspects of the illness are largely ignored and their problems are seen as being due to physiological or neurological dysfunction. Aberrant social behavior is often diagnosed in this group which is said to arise out of faulty learning.

Alcoholism is a most serious problem and constitutes a large percentage of the patient population in the neuropsychiatric dispensaries, in day and night hospitals, and in clinics attached to factories. A determined if not very successful effort is being made by the health authorities on the prophylactic, treatment and rehabilitative levels in order to deal with this immense problem.

Intoxicated persons are picked up by the police and taken to "sobering-up stations" attached to jails, where they are looked after by a team consisting of a physician, aided by a nurse or *feldsher.* An inebriated person either spends the night in this unit and is driven home next day by the police or he is transferred to a hospital. This treatment, unlike any other medical treatment in the Soviet Union, is not free of charge. However, according to present legislation all alcoholics are required to take treatment (National Institute of Mental Health 1969). At the same time the alcoholic's job is kept and his rights are protected. Neuroleptics, chlordiazepoxide, nicotinic acid, vitamins (particularly B complex), and various aversive therapies are widely used. Other therapeutic efforts include individual and marital counselling, group therapy, individual and group hypnosis and social coercive methods (Gorman 1969; National Institute of Mental Health 1969; Portnov and Fedotov 1969).

Child Psychiatry

The organizational set-up is similar to that of adult psychiatry. The theoretical orientation is decisively organic, almost to the total exclusion of possible psychological or interpersonal factors. In all the neuropsychiatric dispensaries great emphasis is placed on speech disorders and a logotherapist is a consistent figure on the staff of these facilities. Long-term treatment of more severe cases is carried out in mental hospitals specifically designated for children.

Child psychiatrists in the Soviet Union have to be graduates of a pediatric post-graduate training and they are not accepted for this course until they have at least three years of practice as pediatricians. There is no prescribed duration for training in child psychiatry but it usually lasts one to two years.

Continuity of followup is one of the hallmarks of the Russian child psychiatric system. The psychiatrist is expected to follow up his patient from the day of contact until the child reaches fifteen years of age. At that age the patient's file is transferred to an adjacent special neuropsychiatric clinic for adolescents, where further after-care is assured until the patient reaches the age of eighteen, when the file is transferred to the closest adult neuropsychiatric dispensary (Gorman 1969).

Forensic Psychiatry

In the forensic psychiatry judiciary in the Soviet Union there is no place for the adversary system. The psychiatrist wields decisive power, both in criminal and civil proceedings. The lawyer and the judge act as mere adjuncts to the psychiatrist or the hospital administration. In the dispensaries and polyclinics lawyers look after the patient's pension, job situation, and his insurance rights regarding disabilities. They act like legal social workers (Bazelon 1968). The judge basically invokes the specific legal consequences of the patient's behavior in relevance to the psychiatrist's decision regarding the culpability of the patient.

The Russian view of criminal responsibility is similar to the one accepted in Canada and the United States. Basically it implies the accused's knowledge and/or control of his action at the time of the deed. Emphasis is laid on organic evidence or other quantifiable physiological and psychological changes (Bazelon 1968). On medicolegal psychiatric commissions no lawyers are included. If the accused is found to be nonimputable he is subjected to compulsory treatment, which is similar to a civil commitment to a mental hospital in the vicinity of his residence. The patient under compulsory treatment is entitled to be reexamined every six months to determine whether he should be transferred to another facility or even released.

The Soviet view of voluntary hospitalization is much wider than in the West. It includes requests by the patient's family, his colleagues at work, his trade union and the physician at the polyclinic or neuropsychiatric dispensary (Bazelon 1968; National Institute of Mental Health 1969). The rationale behind this generous interpretation has to do with the Russian notion that if a patient had been able to make a logical decision he would have asked for the hospitalization himself. In the context it is important to realize that the concept of schizophrenia in the Soviet Union is also quite wide (Ziferstein 1966a). A large number of personality disorders and mentally non-ill people exhibiting politically undesirable behavior are included in this category. Their ideological and social aberrations are seen as signs of a severe maladjustment of a possible psychotic extent.

The Russian criteria for involuntary commitment are similar to those used in Canada and the United States, that is that the patient as a result of his mental disturbance must be dangerous to himself or others. In the Soviet Union a patient can be certified only by a psychiatrist. Within 24 hours after the patient's admission to hospital he has to be reviewed by a commission, consisting of three psychiatrists who will determine whether further involuntary commitment is necessary. This commission is governed by directions issued by the Ministry of Health, which in turn has been coordinated with the Ministry of Internal Affairs. The latter's instructions allow for commitment of a citizen even if he is not visibly dangerous, pointing out that some mental illnesses "which contain doubtless social dangers may be accompanied by extremely correct behavior and dissimulation" (National Institute of Mental Health, 1969). Although the patient is entitled to a reexamination by a three-man panel at least once a month, this is an obivous loophole for the authorities and collaborating psychiatrists to abuse the wide interpretation issued by the Ministries of Health and Internal Affairs. There is no doubt that having legal backing and being a product of a strongly collective oriented society, where adherence to the common norms and values are of preeminent importance, some Soviet psychiatrists will find the above ruling applicable to not a few political dissidents. It should also be kept in mind that the alternative to an involuntary commitment is frequently a confinement to a remote labor camp for several years. Thus, the Soviet colleagues might at times choose what they regard as the lesser evil.

If and when the psychiatric committee finds the patient improved and no longer dangerous to himself or to the public, he is discharged to the custody of his family or to a guardian, and will be followed up by the local neuropsychiatric dispensary.

In Soviet legislation there is no provision for a judiciary review of civil commitment proceedings. Although the Russians maintain that the Ministry of Health keeps a constant watch over the civil commitment system and that the patient's family, colleagues, and party organization would protest if he were improperly committed, one certainly cannot but agree with Bazelon's concern about the dubious effectiveness of such a system (Bazelon 1968).

Alcoholism and drug addiction are not considered to be mental illnesses and therefore cannot be dealt with by civil commitment procedures.

Conclusions

The relevance of Soviet psychiatry to the North American scene is of a complex nature and is likely to be a matter of considerable controversy. As some of the basic assumptions differ in these two settings, conclusions will have to be drawn with care. A Marxist-Leninist society, which subjugates the individual to the common benefit, will have a concept of mental health care delivery unlike that of a social system where a person's rights have priority *vis-à-vis* society at large. The introduction and maintenance of treatment methods and facilities in the Soviet Union is usually made independently of the community and citizen groups, while in our society there is considerable feedback from those sources. The immobility of the Soviet population (due to a severe housing shortage) *versus* the high mobility in North America is another crucial variable which has to be taken into account. It seems that a simple transplantation of the Soviet system of psychiatric care delivery, even with slight modifications, would have deleterious effects in a different environment.

Acknowledgment

The author wishes to express his acknowledgement to Professors Dr. Vartanian and Dr. Sternberg from the Moscow Institute of Psychiatry, and to Professor Dr. Saarma from the University of Tartu for their help in providing him with valuable information, and to Mrs. C. Wright for her administrative efforts.

29

Psychiatric Training and Practice in the People's Republic of China

Philip D. Walls, Lichun Han Walls, and Donald G. Langsley

The millennia of China's existence give this large country a cultural experience that has no equivalent in the Western world. On top of this, its development since 1949 as a socialist country along unique political and philosophical paths has created a fascinating social atmosphere, which in recent years has attracted flocks of observers from the West.

Psychiatry as an institution in China is inscribed within its socialist system where communal goals are paramount, and correspondingly has incorporated such social tenets, along with biological factors, in the conceptualization of the etiology of mental disorders and in the methodology for dealing with them. It has done this at the same time as facing the challenge presented by the mental health needs of a population of almost a billion people.

In the following article, two U.S. psychiatrists (P. D. Walls and D. G. Langsley) and a Native Chinese biochemist (L. H. Walls) present their impressions on the history and current status of psychiatric theory, methods, organization, and professional training in China, taking advantage of a recent visit made by the Walls to that country.

ALTHOUGH A number of American physicians have visited the People's Republic of China since 1972, when travel restrictions were relaxed, there are few firsthand reports about psychiatry and mental hospitals in China. Two of us (P. D. Walls and L. H. Walls) visited China from August 8 to October 21, 1973, to gather and exchange information about medical and psychiatric education and practice. L. H. Walls, a biochemist, is a native of China and is fluent in Mandarin Chinese, as well as being familiar with psychiatric terminology and practice in the United States by virtue of her marriage to a psychiatrist.

The itinerary included Canton, Shanghai, Hangchow, Nanking, and Peking and a visit to a medical school in each of these cities. We met with practicing psychiatrists in Nanking, and in Shanghai we were able to visit psychiatrists and to tour the Shanghai Psychiatric Institute. Visits to a commune near Shanghai and to one near Peking were also arranged, as were visits to various factories, hospitals, clinics, a nursery, a kindergarten, a youth recreation center, and many exhibitions and sights in these cities. All such arrangements were made in each city through local offices of the International Travel Agency of the People's Republic of China, whose agents were courteous and helpful in the handling of so many requests. Our trip was not sponsored by any groups inside or outside China.

We submitted requests in each city visited, and although it was not convenient for all of them to be granted, we received a great deal of cooperation and enjoyed considerable freedom. We were always permitted to take notes during interviews, and we routinely received permission to tape-record the interviews. The tapes were transcribed verbatim into English as soon as possible after each interview in order to avoid misquotations and imperfect recollection. We conducted interviews with groups rather than individuals. At a hospital the group might include an administrator (usually the chairman of the Revolutionary Committee of the hospital), several physicians, and nurses. After introductory remarks had been presented, there was a tour of the facilities and an exchange of questions and answers. The meetings usually lasted a whole morning or afternoon, but only one meeting could be arranged with any one group. This restriction must be due in part to the increasing numbers of visitors, who would consume too much of the working staffs' time if all received repeated appointments.

Psychiatry in Traditional Medicine

Mental illness has been recognized in China for over 2,000 years. Paralysis, epilepsy, and hysteria were mentioned in early texts and were described as maladies of "wind" (Lee et al. 1962). In China the concepts of "breath" and "wind" are still popularly believed to affect health. "Breath" is comparable to very early Greek and Roman notions of "psyche" (from the Greek *psychein,* to breathe, to blow) and of "spirit" (from the Latin *spirare,* to breathe). Specialization in psychiatry existed in the eleventh century, when one Chinese medical school had established a separate department of nervous and mental disorders with 30 students.

In the first decade of the seventeenth century, observation and classification of mental disorders had progressed to the extent that a famous doctor of traditional Chinese medicine, Wang K'en-T'ang, wrote on insanity, mania, and fits (Lee 1958). His description of insanity fits schizophrenia very well, and mania and grand mal seizures are also well characterized. Wang noted that the insane got no better even after years of illness. He believed that these patients had "wind in the mind," and he offered the explanation that "those with frustrated ambition are likely to be so affected." Chang Chieh-Pin, a contemporary of Wang's, pointed out that insanity resulted in progressive deterioration. Chang also alluded to the phenomenon of febrile delirium, and he commented on the lack of childhood cases of insanity (Lee 1958). Acupuncture, herbal preparations, exercises of various kinds, and other traditional methods were used in the treatment of mental illness. However, little change in classification or treatment seemed to develop inside China after the seventeenth century.

Some of the reasons for this slow development of mental health sciences may be related to factors described by Ilza Veith (1955). She suggested that the Chinese were traditionally less concerned about mental illness than the Europeans, although, as Bowman (1948) has confirmed, mental illness was as common in China as in other countries. The tradition of respect for elders (filial piety) and the practice of using go-betweens in potentially embarrassing situations (part of the tradition of saving face) may have done much to lessen the impact and importance of mental disturbance in individual cases. Veith (1955) also pointed out that in China mental illness was never associated with any religious stigma, such as that which stimulated much controversy and theoretical discussion in the West.

Psychiatry in Modern Times (1900–1949)

Western psychiatric ideas were introduced in China about 75 years ago when the first Western-style mental hospital to receive patients was established in 1897 in Canton province. A course in psychiatry was taught at the Peking Union Medical College for the first time in 1922. The practice of psychiatry continued to make slow gains over the 50 years from the establishment of the first asylum for the insane to the inauguration of the People's Republic of China in 1949 (Wong 1950). At that time only four psychiatric hospitals may have been in operation in all of China (Wong 1950; Cerny 1965) with a total capacity of 1,000 to less than 6,000 psychiatric beds and 50 to 60 practicing psychiatrists (Bowman 1948; Cerny 1965). In regard to psychiatric theory, Cerny (1965) has stated that "the teachings of Adolf Meyer were widely accepted in Chinese psychiatry" until 1949.

A report of a brief visit to Peking's An Ding mental hospital provides a glimpse of conditions during the pre-1949 period. This hospital, founded in 1917, was said to have been under police control and neglected for 30 years. There were allusions to experimentation on patients during those years. The hospital had 50 beds in 1949 and was until then being supervised by a non-psychiatric physician who worked only part-time (Thomson et al. 1967).

Psychiatry After 1949

The facilities for psychiatric care and the number of psychiatrists in the People's Republic of China grew rapidly after 1949. The number of beds for psychiatric patients increased from approximately 1,000 to a total of 5,000 in 1955 (Williams 1957) and 20,000 by 1957 (Cerny 1965). There do not seem to be any data on the number of psychiatric beds after 1957, but a reasonable estimate for the present number is about 60,000. Sixty new mental institutions had been built by 1959, and clinics had been set up in the cities (Chin and Chin 1969). The People's Republic of China has 29 administrative districts at the provincial level on the mainland, and this means an average of about two mental hospitals per province. The municipalities and environs of Shanghai and Peking comprise two of these provinces. In 1957 Fox (1957) reported that 600 psychiatric beds were needed for a medical complex in Shanghai; it appears that by 1966, two psychiatric hospitals with a total of 400 beds had been built (Best 1966). A recent study quoted a combined total figure of close to 2,000 beds for the two Shanghai hospitals (Taipale and Taipale 1973). It has been reported that there were a total of 1,500 psychiatric beds in Peking in 1966 (Thomson et al. 1967). An approximation of 2,000 beds per province suggests a figure of about

60,000 beds for the entire country, a number that can also be determined by alternative methods (see following paragraphs).

The meager number of psychiatrists in 1949 grew to 100 in 1952 and to 400 in 1957 (Cerny 1965). Lazure (1964) was told in 1959 that there were 15 times the number of psychiatrists as in 1949, or about 900 judging from Cerny's quoted figure (Cerny 1965).

Although no official figures are reported for the number of psychiatrists after 1959, there are several ways to make a current estimate, and each one produces a similar total. One method takes note of the 61 psychiatrists in one of the two Shanghai mental hospitals. This figure was given to us during our visit and to three others (Taipale and Taipale, 1973; Ratnavale 1973; R. Sidel 1972). If the two Shanghai mental hospitals have similar staffs, there are about 120 practicing psychiatrists in that province and about 3,500 in all 29 provinces. Alternatively, 60 mental institutions were operating in 1959, and if these are now of comparable size to the present Shanghai units, then there are about 3,600 psychiatrists (60 hospitals times 60 psychiatrists is 3,600). Finally, an increase of about 40,000 Western-style physicians was reported in the People's Republic of China from 1949 to 1959 (Lazure 1964; Orleans 1969; Worth 1963), of whom about 900 were psychiatrists, which is a ratio of approximately 1:50. If this ratio held for the next seven years, and 150,000 (V. Sidel 1972) to 180,000 (Thomson et al. 1967) Western-style doctors were reported, this would suggest a figure of about 3,500 psychiatrists and about 60,000 psychiatric beds, extrapolating from the ratio of psychiatrists to beds in Shanghai.

Due to the reorganization of the Cultural Revolution in China (1966-1970), few additional doctors have been trained since that time. The first classes of newly trained physicians graduated from some of the medical colleges in 1974 (Walls et al., in press).

The 10 years after 1949 showed great growth and change in the mental health field in China. A Society of Neurology and Psychiatry was founded in 1952, and the *Chinese Neurology and Psychiatric Journal* was published from 1955 (Cerny 1965) until the Cultural Revolution. Williams commented that the psychiatrists with whom he spoke "were undoubtedly capable and extremely busy with treatment and teaching" and that "psychiatry is given a place in the medical curriculum quite as high as in most Australian universities" (Williams 1957). Each of the 50 medical colleges operating in 1960 had departments of psychiatry (Lazure 1964).

A movement to humanize the mental hospitals took place in these early years, especially during the Great Leap Forward of 1958, when an attitude was developed that "humane considerations were to govern the handling of patients" (Chin and Chin 1969). In 1957 chains, isolation, and psychosurgery had been prohibited in Shanghai (Cerny 1965). The use of chains and confinement was discontinued in Peking's An Ding Hospital in 1958 (Thomson et al. 1967). Reviews and reports have provided little knowledge of the day-to-day interaction between doctors, nurses, and their patients. There does not seem to be any information on facilities for the mentally ill from 1959 to 1966 (Chin and Chin 1969). In 1966, however, the physical structure of An Ding Hospital was described. "Not many frills were noted, but then there are very few frills in the Chinese life of today. There was evidence, however, of a good general attitude towards mental illness and there was a sound approach towards rehabilitation" (Thomson et al. 1967: p 352). There is no indication of whether patients in rural areas were managed similarly or differently from those in the cities.

Most patients classified as needing psychiatric care are referred to regional hospitals for treatment. Inpatient and outpatient care is available. The range of diagnoses given to hospitalized patients is similar to that in this country. From 60 to 80 percent of the patients in three separate reports were classified as schizophrenics (Thomson et al. 1967; Taipale and Taipale 1973; Casey 1973). The remainder of diagnoses were divided among manic-depressive psychoses, organic brain syndromes, depression, and severe neuroses. The average length of hospital stay varied from three months (Thomson et al. 1967) to 70 to 84 days (Ratnavale 1973; Sidel and Sidel 1972).

Psychiatric Treatment

Treatment for hospitalized patients covers a variety of Western and indigenous methods. For years, persistent efforts have been made to combine Western and Chinese modes of treatments in the field of mental health care as well as in other areas of medicine. Work therapy (Cerny 1965; Lazure 1964), insulin coma therapy, ECT, sleep therapy, and tranquilizers, but not hypnotherapy or psychosurgery, were used through the early 1960s (Cerny 1965). Chlorpromazine was the principal medication for schrizophrenia at An Ding Hospital in Peking in 1966, and depressed patients usually received insulin coma or subcoma therapy. Imipramine had been used previously, but "there had been no great demand" for antidepressants at that time (Thomson et al. 1967). A report of the treatment of mental illness at the Third Peking Hospital in 1972 indicated that schizophrenia was managed with "customary drug therapy" (usually chlorpromazine) and insulin coma therapy and that depression was treated with antidepressant medication (Casey 1973). Moreover, psychiatrists in Nanking told us that "insulin shock and ECT are used in schizophrenia, insulin more than ECT, if regular measures fail in a given case. It is not used in depression since cases get better with drugs as a rule." According to two reports, insulin coma therapy and ECT have not been used in at least one Shanghai mental hospital since 1970 (Taipale and Taipale 1973; R. Sidel 1972), although this may not yet be the case in general. Currently, the usual treatment for depression seems to be antidepressant medications. Lithium carbonate is used in the treatment of mania (Taipale and Taipale 1973).

Taipale and Taipale (1973) and Ratnavale (1973) reported that the maximum daily dosages of chlorpromazine in the treatment of schizophrenia were 200 mg and 250 mg, respectively. We were told that the maximum daily in-hospital dosage was about 600 mg at the Shanghai Psychiatric Institute. The tendency to use increasing doses of phenothiazines in the treatment of schizophrenia seems to have occurred in China as it has in the West.

In addition to drug therapy for mental patients, the Chinese use acupuncture, group therapy in political study groups, counseling by other patients, and appropriate job modification after discharge (Sidel 1973). Psychotherapy is described in various sources. The Chinese literature increasingly discussed "psychogenic factors" in the etiology of mental illness between 1956 to 1966, when Pavlovian psychology was influential in placing emphasis on psychotherapy (Chin and Chin 1969). Heart-to-heart talks between patients and nurses and doctors have become a prominent part of the treatment process (Taipale and Taipale 1973; Ratnavale 1973; R. Sidel 1972).

A major therapeutic device is to help patients merge their egos with the collective ego of the state. Patients are presented with the concept of nationalism (Sidel 1973), consisting of exhortation for increased devotion to the community and the state, as a stimulus to generate inner strength with which to overcome mental illness. Point-by-point confrontation of delusional ideas is another part of the interaction between therapists, group members, and the patient (Kagan 1972). Patients may return to the hospital to talk with their nurse (Taipale and Taipale 1973), or a doctor or nurse may make home visits (Sidel 1973). Group discussions of political works, such as Mao's writings, are held regularly in the hospital with doctors and nurses. Work group discussions of politics are also a regular feature of life for every Chinese citizen, and the use of this mechanism in the hospital is not a novelty.

Sidel visited the "Shanghai Mental Hospital" in 1971 and 1972 (R. Sidel 1972; Sidel and Sidel 1972; Sidel 1973); Taipale and Taipale visited the "Central Mental Hospital" of Shanghai in 1972 (Taipale and Taipale 1973); and Ratnavale visited the "Shanghai Psychiatric Institute" in early 1973 (Ratnavale 1973). Our guide used the name "Shanghai Psychiatric Institute" during our visit, but a more literal translation would be "Shanghai Municipal Psychiatric Preventive and Treatment Center." A close comparison of the information reported by the four groups showed that all visited the same hospital. This confusion in names is an excellent example of the potential difficulties involved in the translation of even simple matters from Chinese to English. (We will use the name "Shanghai Psychiatric Institute" in further references to this hospital.) Visitors have reported that the institute has 61 psychiatrists on its staff (Taipale and Taipale 1973; Ratnavale 1973; R. Sidel 1972), 916 beds (Taipale and Taipale 1973; R. Sidel 1972), and 13 wards (Ratnavale 1973; R. Sidel 1972). We were told that it had 14 wards, 974 beds, and a total staff of 583, including 61 doctors and 213 nurses. This appears to mark an increase in the overall size of the hospital since previous visits.

Little is known about the psychiatric treatment used in outpatient clinics. Cerny (1965) reported that acupuncture and other traditional techniques (herbs, exercises, and moxabustion, which is the application of heat to acupuncture points), as well as psychotherapy and pharmacotherapy are used in the treatment of neurotics. Sidel mentioned that chlordiazepoxide, diazepam, acupuncture, herbs, lectures, and individual and group therapy are given to neurotic outpatients (Sidel 1973). Ratnavale wrote that most of the 400 outpatients seen daily at the Shanghai Psychiatric Institute suffered from neurotic and psychosomatic conditions (Ratnavale 1973), but this contrasts with information from our visit. An introductory speech at the Shanghai Psychiatric Institute included the comment, "Most of the outpatients are those who have received inpatient treatment here. In some cases the outpatients suffer from neurasthenia or epilepsy." However, in still another reference, Chin and Chin reported that 60 percent of the patients treated in the Peking Medical College outpatient mental health department in 1959 were neurasthenics (Chin and Chin 1969). They also pointed out that no statistics are available on the incidence of neurotic illness in the People's Republic of China. Paul T. K. Lin, in a paper presented at the 1973 annual meeting of the American Psychiatric Association, commented that neuroses are practically nonexistent in China (Lin 1973).

Psychiatric Theory

The theory of mental illness in the People's Republic of China appears to be no less controversial than the statistics, although of course this statement is equally true of Western schools. Pavlovian psychology was a powerful influence up to and probably beyond the Sino-Soviet rift, which took place in 1960. On the one hand, the biological determinants of mental disorder may be stressed in theory and practice, and on the other hand, sociopolitical factors may take the limelight. At different times and in different places, one or the other orientation has been given emphasis. Chin and Chin have outlined the development and progress of this controversy up to 1966 in their excellent book (Chin and Chin 1969).

The controversy continues to the present. In reply to our questions about the etiology of schizophrenia, Nanking psychiatrists cited their belief in genetic and organic origins. Kagan's report from Tientsin (Kagan 1972) seems to show a bias toward social factors there, although the point that biological and social factors are not mutually exclusive is also made. In Shanghai a middle ground seems to be taken. Most patients appeared to be receiving one or more medications or somatic treatments, and all but the most agitated and disorganized patients joined in group therapy. Works of Mao, Marx, and Lenin and current affairs were common topics of conversation. When we asked whether discussions with patients regarding their illness centered around the content of their thinking, the reply was,

> If some patients suffer from delusion, we hold that it may be due to a confusion of the logic in their minds. Therefore, we try to educate them to think in a correct way. We arm their minds with Marxist-Leninist philosophical thinking. Chairman Mao's philosophical works will be assigned for them to read in order to let them know where the correct thinking comes from. So we do not give the patients any sex analysis or psychoanalysis.

All of the foregoing is consistent with the Pavlovian notion of "correct" thought leading to "correct" processing by the mind's second signal system, which in turn leads to "correct" behavior. It is basic in the thinking of the new China that change and improvement are almost always possible, given enough effort and the right kind of mutual help. Freud's concept of the unconscious, a part of the mind hidden from and inaccessible to direct confrontation and change but still able to influence behavior, is not compatible with the Chinese view. Moreover, Freudian psychology is seen as based on

Western idealism, a philosophy with which the dialectical materialism of Communism is in opposition. Freud emphasized the individual, the self, and this finds little harmony in the Chinese state, which emphasizes the group, the nation, and the family. A thorough understanding of Freudian psychology requires years of study and practice, tending to create an elite group of doctors, and elite groups are anathema in the People's Republic. Finally, the subject of sexual drive is simply not felt to be important in the etiology of mental illness.

It is important that Freudian-trained readers consider these differences in opinion and interpretation when trying to follow the Chinese points of view and practice. They explain the laughter that followed the Sidels' question about Freud's influence in Chinese psychiatry (Sidel and Sidel 1972). When we asked if Chinese psychiatrists believed in the developmental theory of mental illness, our Nanking hosts said flatly that they did not. "Under Chairman Mao's guidance, after Liberation [1949], everyone believes in dialectical materialism and everyone is happy. There is no conflict for the children." In response to the same question, Shanghai psychiatrists answered,

> We have not yet arrived at a unified explanation as to the causes of [mental] disease. Some people hold that the role is played by chemical changes in the brain or genetic factors. We think that a reasonable social system will reduce the environmental causes of mental diseases. But will it also be effective in reducing the occurrence of schizophrenia? Well, there are still some disputes.

One 1957 statistic cited for the prevalence of schizophrenia in the People's Republic puts it at one-tenth of Western countries (Taipale and Taipale 1973).

The place that neurosis currently holds in Chinese psychiatric theory is especially hard for Western observers to discern, for although Freudian views are rejected, some similar terms with perhaps different connotations are maintained. Diagnoses of neurotic patients include such terms as neurasthenia, hysteria, phobia, and obsessive-compulsive neurosis. The most prevalent diagnosis is neurasthenia, a nonspecific term without an English equivalent. Common symptoms of neurasthenia are insomnia, headache, dreams, and pains (Chin and Chin 1969). It is difficult to find detailed descriptions of the other diagnostic categories as the Chinese use them.

Psychiatry in Nanking and Shanghai

Diagnosis

Our interviews with psychiatrists in Nanking and Shanghai confirmed much of the material already discussed and added some new information. In Nanking, hospitalized patients were classified as having schizophrenia, manic-depressive psychosis, involutional psychosis, organic psychosis, symptomatic psychosis (after Mayer-Gross et al.'s definition (1960), which includes various organic diseases that present with psychosis), and psychogenic psychosis, which includes hysterical psychosis and depression. Diagnostic categories for nonpsychotic disorders included neurasthenia, obsessive-compulsive neurosis, hysteria, and phobia. No detailed statistics were available for the frequency of these diagnoses in the neuropsychiatric hospital in Nanking, but schizophrenia was diagnosed in more than 50 percent of the patients. In Shanghai, additional diagnostic classifications of hospitalized patients included postpartum psychosis, encephalitis, senile psychosis, cerebral atherosclerosis, and mental disturbances secondary to stroke. According to psychiatrists with whom we spoke, about 60 percent of the patients at the Shanghai Psychiatric Institute are diagnosed as schizophrenic, with the remaining 40 percent given various other diagnoses.

No classification for childhood mental illness was given in Nanking, but one 10-year-old girl with "childhood schizophrenia" was seen at the Shanghai Psychiatric Institute. The only child in the hospital at the time, she was being treated on a ward for women. There has been a general lack of demand for psychiatric facilities for children in China, and there does not appear to be a subspecialty of child psychiatry. A unit for the treatment of children under 13 or 14 years of age was in operation at the Shanghai Psychiatric Institute prior to 1966, but it was closed after the Cultural Revolution because it was relatively unused. One or two of the hospital psychiatrists with the most experience in treating children were called upon when the need arose.

Personality disorder was recognized as a diagnostic entity, but the cases were said to be few and the patients were not usually treated in a mental hospital. In Shanghai this was felt to be a job for "reeducation" and was done at some other, unspecified, place.

Personality disorder accompanying schizophrenia or epilepsy was treated by the hospital staff. A nonpsychiatric physician commented that in the early years after 1949, sedatives and "some treatment" of an undefined sort were given to homosexuals who suffered from anxiety, but that not many such patients had been seen in recent years. One reason suggested for this decline was that it might be due to the change in the social system and the radical change in the moral standards of the society.

Treatment

The average length of stay at the neuropsychiatric hospital in Nanking was three to four months. The figure given at the Shanghai Psychiatric Institute was 70 days, the same as quoted in earlier reports (Ratnavale 1973, Sidel and Sidel 1972).

Schizophrenia was treated with drugs, herbs, electroacupuncture, and regular acupuncture in both cities. The use of ECT and insulin coma therapy in Nanking has already been described, along with the use of medications for depression. Insulin coma therapy and ECT have not been used at the Shanghai Psychiatric Institute since 1970. The combined use of Chinese and Western modes of therapy was emphasized. Psychiatrists had the clinical impression that the dosage of Western drugs needed to bring about recovery was reduced by half when acupuncture and/or herbs were used concurrently.

Maximum dosages of medications for hospitalized patients in Nanking were as follows: chlorpromazine, 450 mg a day; trifluoperazine, 20 to 30 mg a day; perphenazine, 30 mg a day; and chlorprothixene, 450 mg a day. The following were the maximum daily dosages given to outpatients; chlorpromazine, 100 to 150 mg a day; trifluoperazine, 10 mg a day; perphenazine, 6 to 10 mg a day; and chlorprothixene, 100 to 150 mg a day. Imipramine for depressed patients was given in a dosage of 150 to 300 mg a day for two to four weeks and then discontinued if there was no improvement. In Shanghai the maximum daily dosage of chlorpromazine for inpatients was 600 to 700 mg when used alone and about 300 mg when combined with acupuncture and herbs.

We saw a variety of therapies at the Shanghai Psychiatric Institute. Group meetings of patients and staff seemed to be held regularly. A type of day care center in the form of a large recreation room was available for use by any patients who wished to go there. Carnival-style games, music, dance performances, and songs were held daily, with the patients themselves as the participants on stage and in the audience. Ping-pong and chess were played on the wards. Work was a regular activity. Jobs consisted of simple manual tasks: some patients wove small items, some put small paper fillers into toothpaste caps, and others worked in the hospital garden or helped with grounds maintenance. Articles made in the hospital were sold to factories, and proceeds went to buy recreational materials, books, ink, etc., for the patients' use.

Neuropsychiatric patients in Nanking were given "discharge papers" upon their release from the hospital. These papers contained a list of medications, dosages, and the time and place of follow-up visits. Patients would usually return to the hospital to keep appointments. A different group of doctors and nurses from those who treated inpatients saw the patients in the outpatient department. The same therapist saw the patient on each visit, since the relationship between the therapist and the patient was felt to be important. Acupuncture was given to discharged hospital patients in the outpatient department, in contrast to its use in the treatment of neurosis in various outpatient settings. Most relapses occurred within two years, and patients were advised to take their medications for a least that long after discharge.

At the Shanghai Psychiatric Institute, discharged patients returned to the hospital after two weeks to see the same doctor who had treated them on the ward. More visits could be scheduled as necessary. The doctor could help the patient in his readjustment at home and at work and would sometimes make visits to the factory or neighborhood on the patient's behalf. There was no social worker on the staff. Nurses worked with doctors in the outpatient department, but their role was not clarified. Unlike doctors, the nurses did not seem to alternate between the inpatient and outpatient departments.

Outpatient Care

Some mental health clinics in the cities were operated away from the hospital grounds, but little is known about them. An administrator of a local hospital in Shanghai informed us,

> Only an occasional mental patient is treated here [at this neighborhood hospital], and only on a temporary basis. Most of the follow-up is

done in the district mental "prevention" clinics, which are open two to three days per week. These do outpatient follow-up and are staffed by the doctors and nurses from the mental hospital. The patients discharged from the mental hospital are given "trial discharges" and they return weekly for follow-up. They may be seen in the local hospitals like this one only for medicines or occasionally for emergencies. Those who need the closest outpatient supervision are given aftercare at the mental hospital instead of the district clinics.

In Nanking, neurotic outpatients were treated with sedatives, acupuncture, or other traditional techniques. There were no data on the number of neurotic patients, but they were said to be "very few." The diagnostic category of neurosis was broad and included symptoms like headache and "nerve pain." In general medical clinics, patients who were recognized as having no organic basis for their symptoms could be treated by internists or neurologists without requests for psychiatric referral. A physician in a general hospital in Peking stated, "Internists and other doctors treat neurotics in regular hospitals. They are treated with drugs and acupuncture. They are not admitted to the psychiatric hospitals." Bromides seemed to be commonly prescribed for nonspecific ailments. Phenobarbital was used frequently in factory and neighborhood health stations. A factory doctor and one of our guides each mentioned that they took small doses of perphenazine as often as several times a week to relieve tension.

Consultations were held between nonpsychiatric hospital personnel and staff from the mental hospital in Nanking. The consultations were reciprocal and seemed to be strictly case oriented.

Rehabilitation

The Chinese social structure appears to be very supportive of the mentally ill. Cooperation and the dignity of each citizen as part of the group are emphasized. The duties of the psychiatrist seem oriented toward enabling the patient to regain his position in his family and job. The whole matter appears capable of careful planning and execution from the time of the patient's original referral to a mental hospital to his reintegration in the community. Two case histories related by a physician at the Shanghai Psychiatric Institute illustrate this point.

> After a patient left our hospital and went back to his working unit, the authorities of that unit, in consideration of his health, shifted him to another workshop to do another kind of job. However, he took this in the

wrong way. He thought that the administrator of this work unit might have some kind of prejudice against him, and he became very disappointed and returned to the hospital to ask the doctor's help. The doctor went to the working unit to learn about the whole process and to explain to the patient. The man gradually understood why his work was shifted, his disappointment disappeared, and he worked very well and was very pleasant.

In another instance a patient had been a shop assistant in a department store. When he recovered and returned to his store, his leaders failed to understand him very well, and he was assigned to his original job. However, he was unable to adapt to the original job because the medicine interfered with his memory. Thus, he could not do accounts very well. When he came back to the hospital to ask for the doctor's help, the doctor went to this store and got the leaders to shift the patient's work. He became a warehouse keeper for a half year. His memory then recovered and he asked to do the same job he had held before.

Mobile Teams

One-third of the staff at the Shanghai Psychiatric Institute toured the surrounding countryside in mobile teams. This practice is common in all types of hospitals, general and specialized, and it represents an attempt to bring care closer to the people. The mental hospital teams consisted of three doctors and seven nurses. The whole staff took turns on mobile teams. An important duty of these groups was to train "barefoot doctors" in the management of acute psychiatric problems. Often the barefoot doctors could not immediately send psychiatric patients to the mental hospital, and they thus had to learn about drug and acupuncture treatment for such situations. One doctor reported, "The mobile team of the mental hospital came to our hospital a year ago. They gave two days of lectures at the hospital and worked in the clinics one week more to take measurements on rates of mental diseases."

It is apparent that much of the theory and practice of Chinese psychiatry is based on hospital practice. Almost all patients are sent to the hospital for treatment; follow-up care and community support for discharged patients is organized from the hospital. The hospital staff runs the outpatient departments and the outlying clinics and supplies the mobile teams that disseminate information on psychiatry to neighborhood and commune medical units. Private practice does not exist, and clinical research and training is hospital based.

Training

Chinese medical students now receive instruction in neurology and psychiatry during a two-week series of lectures and visits to neuropsychiatric hospitals in their second year of medical college. Since the Cultural Revolution, medical students have had a three-year curriculum. Prior to the Cultural Revolution they studied for five or six years and received two weeks of psychiatric training in their fourth year (Lazure 1964). At present, psychiatry is part of the course in internal medicine, and lectures seem to be given by internists or neurologists. The departments of psychiatry that had formerly been a regular feature of medical colleges (Williams 1957; Lazure 1964) were suspended during the Cultural Revolution and have not yet been reinstated. It is not known whether separate departments of psychiatry will be reestablished in medical colleges. The whole field of psychiatry may be continuing its Cultural Revolution even though many other medical specialties have reorganized.

After they graduate from medical school, most doctors may have no further exposure to training in psychiatry until they come into contact with a mobile team from a regional mental hospital. The only literature we found in bookstores that dealt with psychiatry for non-psychiatrists consisted of manuals written for barefoot doctors. Several of these included concise descriptions of common manifestatons of epilepsy, psychoses, and neurasthenia. The use of phenothiazines, barbiturates, and bromides was covered briefly. The manuals provided a picture of symptoms and of routine treatment. A small section of a recent manual for barefoot doctors discussed mental illness in this fashion. The section also discussed the concept that some mental illnesses are a reaction to an unspecified underlying disorder, perhaps recalling the pre-1949 influence of Adolf Meyer (Kirin Medical College 1973).

Psychiatrists receive their training in the mental hospitals. Graduates from the medical colleges are assigned to work in mental hospitals, apparently in numbers planned to fit the country's projected need for psychiatrists. The basic course lasts from 6 to 12 months, according to sources in Nanking and Shanghai. Taipale and Taipale (1973) reported that two or three years of training were required, but this difference may indicate that the period of formal training in psychiatry has been reduced from what it was in 1972. Another explanation may be that the shorter period refers to the organized system of lectures and that the longer period refers to the total time required before a resident is felt by his peers and supervisors to be capable of fully independent work.

At the Shanghai Psychiatric Institute the psychiatry residents learned through practice, supervision, readings, and seminars. One doctor at the institute reported, "When the residents first come here, their psychiatric knowlege is quite limited, so we give them training for one-half to one year. In this period of time experienced doctors will give them guidance. They will acquire knowledge mainly through practice. They are assigned some books and literature to read, and through practice they will gradually be capable of doing independent work." The reading assignments consisted of compilations prepared by the teaching staff; students who read English were also assigned selections from texts such as those by Mayer-Gross et al. (1960), Henderson and Gillespie (1956), and Noyes and Kolb (1968). The lectures for residents included topics such as neurology, neuropathology, neurobiochemistry, and psychopharmacology. Psychologists from the university were invited to present lectures from time to time, but they did not practice in the mental hospitals. This has been the case for many years (Lazure 1964).

Some foreign journals available to psychiatrists included *The American Journal of Psychiatry, Archives of General Psychiatry, Journal of Nervous and Mental Disease, British Journal of Psychiatry,* and *Acta Psychiatrica Scandinavica.*

Research efforts were directed toward examination of the effectiveness of therapy. A popular research topic seemed to be a search for the effects of combining Western and traditional Chinese methods of treatment. Chinese psychiatrists seemed uniformly interested in the current trends of basic laboratory research in the United States.

Conclusions

We have attempted to trace some developments in the history of psychiatry in China and to present a picture of the practice of and education of psychiatry as it has been applied in the People's Republic of China. The Chinese approach has had to deal with several large problems. One of these has been the need to expand services to meet the needs of the vast population. This has been approached by increasing the numbers of psychiatrists and mental hospitals to accommodate the severely mentally ill. Personnel and facilities had not existed in adequate numbers before 1949. Outpatient clinics have been developed, but little is known about them. The existing social structure has been used to advantage to help in the rehabilitation of discharged patients. Available psychiatric doctors and nurses are being used to train other medical practitioners in basic concepts and methods so as to increase the availability of care.

Another problem has been to develop a consistent theoretical approach to psychiatry, a difficulty not peculiar to the People's Republic of China. The special approach adopted by the Chinese emphasizes sociopolitical factors whenever possible in theoretical formulations about psychiatry. Research has been pursued mainly in clinical studies, but these could be of great significance when published if they support the claim of decreased prevalence and incidence of almost all kinds of functional mental illness in the People's Republic.

Clearly, the available information about psychiatric practice in the People's Republic of China gives only a hint of the differences between our two systems. There has only been a preliminary and incomplete exchange of information to date, by travelers who cannot fully represent so complex a subject after relatively brief exposures. As West and East observe each other in the future, more exchanges and greater depth of contact may be expected to stimulate greater mutual interest and benefits.

30

Psychiatry in Latin America

Carlos A. León

Latin American countries share an Iberian heritage and an indigenous background, as well as having in common a number of sociocultural characteristics including industrial underdevelopment and political instability. At the same time, these countries exhibit national identities based to a large extent on specific ethnic compositions and degree of miscegenation between European and Indian stocks. Most Latin American countries are quite rich in natural resources which are frequently the property of small segments of the population and are often exploited by multinational corporations through arrangements that do not appear to benefit the majority of the people. In line with this, Latin America presents some of the world's highest rates of illiteracy, morbidity, and mortality.

Under these circumstances, psychiatry as the institution through which society deals with mental health and mental illness faces great challenges. In the same region of such pioneering neuropsychiatric achievements as the sophisticated and successful cranial trephinings performed by the Incas, and the founding in Mexico in 1566 of the first psychiatric hospital of the American continent, mental health services are now grossly neglected because of the priority that has to be given to tremendous malnutrition and infectious disease problems.

In the following article, C. A. León, professor of psychiatry at the Universidad del Valle in Cali, Colombia and principal investigator for one of the centers of the WHO International Pilot Study of Schizophrenia, describes and discusses the present status of psychiatry in Latin America. In his well-documented review the author covers salient aspects of the socioeconomic and health conditions prevailing in the

area, and discusses the history of psychiatry, the status of professional resources and clinical services, research, education, and the need for better epidemiological information.

I. The Area, the People

FOR THE purposes of the present report we will include under the generic term of Latin America a group of 20 countries with geographic, historical, political and cultural common links, which because of being former colonies of Spain and Portugal might better be called Iberoamerica. Tied together in regional groups during colonial days, they became independent at the beginning of the last century and initiated their republican life as separate countries. In almost all of them Spanish is spoken as the exclusive or major language, the two exceptions being Brazil and Haiti.

Whereas there may be common characteristics leading to the identification of the "Latin" element in each one of these countries, they are better defined by their differences and the heterogeneous nature of their national idiosyncrasies. Most of these are probably related to the following four main variables: cultural status of the aboriginal population before European domination, contribution of the African element, attitude towards the mother country, and migratory currents after independence. Thus, the countries which were part of the Inca or Aztec empires kept a well-defined aboriginal physiognomy such as is seen today in Mexico, Peru, Bolivia, and Ecuador, while the lack of a well-established cultural or political system in the aboriginal population of Argentina determined an easier penetration of the European patterns which were later reinforced by successive waves of European immigration. Brazil, on the other hand, smothered its weak aboriginal influence with the introduction of a strong African component, and because of consistently friendly relations with its mother country, Portugal, attracted an abundant European immigration before and after independence.

The geographic aggregate of Latin America has an extension of about 20 million square kilometers and a population of approximately 274 million inhabitants (table 30.1).

Its population doubled in the period 1925–1960, and with an average annual growth rate of 3.1 percent (1968), regarded as the largest in the world, it will soon double again. It is a predominantly

Table 30.1 Population and area of 20 Latin-American countries (1969)

Countries	*Population (Inhab.)*	*Area (in square kilometers)*
Argentina	24,727,000	2,776,655
Bolivia	4,804,000	1,098,581
Chile	10,000,000	756,945
Colombia	21,118,000	1,136,167
Costa Rica	1,706,115	50,900
Cuba	8,250,000	114,524
Dominican Republic	4,174,000	43,442
Ecuador	6,177,125	270,670
El Salvador	3,390,000	21,393
Guatemala	5,200,000	108,889
Haiti	4,768,000	27,844
Honduras	2,718,044	112,088
Mexico	48,313,438	1,927,545
Nicaragua	1,953,000	127,664
Panama	1,463,500	75,650
Paraguay	2,303,000	406,752
Peru	13,586,300	1,285,215
Uruguay	2,852,000	186,926
Venezuela	10,204,000	912,050
Total	273,923,122	19,956,865

Source: Data adapted from the United Nations Demographic Year Book, 1969.

young population; 40 percent under 15 years of age and only 5 percent over 60 years.

Although the number and variety of natural resources are immense, physical obstacles for their development and adverse social and political conditions have successfully interfered with their use and brought about a chronic state of poverty for large sections of the population. There are those who see in this state of affairs the results of a feudal system of land tenure operating since colonial days, when the Crown bestowed huge extensions of land on a handful of favorites who in turn enslaved the natives for labor in farming and mining. The descendants of this elite became the possessors of most of the riches, to the extreme that according to estimates 10 percent of the population owns 90 percent of the wealth in some countries.

Social conditions evolved in such a way that the indigenous population was dispossessed and thoroughly subdued by the colonizers and their descendants. It should be clear why this must have generated intense feelings of frustrated anger, hopelessness and inferiority among the Indians, who took refuge in isolation and restriction of contacts with the white population. However, because of extensive and promiscuous miscegenation, there soon emerged the "mestizo" and "mulatto" groups which now constitute the predominant ethnic element in most countries. In Bolivia, Peru and Ecuador there is a noticeable preponderance of the Indian element in the population, with varying degrees of mixture with the white; whereas in Argentina and Uruguay it is estimated that more than 90 percent of the population is white. In extensive regions of Brazil and the Caribbean there is a predominance of the African stock.

II. Impressions, Contrasts, Misconceptions, Problems

The stereotyped image of Latin America as a land of romance where people lead carefree, hedonistic lives in luscious tropical surroundings and the mirage of luxurious hotels, inviting beaches, and charming tourist resorts is shattered when a closer observation reveals the dismal picture of squalor, hunger, crime, and disease in the ubiquitous slums of the Latin-American cities (Lewis 1959b; De Jesús 1963; Mangin 1965; Rogler 1967) and the misery of huge rural areas where peasants literally die of hunger, or barely exist, fighting a losing battle against a merciless nature in a barren land (De Castro 1946). To those who remark cynically that these are means of maintaining an ecological balance against the inordinate rate of growth of the population it must be pointed out that the rate of infant mortality is decreasing in most Latin-American countries, and also that there is evidence that children who survive infant malnutrition may carry permanent central nervous system damage and make submarginal levels of adaptation (Cravioto 1964).

The per-capita income of some of the Latin-American countries is among the lowest in the world (table 30.2), and it has been estimated that at the present rate of development it may take hundreds of years for some Latin-American countries to reach standards comparable to those in the U.S.A. and other developed countries today (Kann and Wiener, quoted by Bryant 1969).

The obstacles in the way of improving health standards in the face of these problems seem unsurmountable, and the prospect of even harsher conditions for the future tends to stifle any incipient effort.

Table 30.2 Per-capita income and illiteracy rate in 20 Latin-American countries (1969)

Countries	*Per-capita income in U.S. dollars*	*Illiteracy Percent*
Argentina	818	8
Bolivia	135	60
Brazil	290	30
Chile	510	11
Colombia	334	27
Costa Rica	450	15
Cuba	540	?
Dominican Republic	275	35
Ecuador	231	32
El Salvador	280	51
Guatemala	310	62
Haiti	84	80
Honduras	250	52
Mexico	560	22
Nicaragua	360	50
Panama	565	23
Paraguay	244	25
Peru	300	38
Uruguay	590	9
Venezuela	915	24
Average:	401	34.5

Source: Data adapted from the United Nations Demographic Year Book, 1969.

One of the most active factors increasing social problems in Latin America seems to be the massive migration from rural areas to the cities, which contributes to overcrowding, congestion of public services and breakdown of environmental sanitation as well as to the appearance of physical and mental diseases produced by disadaptation (Seguín 1956; Hauser 1961; Rotondo et al. 1962; Valdivia-Ponce 1970). The extremely low sociocultural conditions of these great masses of population are evidenced by the high rate of illiteracy which conspires against the possibility of their cultural and technical development. However, these very same people are exposed to the so-called "information explosion" of our age, since they have ready access to the influence of transistor radio and television which make them even more painfully aware of their own misery and of the differences that separate them from other layers of the population living under the standards of an affluent society. In turn the resentment and frustration created by these confrontations is systematically exploited by the strategists of the new social revolution who advocate violent and incessant attack on the established regime by all sorts of unorthodox means (Debray 1967; Romeo 1969; Guevara 1969).

The endemic manifestations of violence in Latin America can hardly be surpassed by those in any other part of the world. The homicide rates per 100,000 inhabitants of all ages were estimated at 36 and 25 for two Latin-American countries in 1962, and homicide occupied the 8th and 9th place respectively among the causes of death for the general population. For the population between the ages of 15 and 44 in the same countries homicide was the *first* cause of death, with rates of 61 and 47 per 100,000 respectively (W.H.O. 1967).

At the individual, as well as the social behavioral level, violence is a constant feature in Latin American life. "The popular image of Latin America as an area of endemic revolution is warranted. The resolution of succession problems by methods not authorized by constitutional prescription is a recurring phenomenon, and the replacement of leading personnel, notably Presidents, by acts of violence is common" (Kling 1969). Between 1950 and 1965, 40 successful revolutions took place in Latin America, and 3,500 insurgency or insurgency-related events occurred during the period 1946–1963 (Kling 1969). Rather than an aberrant type of behavior, violence is a pervading phenomenon which is capable of becoming a self-perpetuating style of political behavior (Kling 1969).

One of the main ingredients for nurturing violence in Latin America is "machismo," a very prevalent attitude in the male population ("macho" = male) characterized by an exaggerated emphasis in virility as expressed through both aggressive and sexual manifestations. A "macho" is a man who displays his masculinity in an overt manner and relishes his ability for aggression or for sex. He is also very sensitive, has a keen sense of his own "dignity," and is always ready to respond to any real or fancied offense. In aberrant forms of violence, which exceed by far the most relaxed limits of local tolerance, one can detect the presence of clear reparative mechanisms against feelings of rage due to thwarted self-assertion, which under favorable circumstances may explode with unsuspected strength (Leon 1969). Lifelong experiences of misery, oppression and continuous fear may generate deep feelings of envy, resentment and hatred which only await an opportunity to overflow.

Only a small proportion of people in some Latin-American countries have access to adequate health services and medical care. Magical notions about health and disease, folk remedies, and traditional ways of healing such as the practices of "curanderismo" and spiritualism, are widely followed and in some areas involve large segments of the population (Sal y Rosas 1958; Gutierrez de Pineda 1961; Bustamante 1961; Rogler and Hollingshead 1961; Silva et al., 1966; Alvarado 1965; Adis Castro, C. 1967; León 1968; Chiappe 1970). Many of these practices are the residue of aboriginal beliefs and customs; but in some countries they also became enriched by the introduction of African elements which at present are prevalent in large regions of Brazil and the Caribbean (Bastide 1967).

There is a vicious-circle relationship between lack of adequate health services and magical or folk practices of medicine. The absence or inaccessibility of medical services forces the population to use the readily available popular substitutes, and these in turn reinforce magical notions and foster mistrust and rejection of professional medical services even when they may be available.

Of all the misconceptions about Latin America and other underdeveloped areas of the world, perhaps the most fallacious is the belief that since people are not submitted to the excessive demands and pressures imposed by technological development they are free from stress and therefore free from emotional problems and mental disorders. Despite the relative lack of adequate epidemiological studies, wherever prevalence of mental disorders has been explored in Latin America it has been found that rates are comparable to those in other parts of the world (Rotondo et al., 1963; León 1967; Mariátegui et al. 1979; Tarnopolski 1970; Adis Castro, G. 1968; Marconi & Muñoz 1970). Although these studies have used different methodologies, adjustment of data shows that "the proportion of mental disorders in metropolitan urban zones in Latin America fluctuates between 17 and 18 per cent of the general population at risk" (Mariategui and Adis Castro, G. 1970). Furthermore, when common methodologies are used, the results are quite similar to those found in developed countries (Adis Castro, G. 1968; Leon, Climent, Jaramillo, and Estrada 1970). It is therefore a sad reality that Latin-American countries, without having even partially solved their health problems in the areas of communicable diseases, malnutrition, parasitosis, and environmental sanitation, also have to confront the very serious problem of mental disease in similar proportion to that existing in developed countries and without even a small fraction of their resources. There are indeed a bewildering plurality of fronts which have to be attacked in order to bring some badly needed relief to this part of the world.

III. Brief Historical Overview

A comprehensive paper by Roselli (1970) gives an excellent picture of the historical development of psychiatry in Latin America from its aboriginal beginnings to our day. According to this author, there is evidence that more than 200 aboriginal ethnic families existed in Latin America in the pre-columbian era, ranging from very primitively organized tribes to the highly developed cultures of the Aztecs, Mayans, Chibchas, and Incas. Information about their medical and psychiatric practices is very scarce, and the only valid sources are monuments, archaeological findings, reports by Spanish chroniclers, a few transliterated codexes, anthropological research on traditional beliefs, and observation of surviving folk practices and rituals.

Therapeutic procedures included shamanistic practices, priestly rituals, and botanical remedies. Central to all practices seems to have been the notion that disease is either produced by loss of the soul or by the introduction into the organism of a disturbing foreign element through sorcery. Cranial trephining for medical or magico-ritual reasons, sometimes with replacement of the bone fragments by metal plates, was practiced in Mexico and Central America, and especially in Peru, where it attained high levels of sophistication.

The use of psychotropic and hallucinogenic plants was widespread in pre-columbian times, and in several regions the practice has survived to our own day. Cocâ *(Eritroxilon coca)* "Chamico" *(Datura tatula)* and "Ayahuasca," "Capi" or "Yage" (several species of *Banisteriopsis)* were used as trance-inducing elements for divination and therapeutic purposes in extensive areas of South America. It has been found that "Chamico" contains hyoscyamine, and "Yage" harmine. Two species of cactus, "Peyotl" *(Lophoia willamsii)* and "Agua-colla" or "San Pedro" *(Trichocerens pachamoi)* are rich in mescaline and are still widely used in Central America and in Peru and Chile, respectively. Several varieties of mushrooms such as the "Teonnacatl" *(Psylocibe mexicana)* used in Mexico and Guatemala, contain psylocibine. "Olioluqui" *(Ipomera violacea),* also used in Central America, contains active principles similar to LSD. Indians from some areas in the Caribbean and South America also used a variety of hallucinogenic snuff powders prepared from seeds or bark of trees such as "Cebil" *(Piptadenia macrocarpa)* and "Epena" *(Virola calophylloidea).*

It has been found that both species are rich in potent indole alkaloids (Naranjo 1969).

The most frequent purpose of the use of hallucinogens in therapeutic and religious practices was that of trying to establish contact with the gods, who would answer transcendental questions and give advice on the nature of the disease and how to treat it.

Since time immemorial there has been in Latin America a body of knowledge about entities such as "jani," "susto," "espanto," conditions characterized by a variety of symptoms such as anxiety, depression, and somatic complaints. The essential cause of these ailments is believed to be the loss of the soul and its replacement by evil spirits, noxa or evil humors in the body of the victim. The most effective treatment is a shamanistic ritual aimed at "cleansing" the body and bringing back the soul (Gillin 1956; Sal y Rosas 1958; León 1963; Rubel 1964).

For treating mental disorders the Incas used balneotherapy, bloodletting and individual or collective confession. Either individuals or entire communities were submitted to a period of fasting which lasted up to five days, after which the priests listened to the penitents in confession; then they proceeded to strike their backs lightly with stones; and finally priest and penitent together spat on a handful of grass which was thrown into a river. This might have been a symbolic way of washing away the sins (Metraux 1962).

Mental disorders were well known to Mexican aborigines; they used different terms for excited and quiet patients and attributed most of the disorders to exotoxic causes (Calderón, quoted by Roselli 1970).

The use of hallucinogenic plants was generally restricted to shamans, priests and civil authorities, to see the future, to see at a distance, to interpret dreams, and to discover the cause of illness. For the common man they were usually forbidden, since they could lead to chronic insanity or death. The Spanish conquerors learned the hard way how some of these plants could produce acute insanity—as reported by the Spanish chronicler Joaquín Acosta in describing what befell the troops of Gonzalo Jimenez de Quesada during the invasion of the kingdom of the Chibchas: "40 of Quesada's soldiers who marched from Bogotá to Chocontá temporarily went out of their minds when they arrived at a place where some Indian women mixed their food with the seeds of a plant called 'Borrachero' *(Datura arborea)*" (quoted by Roselli 1968). Another chronicler mentions that eating wild mandioc made some soldiers "walk around as if drunk or insane" (Juan de Castellanos, quoted by Roselli 1968).

Most of the aboriginal methods for treating mental disorders, or inducing them, came to an abrupt end with the establishment in the New World of tribunals of the Inquisition in the viceroyalties of Lima 1570, New Spain (Mexico) 1571, and New Granada (Cartagena), 1610. According to a chronicler "what startled the Inquisitors more than anything was the infinite number of witches and sorcerers who swarmed in the New Kingdom" (Llinas, quoted by Roselli 1968).

The first insane asylum in the New World was founded in Mexico in 1566 by the Spaniard Bernardino Alvarez, who although having been in his youth an "adventurer, gambler and escaped convict" later became a devoted protector of the mentally ill. One year after he had founded the hospital in Mexico he established in Oaxtepec a rural colony for chronic patients. A hundred years later, José Sayago, a carpenter, and his wife, founded in Mexico the Hospital Real del Divino Salvador for women mental patients (Muriel, quoted by Roselli 1970). In colonial days some of the general hospitals had sections for the care of the mentally ill, but in most places patients were imprisoned in cells or dungeons where they lay naked chained down to the floor, and submitted to a barbarous routine of whippings and cold showers. Unfortunately, this state of affairs prevailed in some places in Latin America for many years, and it is only in recent decades that the last remnants of these abhorrent practices have been eradicated. After independence from Spain was secured, France began to exert a lasting cultural influence on all Latin American countries. Most of the prominent physicians were trained in Paris, and this fashion continued until the Second World War, when the center of influence was shifted to the U.S.A.

During the nineteenth century we witness a period of increasing enlightenment in the attitudes towards the mentally ill, as reflected by the teaching of mental pathology in medical schools and the passing of special laws for the protection and care of the patients. The first chairs of psychiatry as an independent discipline were created at the end of the century in Buenos Aires and Rio de Janeiro. The first open-door hospital was inaugurated in Brazil by Azevedo Riveira in 1907 and Franco Da Rocha initiated in São Paulo the first system of foster-home care for the mentally ill in 1908.

The first out-patient clinic for psychiatric patients was created at Hospital Santa Ana in Lima in 1915. Baltazar Caravedo Prado, the initiator of the mental health movement in Peru, started the first private psychiatric clinic in partnership with Herminio Valdizán in 1919. In 1941 Carlos A. Seguín started the first psychiatric unit in a general hospital at Hospital Obrero in Lima. The first psychiatric journal, *Archivos de Psiquiatría y Criminología* was published in Buenos Aires by José Ingenieros in 1902. The Sociedad de Psicologia de Buenos Aires, founded in 1908, was the first professional association in the area of psychology in Latin America. The Sociedad Brasileira de Neurologia, Psiquiatria y Medicina Legal was founded in Brazil in 1909. The first Latin American conference on Neurology, Psychiatry and Forensic Medicine met in Buenos Aires in 1928.

Honorio Delgado, an outstanding Peruvian psychiatrist, published his doctoral thesis on psychoanalysis in 1915, and was the first Latin American to become a member of the International Psychoanalytic Association, though he later abandoned this orientation. Angel Gama, Celes E. Carcamo, Enrique Pichon-Riviere, Arnaldo and Luis Raskowsky, and Marie Langer founded the Asociacion Psicoanalitica Argentina in 1942. At present there are psychoanalytic associations in Montevideo, Rio de Janeiro, Santiago, Porto Alegre, Mexico, Bogota and Caracas. A coordinating organization of Latin-American psychoanalytic associations (COPAL) was founded in Santiago in 1960.

A group of prominent Latin American psychiatrists attending the First World Congress of Psychiatry in Paris (1950) conceived the idea of creating the Latin-American Psychiatric Association (APAL). It was through the untiring efforts of Gregorio Bermann, José Angel Bustamante, Guillermo Davila, Raul Gonzalez-Henriquez, Antonio Carlos Pacheco e Silva, and Carlos A. Seguin that this Association, which brings together 14 national psychiatric societies in Latin America, was formed. There have been congresses in Caracas (1961), Mexico City (1962), Lima (1964), Buenos Aires (1966), Bogotá (1968) and São Paulo (1970).

The Inter-American Council of Psychiatric Associations (IACPA) which coordinates the Latin American Psychiatric Association (APAL) with the American Psychiatric Association and the Canadian Psychiatric Association was founded in 1965 under the aegis of Daniel Blain, Guillermo Dávila and Carlos A. Seguín. Under the auspices of IACPA, the first Conference for Mental Health in the Americas took place in San Antonio, Texas, in 1968, attended by an enthusiastic group of psychiatrists from the hemisphere. This was a unique opportunity for assessing the present and future of psychiatry in terms of existing services, needs, resources, education, research and planning. A wealth of information was collected in working papers prepared by several commissions, circulated among participants and discussed during the meetings. From the discussions a series of recommendations were formulated and presented in a final report (Brody 1969). Material presented at the conference has been of great value in the preparation of this paper.

IV. Resources

The Psychiatrist

Because of overwhelming difficulties in obtaining reliable and comparable information about the different types of professionals involved in psychiatric activities in Latin America, we will restrict our discussion to psychiatrists. According to a 1968 estimate there were in Latin America about 3,350 psychiatrists.

A previously published Provisional Directory of Latin American Psychiatrists (PAHO 1967) lists 3,445 professionals. However, its accuracy is questionable, because of overrepresentation in some countries and underrepresentation in others.

The distribution of psychiatrists according to countries is quite uneven, ranging between rates of 0.08 and 4.1 per 100,000 inhabitants, with an average for the whole region of 1.52. It is evident that even in the best of situations the number of psychiatrists falls short of the minimal proportion recommended by WHO (5 psychiatrists per 100,000 inhabitants). Furthermore, because of the high concentration of psychiatrists in the big cities, and the difficulties in transportation and communication, there are extensive areas in which many people are entirely deprived of psychiatric services and even of general medical services. Because of inadequate systems of public medical care, large sections of the population who cannot afford private fees never have the opportunity to receive psychiatric care, short of admission to a public psychiatric hospital during an acute psychotic episode.

A study made in 1966–67 on a sample of Latin-American psychiatrists, stratified by country (León 1970a) showed that the largest proportion of Latin-American psychiatrists are engaged in private practice as their main professional activity, followed by hospital work with in-patients, and teaching (table 30.3).

With regard to scientific orientation it was found that the predominant type is the "eclectic," followed by the "psychodynamic," while the "reflexological" and "behavoristic" orientations have a minimal representation (table 30.4).

The average period of psychiatric training for this group of professionals is two years. Most of them (74 percent) were trained in their own countries, but some spent at least one year in training

Table 30.3 Main professional activity of a sample of Latin-American psychiatrists (1966-1967)

Main professional activity	*N*	*Percent*
Private practice	42	34.2
Hospital work with in-patients	20	16.3
Teaching	12	9.8
Hospital work in out-patient clinics	9	7.3
Work in health centers	2	1.6
Research	2	1.6
Several concomitant (rather than one main activity)	33	26.8
Others	3	2.4
Total	123	100.0

Source: Data from Leon (1970a).

abroad, mostly in the U.S.A. (17 percent), France (5 percent) or the United Kingdom (4 percent).

In a very perceptive profile of some of the characteristics of Latin-American psychiatrists, Martins describes the senior professionals working for public institutions as usually engaged in bureaucratic or administrative activities, very often sceptical of the initiatives for institutional change and disdainful of the use of sociotherapeutic methods. On the other hand the young psychiatrist is

Table 30.4 Predominant scientific orientation of a sample of Latin-American psychiatrists (1966-1967)

Scientific orientation	*N*	*Percent*
Eclectic	41	33.3
Psychodynamic	27	22.0
Psychoanalytic	20	16.3
Biologic	12	9.8
Phenomenologic	6	4.9
Existential	2	1.6
Behavioristic	1	0.8
Reflexologic	1	0.8
Several concomitant	4	3.2
Other	7	5.7
No answer	2	1.6
Total	123	100.0

Source: Data from Leon (1970a)

described as the product of one or two years of training in a psychiatric hospital or rarely in a university department of psychiatry; usually he has been unable to receive good training because of financial difficulties or lack of regional facilities, and looks forward to the opportunity of obtaining a fellowship to study abroad where he hopes to have the training he has idealized. If he leaves the country he may not return, and if he does it is quite likely that he will be unable to adjust to institutional work and will turn exclusively to private practice (Martins 1970).

The Services

The traditional neglect of public office everywhere in matters relative to the psychiatric care of the population truly reaches alarming proportions in the underdeveloped countries. After adequately solving the basic problems of communicable diseases and environmental sanitation, the developed countries have gradually turned their attention to the psychiatric coverage of the population by increasing the number and quality of their facilities. It is only in the last decades that an incipient awareness has developed in Latin America with regard to the tremendous social and economic impact of mental disorders on a community. This is understandable in an area where the resources for public health have always been acutely insufficient to face such problems as tuberculosis, malnutrition, infectious and parasitic diseases. Only to the extent that these problems have been successfully confronted has the need to do something about mental disorders begun to emerge.

The traditional means of dealing with psychiatric problems has been the large hospitals for custodial care of overtly psychotic patients. Large buildings crowded with patients, the number almost always greater than the number of beds, where in an indiscriminate mixture one can see patients representing the whole gamut of degenerative neurological disorders, psychoses and mental deficiency, and care provided by an absurdly insufficient number of doctors and nurses who often lack even an elementary type of training. In our very day, there are only a few countries in which the number of psychiatric hospitals and the number of beds (table 30.5) reach the proportions considered as minimal by WHO, and in some cases the shortage can hardly be matched elsewhere in the world.

As a general rule, the physical facilities of the hospitals are overtaxed by the great number of patients, and the conditions of

Table 30.5 Distribution of public psychiatric hospitals[a], number of psychiatric beds and rate per 10,000 inhabitants[b] in 20 Latin-American countries

Countries	*Public psychiatric hospitals*	*Total number of psychiatric beds*	*Rate of beds per 10,000 inhab.*
Argentina	91	29,294	12.2
Bolivia	4	630	1.3
Brazil	56	62,882	7.7
Chile	5	8,970	11.2
Colombia	13	7,490	3.8
Costa Rica	1	1,081	6.7
Cuba	14	6,206	9
Dominican Republic	2	715	2
Ecuador	3	1,702	3
El Salvador	1	496	1.5
Guatemala	1	1,172	2.6
Haiti	2	20	0.06
Honduras	2	190	0.8
Mexico	33	8,405	2
Nicaragua	1	1,150	6
Panama	4	1,200	8.1
Paraguay	1	665	3
Peru	3	2,010	1.7
Uruguay	2	5,000	1.8
Venezuela	14	4,527	4.5

[a] Source: A Directory of World Psychiatry compiled by Dr. John Gunn on behalf of the World Psychiatric Association, 1971.

[b] Source: Working papers for the Conference on Mental Health in the Americas–San Antonio, 1968.

hygiene, comfort, food and professional care could hardly be worse.

Mexico, the first country of Latin America where a psychiatric hospital was founded, continues to be in the vanguard of progress in the provision of services through an institutional network which incorporates the most recent advances in design, comfort and therapeutic facilities (Calderón-Narváez 1970).

During recent years, in conjunction with marked improvements in the teaching of psychiatry and the training of specialists, we are witnessing a progressive increment in several countries of the number and quality of psychiatric facilities and personnel, as well as the adoption of "modern" patterns of psychiatric care: open-door hospitals, psychiatric units in general hospitals, out-patient clinics, mental health centers, sheltered workshops, and various forms of community care (Lucero-Kelly 1968; Brum-Butler 1968; Argandoña 1969; Esquibel 1969; Carrizosa et al. 1970; Moraes Andrade 1970; Cabral 1970).

There has been a gradual shift in some countries towards a criterion of crisis intervention, delegation of responsibilities to paramedical personnel, and community work aimed at the removal of the stigma attached to mental disorders, and increased contact between staff, patients and relatives. A few of the psychiatric hospitals and psychiatric units in general hospitals are evolving into centers for community mental health (Sisto 1970).

In comparing data from two reports published in 1963 on the state of psychiatric services in Latin America (Velasco-Alzaga 1963; Bermann 1963) with those available for the 1968 Conference on Mental Health in the Americas, one can find a definite trend towards improvement, which although not shared in equal proportion by all countries points to progress in the provision of services for the mentally ill.

A report of the early sixties describing the recently changed conditions of a Latin American psychiatric hospital reads as follows: "The only place where clinical teaching could be conducted was in the so called 'asilo' (asylum) since no other facilities existed in the city for the care of psychiatric patients. In previous years the patients had been gathered in vacant lots surrounded by barbed wire fences where they idled naked and in utter promiscuity. Diagnostically they included psychotics, epileptics, mental defectives, as well as beggars, cripples, and invalids of all kinds. At this "asilo" the historical span of progress in the care of psychiatric patients is much narrower than that of Europe or the United States. The institution has moved 200 years during the past eight years. Eight years ago, it was a human garbage pail for the unwanted mentally ill and mentally defective human beings of the region. Here the police literally dumped these disabled people over the wall into the enclosed compound of the hospital. Often bones were broken in the fall to the ground. Acutely disturbed patients were chained to the floor of dirty cells or placed in strait-jackets and given cold showers with hoses. The emphasis was directed toward protecting the personnel rather than toward protecting the patients. Care was custodial, with enforced incarceration under the most unsanitary conditions and minimal emphasis on therapeutic rehabilitation. The philosophy of care was based on the old adage: 'Where there is no sense, there is no feeling' (Leon quoted by Romano 1967). Fighting the formidable obstacles of a very inadequate budget and the inertia of tradition, a small group of professionals in a resolute move gained access to this institution and after re-naming it Hospital Psiquiatrico, abolished restraints, enforced a set of humane rules and regulations dealing with all aspects of patient handling, from admission to discharge, and secured the active participations of medical students and interns in the care of patients as an integral part of their medical training. At the same time, with the enthusiastic backing of a remotivated board of trustees, they carried on a very active campaign to build a new hospital which was completed by 1961."

V. Research

As can be seen in table 30.4, only a minimal proportion of psychiatrists in Latin America are engaged in research as their main activity. Indeed, there is very little tradition for this kind of work, and only in recent years has it begun to develop.

Among the possible adverse factors in the establishment of research programs and activities in Latin America we can readily identify the following: (a) Teaching and learning methods, with emphasis on memorizing of information, on a bookish type of erudition and on ability in rhetoric rather than on empirical scientific work, have seriously interfered with research activities, since neither teachers nor students have had opportunities for inductive thinking, systematic application of empirical observation or the use of statistical methods of analysis, (b) the meager amount of local funds for financing research prevents professionals from devoting themselves full time to research activities, (c) the lack of a tradition for coordinated group work creates enormous problems in building up a research team.

Most of the recent psychiatric research deals with epidemiological, social, or transcultural aspects of psychiatry. This is understandable, because there are so many fascinating unanswered questions in these areas. There has been a gradual accumulation of information about prevalence of mental disorders and related problems (Marconi 1955; Horwitz et al. 1958; Spinola and Velasco-Alzaga 1960; Rotondo et al. 1963; Pages-Larraya et al. 1966; Marconi and Muñoz 1970; Bermann 1970; G. Adis Castro et al. 1968; Moya et al. 1969; Mariátegui and Adis Castro 1970; Mariátegui, Alva and DeLeon 1970; Cabildo 1970; Bachini et al. 1970; Tarnopolski et al., 1970).

The acute lack of well-trained personnel, laboratory facilities and funds has been a serious handicap in the implementation of research activities in the basic sciences related to psychiatry. In this area there is very little work indeed.[1]

Clinical research dealing with therapeutic methods has increased during recent years, especially in relation to the periodic appearance of new psychotropic drugs. Lately, there has been increasing interest in operations research and systems analysis, primarily directed at the analysis of cost-benefit in psychiatric services and the exploration of alternative models for the provision of health care.

A total of 53 journals dealing with psychiatry and related disciplines are published in Latin America (table 30.6). Unfortunately a good many of them do not appear with strict regularity and only have national circulation, being virtually unknown in other countries. In spite of the great effort made by organizations such as the Latin American Psychiatric Association (APAL) and the Pan-American Health Organization, communication between psychiatrists in Latin America is at best sporadic and restricted, and a great deal more is known about psychiatry and psychiatrists in Europe or U.S.A. than about what goes on in neighboring countries. Under these circumstances it is encouraging to note that at least one journal, *Acta Psiquiátrica y Psicológica de America Latina,* enjoys a wide circulation and has become a forum for diffusion of psychiatric ideas and knowledge. It is edited under the dynamic direction of Guillermo Vidal and is sponsored by ACTA, Fondo para la Salud Mental. This foundation also sponsors the publication of monographs which deal with crucial problems of Latin-American psychiatry.

VI. Education

Traditionally the teaching of psychiatry as a subject in medical schools consisted of a very brief period at the end of the clinical

1. However, it is fitting to remark on the very high quality of some of this research such as that of Hernandez Peon and Castellanos in Mexico, Fernandez Moran in Venezuela, Rocha e Silva in Brazil and Naranjo in Ecuador, to mention only a few.

Table 30.6 Distribution of university departments of psychiatry, psychiatric journals and psychiatric societies in 20 Latin-American countries

Countries	*University departments of psychiatry*	*Psychiatric journals*	*Psychiatric societies*
Argentina	10	12	3
Bolivia	3	1	1
Brazil	10	12	4
Chile	4	2	2
Colombia	6	2	1
Costa Rica	1	1	1
Cuba	3	3	1
Dominican Republic	1	1	1
Ecuador	2	1	1
Guatemala	1	1	1
Haiti	4	1	1
Honduras	1	1	1
Mexico	1	6	2
Nicaragua	1	1	1
Panama	3	1	1
Paraguay	1	1	1
Peru	7	3	2
Uruguay	1	1	1
Venezuela	6	1	1
Totals	68	53	28

Source: 'A Directory of World Psychiatry', compiled by Dr. John Gunn on behalf of the World Psychiatric Association, 1971.

years during which a summary review of the major mental disorders was presented through a series of lectures, usually divorced from any form of clinical practice. The abrupt confrontation with clinical entities, for the understanding of which the student had neither basic knowledge nor objective experience, must have been responsible for the general attitude of regarding psychiatry as an esoteric discipline rather than as a crucial element in the making of a doctor. On the other hand, psychiatric training for specialists consisted of variable periods of affiliation of the candidate to the medical personnel of asylums, where without any sort of formal instruction or supervision and only guided by indiscriminate reading he started the formidable task of finding his way through a field plagued by uncertainties, vagueness, and controversy. Only the very lucky could benefit from personal contact with a teacher and enjoy the privilege of tutorial apprenticeship. Furthermore, the conventional type of Latin American senior psychiatrist was far removed from the ideal of a benevolent teacher. In fact, we often see him as a confused mixture of speculative philosopher and bohemian: witty, sharp, and sarcastic, always prompt to engage in polemics with his medical colleagues; bold in his conceptions, brilliant and imaginative, but utterly unproductive in systematic and disciplined work; acutely sensitive to criticism, always armed with irony and cynicism and a heavy load of overvalued ideas; argumentative and eloquent, assiduous reader and skillful speaker, but because of a selfish and sceptical individualism incapable of attracting students or creating an academic atmosphere.

It is a heavy task for present-day psychiatrists to erase this image from popular conception and substitute for it that of a professional person scientifically sound and with enough emotional stability to relate harmoniously with his fellow men and to serve them as an expert in the solution of their problems. However, the gradual emergence of an increasing number of psychiatrists with adequate personal and professional qualities seems to indicate that the situation is improving and that training programs are making efforts in this direction.

At present there are in Latin America 154 medical schools, and in each of them psychiatry is taught as an independent subject. However, there is a wide variation between different places in the number of hours devoted to psychiatry in the curricula, and whether teaching involves clinical work or not. The range goes from 15 to more than 600 hours, at one extreme consisting exclusively of lectures on clinical psychiatry and at the other of complete courses in medical psychology, psychopathology and clinical psychiatry, plus four weeks of clinical clerkship and four weeks of internship (León 1959). During the last two decades a great deal of concern has been expressed for improving the teaching of psychiatry, and several important publications bear testimony to this concern (Etchegoyen et al. 1960; Matte-Blanco 1961; Leme-Lopes 1961, 1962; Seguín 1964; Queról 1965). The Pan-American Health Organization sponsored a seminar on the teaching of Psychiatry and Mental Health in Medical Schools which met in Lima in 1967, producing a series of recommendations for improvement in this field.

Currently there are 68 Departments of Psychiatry (table 30.6) in Latin America, most of which offer teaching at both the undergraduate and the graduate level. It is estimated that there are a total of about 90 institutions for the training of psychiatrists. In some places this training takes a period of three years and is modelled after the American system of residency with full-time clinical and academic work, while others have an on-the-job type of training. Even though the differences between institutions is very great, there is reason for optimism because of the emergence of several centers which share the common characteristics of an intense devotion to their task and a vigorous enthusiasm for improving existing conditions (Gonzalez and Gallegos 1964; De La Fuente 1965; Vidal 1965; Goldenberg 1966; Pacheco e Silva 1966; Perdomo 1968). A full-time faculty and facilities for research and service have allowed a few medical schools in Latin America to create favorable conditions for the teaching of medicine and the training of specialists. Systems for selection which limit the number of students guarantee an optimal use of teaching facilities, and although these types of institutions are still scarce the effort and initiative seems to have brought about a process of healthy emulation which is gradually extending to other centers.

An important aspect of the training of Latin-American psychiatrists is the fact that a sizable number tend to travel abroad for specialization. Before World War II Europe, and more specifically France, was the place of preference; but since the early forties the U.S.A. has become the goal for many, and there is a steady migration of Latin-American doctors seeking graduate studies in psychiatry. In general, for those who go to Europe, the United Kingdom now seems to be the place of choice for training.

This fact, which in general terms could be regarded as desirable for the development of Latin-American psychiatric potential, may, however, be diminished in net value because of certain adverse factors, of which two stand out. The first has to do with the reluctance of the young professional to go back to his country of origin upon completion of his training. The well publicized problem of the brain drain seems to apply to our countries and is justifiable in most cases because of the excellent working opportunities and high payment found in the host country, in contrast with the difficulties existing at home. Secondly, the type of training received and the cultural context in which this occurs may not be related to conditions in the country of origin. In fact, it is quite possible for the candidate to be submitted to a type of training the operative value of which may depend on ethnic, social, economic and cultural conditions quite different from those at home. Moreover, his clinical experience may be inadequate or insufficient when it is acquired with patients from a different culture. In order to avoid these pitfalls, psychiatric training in a foreign country may need to be preceded by a solid conceptual background and clinical experience acquired at home.

To maximize the advantages of training abroad, a select group of candidates could undergo a period of special preparation in their own institutions and then be sent to foreign centers to be trained in technical matters or specialized fields. People with such training might then become the academic core for teaching and research activities at local institutions. Likewise, foreign centers might send their trainees for prescribed periods of study and research in Latin America under adequate local supervision.

This double current of young people in training might help to emphasize their mutual needs and reinforce both programs by creating an effective basis for cooperation.

Finally, there is the possibility of creating international centers in one or more regions of Latin America which could operate as institutions for advanced training for select groups of professionals under the sponsorship of international agencies.

In a proposal which goes a step beyond the above described cooperative program, a system has been envisioned for reviewing and information exchange in psychiatry for the Americas which would eventually lead to the formulation of standards and guidelines, and finally to the establishment of an Inter-American accrediting and certifying Board. Such action would hopefully provide "a powerful impetus in the direction of producing competent psychiatrically trained physicians whose credentials would be acceptable throughout the hemisphere" (Brody 1970).

VII. Final Comments

An effort has been made to present a panoramic view of psychiatry in Latin America. The main obstacle to the successful completion of this task has been the serious lack of accurate information regarding facts in each one of the countries. It is a well-known but often overlooked fact that one of the surest signs of underdevelopment is the inability to *measure* problems, needs and resources. The 1968 Conference on Mental Health in the Americas was conceived as an opportunity for gathering and exchanging information which would enable countries to have a clearer image of their realities and visualize possible actions for improving them. Although great efforts were made to obtain accurate and comparable information, the goal was only partially fulfilled. Yet it was possible to base most of the discussions on factual matters rather than on hypothetical issues. For this reason, and because they touch upon salient problems described in the text of this report, it may be worthwhile to state some of the recommendations made by the Conference (Brody 1969) as valuable guidelines for needed action:

> It is recommended that governments and public institutions take steps to facilitate an appropriate distribution of time and effort between public and private psychiatric or other mental health practice. Possible approaches include improved recompense for public work, scholarships or fellowships awarded on the basis of agreements for later public service, improved programmes of health insurance, and liberalized regulations permitting combined private and public practice.
>
> It is recommended that the Pan-American Health Organization consider the possibility of establishing agreements with member governments regarding mental health programmes similar to those which have previously been established regarding programmes of infectious disease control.
>
> It is recommended that the initial emphasis of research departments be placed on epidemiological, social, treatment evaluation and data utilization studies. These require a minimum of specialized equipment and permit a maximum of practical and locally relevant application of findings.
>
> The following areas, as well as studies aimed at particular clinical categories, are recommended for investigation:
>
> 1. The development of common international criteria for the classification of mental illness, the description of symptoms, and the estimate of morbidity. This includes the development of indices of social as well as individual morbidity.
>
> 2. The development of an integrated international system for data reporting.
>
> 3. Studies of population dynamics in relation to behaviour. These might include attitudes toward family planning, factors involved in out-of-wedlock births in adolescents, socio-psychological correlates of family size, the influence of population density, and related issues.
>
> 4. Studies of naturally occurring community sources of support, community social control systems, and community solutions to mental health problems such as alcoholism. These should include the study of the concepts, beliefs, and practices about psychiatric conditions and their treatment carried on in each culture through popular tradition (folklore).
>
> It is recommended that steps be taken toward the establishment of one or more regional centres within Latin America located at already

established universities or hospitals. Such centres might be concerned primarily with education, including programme demonstration, research, including research training, or both. They would provide sites for future international conferences. They would foster the retention of scholars in the area and encourage the development of studies with local or regional relevance. The centres should be developed whenever possible with multinational representation and financing. A system of grants and scholarships may be used to support the attendance of students and scholars from other countries.

It is recommended that steps be taken toward the establishment of a mental health information centre or clearing house in Latin America, utilizing if possible already existing personnel and facilities.

After this succinct review of the prevailing conditions in Latin America it is evident how the meager resources and facilities for dealing with mental health problems can only take care of a small proportion of the universe of patients and only offer help in the area of treatment of acute disorders, but practically nothing in the fields of prevention or rehabilitation. Furthermore, in countries where unemployment in otherwise healthy young people is so high, it is quite unrealistic to expect that with the help of a rehabilitation program an ex-mental patient could successfully compete with those who never were ill.

Problems in the area of mental health cannot be divorced from problems in public health, education, social security and welfare. The solution to these problems seems to demand a joint mobilization of social, economic and political forces which could bring about substantial changes in government, education, health, and economic development in each country. In addition there is a great need for an effective system of international cooperation which could be instrumental for the development of human resources and the improvement of facilities.

Latin American psychiatrists confront extremely difficult situations when they decide to extend their range of activities from individual clinical work to the community or social areas. Yet this possibility may represent a great challenge and a unique opportunity for contributing in some degree to orienting the process of change in these countries. In a sense, the whole of Latin America may be regarded as a vast psychosocial laboratory, opened both to the inquiries of the researcher and to the creative impulse of the man of action.

Annotated Additional Readings

a) **Allen, M. G. 1973.** Psychiatry in the United States and the USSR: A comparison. *American Journal of Psychiatry* 130:1333–1337.
The goals, service organization and techniques of psychiatric care in the U.S. are compared with those in the Soviet Union, on the basis of a review of the literature and a visit to the USSR by the author, a U.S. psychiatrist. Twenty features differentiating the psychiatric systems of these two countries are listed. Among these are the prominence of psychodynamic psychotherapy in the U.S. vs the emphasis on somatic therapy and behavioral, directive, and supportive psychotherapies in the USSR, where, in contrast to the U.S., psychiatric care is a state responsibility carried out through a centralized and standardized system which characteristically involves widely available emergency mobile psychiatric services, socially productive work as therapy, continuity of care, and a much larger proportion of female over male psychiatrists. This report is a useful complement to article 28.

b) **Carstairs, G. M. 1973.** Psychiatric problems of developing countries. *British Journal of Psychiatry* 123:271–277.
The term "developing" is used largely to identify a large number of countries located mainly in Asia, Africa, and Latin America which are characterized by very low socioeconomic, educational, and health levels and by their marked dependence on industrialized countries. The latter feature is an escalating phenomenon, as "developed" nations consistently grow at a higher rate than their "developing" counterparts, which make the latter, in comparative terms, increasingly underdeveloped.

Carstairs at the time of writing head of the psychiatry department at the University of Edinburgh, presents his perception of the problems of psychiatry in developing countries. He discusses the impact of centralization, internal migration, and population growth on socioeconomic and health conditions, the relationship between Westernized and folk health systems, and the challenges imposed on the organization of clinical services by the rural conditions and the severe limitations in manpower and budget prevailing in these areas.

c) **Brody, E. B. 1973.** Psychiatric implications of industrialization and rapid social change. *Journal of Nervous and Mental Disease* 156:300–305.
A U.S. psychiatrist and educator well recognized for his Pan-American studies examines ways in which psychiatric problems and services in underdeveloped countries are determined by political and sociocultural factors. The author first reviews the "persistent poverty" of these countries, the roles that industrialized nations and small internal elites play to maintain it, and the effects of this situation on the development of resources for mental health services. He notes that industrialization provides new opportunities for upward social mobility as well as increased possibilities for discrepancy between aspirations and

achievement. Finally, the author reviews the specific influence of migration, literacy, local folk medicine, and status of the family on the nature of mental health problems and services. This paper provides views alternative to those of Carstairs.

d) Lippman, D. 1976. Psychiatry in Ethiopia. *Canadian Psychiatric Association Journal* 21:383–388.

A description of the author's experiences. He is a North American psychiatrist who worked for six months in Addis Ababa. He noted that although Ethiopia's population was at that time about 27 million, it had only six psychiatrists and two psychiatric hospitals. Amanuel Psychiatric Hospital, the largest in Ethiopia, had 300 beds available and an average census of about 550 patients, which required that most patients double up. Treatment modalities included mainly psychotropic medication and to a lesser extent brief psychotherapy and ECT, which was given to both inpatients and outpatients. The physicians ordinarily worked with the assistance of interpreters who were acquainted with one or more of the 27 Ethiopian languages. The author also reports on a survey of the demographic and psychiatric features of the 281 outpatients seen in one 5 ½ day week. He found that most patients had previously consulted with folk healers and used religious procedures as potential remedies. The diagnostic distribution showed that about one third of the patients had epilepsy or other neurological disorders and that depression was very rare (which should be considered cautiously given the difficulties on the identification of depression reported in Africa, as discussed in article 20).

e) Chang, S. C. and Kim, K. I. 1973. Psychiatry in South Korea. *American Journal of Psychiatry* 130:667–669.

Two Korean psychiatrists, the first of them working in the U.S. and the second in Seoul, review the history of psychiatry in Korea from the period of Japanese occupation (1910–1945), during which preventive and curative elements were essentially those provided by the indigenous cultural tradition (shamanism, Buddhism, Confucianism, and folk medicine), to the post-World War II era during which the influence of U.S. psychiatry on South Korea has become prominent. They then review the status of psychiatry in the early 1970s, including manpower, hospital facilities (which use psychotropic medication as the main form of treatment, along with ECT and psychotherapy), and the distribution of psychiatric disorders (which suggests that the incidence of hysteria is higher and of senile psychosis lower than in the West, for which the authors offer cultural explanations).

f) Neki, J. S. 1973. Psychiatry in South-East Asia. *British Journal of Psychiatry* 123:257–269.

The author, a professor at the All-India Institute of Medical Sciences in New Delhi, examines in this article the historical and geographical context and the current status of psychiatry in Southeast Asia. He particularly deals with the organization of clinical services, professional resources and training, folk psychiatry, and local patterns of descriptive psychopathology.

g) Kermani, E. J. 1966. Psychiatry in Iran. *American Journal of Psychiatry* 122:949–952.
An overview of Iranian psychiatry in the mid-1960s as perceived by Ebrahim Kermani, an Iranian-born physician trained as a psychiatrist in the U.S. After presenting a geographical and demographic sketch of the country, the author reviews the history of psychiatry in Iran. He notes that according to the writings of the Persian scientists and physicians, Avicenna and Rhazes in the ninth and tenth centuries, psychotic patients were already called "mentally ill" in ancient Iran, at the time when they were labeled as "lunatic" in Europe. He also notes that in the city of Yazd, there was as early as 1280 a state clinic named "The Home for Sick People," with an "Unsound Mind Division." The author then outlines the contemporary limitations in the number of psychiatrists and of psychiatric beds, which is in line with the very restricted economic resources allocated to mental health services. He points out that the number of male psychiatric inpatients clearly outnumbers the females, a distribution which appears to be common in Eastern countries in contrast to patterns in the West.

h) Ucer, E. 1968. Psychiatry in Turkey. *Mental Hygiene* 52:27–33.
A review of the roots and recent status of psychiatry in Turkey prepared by a graduate of the medical school of the University of Istanbul who was trained and works as a psychiatrist in North America. He first outlines the Turkish socioeconomic and geographic situation. Upon reviewing psychiatric history in that country, he notes that general hospitals were established first in 1205 and that the first mental hospitals were built in Istanbul in 1470 and shortly thereafter in Edirine, where agitated patients were restrained by gold or silver chains according to their severity. It is recorded that in the thirteenth century certain mental patients were placed over deep, sulfurous fume-producing holes and when they were on the verge of losing consciousness a healer would question them, a procedure which may be construed as a forerunner of psychoanalysis. The author also notes that the Koran states that the mentally ill should be kept clean, be well fed, and not be blamed for their actions. In its last section, Ucer reviews the evolution of psychiatry since the Republic was established in 1923, and the currently existing limitations in psychiatric manpower and facilities.

References

Aall-Jilek, L. 1964. Geisteskrankheiten und Epilepsie im tropischen Afrika. *Neurologie-Psychiatrie* 32:213–259,

Abel, T. M. and R. A. Calabrisi. The people from their Rorschach tests. In O'Lewis, *Life in a Mexican Village*. Urbana, Illinois: University of Chicago Press.

Abernethy, V. 1976. Cultural perspective on the impact of women's changing roles on psychiatry. *American Journal of Psychiatry* 133:657–661.

Ablon, J. 1961. Relocated American Indians in the San Francisco Bay Area: Social interaction and Indian identity. *Human Organization* 23:296.

Ablon, J. 1965. American Indian relocation: Problems of dependency and management in the city. *Phylon* 26:362.

Abraham, J. J. 1912. Latah and Amok. *British Medical Journal* 1:438:439.

Abraham, K. 1960. Notes on the psychoanalytic investigation and treatment of manic depressive insanity and allied conditions. In *Selected Papers on Psychoanalysis*, pp. 137, 56. New York: Basic Books.

Adams, A. R. D. 1950–1952. Amok. In *British Encyclopedia of Medical Practice*. London: Butterworth.

Ader, R. 1973. Early experiences and susceptibility to disease. In S. A. Barnett, ed. *Ethnology and Development*. London: Heinemann.

Adis Castro, G. and R. Hernández-Ureña. 1967. Causas de enfermedad mental: Conceptos populares. *Revista Interamericana de Psicologia* 1:297–312.

Adis Castro, G., R. A. Hernandez-Urena, C. Viquez Carsajal, and F. Alvarenga Bianco. 1968. *Prevalencia de problemas de salud mental en Costa Rica*. Centro de Investigaciones Psicológicas, Universidad de Costa Rica.

Adorno, T. W., E. Frenkel-Brunswik, D. J. Levinson, R. N. Sanford. 1950. *The Authoritarian Personality*. New York: Harper.

Ainsworth, M. D. 1967. *Infancy in Uganda*. Baltimore: Johns Hopkins University Press.

Alexander, F. and T. M. French. 1948. *Studies in Psychosomatic Medicine*. New York: Ronald Press.

Alexander, F. G. and S. Selesnick. 1966. *The History of Psychiatry.* New York: Harper and Row.

Allen, M. G. 1973. Psychiatry in the United States and the USSR: A comparison. *American Journal of Psychiatry* 130:12, 1333–1337.

Alvarado, J. M. 1965. Supersticiones y mitos en la psiquiatria indigena de Bolivia. *Acta Psiquiatrica y de America Latina.* 2:24–35.

American Psychiatric Association. 1968. *Diagnostic and Statistical Manual of Mental Disorders,* 2d ed. Washington, D.C.: APA.

American Psychiatric Association. 1980. *Diagnostic and Statistical Manual of Mental Disorders,* 3d Edition. Washington, D.C.: American Psychiatric Association.

Amir, M. 1939. Over eenige gevallen van amok uit Noord Sumartra. *Geneek T Med-Ind* 79:2786–2798.

Amir, Y., S. Sharan, and Y. Kovarsky. 1968. Birth order, family structure, and avoidance behavior. *Journal of Personality and Social Psychology* 10 (3):271–278.

Ancherson, P. 1964. Discussion. In E. Beresford Davies, ed. *Depression: A Cambridge Postgraduate Course.* Cambridge University Press.

Anderson, O. and R. Andersen. 1972. Patterns of use of health services. In Howard Freeman et al. eds. *Handbook of Medical Sociology,* 2d ed., pp. 386–406. Englewood Cliffs: Prentice-Hall.

Antonovsky, A. 1972. A model to explain visits to the doctor: With specific reference to Israel. *Journal of Health and Social Behavior* 13:446–454.

Appel, L. F., R. G. Cooper, N. McCarrell, J. S. Knight, S. R. Yussen, and J. H. Flavell. 1971. The Developmental acquisition of the distinction between perceiving and memory. Unpublished manuscript, University of Minnesota, Minneapolis.

Argandoña, M. 1969. El Guabal—Social psychiatry in Latin America. Unpublished.

Arieti, S. 1959. Manic depressive psychosis. In S. Arieti, ed. 1959:1:419–454.

Arieti, S., ed. 1959. *American Handbook of Psychiatry.* New York: Basic Books, 2d ed. 1974.

Arieti, S. and J. M. Meth. 1959. Rare, unclassifiable, collective, and exotic psychotic syndromes. In S. Arieti, ed. 1959.

Asch, S. E. 1951. Effects of group pressure upon the modification and distortion of judgments. In H. Guetzkow, ed. *Groups, Leadership and Men.* Pittsburgh: Carnegie Press.

Asch, S. E. 1956. Studies of independence and conformity. *Psychological Monographs* 70 (9).

Astrup, C. and O. Odegaard. 1960. Internal migration and mental disease in Norway. *Psychiatric Quarterly* 34:116.

Asuni, T. 1962. Suicide in Western Nigeria. *British Medical Journal* 2:1091.

Asuni, T. 1969. Sociopsychiatric problems in transitional Nigeria. Paper presented at the International Meeting on African Studies. Montreal.

Ayllon, T. and J. Michael. 1959. The psychiatric nurse as a behavioral engineer. *Journal of the Experimental Analysis of Behavior* 2:323–334.

Azima, H. and G. J. Sarwer-Foner. 1961. Psychoanalytic formulations of the effect of drugs in pharmacotherapy. *Review of Canadian Biology* 20:603–614.

Bachini, O., D. Zabala, D. Murguia, C. Tobler, H. Pupo, D. Vaghi, and J. Seigal. 1970. Estudios epidemiologicos en psiquiatria en el Uruguay. In Roselli, ed. 1970.

Bacon, M. K. 1973. Cross-cultural studies of drinking. In P. G. Bourne and R. Fox, eds. *Alcoholism: Progress in Research and Treatment.* New York: Academic Press.

Bagadia V. N., D. V. Jesta, K. P. Dave, S. U. Doshi, and L. P. Shah. 1970. A prospective epidemiological study of 233 cases of depression. *Indian Journal of Psychiatry* 12:190.

Bagley, C. 1965. Juvenile delinquency in Exeter: An ecological and comparative study. *Urban Studies* 2:39–50.

Bagley, C. 1968. Migration, race and mental health: A review of some recent research. *Race* 9:343–356.

Bagley, C. 1969a. A comparative study of mental illness amongst immigrants in Britain. In proceedings of the Anglo-French Conference on Race Relations, Sussex, 1968, The Hague: Mauton.

Bagley, C. 1969b. *The Cost of a Child: Problems in the Relief and Measurement of Poverty.* London: Joseph Rowntree Memorial Trust.

Bagley, C. 1969c. *Social Structure and Prejudice in Five English Boroughs.* London: Institute of Race Relations.

Bagley, C. 1969d. Race relations and theories of status consistency. *Race* 11:267–288.

Bagley, C. 1969e. Alienation and human fulfillment: A case study of South Africa. *Journal of Human Relations* 17:12–25.

Bagley, C. 1971. The social etiology of schizophrenia in immigrant groups. *International Journal of Social Psychiatry* 17:292, 305.

Bagley, C. 1973. Occupational class and symptoms of depression. *Social Science and Medicine* 7:327.

Bagley, C. and A. Binitie. 1969. Alcoholism and schizophrenia in Irishmen in London. *British Journal of Addiction* 65:3–7.

Bakker, D. J. 1972. *Temporal Order in Disturbed Reading.* Rotterdam: Rotterdam University Press.

Bales, R. F. 1946. Cultural differences in rates of alcoholism. *Journal of Studies on Alcohol* 6:480–499.

Balint, M. 1957. *The Doctor, His Patient and the Illness.* New York: International Universities Press.

Bart, P. 1968. Social structure and vocabularies of discomfort: What happened to female hysteria. *Journal of Health and Social Behavior* 9:188–193.

Barthol, R. R. and R. Demille. 1969. *Project Echo, Final Report.* Santa Barbara, California: General Research Corp.

Bastide, R. 1967. Les Ameriques Noires: Les civilisations africaines dans le Nouveau Monde. Paris: Editions Payor.

Bateson, G., D. D. Jackson, J. Haley, and J. Weakland. 1956. Toward a theory of schizophrenia. *Behavioral Science* 1:251–264.

Bateson, G. 1936. *Naven.* London: Cambridge University Press.

Baxter, B. L. 1966. Effect of visual deprivation during postnatal maturation on the electroencephalogram of the cat. *Experimental Neurology* 14:224–237.

Bazelon, D. L. 1968. Impressions of Soviet psychiatry: The law and the mentally ill. *American Journal of Psychiatry* 125:665–669.

Bazzoui, W. 1970. Affective disorders in Iraq. *British Journal of Psychiatry* 117:195.

Beaglehole, E. 1939. Some Hawaiians: Culture and psychosis in Hawaii. University of Hawaii Research Publication no. 19, Appendix B.

Becker, S. W., M. J. Lerner, and J. Carroll. 1966. Conformity as a function of birth order and type of group pressure: A verification. *Journal of Personality and Social Psychiatry* 3:242–244.

Beetham, D. 1967. *Immigrant School Leavers and the Youth Employment Service in Birmingham.* London: Institute of Race Relations.

Beiser, M., W. Burr, J. Ravel, and H. Collomb. 1973. Illness of the spirit among the Serer of Senegal. *American Journal of Psychiatry* 130:881–886.

Bellak, L. 1969. Soviet psychiatric lag. *American Journal of Psychiatry* 125:9, 1267.

Bellak, L. and L. Loeb, eds. 1969. *Schizophrenia: A Review of the Syndrome.* New York: Grune and Stratton.

Benedict, P. K. 1958. Cultural factors in schizophrenia. In L. Bellack, ed. *Schizophrenia: Review of the Syndrome,* New York: Logos Press.

Benedict, P. K. and I. Jacks. 1954. Mental illness in primitive societies. *Psychiatry* 17:377–389.

Benedict, R. 1934. *Patterns of Culture.* Boston: Houghton Mifflin.

Benedict, R. 1946. *The Chrysantheman and the Sword.* Boston: Houghton Mifflin.

Benoist, A. 1964. Valeurs culturelles et depression: Les Canadians Français de Montreal. Paper read at the first International Congress of Social Psychiatry, London.

Benoist, A., M. Roussin, M. Fredette, and S. Rousseau. 1965. La depression chez les Canadiens Français de Montreal. *Transcultural Psychiatric Research Review* 2:52.

Benoit, G. 1964. Qu'est-ce que la psychiatrie transculturelle. *Information Psychiatrique.* 40:592.

Bente, D., et al. 1968. Extrapyramidal-motorische und electroenzephalographische Reaktivitat unter neuroleptischer Medikation. *Pharmakopsychiatrie* 1:27–45.

Bermann, S. 1963. La asistencia psiquiatrica en Latino-américa. *Acta Psiquiat. Psicol. Arg.* 9:56–71.

Bermann, S. 1970. Problemas actuales de la epidemiologia psiquiatrica en America Latina. In Roselli, ed. 1970. *Psiquiatria en la America Latina.* Bogota: Tercer Mundo.

Berne, E. 1960. The cultural problem: Psychopathology in Tahiti. *American Journal of Psychiatry* 116:1076.

Berry, J. W. 1969. On cross-cultural comparability. *International Journal of Psychology* 4:119–128.

Bernstein, B. 1958. Some sociological determinants of perception. *British Journal of Sociology* 9:159–174.

Best, J. B. 1966. Impressions on a recent visit to China. *Medical Journal of Australia* 2:1242–1245.

Birdwhistell, R. 1952. *Introduction to Kinesics.* Louisville: University of Louisville Press.

Blalock, H. M. Jr. 1961. *Causal Inferences in Nonexperimental Research.* Chapel Hill: University of North Carolina Press.

Blanc, H. 1956. Multilingual interviewing in Israel. *American Journal of Sociology* 62:205–209.

Blau, P. M. 1956. Social mobility and interpersonal relations. *American Sociological Review* 21:290.

Blishen, B. R. 1964. The construction and use of an occupational class scale. In B. R. Blishen et al., eds. *Canadian Society.* Toronto: Macmillan.

Blum, R. et al. 1959. *Drugs and Society,.* vol. 1. Stanford: Jossey-Bass.

Bohannan, P. 1954. "Translation—A problem in anthropology." *The Listener,* pp.814–816.

Boissevain, J. 1974. *Friends of Friends—Networks, Manipulators and Coalitions.* New York: St. Martin's.

Bolman, W. M. 1968. Cross-cultural Psychotherapy. *American Journal of Psychiatry* 124:1237.

Bonner, J. T. 1974. *On Development: The Biology of Form.* Cambridge: Harvard University Press.

Book, J. A. 1953. A genetic and neuropsychiatric investigation of North Swedish population. *Acta Genetica* 4:345.

Bordeleau, J. M. 1963. Medicine et psychiatric haitiennes. *Transcultural Psychiatric Research Review* 15:58.

Bosco, J. 1972. The visual information processing speed of lower middle class children. *Child Development* 43:1418–1422.

Bourguignon, E. 1973. Epilogue: Some notes on contemporary Americans and the Irrational. In Bourguignon, ed. *Religion, Altered States of Consciousness and Social Change.* Columbus: Ohio State University Press.

Bowman, K. M. 1948. Psychiatry in China. *American Journal of Psychiatry* 105:70–71.

Boyce, R. M. and D. S. Barnes. 1966. Psychiatric problems of university students. *Canadian Psychiatric Association Journal* 11:49–56.

Bremer, J. 1951. A social psychiatric investigation of small community in Northern Norway. *Acta Psychiatrica et Neurologica, Scandinavica.* Supp. 62.

Brislin, R. W. 1970. Back-translation for cross-cultural research. *Journal of Cross-cultural Psychology* 1:185–216.

Brislin, R. W., W. J. Lonner, and R. N. Thorndike. 1973. *Cross-Cultural Research Methods.* New York: John Wiley.

Brockington, L., L. Phillips, J. G. Draguns, and A. J. Marsella. 1969. Ethnic descent and psychiatric symptomatology. In *Proceedings of the Eleventh Interamerican Congress of Psychology.* 1:83.

Brod, T. M. 1975. Alcoholism as a mental health problem of native Americans. *Archives of General Psychiatry* 32:1385–1391.

Brody, E. B. 1964. Some conceptual and methodological issues involved in research of society, culture and mental illness. *Journal of Nervous and Mental Disease* 139:62.

Brody, E. B. 1966. Recording cross-culturally useful interview data: Experience from Brazil. *American Journal of Psychiatry* 123: 446–456.

Brody, E. B. 1969. *Mental Health in the Americas.* (Report of the first Working Conference in Mental Health in the Americas.) Washington: American Psychiatric Association.

Brody, E. B. 1970. Psychiatric education in the Americas. Presented to the Conference of the Interamerican Council of Psychiatric Associations, Halifax (mimeographed copy).

Brody, H. 1973. The systems view of man: Implications for medicine, science and ethics. *a Perspectives in Biology and Medicine.* 16:71.

Bronfenbrenner, U. 1961a. The changing American child. *Merrill-Palmer Quarterly* 7:73–84.

Bronfenbrenner, U. 1961b. Toward a theoretical model for the analysis of parent-child relationships in a social context. In J. D. Glidewell, ed. *Parental Attitudes and Child Behavior.* Springfield, Ill.: Charles C. Thomas.

Bronfenbrenner, U. 1962. Soviet methods of character education. *American Psychologist* 17:550–564.

Bronfenbrenner, U. 1967. Response to pressure from peers versus adults among Soviet and American school children. *International Journal of Psychology* 2:199–207.

Bronfenbrenner, U. 1970a. Reaction to social pressure from adults versus peers among Soviet day school and boarding school pupils in the perspective of an American sample. *Journal of Personality and Social Psychology* 15:179–189.

Bronfenbrenner, U. 1970b. *Two worlds of childhood: U.S. and USSR.*New York: Russell Sage Foundation.

Broverman, I. K., S. R. Vogel, and D. M. Broverman. 1972. Sex-role stereotypes. *Journal of Social Issues* 28:59–78.

Brown, G. W. and J. L. T. Birley. 1968. Crises and life changes and the onset of schizophrenia. *Journal of Health and Social Behaviour* 9:203–214.

Brown, G. W., J. Bone, G. Dalison, and J. K. Wing. 1966. *Schizophrenia and Social Care.* London. Oxford University Press.

Brown, R. W. 1956. Language and categories, in a Study of Thinking (by Bruner, J. S., Goodnow, J. J., and Austin, G. A.). New York.

Brum-Butler, J. L. 1968. The collective state of mental health in Uruguay. Working paper for the Conference on Mental Health in the Americas, San Antonio, Texas (mimeographed copy).

Bryant, J. 1969. *Health and the Developing World.* Ithaca: Cornell University Press, p. 28.

Buber, M. 1970. *I and Thou.* New York: Scribner's.

Buerkle, J. V. and R. J. Kleiner. 1966. *The North Philadelphia Community: Aspirations and Values.* Philadelphia: Commission on Human Relations.

Burma, J. H. 1954. *Spanish Speaking Groups in the United States.* Durham: Duke University Press.

Burton-Bradley, B. G. 1965. *Psychiatric Examination of the Papua and New Guinea Indigene.* Noumea, New Caledonia: South Pacific Commission.

Burton-Bradley, B. G. 1968. The amok syndrome in Papua and New Guinea. *Medical Journal of Australia* 1:252–256.

Burvill, P. Q., M. G. McCall, T. A. Reid, and N. S. Stenhouse. 1973. Methods of suicide in English and Welsh immigrants in Australia. *British Journal of Psychiatry* 122–220.

Burvill, P. W., M. G. McCall, N. S. Stenhouse, and T. A. Reid. 1972. Deaths from suicide, motor vehicle accidents, and all forms of violent death among migrants in Australia, 1962–66. *Acta Psychiatrica Scandinavica* 48:136.

Bustamante, J. A. 1961. Importancia del folklore en la psiquiatría. In *Proceedings of the Third World Congress of Psychiatry* 1:222–228. University of Toronto Press.

Cabildo, H. A. 1970. Investigación epidemiológica en México. In J. Mariátegui and G. Adis Castro, eds. *Estudios sobre Epidemiología Psiquiátrica en America Latina.* Buenos Aires: Acta.

Cabral, C. A. 1970. Dispensarios de salud mental en comunidades de bajo nivel economico. In Roselli, ed. 1970.

Cade, J. F. J. and J. Krupinski. 1962. Incidence of psychiatric disorders in Victoria in relation to country of birth. *Medical Journal of Australia* 1:400.

Cairns, R. B. and J. S. Nakelski. 1971. On fighting in mice: Ontogenetic and experiential determinants. *Journal of Comparative and Physiological Psychology* 74:354–364.

Calder, B. J. and M. Ross. 1973. *Attitudes and Behavior.* Morristown, N.J.: General Learning Press.

Calderón-Narvaez, G. 1970. Las instituciones hospitalarias y su importancia en la asistencia psiquiátrica. In Roselli, ed. 1970.

Campbell, D. T. 1960. Recommendations for APA test standards regarding construct, trait, or discriminant validity. *American Psychologist* 15:546–553.

Campbell, D. T. 1963. Social attitudes and other acquired behavioral dispositions. In S. Koch, ed. *Psychology: A study of a Science,* pp. 94–172. New York: McGraw-Hill.

Campbell, D. T. 1969. Reforms as experiments. *American Psychologist* 24:409–429.

Campbell, D. T. and D. W. Fiske. 1959. Convergent and discriminant validation by the multitrait-multimethod matrix. *Psychological Bulletin* 56:81–105.

Caplan, G. 1974. *Support Systems and Community Mental Health.* New York: Behavioral Publications.

Carmichael, L. 1926. The development of behavior in vertebrates experimentally removed from the influence of external stimulation. *Psychological Review* 33:51–58.

Carothers, J. C. 1945. A study of mental derangement in Africans and an attempt to explain its peculiarities. *Psychiatry* 2:47.

Carothers, J. C. 1947. A study of mental derangement in Africans. *Journal of Mental Science* 93:548–597.

Carothers, J. C. 1953. *The African Mind in Health and Disease: A Study in Ethnopsychiatry.* WHO monograph series. 17.

Carrizosa, A., A. Rivarola, P. Marin, R. Ayala, D. Barrios, and N. De Alvarenga. 1970. Asistencia psiquiátrica desde una clínica de salud mental en un centro de salud. In Roselli, ed. 1970.

Carroll, J. B. and J. B. Casagrande. 1958. The function of language classification in behavior. In E. Maccoby et al., eds. *Readings in Social Psychology,* 3d ed., pp. 18–31. New York: Holt, Rinehart and Winston.

Carstairs, G. M. 1956. Hinira and Jiryan: Two derivatives of Hindu attitudes to sexuality. *British Journal of Medical Psychology* 29:128.

Casagrande, J. B. 1954. The ends of translation. *International Journal of American Linguistics* 20:335–340.

Casey, E. C. 1973. Observations on some medical procedures in the People's Republic of China. *Journal of the National Medical Association* 65:11–13.

Cassel, J. 1964. Social science theory as a source of hypotheses in epidemiological research. *American Journal of Public Health* 54:1482.

Castaneda, C. 1968. *The Teachings of Don Juan: A Yaqui Way of Knowledge.* Berkeley: University of California Press.

Castaneda, C. 1971. *A Separate Reality: Further Conversations with Don Juan.* New York: Simon and Schuster.

Castaneda, C. 1972. *Journey to Ixtlan.* New York: Simon and Schuster.

Castaneda, C. 1974. *Tales of Power.* New York: Simon and Schuster.

Castro De La Mata, R. 1970. La medicina popular en la enseñanza de la medicina. In Roselli, ed. 1970.

Catford, J. C. 1965. *A linguistic theory of Translation: An Essay in Applied Linguistics.* London: Oxford University Press, p. 20.

Cattell, R. B. 1968. Are I.Q. tests intelligent? *Psychology Today* 1:56.

Caudill, W. 1959. Observations on the cultural context of Japanese Psychiatry. In Opler, ed. 1959.

Caudill, W. and T. Lin, eds. 1969. *Research on Mental Health in Asia and the Pacific.* Honolulu: University of Hawaii Press.

Cederbad, M. 1968. A child psychiatric study on Sudanese Arab children. *Acta Psychiatrica Scandanavica.* Supp. 200.

Cerny, J. 1965. Chinese psychiatry. *International Journal of Psychiatry* 1:229–247.

Chakraborty, A. 1971. Origin of a common psychiatric symptom among Indian patients: Study of a myth with reference to Ayurveda. Paper presented at the 5th World Congress of Psychiatry, Mexico.

Chance, N. A. 1964. A cross-cultural study of social cohesion and depression. *Transcultural Psychiatric Research Review* 1:19.

Chapple, E. D. 1970. *Culture and Biological Man.* New York: Holt, Rinehart and Winston.

Chiappe, M. 1970. El curanderismo en la costa norte del Peru. In Roselli, ed. 1970.

Child, I. 1943. *Italian or American?* New Haven: Yale University Press.

Chin, R. and A. S. Chin. 1969. *Psychological Research in Communist China.* 1949–1966. Cambridge: MIT Press.

Chow, K. L. and D. L. Stewart. 1972. Reversal of structural and functional effects of longterm visual deprivation in cats. *Experimental Neurology* 34:409–433.

Chu, L. W. and M. C. Lin. 1960. Mental diseases in Peking between 1933 and 1943. *Journal of Mental Science* 106:274.

Clark, M. 1959. *Health in the Mexican-American Culture.* Berkeley: University of California Press.

Clark, R. E. 1948. The relationship of schizophrenia to occupational income and occupational prestige. *American Sociological Review.* 13:325.

Clausen, J. and M. L. Kohn. 1959. Relation of schizophrenia to the social structure of a small city. In B. Pasamanick, ed. *Epidemiology of Mental Disorder,* pp. 69–86. Washington, D.C.: American Association for the Advancement of Science.

Clausen, J. and M. R. C. Yarrow. 1955 . Paths to the mental hospital. *Journal of Social Issues* 11:25–32.

Cleveland, E. J. and W. D. Longaker. 1967. Neurotic patterns in the family. In Gerald Handel, ed. *The Psychosocial Interior of the Family,* pp. 159–185. Chicago: Aldine.

Cohen, L. B., E. R. Gelber, and M. A. Lazar. 1971. Infant habituation and generalization of differing degrees of novelty. *Journal of Experimental Child Psychology* 11:379–389.

Cohen, Y. A. 1961. *Social Structure and Personality.* New York. Holt, Rinehart, Winston.

Cole, M., J. Gay, J. A. Glick, and D. W. Sharp. 1971. *The Cultural Context of Learning and Thinking.* New York: Basic Books.

Collomb, H. 1965. Assistance psychiatrique en Alrique: Experience Senegalaise. *Psychopathologie Africaine* 1:11.

Collomb, H. 1967. Methodological problems in cross-cultural research. *International Journal of Psychiatry.* 3(1):1.

Commonwealth Immigration Advisory Council. 1961. The Incidence of Mental Illness among Migrants. Department of Immigration, Canberra.

Cooper, J. E. 1970. The use of a procedure for standardizing psychiatric diagnosis. In Hare and Wing, (eds.)-1970: 109–131.

Cooper, J. E. 1972. *Psychiatric Diagnosis in New York and London: A Comparative Study of Mental Hospital Admissions.* London: Oxford University Press.

Cooper, J. E., et al. 1969. Cross-national study of diagnosis of the mental disorders: Some results of the first comparative investigation. *American Journal of Psychiatry* 125:21–29.

Cooper, J. E., R. E. Kendell, B. J. Gurland, L. Sharpe, J. R. M. Copeland, and R. Simon. 1972. *Psychiatric Diagnosis in New York and London.* London: Oxford University Press.

Copeland, J. R. M., J. E. Cooper, R. E. Kendell, et al. 1971. Differences in usage of diagnostic labels amongst psychiatrists in the British Isles. *British Journal of Psychiatry* 118:629–640.

Coppen, A. and L. Walk, eds. 1968. *Recent Developments in Affective Disorders.* Ashford, England: Headley.

Cordova-Rios, M. 1971. *The Wizard of the Upper Amazon.* New York: Atheneum.

Crandell, D. L. and B. P. Dohrenwend. 1967. Some relations among psychiatric symptoms, organic illness, and social class. *American Journal of Psychiatry* 123:1527–1538.

Cravioto, J. 1964. Malnutrition and behavioral development in the pre-school child: An International Conference on Pre-School Child Malnutrition Primary deterrent to human progress. Publication 1282, National Academy of Science-National Research Council.

Cronbach, L. J. 1957. The two disciplines of scientific psychology. *American Psychologist* 12:671–684.

Crow, J. and J. Felsenstein. 1968. The effect of assortive mating on the genetic composition of a population. *Eugenics Quarterly* 15(2):85–97.

Cuevillas, F. N. A. 1967. Sociología argentina e iberoamericana. Córdoba: Macci.

Cumming, E. and J. H. Cumming. 1957. *Closed Ranks.* Cambridge: Harvard University Press.

Cumming, J. 1961. The family and mental disorder: An incomplete essay. *Milbank Memorial Educational Quarterly* 39:185.

Dalgard, O. S. 1967. *Migration and Functional Psychoses in Oslo.* Oslo: Universitetsforlaget.

Dalgard, O. S. 1969. Status inconsistency and functional psychoses in Oslo. *Acta Sociomedica Scandinavica* 1:55.

Dalgard, O. S. 1971. Social Mobility and Mental Illness in Oslo. Paper presented to the World Congress of Psychiatry, Mexico City, Mexico.

Damon, A. ed. 1975. *Physiological Anthropology.* New York: Oxford University Press.

D'Andrade, R. G. 1967. Testing and training procedures at Bassawa, paper 4. Ethiopia. Ahmadu Bello University Institute of Education (processed).

Darwin, C. 1872. *The Expression of the Emotions in Man and Animals.* London.

Dasen, P. R. 1972. Cross-cultural Piagetian research: a summary. *Journal of Cross-Cultural Psychology* 3:23–39.

Davis, F. 1963. *Passage through Crisis.* Indianapolis: Bobbs-Merrill.

Davison, R. 1966. *Black British.* Oxford University Press.

Davison, K. and C. Bagley. 1969. Schizophrenia-like Psychoses Associated with Organic Disorders of the Central Nervous System. Monograph supplement to *British Journal Psychiatry.*

Davitz, J. R. 1969. *The Language of Emotion.* New York and London.

De Castro, J. 1946. Geografia da fome. In O. Cruzeiro, ed. A fome no Brasil Rio de Janeiro.

Degenhardt, T. 1973. Psychiatrie in der Sowjet Union. *Deutsch Gesundheitswesen* 28:10, 443–446.

De La Fuente, R. 1965. Curso de psiquiatría para graduados. División de Estudios Superiores, Facultad de Medicina. Universidad Nacional Autónoma de Mexico, Mexico D.F.

Debray, R. 1967. *Revolution in the Revolution.* New York: Grove Press Inc.
Deikman, A. F. 1973. Biodal consciousness. In R. E. Ornstein, ed.*The Nature of Human Consciousness.* San Francisco: W. H. Freeman.
De Jesús, C. M. 1963. *Child of the Dark* (Translated from the Portuguese by David St. Clair) New York: Signet .
Delgado, H. 1967. Psychiatric report from South America. In Petrilowitsch, ed. 1967.
Denber, H. C. B., et al. 1961. "Wirkungsunterschiede von Butyrlperazin bei einer amerikanischen und deutschen Patientengruppe." *Medicina Experimentalis* 5:271–279.
Denber, H. C., D. Bente, and P. Rajotte. 1962. Comparative analysis of the action of butyrylperazine at Manhattan State Hospital and the University Psychiatric Clinic at Erlangen. *American Journal of Psychiatry* 119:203–206.
Denber, H. C. and J. Collard. 1962. Differences de bioreactivite au Haloperidol entre deux groupes de psychotiques, americain et europeen. *Acta Neurologica Psychiatrica Belgica* 62:577–588.
Dennis, W. and P. Najarian. 1957. Infant development under environmental handicap. *Psychological Monographs* 71 (7).
Dennis, W. 1973. *Children of the Creche.* New York: Appleton-Century-Crofts.
Denzin, N. 1968. The self-fulfilling prophecy and patient-therapist interaction. In S. Spitzer and N. Denzin, eds. *The Mental Patient: Studies in the Sociology of Deviance.* New York: McGraw-Hill.
Denzin, N. and S. Spitzer. 1966. Paths to the mental hospital and staff predictions of patient role behavior. *Journal of Health and Human Behavior* 7:265–271.
de Rios, M. D. 1974. The influence of psychotropic flora and fauna on Maya religion. *Current Anthropology* 15(2):147–164.
de Rios, M. D. 1975a. The non-western use of hallucinogenic agents. In *Drug Use in America: Problem in Perspective.* Washington, D.C.: Second Report of the National Commission on Marihuana and Drug Abuse.
de Rios, M. D. 1975b. Man, culture and hallucinogens: An overview. In V.Rubin, ed. *Cannabis and Culture,* The Hague: Mouton.
de Rios, M. D. Plant hallucinogens and the religion of the Mochicaan ancient Peruvian people. *Economic Botany* (in press a).
de Rios, M. D. Suggestive hallucinogenic-derived motifs from New World massive earthworks. In B. duToit, ed. *Drugs, Ritual and Altered States of Consciousness.* Amsterdam (in press b).
de Rios, M. D. 1977. *The Wilderness of Mind: Sacred Plants in Cross-Cultural Perspective.* Beverly Hills: Sage Publications.
de Rios, M. D., and F. Katz. 1975. Some relationships between music and hallucinogenic ritual: The "Jungle Gym" in the consciousness. *Ethos* 3(1):64–76.
Despinoy, M. and A. Camelio. 1967. La psychopathologie aux Antilles et ses relations avec les structures sociales. In Petrilowitsch, ed. 1967.

Deutscher, I. 1966. Asking Questions cross-culturally: Some Problems in Semantic Comparability—and some solutions. Syracuse: unpublished manuscript.

Deutscher, I. 1973. *Why do they say one thing, do another?* University Programs Modular Studies. Morristown, N.J.: General Learning Press.

Devereaux, G. 1961. Mohare ethnopsychiatry and suicide: The psychiatric knowledge and the psychic disturbances of an Indian tribe. Smithsonian Institution. Bureau of American Ethnology Bulletin 175. Washington.

Devereux, E. C., R. Shouval, U. Bronfenbrenner, R. R. Rodgers, S. Kav Venaki, E. Kiely, and E. Karson. 1974. Socialization practices of parents, teachers, and peers in Israel: The kibbutz versus the city. *Child Development* 45:269–281.

Díaz Guerrero, R. 1955. Neurosis and the Mexican family structure. *American Journal of Psychiatry* 112:411–417.

Díaz Guerrero, R. 1967. Socio-cultural premises, attitudes and cross-cultural research. *International Journal of Psychology* 2:79–88.

Díaz Guerrero, R. and R. F. Peck. 1967. Estilo de confrontación y aprovechamiento. Un programa de investigacion. *Revista Interamericana de Psicologiá* 1:127–136.

Dick, D. H. 1969. The measurement of aggression and other attitudes in psychosomatic research by means of the Semantic Differential. *Journal of Psychosomatic Research* 13:299–305.

DiMascio, A. 1968. Paradoxical drug effects: The role of the personality. *Proceedings, Fourth World Congress of Psychiatry* (Amsterdam) 4.

DiMascio, A., R. E. Meyer, and L. Stifler. 1967. Effects of Imipramine on individuals varying in level of depression. *American Journal of Psychiatry* 124:55–57.

Dingman, H. F., M. J. Paulson, R. K. Eyman, and C. R. Miller. 1969. The Semantic differential as a tool for measuring programs in therapy. *Psychological Reports* 25:271–279.

Dinitz, S., 1962. Instrumental role expectations and post-hospital performance of female mental patients. *Social Forces* 40: 248–254.

Dinitz, S., M. Lefton, S. Angrist, and B. Pasamanick. 1961. Psychiatric and social attributes as predictors of case outcome in mental hospitalization. *Social Problems* 8:322–328.

Diop, M. 1967. La depression chez le noir Africaine. *Psychopathologie Africaine* 3:183.

Dohrenwend, B. P. 1964. Some indications of methodological malaise in social psychiatric research. Paper read at the First International Congress of Social Psychiatry, London.

Dohrenwend, B. P. 1966. Social status and psychological disorders: An issue of substance and an issue of method. *American Sociological Review* 31:14 -34.

Dohrenwend, B. P., E. T. Chin-Shong, G. Egri, F. S. Mendelsohn, and J. Stokes. 1970. Measures of psychiatric disorder in contrasting class and ethnic groups: A preliminary report of ongoing research. In Hare and Wing, eds. 1970:179.

Dohrenwend, B. P. and B. S. Dohrenwend. 1969. *Social Status and Psychological Disorder.* New York: Wiley-Interscience.
Dohrenwend, B. P. and B. S. Dohrenwend. 1974. Social and cultural influences on psychopathology. *Annual Review of Psychology* 25:417–452.
Doi, L. T. 1962a. Amae—A key concept for understanding Japanese personality structure. *Psychologia* 5:1.
Doi, L. T. 1962b. Morita therapy and psychoanalysis. *Psychologia* 5:117.
Dorrance, D., O. Janiger, and R. L. Teplitz. 1975. Effects of peyote on human chromosomes; Cytogenetic study of the Huichol Indians of Northern Mexico. *Journal of the American Medical Association* 234:299–302.
Draguns, J. G., M. Knobel, T. A. de Fundia, I. K. Broverman, and L. Phillips. 1964. Social competence, psychiatric symptomatology, and culture. In Proceedings of the Ninth Interamerican Congress of Psychology, pp. 610–615. Miami: Interamerican Society of Psychology.
Draguns, J. G., M. Knobel, T. A. de Fundia, I. K. Broverman, and L. Phillips. 1966. Sintomatologia psiquiatricia y cultura: Investigacion intercultural. *Psiquiatrica y Psicologica de America Latina* 12:77–83.
Draguns, J. G., I. Nachshon, I. K. Broverman, and L. Phillips, 1967. Ethnic differences in psychiatric symptomatology: A study of an Israeli child guidance clinic population. Paper presented at the Eastern Psychological Association. Boston.
Draguns, J. G., L. Phillips, I. K. Broverman, W. A. Caudill, and S. Nishimae. Symptomatology of hospitalized psychiatric patients in Japan and in the United States: A study of cultural differences. *Journal of Nervous and Mental Disease* (in press).
Draguns, J. G., L. Phillips, I. K. Broverman, W. A. Caudill, and S. Nishimae. 1970. Social competence and psychiatric symptomatology in Japan: A cross cultural extension of earlier American findings. *Journal of Abnormal Social Psychology* 75:68–73.
Dube, K. S. 1964. Survey of mental morbidity in India at Mental Hospital. Agra. *Indian Journal of Psychiatry* 6, 98, 1964.
Dube, K. C. 1971. Personal communication.
Dublin, L. I. 1963. *Suicide.* New York: Ronald Press.
Dublin, L. I. and B. Bunzel. 1933. *To be or not to be: A study of suicide.* New York: Smith & Hass.
Dubois, C. 1944. *The People of Alor.* Minneapolis: University of Minnesota Press.
Dubos, R. 1959. *Mirage of Health.* New York: Harper & Row.
Dubos, R. 1965. *Man Adapting.* New Haven: Yale University Press.
Dubos, R. 1970. *Reason Awake* New York: Columbia University Press.
Duff, R. S. and A. B. Hollingshead. 1968. *Sickness and Society.* New York: Harper and Row.
Duncan, H. D. 1967. The search for a social theory of communication. In F. X. Dance, ed. *Human Communication Theory,* pp. 236–263. New York: Holt, Rinehart, and Winston.
Dunham, H. W. 1961. Social class and schizophrenia. In the Milbank Memorial Fund, ed. *Causes of Mental Disorders: A Review of Epidemiological*

Knowledge. New York: The Fund. Also in *American Journal of Orthopsychiatry* 34:265.

Dunham, H. W. 1961. Social structures and mental disorders: Competing hypotheses of explanation. *Milbank Memorial Fund Quarterly* 39:259-311.

Dunham, H. W. 1964. Social class and schizophrenia. *American Journal of Orthopsychiatry* 34:634–642.

Dunham, H. W. 1965. *Community and Schizophrenia—An Epidemiological Analysis*. Detroit: Wayne State University Press.

Dunham, H. W., P. Phillips, and B. Srinivasan. 1966. A research note on diagnosed mental illness and social class. *American Sociological Review* 31:223–227.

Dunham, H. W. 1976. Society, culture, and mental disorder. *Archives of General Psychiatry* 33:147–156.

Durkheim, E. 1951. *Suicide*. Glencoe, Ill: Free Press.

Eaton, J. W. and R. J. Weil. 1955. *Culture and Mental Disorders: A Comparative Study of the Hutterites and Other Populations*. Glencoe: Free Press.

Edgerton, R. 1969. On the "recognition" of mental illness. In Plog and Edgerton, eds. 1969.

Edwards, J. E. and F. A. Whitlock. 1968. Suicide and attempted suicide in Brisbane. *Medical Journal of Australia* 1:989.

Eisenstadt, S. N. 1951. Youth, culture and social structure in Israel. *British Journal of Sociology* 2:105–114.

Eisenstadt, S. N. 1967. *Israeli society*. New York: Basic Books.

Eitinger, L. 1958. Psykiatriske undersokelser blant flytinger Norge. Universitetsforgleget. Quoted by H. S. Halevi. 1963. *International Journal of Social Psychiatry* 9:268.

Eitinger, L. 1959. The incidence of mental disease among refugees in Norway. *Journal of Mental Science* 105:326.

Eitinger, L. 1960a. The symptomatology of mental disease among refugees in Norway. *Journal of Mental Science* 106:947.

Eitinger, L. 1960b. Psychiatric investigations among refugee patients in Norway. *Mental Hygiene* 44:91.

Ekman, P. and W. V. Friesen. 1968. Non-verbal behavior in psychotherapy research. *Research in Psychotherapy* 3:179-216.

Ekman, P., E. R. Sorenson, and W. V. Friesen. 1969. Pancultural elements in facial displays of emotion. *Science* 164:86–88.

Eliade, M. 1957. *Sacred and Profane*. New York: Harcourt.

El-Islam, F. M. 1969. Depression and guilt: A study at an Arab psychiatric clinic. *Social Psychiatry* 4:56.

Ellenberger, H. 1960. Cultural aspects of mental illness. *American Journal of Psychotherapy* 14:158-173.

Ellis, W. G. 1893. The amok of the Malays. *Journal of Mental Science* 39:325–342.

Ellis, W. G. 1901. Some remarks on asylum practice in Singapore. *Journal of Tropical Medicine* 4:411–414.

Elnager, M. N., P. Maitra, and M. N. Rao. 1971. Mental health in an Indian rural community. *British Journal of Psychiatry* 118:499.

Elsarrag, M. E. 1968. Psychiatry in the Sudan: A study of comparative psychiatry. *British Journal of Psychiatry* 114–945.

Engel, G. L. 1953. In R. Grinker, ed. *Midcentury Psychiatry,* p. 33. Springfield, Ill.: Thomas.

Engel, G. L. 1960. A unified concept of health and disease. *Perspectives in Biology and Medicine* 3:459-485.

Engel, G. L. 1961. Is grief a disease? A challenge for medical research. *Psychosomatic Medicine* 23:18-22.

Engel, G. L. 1962. *Psychological Development in Health and Disease.* Philadelphia: Saunders.

Engel, G. L. 1967. Medical education and the psychosomatic approach. *Journal of Psychosomatic Research* 11:77–85.

Engel, G. L. 1972a. The education of the physician for clinical observation. *Journal of Nervous and Mental Disease* 154:159-164.

Engel, G. L. 1972b. In R. Porter and G. Knight, eds. *Physiology,* p. 384. Amsterdam: Elsevier.

Engel, G. L. 1973. Enduring attributes of medicine relevant for the education of the physician. *Annals of Internal Medicine* 78:587–593.

Engel, G. L. 1974. Memorial lecture: The psychosomatic approach to individual susceptibility to disease. *Gastroenterology* 67:1085–1093.

Engel, G. L. 1976a. Are medical schools neglecting clinical skills? *Journal of the American Medical Association* 236:861–863.

Engel, G. L. 1976b. Too little science: The paradox of modern medicine's crisis. *Pharos* 39:127–131.

Engel, G. L. and L. Salzman. 1973. Enduring attributes of medicine relevant for the education of the physician. *Annals of Internal Medicine* 78:587.

Erikson, E. 1950. *Childhood and Society.* New York: Norton.

Erikson, E. 1959. Identity and the life cycle: Selected papers. *Psychological Issues Monograph* 1(1):129-132. New York: International Universities Press.

Ervin, S. M. 1964. Language and TAT content in bilinguals. *Journal of Abnormal and Social Psychology* 68:500–507.

Esquibel, A. and P. Perez Upegui. 1969. Servicios de psiquiatría en los hospitales generales. *Acta Psiquiátrica y Pscicólogíca de America Latina* 15:75–81

Essen-Möller, E. 1961. On classification of mental disorders. *Acta Psychiatrica Scandinavica* 37:119-126.

Esser, A. H. 1961. Social character as a transcultural approach to neurosis. In *Proceedings of the Third World Congress of Psychiatry.* Montreal: University of Toronto Press, 2:1140–1144.

Etchegoyen, R., O. Lazarte, and E. D'Accurzio. 1960. Grupos operativos en la enseñanza médica'. Presented to II Congreso Latinoamericano de Psicoterapia de Grupo, Santiago de Chile (printed copy).

Everett, M. W., J. P. Waddell, and D. B. Heath, eds. 1976. *Cross-Cultural Approaches to the Study of Alcohol.* Chicago: Aldine.

Ewing, S. M. P., C. Myers, and M. A. Simpson. 1971. Attempted suicide in the Perth metropolitan area for 1969 (unpublished report).

Fabrega, H. 1969. Social psychiatric aspects of acculturation and migration: a general statement. *Comprehensive Psychiatry* 10:314.

Fabrega, H. 1974a. *Disease and Social Behavior.* Cambridge: MIT Press.

Fabrega, H. 1974b. Problems implicit in the cultural and social study of depression. *Psychosomatic Medicine* 36:377.

Fabrega, H. 1975a. The position of psychiatry in the understanding of human disease. *Archives of General Psychiatry* 32:1500–1512.

Fabrega, H. 1975b. The need for an ethnomedical science. *Science* 189:969.

Fabrega, H. 1977. Disease viewed as a symbolic category. In Engelhardt and Spicker, eds. *Mental Health: Philosophical Perspectives.* Dordrecht: D. Reidel.

Fabrega, H. and P. K. Manning. 1973. An integrated theory of disease: Ladino-mestizo views of disease in the Chiapas highlands. *Psychosomatic Medicine* 35:223.

Fabrega, H. and C. A. Wallace. 1967. How physicians judge symptom statements: A cross-cultural study. *Journal of Nervous and Mental Disease* 145:486–491.

Fallers, L. H. and M. C. Fallers. 1960. Homicide and suicide in Busoga. In P. Bohannan, ed. *African Homicide and Suicide.* Princeton: Princeton University Press.

Faris, R. and H. W. Dunham. 1939. *Mental Disorders in Urban Areas.* Chicago: University of Chicago Press.

Favazza, A. 1974a. Oedipus interruptus: A psychiatric-anthropological interface. *Journal of Operational Psychiatry* 5(2):37–51.

Favazza, A. 1974b. A critical review of studies of national character. *Journal of Operational Psychiatry* 6(1):3–30.

Favazza, A. and M. Oman. 1977. *Anthropological and Cross-Cultural Themes in Mental Health.* Columbia: University of Missouri Press.

Favazza, A. R. and M. Oman. 1980. Anthropology and psychiatry. In H. I. Kaplan et al., eds. 1980.

Fernando, S. J. M. 1966. Depressive illness in Jews and non-Jews. *British Journal of Psychiatry* 112:991.

Fernando, S. J. M. 1969. Cultural differences in the hostility of depressive patients. *British Journal of Medical Psychology* 42:67.

Field, M. G. and J. Aronson. 1965. Soviet community mental health services and work therapy: A report of two visits. *Community Mental Health Journal* 1:81–90.

Field, M. J. 1960. *Search for Security: An Ethno-Psychiatric Study of Rural Ghana.* Evanston, Illinois: Northwestern University Press.

Field, P. B. 1962. A new cross-cultural study of drunkenness. In D. J. Pittman and C. R. Snyder, eds. *Society, Culture and Drinking Patterns,* pp 48-74. New York: Wiley.

Fitzgerald, R. D. 1923. A thesis on two tropical neuroses (amok and latah) peculiar to Malaya. In the Far Eastern Association for Tropical Medicine. *Transactions of the Fifth Biennial Congress, Singapore* 5:148-161. London: John Bale Sons and Danielson Ltd.

Fitzpatrick, J. P. and R. E. Gould. 1970. Mental illness among Puerto Ricans in New York: Cultural condition or intercultural misunderstanding? *American Journal of Orthopsychiatry* 40:238-239.

Fletcher, W. 1908. Latah and crime. *Lancet* 175:254–255.

Foster, F. H. 1962. *Maori Patients in Mental Hospitals*. Dept. of Health (Mental Statistics Branch). Wellington, New Zealand.

Foster, G. M. 1976. Disease etiologist in non-Western medical systems. *American Anthropologist* 78:773–782.

Foulks, E. 1972. *The Arctic Hysterias of the North Alaskan Eskimos*. Washington, D.C. American Anthropological Association.

Foulks, E. et al. 1977. *Current Perspectives in Cultural Psychiatry*. New York: Spectrum Publications.

Fox T. F. 1957. The new China: Some medical impressions. *Lancet* 2:935–939, 995–999, 1053–1057.

Frake, C. O. 1961. The diagnosis of disease among the Subanum of Mindanao. *American Anthropologist* 63:113–132.

Frank, J. D. 1972. Common features of psychotherapy. *Australian and New Zealand Journal of Psychiatry* 6:30.

Frankenhaeuser, M. 1971. Experimental approaches to the study of human behavior as related to neuroendocrine functions. In L. Levi, ed. *Society, Stress and Disease*. London: Oxford University Press.

Frazier, E. F. 1957. *Black Bourgeoisie*. Glencoe: Free Press.

Freeman, H., O. Simmons. 1958. Mental patients in the community. *American Sociological Review* 23:147–154.

Freeman, H. and O. Simmons. 1963. *The Mental Patient Comes Home*. New York: John Wiley.

Freud, S. 1925. Mourning and melancholia. In *Collected Papers* IV. London: Hogarth.

Freud, S. 1913. Totem and taboo. In J. Strachey, ed. and trans. *Complete Psychological Works* 13:1–161.

Fried, J. 1959. Acculturation and mental health among Indian migrants in Peru. In M. K. Opler, ed. 1959: 119–137.

Fromm-Reichmann, F. 1959. *Psychoanalysis and Psychotherapy*. Chicago: University of Chicago Press.

Frostad, A., G. Forrest, and C. B. Bakker. 1966. Influence of personality type on drug response. *American Journal of Psychiatry* 122:1153–1158.

Gaitonde, M. R. 1958. Cross-cultural study of the psychiatric syndromes in outpatient clinics in Bombay, India, and Topeka, Kansas. *International Journal of Social Psychiatry* 2:98–104.

Galloway, D. J. 1923. On amok: Far Eastern Association for Tropical Medicine. *Transactions of the Fifth Biennial Congress, Singapore* 5:162–171. London: John Bale Sons and Danielson Ltd.

Gamble, S. A. and J. S. Burgess. 1921. *Peking: a Social Survey*. New York: Doran.

Garbarino, J. and U. Bronfenbrenner. In press. The socialization of moral judgment and behavior in cross-cultural perspective. In T. Lickona, ed.,

Morality: A Handbook of Moral Development and Behavior. New York: Holt, Rinehart & Winston.

Gardner, E. 1970. Emotional problems in medical practice. *Annals of Internal Medicine* 73:651–652.

Gattozzi, A. A. 1970. Lithium in the treatment of mood disorders. National Clearinghouse for Mental Health Information, Publication No. 5033, U.S. Government Printing Office. pp. 23–24.

Geertz, H. 1961. Modified TAT's of thirty-three Japanese men and women. In B. Kaplan, ed. *Primary Records in Culture and Personality*. Madison: University of Wisconsin Press, vol. 2. (As cited in Bert Kaplan, *Studying Personality Cross-Culturally*. New York: Harper and Row.)

German, G. A. 1972. Aspects of clinical psychiatry in sub-Saharan Africa. *British Journal of Psychiatry* 121:461–479.

Gersten, J. C., T. S. Langner, J. G. Eisenberg, L. Orzeck. 1974. Child behavior and life events: undesirable change or change per se? In B. S. Dohrenwend and B. P. Dohrenwend, eds. *Stressful Life Events: Their Nature and Effect*. pp 159–170. New York: Wiley.

Gibson, G. 1964. The Mexican-American Family. Paper read at the Symposium on Mexican-American Personality. Tucson, Arizona.

Gillin, J. 1956. El temor mágico. In *Culture Indígena de Guatemala, Ensayos de Antropología Social* (ed. del Ministerio de Educación Pública). Guatemala.

Gillis, L. S., J. B. Lewis, and Shubbert, M. 1968. Psychiatric disorder amongst the coloured people of the Cape Peninsula. *British Journal of Psychiatry* 114:1575.

Gimlette, J. D. 1901. Notes on a case of amok. *Journal of Tropical Medicine and Hygiene*. 4:195–199.

Glass, A. J. 1958. Observations upon the epidemiology of mental illness in troops during warfare. In Symposim on Preventive and Social Psychiatry, pp. 185–206. Washington, D.C.: Walter Reed Army Institute of Research.

Glick, L. B. 1967. Medicine as an ethnographic category: The Gimi of the New Guinea highlands. *Ethnology* 6:31–56.

Gobar, A. H. 1970. Suicide in Afghanistan. *British Journal of Psychiatry* 116:493.

Goffman, E. 1961. *Asylums: Essays on the Social Situation of Mental Patients and Other Inmates*. Chicago: Aldine.

Gold, M. 1958. Suicide, homicide and aggression. *American Journal of Sociology* 63:651.

Goldberg, E. M. and S. L. Morrison. 1963. Schizophrenia and social class. *British Journal of Psychiatry* 109:785.

Goldberg, S. C., G. L. Klerman, and J. O. Cole. 1965. Changes in schizophrenic psychopathology and ward behavior as a function of phenothiazine treatment. *British Journal of Psychiatry* 111:120–133.

Goldenberg, M. 1966. Programa de los cursos de especialización en psiquiatría lo. y 2o. años. Servicio de psicopatología del Policlínico Prof. C. A. Alfaro (mimeographed copy).

Gonzalez, M. G. and C. A. Gallegos. 1964. Pian de entrenamiento de residentes en psiquiatría, Hospital Psiquiátrico M. A. Chapui, San José, Costa Rica. Marzo (mimeographed copy).

Goodenough, W. H. 1963. *Cooperation and Change.* New York: Russell-Sage.

Goodenough, W. H. 1970. *Description and Comparison in Cultural Anthropology.* Chicago: Aldine Publishing Co.

Gordon, H. L. 1934. Psychiatry in Kenya Colony. *Journal of Mental Science* 80:167.

Gorer, G. 1943. Themes in Japanese culture. *Transactions of the New York Academy of Science* 5:106–124.

Gorman, M. 1969. Soviet psychiatry and the Russian citizen. *International Journal of Psychiatry* 8:841–854.

Gough, H. G. 1957. *California Psychological Inventory Manual.* Palo Alto: Consulting Psychologists Press.

Gough, H. G., and H. S. Sandhu. 1964. Validation of the CPI Socialization Scale in India. *Journal of Abnormal and Social Psychology* 68:544.

Gould, R. E. 1975. Socio-cultural roles of male and female. In *Comprehensive Textbook of Psychiatry.* 2nd ed., 2:1460–1466. A. M. Freedman et al., eds. Baltimore: Williams & Wilkins.

Gove, W. R. and J. F. Tudor. 1973. Adult sex roles and mental illness. *American Journal of Sociology* 78:812–835.

Grant, E. C. 1970. An ethological description of non-verbal behavior during interviews. In S. J. Hutt and C. Hutt, eds. *Behaviour Studies in Psychiatry.*

Granville-Grossman, K. L. 1968. The early environment in affective disorder. In A. Coppen and A. Walk, eds. *Recent Developments in Affective Disorder,* pp. 65–79. British Journal of Psychiatry Special Publication.

Greenbaum, J. and L. I. Pearlin. 1953. Vertical mobility and prejudice: A social psychological analysis. In R. Bendix and S. M. Lipset, eds. *Class, Status and Power,* pp. 480–491. Glencoe: Free Press.

Greenley, J. and D. Mechanic. 1975. Patterns of seeking care for psychological problems. Publ. 16–74, Research and Analytic Series. Center for Medical Sociology and Health Services Research. Madison: University of Wisconsin.

Gruenberg, E. M. 1963. A review of mental health in the metropolis—the Midtown Manhattan Study. *Millbank Memorial Fund Quarterly* 41:77.

Guevara, E. 1969. Message to the Tricontinental. In Horowitz et al., eds. 1969.

Gumperz, J. J. 1974. Linguistic anthropology in society. *American Anthropologist* 76:785–798.

Gurin, G., J. Veroff, and S. Feld. 1960. *Americans View Their Mental Health.* New York: Basic Books.

Gurland, B. J., et al. 1970. Cross-national study of diagnosis of mental disorders: Hospital diagnoses and hospital patients in New York and London. *Comprehensive Psychiatry* 11:18–25.

Guthrie, G. M. 1970. A culture-fair test of intelligence. Tech. Rep. No. 8. The Impact of Modernization in the Philippines. Pennsylvania State University.

Guthrie, G. M. and F. M. Azores. 1968. Philippine interpersonal behavior patterns. In W. F. Bello and A. de Guzman, eds. *Modernization: Its Impact on the Philippines.* Ateneo de Manila University, IPC Papers No. 6. Quezon City, Philippines.

Guthrie, G. M. and P. J. Jacobs. 1966. *Child Rearing and Personality Development in the Philippines.* University Park, Pa.: Pennsylvania State University Press.

Guthrie, G. M., H. W. Sinaiko, and R. Brislin. 1971. Nonverbal abilities of Americans and Vietnamese. *Journal of Social Psychology* 84:183–190.

Guthrie, G. M., A. Tayag, and P. J. Jacobs. 1969. The Philippine Nonverbal Intelligence Test. *Journal of Social Psychology.* In Press.

Gutierrez de Pineda, V. 1961. La Medicina popular en Colombia, Razones de su Arraigo. Monografía Sociologíca. No. 8, Bogotá.

Gwee, A. L. 1971. Traditional Chinese methods of treatment. In Wagner and Tan, eds. *Psychological Problems and Treatment in Malaysia.* Kuala Lumpur: University of Malaya Press.

Halevi, H. S. 1963. Frequency of mental illness among Jews in Israel. *International Journal of Social Psychiatry* 9:268.

Hall, E. T. 1959. *The Silent Language.* New York: Doubleday.

Hall, E. T. 1966. *The Hidden Dimension.* New York: Doubleday.

Hall, P. 1966. Some clinical aspects of moving house as an apparent precipitant of psychiatric symptoms. *Journal of Psychosomatic Research* 10:59.

Halliday, M. A. K. 1976. Anti-languages. *American Anthropologist* 78:570–584.

Hallowell, A. I. 1952. Ojibwa personality and acculturation. In Sal Toxj, ed. *Acculturation in the Americas.* Proceedings and Selected Papers of the 29th International Congress of Americanists.

Hallowell, A. I. 1954. *Culture and Experience.* Philadelphia: University of Pennsylvania Press.

Hamilton, M. 1967. Development of a rating scale for primary depressive illness. *Journal of Clinical Social Psychology* 6:278.

Hanks, L. M. 1961. Modified TAT's of forty-seven Thai children and adults. In B. Kaplan, ed. *Primary Records in Culture and Personality.* Madison: University of Wisconsin Press. As cited in B. Kaplan, *Studying Personality Cross-Culturally.* New York: Harper and Row.

Hare, A. P. 1969. Cultural differences in performance in communication networks in Africa, the United States and the Philippines. *Sociology and Social Research.* 54:25–41.

Hare, E. H. 1956. Mental illness and social conditions in Bristol. *Journal of Mental Science.* 102:349.

Hare, E. H. 1966. Mental health in new towns: What rent? *Journal of Psychosomatic Research* 10:53.

Hare, E. H. and G. K. Shaw. 1965. *Mental Helath in a New Housing Estate.* Maudsley Monograph No. 12. London: Oxford University Press.

Hare, E. H. and J. K. Wing, eds. 1970. *Psychiatric Epidemiology: An International Symposium.* London: Oxford University Press.

Haring, D. 1956. Japanese national character: Cultural anthropology, psychoanalysis, and history. In D. Haring, ed. *Personal Character and Cultural Milieu,* pp. 424–437. Syracuse: Syracuse University Press.

Harlow, H. F., K. A. Schiltz, and M. K. Harlow. 1969. The effects of social isolation on the learning performance of rhesus monkeys. In C. R. Carpenter, ed. *Proceedings of the Second International Congress of Primatology.* Vol. 1. New York: Karger.

Harner, M., ed. 1973. *Hallucinogens and Shamanism.* New York: Oxford University Press.

Harris, G. W. 1963. *Problems in Measuring Change.* Madison: University of Wisconsin Press.

Hartman, H., E. Kris, and R. M. Lowenstein. 1951. Some psychoanalytic comments on "Culture and Personality." In G. B. Wilbur and W. Munsterberger, eds. *Psychoanalysis and Culture.* New York: International Universities Press.

Hashmi, F. 1969. Racial Conflict and Emotional Stress. In Proceedings of the Anglo-French Conference, Sussex, 1968, The Hague, Mauton.

Hasuzawa, T. 1963. Chronological observations of delusions in schizophrenics. Presented at the joint meetings of the Japanese society of Psychiatry and the American Psychiatric Association, Tokyo.

Haugen, E. 1956. *Bilingualism in the Americas: A Bibliography and Research Guide.* University of Alabama.

Haugen, E. 1966. "Semicommunication: The language gap in Scandinavia. *Sociological Inquiry* 36:280–297.

Hauser, P. M. 1961. *Urbanization in Latin America.* New York. Columbia University Press.

Havighurst, R. J., M. E. DuBois, M. Csikszentmihalyi, and R. Doll. 1963. Las actitudes personales y sociales de adolescentes de Buenos Aires y de Chicago—Estudio comparado. Washington: Union Panamericana.

Heilizer, F. 1960. A critical review of some published experiments with chlorpromazine in schizophrenic, neurotic and normal humans. *Journal of Chronic Diseases* 2:102–148.

Hein, G. 1968. Social psychiatric treatment of schizophrenia in the Soviet Union. *International Journal of Psychiatry* 6:346–361.

Heller, C. 1967. *Mexican-American Youth.* New York: Random House.

Heller, C. 1970. Class as an explanation of ethnic differences in mobility aspirations. In J. H. Burma, ed. *Mexican Americans in the United States.* New York: Holt, Rinehart & Winston.

Helmchen, H. 1975. Schizophrenia: Diagnostic concepts in the ICD-8. In M. H. Lader, ed. *Studies in Schizophrenia.* British Journal of Psychiatry, Special Publication No. 10, 10–18.

Henderson, D., R. D. Gillespie, and I. R. C. Batchelor. 1956. *A Textbook of Psychiatry for Students and Practitioners,* 8th ed. New York: Oxford University Press.

Henderson, S. 1977. The social network, support and neurosis. *British Journal of Psychiatry* 131:185–191.

Hendin, H. 1960. Suicide in Denmark. *Psychoanalytic Quarterly* 34.

Hendin, H. 1964. *Suicide and Scandinavia: A Psychoanalytic Study of Culture and Character*. New York: Grune & Stratton.

Hendrie, H. and D. Hanson. 1972. A comparative study of the psychiatric care of Indian and Metis. *American Journal of Orthopsychiatry* 42:480–489.

Heninger, G., A. Dimascio, and G. Klerman. 1965. Personality factors in variability of response to phenothiazines. *American Journal of Psychiatry* 121:1091–1094.

Hennes, J. D. 1972. The measurement of health. *Mental Care Review* 29:1268–1288.

Henry, W. E., J. H. Sims, and S. I. Spray. 1968. *Public and Private Lives of Psychotherapists*. San Francisco: Jossey-Bass.

Hereford, C. F., N. Selz, W. Stenning, and L. Natalicio. 1969. A cross-cultural comparison of the active-passive dimension of social attitudes. *Revista Interamericana de Psicologia* 1:33–40.

Hertzler, J. O. 1965. *A Sociology of Language.* New York: Random House, pp. 128–131.

Hes, J. P. 1960. Manic depressive illness in Israel. *American Journal of Psychiatry* 116:1082.

Hinde, R. A., ed. 1972. *Non-Verbal Communication.* London: Cambridge University Press.

Hitson, H. M. and D. H. Funkenstein. 1959. Family patterns and paranoidal personality structure in Boston and Burma. *International Journal of Social Psychiatry* 5:182.

Hoch, E. 1959. Psychiatrische Beobachtugen und Erfahrungen an indischen Patienten. *Praxis Nev.* 48:1051–1057.

Hoch, E. 1963. Contents of depressive ideas in Indian patients. *Transcultural Psychiatric Research Review* 13:20.

Hoch, P. and P. Polatin. 1949. Pseudoneurotic forms of schizophrenia. *Psychiatric Quarterly* 23:248–276.

Hoch, P. H. and J. Zubin, eds. 1954. *Depression.* New York: Grune and Stratton.

Hollingshead, A. B., R. Ellis, and E. Kirby. 1954. Social mobility and mental illness. *American Sociological Review* 19:577.

Hollingshead, A. B. and F. C. Redlich. 1954. Schizophrenia and social structure. *American Journal of Psychiatry* 110:695.

Hollingshead, A. B. and F. C. Redlich. 1958. *Social Class and Mental Illness.* New York: Wiley.

Holman, H. R. 1976. The "excellence" deception in medicine [Editorial] *Hospital Practice* 11:11.

Honigmann, J. J. 1954. *Culture and Personality.* New York: Harper & Row.

Honigmann, J. J. 1973. Personality in culture. In Naroll and Naroll, eds. 1973: 217–245.

Honigmann, J. J. 1976. The personal approach in cultural anthropological research. *Current Anthropology* 17:243–262.

Horowitz, I. L., J. De Castro, and J. Gerassi, eds. 1969. *Latin American Radicalism: A Documentary Report on Left and Nationalist Movements.* New York: Random House.

Horton, S. 1943. The functions of alcohol in primitive societies. *Quarterly Journal of Studies on Alcoholism* 4:199–311.

Horwitz, J. et al. 1958. Investigaciones epidemiologicas acerca de morbilidad mental en Chile. *Revista del Servicio Nacional de Salvo* 3:277–291.

Hudson, W. 1960. Pictorial depth perception in subcultural groups in Africa. *Journal of Social Psychology* 52:183–208.

Hughes, C. C., M. A. Tremblay, R. N. Rapoport, and A. H. Leighton. 1960. *People of Cove and Woodlot: Communities from the Viewpoint of Social Psychiatry.* Vol. 2. Stirling County Study of Psychiatric Disorder and Social Environment. New York: Basic Books.

Hunt, W. L., W. W. Crane, and J. C. Wahlke. 1964. Interviewing political elites in cross-cultural comparative research. *American Journal of Sociology* 70:66.

Hymes, D. 1964. *Language in Culture and Society.* New York: Harper & Row.

Itil, T. M., A. Keskiner, and M. Fink. 1966. Therapeutic studies in "therapy-resistant" schizophrenic patients. *Comprehensive Psychiatry* 7:488–493.

Jaco, E. G. 1954. The social isolation hypothesis and schizophrenia. *American Sociological Review* 19:567.

Jaco, E. G. 1959. Mental health of the Spanish-American in Texas. In Opler, ed. 1959.

Jaco, E. G. 1959. Social stress and mental illness in the community. In M. B. Sussman, ed. *Community Structure and Analysis,* pp. 388–409. New York: Crowell.

Jacobson, E. 1954. Methods used for producing comparable data in the O.C.S.R. Seven-Nation Attitude Study. *Journal of Social Issues* 10:40–51.

Jackson, E. F. and P. J. Burke. 1965. Status and symptoms of stress: Additive and interaction effects. *American Sociological Review* 30:556.

Jaffee, D. T. and T. Claude, eds. 1964. *Worlds Apart: Young People in Drug Programs.* New York: Vintage.

Jaffe, J. 1975. *Drug Addiction and Drug Abuse: The Pharmacological Basis of Therapeutics.* New York: Macmillan.

Jakovljevic, V. 1963a. Milieu culturel et nevroses. *Annales Medico-Psychologicues* 120(1): 470–481.

Jakovljevic, V. 1963b. Transkulturno-psihijatriska proucavanja u. *Gvineji. Neuropsihijatrija* 11:21–38.

Jelik, W. G. and L. Jelik. 1970. Transient psychoses in Africans. *Psychiatria Clinica* 3:337–364.

Jilek, W. G. and L. Jilek-Aall. 1971. Transcultural Psychotherapy with Salish Indians. *Proceedings of the Fifth World Congress of Psychiatry.* Mexico City.

Jilek, W. 1974. *Salish Indian Mental Health and Culture Change.* Toronto: Holt, Rinehart and Winston.

Johnson, D., and C. Johnson. 1965. Totally discouraged: a depressive syndrome of the Dakota Sioux. *Transcultural Psychiatric Research Review* 2:141.

Jones, E. 1925. Mother-right and the sexual ignorance of savages. *International Journal of Psycho-Analysis* 6:109–127.

Juel-Nielsen, N., M. Bille, J. Flygenring, and T. Helgason. 1961. Frequency of depressive state within geographically delimited population groups—3:Incidence (The Aarhus County Investigation). *Acta Psychiatrica Scandinavica Suppl.* 162(37):69.

Jung, C. G. 1967. Symbols of transformation. *Collected Works.* Vol 5, 2d ed. Princeton, N.J.: Princeton University Press.

Jung, C. G. 1968. *Archetypes of the Collective Unconscious.* Princeton, N.J.: Princeton University Press.

Kadushin, C. 1962. Social distance between client and professional. *American Journal of Sociology* 67:517–531.

Kadushin, D. 1969. *Why People Go to Psychiatrists.* New York: Atherton.

Kagan, J. 1971. *Change and Continuity in Infancy.* New York: Wiley.

Kagan, J. 1972. Do infants think? *Scientific American* 226(3):74–82.

Kagan, J., R. E. Klein, M. M. Haith, and F. J. Morrison. 1973. Memory and meaning in two cultures. *Child Development* 44:221–223.

Kagan, J. and H. Moss. 1962. *From Birth to Maturity.* New York: Wiley.

Kagan, L. 1972. Report from a visit to the Tientsin Psychiatric Hospital. *China Notes* 10:37–39.

Kahl, J. A. 1968. *The Measurement of Modernism.* Austin: The University of Texas Press.

B. Kaplan. 1954. Study of Rorschach responses in four cultures. *Papers Peabody Museum* 2:42.

Kaplan, B. 1955. Reflections of the acculturation process in the Rorschach test. *Journal of Projective Techniques* 112:411.

Kaplan, B. 1956. An attempt to sort Rorschach records from four cultures. *Journal of Projective Techniques* 20:2.

Kardiner, A. 1939. *The Individual and His Society.* New York: Columbia Univ. Press.

Kardiner, A. 1945. *The Psychological Frontiers of Society.* New York: Columbia University Press.

Karno, M. and R. B. Edgerton. 1970. Perception of mental illness in a Mexican-American Community. In J. H. Burma, ed. *Mexican Americans in the United States.* New York: Holt, Rinehart & Winston.

Katchadourian, H. A. 1974. A comparative study of mental illness among the Christians and Moslems of Lebanon. *International Journal of Social Psychiatry* 27:50.

Katchadourian, H. and J. Racy. 1969. The diagnostic distribution of treated psychiatric illness in Lebanon. *British Journal of Psychiatry,* p. 1309.

Kato, M. 1969. Psychiatric epidemiological surveys in Japan: the problem of case finding. In W. Caudill and T. Lin. *Mental Health Research in the Pacific,* pp. 92–104. Honolulu: East-West Centre.

Katz, M., J. O. Cole, and H. A. Lowery. 1969. Studies of the diagnostic process: The influence of symptom perception, past experience and ethnic background on diagnostic decisions. *American Journal of Psychiatry* 125:937–947.

Katz, S. and E. Foulks. 1969. Mineral metabolism and behavior: Abnormalities of calcium homeostasis. *American Journal of Physical Anthropology* 32:229–304.

Kelvin, P. 1971. Socialization and conformity. *Journal of Child Psychology and Psychiatry* 12:211–222.

Kendall, M. 1955. *Rank Correlation Methods.* New York: Hafner.

Kendall, P. 1954. *Conflict and Mood.* Glencoe: The Free Press.

Kendell, R. E. 1970. Relationship between aggression and depression. *Archives of General Psychiatry* 22:308.

Kendell, R. E., B. Everitt, J. E. Cooper, N. Sartorius, and M. E. David. 1968. The reliability of the present state examination. *Social Psychiatry* 3:123–129.

Kennedy, J. G. 1973. Cultural psychiatry. In J. J. Honigmann, ed. *Handbook of Social and Cultural Anthropology,* pp. 1119–1198. Chicago: Rand McNally.

Kessen, W., M. M. Haith, and B. H. Salapatek. 1970. Human infancy: A bibliography and guide. In P. H. Mussen, ed. *Carmichael's Manual of Child Psychology.* 3d ed. Vol. 1. New York: Wiley.

Kety, S. 1974. From rationalization to reason. *American Journal of Psychiatry* 131:957–963.

Kety, S. 1976. Recent genetic and biochemistry approaches to schizophrenia. In L. L. Simpson, ed. *Drug Treatment of Mental Disorders.* New York: Raven Press.

Kidorf, I. W. 1963. Jewish tradition and the Freudian theory of mourning. *Journal of Religion and Health* 2:248.

Kidson, M. A. 1967. Psychiatric disorders in the Walbiri, Central Australia. *Australian and New Zealand Journal of Psychiatry* 1:14.

Kidson, M. A., and I. H. Jones. 1968. Psychiatric disorders among aborigines of the Australian descent. *Archives of General Psychiatry* 4:413.

Kiev, A., ed. 1964. *Magic, Faith, and Healing.* New York: Free Press.

Kiev, A. 1968a. *Curanderismo: Mexican-American Folk Psychiatry.* New York: Free Press

Kiev, A. 1968b. *Psychiatry in the Communist World.* New York: Science House, p. 17.

Kilham, W. and L. Mann. 1974. Level of destructive obedience as a function of transmittor and executant roles in the Milgram obedience paradigm. *Journal of Personality and Social Psychology* 29:696–702.

Kimura, B. 1965. Vergleichende Untersuchungen uber depressive Erkrankungen in Japan und in Deutschland. *Fortschritte Der Neurologie Psychiatirie und Ihrer Grenz-Gebieie* 33:202–215.

Kimura, B. 1972. Personal communication.

Kinsey, A. C., W. B. Pomeroy, and C. E. Martin. 1948. *Sexual Behavior in the Human Male.* Philadelphia: W. B. Saunders.

Kinsey, A. C., W. B. Pomeroy, C. E. Martin, and P. H. Gebhard. 1953. *Sexual Behavior in the Human Female*. Philadelphia: W. B. Saunders.

Kinzie, J. D., J. Ryals, F. Cottington, and J. E. McDermott. 1973. Cross-cultural study of depressive symptoms in Hawaii. *Social Psychiatry* 19:19.

Kirin Medical College, 1973. *Teaching Manual for Retraining Barefoot Doctors*. Peking: People's Health Publishing Co.

Kleiner, R. J., and S. Parker. 1969. Social mobility, anomie, mental disorder. In Plog and Edgerton, eds. 1969.

Kleiner, R. J., and S. Parker. 1969. Social-psychological aspects of migration and mental disorder in a Negro population. In E. B. Brody, ed. *Behavior in New Environments*, pp. 353–376. Beverly Hills, Calif.: Sage Productions.

Kleiner, R. and Parker, S. 1966. *Mental Illness in the Urban Negro Community*. New York: The Free Press.

Klerman, G., et al. 1959. The influence of specific personality patterns on the reactions to phrenotropic agents. In J. Masserman, ed. *Biological Psychiatry*. New York: Grune and Stratton.

Kline, L. Y. 1969. Some factors in the psychiatric treatment of Spanish-Americans. *American Journal of Psychiatry* 125:1674–1681.

Kline, N. S. 1963. Psychiatry in Indonesia. *American Journal of Psychiatry* 119:809–815.

Kline, N. S. and M. G. Field, and J. Aronson. 1961. Soviet psychiatric nomenclature. *American Journal of Psychiatry* 118:178–180.

Kling, M. 1969. Violence and politics in Latin-America. In Horowitz et al., eds. 1969.

Kluckhohn, C. and and D. Leighton. 1946. *The Navaho*. Cambridge: Harvard University Press.

Kluckhohn, F. R., and F. L. Strodtbeck. 1961. *Variations in Value Orientations*. New York: Harper & Row.

Kohn, M. 1968. Social class and schizophrenia: A critical review. *Journal of Psychiatric Research* 6(suppl. 1):155–173.

Kolb, L. C. 1966. Soviet psychiatric organization and the community mental health center concept. *American Journal of Psychiatry* 123:(4)433–439.

Konnor, M. J. 1973. Development among the Bushmen of Botswana. Doctoral dissertation, Harvard University.

Kraepelin, E. 1921. *Manic-Depressive Insanity and Paranoia*. R. M. Barcley, trans. Edinburgh: E & S Livingston.

Kramer, M. 1961. Some problems for international research suggested by observations on differences in first admission rates to the mental hospitals of England and Wales and of the United States. In *Proceedings of the Third World Congress of Psychiatry*. 3:153–160. Montreal: McGill University Press.

Kramer, M., E. S. Pollack, and R. W. Redick. 1961. Studies of the incidence and prevalence of hospitalized mental disorders in the United States: Current status and future goals. In P. H. Hoch and J. Zubin, eds. *Comparative Epidemiology of the Mental Disorders*, New York: Grune & Stratton. pp 56–100.

Krapf, E. D. 1959. *Medicine et Hygiene* (Geneva) 17:123. (Quoted by Wittkower and Hugel 1968.)
Kraus, J. 1969a. Some social factors and rates of psychiatric hospital admissions of immigrants in New South Wales. *Medical Journal of Australia* 2:17.
Kraus, J. 1969b. The relationship of psychiatric diagnoses, hospital admission rates, and size of age structure of immigrant groups. *Medical Journal of Australia* 12:91.
Kraus, R. E. 1968. Cross-cultural validation of psychoanalytic theories of depression. *Pennsylvania Psychiatric Quarterly* 8(3):24.
Kreisman, J. J. 1975. The curandero's apprentice: A therapeutic integration of folk and medical healing. *American Journal of Psychiatry* 132:81–83.
Kroeber, A. L. and C. K. Kluckhohn. 1952. *Culture: A Critical Review of Concepts and Definitions.* Cambridge: Massachusetts, Peabody Museum.
Krou, M. H. 1939. Typical behavior patterns in twenty-six ordinal positions. *Journal of Genetic Psychology* 55:3–30.
Krupinski, J. 1967. Sociological aspects of mental ill-health in migrants. *Social Science and Medicine* 1:267–281.
Krupinski, J. 1973. Personal Communication.
Krupinski, J., P. Polke, and A. Stoller. 1967. Psychiatric disturbances in attempted and completed suicide in Victoria during 1963. *Medical Journal of Australia* 2:773.
Krupinski, J. and A. Stoller. 1962. Survey of institutionalized mental patients in Victoria, Australia, 1882 to 1959: I. Admissions to and residents in mental hospitals. *Medical Journal of Australia* 1:269.
Krupinski, J. and A. Stoller. 1965. Incidence of mental disorders in Victoria, according to country of birth. *Medical Journal of Australia.* 2:265.
Krupinski, J., A. Stoller, A. G. Baikie, and J. E. Graves. 1970. A Community Study Health Survey of the Rural Town of Heyfield, Victoria. Australia. Mental Health Authority Special Publication No. 1, Melbourne.
Krupinski, J., A. Stoller, and L. Wallace. 1973. Psychiatric disorders in East European refugees now in Australia. *Social Science and Medicine* 7:31.
Krupinski, J., F. Schaechter, and J. Cade. 1965. Factors influencing the incidence of mental disorders among migrants. *Medical Journal of Australia* 2:269.
Kubany, E. S., R. Gallimore, and J. Buell. 1970. The effects of extrinsic factors on achievement-oriented behavior: A non-Western case. *Journal of Cross-Cultural Psychology* 1:77–84.
Kunitz, S. 1970. Equilibrium theory in social psychiatry: The work of the Leightons. *Psychiatry* 33:312–328.
LaBarre, W. 1945. Some observations on character structure in the Orient: the Japanese. *Psychiatry* 8:326–342.
LaBarre, W. 1975. Anthropological perspectives on hallucination and hallucinogens. In R. K. Siegel and L. J. West, eds. *Hallucinations: Behavior, Experience and Theory*. New York: John Wiley.
Labov, W. 1972. *Language in the Inner City: Studies in the Black English Vernacular*. Philadelphia: University of Pennsylvania Press.

Labov, W. and D. Fanshell. 1977. *Therapeutic Discourse.* New York: Academic Press.

Lacey, J. I. 1967. Somatic response patterning in stress: Some revisions of activation theory. In M. H. Appley and R. Trumbull, eds. *Psychological Stress: Issues in Research.* New York: Appleton-Century-Crofts.

LaFave, H. G., J. Rootman, D. Sydiaha, and R. Duckworth. 1967. The ethnic community and the definitions of mental illness: A comparative study of French and non-French Canadian towns. *Psychiatric Quarterly* 41:211.

Lagmay, A. 1966. The Philippines Thematic Apperception Test. Manila: University of the Philippines Press.

Lambert, W. E. 1955. Measurement of the linguistic dominance of bilinguals. *Journal of Abnormal and Social Psychology* 50:197–200.

Lambert, W. E., J. Havelka, and C. Crosby. 1958. The influence of language-aquisition content on bilingualism. *Journal of Abnormal and Social Psychology* 56:239–244.

Lambert, W. E., J. Havelka, and C. Crosby. 1961. The influence of language-acquisition context on bilingualism. *Journal of Abnormal and Social Psychology* 56:239–244. Reprinted in Sol Saporta, ed. *Psycholinguistics: A Book of Readings,* pp. 407–414. New York: Holt, Rinehart and Winston.

Lambo, T. A. 1960. Further neuropsychiatric observations in Nigeria. *British Medical Journal* 2:1696.

Lambo, T. A. 1966. Patterns of psychiatric care in developing African countries: The Nigerian Village Program. In H. P. David, ed. *International Trends in Mental Health,* pp. 147–153. New York: McGraw Hill.

Lamont, A. M. 1951. Affective types of psychotic reactions in Cape coloured persons. *South African Medical Journal* 25:40.

Lancer, I. 1962. *Culture and Psychopathology.* Israel: Bar-Ilan University. (Master's thesis)

Langner, T. S. 1962. A twenty-two-item screening score of psychiatric symptoms indicating impairment. *Journal of Health and Human Behavior* 3:269–276.

Langner, T. S. and S. T. Michael. 1963. *Life Stress and Mental Health:* The Midtown Manhattan Study, Vol. 2. New York: Free Press.

Lapouse, R., M. A. Monk, and M. Terris. 1956. The drift hypothesis and socio-economic differentials in schizophrenia. *American Journal of Public Health* 46:978.

Laszlo, E. 1972. *The Relevance of General Systems Theory*. New York: Braziller.

Laubscher, B. J. F. 1937. *Sex, Custom, and Psychopathology: A Study of South African Pagan Natives.* London: Routledge & Kegan Paul.

Laughlin, D. C. and E. G. D'Aquili. 1974. *Biogenetic Structuralism.* New York. Columbia University Press.

Lauter, H. and W. Schon. 1965. Ober Stilwandlungen endogener Depressionen in den letzten 50 Jahren, *Transcultural Psychiatric Research Review* 11:62ff.

Lawlor, M. 1955. Cultural influences on preference for design. *Journal of Abnormal and Social Psychology* 51:690–692.

Lazarus, J., B. Z. Locke, and D. S. Thomas. 1963. Migration differentials in mental disease. *Milbank Memorial Fund Quarterly* 41:25.

Lazure, D. 1964. Politics and mental health in new China. *American Journal of Orthopsychiatry* 34:925–933.

Leading Article. 1967. Some complexities of migration. *Medical Journal of Australia.* 1:661.

Lebensohn, Z. M. 1962. The organization and character of Soviet psychiatry. *American Journal of Psychotherapy* 16:295–301.

Lederer, W. 1959. Primitive psychotherapy. *Psychiatry* 22:255.

Lee, E. S. 1957. Migration and mental disease, New York State, 1949–1951. In *Selected Studies of Migration since World War II.* New York: Milbank Memorial Fund.

Lee, E. S. 1963. Socioeconomic and migration differentials in mental disease. New York State, 1949–1951. *Milbank Memorial Fund Quarterly* 41:249.

Lee, T. 1958. Chinese medicine during the Ming Dynasty (1368–1644 AD). *Chinese Medical Journal* 76:178–198, 285–304.

Lee, T., C. Ch'eng, and C. S. Chang. 1962. Some early records of nervous and mental disease in traditional Chinese medicine. *Chinese Medical Journal* 81:55–92.

Lehmann, H. E. 1967. Unusual psychiatric disorders and atypical psychoses. In A. M. Freedman and H. I. Kaplan, eds. *Comprehensive Textbook of Psychiatry,* pp. 1150–1161. Baltimore: Williams and Wilkins.

Leighton, A. H. 1959a. Mental illness and acculturation. In I. Gladston, ed. *Medicine and Anthropology,* pp. 108–128. New York: International Universities Press.

Leighton, A. H. 1959b. *My Name Is Legion: Foundation for a Theory of Man in Relation to Culture,* Vol. 1, Stirling County Study of Psychiatric Disorder and Sociocultural Environment. New York: Basic Books.

Leighton, A. H. 1965. Culture change and psychiatric disorder. In A. V. S. de Reuch and R. Porter, eds. *Transcultural Psychiatry,* pp. 216–235. Boston: Little, Brown.

Leighton, A. H. 1968. Introduction: The mental health of the American Indian. *American Journal of Psychiatry* 125:217.

Leighton, A. and J. K. Hughes. 1961. Cultures as causative of mental disorder. In Milbank Memorial Fund. *Causes of Mental Disorder: A Review of Epidemiological Knowledge,* p. 341–366. New York: The Fund.

Leighton, A. H., T. A. Lambo, C. C. Hughes, D. C. Leighton, J. M. Murphy, and O. B. Macklin. 1963. *Psychiatric Disorder Among the Yoruba.* Ithaca: Cornell University Press.

Leighton, D. C., J. S. Harding, D. B. Macklin, A. M. MacMillan, and A. H. Leighton. 1963. *The Character of Danger: Psychiatric Symptoms in Selected Communities.* New York: Basic Books.

Leme-Lopes, J. 1961. Ensino de psiquiatria na escola de medicina. *J. Bras. Psiq.* 10(2):115–132.

Leme-Lopes, J. 1962. A formacao do estundante de medicina em psiquiatria e psicologia medica. *Journal Brasil Psiq.* 11:144–164.

Lemert, E. M. 1951. *Social Pathology.* New York. McGraw-Hill.

Lemert, E. M. 1967. *Human Deviance, Social Problems, and Social Control.* Englewood Cliffs: Prentice-Hall.

Lenski, G. 1954. Status crystalization: A non-vertical dimension of social status. *American Soiological Review* 19:405.

Lenski, G. 1967. Status inconsistency and the vote: A four nation test. *American Sociological Review* 32:298.

Lenz, H. 1964. *Vergleichende Psychiatrie, Elne Studie uber die Beziehung von Kultur, Soziologie und Psychopathologie.* Vienna: Wilhelm Mandrich Verlag.

León, C. A. 1959. Teaching of undergraduate psychiatry at the Universidad del Valle Medical School. *Journal of Medical Education* 34:1093–1097.

León, C. A. 1963. El Espanto: sus implicaciones psiquiátricas. *Acta Psiquiátrica y Psicológica Argentina* 9:207–217.

León, C. A. 1965. El espanto: sus implicaciones psiquiátricas. *Transcultural Psychiatric Research Review* 11:45–48.

León, C. A. 1967. Prevalencia de trastornos mentales en un sector urbano de Cali. *Revista Colombiana de Psiquiatriá* 2:24–36.

León, C. A. 1969. Unusual patterns of crime during 'La Violencia' in Colombia. *American Journal of Psychiatry* 125:118–129.

León, C. A. 1970. Actitudes de Psiquiatras Latinoamericanos hacia la clasificación de trastornos mentales. In Roselli, ed. 1970.

León, C. A. and C. E. Climent. 1968. Anotaciones sobre el ojo en Cali. *Acta Psiquiátrica y Psicológica de América Latina* 14:23–34.

León, C. A., C. E. Climent, R. Jaramillo, and H. Estrada. 1970. Evaluación de instrumentos para el estudio de la prevalencia de trastornos mentales. In J. Mariategui and B. Adis Castro, eds. *Estudios sobre Epidemiología Psiquiátrica en Latino-America.* Buenos Aires: Acta.

León, R. L. 1968. Some implications for a preventive program for American Indians. *American Journal of Psychiatry* 125:232.

LeVine, R. 1973. *Culture, Behavior and Personality.* Chicago: Aldine.

Levinger, G. 1960. Continuance in casework and other helping relationships: A review of current research. *Social Work* 5:40–51.

Levinson, D. J. and P. E. Huffman. 1955. Traditional family ideology and its relation to personality. *Journal of Personality* 23:251–273.

Levi-Strauss, C. 1958. *Anthropologie Structurale.* Paris: Ed. Plon, p. 392.

Lewis, A. 1967. Problems presented by the ambiguous word "anxiety" as used in psychopathology. *Israel Annals of Psychiatry and Related Disciplines* 5:105–121.

Lewis, C. 1975. Child initiated care: A study of the determinants of the illness behavior of children. Unpublished report. Center for Health Sciences. Los Angeles: University of California.

Lewis, M. and R. Freedle. 1972. Mother-infant dyad: The cradle of meaning. Research Bulletin RB72–22. Princeton, N.J.: Educational Testing Service.

Lewis, M., S. Goldberg, and H. Campbell. 1970. A developmental study of learning within the first three years of life: Response decrement to redundant signal. *Monograph of the Society for Research in Child Development* 34(133).

Lewis, N. D. C. and Z. A. Piotrowski. 1954. Clinical diagnosis of manic depressive psychosis. In Hoch and Zubin, eds. 1954:25–38.

Lewis, O. 1949. Husbands and wives in a Mexican village: A study of role conflict. *American Anthropologist* 51:602–610.

Lewis, O. 1951. *Life in a Mexican Village: Tepozlan Restudied.* Urbana, Illinois: University of Illinois Press.

Lewis, O. 1959a. Family dynamics in a Mexican village. *Marriage and Family Living* 21:218–226.

Lewis, O. 1959b. *Five Families: Mexican Case Studies in the Culture of Poverty.* New York: Basic Books.

Lewis, O. 1961. *Five Families: Case Studies in the Culture of Poverty.* New York: Basic Books.

Lewis, O. 1964. *Pedro Martinez.* New York: Random House.

Lin, P. T. K. 1973. APA lecturer says neuroses non-existent in mainland China. *Psychiatric News,* pp 1–13.

Lin, T. Y. 1953. A study of the incidence of mental disorders in Chinese and other cultures. *Psychiatry* 16:313–336.

Lin, T. Y. 1959. The epidemiological study of mental disorders. *WHO Chron.* 21:509–516.

Lin, T. Y. 1967. The epidemiological study of mental disorders by WHO. *Social Psychiatry* 1:204–205.

Lin, T. Y. 1969. Mental disorders in Taiwan, 15 years later. A preliminary report. In Caudill and Lin, eds. 1969.

Lin, T. Y. and C. Standley. 1962. Geneva: World Health Organization. Public Health Papers, no. 16.

Lindemann, F. 1944. Symptomatology and management of acute grief. *American Journal of Psychiatry* 101:141.

Lindzey, G. 1961. *Projective Techniques and Cross-Cultural Research.* New York: Appleton-Century-Crofts, p. 73.

Linn, L. S. 1967. Social characteristics and social interaction in the utilization of a psychiatric outpatient clinic. *Journal of Health and Social Behavior* 8:3–14.

Linton, R. 1945. *The Cultural Background of Personality.* Appleton Century Crofts. New York.

Lion, E. G. 1942. Anancastic depressions: obsessive-compulsive symptoms occurring during depressions. *Journal of Nervous and Mental Diseases* 95:730–738.

Lipkin, K. M., J. Dyrud, and G. G. Meyer. 1970. The many faces of mania. *Archives of General Psychiatry* 22:262–267.

Lipset, S. M. and R. Bendix. 1963. *Social Mobility in Industrial Society.* Berkeley: University of California Press, pp 64–72, 251–252.

Litwak, E. 1956. Conflicting values and decision-making. Doctoral dissertation, Columbia University.

Locke, B. Z., M. S. M. Kramer, and B. Pasamanick. 1960. Immigration and insanity. *Public Health Reports* 75:301.

Lopreato, J. 1967. Upward social mobility and political orientation. *American Sociological Review* 32:586.

Lorr, M. and C. J. Klett. 1967. *Inpatient Multidimensional Psychiatric Scale*. Palo Alto, Calif.: Consulting Psychologists Press.

Lövaas, I. O. 1958. Social desirability ratings of personality variables by Norwegian and American college students. *Journal of Abnormal and Social Psychology* 57:124–125.

Lowenthal, D. 1967. Race and colour in the West Indies. *Daedalus* (Spring): 580–626.

Lubchansky, I., G. Egri, and J. Stokes. 1970. Puerto Rican spiritualists view mental illness: The faith healer as a paraprofessional. *American Journal of Psychiatry* 127:312–321.

Lucero-Kelly, C. 1968. Inventory of human physical and economic resources for mental health in Argentina. Working paper for the Conference on Mental Health in the Americas, San Antonio, Texas (mimeographed copy).

Ludwig, A. M. 1975. The psychiatrist as physician. *Journal of the American Medical Association* 234:603–604.

Lystad, M. 1957. Social mobility among selected groups of schizophrenic patients. *American Sociological Review* 12:288–292.

MacAndrew, C. and R. B. Edgerton. 1969. *Drunken Comportment*. Chicago: Aldine.

Macgregor, G. 1961–62. Community development and social adaptation. *Human Organization* 20:238.

Madsen, W. 1964. Value conflicts in cultural transfer. In Worchel and Byrne, eds. *Personality Change,* p. 470–489. New York: Wiley.

Madsen, W. 1965. *The Mexican-Americans of South Texas*. New York: Holt, Rinehart and Winston.

Maduro, R. J. and C. F. Martinez. 1974. Latino dream analysis: Opportunity for confrontation. *Social Casework* 55:461–469.

Makarenko, A. S. 1952. O kommunisticheskom vospitanii (On communist upbringing). Moscow: Gosudarstvennoe Uchebno-pedagogicheskoye Izdatel'stvo.

Makarenko, A. S. 1955. *The Road to Life*. Moscow: Foreign Languages Publishing House.

Makela, T. 1967. Personality and the extrapyramidal side-effects of Perphenazine. *Nord. Psykiat.* 21:136–144. (In Norwegian).

Malinowski, B. 1927. *Sex and Repression in Savage Society*. New York: Harcourt Brace.

Malzberg, B. 1940. *Social and Biological Aspects of Mental Disease*. Utica, New York: Utica State Hospital Press.

Malzberg, B. 1955. Mental disease among native and foreign-born white populations of New York State, 1939–41. *Mental Hygiene* 39:545.

Malzberg, B. 1959. Statistical data about mental illness. In Arieti, ed. 1959 1:161–174.

Malzberg, B. 1962. The distribution of mental disease according to religious affiliation in New York State, 1949–1951. *Mental Hygiene* 46:510.

Malzberg, B. 1964. Mental disease among foreign-born in Canada, 1950–52, in relation to period of immigration. *American Journal of Psychiatry* 120:971.

Malzberg, B. 1967. Internal migration and mental disease among the white population of New York State, 1960–61. *International Journal of Social Psychiatry* 13:184.

Malzberg, B. and E. S. Lee. 1956. *Migration and Mental Disease: A study of First Admissions to Hospitals for Mental Disease, New York, 1939–41.* New York: Social services research council.

Mandelbaum, D. 1949. *Selected Writings of Edward Sapir.* Berkeley: University of California Press.

Mandelbaum, D. 1965. Alcohol and culture. *Current Anthropology* 6(3):281–293.

Mangin, P. 1965. Mental health and migration to cities: A Peruvian case. In Heath and Adams, eds. *Contemporary Cultures and Societies of Latin America.* New York: Random House.

Manis, J., M. Brawer, C. L. Hunt, and L. Kercher. 1963. Validating a mental health scale. *American Sociological Review* 28:108–116.

Maoz, M. D., S. Levy, N. Brand, and H. S. Halevi. 1966. An epidemiological survey of mental disorders in a community of newcomers to Israel. *J. Coll. Gen. Practit.* 11:267.

Marconi, J. 1955. A survey on the prevalence of alcoholism among the adult population of a suburb of Santiago. *Quarterly Journal of Studies on Alcoholism* 16:438–446.

Marconi, J. and L. Muñoz. 1970. Visión general de la investigación epidemiológica en salud mental en Chile. In Roselli, ed. 1970.

Marcos, L. R. and M. Alpert. 1976. Strategies and risks in psychotherapy with bilingual patients. *American Journal of Psychiatry* 133:1275–1281.

Mariátegui, J., V. Alva, and O. DeLeón, 1970. Prevalencia de desórdenes mentales en un distrito urbano de Lima. In Roselli, ed. 1970.

Mariátegui, J. and G. Adis Castro, eds. 1970. *Estudios sobre Epidemiología Psiquiátrica en América Latina, p. 193.* Buenos Aires: Acta.

Marinko, B. P. 1966. Psychosis in Ethiopia. *Transcultural Psychiatric Research Review* 111:152.

Marsella, A. S., M. D. Murrat, and C. Golden 1974. Ethnic variations in the phenomenology of emotions. *Journal of Cross-Cultural Psychology* 5:312–328.

Marsh, J. F.and C. Chemtob. 1974. Marihuana smoking: Asymmetric hemisphere effects and intellectual performance. Unpublished manuscript.

Marsh, R. M. 1967. *Comparative Sociology: Toward the Codification of Cross-Societal Analysis.* New York: Harcourt.

Martin, F., J. H. F. Brotherston, and S. Chave. 1957. The incidence of neurosis on a new housing estate. *British Journal of Preventive and Social Medicine* 11:196.

Martin, H. W., S. S. Sutker, R. L. Leon, and W. M. Hales. 1958. Mental health of Eastern Oklahoma Indians: An exploration. *Human Organization* 27:308.

Martínez, C. 1973. Community mental health and the Chicano movement. *American Journal of Orthopsychiatry* 43:595–601.

Martins, C. 1970. Reflexoes sobre a assistencia psiquiatrica na America Latina. In Programas e Relatorios Officiais. VI Congreso Latino-Americano de Psiquiatria. I Congreso Brasilerio de Psiquiatria. Sao Paulo, Brasil.

Matte-Blanco, I. 1961. The place of psychiatry and mental health in medicine and in the medical curriculum. In *Teaching of Psychiatry and Mental Health,* W.H.O. Public Health Papers No. 9.

Matza, D. 1969. *Becoming Deviant.* Englewood Cliffs: Prentice-Hall.

Mayer-Gross, W., E. Slater, and M. Roth. 1960. *Clinical Psychiatry.* 2d ed. London: Cassell.

Mayer-Gross, W., E. Slater, and M. Roth. 1969. *Clinical Psychiatry.* 3d ed. London: Cassell.

Mayr, E. 1961a. Behavior and systematics. In A. Roe and G. G. Simpson, eds. *Behavior and Evolution,* p. 341. New Haven: Yale University Press.

Mayr, E. 1961b. Cause and effect in biology. *Science* 1501–1508.

Mayr, E. 1974. Behavior programs and evolutionary strategies. *American Scientist* 62:650–659.

Mazer, M. 1976. *People and Predicaments.* Cambridge: Harvard University Press.

McDonald, R. L. 1967. Influence of personality type on drug response: A critical reply. *Journal of Psychology* 65:123–129.

McDonald, R. L. 1967. The effects of personality type on drug response. *Archives of General Psychiatry* 17:680–686.

McGinnis, J. M. 1976. Editorial: The rising costs of hospital care: Mandate for academic introspection. *Journal of Medical Education* 51:602–604.

McGough, W. E., E. Williams, and J. Blackley, 1966. Changing patterns of psychiatric illness among Negroes of the southern United States. 4th World Congress of Psychiatry, Madrid. Abstracts, *International Congress Series Excerpta Medica Foundation* (Amsterdam). 117:304–305.

McGraw, M. B. 1935. *Growth: A Study of Johnny and Jimmy.* New York: Appleton-Century.

McKinlay, J. B. and D. Dutton 1974. Social-psychological factors affecting health service utilization. In S. Mushkin, ed. *Consumer Incentives for Health Care,* pp. 251–303. New York: Prodist.

Mead, M. 1935. *Sex and Temperament in Three Primitive Societies.* New York: Morrow.

Mead, M. 1952. Some relations between social anthropology and psychiatry. In E. Alexander and H. Ross, eds. *Dynamic Psychiatry,* p. 448. Chicago: University of Chicago Press.

Mead, M. 1970. *Culture and Commitment.* New York: Natural History Press.

Mead, M. 1972. *Blackberry Winter.* New York: Morrow.

Mead, M. 1976. Towards a human science. *Science* 191:903.

Mead, M. and F. C. MacGregor. 1951. *Growth and Culture: A Photographic Study of Balinese Childhood.* New York: Putnam.

Meadow, A. and D. H. Stoker 1965. Symptomatic behavior of hospitalized patients: A study of Mexican-American and Anglo-American patients. *Archives of General Psychiatry* 12:267–277.

Meadow, A., D. H. Stoker and L. A. Zurcher. 1967. Sex role and schizophrenia: A cross cultural study. *International Journal of Social Psychiatry.*

Mechanic, D. 1964. The influence of mothers on their children's health attitudes and behavior. *Pediatrics* 33:444–453.

Mechanic, D. 1968. *Medical Sociology: a Selective View.* New York: Free Press.

Mechanic, D. 1969. *Mental Health and Social Policy.* Englewood Cliffs: Prentice-Hall.

Mechanic, D. 1972. Social psychologic factors affecting the presentation of bodily complaints. *New England Journal of Medicine* 286:1132–1139.

Mechanic, D. and E. H. Volkart, 1961. Stress, illness behavior and the sick role. *American Sociological Review* 26:51–58.

Meehl, P. E. 1954. *Clinical Versus Statistical Prediction: A Theoretical Analysis and a Review of the Evidence.* Minneapolis: University of Minnesota Press.

Menninger, K. 1948. Changing concepts of disease. *Annuals of Internal Medicine* 29:318–325.

Menninger, K. 1963. *The Vital Balance.* New York: Viking.

Merton, R. K. 1957. Social theory and social structure, rev. ed. Glencoe, Ill.: Free Press.

Metraux, A. 1962. *Les Incas, p. 133.* Paris: Editions du Seuil.

Meyer, A. 1917. Progress in teaching psychiatry. *Journal of the American Medical Association* 69:861–863.

Mezey, A. G. 1960a. Personal background, emigration and mental disorder in Hungarian refugees. *Journal of Mental Science* 106:618.

Mezey, A. G. 1960b. Psychiatric illness in Hungarian refugees. *Journal of Mental Science* 106:628.

Mezzich, J. E. 1979. Patterns and issues in multiaxial psychiatric diagnosis. *Psychological Medicine* 9:125–137.

Mezzich, J. E. 1980. Multiaxial Diagnostic Systems in Psychiatry, In Kaplan, et al., eds. 1980.

Milgram, S. 1964. Group pressure and action against a person. *Journal of Abnormal and Social Psychology* 69:137–143.

Miller, J. 1967. In Petrilowitsch. 1967: vol. 6.

Mischel, W. 1970. Sex typing and socialization. In P. H. Mussen, ed. *Carmichael's Manual of Child Psychology. 3d ed.* New York: Wiley.

Mischel, W. 1973. Toward a cognitive social learning reconceptualization of personality. *Psychological Review* 80:252–283.

Mishler, E. G. and N. A. Scotch 1963. Socio-cultural factors in the epidemiology of schizophrenia: A review. *Psychiatry* 26:315–350.

Mitchell, J. C., ed. 1971. *Social Networks in Urban Situations: Analyses of Personal Relationships in African Towns.* Manchester, England: Manchester University Press.

Mitchell, R. E. 1965. Survey materials collected in the developing countries: Sampling, measurement, and interviewing obstacles to intra- and international comparisons. *International Social Science Journal* 17:677.

Moffson, A. 1954. Schizophrenia in male Bantu admissions to West Kooppies Hospital. *South African Medical Journal* 28:662.

Montagu, A. 1967. Culture and mental illness. Presented at 1967 Winter Symposium on mental depression. Washington Psychiatric Society and Department of Psychiatry. Georgetown University School of Medicine. Washington, D.C.

Montagu, A., ed. 1968. *Man and Aggression.* New York: Oxford University Press.

Montesinos, A. 1965. Metabolism of cocaine. *Bulletin on Narcotics* 17(2):11–17.

Moore, J. W. and A. Cuellar. 1970. *Mexican Americans*. Englewood Cliffs: Prentice-Hall.

Moraes Andrade, O. 1970. Saude mental e assistencia psiquiatrica no Brasil. In Programas e Relatorios Oficiais. VI Congreso Latino-Americano de Psiquiatria. I Congreso Brasilerio de Psiquiatria. Sao Paulo.

Morris, J. N. 1959. Health and social class. *Lancet* 1:303.

Moya, L., J. Marconi, J. Horwitz, L. Munoz, A. Bahamondes, H. y Saint Jean 1969. Prevalencia de desordenes mentales en el area norte de Santiago de Chile. *Acta psiquiatrica y Psicologica de America Latina* 15:137–151.

Munsterberger, W. 1968. Address at the American Psychoanaytic Association, regular meetings. New York.

Murdock, G. P. 1965. *Social Structure.* New York: Free Press.

Murdock, G. P. 1967. *Ethnographic Atlas.* Pittsburgh: University of Pittsburgh Press.

Murdock, G. P. et al., eds. 1971. *Outline of Cultural Materials*. 4th ed. New Haven: Human Relations Area File Press.

Murdock, G. P., ed. 1975. *Outline of World Cultures.* 5th ed. New Haven: Human Relations Area File Press.

Murphy, H. B. M. 1954. The mental health of Singapore Part. I—Suicide. *Med. J. Malaya* 9:1.

Murphy, H. B. M. 1955. *Flight and Resettlement.* Paris: UNESCO.

Murphy, H. B. M. 1959a. Culture and mental disorder in Singapore. In Opler, ed. 1959: 291–316.

Murphy, H. B. M. 1959b. Cultural factors in the mental health of Malayan students. In D. H. Funkenstein, ed. *The Student and Mental Health: An International View.* London: World Federation for Mental Health.

Murphy, H. B. M. 1961. Social change and mental health. In *Causes of Mental Disorder: A Review of Epidemiological Knowledge,* pp. 280–329. New York: Milbank Memorial Fund.

Murphy, H. B. M., E. D. Wittkower, J. Fried, and H. Ellenberger. 1963. A cross-cultural survey of schizophrenic symptomatology. *International Journal of Social Psychiatry* 9:237–249.

Murphy, H. B. M. 1965a. Migration and major mental disorders: A reappraisal.

In M. B. Kantor, ed. *Mobility and Mental Health.* Springfield, Illinois: C. C. Thomas.

Murphy, H. B. M. 1965b. The epidemiological approach to transcultural psychiatric research. In De Reuck and Porter, eds. *Transcultural Psychiatry: A Ciba Foundation Symposium.* London: Churchill.

Murphy, H. B. M. 1969a. Ethnic variations in drug response: results of an international survey. *Transcultural Psychiatric Research Review* 6:5–23.

Murphy, H. B. M. 1969b. Handling the culture dimension in psychiatric research. *Social Psychiatry* 4:11–15.

Murphy, H. B. M. 1971. History and evolution of syndromes: The striking case of "latah" and "amok." In M. Hammer et al., eds. *Psychopathology: Contributions from the Biological, Behavioral and Social Sciences.* New York: Wiley-Interscience.

Murphy, H. B. M. 1972. Chronicity, community and culture. Paper presented at the Colloque sur Traitements au long cours des etats psychotiques. Paris, France. Mimeo.

Murphy, H. B. M. and A. C. Raman. 1971. The chronicity of schizophrenia in indigenous tropical peoples: Results of a twelve-year follow-up survey in Mauritius. *British Journal of Psychiatry* 118:489–497.

Murphy, H. B. M., E. D. Wittkower and N. A. Chance. 1967. Cross-cultural inquiry into the symptomatology of depression: A preliminary report. *International Journal of Psychiatry* 3:6–15.

Murphy, H. B. M., E. D. Wittkower, J. Fried, and H. Ellenberger. 1963. A cross-cultural survey of schizophrenic symptomatology. *International Journal of Social Psychiatry* 9:237–249.

Murphy, J. M. 1964. Psychotherapeutic aspects of shamanism on St Lawrence Island, Alaska. In Kiev, ed. 1964.

Murphy, J. M. and A. H. Leighton, eds. 1965. *Approaches to Cross-Cultural Psychiatry.* Ithaca: Cornell University Press.

Myasishev, V. N. In Lebedinskii, M. S. Voprosi Psychoterapii. 1958. (Problems in Psychotherapy). Moscow: Medgiz. Quoted in I. Ziferstein, *Cultural Determinants of the Therapist-Patient Interaction.*

Myers, J. and L. Bean. 1968. *A Decade Later: A Follow-Up of Social Class and Mental Illness.* New York: Wiley.

Myers, J. K. and B. H. Roberts. 1959. *Family and Class Dynamics in Mental Illness.* New York: Wiley.

Myers, J. K. and L. Schaffer. 1954. Social stratification and psychiatric practice: a study of an out-patient clinic. *American Sociological Review 19:307–310.*

Nachshon, I., J. G. Draguns, I. K. Broverman, and L. Phillips. 1972. A reflection of acculturation in psychiatric symptomatology. A study of Israeli child guidance clinic population. *Social Psychiatry.* 7:109–118.

Naranjo, P. 1969. Etnofarmacología de las plantas psicotropas de America. *Terapia* 25:5–62.

Naroll R. 1965. Thwarting disorientation and suicide: A cross-cultural survey. *Transcultural Psychiatric Research Review* 2:89.

Naroll, R. 1973. Holocultural theory tests. In Naroll and Naroll, eds. 1973: 309–384.
Naroll, R. and F. Naroll, eds. 1973. *Main Currents in Cultural Anthropology.* New York: Appleton-Century-Crofts.
Naumburg, M. 1957. Art as symbolic speech. In Ruth Anshen, ed. *Language: An Enquiry into its Meaning and Function.* New York: Harper.
National Institute of Mental Health. 1969. The First U.S. Mission on Mental Health to the USSR. U.S. Department of Health, Education and Welfare.
National Institute of Mental Health. 1972. *Schizophrenia: Is There an Answer?* DHEW Publication No. (HSM) 73–9086.
Nelson, S. H. and E. F. Torrey. 1973. The religious functions of psychiatry. *American Journal of Psychiatry* 43:362–367.
Niedermeyer, E. 1967. Depression—a comparison of American and German concepts. *Bibliotheca Psychiatrica et Neurologica* 133:1.
Norbeck, E. 1954. *Takashima: A Japanese Fishing Community.* Salt Lake City: University of Utah Press.
Noreich, K. 1965. Hospitalized psychoses among wandering people in Norway. *Acta Psychiatrica Scandinavica* 41:157.
Norris, H. 1849. Sentence of death upon a Malay convicted of running amuck. *Journal of Indonesian Archipelago* 3:460–463.
Noyes, A. B. and L. C. Kolb. 1968. *Modern Clinical Psychiatry.* 7th ed. Philadelphia. W. B. Saunders Co.
Nutall, R. and L. Phillips. 1969. Social class and pathological behavior style. In *Proceedings of the Eleventh Interamerican Congress of Psychology.* L. Natalicio, ed. 1:84:1–20.
Obeyesekere, G. 1969. The ritual drama of the Sanni demons: Collective representations of disease in Ceylon. *Comparative Studies in Social History* 11:174–216.
Odegaard, O. 1932. Emigration and insanity: A study of mental disease among the Norwegian-born population of Minnesota. *Acta Psychiatrica Scandinavica* (Kbb.) Supplement 4.
Odegaard, O. 1936. Emigration and mental health. *Mental Hygiene* 20:546–553.
Odegaard, O. 1945. Distribution of mental diseases in Norway: Contribution to ecology of mental disorder. *Acta Psychiatrica et Neurologica Scandinavica* 20:247.
Okasha, A. 1968. Psychiatric observations in Egypt. *Transcultural Psychiatric Research Review* 5:149.
Opler, M. K. 1945. Themes as dynamic forces in culture. *American Journal of Sociology* 51:198–206.
Opler, M. K. 1956. *Culture, Psychiatry and Human Values.* Springfield, Ill.: C. C. Thomas.
Opler, M. K. 1959. Cultural differences in mental disorders: An Italian and Irish contrast in the schizophrenia. In Opler, ed. 1959.
Opler, M. K. 1967. *Culture and Social Psychiatry.* New York: Atherton.

Opler, M. K., ed. 1959. *Culture and Mental Health.* New York, Macmillan.

Orleans, L. A. 1969. Medical education and manpower in Communist China. In C.T. Hu, ed. *Aspects of Chinese Education.* New York: Teachers College Press of Columbia University.

Osgood, C. E., W. K. Archer, and M. S. Miron. 1962. The cross-cultural generality of meaning systems. Appendices to a proposal submitted to the National Science Foundation. Urbana: Institute of Communications Research, University of Illinois, mimeo.

Osgood, C. E. and T. A. Sebeok. 1965. Psycholinguistics: A survey of theory and research problems, a Morton Price memorial supplement to the *Journal of Abnormal and Social Psychology 45.* Expanded and reissued in book form by Indiana University Press, at Bloomington.

Osgood, E. C., C. J. Suici, and P. H. Tannenbaum. 1957. *The Measurement of Meaning.* Urbana. University of Illinois Press.

Osterreicher, W. 1950. Manisch depressive psychose bij een Soendanese. *Med. Maandbl. Djakarta* 3:173.

Ottosson, J. O. and C. Perris. 1973. Multidimensional classification of mental disorders. *Psychological Medicine* 3:238–243.

Overall, J. E. et al. 1969. Extrinsic factors influencing responses to psychotherapeutic drugs. *Archives of General Psychiatry* 21:89–94.

Oxley, J., 1849. Malay amoks. *Journal of the Indonesian Archipelago* 3:532–533.

Pacheco E. Silva, A. C. 1960. Mental hygiene in underdeveloped countries. *Revista archivos de Neurología y Psichiatría* 10:5–15.

Pacheco E. Silva, A. C. 1966. Curso para o grupo de Residentes, Bolsistas e Estagiarios (Bienio), Departamento de Psiquiatria, Facultad de Medicina, Universidad de Sao Paulo (mimeographed copy).

Page, J. D. 1966. Cross-cultural similarities in symptomatology among recent admissions to mental hospitals. Paper presented at Eastern Psychological Association. New York.

Pages-Larraya, F., et al. 1966. Estudio piloto de la distribución de las principales enfermedades psiquiátricas en una zona de la ciudad de Buenos Aires. Coloquio ACTA sobre Epidemiología de las Enfermedades Mentales en América Latina. Buenos Aires (mimeographed copy).

Palmer, S. 1966. Murder and suicide in 40 non-literate societies. *Transcultural Psychiatric Research Review* 3:96.

Pan American Health Organization. 1966. Mental health information Center on Latin America. Provisional Directory of Psychiatrists in Latin-America.

Paredes, J. A. and M. J. Hepburn. 1976. The split brain and the culture-and-cognition paradox. *Current Anthropology* 17:121–127.

Parhad, L., 1965. The cultural-social conditions in a psychiatric outpatient department in Kuwait. *International Journal of Social Psychiatry* 2:14–19.

Parker, S. and R. J. Kleiner 1966. *Mental Illness in the Urban Negro Community.* Glencoe: Free Press.

Parker, S., R. J. Kleiner, and B. Needelman. 1969. Migration and mental illness:

Some reconsiderations and suggestions for further analysis. *Social Science and Medicine* 3:1.

Parres, R. 1979. Ethnocentricity among North American psychiatrists. Paper presented at the 132nd Annual Meeting of the American Psychiatric Association, Chicago.

Parsons, A. 1961. Some comparative observations on ward social structure: Southern Italy, England, and the United States. *Transcultural; Psychiatric Research Review* 10:65–67.

Parsons, T. 1951. *The Social System.* Glencoe: Free Press.

Pattison, E. M. 1977. Psychosocial interpretations of exorcism. *Journal of Operational Psychiatry* 8:5–21.

Payet, M., P. Sankaie, O. Pene, M. Bao, M. Mouianier, A. M. Sow, and I. Seck. 1965. Le Contexte Psychosomatique de l'Ulcere Gastroduodenal chez le Noir Africain. *Bulletin de la Societe Medicale d'Afrique Noire de Langue Francaise* 7:444–450.

Pattison, E. M. A theoretical-empirical base for social systems therapy. In Foulks et al. 1977.

Pease, D., L. Wolins, and D. F. Stockdale. 1973. Relationship and prediction of infant tests. *Journal of Genetic Psychology* 122:31–35.

Pelz, D. C. and F. M. Andrews. 1964. Detecting causal priorities in panel study data. *American Sociological Review* 29:836–854.

P.E.P. 1967. Racial discrimination. London: Political and Economic Planning.

Perdomo, R. 1968. Experiencia en la enseñanza de la psiquiatría como especialidad. *Educación Médica y Salud* 2:306–324.

Petrilowitsch, N., ed. 1967. *Contributions to Comparative Psychology,* part 1. Basel: Karger.

Pfeiffer, W. M. 1966. Psychiatric peculiarities in Indonesia. *Transcultural Psychiatric Research Review* 3:116.

Pfeiffer, W. M. 1970. *Transkulturelle Psychiatric. Ergebnisse und Problems.* Stuttgart: G. Thieme.

Pfeiffer, W. M. 1971. *Transkulturelle Psychiatrie.* Stuttgart: G. Thieme.

Pfeiffer, W. M. and E. Gebelein. 1969. Vergleich der Wirkung des Fluphenazin bei einer indonesischen and einer deutschen Patient-engruppe. *Transcultural Psychiatric Research Review* 6:155–157. (Abstract).

Pfister-Ammende, M. 1955. In H. B. M. Murphy. 1955.

Phillips, D. L., and K. J. Clancy. 1970. Response biases in field studies of mental illness. *American Sociological Review* 35:503–515.

Phillips, H. P. 1959–1960. Problems of translation and meaning in field work. *Human Organization* 18:184–192.

Phillips, H. P. 1966. *Thai Peasant Personality.* Berkeley: University of California Press.

Phillips, L. 1968. *Failures of Human Adaptation.* New York: Academic Press.

Phillips, L., I. K. Broverman, and E. Zigler. 1966. Social competence and psychiatric diagnosis. *Journal of Abnormal Psychology* 71:209–214.

Phillips, L., I. K. Broverman, and E. Zigler. 1968. Sphere dominance, role orientation, and diagnosis. *Journal of Abnormal Psychology* 73:306–312.

Phillips, L., and J. G. Draguns. 1969. Some issues in intercultural research on psychopathology. In Caudill and Lin, eds. 1969:21–32.

Pichot, P. 1966. Problemes methodologiques de la classification en psychiatrie. *Annales Medico-Psychologiques* 124(2):486–491.

Pike, K. 1966. *Language in Relation to a Unified Theory of the Structure of Human Behavior.* The Hague: Mouton.

Plog, S., and R. Edgerton. 1969. Changing Perspectives in Mental Illness. New York: Holt.

Portnov, A. A. and D. D. Fedotov. 1969. *Psychiatry.* Moscow: Mir.

Post, F. 1968. The factor of aging in affective illness. In Coppen and Walk, eds. 1968: 105–116.

Prince, R. 1964. Indigenous Yoruba psychiatry. In Kiev, ed. 1964.

Prince, R. 1967. The changing picture of depressive syndromes in Africa. *Canadian Journal of African Studies.* 1:171.

Queról, M. 1965. Humanización de la enseñanza de la psiquiatriá. *Acta Psiquiátrica y Psicológica de American Latina* 2:127–134.

Racy, J. 1970. Psychiatry in the Arab East. *Acta Psychiatrica Scandinavica.* Supplement, 211.

Raman, A. C. and H. B. M. Murphy. 1972. Failure of traditional prognostic indicators in Afro-Asian psychotics: Results of a long-term follow-up survey. *Journal of Nervous Mental Disease* 154:238–247.

Ramírez, M. 1967. Identification with Mexican family values and authoritarianism in Mexican-Americans. *Journal of Social Psychology* 73:3–11.

Ramírez, S. 1960. El Mexicano: Psicologia de Sus Motivaciones. Republic Argentina 9: Editorial Pax-Mexico, S. A.

Random House Dictionary. 1971. New York: Random House.

Rao, A. V. 1966. Depression in Southern India. Fourth world congress of psychiatry. Madrid. September 5–11, 1966. Abstracts. International congress Series No. 117. Excerpta Medica Foundation. Amsterdam.

Rao, A. V. 1970. A study of depression as prevalent in South India. *Transcultural Psychiatric Research Review* 7:166.

Rappaport, R A. 1971. Ritual, sanctity, and cybernetics. *American Anthropologist* 73:59–76.

Rasch, C. 1894. Uber "amok." *Neurol. Zenir. Bl.* 13:550–554.

Rasmussen, H. 1975. Medical education—Revolution or reaction. *Pharos* 38:53–59.

Ratnavale, D. N. 1973. Psychiatry in Shanghai, China: Observations in 1973. *American Journal of Psychiatry* 130:1082–1087.

Rawnsley, K. 1967. An international diagnostic exercise In *Proceedings of the Fourth World Congress of Psychiatry. Amsterdam: Excerpta Medica Foundations.* 4:2683–2686.

Rawnsley, K. 1968. Epidemiology of affective disorder. In Coppen and Walk, eds. 1968: 27–36.

Registrar General. 1964. *Statistical Review of England and Wales 1960.* Supplement on Mental Health. H.M.S.O. London.

Resnik, H. L. P. and L. H. Dizmang 1971. Observations on suicidal behavior among American Indians. *American Journal of Psychiatry* 127:882.

Rennie, T. A. C., L. Srole, M. K. Opler, and T. S. Langner 1957. Urban life and mental health. *American Journal of Psychiatry* 113:831.

Resnick, H. L. and L. H. Dizmang. 1971. Observations on suicidal behavior among American Indians. *American Journal of Psychiatry* 127:882–887.

RF Illustrated. 1976. 3:5.

Rin, H. 1963. Koro: A consideration on Chinese concepts of illness and case illustrations. *Transcultural Psychiatric Research Review.* 15:23–30.

Rin, H. and T. Lin. 1962. Mental illness among Formosan aborigines as compared with the Chinese in Taiwan. *Journal of Mental Science* 108:134–146.

Rinehart, J. W. 1966. On diagnosed mental illness and social class (II). *American Sociological Review* 31:545–546.

Roberts, B. H., and J. K. Myers. 1954. Religion, national origin, immigration and mental illness. *Amercian Journal of Psychiatry* 110:759.

Rogler, L. H. 1967. Slum neighborhoods in Latin America. *Journal of Inter-American Studies.* 9:507–528.

Rogler, L. H. and A. Hollingshead. 1961. The Puerto Rican spiritualist as a psychiatrist. *American Journal of Sociology* 67:17–21.

Rogler, L. H. and A. B. Hollingshead. 1964. *Trapped: Families and Schizophrenia.* New York: John Wiley & Sons p. 260.

Roheim, G. 1950. *Psychoanalysis and Anthropology.* New York, International Universities Press.

Rollins, N. 1974. Soviet and American youth in a changing world. *Australia & New Zealand Journal of Psychiatry,* 8:149–153.

Romano, J. 1950. Basic orientation and education of the medical student. *Journal of the American Medical Association* 143:409–412.

Romano, J. 1967. Psychiatry, the university and the community. In E. L. Cowan et al, eds. *Emerging Approaches to Mental Health Problems.* New York: Appleton-Century.

Romeo, C. 1969. Revolutionary practice and theory in Latin-America. In Horowitz et al., eds. 1969.

Rootman, I. D. Sydiaha, and H. G. Lafave. 1968. The ethnic community and the expression of mental illness: A comparative epidemiological study of French and non-French Canadian towns. *Psychiatric Quarterly* 42:235.

Rose, A. M., ed. 1955. *Mental Health and Mental Disorder,* ch. 10. New York, W. W. Norton.

Roselli, H. 1968. *Historia de la Psiquiatriá en Colombia.* Vol. I. Bogota: Editorial Horizontes.

Roselli, H. 1970. Antecedentes y desarrollo de la psiquiatría en latinoamérica. Presented to the VI Congreso Latinoamericano de Psiquiatria. Sao Paulo (mimeographed copy).

Roselli, H. ed. 1970. *Psiquiatría en la América Latina.* Bogota: Tercer Mundo.

Rosen, R. 1972. Some systems theoretical problems in biology. In Laszlo 1972:45.

Rosenhan, D. 1973. On being sane in insane places. *Science* 179:250–258.

Rotondo, J., L. P. Aliaga, and C. García-Pacheco. 1963. Estudios de morbilidad psiquiátrica en la población urbana de Mendocita. In Caravedo, et al., eds. *Estudios de Psiquiátrica Social en el Perú*. Lima: Ediciones Del Sol.

Rotondo, J., G. Mariátegui, C. Bambarén, and P. García Pacheco y Aliaga. 1962. Personalidad básica, migración y salud mental. *Boletin Oficina Sanitaria Panamericana* 3:140–142.

Royes, K. 1961. The incidence and features of psychoses in a Caribbean community. In *Proc. 3rd World Cong. Psychiat.* 2:1121–1125.

Rubel, A. J. 1964. The epidemiology of a folk illness: Susto in Hispanic America. *Ethnology* 3:268–283.

Rubin, V. 1959. Approaches to the study of national characteristics in a multicultural society. *International Journal of Social Psychiatry* 5:20.

Ruesch, J. 1946. *Chronic Disease and Psychological Invalidism: A Psychosomatic Study*. New York: American Society for Research in Psychosomatic Problems, pp. 104–124.

Ruesch, J. and G. Bateson. 1968. Communication: The Social Matrix of Psychiatry, 2d ed. New York: Norton.

Reusch, J., A. Jacobson, and M. B. Loeb. 1948. Acculturation and illness. *Psychological Monographs* 62:1.

Ruiz, P. and J. Langrod. 1976. Psychiatry and folk healing: A dichotomy. *American Journal of Psychiatry* 133:95–97.

Runciman, W. and C. Bagley. 1969. Relative deprivation, status consistency, and attitudes to immigrants. *Sociology* 3:359–375.

Russell, B. 1929. *Mysticism and Logic*. New York: Norton.

Rutter, M., D. Shaffer, and C. Sturge. 1975. *A Guide to a Multiaxial Classification Scheme for Psychiatric Disorders in Childhood and Adolescence*. London: Institute of Psychiatry.

Rwegellara, G. 1969. Personal Communication. London: Institute of Psychiatry.

Saenger, G. 1968. Psychiatric out-patients in America and the Netherlands: A transcultural comparison. *Social Psychiatry* 3(4):149.

Sainsbury, M. 1974. Psychiatry in the People's Republic of China. *Medical Journal of Australia* 1:669.

Sainsbury, P. 1968. Suicide and depression in Coppen and Walk, eds. 1968:1-13.

Saks, M. J., J. Edelstein, J. G. Draguns, and T. A. Fundia. 1970. Social class and social mobility in relation to psychiatric symptomatology in Argentina. *Revista Interamericana de Psicologia* 4:105–121.

Sal Y Rosas, F. 1958. El mito del jani o susto de la medicina indígena del Perv. *Revista de Sanidad de Policía* 18:167–189.

Sanchez, R. B. 1979. Politics: Hispanic priority in mental health. Paper presented at the Symposium "Psychiatry: Relevant for hispanics in the 80's" at the 132d Annual Meeting of the American Psychiatric Association.

Sandifer, M. G., A. Hordern, G. C. Timbury, and L. M. Green. 1968. Psychiatric diagnosis: A comparative study in North Carolina, London and Glasgow. *British Journal of Psychiatry* 114:1–9.

Sandifer, M. S., Jr., A. Hardern, G. C. Timbury, and L. A. Green. 1969. Similarities and differences in patient evaluation by U.S. and U.K. psychiatrists. *American Journal of Psychiatry* 126:206–212.

Santoso, R. S. I. 1959. The social conditions of psychotherapy in Indonesia. *American Journal of Psychiatry* 115–798.

Sanua, V. D. 1961. Sociocultural factors in the families of schizophrenics. *Psychiatry* 24:246.

Sanua, V. D. 1966. Socio-cultural aspects of psychotherapy and treatment: A review of the literature. In L. E. Abt and B. F. Reiss, eds. *Progress in Clinical Psychology*. New York: Grune and Stratton, 1966.

Sanua, V. D. 1969. The socio-cultural aspects of schizophrenia: A review of the literature. In Bellak and Loeb, eds. 1969. New York: Grune and Stratton.

Sapir, E. 1927. Central and North American languages. *Encyclopedia Brittanica.* 14th ed. 5:139–141.

Sapir, E. 1963. Cultural anthropology and psychiatry. In D. G. Mandelbaum, ed. *Selected Writings of Edward Sapir in Language, Culture and Personality,* pp. 509–532. Berkeley: University of California Press.

Sartorius, N., E. M. Brooke, and T. Lin. 1970. Reliability of psychiatric assessment in international research. In Hare and Wing, eds. 1970.

Sarwer-Foner, G. J. 1970. Recognition and management of drug-induced extapyramidal reactions and "paradoxical" behavioral reactions in psychiatry. *Canadian Medical Association Journal* 83:312–318.

Saslow, H. L. and M. Harrover. 1968. Research on psychosocial adjustment of Indian youth. *American Journal of Psychiatry* 125:224.

Savory, T. 1957. *The Art of Translation,* London: Jonathan Cape. p. 14.

Scadding, J. G. 1963. Meaning of diagnostic terms in broncho-pulmonary disease. *British Medical Journal* 2:1425–1430.

Schachter, S. 1954. Interpretive and methodological problems of replicated research. *Journal of Social Issues* 10(4):52–60.

Schachter, S. and J. E. Singer. 1962, Cognitive, social and physiological determinants of emotional state. *Psychological Review* 69:379–399.

Schachter, S. and L. Wheeler. 1962. Epinephrine, chlorpromazine and amusement. *Journal of Abnormal and Social Psychology* 65:121–128.

Schaechter, F. 1965. Previous history of mental illness in female migrant patients admitted to Psychiatric Hospital, Royal Park. *Medical Journal of Australia* 2:277.

Schaefer, E. S. and R. Q. Bell. 1958. Development of a parental attitude research instrument. *Child Development* 29:339–361.

Scheff, T. J. 1966a. Users and non-users of a student psychiatric clinic. *Journal of Health and Social Behavior* 7:114–121.

Scheff, T. J. 1966b. *Being Mentally Ill: A Sociological Theory*. Chicago: Aldine.

Scheff, T. J. 1968. Negotiating reality: Notes on power in the assessment of responsibility. *Social Problems* 16:3–17.

Scheflen, A. E. 1972. *Body Language and the Social Order.* Englewood Cliffs: Prentice-Hall.

Schmale, A. H., W. A. Greene, M. Kehoe, and G. L. Engel. 1964. *Advances in Psychsomatic Medicine* 4:4.

Schooler, C. and W. Caudill. 1964. Symptomatology in Japanese and American schizophrenics. *Ethnology* 3:172–177.

Schultes, R. E. 1972. An overview of hallucinogens in the western hemisphere. In P. Furst, ed. *Flesh of the Gods.* New York: Praeger.

Schur, E. 1971. *Labeling deviant behavior: Its sociological implications.* New York: Harper.

Schwab, J. J., M. Bialow, C. E. Holzer, J. M. Brown, and B. E. Stevenson. 1967. Sociocultural aspects of depression in medical in-patients. Parts I & II. *Archives of General Psychiatry* 17:533–543.

Schwab, J. J., J. M. Brown, C. E. Holzer, and M. Sokolof. 1968. Current concepts of depression: The sociocultural. *International Journal of Social Psychiatry* 226.

Scott, M. S. 1973. The absence of interference effects in pre-school children's picture recognition. *Journal of Genetic Psychology* 122:121–126.

Sears, R. R., E. E. Maccoby, and H. Levin. 1957. *Patterns of Child Rearing.* New York: Harper.

Sears Roebuck and Co. 1955. Psychological testing staff, National Personnel: A comparison of the Spanish and English Versions of the Sears Executive battery, mimeo.

Sechrest, L., T. L. Fay, and S. M. H. Zaidi. 1972. Problems of translation in cross-cultural research. *Journal of Cross-Cultural Psychology* 3:41–56.

Sechrest, L. 1963. Incremental validity: A recommendation, *Educational and Psychological Measurement* 23:153–158.

Segall, M.H., D. T. Campbell, and M. J. Herskovits. 1966. *The Influence of Culture on Visual Perception.* Indianopolis, Bobbs-Merrill.

Seguín, C. A. 1956. Migration and psychosomatic disadaptation. *Psychosomatic Medicine* 13:404–409.

Seguín, C. A. 1964. La preparación psicológica del estudiante de medicina. Lima: Universidad de San Marcos.

Seiler, L. 1973. The 22-item scale used in field studies of mental illness. *Journal of Health and Social Behavior 14:252.*

Seligman, C. G. 1929. Temperament, conflict and psychosis in a stone age population. *British Journal of Medical Psychology* 9:187.

Sellers, M. J., R. E. Klein, J. Kagan, and C. Minston. 1972. Developmental determinants of attention: A cross-cultural replication. *Developmental Pscyhology* 6:185

Selvin, H. 1957. A critique of tests of significance in survey research. *American Sociological Review* 22:519–527.

Sethi, B. B., and S. C. Gupta. 1970. An epidemiological and cultural study of depression. Indian Journal of Psychiatry 12:18.

Seymour, J. M. 1974. The rural school as an acculturating institution: The Iban of Malaysia. *Human Organization* 33:277–290.

Shafer, E. S. and R. Q. Bell. 1958. Development of a parental attitude research inventory. *Child Development* 29:339–361.

Sheldon, A. 1970. Toward a general theory of disease and medical care. A. Sheldon et al. eds. *Systems and Medical Care.* Cambridge: MIT Press.

Shelley, H. M., and W. H. Watson. 1936. Investigation concerning mental disorder in Nyasaland natives with special reference to primary aetiological and other contributory factors. *Journal of Mental Science* 82:701.

Shepherd, M., B. Cooper, A. C. Brown, and G. Kalton. 1966. *Psychiatric Illness in General Practice.* London: Oxford University Press Inc.

Shepherd, M., E. M. Brooke, J. E. Cooper, and L. Tusungyi. 1968. An experimental approach to psychiatric diagnosis. *Acta Psychiatrica Scandinavica,* suppl 201.

Sheridan, C. L., and R. G. King. 1972. Obedience to authority with an authentic victim. *Proceedings of the 80th Annual Convention of the American Psychological Association* 7:165–166 (summary).

Sherif, M. 1937. An experimental approach to the study of attitudes. *Sociometry* 1:90–98.

Sidel, R. 1972. Mental diseases and their treatment. In J. R. Quinn, ed. *Medicine and Public Health in the People's Republic of China,* pp. 289–304. Washington, D. C.: US Government Printing Office.

Sidel, R. 1973. The role of revolutionary optimism in the treatment of mental illness in the People's Republic of China. *American Journal of Orthopsychiatry* 43:732–736.

Sidel, R., and V. W. Sidel. 1972. The human services in China. *Social Policy* 2:25–34.

Sidel, V. W. 1972. The barefoot doctors of the People's Republic of China. *New England Journal of Medicine* 286:1292–1300.

Siegel, S. 1956. *Nonparametic Statistics for the Behavioral Sciences.* New York: McGraw-Hill.

Silva, M., R. Morales, R. de Silva, and T. Del Pozo. 1966. El curanderismo en Lima. In C. A. Seguín and R. Ríos-Carrasco, eds. *Anales del III Congreso Latinoamericano de Psiquiatría.* Lima. Talleres Gráficos Villanueva.

Silverman, C. 1968. *The Epidemiology of Depression.* Baltimore: Johns Hopkins, p. 84.

Silverman, S. 1966. An ethnographic approach to social stratification. *American Anthropologist* 68:889–921.

Simon, H. A. 1957. *Models of Man.* New York: Wiley.

Simpson, G. G. 1963. Biology and the nature of science. *Science* 139:81–87.

Singer, K. 1972. Unpublished data.

Singer, K. 1974. Society and rights of the mentally ill: A historical retrospective in the Chinese. *Mental Health Society* 1:49.

Singer, M. 1972. *When a Great Tradition Modernizes: An Anthropological Approach to Indian Civilization.* New York: Praeger.
Singer, P. 1969. The psychiatrist-nurse team and home care in the Soviet Union and Amsterdam. *American Journal of Psychiatry* 125(9):1198–1202.
Sisto, C. 1970. Transformación de un establecimiento tradicional en un hospital psiquiátrico moderno. Proceso de cambio. In Roselli ed. 1970.
Skea, S., J. G. Draguns, and L. Phillips. 1969. Ethnic characteristics of psychiatric symptomatology within across regional groupings: A study of an Israeli child guidance clinic population. *Israel Annals of Psychiatry and Related Disciplines* 7:31–42.
Skoog, G. 1969. The anancastic syndrome and its relation to personality attitudes. *Acta Psychiatrica Scandinavica.* Supplement 134.
Slater, P. 1971. *Pursuit of Loneliness.* Boston: Beacon.
Slater, P. and R. Kastenbaum. 1966. Paradoxical reactions to drugs: Some personality and ethnic correlates. *Journal of American Geriatrics Society* 14:1016–1034.
Smartt, C. G. F. 1956. Mental adjustment in the East Africans. *Journal of Mental Science* 102:441.
Smith, A. G., ed. 1966. *Communication and Culture.* New York: Holt, Rinehart and Winston.
Smith, D. E. 1975. Special treatment and service needs of youthful drug abusers. In *Final Report: A Survey of New Techniques for the Treatment of Drug Abusers.* Vol. 2. Washington, D. C.: METCOR.
Sommers, V. S. 1964. The impact of dual-cultural membership on identity. *Psychiatry* 27(4):332–344.
Spiegel, J. P. 1959. Some cultural aspects of transference and counter-transference. In J. H. Masserman, ed. *Science and Psychoanalysis.* Vol 2. *Individual and Family Dynamics,* pp 160–182. New York: Grune & Stratton.
Spiegel, J. P. 1976. Cultural aspects of transference and counter-transference revisited. *Journal of the American Academy of Psychoanalysis* 4:447–467.
Spiegel, J. P. and P. Machotka. 1974. *Messages of the Body.* New York: Free Press.
Spilka, I. V. 1968. On translating the mental status schedule. *Meta* 13:4.
Spindler, G. D. 1955. Sociocultural and psychological processes. In *Menomini acculturation.* University of California Publications in Culture and Society. Vol. 5. Berkeley: University of California Press.
Spindler, G. D. and W. Goldschmidt. 1952. Experimental design in the study of culture change. *South-western Journal of Anthropology* 8:68.
Spinola De Galviz, L. M. and J. Velasco Alzaga. 1960. Epidemiología del suicidio en la República Mexicana. *Anales del Instituto Nacional de Antropología e Historia* 12(41).
Spitzer, H. M. 1947. Psychoanalytic approaches to the Japanese character. In G. Roheim, ed. *Psychoanalysis and the Social Sciences,* Vol. 1. New York: International Universities Press.

Spitzer, R. L., J. Endicott and E. Robins. 1978. Research diagnostic criteria. *Archives of General Psychiatry* 35:773–782.

Srole, L., T. S. Langner, S. T. Michael, M. K. Opler and T. A. C. Rennie. 1962. *Mental Health in the Metropolis—The Midtown Manhattan Study*. New York: McGraw-Hill.

Staewen, C., and F. Schonberg. 1970. *Culture Change and Anxiety Development in the Yoruba of West Africa*. Munich: Weltforum.

Stainbrook, E. 1952–1953. Some characteristics of the psychopathology of schizophrenic behavior in Bahian society. *American Journal of Psychiatry* 109:330–335.

Stainbrook, E. 1954. A cross-cultural evaluation of depressive reactions. In Hoch and Zubin, eds. 1954.

Steinberg, G. 1973. Verbal communication.

Stoker, D. H. 1963. A comparison of the symptomatic behavior of Spanish-American and Anglo-American hospital patients. Masters' Thesis: The University of Arizona.

Stoker, D. H., L. A. Zurcher, and W. Fox. 1969. Women in psychotherapy: A cross-cultural comparison. *International Journal of Social Psychiatry* 3:227.

Stoller, A. 1969. Urbanization and mental health. *Medical Journal of Australia* 23–228.

Stoller, A. and J. Krupinski. 1969. Mental health of immigrants. *Medical Journal of Australia* 2:365.

Straus, J. H. and M. A. Straus. 1953. Suicide, homicide and social structure in Ceylon. *American Journal of Sociology* 58:461.

Strauss, J. S. 1975. A comprehensive approach to psychiatric diagnosis. *American Journal of Psychiatry* 132:1193–1197.

Summers, G. F. 1971. Psychiatric symptoms: Cross-validation with a rural sample. *Rural Sociology* 36:367–377.

Sundberg, N. D. 1956. The use of the MMPI for cross-cultural personality study: A preliminary report on the German translation. *Journal of Abnormal and Social Psychology* 52:281–283.

Sunier, A. 1956. Mental illness and psychiatric care in Israel. Quoted by Murphy, H.B.M. (1961). Social change and mental health. *Milbank Memorial Fund Quarterly* 39:385.

Suomi, S. J. and H. F. Harlow. 1972. Social rehabilitation of isolate reared monkeys. *Developmental Psychology* 6:487–496.

Swanson, E. E., T. M. Mewcomb, and E. L. Hartley, eds. 1952. *Readings in Social Psychology*. New York: Holt.

Szasz, T. S. 1961. *The Myth of Mental Illness*. New York: Harper & Row.

Szasz, T. S. 1975. *Ceremonial Chemistry. The Ritual Persecution of Drugs, Addicts, and Pushers*. New York: Doubleday.

Taipale, V. and I. Taipale. 1973. Chinese psychiatry: A visit to a Chinese mental hospital. *Archives of General Psychiatry* 29:313–316.

Tarnopolski, A., G. Del Olmo, and D. Valdemarin. 1970. Prevalencia de enfer-

medades mentales en el partido de Lanus. In Mariátegui and Adis Castro, eds. 1970.
Taylor, L. and S. Chave. 1964. *Mental Health and Environment.* London: Longmans.
Teja, J. S., R. L. Narang, and A. K. Aggarwal, 1971. Depression across the cultures. *British Journal of Psychiatry* 119:253–260.
Tewfik, G. I. 1958. Psychoses in Africa. In *Mental Disorders and Mental Health in Africa South of the Sahara.* CCTA/CSA-WFMH-WHO Meeting, London.
Thomas, A. and S. Sillen. 1968. *Racism and Psychiatry.* New York: Oxford University Press.
Thomas, D. S. 1956. In Malzberg and Lee 1956 (introduction).
Thomason, D. S. and B. Z. Locke. 1963. Marital status, education and occupational differentials in mental disease. *Milbank Memorial Fund Quarterly* 41:145.
Thompson, L. 1950. *Culture in Crisis.* Chicago: University of Chicago Press.
Thomas, R. K. C., W. C. MacKenzie, and A. F. W. Peart. 1967. A visit to the People's Republic of China. *Canadian Medical Association Journal* 97:349–360.
Tietze, C., P. Lemkau, and M. Cooper. 1941. Schizophrenia, manic-depressive psychosis, and social-economic status. *American Journal of Sociology,* 47:167.
Tietze, C., P. Lemkau and M. Cooper 1942. Personality disorder and spatial mobility. *American Journal of Sociology* 48:29.
Toffler, A. 1970. *Future Shock.* New York: Random House.
Tongyonk, J. 1972. Depressions in Thailand in the perspective of comparative transcultural psychiatry. *Journal of the Psychiatric Association of Thailand* 17:44.
Tonks, C. M., E. S. Parykel, and G. L. Klerman. 1970. Clinical depression among Negroes. *American Journal of Psychiatry* 127:329.
Tooth, G. 1950. *Studies in Mental Illness in the Gold Coast.* Research Publications No. 6: London: Her Majesty's Stationary Office.
Torrey, E. F., ed. 1966. *An Introduction to Health and Health Education in Ethiopia.* Addis Ababa: Berhanena Selam Printing Press.
Torrey, E. F. 1971. Emergency psychiatric ambulance services in the USSR. *American Journal of Orthopsychiatry* 128:2, 153–157.
Torrey, E. F. 1972a. What western psychotherapists can learn from witch doctors. *American Journal of Orthopsychiatry* 42:69–76.
Torrey, E. F. 1972b. *The Mind Game: Witch Doctors and Psychiatrists.* New York: Emerson Hall.
Torrey, E. F. 1974. *The Death of Psychiatry.* Radnor, Pennsylvania: Chilton.
Tousignant, M., G. Denis, and R. Lachapelle. 1974. Some considerations concerning the validity and use of the health opinion survey. *Journal of Health and Social Behavior* 15:241–252.
Triandis, H. C. 1972. *The Analysis of Subjective Culture.* New York: Wiley.
Tsur, M. 1972. *What Is Kibbutz?* Oranim, Israel: Federation of Kibbutzim in Israel.

Turner, R. J., and M. O. Wagenfeld. 1967. Occupational mobility and schizophrenia: An assessment of the social causation and social selection hypotheses. *American Sociological Review.* 32:104–113.

Tyler, S. A., ed. 1969. *Cognitive Anthropology.* New York: Holt, Rinehart and Winston.

Unwin, J. R. 1970. Contemporary misuse of psychoactive drugs by youth. In S. Arieti, ed. *World Biennial of Psychiatry.* New York: Basic Books.

Univ. Rochester Med. Rev. 1971–1972. p. 10.

Univ. Rochester Med. Rev. 1976. *Pharos* 39:127.

Useem, J. 1963. Notes on the sociological study of language. *Social Science Research Council Items* 17:29–31.

Valdivia-Ponce, O. 1970. Migración interna a la metrópoli. (Contraste cultural, conflictc y desadaptación.) Universidad Nacional Mayor de San Marcos, Lima.

Van Hover, K. I. S. 1971. A developmental study of three components of attention. Doctoral dissertation, Harvard University.

Van Wulfften-Pathe, P. M. 1933. Amok. *Med. J. Geneesk* 77:983–991.

Van Wulfften-Pathe, P. M. 1936. In C. D. de Langen and A. Lichtenstein, eds. *A Clinical Textbook of Tropical Medicine,* p. 225.

Van Loon, F. G. H. 1927. Amok and Latah. *Journal of Abnormal and Social Psychology* 21:434–444.

Varga, E. 1968. Changes in the symptomatology of psychotic patterns. *Transcultural Psychiatric Research Review* 5:93.

Veith, I. 1955. Psychiatric thought in Chinese medicine. *Journal of the History Medicine* 10:261–268.

Velasco-Alzaga, J. 1963. La salud mental en las Américas. Organización Panamericana de la Salud. Publicaciones Científicas No. 81.

Verhaegen, F. 1972. Mental health in foreign workers. Proceedings of the 7th annual meeting of the International Committee on Occupational Mental Health, Leuven. Quoted by Leading Article. *Lancet* 1:1276.

Vermeulen, C. J. J. and A. De Ruijter. 1975. Dominant epistemological presuppositions in the use of the cross-cultural survey method. *Current Anthropology* 16(1):29–52.

Vesell, E. S. 1969. Recent progress in pharmacogenetics. *Advances in Pharmacology & Chemotherapy* 7:1–52.

Vidal, G. 1965. Curso de Psiquiatriá. Instituto Grondona (mimeographed copy).

Vincent, J. 1971. Scaling the universe of states on certain useful multivariate dimensions. *Journal of Social Psychology* 85:261–283.

von Bertalanffy, L. 1952. *Problems of Life.* New York: Wiley.

von Bertalanffy, L. 1968. *General Systems Theory.* New York: Braziller

von Bertalanffy, L. 1972. *The Systems View of the World.* New York: Braziller.

Wallace, A. F. C. 1959. Cultural determinants of response to hallucinatory experience. *Archives of General Psychiatry* 1:58–69.

Wallace, A. F. C. 1961. *Culture and Personality.* New York: Random House.

Wallace, A. F. C. 1970. *Culture and Personality.* 2d ed. New York: Random House.
Wallace, E. L. 1955. Measurement of the linguistic dominance of bilinguals. *Journal of Abnormal and Social Psychology.* 50:197–200.
Walls, P. D., L. H. Walls, and D. G. Langsley. 1975. Medical education in the People's Republic of China. *Journal of Medical Education* 50:371–383.
Warner, L. W. 1937. The society, the individual, and his mental disorders. *American Journal of Psychiatry* 94:274.
Warner, W. L., M. Meeker and K. Eels. 1960. *Social Class in America.* New York: Harper.
Washburn, C. 1961. *Primitive Drinking.* New York: College and University Press.
Wasson, G. R. and V. Wasson. 1957. *Russian, Mushrooms and History.* New York: Atheneum.
Wax, M. L. 1971. *Indian Americans: Unity and Diversity.* Englewood Cliffs: Prentice-Hall.
Waxler, N. E. 1972. Social change and psychiatric illness in Ceylon: An investigation of traditional and modern conceptions of disease and treatment. In W. Lebra, ed. *Mental Health in Asia and the Pacific.* Honolulu: University of Hawaii Press.
Wechsler, H. 1961. Community growth, depressive disorders and suicide. *American Journal of Sociology* 67:9.
Weidman, H. H. and J. N. Sussex. 1971. Cultural values and ego functioning in relation to the atypical culture-bound reactive syndromes. *International Journal of Social Psychiatry* 17:83–100.
Weil, A. 1973. *The Natural Mind: Another Way of Looking at Drugs and the Higher Consciousness.* Boston: Houghton-Mifflin.
Weinberg, S. K. 1965. Cultural aspects of manic-depression in West Africa. *Journal of Health and Human Behavior* 6:247.
Weinreich, U. 1966. *Languages in Contact.* The Hague: Mouton.
Welsh, G. S. 1959. *Preliminary Manual: Welsh Figure Preference Test.* Research Edition. Palo Alto: Consulting Psychologists Press.
Weppner, R. 1973. An anthropological view of the street addict's world. *Human Organization* 31:11–121.
Werner, O. and D. T. Campbell. 1970. Translating, working through interpreters, and the problem of decentering. In R. Naroll and R. Cohen, eds. *A Handbook of Method in Cultural Anthropology.* New York: The Natural History Press.
West, L. J. 1967. Dissociative reaction. In A. M. Freedman and H. I. Kaplan, eds *Comprehensive Textbook of Psychiatry,* pp. 885–898. Baltimore: Williams & Wilkins.
Westermeyer, J. 1971. Grenade-amok: Modern violence in Laos. In the Proceedings of the fifth world congress of psychiatry, Mexico City.
Westermeyer, J. 1972. A comparison of amok and other homicide in Laos. *American Journal of Psychiatry* 129:703–709.

Westermeyer, J. 1974. Alcoholism from the cross-cultural perspective. *American Journal of Drug and Alcohol Abuse* 1:89–105.

Westermeyer, J., ed. 1976. *Anthropology and Mental Health.* Chicago: Aldine.

Westermeyer, J. 1973. Grenade-amok in Laos: A psychosocial perspective. *International Journal of Social Psychiatry.* 19:251–260.

Westermeyer, J. and W. Hausman. 1974. Cross-cultural consultation for mental health planning. *International Journal of Social Psychiatry* 20:34–38.

White, S. H. 1970. Some general outlines of the matrix of developmental changes between 5 and 7 years. *Bulletin of the Orton Society* 21:41–57.

Whiting, B. B., ed. 1963. *Six Cultures—Studies in Child Rearing.* New York: Wiley.

Whiting, J. M. 1959. Sorcery, sin and super-ego: Some cross-cultural mechanisms of social control. In *Nebraska Symposium on Social Motivation* 7:174.

Whiting, J. M. 1961. Socialization process and personality. In F. Hsu, ed. *Psychological Anthropology* Homewood, Ill: Dorsey Press.

Whiting, J. M. 1964. Effects of climate in certain cultural practices. In W. Goodenough, ed. *Exploration in Cultural Anthropology.* New York: McGraw-Hill.

Whiting, J. and I. Child. 1953. *Child Training and Personality: A Cross-Cultural Study.* New Haven: Yale University Press.

Whitlock, F. A. 1971. Migration and suicide. *Medical Journal of Australia* 1:840.

Whorf, B. L. 1956. *Language, Thought and Reality* New York: Wiley.

Wilbur, G. B. and W. Munsterberger. 1951. *Psychoanalysis and Culture.* New York: International Universities Press.

Williams, J. 1957. Child health and psychiatry in China today. *Medical Journal of Australia* 44:630–631.

Williams, T. R. 1972. *Introduction to Socialization: Human Cultures Transmitted.* St. Louis: C. V. Mosby Co.

Williams, T. R., ed. 1976. *Psychological Anthropology.* Chicago, Aldine.

Wilner, D. M., R. P. Walkley, J. M. Schram, T. C. Pinkerton, and M. Tayback. 1960. Housing as an environmental factor in mental health. *American Journal of Public Health* 50:55.

Wilson, P. D. and A. H. Riesen. 1966. Visual development in rhesus monkeys neonatally deprived of patterned light. *Journal of Comparative and Physiological Psychology* 61:87–95.

Wing, J. K. 1974. Psychiatry in the Soviet Union. *British Medical Journal* 1:433–436.

Wing, J. K., J. L. T. Birley, J. E. Cooper, P. Graham, and A. D. Isaacs. 1967. Reliability of a procedure for measuring and classifying present psychiatric state. *British Journal of Psychiatry.* 113:499–515.

Wing, J. K., J. E. Cooper, and K. Sartorius. 1974. *The Measurement and Classification of Psychiatric Symptoms.* London: Cambridge University Press.

Wing, L. 1970. Observations on the psychiatric section of the International Classification of Diseases and the British Glossary of Mental Disorders. *Psychological Medicine* 1:79–85.

Wing, L., J. K. Wing, and A. Hailey. 1967. The use of psychiatric services in three urban areas: An international case register study. *Social Psychiatry* 2:158–167.

Wing, L., C. Bramley, A. Hailey, and J. K. Wing. 1968. Camberwell cumulative psychiatric case register. Part I: Aims and methods. *Social Psychiatry* 3:5–123.

Wittkower, E. D. 1971. Sociocultural factors in the prevention of mental illness. Paper presented at the Fifth World Psychiatric Congress, Mexico.

Wittkower, E. D. and R. Hugel. 1968. Transcultural aspects of the depressive syndrome. Paper presented at Workshop on "Dus depressive syndrom." Freie Cluio. Berlin.

Wittkower, E. D. and H. Rin. 1965. Transcultural psychiatry. *Archives of General Psychiatry* 13:387.

Wittkower, E. D. and R. Prince. 1974. A review of transcultural psychiatry. In Arieti, ed. (1959) 1974:2:535–550.

Wolff, H. G. ed. 1960. *An Outline of Man's Knowledge.* New York: Doubleday,

Wolff, H. 1964. Intelligibility and inter-ethnic attitudes. In D. Hymes, ed. p. 41. *Language in Culture and Society,* pp. 440–445. New York: Harper.

Wolff, P. H. 1972. Ethnic differences in alcohol sensitivity. *Science* 175:449–450.

Wong, K. C. 1950. A short history of psychiatry and mental hygiene in China. *Chinese Medical Journal* 68:44–48.

World Health Organization. 1959. Report of the W. H. O. Study Group on Schizophrenia. *American Journal of Psychiatry* 115:865–872.

World Health Organization. 1967. *Epidemiological and Vital Statistics Report.*

World Health Organization. 1973. *The International Pilot Study of Schizophrenia.*

Worth, R. M. 1963. Health in rural China: From village to commune. *American Journal of Hygiene* 77:228–239.

Wortis, J. and D. Freundlich. 1964. Psychiatric work therapy in the Soviet Union. *American Journal of Psychiatry.* 121:123–128.

Yamamoto, J., Q. C. James, M. Bloombaum, and J. Hattem. 1967. Racial factors in patient selection. *American Journal of Psychiatry* 124:630–636.

Yap. P. M. 1958. *Suicide in Hong Kong.* London: Oxford University Press.

Yap, P. M. 1965. Phenomenology of affective disorder in Chinese and other cultures (Ciba Foundation Symposium). In A. V. S. de Reuck and R. Porter, eds. *Transcultural Psychiatry,* pp. 84–105. London: J. & A. Churchill.

Yap, P. M. 1971. Guilt and shame. Depression and culture: A psychiatric cliche re-examined. *Comm. Contemp. Psychiat.* 1(2):35.

Yolles, S. F. 1968. Impressions of Soviet psychiatry. Impressions of the U.S. mission on mental health: Conclusions and recommendations. *American Journal of Psychiatry.* 125(5):670–674.

Yolles, S. and M. Kramer. 1969. Vital statistics of schizophrenia. In Bellak and Loeb, ed. 1969.

Yoo, P. S. 1961. Mental disorders in Korean rural communities. *Proceedings of 3d World Congress of Psychiatry,* p. 1305.

Young, L. 1975. Changes in the postdoctoral education of internists. *Annals of Internal Medicine* 83:728–730.

Zaguirre, J. C. 1957. *J. Philippine Federation of Private Medical Practitioners.* 6:1138–1149.

Zeisel, H. 1957. *Say It with Figures.* New York: Harper and Row.

Zern, D. 1976. Further evidence supporting the relationship between nurturer/infant contact and later differentiation of the social environment. *Journal of Genetic Psychology* 129:169–170.

Ziferstein, I. 1966a. The Soviet psychiatrist's concept of society as a therapeutic community. *Current Psychiatric Therapies* 6:367–373.

Ziferstein, I. 1966b. The Soviet psychiatrist: His relationship to his patients and his society. *American Journal of Psychiatry* 123:440–446.

Ziferstein, I. 1968. Pathogenic (dynamic) psychotherapy in the Soviet Union. *American Journal of Psychiatry* 125:(5) 667–678.

Ziferstein, I. 1969. Soviet psychiatry and the American citizen. *International Journal of Psychiatry* 8:858–861.

Ziferstein, I. 1972. Group psychotherapy in the Soviet Union. *American Journal of Psychiatry* 129:595–600.

Zigler, E. and L. Phillips. 1960. Social effectiveness and symptomatic behaviors. *Journal of Abnormal Social Psychology* 61:231–238.

Zigler, E. and L. Phillips. 1962. Social competence and the process-reactive distinction in psychopathology. *Journal of Abnormal and Social Psychology,* 65:215–222.

Zola, I. K. 1963. Socio-cultural factors in the seeking of medical care. *Transcultural Psychiatric Research* 1 4:62–65.

Zubin, J. 1972. Ecological vs clinical fallacies in personality research. Annual convention of the American Psychology Association, Honolulu.

Zubin, J. and M. L. Kietzman. 1966. A crosscultural approach to classification in schizophrenia and other mental disorders. In P. H. Hoch and J. Zubin, eds. *Psychopathology of Schizophrenia.* New York: Grune & Stratton.

Zwingmann, C. A., M. Pfister-Ammende, eds. 1973. *Uprooting and After.* New York: Springer-Verlag.

Index of Names

Index of Subjects